Advanced Abnormal
Child Psychology

Second Edition

Advanced Abnormal Child Psychology

Second Edition

Edited by

Michel Hersen
Pacific University

Robert T. Ammerman
Children's Hospital and Medical Center, Cincinnati

2000

LAWRENCE ERLBAUM ASSOCIATES, PUBLISHERS
Mahwah, New Jersey   London

Lawrence Erlbaum Associates, Inc., Publishers
10 Industrial Avenue
Mahwah, NJ 07430

Cover design by Kathryn Houghtaling Lacey

Library of Congress Cataloging-in-Publication Data

Advanced abnormal child psychology / edited by Michel Hersen,
Robert T. Ammerman. — 2nd ed.

    p. cm.

Includes bibliographical references and index.
ISBN 0-8058-2866-4 (cloth : alk. paper) —
 ISBN 0-8058-2867-2 (pbk : alk. paper)
1. Child psychopathology. 2. Child psychiatry. I. Hersen, Michel.
II. Ammerman, Robert T.
[DNLM: 1. Mental Disorders—Child. 2. Mental Disorders—Infant.
3. Child Psychology. WS 350 A2438 1999]
RJ499.A327   1999
618.92'89 —dc21
DNLM/DLC
for Library of Congress   99-38242
                                                               CIP

Books published by Lawrence Erlbaum Associates are printed
on acid-free paper, and their bindings are chosen for strength and
durability.

Printed in the United States of America
10 9 8 7 6 5 4 3 2

Contents

PART II: ASSESSMENT AND TREATMENT

PART III: DESCRIPTION OF THE DISORDERS

Preface

There was a time when abnormal child psychology was the stepchild of abnormal psychology, with perhaps one or two chapters in an entire advanced textbook devoted to children. Given the explosive amount of new research on child development in general since the 1980s, the "stepchild" is obviously no longer a valid characterization. Indeed, in the last 15 years, many new journals devoted to childhood problems have made their appearance on library bookshelves. Although several books reviewing childhood problems were published, none, in our opinion, had sufficient breadth to show the advanced undergraduate and beginning graduate student the extent of our existing knowledge base concerning the disorders that manifest themselves early in development. Therefore, we undertook the task of assembling the first edition of this text, in an effort to integrate the empirical and clinical literatures. Since its publication in 1995, a great deal more work has been done.

This revised and expanded second edition includes much new material from the first edition authors and from three new ones, all respected experts in the field. It is divided into three parts, each preceded by a unifying introduction based on material in the chapter and the authors' conclusions. In Part I, General Issues, students are given a firm grounding and meaningful context for the information presented in parts II and III. Chapter 1 (Historical Overview) reviews the historical developments, essentially documenting both the neglect and abuse that children suffered at the hands of society well into the 20th century. Chapter 2 (Diagnosis and Classification) reviews the salient issues relating to classification and diagnosis of childhood disorders, including new developments in the *Diagnostic and Statistical Manual of Mental Disorders* (4th ed.). Chapter 3 (Epidemiologic Considerations) familiarizes the student with epidemiologic principles. Chapter 4 (Development and Psychopathology) underscores how developmental psychopathology provides a theoretical framework that can guide research and clinical efforts. Chapter 5 (Psychophysiological Research on Childhood Psychopathology) looks at psychophysiological determinants of behavior, with special attention focused on childhood autism, attention deficit disorder, and antisocial/conduct disorder. Chapter 6 (Familial Determinants) carefully looks at the evidence detailing familial factors that are contributory to child psychopathology. Chapter 7 (Research Strategies in Child Psychopathology) reviews the theoretical, methodological, and practical considerations involved in determining the course a researcher will take when investigating a problem in child psychopathology. Finally, chapter 8 (Psychological Aspects of Pediatric Disorders) details reactions of children, families, and society to complex and diverse child health problems.

As the title indicates, Part II focuses on assessment and treatment foundational issues often given short shrift in textbooks; here, they are discussed thoroughly from an empirical perspective. Chapter 9 (Intellectual and Cognitive Assessment), with a particular emphasis on traditional intelligence tests, provides an in-depth coverage of test development, administration, and interpretation of results. Chapter 10 (Behavioral Assessment) contrasts the philosophical and procedural differences between behavioral and other forms of psychological assessment. Chapter 11 (Behavioral Treatment) reviews the most commonly used behavioral techniques. Multiple case examples are provided to illustrate how behavioral treatments are implemented. Chapter 12 (Psychopharmacological Treatment) examines specific psychiatric disorders for which pharmacotherapy shows promise, including conduct disorder, depression, and developmental disorders. The final chapter in Part III (Community, Prevention, and Wellness) reviews various types of preventative interventions, concluding with an illustration of prevention principles involving conduct disorder and major depression.

In part III, Description of the Disorders, a common organizational format for the discussion of numerous case examples facilitates students' comprehension and sparks their interest. This is the general format for each chapter in Part III:

1. Clinical Description
2. Causes of the Disorder(s)
3. Course of the Disorder(s)
4. Familial Contributions
5. Psychophysiological and Genetic Influences
6. Current Treatments (with Case Illustrations)
7. Summary

In light of the wealth of information to which we are attempting to do justice, we opted to have experts in each area contribute to the effort. We thank our eminent contributors and colleagues for sharing with us and readers their views on what has been accomplished and where the field now is going. Next, we thank Carole Londerée, Alexander Duncan, and Erika Qualls for their technical contributions to the book. Finally, but hardly least of all, we thank our friends at Lawrence Erlbaum Associates for their encouragement and good cheer throughout the process of bringing to fruition this multiauthored textbook.

—Michel Hersen
—Robert T. Ammerman

PART I

General Issues

When compared to the rest of abnormal psychology, the history of abnormal child psychology is relatively brief. Indeed, the major findings in the field only can be traced to the last three to four decades. And within that time span, the most exciting developments have taken place since the 1970s. Although abnormal child psychology is a relatively new subdiscipline, it already has had numerous influences, including developmental psychology; epidemiology; psychophysiology; genetics; psychopathology; and the data-based approaches to assessment, diagnosis, and treatment. Overall, the influences have been of an empirical nature. In a very short time, the exponential growth of this subdiscipline has made the area complex. Given the extent of such complexity, we believe that the student requires a firm grounding in the basics before she or he can have a full understanding of the nuances of psychopathology and its treatment interventions.

In this part of the text, we provide the reader with an overview of advanced abnormal child psychology, outlining the contributions from a variety of directions. First, in chapter 1, Brad Donohue, Michel Hersen, and Robert T. Ammerman review the historical developments, essentially documenting both the neglect and abuse that children suffered at the hands of society well into the 20th century. The authors describe historical antecedents that led to the discipline of child psychology, consider the status of contemporary psychotherapies, review the short history of child psychopharmacology, and look at the progression of diagnostic and empirical classification.

In chapter 2, Joseph R. Scotti and Tracy L. Morris review the salient issues relating to classification and diagnosis of childhood disorders, including new developments in the *Diagnostic and Statistical Manual of Mental Disorders* (4th ed.). Criticisms of the psychiatric diagnostic scheme are considered, and the authors document the improvements in reliability and validity of *DSM–III* and *DSM–III–R*. Also discussed are the relations among diagnostic entities and the best methods for evaluating categorization of children at the empirical level.

In chapter 3, Gale A. Richardson and Nancy L. Day familiarize the student with epidemiologic principles. Classic studies in the field are reviewed. Critical issues in child psychiatric epidemiology are addressed, such as comorbidity (i.e., multiple diagnoses), definitions of psychopathology, developmental issues, and use of multiple informants to reach diagnostic conclusions.

In chapter 4, Sally D. Popper, Shelley Ross, and Kay D. Jennings provide an overview of child development and psychopathology. The authors underscore how developmental psychopathology provides a theoretical framework that can guide research and clinical efforts. Throughout this chapter, the importance of defining normal and abnormal behavior from an age perspective, adaptation and maladaptation, and continuity and discontinuity is emphasized.

In chapter 5, Rafael Klorman looks at psychophysiological determinants of behavior, with special attention focused on childhood autism, attention deficit disorder, and antisocial/conduct disorder. Autonomic measures most frequently studied have been heart rate and skin conductance. Researchers have studied autonomic reactivity to classify subjects on a continuum (e.g., sleep–drowsiness to alertness–excitement). Also, studies have examined moment-to-moment reaction of subjects to specific stimuli, looking at the emotional significance of such stimuli. The author brings the reader's attention to the exciting developments in the field, such as the recent finding that antisocial respondents may display heightened information processing.

In chapter 6, G. Stennis Watson and Alan M. Gross carefully look at the evidence detailing familial factors that contribute to child psychopathology. In so doing, they dispel myths about the field and point out the myriad of anthology, alcohol and drug abuse, divorce, and extrafamilial stressors. Given the age of the child, his or her vulnerability to such stressors will differ. The authors underscore how, in the future, additional studies will be required to disentangle parental factors and child characteristics that produce psychopathology.

In chapter 7, Eric J. Mash and Gloria L. Krahn review the theoretical, methodological, and practical considerations involved in determining the course a researcher will take when investigating a problem in child psychopathology. The research endeavor has been likened to a process that follows a number of stages. Included are considerations of sampling, design selection, measurement, and data analysis, in addition to pragmatic concerns. Research areas most often studied involve the determinants of childhood disorders, risk and protective factors, and treatment and prevention.

Finally, in chapter 8, Kenneth J. Tarnowski and Ronald T. Brown examine psychological aspects of pediatric disorders. The authors address the psychological consequences of pediatric illness and injury, as well as psychological and behavioral contributions to illness. They then review the literature for two types of pediatric disorders: burn injuries and sickle cell disease. In pediatric psychology, assessment is comprehensive, involving both children and their families. Interventions must be tailored to the needs of the child and family to maximize adaptation and recovery.

Historical Overview

Brad Donohue
University of Nevada, Las Vegas

Michel Hersen
Pacific University

Robert T. Ammerman
Children's Hospital and Medical Center

Historically, children have been treated poorly. However, significant events have brought about better treatment for children, including legislation protecting their rights, emergence of child guidance clinics, scientific study of child development, and evaluation of child psychotherapies.

Our introductory chapter (a) examines the history of child abuse and neglect, (b) discusses major historical antecedents that have led to the science of child psychology, (c) briefly examines the etiology and current status of major contemporary psychotherapies, (d) reviews the brief history of child psychopharmacology, and (e) examines the progression of behavioral classification and diagnostic categorizing with children.

HISTORY OF THE TREATMENT OF CHILDREN

In ancient Greece, physical and intellectual strengths were highly esteemed. Philosophers encouraged proper childhood education and training for attainment of maturity and success in later vocation, which helped to create a *Zeitgeist* that stressed education, athletics, and skills training for the brightest and most affluent boys in Greece. Older girls and women in that society assumed a domestic role that was limited to taking care of children and home care. However, children with mental or physical handicaps were tormented publicly. Less frequently, children with mental retardation and psychopathology were put to death or abandoned.

3

Treatment of children during the Roman Empire was essentially the same. Affluent children were educated in art, poetry, and sports, and poor children were treated harshly. Indeed, decisions as to whether the child should be sold as a slave, abandoned, or murdered depended on his or her value to the family.

The importance of development and formal education for most children was overlooked in Europe during the Middle Ages, even for those with great promise. Games and books for children were absent, and paintings of children during those times depicted them in adult clothing with adult mannerisms. Children were legally sold into slavery, and severe beatings were commonly carried out. Many children were abandoned or forced to work in monasteries to pay debts incurred by their parents. Children in middle- to low-income families started to work during their early childhood years, sometimes greater than 13 hours a day. Some girls were forced into marriage contracts during pre-adolescence. The child mortality rate was extremely high due to long hours in poor working conditions, epidemics, malnutrition, childhood disease, and murder (illegitimate and unwanted children usually were murdered).

The Renaissance led to increased sensitivity and humanity toward children. However, changes were slow to develop. Initially, severe physical punishment was widely accepted, and psychopathology was believed to be the result of demonic possession, which resulted in harsh treatment for mentally ill children. However, some important changes did occur during this period. Thomas Phaire's *The Boke of Chyldren* was written in 1545, the first publication to address pediatric problems, such as nightmares. Infanticide was determined to be illegal, although abandonment and residential placement in orphanages or church settings was accepted. Although the latter practice appears more merciful than infanticide, it should be mentioned that most children who were raised in orphanages died very young. Mortality rates were generally high, as one of every three children born during this time did not live to adulthood. By the late 1600's, it became customary for European parents to show affection and play with their children, particularly in affluent populations. However, adults in Colonial America continued to treat children abusively. During colonial expansion of America, children were often imprisoned, punished, or killed if they refused to be transported to America, where they often would be forced to work in harsh conditions or be exploited by male settlers as tobacco "brides." In 1654, the Stubborn Child Law allowed a parent to have "stubborn" children put to death for noncompliance. However, most children died before they were 4 years old from disease, starvation, malnutrition, and severe beatings.

Conditions for children began to improve in the 1700s. However, high morbidity rates and poor treatment were still common among children, particularly indigent children. Poor children living in cities typically worked excessive hours in factories, and children in rural areas worked on farms. Although many bills were opposed, a bill was submitted that prohibited children from the ages of 9 to 13 to work more than 48 hours a week and also prohibited children aged 13 to 18 from working more than 68 hours per week. As judged by contemporary standards this bill appears harsh. However, it was a substantial improvement at that time. Records were published pertaining to the development of children, which helped to bring about understanding as to the importance of using toys and pictures to stimulate physical and intellectual growth during childhood.

During the early 1800s, Benjamin Rush helped to bring about moral treatment of children with the publication of results from his studies of children (i.e., descriptions of the development of cholera in infants). Other developments in the medical field created an environment conducive to change for the betterment of child welfare in the late 1800s. Hospital-based interventions for children's medical and psychological conditions were implemented for the first time. Charles Caldwell wrote the first medical degree dissertation on pediatrics, and the first medical textbooks specializing in child psychopathology were published in Europe. Dorothea Dix formally requested the state legislature to increase federal funding to treatment centers that supported moral treatment of children. Her efforts resulted in approximately 30 new mental hospitals that emphasized moral treatment of mentally ill patients. During this time, G. Stanley Hall originated the Illinois Society of Child Study. He studied the motor and emotional development of children by devising the "baby bibliography." His work consisted of sending questionnaires to parents, teachers, mental health professionals, and children about various areas of child development to obtain normative data. In doing so, he was the first person to examine developmental abilities. He also encouraged others to monitor development of children and to consider the stages of development when assessing children. Hall founded the first scholarly journal devoted to pediatric development, and he wrote a two-volume text entitled *Adolescence: Its Psychology and Its Relations to Physiology, Anthropology, Sociology, Sex, Crime, Religion, and Education*. In this endeavor, Hall was the first person to describe "adolescence" as a unique stage of development.

In addition, the child study movement facilitated growth of compulsory education in the United States. An increase in student enrollment during the early 1900s restricted the time that public school teachers were available to assist students with learning disabilities. This led to development of special education programs that were established to accommodate children who were not able to adapt to regular school programs. The poor and ethnic minorities were disproportionately represented in these alternative schools, and issues related to labeling and discrimination were noted for the first time.

During the late 1800s, Alfred Binet developed an objective and standardized way to detect deviance form normal intellectual functioning. In 1916, this test was modified by Lewis Terman and named the Stanford–Binet Scale. The scale was one of the first standardized instruments to compare each child's performance with standardized norms at different age ranges. Development of this test assisted with identification of learning problems in school. The discriminative ability of the Stanford–Binet test influenced several scientists in the 1920s to begin longitudinal studies, using large numbers of children to produce standard norms on physical, intellectual, emotional, and behavioral characteristics.

Starting in the late 1800s, political organizations that promoted the welfare of children first began to appear. These organizations helped to facilitate federal funding for child mental health treatment centers and helped to establish child protection laws. In 1870, the first child abuse case was processed in court by the American Society for the Prevention of Cruelty to Animals. About this time, the Society for the Prevention of Cruelty to Children was founded. Public responsibility for delinquent children was expedited with correctional institutions in America. In 1909, President Theodore Roosevelt organized the first White House Conference on Children. His political reform movement condemned various cruelties perpetrated by adults toward children. The U.S. government provided funding to initiate the Children's Bureau in 1912 to protect the rights and welfare of children and to provide aid to dependent children. Volunteer services for children (e.g., Child Welfare League of America) also were formed. Federally funded child development institutes in the United States were initiated after the Iowa Child Welfare Research Station was founded in 1916 to study the cognitive and behavioral development of children. In 1922, Adolph Meyer, a member of the National Committee on Mental Hygiene, formally requested that psychiatrists be placed in the school system to work with teachers to prevent problems that would interfere with school performance and healthy psychological development. After the Wages and Hours Bill was passed in 1938, children under 16 years of age were no longer allowed to work in hazardous occupations.

The first psychology clinic was established in 1896 at the University of Pennsylvania by Lightner Witmer. This was the first clinic to assess, treat, and study primarily childhood difficulties relevant to school performance, such as stuttering, spelling, and learning disabilities. Target populations were individuals with mental retardation, gifted children with speech impediments, and those requiring vocational adjustment. These clinics helped to foster the development of child treatment centers that began to emerge in the first decades of the 20th century, focusing on educational problems, social dysfunction, and behavioral disorders. The National Committee for Mental Hygiene was founded in 1909, which, in part, sponsored research surveys on children's mental health issues and paved the way for child guidance clinics. In 1909, William Healy established the Juvenile Psychopathic Institute, which primarily focused on the etiology, prevention, and treatment of juvenile delinquents. He also emphasized the social–affective aspects of development and was largely responsible for the beginning of the child guidance movement. The purpose of these clinics was to diagnose and provide psychological treatment recommendations for children who were referred by the juvenile court system. The court system sent most juvenile offenders to state outpatient clinics but also included referrals to child youth organizations such as the YMCA. These organizations were established to provide juveniles with prosocial activities to reduce delinquency rates that had been exacerbated by increased urbanization. By 1932, there were more than 200 clinics in America. The earliest investigative studies of child psychotherapy effectiveness were performed at child guidance clinics during the 1930s and 1940s. Such investigations revealed that about 75% of children evaluated demonstrated significant improvement. However, these investigations were based exclusively on therapists' judgments of improvement and, of course, they were not controlled comparison conditions. By the early 1930s, many colleges included departments for special education, and some states required certification to teach special education to children with intellectual, behavioral, or physical disabilities. Edouard Sequin became the first person to study the mentally retarded, including methods to teach these individuals. This led to the development of schools that were specifically designed to educate mentally retarded children. Unfortunately, these interventions were largely ineffective.

The Juvenile Justice Delinquency Prevention Act implemented in 1974 was the catalyst for community-based diversion programs. With this act, federal funding was made available to deinstitutionalized juvenile status offenders to remove the stigma of court records, prevent association with other more chronic offenders, and promote rehabilitation. In 1975, the Education for All Handicapped Children Act guaranteed the right of public education for all handicapped children. This law stated that, to receive federal funds supporting special education, a state must provide free education to all handicapped children between the ages of 3 and 21. Currently, most child guidance clinics have been incorporated into broad-based mental health centers. In addition to these centers, there has been a dramatic increase in the number of programs offering training in clinical child psychology, and clinical psychology doctoral programs now routinely offer courses and specialization tracks in child psychology.

EMERGENCE OF CHILD PSYCHOTHERAPY

Psychoanalytic Therapies for Children

In 1915, Hermine von Hug-Hellmuth modified adult psychoanalysis for use with children employing drawings and play techniques. Approximately 10 years later, publication of Anna Freud and Melanie Klein's work established child psychoanalysis as a discipline. Child psychoanalysis was easily adopted by most psychiatrists working in America's child guidance clinics. Differences in basic analytic concepts led to more specialized methods. However, most psychoanalytic therapies for children are aimed at bringing unconscious conflicts into conscious awareness through play and art. With play therapy, the therapist attempts to establish an alliance with the child using toys and games. In this manner, the child feels comfortable expressing feelings without criticism and purportedly learns to manage feelings and develop adaptive abilities, while experiencing self-acceptance. Dynamically oriented child psychotherapists typically perform therapy in "play therapy rooms," but sessions are less frequent than with adult counterparts. From the mid-1950s to the mid-1960s, psychodynamically oriented psychotherapies were considered to be the only accepted strategies in residential settings. However, by the 1980s, behavioral therapies started to become recognized as the psychological intervention of choice due to their efficacy in controlled trials (Gelfand, Jenson, & Drew, 1982). Indeed, behavioral strategies are now routinely applied in clinical settings (see Kendall, 1991; Kratochwill & Morris, 1991).

Behavioral Psychotherapies for Children

Lightner Witmer's emphasis on observed behavior as opposed to inferred internal phenomena paved the way for the empirical evaluation of child psychotherapies, although John Watson's deconditioning of simple fears in young children in the 1920s frequently is considered to be the beginning of the behavioral movement. Other studies, such as Mowrer and Mowrer's investigation with childhood nighttime enuresis, using the "bell-and-pad" technique, brought increased attention to the efficacy of behavioral procedures. However, the established influence of psychoanalytic theories overshadowed reports that appeared from the 1920s to the 1950s on the laboratory-derived principles of behavior.

B. F. Skinner's *Science of Human Behavior* in 1953 was one of the first popular texts to describe the application of empirically derived theories of learning to social issues and human psychology. Based on the fundamentals of Skinner's laboratory studies, Sidney Bijou and his associates (Beer, Wolf, and Risely) at the University of Washington used operant programs in the late 1950s to early 1960s to improve social skills and academic performance with handicapped children. Other behaviorists, such as Ivar Lovaas and Nathan Azrin, employed operant conditioning techniques with autistic and mentally retarded populations in the 1960s. Studies in the 1960s began to demonstrate successful outcomes using behavioral techniques with disorders that appeared to be untreatable with standard approaches (e.g., severe vomiting, physical self-abuse). Less severe problems in children, including bedtime crying, inappropriate classroom behavior, and thumb sucking—also were treated effectively with behavioral interventions,. With the increased study and application of behavioral techniques, behavior therapy journals began to appear in the 1960s and 1970s: *Behaviour Research and Therapy* in 1963, *Journal of Applied Behavior Analysis* in 1968,

Behavior Therapy in 1970, *Journal of Behavior Therapy and Experimental Psychiatry* in 1970, *Behavior Modification* in 1976, and *Child Behavior Therapy* in 1979. During the 1950s to 1960s, clinics and educational settings applying behavioral psychotherapy demonstrated remarkable therapeutic gains. However, follow-up evaluation of concurrent behaviors and generalization of results were lacking. Very few controlled outcome studies with sophisticated experimental designs were extant. In addition, behavioral therapists largely ignored cognitive and developmental factors. By the 1970s, however, behavioral scientists began to incorporate cognitive techniques to facilitate internal control in children successfully and to improve outcome in disorders, such as social withdrawal, aggression, learning disabilities, and hyperactivity. The 1980s brought about recognition of modeling influences (Bandura, 1986) and developmental factors (Forehand & Wierson, 1993) in the treatment of children. Presently, behavioral techniques have been applied to the entire spectrum of childhood disorders. Treatment outcome studies investigating directive therapies are now very sophisticated. Studies routinely include examination of differential treatment responsiveness due to various demographic variables, sampling of subjects with statistically validated power, measures of therapist protocol adherence, and utilization of comprehensive interventions and multiple assessment instruments to measure treatment outcome.

PSYCHOPHARMACOLOGY WITH CHILDREN

Although adult psychopharmacological research has become widespread in the last 20 years, psychopharmacological research with children has lagged behind on a comparative basis. This is due to several factors, including the unique biologic system of the developing child, the relatively few diagnoses that are only specific to children, the inability of children to articulate evaluative comments related to drug response, and the reluctance of some humane research committees to permit pharmacological study of minors.

Children absorb, metabolize, and eliminate drugs at different rates, thereby resulting in distinct reactions to psychotropic medications at various age levels. Prepubescent children have efficient livers that allow them to metabolize drugs rapidly. After puberty, drug metabolism decelerates. These changing rates of metabolism make it difficult to prescribe psychotropic medications in a standardized manner. Reports of children who died after tricyclic antidepressant medication treatments underscore the care and sensitivity clinical researchers must exercise when treating children with psychopharmacologic drugs (Biederman, 1991).

Drug therapy for the treatment of child psychopathology was almost exclusively nonexistent prior to the 1930s. Benzedrine, a stimulant, was the first drug that was systematically studied with children. In a pioneering study, Bradley (1937) demonstrated the effectiveness of benzedrine for the improvement of school performance with children living in the first group home in America. Effectiveness of benzedrine was substantiated when later studies found that this drug improved verbal intelligence scores for adolescents. Although benzedrine continued to be widely used throughout the 1940s, it was gradually replaced with other stimulants (e.g., dextroamphetamine) because of their equally efficacious results at reportedly lower doses. Methylphenidate (Ritalin) was synthesized in 1954 and quickly became one of the most frequently prescribed drugs for children in the 1950s and 1960s.

Stimulant medications have continued to maintain their popularity with psychiatrists today. These medications are currently the most frequently prescribed psychotropic drugs in child psychiatry, with more than 6% of elementary-aged children receiving these medications (Wilens & Biederman, 1992). They are favored by practitioners because they are among the safest and most effective medications for the management of childhood psychiatric disorders, particularly attention-deficit hyperactivity disorder (Gadow, 1992). Approximately 70% to 80% of all children respond favorably to stimulant medication. However, efficacy of stimulants may be short-lived, as their long-term success is not supported in the literature (Greenhill, 1992).

Major Tranquilizers (Neuroleptics)

Major tranquilizers (e.g., chlorpromazine), also known as antipsychotic agents, are the treatment of choice for active psychotic states. Other neuroleptics (e.g., haloperidol) have been used to treat motor and vocal tics. Psychotropic medications were first investigated in the 1950s, but were reported to have unwanted side effects with children and thus were not widely accepted at that time. Major tranquilizers, including the piperazines (e.g., thioridazine, thiothixene, trifluoperazine, fluphenazine, and prochlorperazine) and the piperidine compounds (e.g., thioridazine, thiothixene, & haloperidol) began to be researched with children in the mid-1960s to early 1970s. Recent studies investigating major tranquilizers with children have demonstrated improvements in hyperactivity, learning ability, and aggression. However, adverse side effects resulting from neuroleptic medications (e.g., dyskinesias, sedation, dystonias, & Parkinsonian symptoms) suggest that these medications should only be used in the most severe cases. It is interesting to note that side effects caused by pharmacological drugs with children were first reported during the 1960s. However, recent studies of toxicity have added little to what was originally determined from earlier studies (Gadow, 1992).

Antidepressants

Antidepressant medications (e.g., imipramine, desipramine) also were introduced for use in the 1960s to treat a variety of disorders. Early studies with imipratnine (Tofranil) and amitripyline (Elavil) were encouraging. However, recent studies using controlled double-blind procedures have found antidepressants to be no more effective than placebos for depressed adolescents and prepubertal children (see reviews by Gadow, 1992; Ryan, 1992). Of the few controlled studies that have evaluated use of tricyclic antidepressants with children, the number of participants has been minimal and the results mixed, suggesting the efficacy of the tricyclic antidepressants remains to be demonstrated. Such discouraging lack of confirming data has encouraged study of other medications for childhood depression, including human augmentation and monoamine oxidase inhibitors. However, efficacy of these medications for use with children is uncertain at this time.

The first text on pediatric psychopharmacology (Werry, 1978) and the inauguration of the *Journal of Child and Adolescent Psychopharmacology* reflect the increased attention to biological aspects of child psychiatry in the literature. Presently, there is a trend to evaluate use of medications in a more methodologically sound manner and as a conjoint therapy to facilitate behavioral therapies (Dupaul & Barkley, 1993). The complementary effects of behavior therapy and psychopharmacology also have been acknowledged in the literature (Hersen, 1985). However, dose–response issues are still largely unanswered, thus making it somewhat difficult to evaluate the synergistic effects of behavior therapy and pharmacotherapy.

DIAGNOSTIC AND CLASSIFICATION SYSTEMS WITH CHILDREN

With the vast number of psychotherapists believing in different fundamental principles, it is essential that a commonly espoused diagnostic system define psychological disorders in terms of age-specific symptoms so that observations be reliable. Interestingly, however, it was not until the 20th century that children and adolescents were included in standard classification systems of mental illness. The two most commonly used methods of classification used in child psychopathology are the nosological approach (classification of disease) and the psychometric or empirical approach (measuring the degree to which particular children manifest particular problems).

Nosological Model of Classification

To provide a standardized method of statistically coding psychiatric cases, members of the American Psychiatric Association's Committee of Nomenclature and Statistics established the first *Diagnostic and Statistical Manual of Mental Disorders* (*DSM–I* [1st ed.]; [APA], 1952). This was the first manual of mental disorders to contain a glossary of descriptions of the diagnostic categories. Childhood disorders were represented with a single classification, designated *Transient Situational Personality Disorders*. This novel classification included adjustment reactions of infancy, childhood, and adolescence that were thought to represent acute symptom responses capable of remitting when stress in the environment diminished. Childhood adjustment reactions were divided into three categories that identified habit disturbances (e.g., thumb sucking, enuresis, masturbation, tantrums); conduct disturbances (e.g., truancy, stealing, destructiveness, cruelty, sexual offenses, use of alcohol); and neurotic traits (e.g., tics, phobias, overactivity, somnambulism, stammering). Psychotic reaction in children, including primary autism, were classified as *Schizophrenic reaction, childhood type*. Of all the categories in the *DSM–I*, only the Schizoid Personality category described the progression of pathology from childhood to adulthood: "As children, they are usually quiet, shy, obedient, sensitive and retiring. At puberty, they frequently become more withdrawn, then manifesting the aggregate of personality traits known as introversion, namely, quietness, seclusiveness, "n-ness" and unsociability, often with eccentricity" (APA, 1952, p. 35). Supplementary terms specific to childhood also were coded in this manual but were not described (e.g., enuresis, feeding problems in children, tantrums, and thumb sucking).

In 1966, the Group for Advancement of Psychiatry, primarily as a result of the absence of a child psychopathology classification, developed its own nomenclature in its attempt to be systematic. However, this system relied primarily on clinical judgment and did not have an empirical base. Thus, it suffered from the same flaws as did the *DSM–I* (APA, 1952). Nonetheless, this system did underscore the importance of developing a viable classificatory system for children and adolescents. In 1968, the *DSM* (2nd ed. [*DSM–II*]; APA, 1968) was published as a revision of the *DSM–I* to modify descriptions of many disorders, recognize nomenclature, and encourage the recording of multiple psychiatric diagnoses. Two main categories were included in this manual for use with children. The first category, *Transient Situational Disturbances*, was generally the same as it had been in the *DSM–I*, as it included adjustment reactions of infancy, childhood, and adolescence. A new category, *Behavior Disorders of Childhood and Adolescence*, described childhood disorders that were "more stable, internalized, and resistant to treatment than transient situational disturbances, but less so than psychoses, neuroses, and personality disorders" (APA, 1968). The childhood disorders within this classification included various "reactions of childhood or adolescence" (e.g., hyperkinetic, overanxious, runaway, unsocialized, aggressive, withdrawing, and group delinquent).

In 1980, a revised *DSM* replaced the *DSM–II* as an attempt to provide more objective criteria to assist with categorization. More than four times as many categories specific for use with children were contained in the *DSM–III*. New developments of the *DSM–III* included requirement of a specific number of pathological characteristics to receive a diagnosis, duration of disturbance, and exclusion of related psychological disturbances. The *DSM–III* relied less on psychoanalytic terms than did earlier editions and emphasized observable behavior. For the first time, multiaxial classification system allowed children to be assessed with several distinct dimensions (e.g., physical conditions, global functioning).

Many researchers were dissatisfied with the reliability and validity of numerous *DSM–III* subtypes of childhood disorders, as well as its assumptions that mental illness was stable across time and hierarchical. In 1987, the *DSM–III* was revised in an effort to accommodate new information adduced from contemporary diagnostic studies and to become more atheoretical by avoiding etiological inferences and instead relying on observable (reportable) symptoms (Frances, Pincus, Wideger, Davis, & First, 1994). The *revised edition of the DSM–III* (3rd ed. [*DSM–III-R*]; APA, 1987) and currently used *DSM–IV* (APA, 1994) are much more sensitive to child psychopathology than their predecessors. A fourth axis was developed to incorporate psychosocial stressors and environmental problems for children and adolescents (e.g., rejecting and harsh parents). A new section entitled "Disorders Usually First Diagnosed in Infancy, Childhood, or Adolescence" includes greater detail of common disorders found within these age ranges (e.g., mental retardation, pervasive developmental disorders, disruptive behavior disorders, anxiety disorders, gender identity disorders, and elimination disorders). Advances in the objective study of the personality disorders resulted in the empirically justified inclusion of personality disorders in adolescents. With the exception of occasional features that apply specifically to infants, children, and adolescents, the "essential" features of the Mood Disorders and Schizophrenia categories are considered to be the same in children and adults in the *DSM–III–R* and *DSM–IV*. Modifications from the *DSM–III–R* to *DSM–IV* include denoting some of the disorders "learning disorders" (previously denoted "academic skills disorders"); changing the relation to the time within which symptoms must have been evident prior to diagnosis (e.g., Rett's Disorder); changing the names of some disorders (e.g., "elective mutism" to "selective mutism"); and changing symptom criteria for many disorders (e.g., social phobia, tic disorders, conduct disorder); (see Volkmar & Schwab-Stone, 1996). Relative to previous versions of the *DSM*, the *DSM–IV* committees utilized higher thresholds in making revisions; attended to the needs of a diverse professional audience (e.g., researchers, educators, clinicians); and utilized multiple work groups, consisting of 50 to 100 advisors and participants who had major responsibility in establishing the syndromes (Jenson & Hoagwood, 1997).

Empirical Model of Classification

Historically, diagnostic categories for children have evolved from clinical observation. Using the clinical approach to classification, those familiar with child psychopathology classify behavior problems according to a consensus of experiential rather than empirical validation. Starting in the mid-1900s, however, there has been increased emphasis on the use of sophisticated statistical techniques to determine behavioral correlates, thus forming empirically derived syndromes of deviant behaviors that then may be coded into a classification system. Hewitt and Jenkins (1946) performed the first systematic investigation of children using statistical techniques to isolate interrelated patterns of childhood behavioral problems. These investigations examined intercorrelations of 45 behaviors from the records of 500 children admitted to a child guidance clinic. From their visual inspection of the intercorrelations, the researchers found three syndromes among the behavioral traits (e.g., unsocialized aggressive, socialized delinquent, and overinhibited).

Peterson (1961) performed one of the first studies with factor analysis (a statistical procedure that isolates clusters of behaviors that are interrelated) to classify childhood behavior problems. Peterson examined the records of over 400 children who were treated in a child guidance clinic. The most frequently occurring problems were incorporated into a checklist of 58 items descriptive of deviant behavior. This checklist was given to 831 grammar school children. A factor analysis was able to classify the problem behaviors of these children into either "conduct" (aggressive) or "personality" (withdrawal) syndromes.

Since Peterson's (1961) investigations, there have been dozens of factor analytic studies that have attempted to construct a behavioral taxonomy for disorders of childhood and adolescence. In a review of the behavioral taxonomy literature, Quay (1986) found only a few behavioral classifications that cluster together. A dimension most reasonably labeled "Undersocialized Aggressive Conduct Disorder" (e.g., aggressive, disruptive, noncompliant) was found in over 30% of the 61 studies reviewed. Anxiety–Withdrawal–Dysphoria Disorder (anxious, shy, sad, hypersensitive) was found to be the second-most frequently appearing behavioral cluster of problem behaviors. Immaturity, Attention-Deficit Disorder (e.g., poor concentration, daydreaming, distractible) involves problems of concentration, including both hyper- and hypoactivity. A pattern labeled *Socialized Conduct Disorder* (e.g., having "bad" companions, truancy, stealing in company of others) has emerged less frequently.

As summarized by Achenbach and McConaughy (1996), similarities between nosological approaches (e.g., *DSM–IV*) and empirically based approaches (e.g., Revised Behavior Problem Checklist) include specification of problem behaviors, similar content between some diagnostic categories and empirically-based syndromes, and statistical agreement between some diagnoses (nosological) and syndrome scores (empirically based). There also are several dissimilarities between the two approaches. First, in the nosological approach, problems are judged as absent or present, but in the empirical approach, they are scored quantitatively. Second, in the nosological approach, cutpoints are identical across demographic variables, but in the empirical approach, cutpoints are based on norms. Third, in the nosological approach, judgments are involved in decision making, but in the empirical approach, syndromes are based according to standard forms.

SUMMARY

The scientific study of psychopathology in children has emerged relatively recently after centuries of child neglect and maltreatment. Prior to the 1800s, indifference to high rates of child mortality—due to physical abuse, long hours of employment in poor working conditions, and malnutrition—was reflected in laws that overlooked the welfare of children. In fact, until the 1600s, it was legal to publicly scorn, torture, and kill mentally ill children because of their increased "burden" to society. The harsh treatment of children generally improved in the 1900s due to child protection laws that were encouraged by the mental hygiene and child guidance movements.

As recently as 1982, only one of every nine mental health dollars was spent on services for children and adolescents, despite their representation of almost 50% of the population. Child psychological, psychopharmacological, and diagnostic research is largely a 20th-century phenomenon. Prevention and treatment of child psychopathology, until recently, have been an extrapolation of adult psychopathology, and the field indeed is still not as sophisticated or comprehensive as that found in adult psychopathology.

REFERENCES

Achenbach, T. M., & McConaughy, S. H. (1996). Relations between *DSM–IV* and empirically-based assessment. *School Psychology Review, 25*, 329–341.

American Psychiatric Association. (1952). *Diagnostic and statistical manual of mental disorders.* Washington, DC: Author.

American Psychiatric Association. (1968). *Diagnostic and statistical manual of mental disorders* (2nd ed.). Washington, DC: Author.

American Psychiatric Association. (1980). *Diagnostic and statistical manual of mental disorders* (3rd ed.). Washington, DC: Author.

American Psychiatric Association. (1987). *Diagnostic and statistical manual of mental disorders* (3rd ed., rev.). Washington, DC: Author.

American Psychiatric Association. (1994). *Diagnostic and statistical manual of mental disorders* (4th ed.). Washington, DC: Author.

Bandura, A. (1986). *Social foundations of thought and action: A social cognitive theory.* Englewood Cliffs, NJ: Prentice-Hall.

Biederman, J. (1991). Sudden death in children treated with a tricyclic antidepressant. *Journal of the American Academy of Child and Adolescent Psychiatry, 30*, 495–498.

Bradley, C. (1937). The behavior of children receiving Benzedrine. *American Journal of Psychiatry, 94*, 577–585.

Dupaul, G. J., & Barkley, R. A. (1993). Behavioral contributions to pharmacotherapy: The utility of behavioral methodology in medication treatment of children with attention deficit hyperactivity disorder. *Behavior Therapy, 24*, 117–141.

Forehand, R., & Wierson, M. (1993). The role of developmental factors in planning behavioral interventions for children: Disruptive behavior as an example. *Behavior Therapy, 24*, 117–141.

Frances, A. J., Pincus, H. A., Widiger, T. A., Davis, W. W., & First, M. B. (1994). *DSM–IV*: Work in progress. In J. E. Mezzich, M. R. Jorge, & I. M. Salloum (Eds.), *Psychiatric epidemiology: Assessment concepts and methods* (pp. 116–135). Baltimore: John Hopkins University Press.

Gadow, K. D. (1992). Pediatric psychopharmacotherapy: A review of recent research. *Journal of Child Psychology and Pediatric Psychiatry, 33, 153*–195.

Gelfand, D. M., Jenson, W. R., & Drew, C. J. (1982). *Understanding child behavior disorders.* New York: Wiley.

Greenhill, L. L. (1992). Pharmacologic treatment of attention deficit hyperactivity Disorder. *Psychiatric Clinics of North America, 15*, 1–27.

Hersen, M. (Ed.). (1985). *Pharmacological and behavioral treatment: An integrative approach.* New York: Wiley.

Hewitt, L. E., & Jenkins, R. L. (1946). *Fundamental patterns of maladjustment: The dynamics of their origin.* Springfield: State of Illinois.

Jenson, P. S., & Hoagwood, K. (1997). The book of names: *DSM–IV* in context. *Development and Psychopathology, 9*, 231–249.

Kendall, P. C. (Ed.). (1991). *Child and adolescent therapy: Cognitive behavioral procedures.* New York: Guilford.

Kratochwill, T. R., & Morris, R. J. (1991). *The practice of child therapy* (2nd ed.). Boston: Allyn & Bacon.

Peterson, D. R. (1961). Behavior problems of middle childhood. *Journal of Clinical Psychology, 25*, 205–209.

Phaire, T. (1545). *The boke of chyldren*.

Quay, H. C. (1986). Classification. In H. C. Quay & J. S. Werry (Eds.), *Psychopathological disorders of childhood* (3rd ed., pp. 1–34). New York: Wiley.

Ryan, N. D. (1992). The pharmacologic treatment of child and adolescent depression. *Psychiatric Clinics of North America, 15*, 29–40.

Skinner, B. F. (1953). *Science and human behavior*. New York: Macmillan.

Volkmar, F. R., & Schwab-Stone, M. (1996). Annotation: Childhood disorders in *DSM–IV. Journal of Child Psychology and Psychiatry, 37*, 779–784.

Werry, J. S. (Ed.). (1978). *Pediatric psychopharmacology: The use of behavior modifying drugs in children*. New York: Brunner/Mazel.

Wilens, T. E., & Biederman, J. (1992). The stimulants. *Psychiatric Clinics of North America, 15*, 191–222.

Diagnosis and Classification

Joseph R. Scotti
Tracy L. Morris
West Virginia University

Psychology has been called the science of human behavior (e.g., Hilgard, 1987; O'Donohue & Krasner, 1995; Plaud & Eifert, 1998). As scientists—whether basic or applied—psychologists engage in one of the most fundamental steps common to any scientific endeavor, that of classifying the phenomena of interest. Within psychology, particularly the more applied branches, this activity of classification is more commonly known as *diagnosis*. Scientists typically take one of two approaches to the issue of classification: *inductive*—"bottom-up"—or *deductive*—"top down," (see Cone, 1986, 1988). These two approaches are most closely related, within psychology, to the person-centered and behavior-focused *idiographic* approach, and the group-oriented (or norm-referenced) and trait-focused *nomothetic* approach (see Cone, 1986, 1988), although these distinctions rarely are stated explicitly and typically are highly overlapping. A key difference in these two approaches to the subject matter is that, in the inductive approach, one accumulates multiple observations about typical and atypical behavior and orders them along dimensions of similarity and dissimilarity. The taxonomy that this creates becomes the basis for further observations and eventually leads to the development of theory—in this case, theories of behavior and psychopathology. In the deductive approach, one begins with theory (although this clearly must be based on at least an informal observation of behavior) and seeks to gather data that confirm or disconfirm the theory.

Whether deductively or inductively derived, classification schemes are essentially deductively applied. That is, the amassed clinical data and theoretical conceptualizations that form a scheme of classification and diagnosis are applied by making inferences from the general to the specific case. Eschewing this deductive application of data and theory to the individual case would be tantamount to requiring that practitioners rediscover anew the principles of behavior—normal and pathological—for each case that presents to them. Thus, the categories created in a diagnostic classification scheme (i.e., "syndromes" or "disorders") provide "fundamental guidance" in the initial stages of a functional analysis (Hayes & Follette, 1992, p. 352) that ultimately leads to the identification of an intervention strategy. One begins the diagnostic and classification process at the nomothetic level, deductively applying to the single case what is known about persons who engage in similar patterns of behavior, in terms of response classes and behavioral covariation, etiology and prognosis, and lines of intervention likely to be successful (based on past experience and research).

However one proceeds, the focus is on the classification of behavior that is deemed pathological, deviant, or abnormal along some number of dimensions. That behavior, however, may as often be viewed as symptomatic of underlying disease processes or psychodynamic conflicts, as it is of members of a common, covarying class of responses. This distinction—as with several of the others noted previously (i.e., ideographic vs. nomothetic; inductive vs. deductive)—strikes to the heart of a key distinction within the area of diagnosis and classification: traditional versus behavioral assessment (Barrios & Hartmann, 1986; Cone, 1988; Goldfried & Kent, 1972). What we present in this chapter is our view on the integration of behavioral assessment with more traditional approaches in the classification and diagnosis process. We view classification and diagnosis as an important start to the clinical intervention process—although clearly there are times when these are ends in themselves, such as in the conduct of incidence and prevalence studies. We begin where the classification process must always start, with a consideration of what constitutes the very subject matter itself.

ABNORMAL: BY WHAT CRITERIA?

Clearly, the focus of diagnostic classification schemes within psychology has been on behavior that is considered to be deviant, abnormal, or harmful in some way. Not all classification schemes focus on behavior; some also classify contingencies or environments (Bandura, 1968; McReynolds, 1979, 1986), or even the kind and level (e.g., intermittent, limited, extensive, pervasive) of supports (i.e., resources and strategies, such as people, environments, and assistive technology) that enhance a person's life, for example, independence and interdependence, productivity, community integration, and quality of life (American Association on Mental Retardation, 1992). Generally, however, the focus is on what people do—or fail to do—in ways (i.e., frequency, quality, situational context) that deviate from the norm. Because the *Diagnostic and Statistical Manual of Mental Disorders* (*DSM*), currently in its fourth edition (American Psychiatric Association [APA], 1994), is the system of classification that will be most familiar to and utilized by readers of this volume, we note here the definition of a *mental disorder* as given in that work:

> [It is] a clinically significant behavioral or psychological syndrome or pattern that occurs in an individual and that is associated with present distress (e.g., painful symptoms) or disability (i.e., impairment in one or more important areas of functioning) or with a significantly increased risk of suffering death, pain, disability, or an important loss of freedom. In addition, this syndrome or pattern must not be merely an expectable and culturally sanctioned response to a particular event, for example, the death of a loved one. Whatever its original cause, it must currently be considered a manifestation of a behavioral, psychological, or biological dysfunction in the individual. Neither deviant behavior (e.g., political, religious, or sexual) nor conflicts that are primarily between the individual and society are mental disorders unless the deviance or conflict is a symptom of a dysfunction in the individual, as described above. (APA, 1994, pp. xxi–xxii)

This definition is a useful one, despite the immediate shortcomings inherent in the very term that is defined: *mental disorders*. The term itself, which the *DSM* openly admits to being inadequate (APA, 1994, p. xxi), conjures up two important "bogymen" in the history of psychological diagnosis: (a) the mind–body dualism implied by "mental," and (b) the disease model of behavior pathology implicit in the term "disorder." It is quite clear that there are both "physical" and "mental" aspects to abnormal behavior, whether one considers this from the viewpoint of the relation between physical (i.e., medical) disorders and their underlying physiological basis and resulting psychological disorders (e.g., depression as a disorder of mood with a physical basis, such as insufficient levels of serotonin); or from a triple-response mode perspective in which all disorders have important overt behavioral, covert cognitive–behavioral (of which one may or may not be aware), and potentially measurable physiological components. The traditional disease model that is implicit in the term "disorder" follows on this distinction, as it connotes the action of an underlying physiological disease process for all mental disorders, behavioral disorders, or both. Our own preference for more behavioral terminology (e.g., symptom, syndrome, and system) carries its own baggage.

We would remind readers, however, that the current *DSM* system is descriptive; thus, the categories of disorders reflect a cataloging of the overt behaviors and reportable (but often unverifiable, see Evans, 1986) covert (i.e., cognitive) behaviors that appear to covary with each other (either based on clinical experience or—preferably—statistical analysis; for summaries of such factor analytic work with attention deficit hyperactivity disorder [ADHD] and conduct disorder, see Barkley, 1997; McMahon & Estes, 1997). Referring to these covarying sets of behaviors (more neutral than the term *symptoms* or *syndrome*) in as nonpejorative a manner as possible is desirable in order to lessen the implicit assumption of common cause, be that medical, environmental, or psychodynamic, or whatever. The issue may really be one of levels of analysis, however (see Staats, 1990, 1995). It would be foolish to assert that the etiological and maintaining factors for any *DSM* mental disorder are solely genetic, physiological, or environmental in nature. We must consider the role of each of these factors (and others) and then determine the level (or levels) at which conceptualization and intervention will be most fruitful, that is, one must decide whether the most profitable level of intervention will be pharmacological (for disorders with a physical basis), behavioral or cognitive–behavioral (for disorders with strong environmental influences), or some combination of these and other strategies.

Normal Behavior

In deciding what even constitutes "abnormal" behavior, it is interesting to note that the field did not begin with a conceptualization of what constitutes normal behavior, that is, there is little empirical basis for saying how a particular behavior deviates from a known norm, standard, or baseline (Adams & Cassidy, 1993). Several schemes for classifying normal behavior have been proposed (see Adams & Cassidy, 1993; Buss, 1966). For example, within the positive mental health movement, Jahoda (1958) listed six criteria for mental health and normality, including a balance of psychic forces, self-actualization, resistance to stress, autonomy, competence, and perception of reality. More recently, Adams, Doster, and Calhoun (1977) outlined multiple response systems (e.g., emotional, sensory–perceptual, cognitive, motor, biological needs, acquired biological needs, social, and complex variations) within which normal activity could be specified, thus helping to identify when expected variability became an excessive deviation from the norm. Such systems are not standard practice in psychological classification schemes, however. Instead, the approach generally has been a top-down, deductive one: developing theories of human pathology (based on clinical observations) for which categories and then criteria seem to have been developed in an attempt to garner support (e.g., the "neurosis" as described in psychodynamic theory and later codified in the first edition of the *DSM*).

Criteria for Abnormality

A typical approach to defining abnormal behavior is to evaluate its occurrence within the general population in terms of frequency, duration, or intensity. In such an approach, rarity is equivalent to abnormality—especially when one also can determine that the duration or intensity of the behavior exceeds "normal limits." Adams and Cassidy (1993) described this as the *multivariate model* and noted Costello's (1980) warning that the obverse is not always true, that is, a response pattern may not be normal or socially acceptable simply because it is one that occurs with high frequency within the population (sexual abuse is one such example of a frequent but unacceptable set of behaviors). Epidemiological studies of the incidence (i.e., new cases meeting criteria within a specified timeframe) and prevalence (i.e., whether a case has ever met criteria within a specified time-frame) are the main methods for establishing this criteria for abnormality. However, this is only one step in classifying a behavior pattern as pathological.

Other critical features that have been considered include whether the pattern of behavior: (a) is harmful to the person or others in their environment; (b) differs significantly from some optimal level of performance or competence (such as being different—even bizarre—in quality, quantity, or intensity; or is inefficient or ineffective); or (c) causes distress for the person or important others in their environment (see Barrios, 1988; Buss, 1966; Hawkins, 1986). These features pertain to the *criterion of labeled deviance,* the violation of social norms, and the *criterion of adjustment,* whether behavior is effective in meeting ones social and biological needs (see Adams & Cassidy, 1993). Homosexuality is the classic example of a behavior pattern that was once considered to be a mental disorder, being listed as a sexual deviation in both the first and second editions of the *DSM* (APA, 1952, 1968). Although local norms and conventions still vary widely, the broader society is more generally accepting of homosexual behavior during the 1990s than it was during the 1950s; thus, homosexual behavior no longer meets the criteria of labeled deviance. If, however, a man who engages in homosexual behavior finds his lifestyle and sexual orientation to be an ongoing source of internal (rather than due to external or social pressures) conflict and distress—so much so that it may be interfering with his social and occupational functioning and even may be related to physical symptoms—then the criterion of adjustment still may be met for this individual. Clearly, as more of these criteria are met—that is, frequency, deviance, and adjustment—the more abnormal and pathological a behavioral pattern becomes.

Such considerations often have—implicitly or explicitly—a focus on single behaviors that are deemed abnormal or problematic in and of themselves. In practice, the concern is also with a constellation or class of covarying behaviors that need to be addressed as a system rather than as individual targets or symptoms (Barrios, 1988; Evans, 1985, 1986; Scotti, Evans, Meyer, & DiBenedetto, 1991; Scotti, McMorrow, & Trawitzki, 1993). Such a consideration fits the *class* or *qualitative difference model*

(Adams & Cassidy, 1993), within which one considers the covariation of multiple responses. These responses individually may not be deviant or problematic, but taken as a co-occurring class may be classifiable as pathological. Consider, for example, recurring intrusive thoughts that any person may have from time to time. These are not, in themselves, problematic, unless they are accompanied by subjective distress and perhaps compulsions (in the case of obsessive–compulsive disorder) or avoidance and arousal (in the case of posttraumatic stress disorder). Thus, presence of other members of a class of responses that typically covary with each other and are functionally related becomes a critical issue. Such covariation is also an important concern from the standpoint of intervention, which in the field of behavior therapy has all too often been focused on single, isolated target behaviors and not the complex system of related responses with which clients actually present (Evans, 1985; Evans, Meyer, Kurkjian, & Kishi, 1988; Scotti et al., 1991; Scotti, Morris, McNeil, & Hawkins, 1996; Voeltz & Evans, 1982).

PURPOSES AND PROBLEMS

Purposes

An important question with regard to classification and diagnosis is "What purpose does it serve?" Clearly, at the most fundamental level, scientists classify the phenomena that they study; psychologists are no different. But for psychologists, there needs to be both viable scientific and clinical objectives beyond this basic level. A number of authors have suggested the following, among other objectives (Adams & Cassidy, 1993; Hersen & Bellack, 1988; Mezzich & Mezzich, 1987; Sprock & Blashfield, 1983). First is the development of a nomenclature, that is, a consistent terminology for communication among clinicians and researchers, thereby enhancing their ability to share information and conduct reliable observations, providing a common ground that is independent of theoretical orientation.

Second is the organization and recovery of information for the purposes of clinical decision-making, statistical reporting, and interpretation of archival information. Critical here is the use of such data in incidence and prevalence studies, and evaluations of the course and prognosis for various disorders. Related to this is the issue of *base-rates,* the known rates of a disorder within the general population (i.e., prevalence), but equally important are the rates at which people with certain disorders are seen in different settings. If a particular disorder is represented at very high or very low rates in the population of interest, even the most sensitive diagnostic instrument is unlikely to be any better than simply diagnosing everyone—or no one—with that disorder, thereby making the diagnostic enterprise a rather futile one (see Meehl, 1973). Generally, insufficient attention is paid to the sensitivity and specificity of diagnostic instruments, relying more often on simply whether two administrations of an instrument (i.e., test–retest or interrater) agree. Unfortunately, reliability does not assure accuracy or validity.

Third is a consideration of the differences and similarities across persons with specific disorders that will lead to an understanding of specific symptoms, course, etiology, and the identification of unique treatments. Clearly, it would be useful to understand the functional relations (the "why" of behavior) among sets of covarying symptoms, as well as etiological and maintaining factors, and the course if left untreated. All of these features should have important implications for the selection of intervention strategies. In fact, one would certainly need to question the utility of diagnosis for the practicing clinician if the same intervention package was dispensed across a range of groups regardless of diagnosis or target behavior, or if different packages were not differentially effective for specific problems. Although a variety of intervention packages are well known for their use with specific diagnostic groups (Barkley, 1987; Patterson, Reid, Jones, & Conger, 1975), there is surprisingly little evidence of differential application or efficacy (Eifert, Evans, & McKendrick, 1990; Hersen & Bellack, 1988; Scotti et al., 1993).

A fourth purpose, which is financially motivated, is the very real issue of remuneration for services. In the age of managed-care organizations that increasingly oversee the clinician's every move, reimbursement only comes with a formal diagnosis. Furthermore, the extent of reimbursement for services (i.e., rate or number of sessions) may vary with the organization's perception of the severity of the disorder and the need for specific services.

Problems

Among the most commonly stated reasons for not engaging in the process of diagnostic classification is that of the pejorative nature of diagnostic labels and the reification of disorders. Labels stick. They follow people—especially children—around, being known to employers, health care providers, insurance companies, and school officials and teachers. Labels remain even after clinical improvement has been made, creating an ongoing social stigmatization (Hersen & Bellack, 1988; Sprock & Blashfield, 1983). Diagnoses are also reified, that is, the classification becomes an entity that is seen as causal rather than merely descriptive of behavior. In what has been called a self-fulfilling prophecy, some authors have noted that diagnostic labels remove responsibility and blame for aberrant or undesirable behavior from the patient, placing it instead on the disorder that caused the behavior or that cannot be overcome despite the desire of the person to improve (Laing, 1967; Szasz, 1961). Equally troublesome is the increasing addition of "everyday problems" to the *DSM* (e.g., mathematics disorder, disorder of written expression, and caffeine-induced sleep disorder), running the great risk of medicalizing and pathologizing ever more trivial behaviors that are not true mental disorders (Szasz, 1961; Wade & Tavris, 1998). A special issue of *Cognitive and Behavioral Practice* contained a series of papers that provided an update on the issue of labels and stigmatization, including a model for understanding the impact of stigma on severe mental illness (Corrigan, 1998); personal reflections by Robert Lundin (1998) on his experience with manic-depression; and strategies for coping with stigmas on an individual level (Holmes & River, 1998) and for changing societal attitudes (Dickerson, 1998; Mayville & Penn, 1998).

Cultural Issues.   Diagnostic schemes also have been criticized for largely being Eurocentric and not well representing or even tolerating differences due to culture, ethnicity, language, and socioeconomic status (SES). Classification schemes even have been judged to be racist in nature because minority groups—especially African American males—are overrepresented in the categories of mental retardation and ADHD, to name a few (Adebimpe, 1994; Lawson, Hepler, Holladay, & Cuffel, 1994; Webb-Johnson, 1999). This situation may reflect bias within the diagnostic process or a failure to understand and account for different cultural styles of interacting, attending, expressive skills, and response to authority (Cervantes & Arroyo, 1994; Webb-Johnson, 1999). Lower SES also has been associated with higher rates of psychotic disorders (Kohn, 1973). Whether this represents a diagnostic bias or the downward drift of persons with psychotic disorders, the cause and effect relations continue to remain unclear in such data. Cross-national studies also find differences in the rates of diagnosis of certain disorders—such as schizophrenia being diagnosed at a higher rate in a U.S. sample than in a British sample. Such differences sometimes can be accounted for by adherence to different diagnostic practices (see Butcher, Narikiyo, & Bemis Vitousek, 1993, for a discussion).

Language creates a further problem in that test and interview questions do not always translate well (Okazaki & Sue, 1995), taking on sometimes important psychological differences in meaning in another language, or even in the same language but with a different cultural perspective (e.g., during an interview of an elderly, African American man in Mississippi, the man understood a question about "anxiety" to be a reference to his "nature," that is, his eagerness to have sexual intercourse). Finally, there continues to be evidence of culture-specific disorders that do not readily fit into existing Eurocentric diagnostic categories, such as (a) *koro,* an obsessive fear reported in Chinese men that their penis will withdraw into their abdomen; (b) *susto,* a condition reported in Latin America involving insomnia, apathy, depression, and anxiety, among other features; and (c) *windigo,* a cannibalistic obsession among northeastern Native Americans accompanied by mood disturbance, appetite loss, and homicidal ideation (Butcher et al., 1993; Dana, 1993).

There are two major positions on the issue of cultural differences in diagnosis, an issue that is far from resolved. The first is the *etic* approach, which assumes that there are universal commonalities such that psychiatric disorders have highly similar presentations and causes across cultures. This is a broad nomothetic view that contrasts starkly with the more idiographic and culture-specific *emic* approach. From the emic view, each culture must be understood in its own right, without reference to the perspectives and judgments of other cultures. Clearly, these two views have important implications for the broad application of classification schemes and diagnostic measures. Although there have been attempts to account for cultural difference by devising unbiased, culture-free tests (Anastasi & Urbina, 1997; Dana, 1993), the current movement is away from the construction of special tests and toward a focus on the role of the examiner. The interpretation of test results and other information feeding into the diagnostic process must take into account the examinee's cultural background, SES, cultural and religious beliefs, and life experiences (e.g., recent immigration or refugee status), among other factors. It even has been suggested that a cultural axis be added to the current *DSM* multiaxial system (Dana, 1993).

Reliability and Validity of Diagnostic Classification.

A former criticism of the *DSM* process was that disorders and their criteria were formed by the consensus of a committee of experts. This is less an issue with successive versions of the *DSM*, as there is increasing inclusion of the findings of factor analytic and group studies in the decision process (Frick et al., 1994; Lahey, Loeber, Quay, Frick, & Grimm, 1992), although expert committees still guide the process. The reliability of the diagnostic process also has improved significantly with the greater specification of objective diagnostic criteria and the use of structured clinical interviews based on those criteria.

One problem with determining the relative merit of various classification schemes is the lack of an agreed on "gold standard" for diagnosis (Tsuang, 1993). The following elements have been cited as necessary for a proper classification system: reliability, internal consistency, specificity, external validity, and utility (Quay, 1986; Werry, 1992).

Reliability for specific diagnostic categories appears to be a function of the assessment method used. Interrater reliability is often quite high when structured diagnostic interviews are employed, particularly when evaluators all have been trained by the same source. Internal consistency varies more widely across diagnoses. The criteria for certain disorders specify that only a certain subset of symptoms must be met to qualify for the disorder (e.g., 8 of 14 listed symptoms in the case of ADHD). Thus, children qualifying for a diagnosis of ADHD may represent widely heterogeneous groups, each presenting with a more or less well-defined subconstellation of symptoms. The specificity of disorders often is greater between diagnostic classes than within disorders comprising each class. For example, high rates of comorbidity often are cited for anxiety disorders (March, 1995). External validity relates to the ability of classification to relate meaningfully to issues of etiology and prognosis. Clearly, certain diagnoses are useful summary variables and do indeed relate to substantive bodies of information with respect to etiology and prognosis (e.g., mental retardation). However, continued research is necessary to improve the external validity of the diagnostic classification system as a whole. Finally, summative evaluation of the utility of our current classification systems essentially is a matter left to the consideration of each practicing clinician. As Werry (1992) noted, individuals must ask "What use is the diagnosis in the real world?" (p. 472). As increasing information is available to relate differential diagnosis to differential therapeutics, the answer increasingly will be "Accurate diagnosis allows me to provide more effective treatment to my client."

CLASSIFICATION SYSTEMS

Historical Antecedents to Current Systems

Attempts have been made throughout recorded history to classify human behavior. Early evidence of rudimentary classification systems dates to the 5th and 6th century BCE. Several ancient cultures derived astrological systems that purported to correspond to clusters of personality characteristics. Hippocrates developed a personality classification system, later refined by Galen, based on the dominance of specific bodily humors (i.e., choleric, melancholic, phlegmatic, sanguine). Some of these terms remain in use today, including melancholia (i.e., depression) and hysteria (although this is no longer attributed to a "wandering uterus"). Pythagoras supported the concept of physiognomy—the notion that psychological characteristics correspond to overt physical features. This concept was further extended by Franz Gall in the late 18th to early 19th century through the application of phrenology, an individual assessment procedure based on features of the skull (e.g., shape, bumps). Sullivan produced perhaps the most extensive system of classification based on overt features, this being his system of phenotypes (i.e., mesomorphs, endomorphs, etc.).

Diagnostic systems vaguely reminiscent of those in use today began to appear in the 19th century. In the early 1800s, Pinel proposed a diagnostic system that included the following categories: mania, melancholia, dementia, and idiotism. During this era, rapid advancements were being made in the recognition and specification of mental disorders. By 1899, Emil Kraepelin published the sixth edition of his *Textbook of Psychiatry,* in which 16 major categories of psychopathology were included. The first official diagnostic system developed by the American Psychiatric Association—the *Standard Classified Nomenclature of Diseases* (APA, 1933)---was based on the Kraepelinian classification system and included 24 major categories of psychopathology.

Current Approaches

International Classification of Diseases.   The first *International Classification of Diseases* (*ICD*) was approved in 1893 to provide epidemiologists and practitioners a relatively standard format by which mortality and morbidity data could be presented. However, it was not until the sixth edition of the *ICD* that a formal classification system for mental disorders was developed (World Health Organization [WHO], 1948). The section for mental disorders included 10 diagnostic categories of psychoses; 9 categories of psychoneuroses; and 7 categories for disorders of character, behavior, and intelligence. The *ICD* system has been revised at roughly 10-year intervals. The most recent edition (*ICD*–10, WHO, 1992) is largely compatible with the fourth edition of the *DSM* (APA, 1994), to which we now turn.

Diagnostic and Statistical Manual of Mental Disorders.   The first *DSM* was published by the APA in 1952. Three major categories of psychopathology were delineated: organic brain syndromes, functional disorders, and mental deficiency. The *DSM* was designed by a committee that failed to include any clinicians with special expertise in the area of childhood or adolescence. Only one diagnosis specific to children or adolescents was specified: adjustment reaction of childhood/adolescence, included under the heading of "Transient Situational Disorders." The *DSM* was revised in 1968 (*DSM–II*) to include 11 major diagnostic categories. Increased attention was given to problems of childhood through inclusion of a category titled "Behavior Disorders of Childhood–Adolescence" that consisted of the following diagnoses: hyperkinetic reaction, withdrawing reaction, overanxious reaction, runaway reaction, unsocialized aggressive reaction, and group delinquent reaction.

The third edition of the diagnostic manual (*DSM–III*; APA, 1980) represented a major improvement over the preceding diagnostic systems through the introduction of a multiaxial system, inclusion of explicit criteria, and removal of unsubstantiated theoretical inferences. The multiaxial system was intended to promote a more broad-band assessment of an individual's level of functioning within the context of individual, family, and community systems. The five axes of the *DSM–III* included: (a) Clinical Syndromes, (b) Personality Disorders and Developmental Disorders, (c) Physical Disorders and Conditions, (d) Psychosocial Stressors (severity rating), and (e) Global Assessment of Functioning. Consistent with a trend toward increasing complexity and specification across subsequent versions of the diagnostic classification system, 265 diagnoses were included in the *DSM–III* compared with 182 for the *DSM–II* and 108 for the original *DSM*.

The next revision of the diagnostic system (*DSM–III–R*; APA, 1987) placed more emphasis on the empirical literature with respect to the formulation and specification of operational diagnostic criteria. For the first time, the *DSM–III–R* committee utilized information from field trials with respect to basic reliability analyses to provide support for certain diagnostic categories. Increased attention was given to problems of childhood and adolescence, with the identification of five major categories of "Disorders First Evident in Childhood or Adolescence."

The *DSM–IV* (APA, 1994) was released to coincide with the 10th version of the *ICD* (WHO, 1992). *The DSM–IV* extends the emphasis on empirical findings, initiated with the *DSM–III*. Several diagnostic categories were restructured within *DSM–IV*. In particular, the number of diagnostic categories specific to childhood and adolescence has been reduced, with several diagnoses being subsumed within the corresponding "adult" diagnoses (e.g., overanxious disorder of childhood has been subsumed under generalized anxiety disorder; avoidant disorder of childhood has been subsumed under social phobia). Critics of the *DSM–IV* note that there still remains relatively insufficient emphasis on situational or contextual factors (Scotti et al., 1996).

Supplemental and Alternative Classification Schemes.   Recognizing the need for a classification scheme to address problems relevant to very young children, who largely have been ignored in the *DSM* systems, the National Center for Clinical Infant Programs has developed the Diagnostic Classification: 0–3 (DC: 0–3; Zero to Three/National Center for Clinical Programs, 1994). DC: 0–3 is a multiaxial system for classifying problems during the first 3 to 4 years of life. Similar in structure to the *DSM–IV*, the five axes of the DC: 0–3 include the following: (a) Primary Diagnosis, (b) Relationship Disorder, (c) Medical and Developmental Disorders and Conditions, (d) Psychosocial Stressors, and (e) Functional Emotional Developmental Level. Axis II (Relationship Disorder) considers three aspects of the relationship between infants and children and their caregivers: (a) behavioral quality of the interaction, (b) affective tone, and (c) psychological involvement. Assessment of functional developmental level is based largely on direct observations of child–caregiver interaction. The DC: 0–3 was designed from a developmental perspective and emphasizes the assessment of, and integration of information regarding, multiple domains of functioning (physical, cognitive, emotional, social).

In addition to "categorical" schemes such as the *DSM–IV*, empirically based "dimensional" schemes have been derived through multivariate statistical procedures (e.g., Achenbach, 1985; Quay, 1986). Dimensional approaches typically delineate symptom clusters derived from behavior problem or symptom checklists. A major assumption of the dimensional approach is that independent dimensions of behavior may be identified on which all individuals vary to certain degrees. For example, Achenbach (1991; Achenbach & Edelbrock,1981) has identified two broad-band dimensions, labeled *internalizing behavior problems* and *externalizing behavior problems,* that subsume narrow-band clusters such as *anxious/depressed* and *aggressive behavior.*

ADDITIONAL CONSIDERATIONS

Developmental Considerations

Thorough and accurate assessment requires an understanding of child development. In order to determine whether a given behavior is age-appropriate, one must have an adequate understanding of the behavior and skills that children should demonstrate across various ages (see Garber, 1984; Kavanagh & Hops, 1994). Unfortunately, many clinicians have not received adequate training in "normal" child development and thus have limited ability to evaluate adequately whether certain behaviors are indeed "abnormal." Normative information regarding physical, cognitive, and social development is necessary to place many behaviors in a proper context. Clearly, a 3-year-old child who wets the bed would not be considered in need of treatment for enuresis. In contrast, bed-wetting is considered abnormal for a 13-year-old and would warrant further evaluation and intervention. In addition to age-related factors, attention must be paid to gender differences when determining the normalcy of a given behavior. Drawing again on the example of enuresis, bed-wetting is equally common for boys and girls under age 5. However, a steeper curve with respect to the age at which bed-wetting declines is evident for girls than for boys, such that by age 11 more than twice as many boys continue to wet the bed than do girls. Such differences have led many pediatricians and child clinical psychologists to use different age criteria in determining whether bed-wetting should be a focus of clinical concern for boys versus girls. Such examples are rather straightforward; however, behavioral presentation in clinical settings is rarely so clear.

With respect to diagnostic classification, gender, race, and class differences have been reported for many categories. For example, male-to-female ratios of between 4:1 and 8:1 have been reported for ADHD (Barkley, 1996). Furthermore, differences in the behavioral expression of children meeting criteria for ADHD have been found by gender, with girls evincing more social withdrawal and less aggression than do boys. Prevalence rates for ADHD also have been found to differ across cultures (Taylor, 1994) and socioeconomic groups (Biederman et al., 1995). At this point, it is unclear whether differences across gender, culture, and SES are indeed legitimate or are merely artifacts of the inconsistent application of diagnostic criteria (see Butcher et al., 1993; Dana, 1993). However, research utilizing standardized procedures, such as structured diagnostic interviews, may help determine the validity of differences in prevalence and expression. Cohen et al. (1993) provided epidemiological information, derived from structured interview data, regarding the Age x Gender trajectories of specific disorders. Should such differences consistently be confirmed, analysis of contextual differences between groups may help elucidate relevant etiological factors.

Children Within Context

Comprehensive evaluation also requires examination of the context or contexts in which the presenting problem occurs. It is seldom the case that children refer themselves for diagnostic evaluation. Rather, one or more adults in a child's life make a judgment that the child is in need of assessment and treatment. It is incumbent on evaluators to assess the system or systems in which the presenting problem is said to have arisen. All too often, errors are made by undue focus on the child as an individual target, with failure to examine the family or school context. Issues such as parental psychopathology, interpartner conflict, and educational or economic disadvantage may influence parental perceptions and expectations of child behavior. In many cases, the most appropriate route of intervention may be to provide direct services to improve the overall functioning of the parent or parents and, consequently, the family system.

A significant shortcoming of the *DSM–IV* is the insufficient availability of diagnoses relating to disturbances within family systems. The *DSM–IV* is reflective of the practice of many professionals in which individuals—rather than couples, families, or broader systems—are seen as the focus of treatment. The diagnosis of "parent–child relational problem" is inadequate to represent fully the range of problems to which it is frequently applied. Further work is necessary to devise classification systems that go beyond specification of individual psychopathology.

Furthermore, it is important to note that behavior may vary across situations. A child may engage in extreme oppositional behavior at school, yet not at home, and vice versa. Parents should not be considered the gold standard for all information about their children. Information should be solicited from all relevant parties in the situations in which problem behaviors are reported to occur. Preferably, the evaluator will arrange direct observation of child behavior whenever possible. Additionally, evaluators are cautioned to pay attention to notes in the *DSM–IV* that point out the different presentation of specific symptoms that may occur with children.

Ethical Considerations

The use of diagnostic labels is a matter of controversy. As noted previously, diagnostic labels function as important summary variables. However, critics point to the potentially devastating effects of labeling children (e.g., self-fulfilling prophecy). Such criticisms are compounded by concerns regarding the validity of available taxonomic systems and the consistency with which diagnostic criteria are adhered. It is doubtful that diagnostic labels ever will be rejected in favor of purely idiographic specification of target behaviors, nor are we suggesting that such should be the case (Scotti et al., 1996). Clearly the impetus must be on developing taxonomies that may be employed reliably and that relate directly to differential therapeutics.

A potentially problematic issue is that of how to communicate diagnostic information to clients (Pope, 1992). In the case of children, diagnostic information generally is communicated to parents. However, it is often the case that diagnostic information is requested by school officials or child-care providers. Mere provision of a diagnostic label is insufficient to address the needs of the referral source. Relevant information must be provided with respect to effective intervention strategies available to address the presenting problem or problems, as well as information regarding the nature and course of the disorder. Information must be provided in terms that are easily understood by the person being addressed. One must keep in mind the emotional connotation that many members of the public may have to psychological jargon and the concept of "mental disorders." In fact, many practitioners prefer to focus on the functional aspects of the presenting problem and provide specific diagnostic labels to clients only when absolutely necessary (e.g., school placement).

Assessment Methods

Methods of assessment used to obtain information for diagnostic classification purposes include clinical interviews (Silverman & Albano, 1996); parent- and teacher-completed checklists (Achenbach, 1991; Conners, 1990); child-completed self-report measures (Beidel, Turner, & Morris, 1998; Kovacs, 1992); self-monitoring of behavior (Beidel, Neal, & Lederer, 1991; Shapiro & Cole, 1993), peer-informant data (Coie, Dodge, & Coppotelli, 1982; Masten, Morrison, & Pelligrini, 1985); behavioral performance or challenge tasks (Beidel, 1988; Murphy & Bootzin, 1973); and direct observation of behavior (Dadds & Sanders, 1992; Reid, 1978). Comprehensive assessment will incorporate multiple methods across multiple informants to access information with respect to behavior within multiple contexts. The dangers of relying on a single source of information to assign a diagnosis can not be overly stressed. However, the task of the evaluator is not merely to obtain a large quantity of assessment information. Attention must be paid to the potential relevance of the assessment measures selected. Additionally, when information is found to differ across informants the evaluator should examine potential reasons for disagreement. Mash and Dozois (1996) noted the following potential reasons why multiple informants may present discrepant information: (a) bias or error on the part of one of the informants, (b) variability in child behavior across situations observed by the informants, (c) lack of access to specific behavior (i.e., private events), (d) denial of the problem, or (e) active distortion of information in service of some other goal.

Differential Diagnosis

Theoretically, differential diagnosis would lead to differential therapeutics. Unfortunately, there is little empirical data available to address the issue of the association between differential diagnosis and the provision of effective treatment for the vast majority of diagnostic categories. At a molar level, broad-band categories are generally associated with specific forms of intervention. For example, pharmacotherapy is widely used in the case of psychotic disorders, and contingency management approaches are widely used with disruptive behavior disorders. However, within diagnostic categories (e.g., mood disorders), it is unclear whether the application of a specific diagnostic label (e.g., dysthymia vs. major depressive episode) necessitates a specific therapeutic approach. Despite the limited empirical evidence currently available, accurate differential diagnosis may assist in etiological research and ultimately may lead to identification of effective differential therapeutics.

Importantly, one must acknowledge that the same behavior may have different functions. The case of school refusal is one in which the same presenting behavior may be a component of several different diagnostic classes. Identifying the function of school-refusal behavior assists differential diagnosis. School-refusal behavior commonly occurs in three diagnostic groups (Last & Strauss, 1990). Children may refuse to attend school because they are afraid to read aloud or engage in social interaction with peers (as with social anxiety disorder); they may fear that harm may befall a parent in their absence (as with separation anxiety disorder); or they may evidence a general lack of compliance and resistance to authority (as with oppositional defiant disorder). Differential diagnosis through identification of the function of the school-refusal behavior typically would result in a somewhat different treatment approach with each diagnostic category: social skills training and performance-based exposure therapy for the child with social anxiety disorder; parent–child relationship therapy and separation-based exposure exercises for separation anxiety disorder; and contingency management and environmental supports in the case of oppositional defiant disorder.

INTEGRATING DIAGNOSIS AND INTERVENTION

Diagnostic classification may be an end in itself (e.g., epidemiological studies) but is more likely to be one of the initial steps in the process of case conceptualization and intervention. Hawkins (1979; see also Barrios, 1988; Barrios & Hartmann, 1986) described the assessment process as including a number of steps that are followed in order and which successively move from a relatively broad to a narrow focus. Hawkins referred to this process as the "assessment funnel," with specific types of questions being addressed during each phase. The first several phases of the assessment process, or funnel, include "screening" and "problem identification and analysis." It is at this level that one evaluates whether the target person exhibits a problem requiring further assessment and intervention and begins to identify specific problem areas and target behaviors (i.e., symptoms). A range of behavioral and traditional assessment measures may be employed to determine important environmental and organismic factors in the case. Undoubtedly, particularly if reimbursement is sought through an insurance company or managed-care organization, a formal diagnosis will be assigned. This section of the funnel—a broad level of assessment—is wholly compatible with current *DSM* Axis I and Axis II diagnoses, that is, identifying a child as meeting criteria for a disorder based on formal testing, interviews, and observations, and their similarity to specific diagnostic groups by virtue of meeting symptom criteria.

The subsequent phases of the assessment funnel focus on the identification of specific, clearly defined target behaviors and selecting, implementing, and evaluating interventions designed to address those targets. These are the "target behavior and treatment selection," "monitoring progress," and "follow-up" phases of the process. At these levels, the work is case-specific (i.e., narrow focus), although intervention may be selected based on packages known to be effective with similar cases (i.e., persons with similar diagnoses). Here is the deductive application of a body of knowledge to the individual case, as discussed at the start of this chapter. This also begins an iterative process such that diagnostic and other assessment information leads to the selection of interventions. Assessment then continues throughout treatment, allowing an evaluation of progress and pointing toward needed modifications to the treatment plan. This is the essence of the scientist–practitioner model (Barlow, Hayes, & Nelson, 1984), and it is also the level at which individual functional analyses and systems models can be developed and tested for the case at hand (Evans, 1985; Scotti et al., 1996). A change in diagnostic status is rarely the primary outcome that is sought in therapy; rather, the objective is typically the modification of certain behaviors or interactional styles. However, one could see that real, significant treatment gains should mean real resolution to a disorder, in the sense that the behaviors specified in the diagnostic criteria are no longer evident.

Idiographic functional analyses might take several forms, but a specification of excess and deficit behaviors and skills, as well as their relation to each other, and the psychosocial and environmental resources and deficits that support—or fail to support—current repertoires, would be considered. This level of analysis, however, is clearly not part of classification systems such as the *DSM*. Scotti et al. (1996) have proposed that several axes of the *DSM* system be modified or added, providing clinicians the opportunity to incorporate specific case features into the diagnostic process. These axes might include (a) psychosocial and environmental resources and deficits, and (b) idiographic case analysis (including biological factors and general medical conditions). Currently, the *DSM* requires specification of psychosocial and environmental problems, but a consideration of psychosocial and environmental strengths, assets, and supports is equally important in the treatment planning process. Here, the system of supports outlined in the diagnostic manual of the American Association on Mental Retardation (1992) seems particularly relevant, as it would identify the kind and level of resources and supports needed to address the individual case, including people, environments, assistive technology, educational strategies, and so forth. The idiographic case analysis would formalize the assessment of critical antecedents (both proximal and distal), repertoires, and consequences for the particular case. These might include relevant historical features (e.g., prior suicide attempts, parental sexual abuse); immediate antecedents (e.g., parental demands); current skills or deficits (e.g., good social and vocational skills, but poor math and reading skills); and the consequences of their behaviors (e.g., aggressive behavior results in termination of parental demands; academic success is not valued by the parents). Incorporation of such idiographic information into a classification scheme would bring together the traditional nomothetic aspects and purposes of diagnosis and classification and make that enterprise useful in the description, conceptualization, and treatment of the individual case.

CONCLUSION

The attempt to define and classify abnormal behavior has a long history. We have outlined here a number of the critical features and considerations of diagnostic and classifications systems, including the goals and purposes of classification, decisions concerning the subject matter (i.e., what is "abnormal" behavior?), and the pros and cons of engaging in the diagnostic process. We also have outlined a number of features of past and current systems, providing what we see as important considerations in the use of these systems. Finally, we have discussed briefly the place of classification and diagnosis in the clinical intervention process, stressing the need to consider both the nomothetic and idiographic aspects of the process.

Classification and diagnosis remains an important clinical, research, and epidemiological activity. It is also an activity fraught with negative implications, not the least of which are the political implications of labeling people and their behavior as "deviant," and the requirements to engage in the process for the purposes of financial reimbursement. Because psychology is a science, we can expect that classification and diagnosis will not disappear as a critical enterprise of scientists and practitioners. It will remain necessary, however, that the methods, purposes, and ramifications remain a point of discussion, thereby enhancing the usefulness of this important activity and reducing the likelihood of its misuse.

REFERENCES

Achenbach, T. M. (1985). *Assessment and taxonomy of child and adolescent psychopathology.* Beverly Hills, CA: Sage.

Achenbach, T. M. (1991). *Manual for the Child Behavior Checklist/4–18 and 1991 Profile.* Burlington: University of Vermont, Department of Psychiatry.

Achenbach, T. M., & Edelbrock, C. S. (1981). Behavioral problems and competencies reported by parents of normal and disturbed children ages four through sixteen. *Monographs of the Society for Research in Child Development, 46* (1, Serial No. 188).

Adams, H. E., & Cassidy, J. F. (1993). The classification of abnormal behavior: An overview. In P. B. Sutker & H. E. Adams (Eds.), *Comprehensive handbook of psychopathology* (2nd ed., pp. 3–25). New York: Plenum.

Adams, H. E., Doster, J. A., & Calhoun, K. S. (1977). A psychologically based system of response classification. In A. R. Ciminero, K. S. Calhoun & H. E. Adams (Eds.), *Handbook of behavioral assessment* (pp. 47–78). New York: Wiley.

Adebimpe, V. R. (1994). Race, racism, and epidemiological surveys. *Hospital and Community Psychiatry, 45,* 27–31.

American Association on Mental Retardation. (1992). *Mental retardation: Definition, classification, and systems of supports.* Washington, DC: Author.

American Psychiatric Association. (1933). Notes and comment: Revised classified nomenclature of mental disorders. *American Journal of Psychiatry, 90,* 1369–1377.

American Psychiatric Association. (1952). *Diagnostic and statistical manual: Mental disorders.* Washington, DC: Author.

American Psychiatric Association. (1968). *Diagnostic and statistical manual of mental disorders* (2nd ed.). Washington, DC: Author.

American Psychiatric Association. (1980). *Diagnostic and statistical manual of mental disorders* (3rd ed.). Washington, DC: Author.

American Psychiatric Association. (1987). *Diagnostic and statistical manual of mental disorders* (3rd ed., rev.). Washington, DC: Author.

American Psychiatric Association. (1994). *Diagnostic and statistical manual of mental disorders* (4th ed.). Washington, DC: Author.

Anastasi, A., & Urbina, S. (1997). *Psychological testing.* Englewood Cliffs, NJ: Prentice-Hall.

Bandura, A. (1968). A social learning interpretation of psychological dysfunctions. In P. London & P. Rosenhan (Eds.), *Foundations of abnormal psychology* (pp. 293–344). New York: Holt, Rinehart & Winston.

Barkley, R. A. (1987). *Defiant children: A clinician's manual for parent training.* New York: Guilford.

Barkley, R. A. (1996). Attention deficit/hyperactivity disorder. In. E. J. Mash & R. A. Barkley (Eds.), *Child psychopathology* (pp. 63–112). New York: Guilford.

Barkley, R. A. (1997). Attention-deficit/hyperactivity disorder. In E. J. Mash & L. G. Terdal (Eds.), *Assessment of childhood disorders* (3rd ed., pp. 71–129). New York: Guilford.

Barlow, D. H., Hayes, S. C., & Nelson, R. O. (1984). *The scientist–practitioner: Research and accountability in clinical and educational settings.* New York: Pergamon.

Barrios, B. A. (1988). On the changing nature of behavioral assessment. In A. S. Bellack & M. Hersen (Eds.), *Behavioral assessment: A practical handbook* (3rd ed., pp. 3–41). New York: Pergamon.

Barrios, B., & Hartmann, D. P. (1986). The contributions of traditional assessment: Concepts, issues, and methodologies. In R. O. Nelson & S. C. Hayes (Eds.), *Conceptual foundations of behavioral assessment* (pp. 81–110). New York: Guilford.

Beidel, D. C. (1988). Psychophysiological assessment of anxious emotional states in children. *Journal of Abnormal Psychology, 97,* 80–82.

Beidel, D. C., Neal, A. M., & Lederer, A. S. (1991). The feasibility and validity of a daily diary for the assessment of anxiety in children. *Behavior Therapy, 22,* 505–517.

Beidel, D. C., Turner, S. M., & Morris, T. L. (1998). *The Social Phobia and Anxiety Inventory for Children (SPAI–C).* North Tonawanda, NY: Multi-Health Systems.

Biederman, J., Milberger, S., Faraone, S. V., Kiely, K., Guite, J., Mick, E., Ablon, S., Warburton, R., & Reed, E. (1995). Family–environment risk factors for attention-deficit hyperactivity disorder. *American Journal of Psychiatry, 150,* 1792–1798.

Buss, A. H. (1966). *Psychopathology.* New York: Wiley.

Butcher, J. N., Narikiyo, T., & Bemis Vitousek, K. (1993). Understanding abnormal behavior in cultural context. In P. B. Sutker & H. E. Adams (Eds.), *Comprehensive handbook of psychopathology* (2nd ed., pp. 83–105). New York: Plenum.

Cervantes, R. C., & Arroyo, W. (1994). *DSM–IV:* Implications for Hispanic children and adolescents. *Hispanic Journal of Behavioral Sciences, 16,* 8–27.

Cohen, P., Cohen, J., Kasen, S., Velez, C. N., Hartmark, C., Johnson, J., Rojas, M., Brook, J., & Streuning, E. L. (1993). An epidemiological study of disorders in late childhood and adolescence: I. Age- and gender-specific prevalence. *Journal of Child Psychology and Psychiatry, 34,* 851–867.

Coie, J. D., Dodge, K. A., & Coppotelli, H. (1982). Dimensions and types of social status: A cross-age perspective. *Developmental Psychology, 18,* 557–570.

Cone, J. D. (1986). Idiographic, nomothetic, and related perspectives in behavioral assessment. In R. O. Nelson & S. C. Hayes (Eds.), *Conceptual foundations of behavioral assessment* (pp. 111–128). New York: Guilford.

Cone, J. D. (1988). Psychometric considerations and the multiple models of behavioral assessment. In A. S. Bellack & M. Hersen (Eds.), *Behavioral assessment: A practical handbook* (3rd ed., pp. 42–66). New York: Pergamon.

Conners, C. K. (1990). *The Conners Rating Scales.* North Tonawanda, NY: Multi-Health Systems.

Corrigan, P. W. (1998). The impact of stigma on severe mental illness. *Cognitive and Behavioral Practice, 5,* 201–222.

Costello, C. G. (1980). Childhood depression: Three basic but questionable assumptions in the Hefkowitz and Burton critique. *Psychological Bulletin, 87,* 185–190.

Dadds, M. R., & Sanders, M. R. (1992). Family interaction and child psychopathology: A comparison of two observation strategies. *Journal of Child and Family Studies, 1,* 371–391.

Dana, R. H. (1993). *Multicultural assessment perspectives for professional psychology.* Boston: Allyn & Bacon.

Dickerson, F. B. (1998). Strategies that foster empowerment. *Cognitive and Behavioral Practice, 5,* 255–275.

Eifert, G. H., Evans, I. M., & McKendrick, V. G. (1990). Matching treatments to client problems not diagnostic labels: A case for paradigmatic behavior therapy. *Journal of Behavior Therapy and Experimental Psychiatry, 21,* 163–172.

Evans, I. M. (1985). Building systems models as a strategy for target behavior selection in clinical assessment. *Behavioral Assessment, 7,* 21–32.

Evans, I. M. (1986). Response structure and the triple-response mode concept. In R. O. Nelson & S. C. Hayes (Eds.), *Conceptual foundations of behavioral assessment* (pp. 131–155). New York: Guilford.

Evans, I. M., Meyer, L. H., Kurkjian, J. A., & Kishi, G. S. (1988). An evaluation of behavioral interrelationships in child behavior therapy. In J. C. Witt, S. N. Elliott, & F. N. Gresham (Eds.), *Handbook of behavior therapy in education* (pp. 189–216). New York: Plenum.

Frick, P. J., Lahey, B. B., Applegate, B., Kerdyck, L., Ollendick, T., Hynd, G. W., Garfinkel, B., Greenhill, L., Biederman, J., Barkley, R. A., McBurnett, K., Newcorn, J., & Waldman, I. (1994).

DSM–IV field trials for the disruptive behavior disorders: Symptom utility estimates. *Journal of the American Academy of Child and Adolescent Psychiatry, 33,* 529–539.

Garber, J. (1984). Classification of child psychopathology: A developmental perspective. *Child Development, 55,* 30–48.

Goldfried, M. R., & Kent, R. N. (1972). Traditional versus behavioral personality assessment: A comparison of methodological and theoretical assumptions. *Psychological Bulletin, 77,* 409–420.

Hawkins, R. P. (1979). The functions of assessment: Implications for selection and development of devices for assessing repertoires in clinical, educational, and other settings. *Journal of Applied Behavior Analysis, 12,* 501–516.

Hawkins, R. P. (1986). Selection of target behaviors. In R. O. Nelson & S. C. Hayes (Eds.), *Conceptual foundations of behavioral assessment* (pp. 331–385). New York: Guilford.

Hayes, S. C., & Follette, W. C. (1992). Can functional analysis provide a substitute for syndromal classification. *Behavioral Assessment, 14,* 345–365.

Hersen, M., & Bellack, A. S. (1988). *DSM–III* and behavioral assessment. In A. S. Bellack & M. Hersen (Eds.), *Behavioral assessment: A practical handbook* (3rd ed., pp. 67–84). New York: Pergamon.

Hilgard, E. R. (1987). *Psychology in America: A historical survey.* New York: Harcourt, Brace.

Holmes, E. P., & River, L. P. (1998). Individual strategies for coping with the stigma of severe mental illness. *Cognitive and Behavioral Practice, 5,* 231–239.

Jahoda, M. (1958). *Current concepts of positive mental health.* New York: Basic Books.

Kavanagh, K., & Hops, H. (1994). Good girls? Bad boys? Gender and development as contexts for diagnosis and treatment. *Advances in Clinical Child Psychology, 16,* 45–79.

Kohn, M. L. (1973). Social class and schizophrenia: A critical review and a reformulation. *Schizophrenia Bulletin, 7,* 60–79.

Kovacs, M. (1992). *The Children's Depression Inventory (CDI).* North Tonawanda, NY: Multi-Health Systems.

Lahey, B. B., Loeber, R., Quay, H. C., Frick, P. J., & Grimm, J. (1992). Oppositional defiant and conduct disorders: Issues to be resolved for *DSM–IV. Journal of the American Academy of Child and Adolescent Psychiatry, 31,* 639–646.

Laing, R. D. (1967). *The politics of experience.* New York: Pantheon.

Last, C. G., & Strauss, C. C. (1990). School refusal in anxiety disordered children and adolescents. *Journal of the American Academy of Child and Adolescent Psychiatry, 29,* 31–35.

Lawson, W. B., Hepler, N., Holladay, J., & Cuffel, B. (1994). Race as a factor in inpatient and outpatient admissions and diagnosis. *Hospital and Community Psychiatry, 45,* 72–74.

Lundin, R. K. (1998). Living with mental illness: A personal experience. *Cognitive and Behavioral Practice, 5,* 223–230.

March, J. S. (Ed.). (1995). *Anxiety disorders in children and adolescents.* New York: Guilford.

Mash, E. J., & Dozois, D. J. A. (1996). Child psychopathology: A developmental-systems perspective. In E. J. Mash & R. A. Barkley (Eds.), *Child psychopathology* (pp. 3–62). New York: Guilford.

Masten, A. S., Morrison, P., & Pelligrini, D. (1985). A revised class play method of peer assessment. *Developmental Psychology, 21,* 523–533.

Mayville, E., & Penn, D. L. (1998). Changing societal attitudes toward persons with severe mental illness. *Cognitive and Behavioral Practice, 5,* 241–253.

McMahon, R. J., & Estes, A. M. (1997). Conduct problems. In E. J. Mash & L. G. Terdal (Eds.), *Assessment of childhood disorders* (3rd ed., pp. 130–193). New York: Guilford.

McReynolds, P. (1979). The case for interactional assessment. *Behavioral Assessment, 1,* 237–247.

McReynolds, P. (1986). History of assessment in clinical and educational settings. In R. O. Nelson & S. C. Hayes (Eds.), *Conceptual foundations of behavioral assessment* (pp. 42–80). New York: Guilford.

Meehl, P. E. (1973). *Psychodiagnosis: Selected papers.* New York: Norton.

Mezzich, J. E., & Mezzich, A. C. (1987). Diagnostic classification systems in child psychopathology. In C. L. Frame & J. L. Matson (Eds.), *Handbook of assessment in childhood psychopathology: Applied issues in differential diagnosis and treatment evaluation* (pp. 33–60). New York: Plenum.

Murphy, C. M., & Bootzin, R. R. (1973). Active and passive participation in the contact desensitization of snake fear in children. *Behavior Therapy, 4,* 203–211.

O'Donohue, W., & Krasner, L. (Eds.). (1995). *Theories of behavior therapy: Exploring behavior change*. Washington, DC: American Psychological Association.

Okazaki, S., & Sue, S. (1995). Methodological issues in assessment research with ethnic minorities. *Psychological Assessment, 7*, 367–375.

Patterson, G. R., Reid, J. B., Jones, R. R., & Conger, R. E. (1975). *A social learning approach to family intervention: Vol. 1. Families with aggressive children*. Eugene, OR: Castalia.

Plaud, J. J., & Eifert, G. H. (Eds.). (1998). *From behavior theory to behavior therapy*. Boston: Allyn & Bacon.

Pope, K. S. (1992). Responsibilities in providing psychological test feedback to clients. *Psychological Assessment, 4*, 268–271.

Quay, H. C. (1986). Classification. In H. C. Quay & J. S. Werry (Eds.), *Psychopathological disorders of childhood* (3rd ed., pp. 1–34). New York: Wiley.

Reid, J. B. (1978). *A social learning approach to family intervention: Volume 2. Observation in home settings*. Eugene, OR: Castalia.

Scotti, J. R., Evans, I. M., Meyer, L. H., & DiBenedetto, A. (1991). Individual repertoires as behavioral systems: Implications for program design and evaluation. In B. Remington (Ed.), *The challenge of severe mental handicap: A behaviour analytic approach* (pp. 139–163). London: Wiley.

Scotti, J. R., McMorrow, M. J., & Trawitzki, A. L. (1993). Behavioral treatment of chronic psychiatric disorders: Publication trends and future directions. *Behavior Therapy, 24*, 527–550.

Scotti, J. R., Morris, T. L., McNeil, C. B., & Hawkins, R. P. (1996). *DSM–IV* and disorders of childhood and adolescence: Can structural criteria be functional? *Journal of Consulting and Clinical Psychology, 64*, 1177–1191.

Shapiro, E. S., & Cole, C. L. (1993). Self-monitoring. In T. H. Ollendick & M. Hersen (Eds.), *Handbook of child and adolescent assessment* (pp. 124–139). Needham Heights, MA: Allyn & Bacon.

Silverman, W. K., & Albano, A. M. (1996). *Anxiety Disorders Interview Schedule for DSM–IV, Child Version*. New York: Graywind.

Sprock, J., & Blashfield, R. K. (1983). Classification and nosology. In M. Hersen, A. E. Kazdin, & A. S. Bellack (Eds.), *The clinical psychology handbook* (pp. 289–307). New York: Pergamon.

Staats, A. W. (1990). Paradigmatic behavior therapy: A unified framework for theory, research, and practice. In G. H. Eifert & I. M. Evans (Eds.), *Unifying behavior therapy: Contributions of paradigmatic behaviorism* (pp. 14–54). New York: Springer.

Staats, A. W. (1995). Paradigmatic behaviorism and paradigmatic behavior therapy. In W. O'Donohue & L. Krasner (Eds.), *Theories of behavior therapy: Exploring behavior change* (pp. 659–693). Washington, DC: American Psychological Association.

Szasz, T. S. (1961). *The myth of mental illness*. New York: Hoeber-Harper.

Taylor, E. (1994). Syndromes of attention deficit and overactivity. In M. Rutter, E. Taylor, & L. Hersov (Eds.), *Child and adolescent psychiatry* (pp. 285–307). Oxford: Blackwell Scientific.

Tsuang, M. T. (1993). From *DSM–III–R* to *DSM–IV*: Some reflections on process and method. *Harvard Review of Psychiatry, 1*, 126–128.

Voeltz, L. M., & Evans, I. M. (1982). The assessment of behavioral interrelationships in child behavior therapy. *Behavioral Assessment, 4*, 131–165.

Wade, C., & Tavris, C. (1998). *Psychology* (5th ed.). New York: Longman.

Webb-Johnson, G. (1999). Cultural contexts: Confronting the overrepresentation of African American learners in special education. In J. R. Scotti & L. H. Meyer (Eds.), *Behavioral intervention: Principles, models, and practices* (pp. 449–464). Baltimore: Paul H. Brookes.

Werry, J. S. (1992). Child psychiatric disorders: Are they classifiable? *British Journal of Psychiatry, 161*, 472–480.

World Health Organization. (1948). *International classification of diseases* (6th rev.) Geneva, Switzerland: Author.

World Health Organization. (1992). *International statistical classification of disease* (10th ed). Geneva, Switzerland: Author.

Zero to Three/National Center for Clinical Infant Programs. (1994). *Diagnostic classification of mental health and developmental disorders of infancy and early childhood (Diagnostic classification: 0–3)*. Washington, DC: Author.

Epidemiologic Considerations

Gale A. Richardson
Nancy L. Day
Western Psychiatric Institute and Clinic
University of Pittsburgh School of Medicine

Epidemiology is the study of the patterns of disease in human populations and of the factors that influence these patterns. The focus is on populations rather than on individual cases. In the past, epidemiology dealt with the study of infectious diseases in a population. A single-cause model usually was used to explain the presence of a particular disease (Day, 1992; Verhulst & Koot, 1992). The emphasis of epidemiology gradually has shifted to the study of long-term, chronic diseases, including psychiatric disorders. Most such diseases are determined by more than one cause (e.g., personal characteristics of the individual and environmental factors; Verhulst & Koot, 1992).

The first systematic epidemiologic study in the field of child psychiatry was reported by Lapouse and Monk (1958). These investigators studied the frequency of mother-reported problem behaviors in a random, representative sample of 482 children aged 6 to 12 years old in Buffalo, New York. The authors found a high frequency of emotional and behavioral problems, particularly among the 6- to 8-year-olds. Common problems included fears and worries, nightmares, overactivity, and temper tantrums. Lapouse and Monk's study demonstrated the importance of systematic data collection, the need for examining the prevalence of psychiatric disorders in children, and the high rate of problems among children.

The goals of child psychiatric epidemiology are to estimate the overall prevalence of childhood disorders and to identify the possible causes and correlates of the disorders (Verhulst & Koot, 1992). These data are necessary to provide appropriate treatment for children with psychiatric disorders, to evaluate mental health services, and to implement preventive measures.

SELECTED CLASSIC STUDIES

Five classic studies have been selected to familiarize the reader with child psychiatric epidemiology. These studies are used to illustrate principles throughout the chapter. The following section briefly summarizes the purpose, study design, and major findings of each study.

The first large-scale child psychiatric epidemiologic study was conducted by Rutter and his colleagues (Rutter, Tizard, & Whitmore, 1970). The Isle of Wight Study examined educational and intellectual disorders in a prospective investigation of the entire population of 3,500 children aged 9 to 11 years old who lived on a semirural island off the coast of England. Children also were evaluated for psychiatric and physical disorders a year after the initial interview and again when they were 14 to 15 years old. The aims of the study were to identify the age of onset of psychiatric disorders, examine risk factors associated with disorders, and examine the course of disorders over time. This study had numerous methodologic strengths, including: the use of multiple data sources (parents, teachers, children, school and medical records); a two-stage research strategy (a screening instrument was used to identify high-risk children who then were followed with more extensive assessment); use of standardized interviews; and the use of social impairment as a criterion of severity along with the symptoms of the psychiatric disorder (Rutter, 1989).

Rutter et al. (1970) found that the overall rate of child psychiatric disorders in the 9- to 11-year-olds was 6.8%. However, the rates of specific types of disorders changed with age. For example, depressive disorders were more common at 14 to 15 years than at 10 to 11 years. In addition, psychiatric disorders in adolescence (onset after age 10) had a different set of correlates associated with them than those arising in earlier childhood.

Low agreement was found between parent and teacher reports of children's functioning, demonstrating the importance of obtaining information from multiple sources because children act differently in different settings. The Isle of Wight Study was also important in noting the need to consider the overlap in conditions, or *comorbidity*, where more than one disorder is present at a time.

During a 3-year period in the mid-1950s, the Kauai Pregnancy Study (Werner, Bierman, & French, 1971) recruited more than 2,000 pregnant women in Kauai, Hawaii. The purpose of this prospective study was to compare the relative contributions of perinatal stress (medical problems during pregnancy, labor, or delivery) and the characteristics of the family environment to outcomes such as physical, cognitive, and social development of preschool and school-age children. Over 1,000 of the offspring were seen at 2 and 10 years of age for follow-up evaluations. Werner et al. (1971) found that higher levels of perinatal stress were associated with poorer development at 2 years of age. An inadequate environment exacerbated the effects of perinatal stress, that is, the children with high levels of perinatal stress and a poor environment had the worst outcomes. Furthermore, emotionally unsupportive childrearing practices in the home were related to child behavior problems. By 10 years of age, however, the effect of perinatal stress had diminished and the impact of the environment had increased.

A portion of the original Kauai cohort was followed through adolescence and adulthood: At 32 years of age, 505 adults were interviewed (Werner & Smith, 1992). One of the important findings to emerge from this adult follow-up was that high-risk children who became successful adults tended to be sociable as children; they had a close relationship with a parent substitute (e.g., grandparent, aunt, uncle, neighbor); and they had a support system outside of the family (Werner & Smith, 1992).

The London Epidemiologic Study (Richman, Stevenson, & Graham, 1975) investigated the prevalence of behavior problems among 3-year-old children living in a London borough. A two-stage sampling design was used. A random sample of 705 children was selected and a semistructured screening instrument, the Behavior Screening Questionnaire (BSQ), was used to identify children who were reported by their parents as having behavior problems. The estimated rate of moderate to severe behavior problems in the random sample was 7%; an additional 15% had mild behavior problems. Boys were significantly more likely to be described as being overactive, having more problems with toilet training, and having fewer fears than girls.

Each child identified as having a behavior problem was then matched by gender and social class with a child with no behavior problems to create a behavior problems group and a control group. The two groups of children and their families then received an in-depth interview and developmental assessment. These children were seen again at 4 and 8 years of age. Of the children in the behavior problems group at 3 years of age, 69% and 62% were identified as having behavior problems at 4 and 8 years of age, respectively. This compares with 14% and 22% of the control group who had behavior problems at 4 and 8 years, respectively (Richman, 1977; Richman, Stevenson, & Graham, 1982). Persistence of behavior problems was associated with maternal depression and poor marital relationships.

Earls (1980) replicated the London Epidemiologic Study (Richman et al., 1975) with a sample of 100 children aged 3 years old in a rural U.S. community (Martha's Vineyard, Massachusetts). This sample represented 90% of the entire population of 3-year-olds. Interviews were conducted with both parents, and play interviews were done with the children. The BSQ from the London study (Richman et al., 1975) was used to identify behavior problems. Earls reported that 11% of the children had behavior problems—a rate similar to that reported by Richman et al. (1975), despite differences in geographic locale and sample size. Common behavior problems included sleep problems, fears, and bed-wetting. The children were seen again at 6 to 7 years of age, after they began first grade. Twenty-five percent of those children with behavior problems at 3 years of age were reported by their teachers to have adjustment problems in school (Earls, 1983).

The Ontario Child Health Study (Boyle et al., 1987; Offord et al., 1987) surveyed parents of 2,679 children aged 4 to 16 years old to determine the prevalence of emotional and behavioral disorders among children in Ontario, Canada. Families were randomly sampled from large and small urban areas and rural areas. Parents and teachers completed a behavior problem checklist that asked about conduct disorders (physical violence against people or property); hyperactivity; emotional disorders (anxiety, depression, obsessive–compulsive disorder); and somatization disorders (physical symptoms without organic cause). A subsample of children also received a clinical evaluation by a child psychiatrist. In addition to behavior problems, parents were asked about social and demographic characteristics, family composition, functioning, alcoholism, criminality, stressful life events, social support, and the child's medical history. Nineteen percent of the boys and 17% of the girls had one or more disorders. Conduct disorders and hyperactivity were reported more frequently for boys than for girls. Emotional disorders were more frequent in 12- to 16-year-old girls. In a separate analysis of the 4- and 5-year-olds in the study, predictors of behavior problems included the child's general health, maternal depression, marital status, parent health problems, and number of siblings (Thomas, Byrne, Offord, & Boyle, 1991).

EPIDEMIOLOGIC METHODS

Sample Selection

Research in child psychiatric epidemiology has involved both clinic and community samples (Verhulst & Koot, 1992). *Clinic samples* consist of children who already have been identified as suffering from a disorder and who usually are receiving treatment. Clinic samples differ in demographic characteristics from the general population. In a study of 62 children who were inpatients in a psychiatric hospital, Kazdin, Esveldt-Dawson, Sherick, and Colbus (1985) reported that 82% of the children were males and 82% were White. Clinic samples are also unrepresentative of the general population because of factors associated with referral to treatment, the family's access to health care, and their utilization of health services. Jensen, Bloedau, and Davis (1990) found that family size, marital status, and parental psychopathology were related to utilization of a child psychiatric clinic. An additional limitation of clinic samples is that information regarding the development of the disorder can only be collected retrospectively because the children have the disorder at the beginning of the study.

Community samples are drawn from a more general population and are not limited to children who have developed a disorder or who are in treatment. Each of the five classic studies was a population-based community investigation. To the extent that the population that is sampled yields a random or representative sample, these studies can be used to generate prevalence rates of disorders in the community. Clinic samples cannot be used for this purpose because the subjects are a select group. For example, Kashani, Orvaschel, Rosenberg, and Reid (1989), in a community sample of 8-, 12-, and 17-year-olds, reported that 3% had a depressive disorder, whereas Kazdin et al. (1985) found a 17.7% rate of depressive disorders in a clinic sample.

Both clinic and community samples can be either descriptive or analytic. When there are few data available on the disorder in the population, *descriptive studies* are undertaken. These studies are hypothesis-generating, collecting data on the distribution of psychiatric disorder by age, gender, social class, or geographic variables. These data can then be used to generate specific hypotheses. Once hypotheses are formulated, *analytic studies* test the hypotheses to further the understanding of the causes of the disorder.

Sampling

Although several of the classic studies previously reviewed included an entire population (Earls, 1980; Werner et al., 1971), it is generally not feasible or necessary to enroll the whole population into a study. Rather, a sample of the population is used to generate information about the entire population. The ability to generalize study findings is directly related to the degree to which the sample is representative of the entire population and of other populations to which one might wish to extend the findings. If the sample is derived from a population with special characteristics, generalizability to the entire population will be compromised. For example, clinic samples are already identified with disorders and, therefore, findings will not be comparable to findings from community samples. However, community samples are not exempt from generalizability problems. Characteristics of the sample, such as urban–rural differences, race, gender, and social class, must be similar to those of the population to which one wishes to generalize in order for results to be comparable. The study by Earls (1980), which sampled all 3-year-olds on Martha's Vineyard, has been criticized as being unrepresentative of the larger population of 3-year-olds because of the geographic locale and isolated nature of the island.

There are two methods of sampling: *nonprobability* and *probability*. Nonprobability or "convenience" sampling is subject to the most error. An example of nonprobability sampling would be a study conducted in a clinical setting, such as a pediatrician's office. The children in the office who are surveyed will differ in important ways from potential subjects who are not at the office. For example, factors such as socioeconomic status (Adler et al., 1994), gender (Verhulst, 1995), and availability of transportation (Staghezza-Jaramillo, Bird, Gould, & Canino, 1995) are associated with seeking medical care and, therefore, inclusion in the study. Findings from the study would be limited to people who share similar characteristics with the sample.

By contrast, in probability sampling, each participant in the population has a known probability of selection. Sampling is random, such that the selection of one participant is independent of the selection of other participant. There are several types of probability sampling: simple random, systematic, stratified, cluster, and multistage (see Boyle, 1995; Verhulst & Koot, 1992, for more detail). The London Epidemiologic Study randomly chose one out of every four 3-year-old children who were living in the borough (Richman et al., 1975). Probability sampling enables the investigator to make inferences from the sample to the population from which it was drawn and maintains the representativeness of the sample.

Study Designs

There are several major study designs used in epidemiology. *Cross-sectional study designs* also are referred to as "prevalence studies" or "surveys" (Verhulst & Koot, 1992). The relation between risk factors and disorders is assessed at a single point in time. Most community surveys are cross-sectional designs. For example, the Lapouse and Monk (1958) study was a cross-sectional study, as was the initial phase of the Earls (1980) study on Martha's Vineyard. The cross-sectional design allows the study of variations between individuals, but not within individuals over time. Cross-sectional designs allow the researcher to discuss age differences, but do not allow an interpretation of changes that occur as an individual ages. Although useful for prevalence information and planning of treatment services, the cross-sectional design cannot determine the timing or sequence of the relation between risk factors and onset of the disorder. A longitudinal study design is needed to begin to understand cause-and-effect relationships.

Longitudinal or prospective study designs allow the investigation of changes over time within individuals, of the developmental course of a disorder, and of the factors that influence this course (Verhulst, 1995; Verhulst & Koot, 1992). Longitudinal research is critical in the study of child psychiatric disorders to understand which disorders do and do not persist over time, to understand the causes of a disorder, and to assess the effectiveness of treatment (Verhulst & Koot, 1991).

A specific type of longitudinal design is a *cohort study,* in which a group (cohort) is identified based on exposure to hypothesized risk factors and followed prospectively over time to determine which subjects subsequently develop the disorder of interest. Etiology is studied by comparing the incidence of the disorder in relation to the risk factors. The Kauai Pregnancy Study (Werner et al., 1971) investigated the relative effects of perinatal stress and quality of the home environment on short- and long-term development by using a longitudinal design. One important finding from the study was that effects of parental divorce on the offspring's psychological development extended into adulthood (Werner & Smith, 1992). Rutter (1989) noted that longitudinal studies of family breakup show that it was the family disorganization and disagreement which preceded the breakup, rather than the event of the breakup itself, that were associated with child behavior problems. Findings such as these are only possible with a longitudinal design.

Case-control or retrospective studies define the study population by presence (cases) or absence (controls) of a disorder. The investigator then studies the presence and nature of risk factors in each group through the collection of retrospective data. For example, in the Isle of Wight Study, from the sample of 3,500 children, 110 were identified as having a psychiatric disorder (cases; Rutter et al., 1970). The characteristics of the cases then were compared with those of the controls. More children in the disordered group than in the nondisordered group came from homes characterized by parental separation, divorce, or death.

There are other more complex study designs used in epidemiologic research that are beyond the scope of this chapter. The interested reader is referred to Loeber and Farrington (1995) and Stanger and Verhulst (1995).

Incidence and Prevalence

Epidemiologic studies quantify the occurrence of a disorder by deriving incidence and prevalence rates. *Incidence* is the number of new cases of a disorder within a population in a defined period of time. Only prospective studies can yield true incidence rates, because the population is disease-free at the start of the study. Studying the development of new cases makes it possible to study the relation between the risk factors and the occurrence of the psychiatric disorder.

The *prevalence* rate is the number of cases that exist at a given point in time (point prevalence) or over a specified period of time (period prevalence). Both the Richman et al. (1975) study and the Earls (1980) study determined the prevalence of behavior problems among 3-year-old children. Offord et al. (1987) reported that the 6-month prevalence of one or more disorders was 18% in a group of 4- to 16-year-olds. Factors such as case definition, sample characteristics, and assessment procedures influence the prevalence rate found in a particular study (Offord, 1995).

Several measures of association are derived using these rates. The *relative risk* (RR) is the incidence of the disorder in the exposed group compared with the incidence among those who are not exposed. RR can only be calculated from prospective data. Another statistic, the *odds ratio* (OR), has been developed to estimate the relative risk in cross-sectional and case-control study designs. The RR and OR are interpreted similarly. An exposure is associated with an increased risk if the ratio is greater than one and with a decreased risk if the ratio is less than one. Garrison, Earls, and Kindlon (1984) investigated the relation between the mother's rating of the child's temperament at 3 years of age and the child's adjustment problems in first grade. An OR of 3.5 for school maladjustment was found for children whose mothers rated them as persistent or oppositional compared with children who were not rated as persistent, that is, children who were persistent–oppositional were more than three times as likely to have adjustment problems in school as were children who were not persistent–oppositional.

Correlates of Disorders

Because psychiatric disorders usually are determined by many factors, epidemiologic studies must examine numerous risk factors. E. J. Costello (1989b) summarized some of the demographic correlates associated with child psychiatric disorders. Younger children were generally less likely than older children to have a disorder. Girls were more likely to have emotional, or internalizing, disorders, whereas boys were more likely to have behavioral, or externalizing, disorders. Children from lower social class families were more likely than children from higher social class families to have emotional and behavioral disorders. Other correlates of child psychiatric disorders included cognitive ability, self-esteem, family functioning, and parental psychopathology (E. J. Costello, 1989b). In order to understand the effect of any separate risk factor, it is necessary to consider other correlates of the disorder. For example, a researcher may be interested in whether children from single-parent families develop more behavior problems than do those from two-parent families. If the investigator fails to consider the difference in income levels between one- and two- parent families, an effect on behavior problems may be misattributed to family structure rather than to income level.

ISSUES IN CHILD PSYCHIATRIC EPIDEMIOLOGY

In addition to decisions about sampling techniques and study design, a researcher interested in psychiatric disorders must define the disorder. How to define a case, that is, how to accurately discriminate between normality and pathology or how to tell if a person has a disorder or not, is an issue that still is unresolved in psychiatric epidemiology. The definition of a case can differ across assessment techniques, clinicians, institutions, disciplines, and cultures.

In child psychiatric epidemiology, the issue of defining a case is made even more difficult because of the following issues: comorbidity, recognition of the dimensional nature of child psychopathology, need for a developmental approach, and lack of a consistent method to incorporate and synthesize data from multiple informants (Verhulst & Koot, 1992). Each of these challenges is discussed.

Comorbidity

One consideration in defining a case concerns *comorbidity*, the presence of more than one disorder. Several epidemiologic studies have reported a high level of comorbidity. The Isle of Wight studies found that depressive symptoms were commonly present in conjunction with many other disorders, especially conduct disorders (Rutter, 1989). Bird et al. (1988) reported that 54% of children with attention deficit disorder also had conduct disorder. Poorer long-term outcomes may be more strongly related to the combination of disorders, such as hyperactivity and aggression (Rutter, 1988). Comorbidity also has been shown to be related to the use of mental health services. The use of services increases as the number of disorders increases (Bird, Gould, & Staghezza, 1993). These findings highlight a need for more systematic study of patterns of comorbidity in child psychiatry.

Categorical Versus Dimensional Approaches

Two approaches in psychiatric epidemiology represent divergent views of psychiatric disorders. In the *categorical approach,* cases are based on separate, distinct, and definable disorders. The categorical approach generally represents the biomedical view. This approach in psychiatric epidemiology makes use of a formal taxonomic system, the *Diagnostic and Statistical Manual of Mental Disorders* 4th ed. [*DSM–IV*]; (American Psychiatric Association, 1994), which has explicit criteria to operationalize disorders. Structured interviews also have been created for detecting psychiatric disorders in the community (Brandenburg, Friedman, & Silver, 1990). The Diagnostic Interview Schedule for Children (DISC) and the children's version of the Schedule for Affective Disorders and Schizophrenia (Kiddie–SADS) are examples of instruments scored to derive *DSM* diagnoses.

The DISC (A. J. Costello, Edelbrock, Dulcan, Kalas, & Klaric, 1984) is a highly structured interview developed for use in epidemiologic surveys with 6- to 18-year-olds. Because of its structure, less training and clinical judgment is required, and it can be administered by lay interviewers. The DISC covers a broad range of child behavior and symptoms in both the home and school. Symptom scores correspond to diagnostic constructs such as attention deficit hyperactivity disorder (ADHD), conduct disorder, and depression. The DISC has parallel forms for parent and child.

The Kiddie–SADS (Puig-Antich & Chambers, 1978) is a semistructured interview for 6- to 17-year-olds. The less structured format requires the clinical judgment of a trained interviewer. Both parent and child are interviewed and discrepancies in their reports are resolved by the interviewer. The symptoms of various disorders, such as depression, schizophrenia, ADHD, conduct disorder, and substance use, are evaluated.

In contrast to the categorical approach, the *dimensional approach* views mental health and illness on a continuum and is more consistent with a psychosocial view. Psychopathology is seen as a greater or lesser degree of normality rather than as a separate disorder (Edelbrock & Costello, 1988). Important information about the degree of impairment can be lost if disorders are characterized as present versus absent. In addition, for some disorders, such as behavior problems, there is evidence that there is a continuous distribution of problem severity rather than a clear-cut presence or absence of problems (Edelbrock & Costello, 1988). Empirically derived symptom rating scales measure gradients of disorders rather than provide diagnoses. The most widely used dimensional assessment is the Child Behavior Checklist (CBCL).

The CBCL was developed for children 4 to 18 years of age (Achenbach, 1991). A version also has been developed for use with 2- to 3-year-old children (Achenbach, 1992). The instrument is designed to describe behavior symptoms rather than to provide a diagnosis of a disorder. The CBCL has undergone extensive psychometric testing with national normative samples and clinical samples. The constructs and symptom scores have been derived statistically. Eight syndromes, such as attention problems, aggressive behavior, and delinquent behavior, are normed separately by gender within age groups. Parent, teacher, and youth self-report versions are available. The CBCL is widely used in epidemiologic studies of the prevalence of behavior problems (Bird et al., 1988; Verhulst, Koot, & Berden, 1990).

Boyle et al. (1997) compared administration of a structured interview and a self-administered behavior problem checklist and found little difference in the reliability and validity between the two types of instruments. For a more detailed discussion of the controversy surrounding the utility of categorical versus dimensional approaches, refer to Carson (1991), Frances et al. (1991), Millon (1991), and Offord (1995).

Developmental Approach

Epidemiologists have begun to incorporate a *developmental framework,* which is crucial to the study of abnormal child development. This view argues that deviant behavior must be determined in the context of the child's developmental level, because some behaviors are normal or abnormal, depending on the child's age. The definition of psychopathology is based on an understanding of normal development in normal environments (Masten & Braswell, 1991). For example, if a child is referred to a clinic because she or he is afraid of a monster under her or his bed, it is important to know that fears of ghosts and monsters are common in kindergartners but not in sixth graders (Bauer, 1976). Rutter (1988) described a developmental perspective as a consideration of age with respect to the prevalence, onset, remission, developmental appropriateness, and continuity or discontinuity of a disorder across the life span.

An example of incorporating a developmental perspective is the Isle of Wight Study. The longitudinal design allowed the description of disorders according to age of onset. Different disorders were common at different ages. Depression was more common in teenagers than in preadolescents (Rutter, 1989). In another longitudinal study, Loeber et al. (1993) studied 500 boys in each of the first, fourth, and seventh grades and followed them every 6 months. These investigators showed that there was a development or unfolding of problem behaviors that progressed from minor problem behaviors, such as stubbornness, to severe delinquency. In order to understand the course and causes of a disorder more fully, it is necessary to be aware of developmental issues.

Multiple Informants

Traditionally, only parents reported on a child's problems, but there has been an increasing recognition of the usefulness of multiple informants, each of whom contributes unique information about the child's behavior (Loeber, Green, & Lahey, 1990). Accurately defining whether a child has a disorder is a complex issue in child psychiatric epidemiology because of the necessity of obtaining data from multiple sources, such as parents, teachers, and the child, to evaluate the child's functioning in different settings. However, it is important to collect data from these multiple sources for several reasons. First, child behavior and adjustment problems may be situation-specific. For example, the behavior problem may occur at home but not at school. Second, the reliability of children's reporting of their own behavior has been questioned because of differences in cognitive abilities and in abilities to think about their own behavior (Canino, Bird, Rubio-Stipec, & Bravo, 1995). Finally, different reporters may observe different behaviors. E. J. Costello (1989a) reported that relying on parental reports of problems would have resulted in the misdiagnosis of 50% of the children who had a disorder; relying on the child's reports would have resulted in an equally high rate of misdiagnosis.

An additional issue is that agreement depends on the type of behavior problem. Loeber, Green, Lahey, and Stouthamer-Loeber (1989) interviewed a clinic sample of 7- to 13-year-old boys, their parents, and teachers. They found the highest agreement between informants for oppositional behaviors and conduct disorders and the lowest agreement for hyperactivity–inattention disorders. The children reported the least amount of hyperactive symptoms for themselves compared with the parents' and teachers' reports of the children's hyperactive symptoms. Teachers generally are better reporters of hyperactive–inattention disorders, parents are better reporters of oppositional behaviors, and children are better reporters of behaviors such as worrying, anxiety, and depressive symptoms (Loeber et al., 1990). Thus, each informant has unique information to contribute about the child's functioning. Disagreements among informants about behavior problems also can occur due to factors such as stress in the family and parental psychopathology (Kolko & Kazdin, 1993).

There are several approaches that can be used to integrate data from multiple sources (Verhulst & Koot, 1992). A child can be defined as having a disorder if at least one informant reports symptoms. A more stringent definition is to require that more than one informant report that the child exhibits symptoms in order for him or her to be defined as having a disorder. A third approach is to determine an optimal informant, that is, information from one informant is used for certain symptoms and from another informant for other symptoms. The utility of using data from multiple informants to define pervasive (occurring in multiple settings) and situation-specific disorders was demonstrated by Rutter (1989). Offord et al. (1996) compared different strategies for combining information from different informants and found that the strategy used had important implications for the correlates associated with the disorder. For example, children identified by their parent as having conduct disorder were more likely to have a depressed parent, whereas those identified by the teacher as having conduct disorder were more likely to be boys. The approach used by an investigator to integrate data from multiple informants depends on the nature of the research question. However, several authors have called for researchers to develop a consensus about how to use informant information so that there will be comparable data across studies (Canino et al., 1995; Offord et al., 1996).

SUMMARY

This chapter has introduced the reader to child psychiatric epidemiology by describing classic studies in the field and by outlining basic epidemiologic methods. Important issues that must be considered in child psychiatric research, such as comorbidity, approaches to defining psychopathology, use of a developmental perspective, and multiple informants, were addressed. Child psychiatric epidemiology incorporates numerous research questions that have major implications for clinicians and policymakers. The field has evolved from describing the prevalence of psychopathology to developing and applying diagnostic and conceptual frameworks. However, continued attention should be accorded to developing standardized, reliable assessment tools for defining disorders; using appropriate study designs for investigating causes of disorders; and developing methods to integrate data from multiple informants (Verhulst & Koot, 1992).

REFERENCES

Achenbach, T. M. (1991). *Manual for the Child Behavior Checklist/4-18 and 1991 profile*. Burlington, VT: University of Vermont, Department of Psychiatry.
Achenbach, T. M. (1992). *Manual for the Child Behavior Checklist/2-3 and 1992 profile*. Burlington, VT: University of Vermont, Department of Psychiatry.
Adler, N. E., Boyce, T., Chesney, M. A., Cohen, S., Folkman, S., Kahn, R. L., & Syme, S. L. (1994). Socioeconomic status and health. The challenge of the gradient. *American Psychologist, 49,* 15–24.
American Psychiatric Association. (1994). *Diagnostic and statistical manual of mental disorders* (4th ed.). Washington, DC: Author.

Bauer, D. H. (1976). An exploratory study of developmental changes in children's fears. *Journal of Child Psychology & Psychiatry, 17,* 69–74.

Bird, H. R., Canino, G., Rubio-Stipec, M., Gould, M. S., Ribera, J., Sesman, M., Woodbury, M., Huertas-Goldman, S., Pagan, A., Sanchez-Lacay, A., & Moscoso, M. (1988). Estimates of the prevalence of childhood maladjustment in a community survey in Puerto Rico. *Archives of General Psychiatry, 45,* 1120–1126.

Bird, H. R., Gould, M. S., & Staghezza, B. M. (1993). Patterns of diagnostic comorbidity in a community sample of children aged 9 through 16 years. *Journal of the American Academy of Child & Adolescent Psychiatry, 32,* 361–368.

Boyle, M. H. (1995). Sampling in epidemiological studies. In F. C. Verhulst & H. M. Koot (Eds.), *The epidemiology of child and adolescent psychopathology.* (pp. 66–85). New York: Oxford University Press.

Boyle, M. H., Offord, D. R., Hofmann, H. G., Catlin, G. P., Byles, J. A., Cadman, D. T., Crawford, J. W., Links, P. S., Rae-Grant, N. I., & Szatmari, P. (1987). Ontario Child Health Study. I. Methodology. *Archives of General Psychiatry, 44,* 826–831.

Boyle, M. H., Offord, D. R., Racine, Y. A., Szatmari, P., Sanford, M., & Fleming, J. E. (1997). Adequacy of interviews vs checklists for classifying childhood psychiatric disorder based on parent reports. *Archives of General Psychiatry, 54,* 793–799.

Brandenburg, N. A., Friedman, R. M., & Silver, S.E. (1990). The epidemiology of childhood psychiatric disorders: Prevalence findings from recent studies. *Journal of the American Academy of Child & Adolescent Psychiatry, 29,* 76–83.

Canino, G., Bird, H. R., Rubio-Stipec, M., & Bravo, M. (1995). Child psychiatric epidemiology: What we have learned and what we need to learn. *International Journal of Methods in Psychiatric Research, 5,* 79–92.

Carson, R. C. (1991). Dilemmas in the pathway of the *DSM–IV. Journal of Abnormal Psychology, 100,* 302–307.

Costello, A. J., Edelbrock, C. S., Dulcan, M. K., Kalas, R., & Klaric, S. H. (1984). *Development and testing of the NIMH Diagnostic Interview Schedule for Children in a clinic population: Final report.* Rockville, MD: National Institute of Mental Health.

Costello, E. J. (1989a). Child psychiatric disorders and their correlates: A primary care pediatric sample. *Journal of the American Academy of Child & Adolescent Psychiatry, 28,* 851–855.

Costello, E. J. (1989b). Developments in child psychiatric epidemiology. *Journal of the American Academy of Child & Adolescent Psychiatry, 28,* 836–841.

Day, N. L. (1992). Epidemiology. In L. K. Hsu & M. Hersen (Eds.), *Research in psychiatry: Issues, strategies, and methods* (pp. 293–308). New York: Plenum.

Earls, F. J. (1980). Prevalence of behavior problems in 3-year-old children. *Archives of General Psychiatry, 37,* 1153–1157.

Earls, F. J. (1983). An epidemiological approach to the study of behavior problems in very young children. In S. B. Guze, F. J. Earls, & J. E. Barrett (Eds.), *Childhood psychopathology and development* (pp. 1–15). New York: Raven.

Edelbrock, C., & Costello, A. J. (1988). Convergence between statistically derived behavior problem syndromes and child psychiatric diagnoses. *Journal of Abnormal Child Psychology, 16,* 219–231.

Frances, A. J., First, M. B., Widiger, T. A., Miele, G. M., Tilly, S. M., Davis, W. W., & Pincus, H. A. (1991). An A to Z guide to *DSM–IV* conundrums. *Journal of Abnormal Psychology, 100,* 407–412.

Garrison, W., Earls, F., & Kindlon, D. (1984). Temperament characteristics in the third year of life and behavioral adjustment at school entry. *Journal of Clinical Child Psychology, 13,* 298–303.

Jensen, P. S., Bloedau, L., & Davis, H. (1990). Children at risk: II. Risk factors and clinic utilization. *Journal of the American Academy of Child & Adolescent Psychiatry, 29,* 804–812.

Kashani, J. H., Orvaschel, H., Rosenberg, T. K., & Reid, J. C. (1989). Psychopathology in a community sample of children and adolescents: A developmental perspective. *Journal of the American Academy of Child & Adolescent Psychiatry, 28,* 701–706.

Kazdin, A. E., Esveldt-Dawson, K., Sherick, R. B., & Colbus, D. (1985). Assessment of overt behavior and childhood depression among psychiatrically disturbed children. *Journal of Consulting & Clinical Psychology, 53,* 201–210.

Kolko, D. J., & Kazdin, A. E. (1993). Emotional/behavioral problems in clinic and nonclinic children: Correspondence among child, parent and teacher reports. *Journal of Child Psychology & Psychiatry, 34,* 991–1006.

Lapouse, R., & Monk, M. A. (1958). An epidemiologic study of behavior characteristics in children. *American Journal of Public Health, 48,* 1134–1144.

Loeber, R., & Farrington, D. P. (1995). Longitudinal approaches in epidemiological research of conduct problems. In F. C. Verhulst & H. M. Koot (Eds.), *The epidemiology of child and adolescent psychopathology* (pp. 309–336). New York: Oxford University Press.

Loeber, R., Green, S. M., & Lahey, B. B. (1990). Mental health professionals' perception of the utility of children, mothers, and teachers as informants on childhood psychopathology. *Journal of Clinical Child Psychology, 19,* 136–143.

Loeber, R., Green, S. M., Lahey, B. B., & Stouthamer-Loeber, M. (1989). Optimal informants on childhood disruptive behaviors. *Development & Psychopathology, 1,* 317–337.

Loeber, R., Wung, P., Keenan, K., Giroux, B., Stouthamer-Loeber, M., Van Kammen, W. B., & Maughan, B. (1993). Developmental pathways in disruptive child behavior. *Development & Psychopathology, 5,* 103–133.

Masten, A. S., & Braswell, L. (1991). Developmental psychopathology: An integrative framework. In P. R. Martin (Ed.), *Handbook of behavior therapy and psychological science: An integrative approach* (pp. 35–56). Elmsford, NY: Pergamon.

Millon, T. (1991). Classification in psychopathology: Rationale, alternatives, and standards. *Journal of Abnormal Psychology, 100,* 245–261.

Offord, D. R. (1995). Child psychiatric epidemiology: Current status and future prospects. *Canadian Journal of Psychiatry, 40,* 284–288.

Offord, D. R., Boyle, M. H., Racine, Y., Szatmari, P., Fleming, J. E., Sanford, M., & Lipman, E. L. (1996). Integrating assessment data from multiple informants. *Journal of the American Academy of Child & Adolescent Psychiatry, 35,* 1078–1085.

Offord, D. R., Boyle, M. H., Szatmari, P., Rae-Grant, N. I., Links, P. S., Cadman, D. T., Byles, J. A., Crawford, J. W., Blum, H. M., Byrne, C., Thomas, H., & Woodward, C. A. (1987). Ontario Child Health Study: II. Six-month prevalence of disorder and rates of service utilization. *Archives of General Psychiatry, 44,* 832–836.

Puig-Antich, J., & Chambers, W. (1978). *The Schedule for Affective Disorders and Schizophrenia for School-age Children.* New York: New York State Psychiatric Institute.

Richman, N. (1977). Short-term outcome of behaviour problems in three year old children. In P. J. Graham (Ed.), *Epidemiological approaches in child psychiatry* (pp. 165–179). New York: Academic Press.

Richman, N., Stevenson, J. E., & Graham, P. J. (1975). Prevalence of behaviour problems in 3-year-old children: An epidemiological study in a London Borough. *Journal of Child Psychology & Psychiatry, 16,* 277–287.

Richman, N., Stevenson, J. E., & Graham, P. J. (1982). *Pre-school to school: A behavioural study.* New York: Academic Press.

Rutter, M. (1988). Epidemiological approaches to developmental psychopathology. *Archives of General Psychiatry, 45,* 486–495.

Rutter, M. (1989). Isle of Wight revisited: Twenty-five years of child psychiatric epidemiology. *Journal of the American Academy of Child & Adolescent Psychiatry, 28,* 633–653.

Rutter, M., Tizard, J., & Whitmore, K. (Eds.). (1970). *Education, health, & behaviour.* London: Longman.

Staghezza-Jaramillo, B., Bird, H. R., Gould, M. S., & Canino, G. (1995). Mental health service utilization among Puerto Rican children ages 4 through 16. *Journal of Child and Family Studies, 4,* 399–418.

Stanger, C., & Verhulst, F. C. (1995). Accelerated longitudinal designs. In F. C. Verhulst & H. M. Koot (Eds.), *The epidemiology of child and adolescent psychopathology* (pp. 385–405). New York: Oxford University Press.

Thomas, B. H., Byrne, C., Offord, D. R., & Boyle, M. H. (1991). Prevalence of behavioral symptoms and the relationship of child, parent, and family variables in 4- and 5-year-olds: Results from the Ontario Child Health Study. *Journal of Developmental & Behavioral Pediatrics, 12,* 177–184.

Verhulst, F. C. (1995). The epidemiology of child and adolescent psychopathology: Strengths and limitations. In F. C. Verhulst & H. M. Koot (Eds.), *The epidemiology of child and adolescent psychopathology* (pp. 1–21). New York: Oxford University Press.

Verhulst, F. C., & Koot, H. M. (1991). Longitudinal research in child and adolescent psychiatry. *Journal of the American Academy of Child & Adolescent Psychiatry, 30,* 361–368.

Verhulst, F. C., & Koot, H. M. (1992). *Child psychiatric epidemiology: Concepts, methods, and findings.* Newbury Park, CA: Sage.

Verhulst, F. C., Koot, H. M., & Berden, G. F. (1990). Four-year follow-up of an epidemiological sample. *Journal of the American Academy of Child & Adolescent Psychiatry, 29, 440–448.*

Werner, E. E., Bierman, J. M., & French, F. E. (1971). *The children of Kauai: A longitudinal study from the prenatal period to age ten.* Honolulu: University of Hawaii Press.

Werner, E. E., & Smith, R. S. (1992). *Overcoming the odds. High risk children from birth to adulthood.* Ithaca, NY: Cornell University Press.

Development and Psychopathology

Sally D. Popper
Western Psychiatric Institute and Clinic

Shelley Ross
Kay D. Jennings
University of Pittsburgh

Developmental psychopathology is the "study of the origins and course of individual patterns of behavioral maladaptation" (Sroufe & Rutter, 1984, p. 14). Each part of this definition is significant and has multiple implications. First, developmental psychopathology stresses the factors leading to development, onset, and course of maladaptive behavior. Second, it typically focuses on individual rather than group differences. Third, behavioral maladaptation, rather than diagnosis or classification, is emphasized. As the word maladaptation implies, psychopathology is set within the social and developmental context of the individual, rather than within the individual. In each of these ways, the developmental psychopathology approach differs from the typical approach taken to psychopathology by clinicians and researchers, exemplified in the *Diagnostic and Statistical Manual of Mental Disorders* (4th ed. [*DSM–IV*]; American Psychiatric Association, 1994). The authors of the *DSM–IV* have chosen a system that de-emphasizes origins or causes of disorders and emphasizes symptom clusters that produce a mental disorder that is "considered a manifestation of a behavioral, psychological, or biological dysfunction *in* [italics added] the individual" (pp. xxi–xxii).

Central to the emerging field of developmental psychopathology is the transactional model of development proposed by Sameroff (Sameroff & Chandler, 1975). The model posits that a child's behavior is both influenced by and further influences the behavior of caregivers with consequences that only can be predicted using an ecological, longitudinal approach to assessment. In recent years, the transactional model has been developed further to include our increasing understanding of the complex interplay of genetics and environment in development (e.g., Plomin, 1989).

In this chapter, we further define developmental psychopathology and describe how it is different from other related fields. We discuss how a developmental approach enhances our understanding of psychopathology, and we provide illustrations from both research and clinical work.

Developmental psychopathology, as a separate field, dates from approximately 1984, when a special issue of *Child Development* was devoted to theoretical and research papers on the topic. By that time, it had become clear that many researchers were studying development of psychopathology in young children in longitudinal research projects. Considerable resources were being devoted to the task of identifying protective and risk factors for psychopathology in young children from developmental perspectives (Cicchetti, 1989). The field of developmental psychopathology has enjoyed an explosion of interest since that time, and there recently have been several important reviews of the field (e.g., Achenbach, 1990; Campbell, 1998; Cicchetti & Cohen, 1995; Kazdin, 1989; Sroufe, 1989).

WHAT IS "PSYCHOPATHOLOGY" IN "DEVELOPMENTAL PSYCHOPATHOLOGY"?

Cowan (1988) stated, "Developmental psychopathology shifts our focus from the endless and perhaps fruitless debate about what psychopathology is, to how dysfunction emerges and is transformed over time" (p. 6).

Garber (1984) discussed three definitions of psychopathological disorders, each of which emphasizes the developmental approach. First, such disorders can be viewed as deviations from age-appropriate norms (e.g., being unable to separate from the mother at kindergarten). Second, they can be exaggerations of normal developmental trends (e.g., being rebellious versus engaging in criminal behavior as an adolescent). Third, they can be behaviors that interfere with normal developmental processes (e.g., being so aggressive that friendships with peers cannot develop). As Garber noted, all of these definitions assume some knowledge of normal, adaptive development.

Understanding psychopathology as deviation from age-appropriate norms—Garber's (1984) first definition—is critical because the same behavior may be perfectly normal at one age but an indication of pathology at another. Temper tantrums are expected during toddlerhood but may be seen as pathological in adolescence. Similarly, frequency and intensity of any particular behavior may vary across ages. For example, up to half of preschool and young grade school boys in various studies have been found to be overactive, restless, distractible, or to have short attention spans (Lapouse & Monk, 1958; Rutter, Tizard, & Whitmore, 1970; Werry & Quay, 1971). Obviously, we would not diagnose half of young boys with attention deficit hyperactivity disorder, but we would look for the smaller number who show an unusual level or frequency of symptoms. Likewise, frequent, chronic nighttime enuresis would be considered a problem behavior in a 6-year-old child but not in a 2-year-old child. Infrequent nighttime bed-wetting probably would be overlooked in a 6-year-old but not in a 12 year old. Thus, assigning a diagnosis based on any specific behaviors requires an understanding of age norms for both incidence and frequency.

Psychopathological behavior also can be an exaggeration of normal developmental trends. Thus, negative attitudes and "acting out" are typical of most adolescents, but delinquency is viewed as pathological. Extremes of inhibition, a normal characteristic of young children, are also problematic. Kagan, Rosenbaum, and colleagues have carried out a series of studies indicating that those children who from infancy are extremely inhibited (approximately 15–20% of children) are most likely to develop anxiety disorders later (Rosenbaum et al., 1993).

Finally, behavior can be considered pathologic because it interferes with normal developmental processes. Such behavior is maladaptive, in part, because it will lead to further developmental outcomes that are nonoptimal or lead to a narrowing of choice points for adaptive development later on (Sroufe, 1989). For example, although avoidant, resistant, and disorganized attachment relationships are manifest in different behaviors and are believed to be the results of different dyadic processes, they both place the child at risk for the development of nonoptimal social behaviors with peers and others (Allen, Moore, Kuperminc, & Bell, 1998; Carlson, 1998; Matas, Arend, & Sroufe, 1978; Sroufe, Egeland, & Kreutzer, 1990; Sroufe, Fox, & Pancake, 1983; Wartner, Grossman, Fremmer-Bombik, & Suess, 1994; Waters, Wippman, & Sroufe, 1979).

Avoidance is a good example of this point. Selma Fraiberg (1982), in a compelling article on pathological defenses in infancy, explained how avoidance of the caregiver (which may occur as early as 3 months of age) may result from past experiences of parental deprivation or threat. Avoidance, a maladaptive behavior, is a defense against the "painful affects" associated with experiencing extreme negative parenting behavior and "signifies that the baby has associated the figure of his mother with a threat to his functioning" (Fraiberg, 1982, p. 622). Avoidance is adaptive in that it enables the child to avoid repeated bouts of unbearable anxiety. Avoidance is maladaptive because it prevents corrective experience and clearly signals a failure to develop trust and a secure attachment relationship. Main and Goldwyn (1984) also described avoidance from a similar perspective.

WHAT IS "DEVELOPMENTAL" IN "DEVELOPMENTAL PSYCHOPATHOLOGY"?

In normally developing children, the specific behaviors that indicate adaptive functioning change with age. For example, with peers, the competent 2-year-old silently offers a toy, the 5-year-old suggests a game of hide-and-seek, and the 10-year-old expresses concern when a peer falls down. Thus, within normal development, there are differentiations and transformations of behavior that are adaptive and expected. The same is true for maladaptive behaviors. Clearly, stability in development does not imply that individual behaviors will be exhibited in the same manner over time, but rather that adaptive or nonadaptive patterns of behavior are predictive of similar patterns later in life. Sroufe and Rutter (1984) summarized, "Individual functioning is coherent across periods of discontinuous growth and despite fundamental transformations in manifest behavior" (p. 21). For example, social competence tends to be modestly stable over time and clearly is manifested by different behaviors at different times, such as sharing, altruism, cooperation, assertiveness, conscientiousness, responsibility, and independence (Radke-Yarrow, Zahn-Waxler, & Chapman, 1983). There is also evidence that maladaptive behavior continues over time. Many longitudinal studies have now confirmed that children identified during preschool or early grade school as having severe problems with anger, aggressive behavior, and overactivity tend to continue problematic behaviors in elementary school (Campbell & Ewing, 1990; Campbell, Pierce, Moore, Marakovitz, & Newby, 1996; Moffitt, 1990; Richman, Stevenson, & Graham, 1982); adolescence (Barkley, Fischer, Edelbrock, & Smallish, 1990; Ewing & Campbell, 1995; Gersten, Langer, Eisenberg, Simcha-Fagan, & McCarthy, 1976); and young adulthood (Robins, 1966; Weiss & Hechtman, 1993).

Most models of development include multiple branching points ("trees") and assume that pathways may lead to a variety of outcomes. Pathways may become quite divergent from the normative (i.e., most frequent) paths but then may converge again, that is, different pathways may lead to the same outcome. The main task for researchers is to better understand precursors, outcomes, and the pathways that connect them (Sroufe & Jacobvitz, 1989).

Obviously, there are many factors that determine both the initial path chosen and the later course; two broad categories of factors are genetic–biological determinants and environmental influences. Sroufe (1989, 1991) and Rutter and Quinton (1984) discussed an important third factor: preceding development. An individual's past experiences shape his or her personality and environment and constrain the availability and type of future choices they can make. They also shape the way in which future experiences are interpreted by the individual. Thus, maladaptive behavior does not spring directly from past experience but rather is influenced both by past factors and present circumstances.

In addition to examining developmental paths and transformations in psychopathology, the field of developmental psychopathology examines other ways in which psychopathology may be affected by age or developmental stage. As Rutter (1989) pointed out, the meaning and expression of behavior varies with the age of the child. Thus, a toddler with anxiety may appear hyperactive, whereas an adolescent with the same anxiety may develop panic attacks.

HOW DOES DEVELOPMENTAL PSYCHOPATHOLOGY LINK PATTERNS OF ADAPTATION AND MALADAPTATION OVER TIME?

The contribution of developmental psychopathology to understanding continuity and discontinuity is best illustrated with two examples. The first example is taken from the work of Alan Sroufe and his colleagues at the University of Minnesota. Their project is a longitudinal study of high-risk children (from families in poverty), with an emphasis on attachment and the development of social relations (Arend, Gove, & Sroufe, 1979; Elicker, Englund, & Sroufe, 1992; Matas et al., 1978; Sroufe et al., 1983, 1990; Waters et al., 1979). Sroufe and colleagues have demonstrated that there is continuity in children's adaptation to salient developmental issues over time. Infants with secure attachments to their mothers were more autonomous in solving problems as toddlers. Links to preschool behaviors were also were observed, although the behaviors were dissimilar. For example, children who had exhibited an anxious attachment in infancy were more dependent on their preschool teachers. When the children were 10 to 11 years old, those with a history of secure attachments demonstrated better ego-resiliency, emotional health, social competence, and self-confidence and had resolved dependency issues in more healthy ways. They were less often isolated, less passive in response to aggression, and expressed more positive emotion than did children with a history of anxious attachment. Sroufe's research indicates the underlying coherence of adaptation despite profound developmental changes in the expression of behavior. Clearly, it also indicates the need for theory-driven models (like attachment theory) to make predictions about the underlying processes that drive development.

The second example illustrates discontinuity and comes from research following the relatively recent (i.e., 1970s) acknowledgment of depression as a disorder that can occur in childhood. The current guidelines (*DSM–IV*) for the diagnosis of depression in adults require presence of depressed mood or anhedonia and a number of vegetative and cognitive symptoms (sleep disturbance, appetite disturbance, fatigue, psychomotor agitation or retardation, loss of interest, difficulty concentrating, guilt, and suicidal thoughts or behaviors). However, there are no specific guidelines on adapting these criteria to children. Some of these behaviors may not be symptomatic of depression in children, and the significance of a particular depressive behavior probably varies with age (Digdon & Gotlib, 1985). In addition, base rates of the behavior in the normal population must be considered. For example, it may be particularly difficult to distinguish hyperkinesis in children from psychomotor agitation, and the base rate of hyperkinesis is quite high. Because decreased appetite is a common (and fluctuating) occurrence in children, it may be difficult to determine whether it is a symptom of depression (Digdon & Gotlib, 1985).

There are also developmental changes in how children describe their experience of depression. Children 6 to 8 years of age report sadness and helplessness, whereas children 8 to 11 years of age report feeling unloved and unworthy and 12 to-13-year- old children are more likely than younger children to report feeling guilty (McConville, Boag, & Purohit, 1973). The question of whether these data reflect changes in the children's actual experience of depression or in their report of depression remains unanswered.

PROBLEMS IN DEFINING PSYCHOPATHOLOGY IN CHILDREN

When diagnosing adult psychopathology, self-report instruments and diagnostic interviews are considered reliable sources of information. This is more difficult in children, for several reasons. First, children's self-reports show correlations as low as .22 with reports by others in their environments, such as parents, teachers, and therapists. When looking at agreement among those other reporters, correlations range from .28 to .66 (Achenbach, McConaughy, & Howell, 1987). In addition to these problems, considerable research has identified parental perception of problems to be colored by the parent's own dysfunction, family distress, and parental negative coercive disciplinary styles (e.g., Campbell, Pierce, March, & Ewing, 1991; Emery, 1982; Richman et al., 1982).

THE TRANSACTIONAL MODEL AND DEVELOPMENTAL PSYCHOPATHOLOGY

One of the basic tenets of developmental psychopathology is that psychopathology does not exist solely within the child but is complexly determined by the transactions between the child and his/her environment (Sameroff & Chandler, 1975). Thus, although the environment obviously will influence the child's development, this interaction is not a simple one-way street. The child also changes the nature of the environment (e.g., a confident, easygoing child will tend to attract a supportive peer group, whereas an angry, aggressive child will drive others away or attract similar peers).

The acceptance of the transactional model has led to an emphasis on longitudinal studies of problem behavior in children and a consideration of increasing numbers of environmental and within-child factors, as well as the interaction of those factors. A brief description of recent work on the development of externalizing behaviors (e.g., aggression, defiance, delinquency) and internalizing behaviors (e.g., inhibition, anxiety, depression) over time illustrates this trend.

Externalizing behaviors have been shown to be the result of the interaction of many different variables both within the child and within the environment. Genetic factors and birth complications have been implicated as contributing to externalizing behavior problems and later violent or criminal behavior in interaction with other factors such as maternal rejection (Adams, Hillman, & Gaydos, 1994; Plomin, Rende, & Rutter, 1991; Raine, Brennan, & Mednick, 1994.) Externalizing problems also have been predicted by parental behaviors, such as unresponsiveness to the child's needs; noncontingent, harsh, and rejecting discipline; poor supervision of child activities; and parental depression in interaction with other factors (Campbell, 1995; Campbell et al., 1996; McFadyen-Ketchum, Bates, Dodge, & Pettit, 1996; Patterson, DeBaryshe, & Ramsey, 1989; Shaw et al., 1998; Snyder, 1991). The attachment relationship has been found to predict or interact with other predictors in explaining externalizing behaviors as well as other behavior and emotional difficulties (Allen et al., 1998; Carlson, 1998; Cohn, 1990; Lyons-Ruth, 1992; Speltz, Greenberg, & DeKlyen, 1990; Wartner et al., 1994). Family and community violence have been found to interact further with other factors to predict childhood aggression and anger (Lynch & Cicchetti, 1998; McCloskey, Figueredo, & Koss, 1995; Osofsky, 1995). More general family factors, such as family socioeconomic status, single-parent status, and poor social support add to the prediction of externalizing outcomes (Adams et al., 1994; Moffitt, 1990; Patterson et al., 1989; Sampson & Laub, 1994). The peer group also can have a major influence on shaping child behavior (Elliott, Huizinga, & Ageton, 1985; Harris, 1998; Patterson et al., 1989). Finally, externalizing behaviors have been predicted by an interaction of gender and other factors (McFadyen-Ketchum et al., 1996; Richman et al., 1982; Shaw, Keenan & Vondra, 1994; Shaw et al., 1998; Wall & Holden, 1994). Clearly, our understanding of the etiology and course of externalizing behavior problems must account for a complex web of interacting influences, something that is only possible through the use of a transactional model of development.

Internalizing problems have been the subject of less research than externalizing problems but also provide a good example of the transactional origins of maladaptive outcomes. Internalizing problems in preschool children were found to be predicted by infant negative emotionality, disorganized attachment relationships, negative life events, and parenting difficulties by Shaw and colleagues (Shaw, Keenan, Vondra, Delliquadri, & Giovannelli, 1997). There has been controversy about whether social inhibition in preschoolers is a transient or lasting phenomenon (e.g., Fagot, 1984; Kohn, 1977; Leach, 1972), and whether it has significant effects on child functioning (Rubin, Hymel, Mills, & Rose-Krasnor, 1991). In general, internalizing behaviors appear to present less risk for long-term adverse outcomes than externalizing behaviors (Parker & Asher, 1987). Kagan and colleagues carried out a series of studies of extremely inhibited children and suggested that such inhibition significantly predicts later anxiety disorders (Rosenbaum et al., 1993). Barlow (1988) proposed a model through which the child's inhibition interacts with his or her environment to determine whether an anxiety disorder will develop. Ollendick (1998) further developed Barlow's model to describe the hypothesized developmental etiology of panic disorder. His model suggests interactions among biological vulnerability, separation-related stress, psychological vulnerability in the form of an insecure–ambivalent attachment relationship and internal attributional style in response to negative outcomes, as well as alarms associated with interoceptive cues. Panic disorder is proposed to result from the interaction of this combination of biological, psychological, and environmental factors.

Thus, outcomes such as childhood internalizing or externalizing disorders must be considered in terms of a complex interaction of factors within and between the child and the environment. This, obviously, has profound implications for diagnosis and treatment, as well as for training of clinicians.

SUMMARY

In the area of developmental psychopathology, researchers are attempting to define normal and abnormal behavior, adaptation and maladaptation, and continuity and discontinuity. The tasks are enormous and require both theoretical and methodological advances. However, developmental psychopathology provides an important theoretical framework that will direct both research and clinical efforts. Future directions include (a) continued study of normal development, from both a group perspective that describes typical behaviors at different ages and from an individual perspective that describes links across domains of functioning in one person; (b) further definition and identification of maladaptive development and refinement of classification systems; and (c) understanding developmental transformation, vulnerability, and resilience across the life span.

REFERENCES

Achenbach, T. M. (1990). Conceptualization of developmental psychopathology. In M. Lewis & S. M. Miller (Eds.), *Handbook of developmental psychopathology, pp 3–14.* New York: Plenum.

Achenbach, T. M., McConaughy, S. H., & Howell, C. T. (1987). Child/adolescent behavioral and emotional problems: Implications of cross-informant correlations for situational specificity. *Psychological Bulletin, 101,* 213–232.

Adams, C. D., Hillman, N., & Gaydos, G. R. (1994). Behavioral difficulties in toddlers: Impact of sociocultural and biological risk factors. *Journal of Clinical Child Psychology, 23,* 373–381.

Allen, J. P., Moore, C., Kuperminc, G., & Bell, K. (1998). Attachment and adolescent psychosocial functioning. *Child Development, 69,* 1406–1419.

American Psychiatric Association. (1994). *Diagnostic and statistical manual of mental disorders* (4th ed.).Washington, DC: Author.

Arend, R., Gove, F., & Sroufe, L. A. (1979). Continuity of individual adaptation from infancy to kindergarten: A predictive study of ego-resiliency and curiosity in preschoolers. *Child Development, 50,* 950–959.

Barkley, R. A., Fischer, M., Edelbrock, C., & Smallish, L. (1990). The adolescent outcome of hyperactive children diagnosed by research criteria: I. An 8-year prospective follow-up study. *Journal of the American Academy of Child and Adolescent Psychiatry, 29,* 546–557.

Barlow, D. H. (1988). *Anxiety and its disorders: The nature and treatment of anxiety and panic.* New York: Guilford.

Campbell, S. B. (1995). Behavior problems in preschool children: A review of recent research. *Journal of Child Psychology and Psychiatry, 36,* 113–149.

Campbell, S. B. (1998). Developmental perspectives. In T. H. Ollendick & M. Hersen (Eds.), *Handbook of child psychopathology* (3rd ed., pp. 3–36.). New York: Plenum.

Campbell, S. B., & Ewing, L .J. (1990). Hard-to-manage preschoolers: Adjustment at age nine and predictors of continuing symptoms. *Journal of Child Psychology and Psychiatry, 31,* 871–889.

Campbell, S. B, Pierce, E., March, C., & Ewing, L. J. (1991). Noncompliant behavior, overactivity, and family stress as predictors of negative maternal control in preschool children. *Development and Psychopathology, 3,* 175–190.

Campbell, S. B., Pierce, E. W., Moore, G., Marakovitz, S., & Newby, K. (1996). Boys' externalizing problems at elementary school age: Pathways from early behavior problems, maternal control, and family stress. *Development and Psychopathology, 8,* 701–719.

Carlson, E. A. (1998). A prospective longitudinal study of attachment disorganization/disorientation. *Child Development, 69,* 1107–1128.

Cicchetti, D. (1989). Developmental psychopathology: Some thoughts on its evolution. *Development and Psychopathology, 1,* 1–4.

Cicchetti, D., & Cohen, D. J. (1995). Perspectives on developmental psychopathology. In D. Cicchetti & D. J. Cohen (Eds.), *Developmental psychopathology. Vol. 1: Theory and methods,* (pp. 3–20). New York: Wiley.

Cohn, D. A. (1990). Child–mother attachment of six-year-olds and social competence in school. *Child Development, 61,* 152–162.

Cowan, P. A. (1988) Developmental psychopathology: A nine-cell map of the territory. In E. D. Nannis & P. A. Cowan (Eds.), *New directions for development: No. 39. Developmental psychopathology and its treatment* (pp. 5–29). San Francisco: Jossey-Bass.

Digdon, N., & Gotlib, I. H. (1985). Developmental considerations in the study of childhood depression. *Developmental Review, 5,* 162–199.

Elicker, J., Englund, M., & Sroufe, L. A. (1992). Predicting peer competence and peer relationships in childhood from early parent–child relationships. In R. Parke & G. Ladd (Eds.), *Family–peer relations: Modes of linkage* (pp. 77–106). Hillsdale, NJ: Lawrence Erlbaum Associates.

Elliot, D. S., Huizinga, D., & Ageton, S. S. (1985). *Explaining delinquency and drug use.* Beverly Hills, CA: Sage.

Emery, R. E. (1982). Interparental conflict and the children of discord and divorce. *Psychological Bulletin, 92,* 310–330.

Ewing, L. J., & Campbell, S. B. (1995, April). *Hard-to-manage preschoolers: Social competence, externalizing behavior, and social competence at early adolescence.* Poster session presented at the meeting of the Society for Research in Child Development, Indianapolis, IN.

Fagot, B. (1984). The consequents of problem behavior in toddler children. *Journal of Abnormal Child Psychology, 1,* 248–256.

Fraiberg, S. (1982). Pathological defenses in infancy. *Psychoanalytic Quarterly, 11,* 612–635.

Garber, J. (1984). Classification of childhood psychopathology: A developmental perspective. *Child Development, 55,* 30–48.

Gersten, J. C., Langner, T. S., Eisenberg, J. G., Simcha-Fagan, O., & McCarthy, E. D. (1976). Stability and change in types of behavioral disturbances of children and adolescents. *Journal of Abnormal Child Psychology, 4,* 111–128.

Harris, J. R. (1998). *The nurture assumption: Why children turn out the way they do.* New York: The Free Press.

Kazdin, A. E. (1989). Developmental psychopathology: Current research, issues, and directions. *American Psychologist, 44,* 180–187.

Kohn, M. (1977). *Social competence, symptoms, and under-achievement in childhood: A longitudinal perspective.* Washington, DC: Winston.

Lapouse, R., & Monk, M. A. (1958). An epidemiologic study of behavior characteristics in children. *American Journal of Public Health, 48,* 1134–1140.

Leach, G. M. (1972). A comparison of the social behaviour of some normal and problem children. In N. Blurton-Jones (Ed.), *Ethological studies in child behavior* (pp. 244–284). Cambridge, England: Cambridge University Press.

Lynch, M., & Cicchetti, D. (1998). An ecological–transactional analysis of children and contexts: The longitudinal interplay among child maltreatment, community violence, and children's symptomatology. *Development and Psychopathology, 10,* 235–257.

Lyons-Ruth, K. (1992). Maternal depressive symptoms, disorganized infant–mother attachment relationships and hostile–aggressive behavior in the preschool classroom: A prospective longitudinal view from infancy to age five. In D. Cicchetti & S. Toth (Eds.), *Rochester Symposium on Developmental Psychopathology, Vol. 4. Developmental perspectives on depression* (pp. 131–172). Rochester, NY: University of Rochester Press.

Main, M., & Goldwyn, R. (1984). Predicting rejection of her infant from mother's representation of her own experience: Implications for the abused–abusing intergenerational cycle. *Child Abuse and Neglect, 8,* 203–217.

Matas, L., Arend, R. A., & Sroufe, L. A. (1978). Continuity of adaptation in the second year: The relationship between quality of attachment and later competence. *Child Development, 49,* 547–556.

McCloskey, L. A., Figueredo, A. J., & Koss, M. P. (1995). The effects of systemic family violence on children's mental health. *Child Development, 66,* 1239–1261.

McConville, B. J., Boag, L. C., & Purohit, A. P. (1973). Three types of childhood depression. *Canadian Psychiatric Association Journal, 18,* 133–138.

McFadyen-Ketchum, S. A., Bates, J. E., Dodge, K. A., & Pettit, G. S. (1996). Patterns of change in early childhood aggressive–disruptive behavior: Gender differences in predictions from early coercive and affectionate mother–child interactions. *Child Development, 67,* 2417–2433.

Moffitt, T. E. (1990). Juvenile delinquency and attention deficit disorder: Boys' developmental trajectories from age 3 to age 15. *Child Development, 61,* 893–910.

Ollendick, T. H. (1998). Panic disorder in children and adolescents: New developments, new directions. *Journal of Clinical Child Psychology, 27,* 234–245.

Osofsky, J. D. (1995). The effects of exposure to violence on young children. *American Psychologist, 50,* 782–788.

Parker, J. G., & Asher, S. R. (1987). Peer relations and later personal adjustment: Are low accepted children at risk? *Psychological Bulletin, 102,* 357–389.

Patterson, G. R., DeBaryshe, B. D., & Ramsey, E. (1989). A developmental perspective on antisocial behavior. *American Psychologist, 44,* 329–335.

Plomin, R. (1989). Environment and genes: Determinants of behavior. *American Psychologist, 44,* 105–111.

Plomin, R., Rende, R. D., & Rutter, M. L. (1991). Quantitative genetics and developmental psychopathology. In D. Cicchetti & S. Toth (Eds.), *Rochester Symposium on Developmental Psychopathology: Vol. 2. Internalizing and externalizing expressions of dysfunction* (pp. 155–202). Rochester, NY: University of Rochester Press.

Radke-Yarrow, M., Zahn-Waxler, C., & Chapman, M. (1983). Children's prosocial dispositions and behavior. In P. H. Mussen (Ed.), *Handbook of child psychology: Vol. 4. Socialization, personality, and social development* (pp. 469–546). New York: Wiley.

Raine, A., Brennan, P., & Mednick, S. A. (1994). Birth complications combined with early maternal rejection at age 1 year predispose to violent crime at age 18 years. *Archives of General Psychiatry, 51,* 984–988.

Richman, N., Stevenson, J., & Graham, P. (1982). *Preschool to school: A behavioural study.* New York: Academic Press.

Robins, L. N. (1966). *Deviant children grown up.* Baltimore: Williams & Wilkins.

Rosenbaum, J. F., Biederman, J., Bolduc-Murphy, E., Faraone, S. V., Chaloff, J., Hirshfeld, D. R., & Kagan, J. (1993). Behavioral inhibition in childhood: A risk factor for anxiety disorders. *Harvard Review of Psychiatry, 1,* 2–16.

Rubin, K. H., Hymel, S., Mills, R., & Rose-Krasnor, L. (1991). Conceptualizing different developmental pathways to social isolation in children. In D. Cicchetti & S. Toth (Eds.), *Rochester Symposium on Developmental Psychopathology: Vol. 2. Internalizing and externalizing expressions of dysfunction.* Rochester, NY: University of Rochester Press.

Rutter, M., & Quinton, D. (1984). Parental psychiatric disorder: Effects on children. *Psychological Medicine, 14,* 853–880.

Rutter, M., Tizard, J., & Whitmore, K. (1970). *Education, health, and behavior.* London: Longman.

Sameroff, A. J., & Chandler, M. J. (1975). Reproductive risk and the continuum of caretaking casualty. In F. D. Horowitz (Ed.), *Review of child development research* (Vol. 4., pp. 187–241). Chicago: University of Chicago Press.

Sampson, R. J., & Laub, J. H. (1994). Urban poverty and the family context of delinquency: A new look at structure and process in a classic study. *Child Development, 65,* 523–540.

Shaw, D. S., Keenan, K., & Vondra, J. I. (1994). The developmental precursors of antisocial behavior: Ages 1–3. *Developmental Psychology, 30,* 355–364.

Shaw, D. S., Keenan, K., Vondra, J. I., Delliquadri, E., & Giovannelli. J. (1997). Antecedents of preschool childrens' internalizing problems: A longitudinal study of low-income families. *Journal of the American Academy of Child and Adolescent Psychiatry, 36,* 1760–1767.

Shaw, D. S., Winslow, E. B., Owens, E. B., Vondra, J. I., Cohn, J. E., & Bell, R. Q. (1998). The development of early externalizing problems among children from low-income families: A transformational perspective. *Journal of Abnormal Child Psychology, 26,* 95–107.

Snyder, J. (1991). Discipline as a mediator of the impact of maternal stress and mood on child conduct problems. *Development and Psychopathology, 3,* 263–276.

Speltz, M. L., Greenberg, M. T., & DeKlyen, M. (1990). Attachment in preschoolers with disruptive behavior: A comparison of clinic-referred and non-problem children. *Development and Psychopathology, 2,* 31–46.

Sroufe, L. A. (1989). Pathways to adaptation and maladaptation: Psychopathology as developmental deviation. In D. Cicchetti (Ed.), *Rochester symposium on developmental psychopathology: Vol. 1. The emergence of a discipline* (pp. 13–40). Hillsdale, NJ: Lawrence Erlbaum Associates.

Sroufe, L. A. (1991). Considering normal and abnormal together: The essence of developmental psychopathology. *Development and Psychopathology, 2,* 335–347.

Sroufe, L. A., Egeland, B., & Kreutzer, T. (1990). The fate of early experience following developmental change: Longitudinal approaches to individual adaptation in childhood. *Child Development, 61,* 1363–1373.

Sroufe, L. A., Fox, N. E., & Pancake, V. R. (1983). Attachment and dependency in developmental perspective. *Child Development, 54,* 1615–1627.

Sroufe, L. A., & Jacobvitz, D. (1989). Diverging pathways, developmental transformations, multiple etiologies and the problem of continuity in development. *Human Development, 32,* 196–203.

Sroufe, L. A., & Rutter, M. (1984). The domain of developmental psychopathology. *Child Development, 55,* 17–29.

Wall, J. E., & Holden, E. W. (1994). Aggressive, assertive, and submissive behaviors in disadvantaged, inner-city preschool children. *Journal of Clinical Child Psychology, 23,* 382–390.

Wartner, U. G., Grossman, K., Fremmer-Bombik, E., & Suess, G. (1994). Attachment patterns at age six in south Germany: Predictability from infancy and implications for preschool behavior. *Child Development, 65,* 1014–1027.

Waters, E., Wippman, J., & Sroufe, L. A. (1979). Attachment, positive affect, and competence in the peer group: Two studies in construct validation. *Child Development, 50,* 821–829.

Weiss, G., & Hechtman, L. T. (1993). *Hyperactive children grown up* (2nd ed.). New York: Guilford.

Werry, J. S., & Quay, H. C. (1971). The prevalence of behavior symptoms of younger elementary school children. *American Journal of Orthopsychiatry, 37,* 725–731.

Psychophysiological Research on Childhood Psychopathology

Rafael Klorman
University of Rochester

SCOPE OF THIS REVIEW AND SOME BACKGROUND

This chapter examines autonomic and brain electrical measures of arousal and responsiveness to stimulation in childhood autism, attention deficit hyperactivity disorder (ADHD), and antisocial/conduct disorder. The most commonly studied autonomic measures are heart rate (HR) and skin conductance (electrodermal activity). Electrodermal measures reflect the activity of sweat glands, which are innervated solely by the sympathetic branch of the autonomic nervous system (Fowles, 1993), whereas HR is affected by the balance between the sympathetic and parasympathetic branches of the autonomic nervous system.

Investigators have examined autonomic activity to characterize subjects on a continuum from sleep–drowsiness through alertness to excitement. Arousal of the central nervous system (CNS) is assessed from the electroencephalogram (EEG), the voltages recorded from the scalp. Slow EEG frequency (low number of cycles per second; increased activity in the delta and theta bands) indicates low levels of arousal, whereas fast activity (e.g. faster waves characteristic of the beta band) reflects heightened arousal.

Another focus of research has been on participants' moment-by-moment reactions to discrete stimuli with emotional or task significance. Specifically, investigators are interested in the magnitude of brief increases in skin conductance or slowing of HR, which are evoked by novel or attended stimuli. A conceptually related methodology involves event-related potentials (ERPS), patterns of voltage changes evoked by discrete stimuli like sounds or lights. Averaging over trials is needed to extract ERPS from the background EEG. This chapter focuses on relatively late ERP components (≥ 100 milliseconds) that are affected by cognitive factors and are relevant to abnormalities in attention.

AUTISM

Children with autism are especially handicapped in language skills, so conventional methods for cognitive assessment present difficulties. The noninvasiveness of psychophysiological methods recommend their use with this population.

Arousal: Autonomic Measures

Consistent with clinical impression that autistic children are hyperaroused, researchers have detected abnormally elevated levels of skin conductance (Palkowitz & Wiesenfeld, 1980; Stevens & Gruzelier, 1984); HR (including sustained tachycardia); and blood pressure (BP; D. J. Cohen & Johnson, 1977; James & Barry, 1984; Kootz, Marinelli, & Cohen, 1982; Lake, Ziegler, & Murphy, 1977). However, some studies detected normal HR (Graveling & Brooke, 1978; Hutt, Forrest, & Richer, 1975; MacCulloch & Williams, 1971; Miller & Bernal, 1971; Palkowitz & Wiesenfeld, 1980), skin conductance level, and pupil diameter in autistic children (van Engeland, Roelofs, Verbaten, & Slangen, 1991). Moreover, heightened cardiovascular arousal sometimes was found also among nonautistic psychiatric patients (D. J. Cohen & Johnson, 1977; James & Barry, 1984). In addition, it is possible that sympathetic overarousal might be due to the stress of being tested rather than some enduring abnormality. In fact, investigations that included acclimatization sessions for autistic patients before the actual test found normal HR (Bernal & Miller, 1970; Palkowitz & Wiesenfeld, 1980).

Autonomic Responsiveness: Repeated Stimulation

James and Barry (1984; Barry & James, 1988) reported that, for both normal and mentally retarded children, amplitude of skin conductance responses decreased regularly over five repetitions of visual (squares of two sizes) and auditory stimuli (tones of two loudnesses). This pattern of response diminution with stimulus repetition is a fundamental characteristic of normal autonomic reactions to novel stimuli and was absent among autistic children, who had abnormally large electrodermal responses across all trials. A similar lack of amplitude diminution with repetition was obtained for the respiratory pause and HR deceleration (James & Barry, 1984). Because variations in stimulus intensity (size of the squares and loudness of the tones) increased autonomic responses of autistic and control groups, the findings suggested a specific defect in registration of reduced novelty. Absence of this orienting disturbance in mentally retarded participants implied that it was not secondary to the lower IQ of autistic children. However, autistic children's autonomic insensitivity to stimulus repetition might reflect the elevated arousal of these participants, who were so severely disturbed that the experimenters had to physically restrain their hands to achieve satisfactory recordings.

Despite the consistency of Barry and James' findings across two studies and their use of large sample sizes, other researchers have not observed autonomic hyperresponsivity in autistic youngsters. Some studies found that autistic children have abnormally small skin conductance responses to visual patterns (van Engeland et al., 1991), tones, and lights (Bernal & Miller, 1970). Other workers obtained normal amplitude of skin conductance responses to tones (Palkowitz & Wiesenfeld, 1980; Stevens & Gruzelier, 1984). Most important, none of these investigators found failure of autonomic response diminution with stimulus repetition.

Autonomic Responsiveness: Change in Stimulation

van Engeland et al. (1991) reported that their nonretarded autistic adolescent patients, in comparison to normal and psychiatric controls, were electrodermally underresponsive to an unexpected change in the position of a visual pattern presented repeatedly on a screen. Notably, autistic and control participants were comparable in the extent to which they visually tracked the movement of the pattern. The investigators concluded that autistic patients may have deficits in arousal or in cognitive evaluations of change in the visual field.

van Engeland et al.'s (1991) results contrast with an earlier study by Bernal and Miller (1970), which found no differences between autistic and normal children's electrodermal reactions to an unexpected change in the pitch of a tone or the brightness of a light. However, the type of stimulus change (spatial position vs. pitch or brightness) differed, and Bernal and Miller's participants were more clinically disturbed and younger.

Summary of Studies on Autonomic Arousal. The majority of investigations reported hyporesponsiveness in the electrodermal responses of autistic children. There is contradictory evidence concerning autistic children's sensitivity to changes in stimulation.

Event-related Potentials: Oddball Tasks

A number of studies examined ERPs in the "oddball" task, in which one stimulus (frequent, standard, or nontarget) appears on the preponderance of trials and another cue (target or deviant) is presented unpredictably the rest of the time. In one version of the task, participants are directed to count silently the occurrence of the deviant; in another format, they press a button when the target is presented. Sometimes, there is a second infrequent event (novel) to which no response is required. Finally, there is a passive variant of the task in which participants do not make any overt responses. Oddball task stimuli evoke ERPs with two major components of interest, which have larger amplitude in response to novel and target stimuli than to nontargets (see Fig. 5.1). P3b is a positive wave that reaches maximal amplitude at posterior scalp sites around 300 to 500 milliseconds after the stimulus is presented. The amplitude of P3b has been related to the degree of attentional capacity allocated to a task and extent of information processed (Johnson, 1988). Nc is a somewhat later negative wave with maximal amplitude at frontal scalp. Finally, A/Pcz/300 is a vertex maximum component within the latency of P3b that is evoked by auditory novel stimuli. (Courchesne, Lincoln, Kilman, & Galambos, 1985).

An influential study by Courchesne et al. (1985) investigated ERPs of nonretarded autistic and normal adolescents to visual and auditory stimuli. The auditory oddball task included a frequent semantic stimulus ("me"), an infrequent semantic target ("you"), and novel acoustic patterns. In turn, the visual task consisted of the letter B as the frequent stimulus, the letter "A" as a target, and unrecognizable visual patterns as novels. Both tasks were presented under instructions to (a) merely attend or (b) press a button to the designated target. Figure 5.1 shows that the autistic participants exhibited abnormally small P3b amplitudes to both targets and novels. Reduction of P3b amplitude in autism was significant for only acoustic stimuli, a finding possibly suggesting that autistic patients have a specific abnormality in processing significant auditory (semantic) versus visual (graphic) stimuli. Also, the autistic participants had

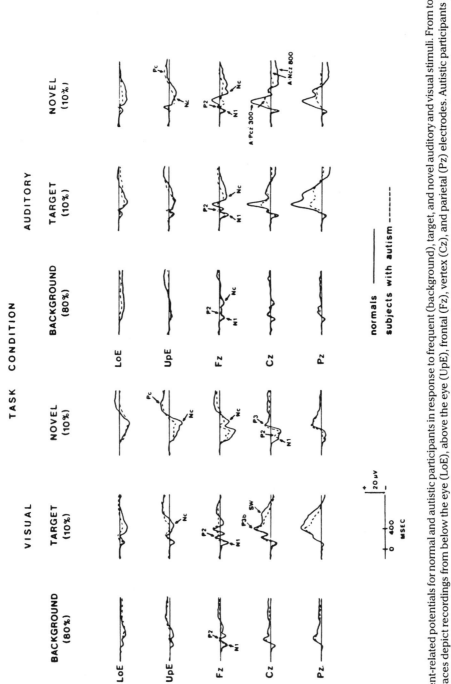

FIG. 5.1. Event-related potentials for normal and autistic participants in response to frequent (background), target, and novel auditory and visual stimuli. From top to bottom, the traces depict recordings from below the eye (LoE), above the eye (UpE), frontal (Fz), vertex (Cz), and parietal (Pz) electrodes. Autistic participants had smaller amplitude of the P3b (especially at Pz and the auditory task) and the Nc components (especially at Fz). From "Event-Related Brain Potential Correlates of the Processing of Novel Visual and Auditory Information in Autism," by E. Courchesne, A. J. Lincoln, B. A. Kilman, and R. Galambos, 1985, *Journal of Autism and Developmental Disorders, 15*, p. 55. Copyright c1985 by Kluwer Academic/Plenum. Reproduced with permission.

smaller amplitude of A/Pcz/300 to novel auditory sounds. Yet, the autistic patients also had smaller Nc waves to *visual* target and novel stimuli than normal participants.

In both the auditory and the visual tasks, unlike normal participants, autistic adolescents lacked larger P3b amplitudes to the visual and auditory infrequent stimuli in the reaction time (RT) task than under passive stimulation. These findings are remarkable, because the autistic participants, although slower than normals, were just as accurate at detecting targets. The results suggest "a limited or selective capacity to orient to novel information, [an ability] critical to cognitive development" (Courchesne et al., 1985, p. 69). However, as noted by the investigators, the autistic patients' ERPs did reflect sensitivity to novelty insofar as several of their ERP components (e.g., P3b) were larger for novels and targets than for frequent or nontarget stimuli.

In a subsequent investigation by Courchesne, Lincoln, Yeung-Courchesne, Elmasian, and Grillon (1989), nonretarded autistic young adults were compared with somewhat younger normal participants and patients with receptive developmental dysphasia, a disorder of language development without the social abnormalities of autism. Auditory and visual oddball tasks were presented, such that the target was defined as either the less frequent of two tone pitches (or colored squares) or as the occasional omission of a single tone (or square) presented at constant intervals. Although the three groups had comparable task performance, autistic participants had smaller P3b amplitude than did normal or dysphasic individuals for both infrequent and deleted targets. Although these differences were found for both modalities, they were greater in the auditory task.

Notably, these two studies detected abnormally small amplitude of Nc and P3b in autistic participants whether the discriminations required were sensory (pitch or color) or linguistic ("you" vs. "me" or A vs. B). Reduction of P3b to the omission of an expected stimulus is especially important, because such events evoke cognitive, but not sensory, reactions. The authors proposed that the diminution of autistic participants' ERPs to target and novel events, despite their normal task performance, suggested aberrant physiological processes or task strategies.

Three other investigations found diminished amplitude of P3b to auditory targets among autistic participants (Dawson, Finley, Phillips, Galpert, & Lewy, 1988; Lincoln, Courchesne, Harms, & Allen, 1993; Novick, Vaughan, Kurtzberg, & Simson, 1980; Oades, Walker, Geffen, & Stern, 1988). One study found nonsignificant trends in the same direction (Niwa, Ohta, &Yamazaki, 1983). In contrast, Erwin et al. (1991) found normal amplitude of P3b by nonretarded autistic adults for prosodic discriminations (e.g., "Bob" as a flat statement or a question).

P3b attenuation in autism has been reported as well for visual stimuli, although less consistently than for the auditory modality (Novick, Kurtzberg, & Vaughan, 1979; Pritchard, Raz, & August, 1987; Verbaten, Roelofs, van Engeland, Kenemans, & Slangen, 1991). Notably, Verbaten et al. (1991) found attenuated visual P3b only for those autistic children with highly erroneous counts of the target and externalizing subjects (who had normal performance). Finally, Strandburg et al. (1993) reported that very highly functioning autistic adults exhibited greater P3b amplitude than did controls in visual oddball and idiom recognition tasks.

Two studies attempted to resolve these issues by studying reactions to stimuli in three modalities by autistic children, normal peers, and psychiatric controls (Kemner, Verbaten, Cuperus, Camfferman, & van Engeland, 1994, 1995). Autistic children had larger P3b amplitude to visual novels (but not targets) than did normal controls, but did not differ from psychiatric controls. For somatosensory targets, autistic children had smaller P3bs that normal, but not psychiatric, controls. Finally, in an auditory oddball test, there were no differences between groups in P3b amplitude. However, consistent with Courchesne et al.'s (1985) report, the autistic children had smaller amplitude of A/Pcz/300 than did any control sample.

Event-Related Potentials: Selective Attention

Ciesielski, Courchesne, and Elmasian (1990) utilized ERPs to determine whether nonretarded autistic young adults are deficient in *selective attention*, the ability to focus more on stimuli central to a task than on task-irrelevant events. Participants were asked to press a button to infrequent green, as opposed to frequent red, flashes and to ignore frequent and infrequent tones of different pitches. (These instructions were reversed in another condition.) To highlight the effects of selective attention, the experimenters subtracted ERPs for frequent tones when tones were not relevant (visual targets) from the corresponding ERPs when tones were targets. (A similar procedure was performed for ERPs for frequent red flashes.) As shown in Fig. 5.2, this method yields a negative wave termed "Nd" (negative difference), or processing negativity. Normal participants exhibited Nd waves of greater amplitude than did autistic patients for both tones and lights, but to a greater extent for auditory stimuli. In addition, as previously found, autistic participants had smaller amplitude of P3b and Nc. A similar study by Ciesielski, Knight, Prince, Harris, and Handmaker (1995) replicated the attenuation of Nc amplitude to infrequent stimuli but not the reduction of Nd and P3b. In fact, autistic participants, unlike normal ones, failed to show an increase in Nc amplitude when the stimulus was more task-relevant. Thus, again, autistic participants displayed smaller ERPs related to task demands despite satisfactory performance. However, further research is needed to verify the stability of findings for Nd, the ERP component linked to selective attention.

Summary of ERP Studies in Autism.   The weight of the evidence indicates that autistic participants have abnormally small amplitude of P3b and Nc to target and novel stimuli, although patients performed comparably to normal participants. In addition, ERPs reflecting selective attention were smaller in autistic patients. These ERP abnormalities were more pronounced for auditory than visual stimuli, a finding consistent with the linguistic deficits of the autistic disorder.

Factors associated with negative findings for P3b and Nc include: (a) use of highly functioning autistic participants, such as adolescents or young adults with a childhood history of autism who might have achieved significant recovery (e.g., Erwin et al., 1991); (b) very small samples (e.g., $N = 5$), which may provide insufficient statistical power; (c) experimental tasks too difficult for the autistic sample (e.g., Niwa et al., 1983); and (d) use of control groups closely matched on IQ with autistic participants (Strandburg et al., 1993) or composed of psychiatric patients (e.g., Pritchard et al., 1987). However, these methodological factors do not fully account for discrepant findings, because they were present in some studies that did obtain ERP abnormalities among autistic participants. Certainly, inclusion of comparison groups with psychiatric and language disorders is important for evaluating the specificity of any findings. Controls for IQ and age (possibly with separate samples) are also important. Finally, although the focus on high functioning autistic persons reduces the influence of mental retardation on results, it is important to extend this research to more impaired autistic participants.

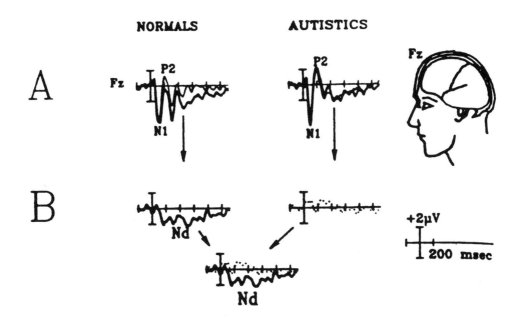

FIG. 5.2. Event-related potentials of normal and autistic Event-related potentials to auditory frequent stimuli (standards) recorded from frontal scalp (Fz). Trace A shows each group's responses to the frequent tones when they were attended (thick lines) and unattended (thin lines). Trace B shows the algebraic difference between the attended and unattended conditions (Nd, or processing negativity) for normal (solid thick line) and autistic participants (dotted line). The lowermost trace superimposes the Nd for normal and autistic participants. Nd was larger for normal persons. From "Effects of Focused Selective Attention Tasks on Event-Related Potentials in Autistic and Normal Individuals," by K. T. Ciesielski, E. Courchesne, and R. Elmasian (1990), *Electroencephalography and Clinical Neurophysiology, 75,* p. 207. Copyright © 1990 by Elsevier Science Publishers. Reproduced with permission.

ATTENTION DEFICIT HYPERACTIVITY DISORDER

Psychophysiological studies have investigated arousal and attentional abnormalities in ADHD. Reviewers (e.g., Sergeant, 1988) have questioned whether apparent deficits in ADHD are due to nonspecific abnormalities of arousal or motivation rather than attention. Investigators also have addressed whether stimulant medications reduce psychophysiological abnormalities of ADHD children as well as their behavior. Such findings would increase our understanding of the psychological processes affected by these substances.

Arousal

This section is focused on EEG results because studies of autonomic arousal have yielded contradictory findings (Zahn, Abate, Little, & Wender, 1975). The prevalent assumption that ADHD children are excessively aroused was challenged by

Satterfield, Cantwell, and Satterfield's (1974) report that these patients have an excess of slow EEG activity and low skin conductance level, both indications of underarousal. In a later report, Satterfield, Schell, Backs, and Hidaka (1984) took advantage of their unusually large ADHD sample ($N = 138$) to analyze the EEG arousal of ADHD children as a function of age. Compared to age-matched normal children, ADHD patients under 7.5 years of age had less energy in all EEG bands (delta, theta, alpha, and beta), whereas older ADHD patients exhibited more power throughout the EEG spectrum. These results are not clearly interpreted in terms of either under- or overarousal.

Satterfield et al.'s (1984) results are consistent with those of three studies involving relatively older ADHD patients (Dykman, Holcomb, Oglesby, & Ackerman, 1982; Grünewald-Zuberbier, Grünewald, & Rasche, 1975; Kuperman, Johnson, Arndt, Lindgren, & Wolraich, 1996). Callaway, Halliday, and Naylor (1983), by contrast, detected less EEG power among ADHD children than among controls, but these researchers recorded EEG for a shorter period (1 minute) than the studies cited previously (45 minutes in Satterfield et al., 1984). Longer recordings may evoke fatigue or decreased motivation, so it would be useful to track EEG arousal as a function of time in the session.

Recently, Chabot and Serfontein (1996) considered EEG arousal in ADHD children ($N = 407$) across an extensive array of electrodes, age range (6–17 years old), and clinical aspects of ADHD (IQ level, learning disabilities, hyperactivity, and clinical severity). This team also found that slow EEG frequencies were more prevalent among ADHD than among control children. However, excess of theta or alpha EEG frequencies was present for both patients with decreased and normal alpha mean frequency (30% and 46%, respectively, of ADHD children). The investigators concluded that these two groups "support the notion that CNS arousal can be abnormally low or high in children with attention problems" (p. 960).

Autonomic Responsiveness

Unlike research on autonomic arousal in ADHD, studies of autonomic responsiveness are relatively consistent. Zahn et al. (1975) reported that ADHD children, in comparison to normal peers, exhibited smaller skin conductance responses to both neutral tones and signals in an RT task. Diminished electrodermal responsiveness sometimes has been reported for nonsignal auditory stimuli (Spring, Greenberg, Scott, & Hopwood, 1974) but there are also negative findings (Cohen & Douglas, 1972; Zahn & Kruesi, 1993). In contrast, the report of reduced skin conductance responses to signal stimuli has been replicated (Cohen & Douglas, 1972; Zahn & Kruesi, 1993), suggesting decreased task involvement by ADHD participants.

Zahn et al. (1975) found that ADHD children had smaller cardiac deceleration to neutral tones but not to RT stimuli. In contrast, Zahn, Little, and Wender (1978) obtained attenuated cardiac deceleration by ADHD children to R T task stimuli.

Summary of Autonomic Responsiveness. The general finding across all of these studies was that skin conductance to significant task stimuli was reduced in ADHD, suggesting deficient involvement in the task. In contrast, results for autonomic reactions to nonsignal stimulation were inconsistent.

Autonomic Responsiveness: Motivational Manipulations

Recent research has related effects of motivational manipulations on autonomic re-actions to Gray's (1982) neurophysiological theory. Gray described a behavioral inhi-bition system (BIS), which processes signals that are novel or associated with past punishment, and a behavioral activation system (BAS), which processes signals re-lated to reward. Quay (1988) proposed that ADHD children have decreased activity in the BIS. In turn, Fowles (1980) suggested that increased HR in response to reward re-flects the BAS, whereas increased skin conductance in response to removal of re-ward tracks the BIS.

To test for an underactive BIS in ADHD, Pliszka, Hatch, Borcherding, and Rogeness (1993) investigated responsiveness to punishment signals in classical conditioning among ADHD children (with and without overanxious disorder) and control partici-pants. Loud white noise (unconditioned stimulus) followed presentations of a partic-ular combination of colored squares and tones (conditioned stimulus) but not a different square–tone arrangement. Because the three diagnostic groups exhibited a comparable degree of autonomic conditioning (HR acceleration and increased skin conductance to the conditioned stimulus and concomitant decreases during extinc-tion), the results did not support the hypothesis of an underactive BIS in ADHD.

In a conceptually related study (Iaboni, Douglas, & Ditto, 1997), monetary rewards were delivered in some phases of a repetitive motor task and withheld in others. In general, ADHD children exhibited less cardiac acceleration or electrodermal arousal to the presentation and withdrawal of reward over trials. The attenuated cardiac re-sponsiveness of ADHD children to reward suggests a somewhat weaker BAS, whereas their faster habituation to reward and reduced reactions to the extinction of reward are consistent with a defective BIS.

ERP Studies: P3b Amplitude.   This section emphasizes cognitive ERPs, because most investigations have yielded null findings in conditions not involving attention, such as passive stimulation (e.g., Oades, Dittmann-Balcar, Schepker, Eggers, & Zerbin, 1996; Winsberg, Javitt, & Shanahan/Silipo, 1997). Several investigations have focused on ERPs during the Continuous Performance Test (CPT), a task in which ADHD children perform deficiently. The CPT is similar to an oddball task; on each trial, one of several letters is presented, and participants press a button to a designated letter or se-quence of letters. ADHD participants performed more poorly on this type of task and had smaller P3b amplitude than did age-matched controls (Holcomb, Ackerman, & Dykman, 1985, 1986; Jonkman et al., 1997b; Kemner et al., 1996; Klorman, Salzman, Pass, Borgstedt, & Dainer, 1979; Loiselle, Stamm, Maitinsky, & Whipple, 1980; Mi-chael, Klorman, Salzman, Borgstedt, & Dainer, 1981; Novak, Solanto, & Abikoff, 1995; Robaey, Breton, Dugas, & Renault, 1992; Satterfield, Schell, & Nicholas, 1994; Satterfield, Schell, Nicholas, Satterfield, & Freise, 1990; Strandburg et al., 1996). In some (e.g., Sunohara, Voros, Malone, & Taylor, 1997; Taylor, Voros, Logan, & Malone, 1993), but not all (Satterfield, Schell, Nicholas, & Backs, 1988; Winsberg et al., 1997), studies that did not replicate P3b diminution in ADHD, ADHD children exhibited nor-mal performance.

As shown in Figure 5.3, Holcomb et al. (1985) found abnormally small P3b ampli-tude in patients with ADHD with and without hyperactivity as well as in non-ADHD reading-disordered children. Other studies also have reported abnormally small am-

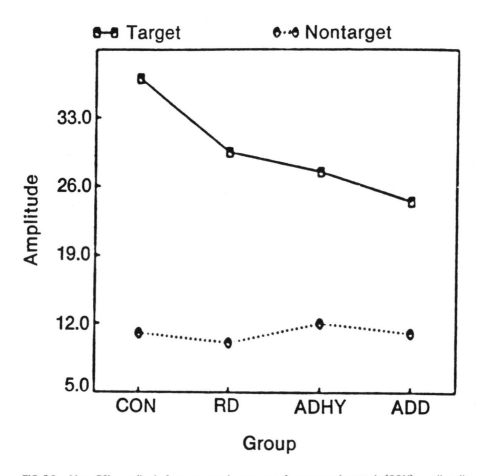

FIG. 5.3. Mean P3b amplitude for targets and nontargets from normal controls (CON), reading disorder (RD), attention deficit disorder with hyperactivity (ADDH), and attention deficit disorder (ADD) children. From "Cognitive Event-Related Potentials in Children With Attention and Reading Deficits" by P. J. Holcomb, P. T. Ackerman, and R. A. Dykman, 1985, *Psychophysiology, 22,* p. 656. Copyright © 1985 by the Society for Psychophysiological Research. Reprinted with permission.

plitude of P3b in learning disorder (e.g., Dainer et al., 1981; Taylor & Keenan, 1990) and, as reviewed previously, in autism. The presence of P3b reduction in such vastly different disorders is probably due to the detection of similar abnormalities in information processing.

ERP Studies: P3b Latency

Extensive research suggests that latency of P3b (timing of peak amplitude) reflects the relative duration of stimulus evaluation, that is, those stages preceding the preparation and execution of motor responses. Thus, it is significant that children with ADHD had slower P3b latency than normal controls (Holcomb et al., 1985; Strandburg et al., 1996; Sunohara et al., 1997; Taylor et al., 1993). Because similar results were found for dyslexic children (Holcomb et al., 1985; Taylor & Keenan, 1990), delays in P3b latency, like reduced P3b amplitude, may not be specific to ADHD.

Klorman, Brumaghim, Fitzpatrick, and Borgstedt (1992) compared ADHD adolescents with age-matched controls in a memory scanning test requiring memorizing lists of one to four numbers (targets). Subsequently, participants viewed one number at a time and pressed one hand-held button if the number was a target and pressed with the other hand if the number was a nontarget. ADHD adolescents made more errors than did normals to targets and lacked the normative tendency for faster P3b latencies to targets (numbers held in memory) than did nontargets (see Fig. 5.4). These findings implied that ADHD participants have a deficit in the stage of stimulus identification, that is, a specific defect of information processing. These results argue against the view that cognitive deficits of ADHD participants are attributable exclusively to nonspecific factors such as arousal or motivational variables.

ERP Studies: Selective Attention

Stamm and colleagues studied adolescents with a history of ADHD (Zambelli, Stamm, Maitinsky, & Loiselle, 1977) and ADHD children (Loiselle et al., 1980) with age-matched controls in a dichotic listening task involving independent sequences of infrequent and frequent tone pips in each ear. The instructions were to press a button when detecting the infrequent tone in one ear and to ignore input to the other ear. As expected, ADHD patients made more errors and responded more slowly than did their normal peers. The research was focused on the N1 component, which is enhanced in focused selective attention. Interestingly, ADHD adolescents and children in these studies lacked their normal peers' pattern of larger amplitude of the N1 component for tones presented to the relevant ear than the corresponding stimuli for the irrelevant ear.

A related question was examined by Satterfield et al. (1988) in a task consisting of an infrequent loud click, a frequent soft click, an infrequent bright light, or a frequent dim light. Instructions in one task were to respond to the infrequent sound, and in another test, to the infrequent light. As shown in Figure 5.5, the ERPs of normal, but not ADHD, children, exhibited the impact of selective attention: greater negativity in response to the frequent click when attention was directed to clicks than when subjects pressed in response to lights.

Satterfield et al. (1990) obtained similar, but less clear-cut, trends of reduced Nd for 6-year-old ADHD children, but this abnormality was absent when the same children were assessed at age 8. Similarly, other investigators replicated diminished Nd to auditory (Jonkman et al., 1997b), but not visual, test stimuli (Jonkman et al., 1997b; Strandburg et al., 1996). Analogous research has focused on the N2 wave, another ERP component sensitive to selective attention. This work found reduced enhancement of N2 amplitude under selective attention in ADHD, but these findings also were limited to auditory stimuli (Jonkman et al., 1997b) or less pronounced for visual stimuli (Satterfield et al., 1994). In addition, there have been reports that, among ADHD children, ERP components sensitive to selective attention were larger (Callaway et al., 1983; Harter, Anllo-Vento, Wood, & Schroeder, 1988) or comparable to those of controls (Novak et al., 1995).

Summary of ERP Studies.   Numerous studies reported that ADHD children have abnormally small amplitude of the P3b component along with concomitant deficits in task performance. However, the abnormal reduction of P3b amplitude is also present in autism and reading disorder. Several studies have reported slower latency of

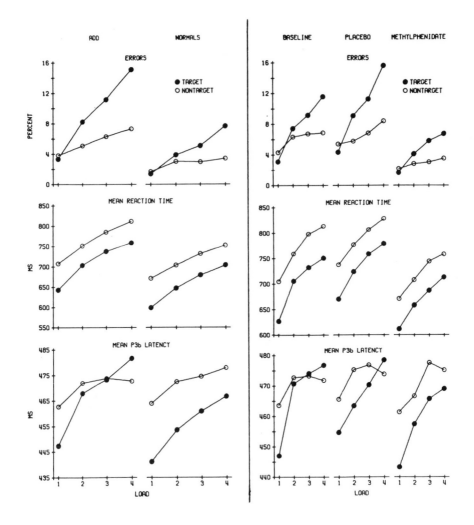

FIG. 5.4.   Left panel: data for unmedicated ADHD and normal adolescents. Right panel: data for ADHD adolescents tested in an off-drug baseline session, placebo, and methylphenidate. Top panel: percentage errors; middle panel: mean reaction time. Bottom panel: mean P3b latency. From "Methylphenidate reduces abnormalities of stimulus classification in adolescents with attention deficit disorder" by R. Klorman, J. T. Brumaghim, P. A. Fitzpatrick, and A. D. Borgstedt, 1992, *Journal of Abnormal Psychology, 101,* p. 130. Copyright © 1992 by the American Psychological Association. Adapted with permission.

P3b in ADHD than in normal controls. ADHD participants had slower P3b latency than did normal children and lacked the normal tendency for faster P3b latency to targets than nontargets, a finding suggesting deficits in stimulus identification. Finally, most research points to smaller amplitudes in ADHD children of negative ERP waves sensitive to selective attention.

Effects of Stimulants: Autonomic Activity

In an influential study (Zahn, Rapoport, & Thompson, 1980), single doses of amphetamine and of placebo were administered to both ADHD and normal children. Amphetamine improved performance, increased HR deceleration, and diminished electrodermal reactivity of both groups. These results contradict the popular belief that ADHD children's reactions to stimulants are paradoxical and indicate similar benefits for attentiveness and associated autonomic changes for ADHD and normal children.

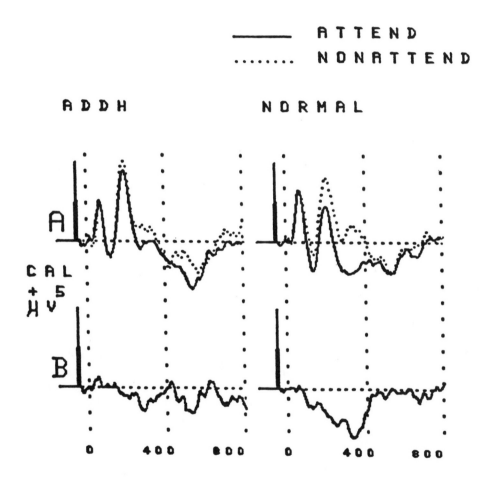

FIG. 5.5.   Panel A: ERPs for nontarget tones when they were relevant to the task (ATTEND, solid line) or not (NONATTEND, dotted line). The data were obtained from Attention Deficit Disorder with Hyperactivity (ADDH) or normal children. Panel B: Nd, that is, difference curves produced by subtracting the ERPs in the Nonattend condition from those in the Attend condition. Nd was larger for normal than for ADDH children. From "Topographic study of auditory event related potentials in normal boys and in boys with attention deficit disorder with hyperactivity" by J. H. Satterfield, A. M. Schell, T. W. Nicholas, and R. W. Backs, 1988, *Psychophysiology, 25,* p. 591. Copyright © 1988 by the Society for Psychophysiological Research. Reproduced with permission.

Effects of Stimulants: P3b Amplitude

In several studies (Fitzpatrick, Klorman, Brumaghim, & Borgstedt, 1992; Klorman et al., 1979; Jonkman et al., 1997a; Michael et al., 1981; Novak et al., 1995; Verbaten et al., 1994; Winsberg et al., 1997), administration of methylphenidate improved ADHD patients' performance and increased the amplitude of P3b, usually to a comparable extent for targets and nontargets. Thus, both performance and P3b were normalized by this medication. Some failures to replicate the enlargement of P3b with stimulants were obtained in studies in which these medications yielded weak or no improvements of performance (Frobel-Smithee, Klorman, Brumaghim, & Borgstedt, 1998; Sunohara et al., 1997; Syrigou-Papavasiliou, Lycaki, & Lewitt, 1988; Taylor et al., 1993). In our work, this phenomenon was found for ADHD patients varying on a variety of potentially biasing factors: (a) age: both ADHD children (Michael et al., 1981) and adolescents (Coons, Klorman, & Borgstedt, 1987; Klorman, Brumaghim, Fitzpatrick, & Borgstedt, 1991; Klorman et al., 1992); (b) history of or lack of previous treatment with stimulants. Thus, P3b enlargement is not an artifact of having studied a sample of patients known to respond to the medication, that is, those selected from currently treated patients; (c) pervasiveness: both children meeting criteria for ADHD at home and school or in only one setting (Klorman, Brumaghim, Fitzpatrick, Borgstedt, & Strauss, 1994; Klorman et al., 1983, 1988); and (d) comorbidity: ADHD children with and without concurrent oppositional/aggressive features (Klorman et al., 1988, 1994). In fact, the same effect was obtained in psychiatrically normal children (Peloquin & Klorman, 1986) and young adults (e.g., Brumaghim & Klorman, 1998 ; Brumaghim, Klorman, Strauss, Lewine, & Goldstein, 1987). The generality of the effects of stimulants on ERPs and autonomic responses (Zahn et al., 1980) contradict the view that ADHD patients' cognitive enhancement by stimulants is unique to ADHD.

Effects of Stimulants: P3b Latency

P3b latencies of ADHD children were shortened by methylphenidate (Klorman et al., 1991; Syrigou-Papavasiliou et al., 1988; Taylor et al., 1993; Winsberg et al., 1997). In addition, treatment with methylphenidate differentially reduced errors to targets over those to nontargets and speeded the latency of P3b to targets for ADHD adolescents (Klorman et al., 1992; see Fig. 5.4) and children (Klorman et al., 1994). These results point to enhancements of specific aspects of information processing. Notably, a speeding of P3b in this task by methylphenidate also was found in normal young adults (Brumaghim et al., 1987), suggesting once again that this impact of stimulants is not diagnostically specific.

Effects of Stimulants: Selective Attention

Methylphenidate increased the early portion of ADHD children's Nd to tones in comparison to their responses under placebo (Klorman et al., 1990); however, stimulant medication did not affect Nd amplitude to lights. In contrast, Jonkman et al. (1997a) reported that methylphenidate enhanced ADHD children's processing negativities (Nd) to both visual and auditory stimuli, although—as described previously—the same patients exhibited abnormally small processing negativities for only the auditory modality. In combination, these results support the conclusion that methylphenidate enhances ERPs associated with selective attention.

Effects of Stimulants: Other Cognitive ERP Components

Studies by Halliday and colleagues (Halliday, Callaway, & Rosenthal, 1984; Halliday, Rosenthal, Naylor, & Callaway, 1976) investigated the effects of stimulants on ADHD children's ERPs in an oddball task involving infrequent dim lights (targets), frequent bright lights, and frequent tones. Halliday et al. (1976, 1984) found that clinical response to methylphenidate treatment was correlated with an increase by this medication of the N1–P2 wave to frequent lights. The replication of these results suggests that this ERP may reflect gains in cognitive processing resulting from stimulant therapy and may have practical value in predicting response to treatment.

Klorman et al. (1983) administered a similar task to ADHD children under placebo and two doses of methylphenidate (0.3 and 0.6 mg/Kg). The stimulant speeded RT but did not affect the visual ERP component identified by Halliday et al. (1976) as sensitive to clinical response to methylphenidate. Rather, the medication increased P3b amplitude to nontarget lights and magnified the increase in N1 to nontarget tones when subjects responded to targets (infrequent lights) as opposed to a condition in which no responses were required. This effect of the drug may reflect the greater salience of tones in the active than the passive task.

Summary of Effects of Stimulants. Stimulant medication may enhance cardiac deceleration to RT task stimuli, but it generally reduces electrodermal responding. Similarly, stimulants improve performance and increase cognitive ERP amplitude. In addition, methylphenidate reduces the slowing of P3b latency in ADHD children and restores the tendency for faster P3b latency to targets than nontargets, findings implicating an impact on stimulus identification. However, these effects of stimulants are not specific to ADHD children.

Enlargement of Nd by stimulants suggests selective attention deficits, but often stimuli were presented sufficiently far apart such that limited selective attention (ignoring irrelevant stimuli) may have been required.

The robustness of stimulant effects on cognitive ERPs has resulted in replicated findings that these changes are related to clinical changes in this therapy.

ANTISOCIAL AND CONDUCT DISORDER

Much research has considered individual differences in psychophysiological responding in individuals with antisocial and conduct disorders. Importantly, most psychophysiological research on ADHD or conduct disorder has not considered the overlap between ADHD and conduct and oppositional disorder. Participants often identified by teacher ratings of antisocial behavior or juvenile delinquency rather than by contemporary definitions of conduct disorder, so I refer to these samples by the admittedly imprecise term of *antisocial*.

Arousal: Autonomic Activity

Because deficits in anxiety have been attributed to some criminals, it is of interest whether antisocial adolescents display abnormal physiological arousal. Notably, several studies related abnormally slow resting HR to antisocial tendencies in adolescence. Raine and Jones (1987) reported that among behaviorally maladjusted children (7–15 years old), a low resting HR was correlated with high self-ratings of conduct disorder and socialized aggression. Similarly, among psychiatrically unselected adolescent students (14–16 years old), Raine and Venables (1984b) obtained an association between slow HR and self- and teacher-rated antisocial behavior. However, this correlation was more pronounced for youngsters from higher than from lower social classes.

Along similar lines, boys classified as refractory by their teachers had lower HRs than did those viewed as cooperative (Davies & Maliphant, 1971). Similarly, adolescent girls classified as refractory also had lower HRs than did their well-behaved peers (Maliphant, Hume, & Furnham, 1990). Rogeness et al.'s (1990) study of 383 male (mean age = 11.8 years) and 106 female psychiatric inpatients (mean age = 12.5 years) is especially interesting, because of its large sample and use of contemporary diagnoses using the *Diagnostic and Statistical Manual of Mental Disorders* (3rd ed., American Psychiatric Association, 1980). For both genders, conduct disorder patients had lower HRs than did patients with other diagnoses. In fact, conduct disorder symptoms were correlated with low HR and low systolic blood pressure, whereas high cardiovascular arousal was correlated with indications of anxiety among male patients. In contrast to the preceding studies, Garralda, Connell, and Taylor (1991) did not find slow HR in conduct disorder outpatients. However, their participants were younger than those in other studies and combined neurotic and conduct disorders.

Several possible interpretations of the association between HR and antisocial behavior were evaluated in an epidemiological study of 1,795 Mauritian children who were 3 years old (Raine, Venables, & Mednick, 1997). Low HR measured at age 3 was associated with parent ratings of aggressive antisocial behavior at age 11. This phenomenon could not be explained by muscle tone at age 3 or by a variety of other possible confounding factors (ethnic background, gender, measures of body size, motor activity, crying during the assessment of HR, time of day at the assessment, physical development, health status, family discord, socioeconomic status, and temperament). Yet, despite the exemplary thoroughness of this investigation, parental reports of aggression at age 11 do not necessarily reflect antisocial acts, which were measured in the studies cited previously.

A question raised in previous sections is relevant to all these studies: Do antisocial adolescents' abnormally low resting levels of autonomic activity reflect a disturbance of arousal or lower reactivity to being evaluated? Davies and Maliphant (1971) attempted to address this concern by assessing HR on four different occasions in a school day, a procedure likely to induce adaptation to the stress of being tested. However, ruling out lesser excitement or greater boredom by antisocial adolescents requires monitoring HR over several days.

Autonomic Responsiveness

A related question is whether antisocial adolescents have lower responsivity to stress, a finding that would be especially compatible with the view that these patients have an anxiety deficit. Interestingly, Davies and Maliphant (1971) found that refractory boys exhibited less HR acceleration than did controls during an RT test involving threat of shock or loss of monetary rewards. Similarly, Maliphant et al. (1990) reported that refractory girls had lower peak cardiac rates when tested on Raven's (1960) Progressive Matrices Test under stress (being rushed to work faster and being told that their results would be compared with the rest of their class). Two studies that obtained discrepant findings employed considerably less noxious stimuli, such as moderately loud tones (Borkovec, 1970; Garralda et al., 1991). Although more extensive research may be required before firm conclusions can be drawn, the evidence for smaller cardiac reactions in antisocial youths seems stronger in studies employing noxious stimuli.

Besides reduced HR reactivity, several studies document diminished electrodermal responsiveness among antisocial youngsters. Abnormally small skin conductance responses to a novel tone were detected in psychopathic juvenile delinquents (Borkovec, 1970) and in highly antisocial incarcerated adolescents (Siddle, Nicol, & Foggit, 1973). Similar results were obtained in samples of noncriminal adolescents: Schoolchildren rated high in antisocial behavior (Raine & Venables, 1984a) and learning-disordered children rated high on conduct disorder and low on tension–anxiety (Delamater & Lahey, 1983).

Autonomic Responsiveness: Subsequent Criminality

Raine, Venables, and Williams (1990a, 1990b, 1990c) reported that those students who had acquired a criminal record by age 24 had lower autonomic arousal in adolescence than did their noncriminal peers, including slower HR, nonsignificantly lower skin conductance level, and lower frequency of spontaneous skin conductance responses. Similarly, low resting HR and skin conductance level also predicted institutionalization in a 2-year follow-up of another sample of children and adolescents with disruptive behavior disorders (Kruesi et al., 1992). In combination with previously reviewed evidence of low autonomic arousal in antisocial adolescents, these prospective studies support the enduring clinical significance of these psychophysiological findings.

Besides low autonomic arousal, the adolescents who became criminals in the sample of Raine et al. (1990b) exhibited lower cortical arousal in adolescence (more power in the theta bands and, nonsignificantly, in the delta and alpha bands) than did adolescents without a subsequent criminal record. Raine et al. (1990a) also linked low frequency of electrodermal responses and small HR reactions to neutral tones in adolescence to subsequent criminality. Such reduced orienting was interpreted as a deficit in the allocation of attentional resources to external stimuli. Thus, these researchers found concordance in autonomic and cortical underarousal for future criminals. In contrast, a similarly designed study by Satterfield and Schell (1984) yielded generally opposite findings. In their longitudinal study of ADHD children, slower EEG and smaller amplitude of the N2 component to clicks was found for patients who did not become delinquents. As a result, Satterfield and Schell (1984) proposed that nondelinquent ADHD children may suffer from a neurological disorder, whereas ADHD children who become delinquent have a disorder based on adverse background. Clearly, studies by Raine et al. (1990b) and Satterfield and Schell differed in the clinical composition of their samples (unselected adolescents vs. ADHD children) and the length of the EEG recording (2 vs. 45 minutes). Further research is needed to resolve these discrepancies.

Summary of Autonomic Research on Antisocial Disorders. Abnormally low resting HR and autonomic hyporeactivity to stimulation among adolescents with antisocial tendencies is compatible with findings of abnormally low resting electrodermal arousal in antisocial adults (Fowles, 1993). There is particularly strong evidence that antisocial adults are electrodermally underresponsive to stressful conditions (e.g., threat of shock) or signal stimuli (e.g., RT cues). However, the cardiac reactions (e.g., HR acceleration to noxious stimulation) of antisocial adults have been found to be of normal or greater than normal amplitude. Fowles (1993) has reconciled these findings by suggesting that HR reflects Gray's (1982) BAS (rewards or avoidance of punishment) and that skin conductance is related to the BIS (negative affect). In this scheme, the antisocial adult has a weak BIS and a dominant BAS.

Evidence on antisocial children and adolescents is partially compatible with Fowles' (1993) position. Evidence for autonomic underarousal and underresponsiveness to noxious stimulation in antisocial children is most convincing for HR, whereas results for antisocial adults are more supportive for the electrodermal system. Still, it is possible to reconcile these apparent discrepancies between developmental and adult studies of antisocial participants. First, studies with children generally have not employed truly noxious stimuli like shock, so that this aspect of adult antisocial underresponsiveness has not been examined sufficiently in childhood and adolescence. Second, few studies of antisocial youngsters have examined HR and electrodermal activity simultaneously, and those that did obtained at least modest associations (Borkovec, 1970; Raine et al., 1990a). Therefore, it has not been possible to determine clearly whether antisocial adolescents exhibit the abnormalities reported for antisocial adults. Third, most of the studies of antisocial adults are based on prisoners, whereas most developmental research involved children and adolescents who were not incarcerated. It would be useful in future research to clarify the importance of these factors. In addition, inclusion of psychiatric comparison groups is important for evaluating deficits in the experience of anxiety or in the behavioral inhibition system. For instance, anxious participants would be expected to exhibit directionally opposite autonomic reactions to anxiety signals in comparison to those of antisocial participants.

ERP Studies

Raine and Venables (e.g., 1987) interpreted the literature on autonomic abnormalities in antisocial persons in terms of abnormal information processing rather than deficient anxiety. In support of this position is these authors' (1984a) finding that electrodermal nonresponding was related to schizoid tendencies. In addition, Raine and Venables (1987) pointed to clinical and empirical findings that antisocial adults do not attend to boring tasks but excel in situations they find interesting. Consistent with this position, these investigators reported that antisocial adolescents had smaller amplitude of the contingent negative variation (CNV) than did prosocial adolescents. (The CNV is a slow negative potential that develops over the interval [1.5 seconds in this instance] between a warning stimulus and the imperative signal to press a button in an RT test. CNV amplitude has been related to cognitive factors like expectancy and attentional capacity.) On the other hand, antisocial adolescents had larger amplitude of the P3b component in response to the warning tone in the same task. Raine and Venables (1987) regarded the P3b findings as evidence of enhanced information processing in their antisocial subjects.

Additional support for the attentional interpretation came from the finding that future criminals had smaller autonomic orienting responses in adolescence than did noncriminals (Raine et al., 1990a). In addition, the future criminals exhibited larger amplitude of the N1 component and earlier latencies of P3b to the warning tone in the RT task (Raine et al., 1990c). These results were interpreted, respectively, as indications of deficits in passive attention and enhanced processing speed. However, the ERP measures sensitive to the original antisocial–prosocial distinction were different from those that predicted future criminality. Thus, this research again reveals a mixed picture, with both diminished and enhanced attention in the antisocial group.

Herning, Hickey, Pickworth, and Jaffe (1989) also found that adolescents with highly delinquent backgrounds, in comparison to peers low in delinquency, had an earlier latency of the N1 wave and smaller amplitude of a late frontal negative slow wave evoked by the target tone in an oddball task performed under noisy conditions. Importantly, the investigators demonstrated that the ERP findings for delinquent adolescents were not dependent on a history of drug use. Although the ERP components implicated by Herning et al. (1989) differ from those identified in Raine et al. (1990b), there were differences in the task (oddball vs. RT) and populations (criminal adolescents vs. adolescents with subsequent delinquency) studied.

SUMMARY

There is inconsistent evidence on whether antisocial adolescents have attentional deficits or, under some circumstances, enhanced information processing. However, there is a need for replication, because several findings are based on a single sample. In addition, except for Herning et al. (1989), investigators have not evaluated the possible confounding effects of drug abuse by antisocial participants. Future research needs to delineate the conditions that elicit deficient and enhanced attentiveness by this population. There is also a need for more extensive ERP research on antisocial disorders in adolescence. Of course, it is important to determine whether any abnormalities in cognitive ERPs are also present in other psychiatric groups.

ACKNOWLEDGMENTS

My work on this chapter was made possible by NIMH grant MH56571 and NICHD grant HD25802. I am grateful to Loisa Bennetto, H. Theresa Chang, Joan T. Brumaghim, Don Fowles, and Marinus N. Verbaten for their comments on earlier drafts.

REFERENCES

American Psychiatric Association. (1980). *Diagnostic and statistical manual of mental disorders* (3rd ed.). Washington, DC: Author.

Barry, R. J., & James, A. L. (1988). Coding of stimulus parameters in autistic, retarded, and normal children: Evidence for a two-factor theory of autism. *International Journal of Psychophysiology, 6*, 139–149.

Bernal, M. E., & Miller, W. H. (1970). Electrodermal and cardiac responses of schizophrenic children to sensory stimuli. *Psychophysiology, 2*, 155–168.

Borkovec, T. D. (1970). Autonomic reactivity to sensory stimulation in psychopathic, neurotic, and normal juvenile delinquents. *Journal of Consulting and Clinical Psychology, 35*, 217–222.

Brumaghim, J. T., & Klorman, R. (1998). Methylphenidate effects on paired-associate learning and event-related potentials of young adults. *Psychophysiology, 35*, 73–85.

Brumaghim, J. T., Klorman, R., Strauss, J., Lewine, J. D., & Goldstein, M. G. (1987). Does methylphenidate affect information processing? Findings from two studies on performance and P3b latency. *Psychophysiology, 24*, 361–373.

Callaway, E., Halliday, R., & Naylor, H. (1983). Hyperactive children's event-related potentials fail to support underarousal and maturational-lag theories. *Archives of General Psychiatry, 40*, 1243–1248.

Chabot, R. J. & Serfontein, G. (1996). Quantitative electroencephalographic profiles of children with Attention Deficit Disorder. *Biological Psychiatry, 40*, 951–963.

Ciesielski, K. T., Courchesne, E., & Elmasian, R. (1990). Effects of focused selective attention tasks on event-related potentials in autistic and normal individuals. *Electroencephalography and Clinical Neurophysiology, 75,* 207–220.

Ciesielski, K. T., Knight, J. E., Prince, R. J., Harris, R. J., & Handmaker, S. D. (1995). Event-related potentials in cross-modal divided attention in autism. *Neuropsychologia, 33,* 225–246.

Cohen, D. J., & Johnson (1977). Cardiovascular correlates of attention in normal and psychiatrically disturbed children. *Archives of General Psychiatry, 34,* 561–567.

Cohen, N. J., & Douglas, V. I. (1972). Characteristics of the orienting response in hyperactive and normal children. *Psychophysiology, 9,* 238–245.

Coons, H. W., Klorman, R., & Borgstedt, A. D. (1987). Effects of methylphenidate on adolescents with a childhood history of Attention Deficit Disorder: II. Information Processing. *Journal of the American Academy of Child and Adolescent Psychiatry, 26,* 368–374.

Courchesne, E., Lincoln, A. J., Kilman, B. A., & Galambos, R. (1985). Event-related brain potential correlates of the processing of novel visual and auditory information in autism. *Journal of Autism and Developmental Disorders, 15,* 55–76

Courchesne, E., Lincoln, A. J., Yeung-Courchesne, R., Elmasian, R., & Grillon, C. (1989). Pathophysiologic findings in nonretarded autism and receptive developmental language disorder. *Journal of Autism and Developmental Disorders, 19,* 1–17.

Dainer, K. B., Klorman, R., Salzman, L. F., Hess, D. W., Davidson, P. W., & Michael, R. L. (1981). Learning-disordered children's evoked potentials during sustained attention. *Journal of Abnormal Child Psychology, 9,* 79–94.

Davies, J. G. V., & Maliphant, R. (1971). Autonomic responses of male adolescents exhibiting refractory behaviour in school. *Journal of Child Psychology and Psychiatry, 12,* 115–127.

Dawson, G., Finley, C., Phillips, S., Galpert, L., & Lewy, A. (1988). Reduced P3 amplitude of the event-related brain potential: Its relationship to language ability in autism. *Journal of Autism and Developmental Disorders, 18,* 493–504.

Delamater, A. M., & Lahey, B. B. (1983). Physiological correlates of conduct problems and anxiety in hyperactive and learning-disabled children. *Journal of Abnormal Child Psychology, 11,* 85–100.

Dykman, R. A., Holcomb, P. J., Oglesby, D. M., & Ackerman, P. T. (1982). Electrocortical frequencies in hyperactive, learning-disabled, mixed, and normal children. *Biological Psychiatry, 17,* 675–685.

Erwin, R., Van Lancker, D., Guthrie, J., Schwafel, J. Tanguay, P., & Buchwald, J. S. (1991). P3 responses to prosodic stimuli in adult autistic subjects. *Electroencephalography and Clinical Neurophysiology, 80,* 561–571.

Fitzpatrick, P. A., Klorman, R., Brumaghim, J. T., & Borgstedt, A. D. (1992). Effects of sustained-release and standard preparations of methylphenidate on Attention Deficit Disorder. *Journal of the American Academy of Child and Adolescent Psychiatry, 31,* 226–234.

Fowles, D. C. (1980). The three arousal model: Implications of Gray's two-factor learning theory for heart rate, electrodermal activity, and psychopathy. *Psychophysiology, 17,* 87–104.

Fowles, D. C. (1993). Electrodermal activity and antisocial behavior: Empirical findings and theoretical issues. In J.-C. Roy, W. Boucseim, D. C. Fowles, & J. Gruzelier (Eds.), *Progress in electrodermal research.* New York: Plenum.

Frobel Smithee, J. A., Klorman, R., Brumaghim, J. T., & Borgstedt, A. D. (1988). Methylphenidate does not modify the impact of response frequency or stimulus sequence on performance and event-related potentials of children with Attention Deficit Hyperactivity Disorder. *Journal of Abnormal Child Psychology, 26,* 233–245.

Garralda, M. E., Connell, J., & Taylor, D. C. (1991). Psychophysiological anomalies in children with emotional and conduct disorder. *Psychological Medicine, 21,* 947–957.

Graveling, R. A., & Brooke, J. D. (1978). Hormonal and cardiac response of autistic children to changes in environmental stimulation. *Journal of Autism and Childhood Schizophrenia, 8,* 441–455.

Gray, J. A. (1982). *The neuropsychology of anxiety: An enquiry into the functions of the septohippocampal system.* New York: Oxford University Press.

Grünewald-Zuberbier, E., Grünewald, G., & Rasche, A. (1975). Hyperactive behavior and EEG arousal reactions in children. *Electroencephalography and Clinical Neurophysiology, 38,* 149–159.

Halliday, R., Callaway, E., & Rosenthal, J. H. (1984). The visual ERP predicts clinical response to methylphenidate in hyperactive children. *Psychophysiology, 21,* 114–121.

Halliday, R., Rosenthal, J. H., Naylor, H., & Callaway, E. (1976). Averaged evoked potential predictors of clinical improvement in hyperactive children treated with methylphenidate: An initial study and replication. *Psychophysiology, 13,* 429–440.

Harter, M. R., Anllo-Vento, L., Wood, F. B., & Schroeder, M. M. (1988). II. Separate brain potential characteristics in children with reading disability and attention deficit disorder: Color and letter relevance effects. *Brain and Cognition, 7,* 54–86.

Herning, R. I., Hickey, J. E., Pickworth, W. B., & Jaffe, J. H. (1989). Auditory event-related potentials in adolescents at risk for drug abuse. *Biological Psychiatry, 25,* 598–609.

Holcomb, P. J., Ackerman, P. T., & Dykman, R. A. (1985). Cognitive event-related brain potentials in children with attention and reading deficits. *Psychophysiology, 22,* 656–667

Holcomb, P. J., Ackerman, P. T., & Dykman, R. A. (1986). Auditory event-related potentials in attention and reading disabled boys. *International Journal of Psychophysiology, 3,* 263–273.

Hutt, C., Forrest, S. J., & Richer, J. (1975). Cardiac arrhythmia and behaviour in autistic children. *Acta Psychiatrica Scandinavica, 51,* 361–372.

Iaboni, F., Douglas, V. I., & Ditto, B. (1997). Psychophysiological response of ADHD children to reward and extinction. *Psychophysiology, 34,* 116–123.

James, A. L., & Barry, R. J. (1984). Cardiovascular and electrodermal responses to simple stimuli in autistic, retarded and normal children. *International Journal of Psychophysiology, 1,* 179–193.

Johnson, R. (1988). The amplitude of the P300 component of the event-related potential: Review and synthesis. *Advances in Psychophysiology, 3,* 69–137.

Jonkman, L. M., Kemner, C. Verbaten, M. N., Koelega, H. S., Camfferman, G., van der Gaag, R.-J., Buitelaar, J. K., & van Engeland, H. (1997a). Effects of methylphenidate on event-related potentials and performance of attention-deficit hyperactivity disorder children in auditory and visual selective attention tasks. *Biological Psychiatry, 41,* 690–702.

Jonkman, L. M., Kemner, C. Verbaten, M. N., Koelega, H. S., Camfferman, G., van der Gaag, R.-J., Buitelaar, J. K., & van Engeland, H. (1997b). Event-related potentials and performance of attention-deficit hyperactivity disorder: Children and normal controls in auditory and visual selective attention tasks. *Biological Psychiatry, 41,* 595–611.

Kemner, C., Verbaten, M. N., Cuperus, J. M., Camfferman, G., & van Engeland, H. (1994). Visual and somatosensory event-related brain potentials in autistic children and three different control groups. *Electroencephalography and Clinical Neurophysiology, 92,* 225–237.

Kemner, C., Verbaten, M. N., Cuperus, J. M., Camfferman, G., & van Engeland, H. (1995). Auditory event-related brain potentials in autistic children and three different control groups. *Biological Psychiatry, 38,* 150–165.

Kemner, C., Verbaten, M. N., Koelega, H. S., Buitelaar, J. K., van der Gaag, R.-J., Camfferman, G., & van Engeland, H. (1996). Event-related brain potentials in children with attention-deficit and hyperactivity disorder: Effects of stimulus deviancy and task relevance in the visual and auditory modality. *Biological Psychiatry, 40,* 522–534.

Klorman, R., Brumaghim, J. T., Fitzpatrick, P. A., & Borgstedt, A. D. (1991). Methylphenidate speeds evaluation processes of attention deficit disorder adolescents during a continuous performance test. *Journal of Abnormal Child Psychology, 19,* 263–283.

Klorman, R., Brumaghim, J. T., Fitzpatrick, P. A., & Borgstedt, A. D. (1992). Methylphenidate reduces abnormalities of stimulus classification in adolescents with attention deficit disorder. *Journal of Abnormal Psychology, 101,* 130–138.

Klorman, R., Brumaghim, J. T., Fitzpatrick, P. A., Borgstedt, A. D., & Strauss, J. (1994). Clinical and cognitive effects of methylphenidate in attention deficit disorder as a function of age and aggression/oppositionality. *Journal of Abnormal Psychology, 103,* 206–221.

Klorman, R., Brumaghim, J. T., Salzman, L. F., Strauss, Borgstedt, A. D., McBride, M., & Loeb, S. (1988). Clinical and cognitive effects of methylphenidate on attention deficit disorder with and without aggressive features. *Journal of Abnormal Psychology, 97,* 413–422.

Klorman, R., Brumaghim, J. T., Salzman, L. F., Strauss, J., Borgstedt, A. D., McBride, M. C., & Loeb, S. (1990). Effects of methylphenidate on processing negativities in patients with Attention-deficit Hyperactivity Disorder. *Psychophysiology, 27,* 328–337.

Klorman, R., Salzman, L. F., Bauer, L. O., Coons, H. W., Borgstedt, A. D., & Halpern, W. I. (1983). Effects of two doses of methylphenidate on cross-situational and borderline hyperactive children's evoked potentials. *Electroencephalography and Clinical Neurophysiology, 56,* 169–185.

Klorman, R., Salzman, L.F., Pass, H. L., Borgstedt, A. D., & Dainer, K. B. (1979). Effects of methylphenidate on hyperactive children's evoked responses during passive and active attention. *Psychophysiology, 16,* 23–29.

Kootz, J. P., Marinelli, B., & Cohen, D. J. (1982). Modulation of response to environmental stimulation in autistic children. *Journal of Autism and Developmental Disorders, 12,* 185–193.

Kruesi, M.J.P., Hibbs, E. D., Zahn, T. P., Keysor, C. S., Hamburger, S. D., Bartko, J. J., & Rapoport, J. L. (1992). A 2-year prospective follow-up study of children and adolescents with disruptive behavior disorders. *Archives of General Psychiatry, 49,* 429–435.

Kuperman, S., Johnson, B., Arndt, S., Lindgren, S., & Wolraich, M. (1996). Quantitative EEG differences in a nonclinical sample of children with ADHD and undifferentiated ADD. *Journal of the American Academy of Child and Adolescent Psychiatry, 35,* 1009–1017.

Lake, C. R., Ziegler, M. G., & Murphy, D. L. (1977). Increased norepinephrine levels and decreased dopamine-b-hydroxylase activity in primary autism. *Archives of General Psychiatry, 34,* 553–556.

Lincoln, A. J., Courchesne, E., Harms, L., & Allen, M. (1993). Contextual probability evaluation in autistic, receptive developmental language disorder, and control children: Event-related brain potential evidence. *Journal of Autism and Developmental Disorders, 23,* 37–58.

Loiselle, D. L., Stamm, J. S., Maitinsky, S., & Whipple, S. C. (1980). Evoked potential and behavioral signs of attentive dysfunctions in hyperactive boys. *Psychophysiology, 17,* 193–201.

MacCulloch, M. J., & Williams, C. (1971). On the nature of infantile autism. *Acta Psychiatrica Scandinavica, 47,* 295–314.

Maliphant, R., Hume, F., & Furnham, A. (1990). Autonomic nervous system (ANS) activity, personality characteristics and disruptive behaviour in girls. *Journal of Child Psychology and Psychiatry, 31,* 619–628.

Michael, R. L., Klorman, R., Salzman, L. F., Borgstedt, A. D., & Dainer, K. B. (1981). Normalizing effects of methylphenidate on hyperactive children's vigilance performance and evoked potentials. *Psychophysiology, 18,* 665–677.

Miller, W. H., & Bernal, M. E. (1971). Measurement of the cardiac response in schizophrenic and normal children. *Psychophysiology, 8,* 533–537.

Niwa, S., Ohta, M., & Yamazaki, K. (1983). P300 and stimulus evaluation process in autistic subjects. *Journal of Autism and Developmental Disorders, 13,* 33–42.

Novak, G. P., Solanto, M., & Abikoff, H. (1995). Spatial orienting and focused attention in attention deficit hyperactivity disorder. *Psychophysiology, 32,* 546–559.

Novick, B., Kurtzberg, D., & Vaughan, H. G. (1979). An electrophysiologic indication of defective information storage in childhood autism. *Psychiatry Research, 1,* 101–108.

Novick, B., Vaughan, H. G., Kurtzberg, D., & Simson, R. (1980). An electrophysiologic indication of auditory processing defects in autism. *Psychiatry Research, 3,* 107–114.

Oades, R. D., Dittmann-Balcar, A., Schepker, R., Eggers, C., & Zerbin, C. (1996). Auditory event-related potentials (ERPs) and mismatch negativity (MNM) in healthy children and those with attention-deficit or tourette/tic symptoms. *Biological Psychology, 43,* 163–185.

Oades, R. D., Walker, M. K., Geffen, L. B., & Stern, L. M. (1988). Event-related potentials in autistic and healthy children on an auditory choice reaction time task. *International Journal of Psychophysiology, 6,* 25–37.

Palkowitz, R. J., & Wiesenfeld, A. R. (1980). Differential autonomic responses of autistic and normal children. *Journal of Autism and Developmental Disorders, 10,* 347–360.

Peloquin, L. J., & Klorman, R. (1986). Effects of methylphenidate on normal children's mood, event-related potentials, and performance in memory scanning and vigilance. *Journal of Abnormal Psychology, 95,* 88–98.

Pliszka, S. R., Hatch, J. P., Borcherding, S. H., & Rogeness, G. A. (1993). Classical conditioning in children with attention deficit hyperactivity disorder (ADHD) and anxiety disorders: A test of Quay's model. *Journal of Abnormal Child Psychology, 21,* 411–423.

Pritchard, W. S., Raz, N., & August, G. J. (1987). Visual augmenting/reducing and P300 in autistic children. *Journal of Autism and Developmental Disorders, 17,* 231–242.

Quay, H. C. (1988). The behavioral reward and inhibition systems in childhood behavior disorders. In L. M. Bloomingdale (Ed.), *Attention deficit disorder* (Vol. 3, pp. 176–186). Elmsford, NY: Pergamon.

Raine, A., & Jones, F. (1987). Attention, autonomic arousal, and personality in behaviorally disordered children. *Journal of Abnormal Child Psychology, 15,* 583–599.

Raine, A., & Venables, P. H. (1984a). Electrodermal nonresponding, antisocial behavior, and schizoid tendencies in adolescents. *Psychophysiology, 21,* 424–433.

Raine, A., & Venables, P. H. (1984b). Tonic heart rate level, social class and antisocial behaviour in adolescents. *Biological Psychology, 18,* 123–132.

Raine, A., & Venables, P. H. (1987). Contingent negative variation, P3 evoked potentials, and antisocial behavior. *Psychophysiology, 24,* 191–199.

Raine, A., Venables, P. H., & Mednick, S. A. (1997). Low resting heart rate at age 3 years predisposes to aggression at age 11 years: Evidence from the Mauritius Child Health Project. *Journal of the American Academy of Child and Adolescent Psychiatry, 36,* 1457–1464.

Raine, A., Venables, P. H., & Williams, M. (1990a). Autonomic orienting responses in 15-year-old male subjects and criminal behavior at age 24. *American Journal of Psychiatry, 147,* 933–937.

Raine, A., Venables, P. H., & Williams, M. (1990b). Relationships between central and autonomic measures of arousal at age 15 years and criminality at age 24 years. *Archives of General Psychiatry, 47,* 1003–1007.

Raine, A., Venables, P. H., & Williams, M. (1990c). Relationships between N1, P300, and contingent negative variation recorded at age 15 and criminal behavior at age 24. *Psychophysiology, 27,* 567–574.

Raven, J. C. (1960). *Guide to the standard progressive matrices.* London: H. K. Lewis.

Robaey, P., Breton, F., Dugas, M. & Renault, B. (1992). An event-related potential study of controlled and automatic processes in 6-8-year-old boys with attention deficit hyperactivity disorder. *Electroencephalography and Clinical Neurophysiology, 82,* 330–340.

Rogeness, G. A., Cepeda, C., Macedo, C. A., Fischer, C., & Harris, W. R. (1990). Differences in heart rate and blood pressure in children with conduct disorder, major depression, and separation anxiety. *Psychiatry Research, 33,* 199–206.

Satterfield, J. H., Cantwell, D. P., & Satterfield, B. T. (1974). Pathophysiology of the hyperactive child syndrome. *Archives of General Psychiatry, 31,* 839–844.

Satterfield, J. H., & Schell, A. M. (1984). Childhood brain function differences in delinquent and non-delinquent hyperactive boys. *Electroencephalography and Clinical Neurophysiology, 57,* 199–207.

Satterfield, J. H., Schell, A. M., Backs, R. W., & Hidaka, K. C. (1984). A cross-sectional and longitudinal study of age effects of electrophysiological measures in hyperactive and normal children. *Biological Psychiatry, 19,* 973–990.

Satterfield, J. H., Schell, A. M., & Nicholas, T. (1994). Preferential neural processing of attended stimuli in attention-deficit hyperactivity disorder and normal boys. *Psychophysiology, 31,* 1–10.

Satterfield, J. H., Schell, A. M., Nicholas, T. W., & Backs, R. W. (1988). Topographic study of auditory event related potentials in normal boys and in boys with attention deficit disorder with hyperactivity. *Psychophysiology, 25,* 591–606.

Satterfield, J. H., Schell, A. M., Nicholas, T. W., Satterfield, B. T., & Freese, T. E. (1990). Ontogeny of selective attention effects on event-related potentials in attention-deficit hyperactivity disorder and normal boys. *Biological Psychiatry, 28,* 879–903.

Sergeant, J. (1988). Functional deficits in attention deficit disorder. In L. M. Bloomingdale (Ed.), *Attention deficit disorder* (Vol. 3, pp. 1–19). Elmsford, NY: Pergamon.

Siddle, D.A.T., Nicol, A. R., & Foggitt, R. H. (1973). Habituation and over-extinction of the GSR component of the orienting response in anti-social adolescents. *British Journal of Social and Clinical Psychology, 12,* 303–308.

Spring, C., Greenberg, L., Scott, J., & Hopwood, J. (1974). Electrodermal activity in hyperactive boys who are methylphenidate responders. *Psychophysiology, 11,* 436–451.

Stevens, S., & Gruzelier, J. (1984). Electrodermal activity to auditory stimuli in autistic, retarded, and normal children. *Journal of Autism and Developmental Disorders, 14,* 245–260.

Strandburg, R. J., Marsh, J. T., Brown, W. S., Asarnow, R. F., Guthrie, D., & Higa, J. (1993). Event-related potential in high-functioning adult autistics: Linguistic and nonlinguistic visual information processing tasks. *Neuropsychologia, 31,* 413–434.

Strandburg, R. J., Marsh, J. T., Brown, W. S., Asarnow, R. F., Higa, J., Harper, R., & Guthrie, D. (1996). Continuous-processing-related event-related potentials in children with attention deficit hyperactivity disorder. *Biological Psychiatry, 40,* 964–980.

Sunohara, G. A., Voros, J. G., Malone, M. A., & Taylor, M. J. (1997). Effects of methylphenidate in children with attention deficit hyperactivity disorder: A comparison of event-related potentials between medication responders and non-responders. *International Journal of Psychophysiology, 27,* 9–14.

Syrigou-Papavasiliou, A., Lycaki, H., LeWitt, P. A. (1988). Dose-response effects of chronic methylphenidate administration on late event-related potentials in Attention Deficit Disorder. *Clinical Electroencephalography, 19,* 129–133.

Taylor, M. J., & Keenan, N. K. (1990). Event-related potentials to visual and language stimuli in normal and dyslexic children. *Psychophysiology, 27,* 318–327.

Taylor, M. J., Voros, J. G., Logan, W. J., & Malone, M. A. (1993). Changes in event-related potentials with stimulant medication in children with attention deficit hyperactivity disorder. *Biological Psychology, 36,* 139–156.

van Engeland, H., Roelofs, J. W., Verbaten, M. N., & Slangen, J. L. (1991). Abnormal electrodermal reactivity to novel visual stimuli in autistic children. *Psychiatry Research, 38,* 27–38.

Verbaten, M. N., Overtoom, C.C.E., Koelega, H. S., Swaab-Barneveld, H., van der Gaag, R.-J., Buitelaar, J., & van Engeland, H. (1994). Methylphenidate influences on both early and late ERP waves of ADHD children in a continuous performance test. *Journal of Abnormal Child Psychology, 22,* 578.

Verbaten, M. N., Roelofs, J. W., van Engeland, H., Kenemans, J. K., & Slangen, J. L. (1991). Abnormal visual event-related potentials of autistic children. *Journal of Autism and Developmental Disorders, 21,* 449–470.

Winsberg, B. G., Javitt, D. C., & Shanahan/Silipo, G. (1997). Electrophysiological indices of information processing in methylphenidate responders. *Biological Psychiatry, 42,* 432–445.

Zahn, T. P., Abate, F., Little, B. C., & Wender, P. H. (1975). Minimal brain dysfunction, stimulant drugs, and autonomic nervous system activity. *Archives of General Psychiatry, 32,* 381–387.

Zahn, T. P., & Kruesi, M.J.P. (1993). Autonomic activity in boys with disruptive behavior disorders. *Psychophysiology, 30,* 605–614.

Zahn, T. P., Little, B. C., & Wender, P. H. (1978). Pupillary and heart rate reactivity in children with minimal brain dysfunction. *Journal of Abnormal Child Psychology, 6,* 135–147.

Zahn, T. P., Rapoport, J. L., & Thompson, C. L. (1980). Autonomic and behavioral effects of dextroamphetamine and placebo in normal and hyperactive prepubertal boys. *Journal of Abnormal Child Psychology, 8,* 145–160.

Zambelli, A. J., Stamm, J. S., Maitinsky, S., & Loiselle, D. L. (1977). Auditory evoked potentials and selective attention in formerly hyperactive adolescent boys. *American Journal of Psychiatry, 134,* 742–747.

Familial Determinants

G. Stennis Watson
Alan M. Gross
The University of Mississippi

Social scientists long have recognized that familial determinants play a decisive role in a child's behavioral, affective, and cognitive functioning. For example, the probability of a diagnosis of schizophrenia, a mood disorder, a pervasive developmental disorder, or alcoholism increases with a family history of these disorders (Carson, Butcher, & Mineka, 1996). Such demographic knowledge may suggest that the role of family influence on child psychopathology can be well defined. However, as Reitman and Gross (1995) noted in the first edition of this volume, social scientists have been able to identify many of the familial determinants, but they have yet to describe the relations among them and the limits to their influence on child functioning in a way that satisfies the demands of a single unified theory. Therefore, the purpose of this chapter remains essentially the same as that of Reitman and Gross, briefly to review historical antecedents and empirical observations concerning familial determinants, to define obstacles to understanding familial determinants, and to describe essential elements of familial influence on childhood mental health.

HISTORICAL ANTECEDENTS

The western view of children—that children are physically, cognitively, emotionally, and socially distinct from adults—is relatively modern. In the Middle Ages, children were viewed as "miniature adults," smaller but not essentially different. During the sixteenth and seventeenth centuries, a notion of childhood began to emerge with a budding awareness of children's religious, educational, and nurturance needs. However, a scientific approach to childhood and developmental processes appeared only in the late nineteenth century, as the work of theorists such as Darwin, Preyer, Hall, Binet, Freud, Terman, and Baldwin took root in the growing science of psychology (see Dixon & Lerner, 1988; McGraw, 1987; Weinert, 1996). Childhood became the subject of investigation, and developmental norms were established. Only then were social scientists able to define child and adolescent abnormal behavior.

It is difficult to estimate the impact of Darwin on developmental psychology. On the one hand, the direct association between Darwin's work and developmental psychology is weak, and his writings are often absent from lists of influential literature (Charlesworth, 1994). On the other hand, Darwin's influence was pervasive in science, and notions of gradual evolutionary change, survival of the fittest, and adaptive functions for behavior (and mental activity) influenced developmental theory (Dixon & Lerner, 1988).

G. Stanley Hall, often credited as "the founder of developmental studies" in the United States (McGraw, 1987, p. 19), published his landmark study *Adolescence* in 1904. His view of adolescence as "storm and stress" has been challenged, and his assertion that postnatal phylogeny recapitulates ontogeny has been rejected outright. Nonetheless, Hall established a research program leading to "a first cooperative 'normal science' of child development," developed a "social–biological conception of childhood," and produced a massive description of adolescence (White, 1994, p. 122). A contemporary of Hall, Sigmund Freud proposed an evolutionary development of personality that has long influenced explanations of childhood, and, like Hall, Freud accepted recapitulation theory. In 1909, Freud visited Hall at Clark University, and a long-term correspondence between Hall and Freud ensued, suggesting a reciprocal influence (Dixon & Lerner, 1988). Freud's theories concerning parental influence on development and his treatment of child and adolescent patients crystalized childhood psychopathology and prepared the way for such life-span theories of personality as that of Erikson.

Concurrently with the work of Hall and Freud, the intellectual assessment movement was defining normal intelligence among children. Laws mandating universal education established public schools, and classes frequently contained children who varied widely in age and ability. To facilitate education, it was thought necessary to identify students who were not able to benefit from regular lessons and to provide special educational opportunities for them. In 1904, the French minister of education commissioned Alfred Binet to develop an examination for selecting children who should be placed in the special education schools being organized in Paris. In 1905, Binet and Theodore Simon published the Binet–Simon Scale, the first practical intelligence test, and in 1908, they published the Binet–Simon Mental-Age Scale, a test designed to assess mental age and to determine mental retardation. In the United States, Lewis Terman published a 1912 English version of the Binet–Simon Scale, and in 1916, Terman's impressive Stanford Revision and Extension of the Binet–Simon Scale (the Stanford–Binet) was published. In addition, Terman conducted "one of the most extensive longitudinal investigations of children," assessing the relations among intellectual, volitional, emotional, aesthetic, moral, physical, and social traits (Sattler, 1992, p. 680). The attempts of Binet, Terman, Wechsler, and others to establish normative descriptions of children's mental abilities were complemented by their attempts to construct useful, theoretically sound, and empirically valid definitions of intelligence (see McGraw, 1987; Sattler, 1992). Furthermore, the assessment of intellectual abilities challenged social scientists to identify the source of intellectual abilities. To the extent that these abilities were learned, family literacy and formal education could change ability levels. To the extent that they were inherited, they would be resistant to the environment. In either case, familial determinants were significant forces in shaping intellectual ability, either by direct inheritance or by the learning environment provided by the family.

Jean Piaget, influenced extensively by John Mark Baldwin, extended the study of children to include a qualitative stage model of cognitive development. Drawing from his background as a biologist, Piaget observed children's interactions with their environment and identified what he considered to be developmentally normative behavioral patterns, or schemas. Piaget's greatest contributions were an awareness of the central role of cognition in a child's development, a rich description of children's behavior, and a clinical method of observation characterized by a high degree of ecological validity. Piaget's theory is marred by a host of weaknesses, including tenuous links between overt behavior and theoretical constructs and an inadequate rational for his stage notion. Yet, it remains influential because Piaget's works evoked a general awareness of an important developmental facet and because he raised intriguing questions about the nature of the child (Perner, 1996; see also Miller, 1989).

This brief review of historical antecedents brings together a variety of issues for familial determinants in child abnormal psychology. The work of Darwin raised the question of genetic influences and adaptation in normal functioning. Freud challenged theorists to explain the role of significant others, especially parents, in personality development and psychopathology. A primary thrust of the intellectual testing movement was to determine the relative contributions of nature and nurture to a child's mental abilities. Thus, history sets the stage for a discussion of familial determinants.

OBSTACLES TO UNDERSTANDING FAMILIAL DETERMINANTS

A variety of obstacles hinder progress toward a unified theory explaining the place of familial determinants in child psychopathology. Some obstacles involve core definitions such as the nature of the family, childhood and adolescence, and psychopathology. Others derive from differences in theoretical perspectives, such as the relative contributions of biology and environment to human functioning. Still other obstacles relate to the difficulties inherent in integrating a large and complex group of observations into a coherent theory. Finally, in a field as extensive as child psychopathology, a number of empirical questions remain unanswered.

What Is a family?

Popular television shows of the past four decades demonstrate the enormous complexity of defining the family. Forty years ago, a typical television family consisted of two biological parents and their offspring living together in a single family dwelling. Since then, television presentations have included single-mother and single-father homes, blended families, adopted children, extended families, families without parents present in the home, and multicultural families. Even with all these variations, the list of possible family structures is not expended. For example, children may be reared in a communal setting where unrelated adults assume parental responsibility or in a home where a same-gender couple shares parental tasks. Based on these anecdotal data, it seems obvious that popular notions of family structure change over time and across cultures.

Furthermore, theoretical perspectives influence a researcher's definition of the family and influence the design and interpretation of studies. If the researcher is exploring the contributions of nature to abnormal child psychology, then defining the family may be relatively easy: A family is determined by genetic relationships. However, from a behavioral perspective, opportunities for reinforcement, classical conditioning, and modeling must enter into the definition of a family, and so proximity rather than biology is given priority. Even when researchers share a common theoretical perspective on family influence, they may focus on different target populations (e.g., genetic researchers examining the incidence of autism or childhood depression in monozygotic twins living apart vs. siblings living together), which may lead to different conclusions about the phenomenon. Currently, it seems impossible to provide a single, invariant definition of the family. Therefore, social scientists must state their assumptions regarding family definition and draw out the limitations of their definition.

What Is Psychopathology?

After Emil Kraeplin developed the first modern system for classifying abnormal behavior (Comer, 1998), many researchers pushed toward a unified and empirically valid nosology. The current edition of the *Diagnostic and Statistical Manual of Mental Disorders* (4th ed. [*DSM–IV*]; American Psychiatric Association, 1994) is an important step in that direction. However, problems are inherent in the process of classification. At the most global level, one must ask about *construct validity*, or the extent to which the system effectively relates measured behavior, etiology, and treatment of abnormal behavior (Carson et al., 1996; see Cronbach & Meehl, 1955). Although the *DSM–IV* enjoys widespread use, not all researchers agree that it possesses adequate construct validity and some advocate alternative classification systems. Although the *DSM–IV* is assumed to be adequate at the global level of classification, it must demonstrate adequate reliability and validity for specific diagnoses if it is to be useful. For example, the *DSM–IV* describes the pervasive developmental disorders (PDD) as a group of discrete disorders (see Volkmar et al., 1994), whereas Gillberg (1990, 1993) argues that the PDDs are continuous (see Watson & Gross, 1997). Thus, even when theorists show a strong commitment to a particular classification system, they can disagree about substantial elements of the system. Lack of diagnostic consensus may lead to a serious problem. Researchers may apply a common label to very different constructs. This, in turn, may lead to widely divergent conclusions about an entity that researchers assume to be a single phenomenon. Therefore, to the extent that researchers diverge from commonly accepted definitions of abnormal functioning, their constructs must be elaborated so as not to confuse further the meanings of labels that already may be ambiguous.

The Role of Nature and Nurture

Few would dispute that children are a product of both biology and learning, a tenet emphasized in the field of behavior genetics (Hewitt & Turner, 1995). In some cases, the genetic loading for a disorder may be extremely high, as in autism (Piven & Folstein, 1994) or Huntington's chorea, and in other cases the loading may be low, as Dadds (1997) suggested for oppositional, conduct, and hyperactivity disorders. In general, both nature and nurture contribute significantly to abnormal functioning, for example, depressive disorders (Mufson & Moreau, 1997); anxiety disorders (Hagopian & Ollendick, 1997); posttraumatic stress disorder (DeBellis, 1997); attention deficit hyperactivity disorder (Anastopoulos, 1997); and eating disorders (Mizes & Palermo, 1997).

The mutual influence of nature and nurture raises the very thorny issue of parsing out the relative contributions of inheritance and learning to a person's functioning. Behavior geneticists assume that variance in a child's phenotype (in this case, abnormal behavior) is explained by genetic sources, environmental sources that the child shares with other family members, environmental sources that are unique to the child, and measurement error. Furthermore, nature and nurture are reciprocal influences, each affecting the course of the other. Epigenetic studies are complicated by the indirect effects of nature and nurture on human functioning, in addition to the effects they exercise directly (see Gottlieb, 1983).

The Role of Theoretical Perspectives

Major theories of abnormal behavior must account for the appearance of childhood psychopathology, often employing widely divergent concepts. For example, behavior therapy emphasizes the role of determinism and learning (classical conditioning, environmental consequences, or modeling) in the emergence of maladaptive behavior. The implications are that psychopathology in children is similar to that in adults, and treatment depends on new learning (See Wilson, 1989). Psychoanalytic thought, although also deterministic, focuses on the special role of parents, forces within the individual, and failure to pass successfully through set developmental courses. Treatment is insight-based and aims at helping the individual move toward a mature balance of intrapsychic forces (see Arlow, 1989). Cognitive therapy proposes that environmental and internal stimuli activate schemata (thought patterns) formed by a person's early experiences. These thought patterns, in turn, lead to abnormal behavior. Cognitive therapy emphasizes the role of thought patterns, rather than learning or developmental issues, and the ability of the person to will change, rather than determinism (see Beck, Rush, Shaw, & Emery, 1979).

Even a cursory comparison of these three theories reveals that theoretical perspectives influence one's view of psychopathology. Abnormal behavior can be seen as an observable or occult phenomenon, as a problem in the environment or the individual, as developmentally related or development-free, as deterministic or in relation to an individual's free will. Treatment can address the environment per se, the individual's response to internal and external events, or the individual's insight. Likewise, the family can be seen as the medium in which a child learns behavior and thought patterns, the model for behavior, or the cause of a child's health or pathology. The perspectives adopted by researchers affect their choice of variables of interest, which often leads to different appraisals of the hypothesized strengths and limits of family variables.

FAMILIAL DETERMINANTS: EMPIRICAL OBSERVATIONS

Familial determinants are a commonly accepted influence in abnormal child psychology, and we could easily (and erroneously) omit an important question, "What is the evidence for asserting that family events are associated with psychopathology?" In a brief literature review, several areas are examined to ensure a firm foundation for stating that abnormal functioning is related to familial determinants.

Parenting Styles

Parenting styles have been shown to affect the quality of an adolescent's interpersonal relationships. African American and Caucasian adolescents reported better interpersonal relationships with their mothers, teachers, and peers when mothers were perceived as authoritative rather than authoritarian or permissive (Hall &

Bracken, 1996). Adolescent children of authoritative parents were better integrated into school and showed better psychological well-being than children of authoritarian or permissive parents (Shucksmith, Hendry, & Glendinning, 1995). When children were rated by their peers, "average" children were more likely than "neglected" or "rejected" children to have positive interactions with peers and to receive more praise, commands, suggestions, and explanations from parents on a cooperative task (Franz & Gross, 1996). Consequently, it appears that authoritative but not authoritarian or permissive parenting styles are associated with positive interpersonal relationships in adolescents.

Suboptimal parenting styles are associated with increased vulnerability for emotional disorders. Preschool boys with hyperactivity and aggressive behavior had more restrictive fathers and mothers who reported more marital conflict than did controls (Stormont-Spurgin & Zentall, 1995). Parental conflict and negativity have been associated with antisocial behavior (Reiss et al., 1995). Parents of psychiatric inpatient youths reported more parental conflicts over childrearing, less father–child interaction, and more severe school behavior problems than did parents of controls (King, Radpour, Naylor, Segal, & Jouriles, 1995). Parenting characterized by the presence of empathy and caring and the absence of intrusion was associated with adolescent well-being (McFarlane, Bellissimo, & Norman, 1995). In families with depressed children, both parents and children perceived parenting practices as more negative than did families without a depressed child (Messer & Gross, 1995). Finally, Palestinian children who perceived parenting as good were less vulnerable to adjustment problems following traumatic events than those who perceived parenting as poor (Punamaki, Qouta, & El Sarraj, 1997).

Parental Psychopathology

When a parent has a psychiatric diagnosis, children may be at greater risk for behavioral disorders. The probability of a childhood psychiatric disorder increased with a parental anxiety or depressive disorder, and a parental anxiety diagnosis is specifically associated with a child's increased risk for an anxiety diagnosis (Beidel & Turner, 1997). Meta-analytic techniques have suggested that the children of parents with bipolar disorders are 2.7 times more likely than controls to develop a mental disorder and 4 times more likely than controls to develop an affective disorder (Lapalme, Hodgins, & LaRoche, 1997).

Evidence suggests a high concordance rate for several disorders among first-degree relatives: depressive disorders (Mufson & Moreau, 1997); anxiety disorders (Hagopian & Ollendick, 1997); and autism (G. S. Watson & Gross, 1997). A reported association between paternal antisocial personality disorder and conduct problems in children did not covary as a function of the father's presence in the child's home (Tapscott, Frick, Wootton, & Kruh, 1996). Adopted children of biological parents with substance abuse and antisocial personality disorder were at increased risk for antisocial–hostile disorders (Ge et al., 1996). A parental diagnosis of mental retardation was associated with increased risk for lowered IQ, lowered school achievement, and behavior problems, especially in male children (Feldman & Walton-Allen, 1997).

Parental alcoholism and substance use are associated with a number of negative outcomes in offspring. Male and female children of alcoholic parents were at higher risks across a variety of psychiatric disorders (Lynskey, Fergusson, & Horwood, 1994). There is mixed evidence that parental substance abuse is associated with adolescent substance use (Havey & Dodd, 1995; Hops, Duncan, Duncan, & Stoolmiller, 1996).

Children of active alcoholic, but not recovering or social drinking, fathers were at increased risk for a variety of cognitive problems, including visuospatial, memory, and attentional tasks and general intellectual functioning (Ozkaragoz, Satz, & Noble, 1997). Children of fathers with substance abuse disorders were at higher risk for disruptive behavior disorders, although parental psychopathology was a greater risk factor than substance use (Clark et al., 1997). Eating disorders may be related to parental alcohol abuse (Chandy, Harris, Blum, & Resnick, 1995). Parental alcohol misuse may be associated with probability and frequency of sexual intercourse and increased risk for pregnancy in adolescent females (Chandy, Harris, Blum, & Resnick, 1994). Among incarcerated juveniles, an increase in family violence and abuse has been associated with substance-abusing families (McGaha & Leoni, 1995). Finally, heavy paternal alcohol use may be associated with poor mother attachment, and attachment security further decreased in the presence of both paternal drinking and maternal depression (Eiden & Leonard, 1996).

Parental Separation and Divorce

Separation and divorce can produce significant distress in the lives of children. Weiner, Harlow, Adams, and Grebstein (1995) reported that paternal and maternal indifference (but not age at the time of divorce, gender, parental conflict, or social support) were significant predictors of the child's adjustment. However, Derdeyn (1994) reported that parental discord may influence children's adjustment more than the divorce itself. The effects of divorce may be different for male and female children (Seltzer, 1994). For example, in single-custodial-mother families, boys were at increased risk for depression, and in stepfamilies, girls were at increased risk for depressive and anxiety disorders (Kasen, Cohen, Brook, & Hartmark, 1996). Based on the (British) National Child Development Survey, divorce was shown to have a moderate, long-term negative effect on adult mental health (Chase-Lansdale, Cherlin, & Kiernan, 1995).

Familial Child Sexual and Physical Abuse

Familial childhood sexual abuse (FCSA) and physical abuse have been associated with increased childhood and adolescent risk for negative emotional and behavioral outcomes (Alpert, Cohen, & Sege, 1997). FCSA appears to increase acute and long-term vulnerability to depression, low self-esteem, and behavioral problems (Tebbutt, Swanston, Oates, & O'Toole, 1997). Wagner (1997) reported that a history of FCSA and physical abuse increased risks for suicide. In a sample of British adolescents who had murdered, family backgrounds were characterized by paternal alcohol abuse and violence and a history of early sexual abuse (Bailey, 1996). Physical abuse has been reported to predict increased global impairment; poor social competence; major depression; agoraphobia; and conduct, oppositional defiant, and overanxious disorders (Flisher, Kramer, Hoven, & Greenwald, 1997). Finally, the effects of FCSA may produce only slightly elevated evidence of distress when compared with extrafamilial abuse (Marcellina, Marton, & LeBaron, 1996).

Homelessness

Childhood homelessness may be related to increased risk for behavior and mental health issues. Homeless children have been reported to have poorer school success (achievement and class behavior) than controls (Masten et al., 1997) and increased problem behaviors and anxiety (Schmitz, Wagner, & Menke, 1995). Homelessness has been associated with lower aspirations (Donahue & Tuber, 1995) and with lower self-concepts and increased deviant behavior (DiBiase & Waddell, 1995). However, the effects of homelessness on children may be produced or influenced by other latent variables. It has been reported that academic and psychological functioning vary as a function of mobility among low-socioeconomic status (SES) families rather than homelessness per se, implicating long-term poverty rather than homelessness as the detrimental influence in children's lives (Ziesemer, Marcoux, & Marwell, 1994). Poor children are less likely than other children to receive routine and preventative medical care (Oberg, Bryant, & Bach, 1995). In homeless children, depression and internalizing and externalizing behaviors have been associated with maternal mental health and substance abuse (Zima, Wells, Benjamin, & Duan, 1996).

Clearly, familial determinants of child psychopathology exist: parenting styles, parental psychopathology and substance abuse, marital conflict, abuse, and homelessness. We might be tempted to "allow the data to speak for themselves." However, empirical observations must be related to a theoretical framework if explanatory and predictive power are to be maximized.

FAMILIAL DETERMINANTS: THEORETICAL ELEMENTS

A model of familial determinants of abnormal child psychology must be, at best, complex. It has to account for the contributions of genes and environment to an individual's functioning, and it has to be flexible enough to explain different relative contributions across a variety of disorders. It has to explain why psychopathology fails to appear in some individuals with seemingly common inheritance and experience, such as monozygotic twins living in the same home and treated virtually identically by parents, siblings, and other social contacts. Furthermore, this model should explain the commonalities among persons who have a common disorder and yet appear to have different inheritances and experiences. At this time, no single theory of abnormal child psychology has integrated these demands in a coherent and parsimonious fashion successfully. Nonetheless, it is possible to identify many elements that ultimately must be integrated into a cohesive theory.

Behavioral and Cognitive Theories

One of the most valuable contributions of psychology is the observation that an organism's behavior is controlled to a great degree by the environment. Behaviorism asserts that humans respond to stimuli because of temporal contiguities (classical conditioning), consequences of a response (operant conditioning), or imitation (modeling). Learning is viewed as adaptive or maladaptive, without having to posit a basic defect in the individual. Abnormal behavior reflects a problem with the learning environment, and treatment of abnormal behavior consists of altering the environment to produce desired responses.

Classical conditioning, first described by Ivan Pavlov, depends on the pairing of two events in time. One event (unconditioned stimulus, or US) naturally elicits a response (unconditioned response) from a child. The second event (conditioned stimulus) does not naturally elicit a response but is made to elicit a response (conditioned response) through temporal association with the US. The "little Albert" study of J. Watson and Raynor (1920, cited in Gerow, 1989) demonstrated the power of temporal association in the generation of fear in a child. "Little Albert," who seemed to be quite comfortable in the presence of a white rat, began to show fear responses to the rat and similar objects (stimulus generalization) when the presence of the rat was paired with a loud noise.

Classical conditioning provides solid explanations for emotional and physiological responses, such as fear, anxiety, anger, or sexual arousal (Carson et al., 1996). For example, children who develop anxious feelings in the presence of their abusive parents may generalize these anxiety responses to other authority figures and thus be diagnosed with internalizing disorders. Alternatively, children who develop angry feelings in the presence of their abusive parents may generalize angry responses to other authority figures and thus be diagnosed with externalizing disorders.

Operant conditioning assumes that behavior is controlled by the consequences of the behavior. Satisfying (appetitive) consequences increase the likelihood that an organism will repeat a behavior, and aversive consequences decrease the likelihood. At the most obvious level, a child who is rewarded for good behavior probably will continue to behave well, and a child who is rewarded for bad behavior probably will continue to behave badly. For example, if a parent rewards a child for good study habits, then the child is likely to continue to study and even may develop an internal reward system that reinforces academic and occupational productivity long past childhood. If parents think that a child's social misbehavior is funny and reward the child for it, then the child is likely to repeat the misbehavior and even may develop an internal reward system that reinforces socially inappropriate behavior long past childhood.

An apparent problem for operant models is the failure of a consequence to produce a predicted behavior. However, in operant conditioning, the value of a reinforcer or punisher is determined empirically, and the failure to facilitate or to inhibit behavior is never seen as a reinforcer–punisher failure. The challenge is to identify the consequence that actually controls the child's behavior. For example, if parents punish a child for fighting with a sibling, they may wonder why the child continues to initiate fights. A functional analysis of the child's behavior may reveal that the child's behavior actually is controlled by parental attention rather than by the punisher. The child has learned to gain attention from the parents by provoking them to punish the child, whom they ignore otherwise. In this case, a therapist may help parents to ignore fighting behavior (withdrawing attention for bad behavior) whenever possible and to reward desirable behaviors with parental attention. Again, abnormal behavior is a function of the consequences controlling the behavior.

Modeling, or social learning theory, suggests that children learn by observation and imitation, as well as by direct experience with a stimulus event (classical conditioning) and appetitive or aversive consequences (operant conditioning). For example, Bandura, Ross, and Ross (1963) exposed children to adults striking a rubber doll; when the children were placed in the presence of the doll, they imitated the adults and struck the doll. According to Bandura (1977), modeling is the most basic form of learning in that imitation provides children with a means for expanding their repertoires to include novel behaviors. Parents, as the earliest strong influences in a child's life, are the first models that the child has. Consequently, parental imitation is a primary force in a child's development. This is immediately apparent to anyone who has observed children use a hammer and a saw, push a lawn mower, or pretend to cook in imitation of their parents. The implications of social learning theory for childhood psychopathology are evident in a dysfunctional family where parents demonstrate some maladaptive behavior (such as spousal abuse, alcohol abuse, a mood disorder, or a psychotic disorder), and the children imitate and incorporate parental behaviors into their own behavioral repertoires.

Modeling is related to classical and operant conditioning in that the environment teaches a child how to behave, but it differs in a very important respect. Conditioning models assume a direct link between the environment and behavior. Social learning requires organism-specific variables for the child to learn a new behavior. The child has to attend to an event, abstract a schematic lesson from the event, translate it into symbols that can be stored and recalled in the future, and retrieve the event to act on it. In short, an observational learning theory assumes cognitive processes (see Miller, 1989). Therefore, social learning theory provides a link between pure learning theories and more explicitly cognitive theories of abnormal behavior.

Beck et al's (1979) cognitive model assumes that irrational thinking and maladaptive assumptions are at the heart of abnormal behavior. Beck et al. argued that humans do not respond to the environment, but they respond to their cognitive representations of the meaning of events, that is, some event occurs, and the event activates thought patterns (schemata) that, in turn, determine the person's response to the event. Beck et al.'s theory explains why one person responds to failure with increased effort and perseverence, and another person responds to the very same event with decreased effort and a negative expectancy. The former person may be acting on a positive schema set: "I can do better. I can succeed. I can control may destiny, at least to some degree." The latter may be acting on a negative schema set: "I am a failure. I will never succeed. Life is never fair and will never go my way."

An important issue in the context of familial determinants is the formation of schemata. According to Beck, schemata are the product of early experience, which lie dormant until they are activated by precipitating events. The predisposition for psychopathology is rooted in learned maladaptive thought patterns. As in learning models, the role of the family, especially parents, is foundational. For example, children may grow up in homes where depressogenic assumptions are communicated: I must be successful to be happy; I must be accepted by everyone; I am a total failure if I make a single mistake; my worth depends on what others think about me. These assumptions lie dormant until they are activated by a series of distressing events, at which time the person becomes depressed. A long period may have elapsed between the depressogenic schema formation and the manifestation of depression, but the depression is still a reaction to family learning.

Other cognitive models of abnormal behavior may also be important, insofar as they are determined by family interactions. For example, Seligman's (1975) model of learned helplessness and attribution theory (Kinderman & Bentall, 1997) have been related to depression and anxiety.

The Role of Attachment and Parenting Styles

In the early twentieth century, two perspectives (psychoanalytic theory and behaviorism) dominated research and descriptions of familial determinants of child development. Psychoanalytic theory emphasized childhood plasticity and the acquisition of essentially immutable traits reflecting intrapsychic forces within the child. Parenting was the central variable in determining child development in that the child internalizes, or introjects, parental figures during development. Behaviorism, as suggested previously, emphasized the role of parents as teachers but did not accord parents the innately critical roles ascribed to them in psychoanalytic theory. Behaviorism envisioned the person as plastic (i.e., responding to environmental demands) throughout life. Since the middle of the century, psychoanalytic and behavioral theories of parental influence on children's development have been complemented by attachment and parenting styles theories (see Maccoby, 1994).

Social referencing, a common childhood event, can illustrate the influence of infant–mother attachment in the social development of children. Two young children are playing in a room while their mothers are reading. A stranger enters the room, and the children look at their mothers' faces for response cues. One mother seems unconcerned, smiles at the child, and ignores the stranger; her child returns to play and ignores the stranger. The second mother appears frightened and attends to the stranger; her child moves closer to mother, cries, and watches the stranger. These two very different child responses to a single stranger are guided by maternal reactions to the stranger rather than by the presence of the stranger per se (see McGraw, 1987).

Attachment theory was defined primarily by John Bowlby and Mary Ainsworth. Bowlby asserted that healthy development requires that "the infant and young child should experience a warm, intimate, and continuous relationship with his mother (or permanent mother substitute) in which both find satisfaction and enjoyment" (Bowlby, 1951, p. 13, cited in Bretherton, 1994, p. 437). An optimal infant–mother attachment relationship facilitates the development of emotional security, which, in turn, promotes independence in the child. According to attachment theory, infants and mothers engage in a variety of instinctive behaviors that serve to bind the two in a special relationship. Mothers talk to their children, smile at them, and hold them; infants smile at, cling to, and follow their mothers. Once the infant–mother attachment has been formed, infants respond dramatically to separation: they protest (first phase), despair (second phase), and engage in denial or despair (third phase; see Bretherton, 1994; Lamb, 1988; McGraw, 1987).

The implication of attachment theory is that a suboptimal infant–mother bond can be causally related to abnormal behavior. First, infant–mother attachment may be absent. Mothers must be able to respond instinctively to their children. To the extent that mothers do not engage in talking, smiling, cuddling, or other nurturance behaviors, the infant–mother bond will fail to evolve. In the extreme, infants may not develop the capacity to attach to significant others. Second, secure attachment is based on maternal sensitivity. Mothers must attend to, interpret, and respond to infant needs. According to Ainsworth (Ainsworth, Blehur, Waters, & Wall, 1978) children whose mothers are optimally sensitive to the children's needs will develop a sense of security marked by reciprocal infant–mother interactions, an ability to be in contact with their mothers, distress at their mother's absence, and interest in contact with their mothers rather than strangers. Suboptimal sensitivity is associated with avoidant or ambivalent behavioral patterns in the infant. Avoidance patterns are marked by children's avoidance of maternal interaction, equivalent treatment of mothers and strangers, and lack of distress on separation from mothers; ambivalence patterns are marked by both approach and avoidance and by "maladaptive" behavior in the presence of strangers (Ainsworth et al., 1978).

A weakness of classical attachment theory is that it is limited to instinctive responses, maternal attachments, and early childhood development. Other theories have expanded the concept of parenting to include older children, fathers as well as mothers, and the roles of nurturance (warmth and coldness), restrictiveness–permissiveness, parental cooperation, parental attitudes, and specific childrearing behaviors (see Maccoby, 1994; McGraw, 1987; Reitman & Gross, 1995).

Baumrind (1967) identified three parenting styles: authoritarian, authoritative, and permissive. As summarized by McGraw (1987), *authoritarian* parents use an absolute standard to shape and assess a child's behavior; traditional values such as obedience and respect are valued, and punitive means of behavior control are employed in discipline. *Permissive* parents allow the child a high degree of freedom and mutuality in negotiating behavior, affirm the child's impulses and desires, and make few demands on the child; reason and not power is the favored means of control. *Authoritative* parents encourage the child's interests, thoughts, and abilities but assume final parental authority. Authoritative parents are high in parental control, communication with children, maturity demands on children, and nurturance. Authoritarian parents are low on nurturance and communication, and permissive parents are low on maturity demands and control.

Baumrind's parenting styles have been associated with positive and negative behavior in children. Baumrind defined the concept of *instrumental competence* as "social responsibility, independence, achievement orientation, and vitality" (1973, p. 4, cited in McGraw, 1987, p. 644). The child or adolescent who is instrumentally competent is socially secure, autonomous, and adaptive. A child or adolescent who is instrumentally incompetent engages in socially maladaptive behavior and lacks goal-directedness. Baumrind's research showed instrumental competence to be associated with authoritative parenting and instrumental incompetence to be associated with authoritarian and permissive parenting.

According to Maccoby (1994), "Baumrind's concept of authoritative parenting has been widely adopted by other students of socialization and has been notably successful in distinguishing effective from ineffective parenting" (pp. 604–605). Recently, other concepts have complemented Baumrind's definition of optimal parenting. Researchers are exploring the roles of degree of parental commitment–disengagement, age-appropriate styles of parenting, and psychological autonomy in the development of normal and abnormal behavior (see Maccoby, 1994).

Nature, Nurture, and Behavior Genetics

Early developmental theorists, such as Gesell, Hall, and Baldwin, emphasized the role of nature in the evolution of the child. A particularly strong form of this position was Hall's assertion that postnatal phylogeny recapitulates ontogeny (see Dixon & Lerner, 1988). The role of nurture in childhood development was at the core of behaviorist theories, enshrined in John B. Watson's dictum that he could train a healthy child, chosen at random, to become "any type of specialist I might select—doctor, lawyer, artist, merchant-chief, and yes, even beggar-man or thief, regardless of his talents, penchants, tendencies, abilities, vocations and race of his ancestor" (J. B. Watson, 1924/1970, p. 104; see Horowitz, 1994, p. 237). The accumulated evidence of the past few decades argues that both nature and nurture contribute to the development of a child and that neither alone can account fully for the emergence of abnormal behavior.

Few modern theorists would challenge the notion that child development is the product of both heredity and environment, but many have not arrived at a comfortable understanding of the relation between the two. One approach has been to ignore one force or the other, or to "wish it away." Behavioral researchers, for example, may admit that genetic structure sets limits on the development of a child and then explore variability only within the confines of genetically imposed limits. This approach decreases the power of science to explain abnormal behavior. A second approach has been to accord genes and environment equal roles and to ask statistical questions about main effects for nature, nurture, and the interaction of the two. This second approach is certainly an advance over the first, but it is too simple to account for complex, real-world phenomena (see Gottlieb, 1983; Hewitt & Turner, 1995; Rowe, 1994).

An increasingly complex epigenetic model of development has emerged in recent years. The basic premise is that genes and learning are both influential in development. However, neither operates independently of the other, and neither simply sets the limits on the other. There is a reciprocal influence between inheritance and learning: Genetic traits can affect an individual's learning history, and experience can affect genetic expression (see McGraw, 1987).

Progestin-induced hermaphroditism, an atypical course of sexual differentiation, illustrates the profound effect that the environment can exert over usual genetically programmed courses of development. A person with progestin-induced hermaphroditism has XX sex chromosomes and thus is female from a strict genetic perspective. However, in utero exposure to diethylstilbestrol (DES) appears to overload the alpha-feto-protein system that protects a female fetus from maternal estrogen, and DES crosses the blood–brain barrier. Even though the child has XX chromosomes, the external genitalia are slightly masculinized, and DES-exposed women may have more "masculine personality traits" than the majority of women never exposed in utero to DES. Therefore, this and other abnormalities in sexual differentiation lead to the conclusion that prenatal experiences can alter gene expression (see Kelly, 1991).

Research designs (e.g., twin, family pedigree, and adoption studies) and statistical techniques (e.g., intraclass correlation and heritability coefficients) have facilitated the exploration of the relative contributions of genes and environment to abnormal behavior (see Carson et al., 1996; Comer, 1998; McGraw, 1987; Rowe, 1994; Turner, Cardon, & Hewitt, 1995). This work should be continued as researchers seek to explain familial determinants of abnormal behavior. A far more complex and challenging task is to explore the reciprocal effects of nature and nurture. In light of progestin-induced hermaphroditism, a potential model for psychopathology is that some disorders represent a maladaptive interference of the environment (or genes) on normative development.

Socioeconomic Status: An Extrafamilial Variable?

At one level, socioeconomic variables can be viewed as general, sociocultural mediators of behavior. For example, income, education, occupation, and drug use typically are described in terms of a community that is defined by ethnicity or geography. However, we must not lose sight of the fact that variables assumed to assess SES are expressed in the family and thus are familial determinants. Being poor may mean that mothers do not have adequate access to prenatal health care; that families are characterized by a sense of despair and hopelessness; and that parents have poor educational backgrounds, must work long hours and spend decreased time with children, live with the stress of employment insecurity, or limit the ability to make academic, vocational, or residential choices. In this situation, poor maternal nutrition and lack of prenatal care can increase the child's vulnerability for mental retardation. If parents must work long hours and be absent from the child, then the infant may miss vital stimulation (situationally induced suboptimal parenting), further increasing the child's vulnerability for mental retardation. Finally, if the parents do not have the academic background to teach the child basic academic skills or the financial resources to hire a tutor, the abilities that the child does have may go underutilized. Based on this chain of events, it is easy to see how a child with innate normal abilities may be debilitated by family determinants that reflect SES (see Bradley & Whiteside-Mansell, 1997).

Theoretical Elements: A Summary

A number of theories address abnormal child psychology. Each of the theories previously discussed offers a useful perspective on normal development and the emergence of abnormal behavior. Learning and cognitive theories emphasize the role of the environment, although they are not essentially family influence theories. Attachment and parenting theories point specifically to the family as the cradle of adaptive or maladaptive behavior, and they explore the reciprocal nature of parent–child interactions. Furthermore, attachment theory (and cognitive developmental theories) presses the case for the role of biology in normal development. Behavior genetics explores the relative contributions of nature and nurture to child development and asks researchers to consider their reciprocal relation in the emergence of abnormal behavior.

Currently, there is no overarching theory that unifies these theories. They may compete with each other in providing explanations of psychopathology, or they may reside together in an uneasy coexistence. A great challenge will be to draw together disparate observations and explanations into a unified theory of child abnormal psychology.

SUMMARY AND FUTURE DIRECTIONS

A century ago, abnormal child psychology found its origins in the works of Freud, Hall, Binet, and Terman. Hall endeavored to found a science of normal development, with special emphasis on adolescence. Freud raised the issue of abnormal development and suggested that the environment, especially parent–child relationships, was the predominant influence. Binet, Terman, and others involved in the intellectual testing movement struggled to define what it meant to have a normal intellect and to describe normative populations. By the middle of the twentieth century, developmental and abnormal child psychology were well established as young sciences seeking to describe normative development in terms of physiology, affect, behavior, and cognitive abilities; exploring statistical and functional models of abnormality; disputing the relative importance of nature and nurture in development; and attempting to formulate theories that would explain and predict the emergence of normal and abnormal phenomena.

A number of obstacles have impeded the progress of abnormal child psychology. Not the least of these is the continuing effort to define and understand abnormal behavior. As the rapid and frequent revision of the *DSM* in recent years illustrates, social scientists still have difficulty agreeing on many of the constructs of abnormal psychology. Adopting a common classification scheme and explaining the emergence of psychopathology go hand-in-hand ("bootstrapping," according to Cronbach & Meehl, 1955), but, as many have observed, a lack of common taxonomies limits the ability of social scientists to generalize across research. Second, social change in the modern Western world is associated with evolving family structures. In order to comprehend familial determinants, social scientists must formulate definitions of the family that include newly evolved family influences as well as more traditional influences. Third, although abnormal psychologists would agree that both nature and nurture affect a child's development, they have not achieved consensus regarding what dual influences mean for normal development and abnormal behavior. Furthermore, for a number of years, behavior geneticists have argued that inheritance and environment are bidirectional influences in development, a concept that is difficult to grasp and to test.

Research data confirm that familial determinants affect normal development and the emergence of abnormal phenomena. Parenting styles affect a child's ability to relate to others: authoritative parenting is associated with better interpersonal relationships than is authoritarian or permissive parenting. Parental psychopathology and substance use are predictive of a number of negative outcomes in children, including anxiety, mood, behavior, developmental, and substance disorders. Marital discord and divorce are associated with adjustment, mood, and anxiety disorders. Physical and sexual abuse in families increase the risk of global impairment, poor social competence, and mood, anxiety, and externalizing behavior disorders. Homelessness—although confounded with poverty—has been associated with anxiety, low self-esteem, low aspirations, poor school success, and problem behavior.

Placing these observations in a theoretical framework has been a challenging process. Learning theories (classical and operant conditioning and modeling) and cognitive theories have exploited environmental causation of abnormal behavior successfully. Parenting styles theory has been particularly effective in explaining the influence of the parent–child social relationship in development. Attachment theory and biologically driven models have identified innate processes that account for normal development and pathology. However, none of theories accounts for an adequate proportion of variance in human development across all disorders and domains of interest in abnormal behavior, and, as yet, a unified, comprehensive theory of child development and abnormal psychology has not been formulated successfully.

A challenge for the future is to continue to explore family determinants of abnormal child psychology in the context of behavior genetics. This means continuing to sort out the extent to which abnormal phenomena are controlled by nature and by nurture. It also implies that bidirectional nature–nurture influences can work together to produce abnormal phenomena. A second challenge for the future is even more daunting: to formulate a unified and coherent theory of child development and abnormal psychology that can embrace the full range of developmental concerns and influences.

REFERENCES

Ainsworth, M.D.S., Blehur, M. C., Waters, E., & Wall, S. (1978). *Patterns of attachment: A psychological study of the strange situation.* Hillsdale, NJ: Lawrence Erlbaum Associates.

Alpert, E. J., Cohen, S., & Sege, R. D. (1997). Family violence: An overview. *Academic Medicine, 72,* S3–S6.

American Psychiatric Association. (1994). *Diagnostic and statistical manual of mental disorders* (4th ed.). Washington, DC: Author.

Anastopoulos, A. D. (1997). Attention-deficit/hyperactivity disorder. In R. T. Ammerman & M. Hersen (Eds.), *Handbook of prevention and treatment with children and adolescents* (pp. 551–571). New York: Wiley.

Arlow, J. A. (1989). Psychoanalysis. In R. J. Corsini & D. Wedding (Eds.), *Current psychotherapies* (4th ed.; pp. 19–62). Itasca, IL: Peacock.

Bailey, S. (1996). Adolescents who murder. *Journal of Adolescence, 19,* 19–39.

Bandura, A. (1977). *Social learning theory.* Englewood Cliffs, NJ: Prentice-Hall.

Bandura, A., Ross, D., & Ross, S. A. (1963). Imitation of film-mediated aggressive models. *Journal of Abnormal and Social Psychology, 66,* 3–11.

Baumrind, D. (1967). Child care practices anteceding three patterns of preschool behavior. *Developmental Psychology Monograph, 4,* 1–103.

Beck, A. T., Rush, A. J., Shaw, B. F., & Emery, G. (1979). *Cognitive therapy of depression*. New York: Guilford.

Beidel, D. C., & Turner, S. M. (1997). At risk for anxiety: I. Psychopathology in the offspring of anxious parents. *Journal of the American Academy of Child and Adolescent Psychiatry, 36,* 918–924.

Bradley, R. H., & Whiteside-Mansell, L. (1997). Children in poverty. In R. T. Ammerman & M. Hersen (Eds.), *Handbook of prevention and treatment with children and adolescents* (pp. 13–58). New York: Wiley.

Bretherton, I. (1994). The origins of attachment theory: John Bowlby and Mary Ainsworth. In R. D. Parke, P. A. Ornstein, J. J. Rieser, & C. Zahn-Waxler (Eds.), *A century of developmental psychology* (pp. 431–471). Washington, DC: American Psychological Association.

Carson, R. C., Butcher, J. N., & Mineka, S. (1996). *Abnormal psychology and modern life* (10th ed.). New York: HarperCollins.

Chandy, J. M., Harris, L., Blum, R. W., & Resnick, M. D. (1994). Female adolescents of alcohol misusers: Sexual behaviors. *Journal of Youth and Adolescence, 23,* 695–709.

Chandy, J. M., Harris, L., Blum, R. W., & Resnick, M. D. (1995). Female adolescents of alcohol misusers: Disordered eating features. *International Journal of Eating Disorders, 17,* 283–289.

Charlesworth, W. R. (1994). Charles Darwin and developmental psychology: Past and present. In R. D. Parke, P. A. Ornstein, J. J. Rieser, & C. Zahn-Waxler (Eds.), *A century of developmental psychology* (pp. 77–102). Washington, DC: American Psychological Association.

Chase-Lansdale, P. L., Cherlin, A. J., & Kiernan, K. K. (1995). The long-term effects of parental divorce on the mental health of young adults: A developmental perspective. *Child Development, 66,* 1614–1634.

Clark, D. B., Moss, H. B., Kirisci, L. Mezzich, A. C., Miles, R., & Ott, P. (1997). Psychopathology in preadolescent sons of fathers with substance abuse disorders. *Journal of the American Academy of Child and Adolescent Psychiatry, 36,* 495–502.

Comer, R. J. (1998). *Abnormal psychology* (3rd ed.). San Francisco: Freeman.

Cronbach, L. J., & Meehl, P. E. (1955). Construct validity in psychological tests. *Psychological Bulletin, 52,* 281–302.

Dadds, M. R. (1997). Conduct disorder. In R. T. Ammerman & M. Hersen (Eds.), *Handbook of prevention and treatment with children and adolescents* (pp. 521–550). New York: Wiley.

DeBellis, M. D. (1997). Posttraumatic stress disorder and acute stress disorder. In R. T. Ammerman & M. Hersen (Eds.), *Handbook of prevention and treatment with children and adolescents* (pp. 455–494). New York: Wiley.

Derdeyn, A. P. (1994). "Parental separation, adolescent psychopathology, and problem behaviors": Comment. *Journal of the American Academy of Child and Adolescent Psychiatry, 33,* 1131–1133.

DiBiase, R., & Waddell, S. (1995). Some effects of homelessness on the psychological functioning of preschoolers. *Journal of Abnormal Child Psychology, 23,* 783–792.

Dixon, R. A., & Lerner, R. M. (1988). A history of systems in developmental psychology. In M. H. Bornstein & M. E. Lamb (Eds.), *Developmental psychology: An advanced textbook* (2nd ed; pp. 3–50). Hillsdale, NJ: Lawrence Erlbaum Associates.

Donahue, P. J., & Tuber, S. B. (1995). The impact of homelessness on children's level of aspiration. *Bulletin of the Menninger Clinic, 59,* 249–255.

Eiden, R. D., & Leonard, K. E. (1996). Paternal alcohol use and the mother–infant relationship. *Development and Psychopathology, 8,* 307–323.

Feldman, M. A., & Walton-Allen, N. (1997). Effects of maternal mental retardation and poverty on intellectual, academic, and behavioral status of school-age children. *American Journal on Mental Retardation, 101,* 352–364.

Flisher, A. J., Kramer, R. A., Hoven, C. W., & Greenwald, S. (1997). Psychosocial characteristics of physically abused children and adolescents. *Journal of the American Academy of Child and Adolescent Psychiatry, 36,* 123–131.

Franz, D. Z., & Gross, A. M. (1996). Parental correlates of socially neglected, rejected, and average children: A laboratory study. *Behavior Modification, 20,* 170–182.

Ge, X., Conger, R. D., Cadoret, R. J., Neiderhiser, J. M., Yates, W., Troughton, E., & Stewart, M. A. (1996). The developmental interface between nature and nurture: A mutual influence model of child antisocial behavior and parent behaviors. *Developmental Psychology, 32,* 574–589.

Gerow, J. R. (1989). *Psychology: An introduction* (2nd ed.). Glenview, IL: Scott, Foresman.

Gillberg, C. (1990). Autism and pervasive developmental disorders. *Journal of Child Psychology and Psychiatry, 31,* 99–119.

Gillberg, C. (1993). Autism and related behaviors. *Journal of Intellectual Disability Research, 37,* 343–372.

Gottlieb, G. (1983). The psychobiological approach to developmental issues. In P. H. Mussen (Series Ed.), M. M. Haith, & J. J. Campos (Vol. Eds.), *Handbook of child psychology: Vol. 2. Infancy and developmental psychobiology* (4th ed., pp. 1–26). New York: Wiley.

Hagopian, L. P., & Ollendick, T. H. (1997). Anxiety disorders. In R. T. Ammerman & M. Hersen (Eds.), *Handbook of prevention and treatment with children and adolescents* (pp. 431–454). New York: Wiley.

Hall, W. N., & Bracken, B. A. (1996). Relationship between maternal parenting styles and African American and White adolescents' interpersonal relationships. *School Psychology International, 17,* 253–267.

Havey, J. M., & Dodd, D. K. (1995). Children of alcoholics, negative life events, and early experimentation with drugs. *Journal of School Psychology, 33,* 305–317.

Hewitt, J. K., & Turner, J. R. (1995). Behavior genetic approaches in behavioral medicine: An introduction. In J. R. Turner, L. R. Cardon, & J. K. Hewitt (Eds.), *Behavior genetic approaches in behavioral medicine* (pp. 3–13). New York: Plenum.

Hops, H., Duncan, T. E., Duncan, S. C., & Stoolmiller, M. (1996). Parental substance use as a predictor of adolescent use: A six-year lagged analysis. *Annals of Behavioral Medicine, 18,* 157–164.

Horowitz, F. D. (1994). John B. Watson's legacy: Learning and environment. In R. D. Parke, P. A. Ornstein, J. J. Rieser, & C. Zahn-Waxler (Eds.), *A century of developmental psychology* (pp. 233–250). Washington, DC: American Psychological Association.

Kasen, S., Cohen, P., Brook, J. S., & Hartmark, C. (1996). A multiple-risk interactional model: Effects of temperament and divorce on psychiatric disorders in children. *Journal of Abnormal Child Psychology, 24,* 121–150.

Kelly, D. D. (1991). Sexual differentiation of the nervous system. In E. R. Kandel, J. H. Schwartz, & T. M. Jessell (Eds.), *Principles of neural science* (3rd ed; pp. 959–973). New York: Elsevier.

Kinderman, P., & Bentall, R. P. (1997). Causal attributions in paranoia and depression: Internal, personal, and situational attributions for negative events. *Journal of Abnormal Psychology, 106,* 341–345.

King, C. A., Radpour, L., Naylor, M. W., Segal, H. G., & Jouriles, E. N. (1995). Parents' marital functioning and adolescent psychopathology. Journal of Consulting and Clinical Psychology, 63, 749–753.

Lamb, M. E. (1988). Social and emotional development in infancy. In M. H. Bornstein & M. E. Lamb (Eds.), *Developmental psychology: An advanced textbook* (2nd ed.; pp. 359–410). Hillsdale, NJ: Lawrence Erlbaum Associates.

Lapalme, M., Hodgins, S., & LaRoche, C. (1997). Children of parents with bipolar disorder: A meta-analysis of risk for mental disorders. *Canadian Journal of Psychiatry, 42,* 623–631.

Lynskey, M. T., Fergusson, D. M., & Horwood, L. J. (1994). The effect of parental alcohol problems on rates of adolescent psychiatric disorders. *Addiction, 89,* 1277–1286.

Maccoby, E. E. (1994). The role of parents in the socialization of children: An historical overview. In R. D. Parke, P. A. Ornstein, J. J. Rieser, & C. Zahn-Waxler (Eds.), *A century of developmental psychology* (pp. 589–615). Washington, DC: American Psychological Association.

Marcellina, M., Marton, P., LeBaron, D. (1996). The effects of sexual abuse on 3- to 5-year-old girls. *Child Abuse and Neglect, 20,* 731–745.

Masten, A. S., Sesma, A., Si-Asar, R., Lawrence, C., Miliotis, D., & Dionne, J. A., (1997). Education risks for children experiencing homelessness. *Journal of School Psychology, 35,* 27–46.

McFarlane, A. H., Bellissimo, A., & Norman, G. R. (1995). Family structure, family functioning and adolescent well-being: The transcendent influence of parental style. *Journal of Child Psychology and Psychiatry and Allied Disciplines, 36,* 847–864.

McGaha, J. E., & Leoni, E. L. (1995). Family violence, abuse, and related family issues of incarcerated delinquents with alcoholic parents compared to those with nonalcoholic parents. *Adolescence, 30,* 473–482.

McGraw, K. O. (1987). *Developmental psychology.* New York: Harcourt Brace.

Messer, S., C., & Gross, A. M. (1995). Childhood depression and family interaction: A naturalistic observation study. *Journal of Clinical Child Psychology, 24,* 77–88.

Miller, P. H. (1989). *Theories of developmental psychology.* San Francisco: Freeman.

Mizes, J. S., & Palermo, T. M. (1997). Eating disorders. In R. T. Ammerman & M. Hersen (Eds.), *Handbook of prevention and treatment with children and adolescents* (pp. 572–603). New York: Wiley.

Mufson, L., & Moreau, D. (1997). Depressive disorders. In R. T. Ammerman & M. Hersen (Eds.), *Handbook of prevention and treatment with children and adolescents* (pp. 403–430). New York: Wiley.

Oberg, C. N., Bryant, N. A., & Bach, M. L. (1995). A portrait of America's children: The impact of poverty and a call to action. *Journal of Social Distress and the Homeless, 4,* 43–56.

Ozkaragoz, T., Satz, P., & Noble, E. P. (1997). Neuropsychological functioning in sons of active alcoholic, recovering alcoholic and social drinking fathers. *Alcohol, 14,* 31–37.

Perner, J. (1996). Cognitive development: An overview of cognitive development. In E. de Corte & F. E. Weinert (Eds.), *International encyclopedia of developmental and instructional psychology* (pp. 263–267). Elmsford, NY: Pergamon.

Piven, J., & Folstein, S. (1994). The genetics of autism. In M. L. Bauman & T. L. Kemper (Eds.), *The neurobiology of autism* (pp. 18–44). Baltimore: Johns Hopkins University Press.

Punamaki, R. L., Qouta, S., & El Sarraj, E. (1997). Models of traumatic experiences and children's psychological adjustment: The roles of perceived parenting and children's own resources and activities. *Child Development, 68,* 718–728.

Reiss, D., Hetherington, M., Plomin, R., Howe, G. W., Simmens, S. J., Henderson, S. H., O'Connor, T. J., Bussell, D. A., Anderson, E. R., & Law, T. (1995). Genetic questions for environmental studies: Differential parenting and psychopathology in adolescence. *Archives of General Psychiatry, 52,* 925–936.

Reitman, D., & Gross, A. M. (1995). Familial determinants. In M. Hersen & R. T. Ammerman (Eds.), *Advanced abnormal child psychology* (pp. 87–104). Hillsdale, NJ: Lawrence Erlbaum Associates.

Rowe, D. C. (1994). *The limits of family influence: Genes, experience, and behavior.* New York: Guilford.

Sattler, J. M. (1992). *Assessment of children* (3rd ed., rev.). San Diego, CA: Sattler.

Schmitz, C. L., Wagner, J. D., & Menke, E. M. (1995). Homelessness as one component of housing instability and its impact on the development of children in poverty. *Journal of Social Distress and the Homeless, 4,* 301–317.

Seligman, M.E.P. (1975). *Helplessness.* San Francisco: Freeman.

Seltzer, J. A. (1994). Consequences of marital dissolution for children. *Annual Review of Sociology, 20,* 235–266.

Shucksmith, J., Hendry, L. B., & Glendinning, A. (1995). Models of parenting: Implications for adolescent well-being within different types of family contexts. *Journal of Adolescence, 18,* 253–270.

Stormont-Spurgin, M., & Zentall, S. S. (1995). Contributing factors in the manifestation of aggression in preschoolers with hyperactivity. *Journal of Child Psychology and Psychiatry and Allied Disciplines, 36,* 491–509.

Tapscott, M., Frick, P. J., Wootton, J., & Kruh, I. (1996). The intergenerational link to antisocial behavior: Effects of paternal contact. *Journal of Child and Family Studies. 5,* 229–240.

Tebbutt, J., Swanston, H., Oates, R. K., & O'Toole, B. I. (1997). Five years after child sexual abuse: Persisting dysfunction and problems of prediction. *Journal of the American Academy of Child and Adolescent Psychiatry, 36,* 330–339.

Turner, J. R., Cardon, L. R., & Hewitt, J. K. (Eds.). (1995). *Behavior genetic approaches in behavioral medicine.* New York: Plenum.

Volkmar, F. R., Klin, A., Siegel, B., Szatmari, P., Lord, C., Campbell, M., Freeman, B. J., Cicchetti, D. V., Rutter, M., Kline, W., Buitelaar, J., Hattab, Y., Fombonne, E., Fuentes, J., Werry, J., Stone, W., Kerbeshian, J., Hoshino, Y., Bregman, J., Loveland, K., Szymanski, L., & Towbin, K. (1994). Field trial for autistic disorder in *DSM–IV. American Journal of Psychiatry, 151,* 1361–1367.

Wagner, B. M. (1997). Family risk factors for child and adolescent suicidal behavior. *Psychological Bulletin, 121,* 246–298.

Watson, G. S., & Gross, A. M. (1997). Mental retardation and developmental disorders. In R. T. Ammerman & M. Hersen (Eds.), *Handbook of prevention and treatment with children and adolescents* (pp. 495–520). New York: Wiley.

Watson, J. B. (1970). *Behaviorism* (Rev. ed). New York: Norton. (Original work published 1924.)

Weiner, J., Harlow, L., Adams, J., & Grebstein, L. (1995). Psychological adjustment of college students from families of divorce. *Journal of Divorce and Remarriage, 23,* 75–95.

Weinert, S. (1996). History of developmental psychology. In E. de Corte & F. E. Weinert (Eds.), *International encyclopedia of developmental and instructional psychology* (pp. 1–7). Elmsford, NY: Pergamon.

White, S. H. (1994). G. Stanley Hall: From philosophy to developmental psychology. In R. D. Parke, P. A. Ornstein, J. J. Rieser, & C. Zahn-Waxler (Eds.), *A century of developmental psychology* (pp. 103–126). Washington, DC: American Psychological Association.

Wilson, G. T. (1989). Behavior therapy. In R. J. Corsini & D. Wedding (Eds.), *Current psychotherapies* (4th ed.; pp. 241–282). Itasca, IL: Peacock.

Ziesemer, C., Marcoux, L., & Marwell, B. E. (1994). Homeless children: Are they different from other low-income children? *Social Work, 39,* 658–668.

Zima, B. T., Wells, K. B., Benjamin, B., & Duan, N. (1996). Mental health problems among homeless mothers: Relationship to service use and child mental health problems. *Archives of General Psychiatry, 53,* 332–338.

Research Strategies
in Child Psychopathology

Eric J. Mash
University of Calgary

Gloria L. Krahn
Oregon Health Sciences University

My 6-year-old son James still wets the bed one or two nights a week. I think it's gotten worse since my husband and I separated 3 months ago. Is this behavior normal?

I just don't understand why my 11-year-old daughter Phyllis is so sad all the time. She's always been a moody child. Is this her personality or is something at home or at school causing her to feel this way?

My 9-year-old son Keith is constantly getting into fights with other children. He also has severe tantrums during which he throws and breaks things. My husband thinks he is just a tough kid, but I'm really worried. Will he outgrow this behavior? What can I do about it?

These are questions that parents frequently ask about their children's problem behaviors; they also exemplify the kinds of questions that research studies in child psychopathology seek to address. Such questions have to do with defining what constitutes normal and abnormal behavior for children of different ages and genders, identifying the causes and correlates of abnormal child behavior, making predictions about long-term outcomes for varying childhood problems, and developing and evaluating methods for the treatment and prevention of abnormal child behavior (Achenbach, 1978; Kazdin, 1998).

When studying childhood disorders, it is crucial that one's choice of research methods and strategies be appropriate to the questions being asked. A research strategy that is effective for answering certain types of questions may prove ineffective for answering other types of questions. In practice, most problems in child psychopathology are best studied through the use of a variety of research methods and strategies. Because there is no one "correct" approach to research in child psychopathology, it is our view that research activities are best conceptualized within a decision-making framework. Such a framework requires an understanding of the theoretical, methodological, and practical considerations that permit the researcher to make informed decisions about when certain research methods and strategies are appropriate, and when they are not.

In this chapter, we provide an overview of selected research issues and strategies in child psychopathology. We begin with a discussion of the kinds of questions that research studies in child psychopathology typically address. We then consider three fundamental issues in child psychopathology research: the relation between theory and research, the role of developmental factors, and the impact of the child's social context. Next, we examine the process of research and highlight issues that are relevant at various stages of this process. These include general approaches to research, sampling considerations, types of research designs, methods of measurement, and approaches to data analysis. Finally, we consider some of the ethical and pragmatic issues encountered in conducting research with disturbed children and families.

COMMON TYPES OF RESEARCH QUESTIONS

Four common and interrelated types of research questions in the study of child psychopathology are questions about (a) the nature of childhood disorders, (b) the determinants of childhood disorders, (c) risk and protective factors, and (d) treatment and prevention.

Questions About the Nature of Childhood Disorders

Questions about the nature of childhood disorders are concerned with how disorders are defined and diagnosed, how they are expressed at different ages and in various contexts, constellations and patterning of symptoms, base rates for various problems and competencies, and natural progressions of problems and competencies over time (Mash & Dozois, 1996). These kinds of questions frequently are addressed through epidemiological or survey studies of the incidence, prevalence, and co-occurrence of childhood disorders and competencies in the general population of children, and in populations of children referred for treatment (Costello, 1990; Costello & Angold, 1995).

In one illustrative epidemiological study, Achenbach, Howell, Quay, and Conners (1991) conducted a national survey in the United States with parents of more than 5,000 children aged 4 to 16. Parents of nonreferred and clinic-referred children completed checklists and were interviewed concerning 216 problem child behaviors (e.g., argues, cheats, is lonely) and 23 child competencies (e.g., number of friends, social activities, school performance). Important differences in problem patterns were found for children of different ages and genders. Regional and ethnic differences were minimal, but children from lower socioeconomic status (SES) background were reported to have more problems and fewer competencies than those from upper-SES levels.

As these and other epidemiological findings indicate, the rate and expression of childhood symptoms and disorders often vary in relation to variables such as: the child's age and gender; the parents' SES (i.e., family income, level of education, and occupational status); ethnicity; geographical region; family size and constellation; and parents' marital or mental health status. Consequently, these variables must be assessed or controlled for in most studies of child psychopathology. Many inconsistent findings in child psychopathology are the direct result of research designs or interpretations of findings that fail to take these important variables into account. For example, it has been reported that physically abused children display more parent-rated problem symptoms than do nonabused children. However, this difference may not be found when groups of abused and nonabused children are well matched with respect to SES (Wolfe & Mosk, 1983). Similarly, although behavior disorders are reported to be more frequent in African American than in White youngsters, this finding is likely an artifact related to SES. Because behavior disorders are more prevalent in low-SES families, and because African American children are overrepresented in such families in North America, it is likely that any link between race and behavior disorders is accounted for by the conditions associated with growing up in a poor family (Lahey et al., 1995).

Questions About the Determinants of Childhood Disorders

Questions about the determinants of childhood disorders ask how biological, psychological, and environmental processes interact to produce the outcomes that are observed over time. Research into biological determinants has focused on possible causes of child psychopathology such as structural brain damage, brain dysfunction, neurotransmitter imbalances, and genetic influences, whereas environmental models have emphasized the role of environmental toxins, sociocultural contexts, disciplinary practices, early experiences, and family constellations and systems. Questions about the causes of childhood disorders are complicated by the following: (a) what qualifies as a cause will vary according to what we are studying, and how far back in time we wish to trace a causal chain; and (b) determinants of childhood disorders seldom involve simple one-to-one cause-and-effect relations (Kazdin & Kagan, 1994).

Childhood disorders are almost always the result of multiple and interacting causes (Mash & Barkley, 1996). For example, genetic factors, family history, child temperament, family management processes, and parental personality all are potential contributors to conduct disorders in children. A challenge for research into the determinants of conduct disorders, as well as for research into other childhood problems, is to identify the relative contributions of each of these factors and how they may combine to produce specific outcomes. For example, neuropsychological deficits and family socialization practices may contribute to a life-course persistent pattern of conduct disorder, but not to conduct problems that occur only during adolescence (Moffitt, 1993). Because simple cause-and-effect relations rarely occur in the study of child psychopathology, causes are more appropriately conceptualized as being necessary, sufficient, necessary and sufficient, or contributory factors in the development of childhood disorders (Achenbach, 1982).

Causes of child psychopathology operate at the molecular (e.g., biochemical events, parent–child interaction) and molar (e.g., cultural values) levels. Therefore, one's research methods and strategies will depend greatly on the particular determinants and level of influence that one is interested in studying. For example, direct observation and sequential analyses of behavior may be the best methods for capturing the moment-to-moment exchanges that occur during parent–child interactions, whereas questionnaires, interviews, and qualitative analysis may be the more appropriate methods for studying parental beliefs and cultural attitudes about children.

Because the etiologies for most childhood disorders are presently unknown, researchers are frequently interested in identifying characteristics and conditions that are associated with a disorder as potential causal factors. For example, the observed association between marital discord and child conduct problems has led to an interest in the possible mechanisms by which marital discord can lead to conduct difficulties (Crockenberg & Covey, 1991; Fincham, Grych, & Osborne, 1994). Because the causes of childhood disorders may operate as direct or indirect influences, marital discord may influence a child directly as a result of his or her exposure to aggression between parents, or indirectly, when such discord interferes with a parents' ability to provide adequate nurturance and consistent discipline. Such findings regarding associated factors raise the important consideration of directionality of effects. For example, although marital discord and childhood problems are known to be associated, discord may represent a cause of difficult child behavior, an outcome of difficult child behavior, or, as is more commonly the case, both a cause and an outcome (i.e., reciprocal influences). The realities of multiple determinants, associated characteristics, direct and indirect effects, and reciprocal influences necessitate that research into the determinants of childhood disorders must rely on design (e.g., longitudinal study) and data analytic strategies (e.g., path analysis) that can distinguish direct and indirect effects, and that can identify, compare, and evaluate alternative pathways and directions of influence.

Illustrative etiologic studies have examined the relation between parental disciplinary practices and children's antisocial behavior (Patterson, Reid, & Dishion, 1992); the impact of sexual abuse on children (Browne & Finkelhor, 1986); the relation between quality of early attachments and the later development of behavior problems (Greenberg, Speltz, Deklyen, & Endriga, 1991); the relation between parental personality disorders and childhood conduct problems (Frick et al., 1992); the heritability of extreme fearfulness in children (Stevenson, Batten, & Cherner, 1992); and the role of specific genes in attention deficit hyperactivity disorder (ADHD; Gill, Daly, Heron, Hawi, & Fitzgerald, 1997).

Questions About Risk and Protective Factors

Some research studies seek to identify characteristics, conditions, or circumstances that place a child at risk for the development of problems. Common risk factors that increase the likelihood that some form and degree of disorder will occur include low child intelligence, childhood illnesses, physical or sexual abuse, separations from parents, low maternal education, and parent criminality. Whether presence of these or other risk factors will result in emergence of childhood psychopathology is influenced by the number of risk factors present and by the presence of protective factors. Protective factors are represented by characteristics, conditions, or circumstances that promote or maintain healthy development. Common protective factors include high child intelligence, contact with a supportive and consistent adult, and the availability of social supports (Werner, 1995).

Research into risk and protective factors often requires that large samples of children be studied and that multiple areas of child functioning (i.e., physical, intellectual, psychosocial) be evaluated over long periods of time. This is necessary because: (a) only a small proportion of children who are at risk for a problem will actually develop the disorder; (b) the areas of child functioning that will be affected, and how they will be affected, are not known in advance; and (c) the points in development at which a disorder may occur or reoccur are also not known in advance. Sometimes the effects of exposure to a risk factor during infancy or early childhood may not be visible until adolescence or adulthood. The possibility that delayed or "sleeper effects" will occur complicates the study of risk and protective factors, because children must be studied for many years if delayed effects are to be detected.

In an illustrative study of risk and protective factors for child maltreatment (Egeland, 1991), 267 first-time expectant mothers who were assessed to be at risk for poor-quality caregiving were recruited during the last trimester of their pregnancy. The mothers' high-risk status was based on their young age, low education, unplanned pregnancy, and single-parent status. Mothers and children were evaluated at regular intervals from the last trimester of pregnancy through the time that the children were in the sixth grade. Evaluations included information about the children, mothers, mother–child interactions, life circumstances, and stresses. When the children were 2 years of age, approximately 16% of these high-risk mothers exhibited one or more forms of maltreatment (e.g., physical abuse, verbal abuse, psychological unavailability, neglect), a proportion that is considerably higher than the base rate of approximately 3% to 5% that would be expected in a community sample of mothers who had not been preselected to be at risk for maltreatment of their children. The at-risk approach in this investigation also enabled the researchers to identify a comparison group of mothers who were at high risk for poor caregiving but who did not later maltreat their children. By comparing high-risk families showing positive childrearing outcomes with those showing negative outcomes, possible protective factors could then be identified and used as the basis for designing prevention programs for child maltreatment.

Questions About Treatment and Prevention

Questions about treatment and prevention are concerned with:

1. Evaluating the immediate and long-term effects of a variety of psychological, environmental, and biological treatments.
2. Comparing the relative effectiveness of differing forms and combinations of treatment.
3. Identifying the basic mechanisms to explain why a particular treatment works.
4. Understanding the factors that influence the referral and treatment process.
5. Understanding how intermediate therapy processes such as client motivation, adherence, parental involvement, or the therapist–client relationship contribute to treatment successes and failures.
6. Assessing the acceptability of equivalent forms of treatment for children and significant adults.
7. Evaluating programs designed to reduce the likelihood that children who are at risk for a disorder will in fact develop the disorder (Conduct Problems Prevention Research Group, 1997).

Kazdin (1988) identified over 200 alternative forms of psychosocial treatment for children and adolescents, the great majority of which have not been evaluated. Although integrative reviews suggest that children who receive treatment are generally better off than children who do not, there is currently a pressing need for research to evaluate and compare the efficacy and effectiveness of specific types and combinations of child intervention and prevention programs as carried out in real-world clinical settings (Kazdin & Weisz, 1998; Weisz, in press).

Several key issues in treatment outcome research are identifying the constructs to be used in assessing treatment outcomes, selecting or developing appropriate measures of these constructs, deciding on which informant or informants will be asked to judge treatment outcomes, evaluating the impact of treatment against known age-related improvements in functioning, and specifying the criteria to be used in determining both the short- and long-term impact of treatment. An important distinction to be made in treatment evaluation research relates to the statistical versus clinical significance of change. Although problem children may show improvements in their behavior as the result of treatment that are statistically significant, their performance may still fall short of normative expectations. For example, Barkley, Guevremont, Anastopoulos, and Fletcher (1992) reported that although the behaviors of adolescents with ADHD improved following family intervention, only a small proportion of these adolescents were functioning in the normative range. In conducting outcome research, it is important that treatment-related changes be evaluated with respect to their clinical relevance as well as their statistical significance (Jacobson & Truax, 1991).

Another important distinction to be made in evaluating treatment outcomes is between treatment effectiveness versus treatment efficacy. Efficacy refers to whether a treatment can produce changes under controlled conditions, whereas effectiveness refers to whether the treatment can be shown to work in actual clinical practice (American Psychological Association Task Force on Psychological Intervention Guidelines, 1995). Treatment effects with children have been generally found to be larger in controlled research settings than in clinic practice (Weisz, Donenberg, Han, & Weiss, 1995).

Illustrative treatment studies have evaluated the impact of child management training for parents of pre-school ADHD children (Pisterman et al., 1989), the effects of parent training and problem-solving skill training for the treatment of antisocial behavior (Kazdin, Siegel, & Bass, 1992), the impact of school-based cognitive–behavioral interventions for aggressive boys (Lochman, 1992), and the effectiveness of cognitive–behavioral treatment for children with anxiety disorders (Kendall et al., 1997). Illustrative prevention studies have evaluated school-based coping and self-esteem-building programs for children in alcoholic families (Roosa, Gensheimer, Short, Ayers, & Shell, 1989), early interventions to minimize the adverse effects of low birthweight (Rauh, Achenbach, Nurcombe, Howell, & Teti, 1988), multi-modal cognitive–behavioral training to prevent adolescent drug abuse (Botvin, 1990), and school-based interventions for adolescents at risk for depression (Clarke et al., 1995).

FUNDAMENTAL ISSUES IN CHILD PSYCHOPATHOLOGY RESEARCH

Theory and Research

The knowledge base of psychology traditionally has developed through the dynamic dialectic of theory and empiricism leading to new information. Theory, often developed from observations, leads to predictions that are empirically supported or refuted. These empirical findings, in turn, lead to refinement, alteration, or abandonment of the theory. Through theoretical formulations, one can integrate related research results and develop meanings that extend beyond the immediate findings. Theory also provides the context to formulate new hypotheses and generalizations. The theoretical model(s) of child development and child psychopathology that the researcher adopts will dictate the variables deemed important to study, the choice of research methods, and the interpretation of research findings.

Several researchers have proposed a hierarchical approach to the conceptualization of child psychopathology (Overton & Horowitz, 1991). From a hierarchical perspective, theory at more general levels can provide an overarching conceptualization of maladaptive behaviors, which then can be examined from a more focused perspective. For example, general theories of development may conceptualize childhood psychopathology in terms of the child's failure to adapt to age-salient developmental tasks. However, more focused theories are then needed to determine the specific adaptations and tasks that are important to study within this general framework. Attachment theory, for example, emphasizes the importance of forming a secure bond with a caregiver as a critical age-salient task during the first two years of development (Bowlby, 1988).

Achenbach (1990) used the term "macroparadigm" to connote a broad perspective that integrates different approaches around common phenomena and questions. He proposed that the conceptual framework of developmental psychopathology (Cicchetti & Cohen, 1995), which considers childhood disorders in the context of maturational and developmental processes, be regarded as a macroparadigm. In contrast, specific theories—such as object relations theory, social learning theory, attachment theory, cognitive–developmental theory, and family systems theory—represent examples of microparadigms under this broader conceptualization. These more focused theories attempt to make immediate empirical reference to the specific domains that they seek to explain (e.g., quality of parent–child relationships, learning of antisocial behavior, social cognition, family processes).

On the other hand, recognizing that broad theories rarely yield testable hypotheses, other researchers have advocated for the development of "minitheories" that are amenable to empirical testing (Kazdin, 1989). Following confirmation of these minitheories, their focus can be expanded and generalized, forming the building blocks for a broader conceptualization of childhood disorders. For example, Gerald Patterson's (1982) "coercion model" proposed a number of family interaction processes to account for the development of antisocial behavior in children. In a series of empirical studies spanning more than 2 decades, Patterson identified specific characteristics and processes that are important in the learning of antisocial behavior (e.g., parental failure to follow through on demands, inadequate monitoring of child behavior, use of harsh discipline) and used these findings to formulate a broader developmental model of how these events unfold over time to produce a variety of antisocial outcomes (Patterson et al., 1992).

Developmental Considerations

Knowledge of normal developmental processes and pathways is critical to our general understanding of child psychopathology (Loeber, 1991; Popper, Ross & Jennings, chap. 4, this volume). Moreover, the rapid changes that are known to occur throughout infancy, childhood, and adolescence present unique conceptual, methodological, and pragmatic challenges to research on childhood disorders. Many childhood difficulties, such as fears and oppositionality, are quite common in young children but are known to decrease in magnitude and to change in form over time. The high frequency of occurrence in the general population for many childhood difficulties makes it difficult to determine which of these problems are predictive of later difficulties.

Many developmental changes are predictable enough by chronological age that normative data from standardized child symptom checklists reveal these patterns of increases and decreases when aggregated across large numbers of children of different ages (Achenbach, 1991; Achenbach et al., 1991). This type of normative–developmental information regarding the base rates of different childhood problems for children of different ages is critical in making judgments about developmental deviation. However, although the timing of developmental changes is related to chronological age, the relationship is far from perfect. Although the child's age often provides an adequate marker for developmental stage, some research questions require use of more functional measures of developmental level, such as gestational age, mental age, or stage of pubertal maturation.

This issue is especially significant in the study of children with known developmental delays, such as mental retardation or language delay. For these populations, comparisons with mental age or linguistic equivalency may provide a partial but not complete solution to the issue of developmental equivalence (see Stoneman, 1989, for a discussion of mental–age matches). Similarly, in research with children born prematurely, use of chronological versus gestational age matches has been debated. If correction is made to chronological age based on the degree of prematurity, then questions arise as to the length of time that such corrections are to be made, and whether age-corrections should be applied uniformly across all domains of functioning. Other studies have found associations between pubertal maturation and parent–child conflict (Steinberg, 1988), and pubertal maturation in girls and panic disorder (Hayward et al., 1992), that would not have been revealed had the less discriminating measure of chronological age been used.

Studies also have shown that the patterning and organization of childhood symptoms and disorders differ as a function of the child's age and developmental stage, and, after about age 3, as a function of the gender of the child (Achenbach, 1985). These qualitative developmental changes in the expression and organization of behavioral displays present unique research problems. For example, aggressive behavior that is evident in the kicks and toy-snatches of a preschooler may be manifest as verbally aggressive behavior during childhood or as covert hostility during adolescence. Do these changes reflect developmental symptom substitution (i.e., a specific symptom may disappear and be replaced by another symptom at a different age), or do they represent separate but linked behaviors on a trajectory of aggressive behaviors, with a greater likelihood of the second behavior occurring given the historical presence of the first? The difference in these views stems from differing theoretical assumptions about aggression as a relatively stable personality trait. Because the frequency and form of childhood problems change over time, the ways in which childhood disorders are defined and measured will, of necessity, differ at different ages. As a result, it may be difficult to determine whether observed changes in problem expression over time reflect "true" developmental progressions, or whether they are the result of variations in how the problem was defined or measured at different ages (i.e., a result of method variance).

The Social Context of the Child

Theory and research in child psychopathology have emphasized the importance of studying children's behavior and development in relation to the child's social context, typically consisting of the family, school, and peers. Children's dependency on significant adults, and the central role that adults play in defining childhood disorders, necessitate that the role of social context be considered in conceptualizing research and in deciding how samples of children are recruited, how data are collected, and how findings are interpreted.

Significantly, most children participating in research on emotional or behavioral problems have been referred for treatment by their parents, or, in the case of teacher referrals, with the agreement of their parents. Rarely do children refer themselves for treatment. Children referred by adults in different settings may not be comparable with respect to the nature or severity of their problems, or with respect to important associated characteristics such as SES or accompanying disorders. As a result, inconsistent research findings may reflect differences in the referral and selection processes that were used to identify children who participated in the research (Mash & Wolfe, 1991).

The likelihood of parents seeking help for their child is influenced by many factors, including the degree to which the child's behavior is noticeable and bothersome, the parents' own mental health and possible treatment history, the perceived benefits of treatment, and the parents' awareness of and access to resources. Unless precautions are taken, these sources of bias may influence the nature of research samples that are drawn from clinic versus nonclinic populations. The reports of parents and teachers also may be biased, for example, in the tendency of parents to see their children with problems in a negative light, even when the child's behavior may not warrant such a view. Such biases may reflect a history of conflictual parent–child interactions or high levels of parental depression and stress.

The question of who will serve as the respondent in providing research data is an important one, especially in research with older children and adolescents where the child's verbal report becomes increasingly reliable as a source of data. The choice of respondent is a critical decision, because rates of agreement between different informants and across different situations are generally poor to modest (Achenbach, McConaughy, & Howell, 1987) and may vary with the age of the child and nature of the problem. Mothers have been found to report less psychiatric disorder of all types in their children than children self-report, with a higher correspondence between mother and child report when mothers were themselves depressed at the time of reporting (Weissman et al., 1987). Research also has suggested that parents may be more accurate reporters of overt child behavioral difficulties than children, but that children may provide more accurate accounts of their own internal thoughts and feelings. Other studies have found that mothers typically report higher rates of problem child behaviors than do fathers.

In an integrative review of a large number of studies in which different informants were used to report on child symptoms, Achenbach et al. (1987) noted average correlations of around .22 between child self-reports of symptoms and the reports of parents, teachers, and mental health workers, average correlations of .60 between similar informants in similar settings (e.g., mothers and fathers, pairs of teachers), and average correlations of .28 between different informants in different settings (e.g., parents and teachers). Verhulst and Van der Ende (1992) found levels of agreement (.54) between parents and adolescents that were higher than those previously reported by Achenbach et al. (1987), suggesting that such levels of agreement may be higher for older children and their parents. These and other findings indicate that the magnitude of agreement among informants may depend on the age, gender, and other characteristics of the child; characteristics of the informant; the method of assessment; the setting in which behavior is rated; and the types of problem behaviors being rated. One way of addressing discrepancies in reporting that avoids searching for a "true" perception has been a validation approach that seeks to determine whose report is the best predictor of particular outcomes.

The child's social context also serves as an important moderator of behavior. Although some severe forms of child psychopathology may be pervasive across settings such as the home, classroom, and playground, more typically, the rate and quality of children's behavior will vary from situation to situation. Such variations may reflect the interaction between particular child characteristics and differences in the expectations, demands, and reinforcement contingencies associated with different settings. From a research standpoint, data that are collected in one setting may not be representative of the child's behavior in other settings. For example, a hyperactive child may exhibit few behavioral or attentional difficulties in a nondemanding unstructured situation such as watching television at home. However, the same child may display difficulties in a more demanding situation such as working on a structured academic task in the classroom. Similarly, children who have been physically abused may show high levels of compliant behavior when observed during interactions with their abusive parent. However, these children may show an opposite pattern of noncompliance and aggressive behavior in other situations where their parent is not present. Although the reasons for cross-setting variability in the expression of child psychopathology are numerous and not yet fully understood, the researcher needs to be cognizant of this variability when sampling behavior and when attempting to evaluate the representativeness and generalizability of research findings.

RESEARCH STRATEGIES

Research activities in child psychopathology can be viewed as a multi-staged decision-making process involving a series of key decisions at various points in this process. The process typically begins with development of hypotheses on the basis of theory and previous findings, and then proceeds to deciding on a general approach to research, identifying the population to be studied, developing a plan for sampling from that population, developing a research design and procedures that balance the pragmatics of implementation with the adequacy of the research to address the hypotheses under investigation, selecting or developing data collection measures, gathering and analyzing the data, and interpreting the results in relation to theory and previous findings. Ethical considerations associated with conducting research with children also must be taken into account at every stage of this process. The following discussion provides examples of some of the issues that may be encountered at various stages of this research process.

General Approaches to Research

Research varies in the degree to which the study uses an experimental versus correlational approach, employs a longitudinal versus cross-sectional strategy, or collects data prospectively or retrospectively. These alternative, but complementary, approaches offer different advantages and disadvantages. The choice of approach frequently depends on the nature of the population and disorder under investigation, the research questions being addressed, and the availability of resources.

Correlational Versus Experimental Research. The basic distinction between correlational versus experimental research reflects the degree to which the investigator can manipulate the "independent variable" or, alternatively, must rely on examining the covariation of several variables of interest. The greater the degree of control that the researcher has over the independent variables, the more the study approximates a true experiment. Conversely, the less control the researcher has in determining who will be exposed to the independent variables, the more correlational the research will be. Most variables of interest in child psychopathology cannot be manipulated directly (e.g., parenting styles, genetic influences). As a result, much of the research in the field has not been experimental, and correlational approaches have been relied on extensively. The primary limitations of correlational research are that interpretations of causality are difficult to make because: (a) a correlation between two variables does not imply that one variable causes the other, and (b) the correlation may occur because the two variables are both measures of some other more fundamental variable.

For example, in studying the effects of an independent variable, such as a specific childhood disorder or parenting behavior, research has identified a relation between ADHD in children and high levels of maternal directiveness (Danforth, Barkley, & Stokes, 1991). Because the variables of ADHD and parenting behavior cannot be randomly assigned, these findings are necessarily correlational in nature and do not lend themselves to making a clear causal interpretation. Common symptoms of ADHD, such as inattention, impulsivity, and noncompliance, may result in the use of greater maternal directiveness. Alternatively, maternal use of high levels of directiveness may provoke inattentive, impulsive, and noncompliant child behaviors. Alternatively, symptoms of ADHD and maternal directiveness both may be the result of some other more fundamental variable such as shared genetic dispositions or common environmental stressors. An experimental approach can be used to clarify these correlational findings, for example, by altering the child's behavior via stimulant medication and examining the subsequent effects on maternal behavior. When children with ADHD were given stimulant medication, it was found that improvements in child behavior as a result of such medication led to concomitant reductions in maternal directiveness (Humphries, Kinsbourne, & Swanson, 1978). These experimental findings support the causal interpretation that higher levels of maternal directiveness are at least in part the result of the difficult-to-manage behaviors of the child with ADHD.

Longitudinal Versus Cross-Sectional Research. In longitudinal research, the same individuals are studied at different ages and stages of development, whereas in cross-sectional research different individuals are studied at different ages and stages of development. Although cross-sectional research can provide suggestive information concerning developmental changes, more definitive answers to questions about continuities and discontinuities in child psychopathology can best be obtained through the use of longitudinal designs.

Longitudinal designs are conducted prospectively, with data collection occurring at specified points in time from the same individuals who were initially selected because of their membership in one or more populations of interest. The prospective longitudinal design allows the researcher to track developmental change within individuals. Because data are collected on the same individuals at Time 1 and Time 2, causal inferences based on temporal ordering can be made. Such inferences of causality cannot be made in cross-sectional designs, where different individuals are assessed at the two time points. Longitudinal designs also allow for identification of individual developmental trends that would be masked by aggregating over individuals. The prepubertal growth spurt exemplifies this, where rapid accelerations in growth occurring at different ages across the population are not reflected in growth measures aggregated across adolescents.

Difficulties associated with longitudinal designs are both design-related as well as pragmatic. Design difficulties relate to the issues of aging effects, cohort effects, and period effects. Aging effects refer to changes that occur because of aging of the participants, such as increases in physical prowess. Cohort effects refer to influences related to membership in a group of individuals born at one time and experiencing a sequence of events at the same time. Persons who regard themselves as "children of the sixties" reflect self-identified membership in a specific cohort. Period effects refer to influences occurring at particular times historically, such as the economic recession or the increased awareness of child abuse in the 1980s. Longitudinal designs confound aging and period effects, whereas cross-sectional designs confound aging and cohort effects (Farrington, 1991). Pragmatic disadvantages of longitudinal designs include the long wait for data, participant attrition, possible changes in diagnostic definitions or measurement instruments, and difficulties in maintaining research funding and resources over many years.

Some of the difficulties associated with longitudinal research can be reduced by using a combined cross-sectional–longitudinal approach in an "accelerated longitudinal design" (Farrington, 1991). With this approach, several cohorts of individuals are followed, each at different but overlapping ages or stages of development. For example, if the hypotheses related to the association between insecure early attachments and subsequent conduct disorder, cohorts of children might be followed from ages 1 to 6, 4 to 10, 8 to 14, and 12 to 18 years. Tracking the same children longitudinally would allow for measurement of aging effects (i.e., the developmental changes that are of interest), whereas use of different samples of children reduces the period effect, and overlap at different ages allows for measurement and control of the cohort effect. This approach assumes that links between early and later events are reflected at intermediate stages. If this assumption is not met, as in the case of delayed effects that only appear at much later ages, the data would fail to reveal these relations. This shortcoming may be particularly problematic in studies of genetic influences where the effects on some characteristics may become increasingly apparent with age. For example, Scarr and Weinberg (1983), in a study of adopted children, found greater correlations between biological parents' and child's IQ at later ages than at earlier ages. Similarly, certain genetic disorders such as Huntington's chorea only become evident in early and middle adulthood.

Retrospective Versus Prospective Research.   Research designs may differ with respect to when the sample is identified and when data are collected. Verhulst and Koot (1991) distinguish among three types of designs. In "real-time" prospective designs, the research sample is identified and then followed longitudinally over time, with data collected at specified time intervals. Disadvantages of this design include sample attrition over time, and the delay in collecting data that reflect changes over time. In "catch-up" designs, a sample of children is identified from records from an earlier time and then located at a second later time. This design provides for faster data collection, but results can be seriously compromised by the unrepresentativeness of individuals who can be located at the later time.

In "follow-back" or retrospective designs, a sample is identified at the current time and asked for information relating to an earlier time period. For example, a sample of young adults with depression might be asked to provide retrospective ratings and descriptions of their early family experiences. Although data are more immediately available in retrospective studies, they are also highly susceptible to bias and distortion in recall. Moreover, retrospective designs fail to identify individuals who were exposed to certain earlier experiences but do not develop the problem. For example, young adults with depression may report more negative early experiences (e.g., Blatt, Wein, Chevron, & Quinlan, 1979). However, based on this finding, we could not conclude that negative early experiences were specific precursors of adult depression, since the retrospective study fails to identify those children whose early experiences were negative, but who did not exhibit depression as young adults.

Sampling Considerations

Sample Definition. A careful definition of the sample of children to be studied is critical if there is to be comparability of findings across studies and clear communication among research investigators. Unfortunately, there has been little consensus on how childhood disorders should be defined, and many studies of childhood disorders have been carried out on poorly defined groups of children given such nonstandardized labels such as "emotionally disturbed" or "clinically maladjusted." Although this situation has improved, there continues to be a great deal of variability in sample definition from study to study. Even when standard diagnostic practices are used, children may differ widely in their pattern and severity of symptoms and associated characteristics.

It is especially important that studies that seek to determine the incidence and prevalence of childhood disorders rely on standardized and well-accepted definitions of these disorders. The failure to apply uniform standards in epidemiological research has led to wide differences in estimated base rates for various childhood disorders. For example, estimates of the incidence of ADHD have ranged from 1% to 20% of the general population, depending on such factors as how one defines ADHD; the use or nonuse of exclusionary criteria (e.g., low intelligence), the population studied; the informant (e.g., parent, teacher, physician); and the geographical locale of the survey (Barkley, 1996).

Categorical Diagnosis. Although an extensive discussion of diagnostic issues is beyond the scope of this chapter (for a discussion of diagnosis and classification see Scotti & Morris, chap. 2, this volume), the quality of any research study in child psychopathology is ultimately dependent on the classification systems that are used to identify the samples of children who participate in the research. The two major approaches that have been used to diagnose mental and emotional disorders in children are represented by the *Diagnostic and Statistical Manual of Mental Disorders* (4th ed. [*DSM–IV*]; American Psychiatric Association, 1994) and the *International Classification of Diseases (ICD–10*; World Health Organization, 1992). These diagnostic systems have been criticized for a variety of reasons, including inadequate reliability and validity, implicit assumptions about etiology, subjective nature of the criteria used to derive categories, lack of empirically derived operational criteria for assignment to categories, developmental insensitivity, lack of relevance for treatment, insensitivity to contextual influences, and insufficient attention to childhood disorders. The most recent revisions of both systems reflect a shift to increasingly greater differentiation of categories for children and adolescents and the use of more operationally and behaviorally specified criteria, with correspondingly less reliance on particular theoretical formulations. In addition, there are efforts under way to develop alternative diagnostic schemes that possess greater sensitivity to the specific developmental, relational, and emotional characteristics of infants and toddlers than do the current diagnostic approaches (Greenspan, Harmon, Emde, Sameroff, & Wieder, 1991). One such system is the *Diagnostic Classification: 0–3* (Zero to Three/National Center for Clinical Infant Programs, 1994).

Dimensional Classification

The question has been debated at length as to whether childhood disorders constitute qualitatively distinct categories or extreme points on continuous dimensions that include adaptive, normal behaviors at other points along these dimensions. Psychotic behavior in children may be categorically distinct from nonpsychotic, whereas severe attentional difficulties may differ only in magnitude from attentional functioning that is regarded as normal for age. Both perspectives may have their place, depending on the disorder under consideration. When the disorder is viewed on a continuum, questions arise as to where the cutpoints that differentiate normal from abnormal functioning are to be located and how those points are to be established. What magnitude of disorder will lead to a diagnosis for one child, but not for another? Frequently, these decisions are based on statistical departures from the average (e.g., greater than two standard deviations from the mean) or other empirically derived criteria (Achenbach, 1985).

The diagnosis of mental retardation provides an illustration of differences in meaning and practical implications based on the cutpoints chosen. Mental retardation is defined as significantly subaverage general intellectual functioning associated with concurrent impairments in adaptive functioning, and these need to be evident during the first 18 years of the individual's life (Grossman, 1983). Prior to 1977, an IQ below 80 met the criterion for subaverage intellectual functioning. In 1977, the American Association on Mental Deficiency changed the cutpoint to an IQ of 68, thereby eliminating from classification as mental retardation the largest category, borderline intellectual functioning (IQ = 69–80). In 1994, the *DSM–IV* (American Psychiatric Association, 1994) designated an IQ of 70 or below for a diagnosis of mental retardation, and in 1992, the AAMR noted that "significantly subaverage" is equivalent to IQ scores of approximately 70 to 75 or below (American Association on Mental Retardation, 1992). Although these differences may appear to be small, given the bell-shaped nature of the IQ distribution, a cutoff score of 75 results in twice as many individuals being eligible for a diagnosis of mental retardation than a cutoff of 70 (MacMillan, Gresham, & Siperstein, 1993).

Comorbidity

The simultaneous occurrence of two or more childhood disorders is far more common than would be predicted from the general population base rates of the individual disorders. For example, for children who are diagnosed as having ADHD, as many as 50% also have a conduct disorder and 20% to 25% a specific learning disability (Barkley, 1996). Rates of comorbidity between other disorders such as anxiety and depression are also quite high (Brady & Kendall, 1992). Several possible explanations have been proposed for the observed high rates of comorbidity. These include shared risk factors, assortative mating, and the possibility that one disorder represents an earlier form of, or predisposes the child to, a second disorder (Caron & Rutter, 1991).

Comorbidity has direct implications for the selection of research participants and interpretation of results. Research samples that are drawn from clinic populations will have a disproportionately high rate of comorbidity because referral for treatment is likely to be based on the combined symptomatology of all disorders. To deal with comorbidity in research samples, some researchers may adopt exclusionary criteria in order to select only participants with single "pure" disorders. This strategy may yield small, atypical samples whose findings do not generalize to other populations. On the other hand, the failure to consider comorbidity may result in an interpretation of findings in relation to one disorder, when these findings are more validly attributed to a second disorder or to the combination of disorders. Research strategies that compare children showing single disorders with those showing comorbid disorders are needed to help disentangle the effects of comorbidity.

Setting and Source of Referral for Research

Research samples of problem and nonproblem children have been selected from a variety of settings that include outpatient psychology and psychiatry clinics, schools, pediatric, developmental, and learning disorder clinics, hospitals, day-care centers, social welfare agencies, youth or church groups, and the general community. Effects related to setting often are confounded with those related to referral source, because across settings, referral sources may include parents, teachers, day-care workers, physicians, or mental health personnel. As sufficiently large samples of children with a particular disorder may not be readily available in a single setting, some studies have included samples that consist of children drawn from different settings and referral sources. This procedure likely will contribute to increased sample heterogeneity and subsequently to increased variance in findings. On the other hand, selection of participants from a single setting may provide potentially unrepresentative findings that are the result of parameters unique to that particular setting.

Samples drawn from different settings and referral sources can be quite different from one another with respect to the nature and severity of the children's problems, and with respect to the children's associated behavioral, learning, and developmental characteristics. Samples from different settings also may show systematic differences with respect to important family characteristics and demographics. To illustrate the effects that referral setting and source can have on research findings, in school-identified samples of children with ADHD, and in samples of children with ADHD drawn from learning disorder clinics, girls with ADHD have been found to exhibit fewer behavioral and conduct problems than boys, and more cognitive and developmental difficulties. However, in psychology and psychiatry clinic samples, where referral often is based on problem severity, such differences between boys and girls with ADHD have not been found (Barkley, 1996). These and other findings reinforce the importance of carefully examining the ways in which the characteristics of specific settings and referral sources may influence research results, and the need to take this into account when attempting to generalize one's findings to other groups of children.

Sample Size

The question of how large a sample size is needed is an important one in any study of child psychopathology. Too often, sample size has been based on subject availability rather than on logical or statistical criteria. Because many childhood disorders occur infrequently (e.g., autistic disorder), many studies have been carried out with very small samples of children. Small sample sizes tend to reduce the likelihood that significant effects will be found, preclude multifactorial analysis of the results, and limit the generalizability of findings.

The concept of statistical power is relevant to any discussion of sample size. The statistical power of a test refers to the probability of detecting a true difference given that certain conditions hold. These conditions include the anticipated effect size, the size of the variance, and the sample size. In general, increasing the sample size increases the power of a test to detect statistically significant differences. Power analyses may be conducted a priori to determine the sample size needed to detect significant effects (see Cohen, 1988, for a discussion of power analysis).

Because a large sample size increases the likelihood of demonstrating statistical significance, studies with very large samples are virtually assured of producing at least some significant findings, even when the magnitude of the effects may be quite small. Consequently, in addition to statistical significance, the researcher also is interested in detecting effect sizes that are large enough to be meaningful. A study of the impact of early intervention on children's later intellectual development illustrates this point (Ramey et al., 1992). With an initial sample of almost 1,000 infants and their families, of which one third were randomly assigned to a treatment condition and two thirds to the control condition, the authors predictably obtained statistically significant findings for treatment effects on children's IQ scores at 3 years of age. The authors also reported indexes that addressed the clinical significance of their findings, including IQ differences between intervention and control groups of 9 points and percentages of children scoring in the borderline range of intellectual functioning or lower (IQ < 70) of 6.9% for the intervention group versus 35.5% for the control group.

Sample Attrition

Sample attrition or drop out is a major problem in child psychopathology research, particularly in longitudinal studies of high-risk populations. Attrition is not a randomly distributed event, because families who drop out of a research study are more likely to have particular characteristics (e.g., multiproblem, low SES, single-parent) when compared with those who remain. Sample attrition results in a reduced sample size, unequal group sizes, and difficulties in generalizing because of a lack of sample representativeness. For example, a study of high-risk mothers may produce misleading findings if, during the course of the study, the most severely impaired mothers were to drop out, and interpretations were based on those mothers who remained. Researchers who conduct studies with high-risk populations have devised a number of methods for keeping families involved in the investigation, including subject payment, flexible research schedules, and provision of information and services. Although these procedures are necessary if high-risk samples are to be studied, the researcher needs to be cognizant of the possibility that such procedures can influence and distort the data that are obtained.

RESEARCH DESIGNS

Case Studies

The study of child psychopathology through intensive observation and analysis of individual cases has a long tradition in abnormal child psychology. Itard's description of

Victor, the Wild Boy of Aveyron, Freud's treatment of a phobia in Little Hans, John Watson's conditioning of a phobic reaction in Albert B, and many other similar case studies have played an influential role in shaping the way we think about child psychopathology. Nevertheless, case studies typically have been viewed as unscientific and flawed because of the uncontrolled methods and selective biases that often characterize them and the inherent difficulties associated with integrating diverse observations and generalizing from single cases. Hence, case studies have been viewed mostly as rich sources of descriptive information that provide a basis for subsequent hypothesis-testing in research with larger samples and using more controlled methods.

On the other hand, it also has been noted that case studies can capture meaningful life events in specific contexts and can serve the scientific goals of: exploration (i.e., revealing rare or previously unrecognized events); description (i.e., formulating theory and providing ideas for further investigation); and explanation (i.e., via hypothesis testing; Mendelson, 1992). There are a number of reasons that systematically conducted case studies are likely to continue to play a useful role in research on childhood disorders. First, many childhood disorders are rare, making it difficult to generate large samples of children for research. Second, the analyses of individual cases may contribute to our understanding of many striking symptoms of childhood disorders that either occur infrequently (e.g., acts of extreme cruelty), or that are covert and therefore difficult to observe directly (e.g., stealing). Third, significant childhood disturbances often develop as the result of naturally occurring extreme events and circumstances (e.g., natural disasters, severe trauma, or abuse) that are not easily studied via controlled methods. Improved methods and technologies for data recording and recent advances in qualitative and content analysis have the potential for removing some of the bias that has characterized clinical case studies and for increasing their scientific respectability. Nevertheless, generalization remains a problem, as does the time-consuming nature associated with the intensive analyses of single cases.

Single-Case Experimental Designs

Single-case experimental designs most frequently have been used to evaluate the impact of a clinical treatment (e.g., reinforcement, stimulant medication) on problem child behavior. The central features of single-case designs include repeated assessment of behavior over time, the replication of treatment effects within the same participant over time, and the participant serving as his or her own control by experiencing all treatment conditions. There are many different types of single-subject designs, the most common being the ABAB, or reversal, design, and the multiple baseline design carried out across behaviors, situations, or individuals.

In an ABAB, or reversal, design, the participant's behavior is monitored repeatedly throughout four successive phases: (a) a baseline phase (A) in which no treatment occurs; (b) an intervention phase (B) in which treatment is introduced and behavior typically is observed to change in the desired direction; (c) a reversal phase (A) or return to baseline in which the treatment is withdrawn; and (d) a final phase (B) in which treatment is reinstituted. If the treatment was responsible for the observed change during the intervention phase, the behavior should revert to its baseline level during the reversal phase, and again should change in the desired direction when the treatment is reinstituted during the final phase.

In a multiple baseline design across behaviors, different responses of the same individual are identified and measured over time to provide a baseline against which changes may be evaluated. Each behavior is then successively modified in turn. If each behavior changes only when it is specifically treated, the inference of a cause–effect relationship between the treatment and the behavior change is made. Other common varieties of multiple baseline designs involve successive introductions of treatment for the same behavior in the same individual across different situations, or for the same behavior across several individuals in the same situation. The critical feature of the multiple baseline approach is that change must occur only when treatment is instituted, and only for the behavior, situation, or individual that is the target of treatment. Concomitant changes must not occur for untreated behaviors, situations, or individuals until the time that each of these, in turn, is targeted for treatment.

There are several advantages and limitations associated with the use of single-case designs. Although preserving the personal quality of the case study, these designs: (a) offer some degree of control for potential confounds such as the effects of maturation, history, statistical regression, instrument decay, and reactivity to observation; (b) provide an objective evaluation of treatment for individual cases; (c) permit for the study of rare disorders; and (d) facilitate the development and evaluation of alternative and combined forms of treatment. On the negative side are the possibilities that specific treatments will interact with individual subject characteristics, limited generality of findings, difficulties in interpretation when observed changes are highly variable, subjectivity and inconsistency that is involved when visual inspection is used as the primary basis for evaluating the data, and limitations associated with specific types of case-study designs (e.g., in the ABAB reversal design, in which ethical concerns surround the return to a baseline condition following effective treatment for undesirable or even dangerous behaviors).

Between-Group Comparison Designs

Rather than comparing an individual with his or her own performance under different conditions, many research designs are based on comparisons between a group of individuals assigned to one condition and other groups of individuals assigned to different conditions. When participants are randomly assigned to groups, and groups are presumed to be equivalent in all other respects, one group typically serves as the experimental group and the other as the control group. Any differences observed between groups are then attributed to the experimental condition. More commonly, the nature of the event (e.g., marital discord) or the disorder of interest (e.g., childhood depression) in studies of child psychopathology precludes random assignment to groups. Comparison groups are then selected to provide contrasting information, but with the recognition that the experimental and comparison groups may vary on dimensions other than those of interest to the researcher. The selection of comparison groups requires careful attention to specific characteristics of the disorder and the inferences one desires to make. The choice of comparison groups is particularly important if one wishes to make inferences as to the specificity of findings to the particular disorder under consideration.

An example from the literature on social interactions illustrates this point. When compared with children of normal intelligence, children with mental retardation of various etiologies long have been known to show dampened affect or a lack of emotional expressiveness during social interactions with their parents and others (e.g., Cicchetti & Serafica, 1981; Yoder & Feagans, 1988). These differences have led to the interpretation that dampened affect is a specific feature of mental retardation. However, it has been also found that children with physical but not mental delays exhibit dampened affect during social interactions (Wasserman, Shilansky, & Hahn, 1986). These findings with children who are not mentally retarded call into question previous interpretations regarding the specificity and possible causes of this symptom and illustrate the importance of careful selection of comparison groups. One strategy to help address this threat to validity is the use of multiple comparison groups. Each group can provide comparative data on a relevant dimension (e.g., general level of distress). For example, in a study of the parent–adolescent interactions of families with an alcoholic father, Jacob, Krahn, and Leonard (1991) used both nondistressed- and depressed-father families as comparison groups.

Multivariate Approaches

As previously discussed, models of child and family functioning are typically complex, with multiple components and multiple pathways of direct, indirect, and reciprocal influences (Mash & Dozois, 1996; Mash & Johnston, 1990; McCubbin & Patterson, 1983; Patterson et al., 1992). Multivariate approaches are needed to test complete or partial versions of these models. In general, multivariate approaches, which include multiple-regression analysis and its many variants (e.g., path analysis), offer several advantages. First, they allow for the simultaneous consideration of multiple variables in combination (i.e., as a system). Multifactorial designs routinely are required to assess the unique effects of salient variables and their interaction effects with other variables. Second, they allow for the simultaneous consideration of multiple outcome measures. In so doing, they identify redundancy or overlapping variance among dependent variables, all of which may be significant because of shared variance with a salient variable; alternatively, they also allow for the potential identification of effects that may only be evident in the combination of dependent variables and not evident in any single variable. Finally, they provide a means for controlling the experimentwise error rate when using numerous dependent variables.

Multivariate designs are particularly well suited for testing predictive models of behavior. In one study of behavioral adjustment in children, Abidin, Jenkins, and McGaughey (1992) examined the contribution of family variables measured during the child's first year of life to predict subsequent behavioral adjustment 4 1/2 years later. Hierarchical regression models indicated that 39% of the variance in mother's ratings of the child's behavioral adjustment could be predicted by child gender, family life stress events, child characteristics, and maternal characteristics. No support was evident for models predicting father or teacher ratings of children's behavioral adjustment.

METHODS OF MEASUREMENT

A variety of measurement methods have been used to assess relevant constructs (e.g., aggression, sociability, temperament, attachment) in child psychopathology (Mash & Terdal, 1997a). The most common of these are direct observation, interviews, and questionnaires. As outlined in the comparisons of methods presented in Table 7.1, these methods vary with respect to several important dimensions.

One major distinction relates to who will make inferences about behaviors—the researcher using observational methods, or the participants through survey methods. The methods used in child psychopathology research have included unstructured and structured interviews, behavioral checklists and questionnaires, rating scales, self-monitoring procedures, formal tests, psychophysiological recordings, and direct observations of behavior (Bellack & Hersen, 1998; Kamphaus & Frick, 1996; Mash &

TABLE 7.1

A Comparison of Three Data-Gathering Methods

	Observation	Interview	Questionnaire
Structure of situation	Situation can be structured or naturalistic	Semistructured or structured	Highly structured
Structure of responses	Data to be recorded can be very inclusive to highly selective	Opportunity for probes, expansion, and clarification	Highly structured, no opportunity for probes or clarification
Resource requirements	Extensive time needed for observing and coding observations	Considerable time needed for interviewing and coding responses	Little experimenter time needed
Sources of bias	Does not rely on participants' disclosure, though will be influenced by reactivity	Relies on participants' perception and willingness to report; responses may be influenced by interviewer characteristics and mannerisms	Relies on participants' perception and willingness to report
Data reduction	What is observed is highly influenced by the observational coding system	Requires analysis of narrative responses or recoding into categories	Little data reduction needed

Terdal, 1997b; Messick, 1983). Because data obtained via different methods may vary as a function of the method used (i.e., method variance), researchers frequently must rely on a multimethod approach to define and assess the constructs of interest. Convergent validity is reflected in the extent to which data obtained via different measures of a construct provide similar information.

One's choice of measures in any research study is the result of a decision process based on a number of factors, and for which there are no hard and fast rules. In addition to the characteristics of the measure itself (e.g., reliability, validity, complexity, training requirements), other factors that will influence one's choice of measures include:

1. The purpose of the research (e.g., epidemiological, treatment evaluation).
2. The nature of the construct being evaluated (e.g., chronic vs. acute, overt vs. covert).
3. Child characteristics (e.g., age, cognitive level, language skills).
4. Family characteristics (e.g., education, SES).
5. Research-setting characteristics (e.g., home, lab).
6. Desired comparability with other research (e.g., use of a new measure vs. an existing one).
7. Characteristics and resources of the researcher (e.g., theoretical preferences, time, and personnel).

Observational Methods

Using direct observational methods, the researcher gathers information under conditions that can range from highly structured tasks completed in a clinic or laboratory to unstructured observations in the child's natural environment (Mash, 1991). Tasks assigned to participants for observational data-gathering purposes typically are structured to elicit behaviors of particular interest. For example, studies of noncompliance in children frequently employ tasks in which increasing demands are placed on the child by the parent, thereby eliciting multiple instances of the parent issuing commands and the child having the opportunity to demonstrate compliance or noncompliance. Structured laboratory or clinic-based observations are cost-effective and offer the advantage of focusing observations on the phenomena of interest. However, questions arise as to whether such observations provide a representative sample of the behaviors of interest.

The ecological validity of observations made in the child's natural environment may be greater than in the clinic or laboratory, but not necessarily so if the degree of intrusiveness associated with observing in the natural environment is also high. Additionally, because observation in the natural environment may require long periods of time to collect a sample of low- frequency behaviors that is large enough to analyze statistically, this form of data collection can become extremely expensive. The settings in which observations are to be conducted in a particular research study depend on a number of factors, many of which are similar to those involved in one's choice of method of measurement.

There are numerous other issues associated with the use of observational methods in research on child psychopathology (for a comprehensive discussion see Foster & Cone, 1986; J. B. Reid, Patterson, Baldwin, & Dishion, 1988). These issues relate to: code system characteristics (e.g., number and complexity of categories); characteristics of the behaviors being observed (e.g., rate, complexity); methods for assessing and calculating reliability; observer characteristics; sources of observer and participant bias; reactivity to observation; and summary and interpretation of observations.

Survey Methods

Survey methods assess the perceptions and opinions of the participants or related others. Questionnaires are popular as an inexpensive means of gathering a defined set of information. Frequently used questionnaires in child psychopathology research include child behavior checklists (completed by the child, parent, or teacher) and measures of personality and affect. The information provided by questionnaires is typically precise but narrow in content. Thus, questionnaires often are used in conjunction with other measures of related variables of interest.

More expensive and time-consuming than questionnaires, interviews serve as another survey method. They allow the researcher to listen and adapt to additional insights or directions that the participants' responses may suggest. Interviews can vary widely in structure, both in the nature and phrasing of questions to be asked and the manner in which responses are recorded (verbatim or precoded categories).

Qualitative Data Measurement

Ethnographic or qualitative research methods are intended to provide a holistic view of a situation through inductive and naturalistic inquiry (Patton, 1990). Rather than beginning from already developed coding systems or assessment tools, ethnographic researchers strive to understand the phenomenon from the participant's perspective. Qualitative data typically are collected through observations or open-ended interviewing and are recorded narratively, as case-study notes, for example. The obtained observations and narrative accounts are examined to build general categories and patterns.

Proponents of qualitative research believe that it provides for an intensive and intimate understanding of a situation that is rarely achieved in quantitative research (e.g., Denzin & Lincoln, 1994; Murphy, 1992). The two methods can be used in complementary ways. Common combinations of these methods are to use the qualitative approach to identify salient dimensions that are developed into a theoretical model that can be tested quantitatively, or to use qualitative case studies to illuminate the meaning of quantitatively derived findings. Miles and Huberman (1984) provide an excellent and readable account of the collection, reduction, and display of qualitative data and strategies for reaching conclusions. Qualitative data ultimately may be analyzed using quantitative methods if the data have been reduced to numbers, such as through word counts or frequency counts of themes.

DATA ANALYSIS

One's choice of research design and data analytic strategy will depend on the hypothesis under investigation and the nature of the data set. Strategies for data analysis are too numerous and varied to be discussed in any great detail here (see Appelbaum & McCall, 1983, for an excellent discussion of design and data analysis issues). However, several analytic approaches that are of particular current interest and applicability to research in child psychopathology are reviewed briefly. These include meta-analysis, structural equation modeling, and growth curve analysis. In the context of child psychopathology research, these approaches are particularly relevant because they offer the potential to: (a) integrate findings across diverse data sets and studies; (b) derive and test models that are sensitive to multiple determinants, direct and indirect effects, and alternative pathways of influence; and (c) conduct analyses that are especially sensitive to the parameters of developmental change.

Meta-analysis is a quantitative method for averaging and integrating the standardized results from a large number of independent studies. Using data from already published studies, meta-analysis provides for the statistical estimation of effect sizes (ES), most typically derived by subtracting the mean of the control group from the mean of the experimental or treatment group and dividing the difference by the standard deviation of the control group. The larger the ES, the greater the effect of the treatment condition. Once ESs from a large number of different studies are calculated, statistical analyses then can be used to answer different questions, for example, comparing different forms of therapy or different levels of therapist experience.

Meta-analyses have been used successfully to determine the efficacy along multiple parameters of psychotherapy with children (Weisz & Weiss, 1993), to identify salient features of successful early intervention programs for young children with developmental disabilities (Shonkoff & Hauser-Cram, 1987), and to determine the relation between marital discord and child behavior problems (W. J. Reid & Crisafulli, 1990). Meta-analysis also has found that adjustment to pediatric physical disorder leaves children vulnerable to both externalizing and internalizing problems (Lavigne & Faier-Routman, 1992).

Meta-analytic studies have been criticized with respect to the criteria used to generate a database for statistical analysis, the inclusion and equal weighting of findings from studies of different quality, and the choice and nonindependence of dependent measures. Although these criticisms of meta-analysis are valid, it is also important to note that many of them are not inherent to meta-analysis per se, but rather reflect inadequacies in the way in which meta-analyses have been conducted. Proponents of meta-analysis believe that integrative interpretations of data are fairer, more objective, and more comprehensive than qualitative literature reviews and that they optimize the possibility of cumulative scientific knowledge (Schmidt, 1992).

A second analysis strategy to enjoy recent popularity in research on child psychopathology is structural equation modeling (SEM). SEM is particularly useful for purposes of causal modeling and validation of measures. A valuable feature that distinguishes SEM (e.g., LISREL) from more traditional factor analyses is that it affords a way to test hypotheses about latent variables or structures. Latent (or unmeasured) constructs are inferred from measurable variables. General applications of SEM are described in Morris, Bergan, and Fulginiti (1991), and specific applications in the context of antisocial behavior are described in Patterson et al. (1992).

Finally, there have been recent advances in the methods used to analyze change. Many of these models and methods are presented by Collins and Horn (1991) and Newman and Howard (1991). Particularly well suited for measuring change, such as developmental changes in longitudinal studies, are growth curve analyses. As an example, Graham, Collins, Wugalter, Chung, and Hansen (1991) applied latent transition analysis procedures to test competing hypotheses about the steps in the development of substance use patterns in a large sample of adolescents. Through these procedures they were able to address the role and identity of "gateway" drugs in the progression to more significant drug abuse in teenagers.

ETHICAL AND PRAGMATIC ISSUES

Researchers have become increasingly sensitive to the possible ethical misuses of research procedures and correspondingly more aware of the need for principles and guidelines to regulate research practices in child psychopathology. Currently, ethical guidelines for research are provided through institutional review boards, federal funding agencies, and professional organizations (e.g., SRCD Ethical Standards, 1990). Ethical guidelines attempt to strike a balance between freedom of scientific inquiry and protecting the rights of privacy and the overall welfare of the research participants.

Informed Consent and Assent

The individual's fully informed consent to participate, obtained without coercion, serves as the single most protective regulation for research participants. Informed consent ensures that all participants be fully informed of the nature of the research and of the research procedures before they agree to participate. In the case of research with children, this is extended to obtaining the informed consent of the parents acting for the child, as well as the assent of the child. Guidelines for obtaining assent of the child include that assent is sought beginning when children enter school or when they are at the developmental level where they can recognize their printed name. Informed consent includes awareness of potential benefits as well as risks, of the option to withdraw from the study at any time, and of the fact that participation or nonparticipation in the research does not affect eligibility for other services.

In some instances, obtaining informed consent poses formidable challenges. For example, in research with uneducated individuals, special efforts must be taken to insure that they fully comprehend the research procedures. Research on child maltreatment often informs parents that the purpose of the study is to examine a range of caregiving practices. If parents were fully informed that the researchers were studying abuse, the research likely could not be conducted. In studying "street kids," minors who are generally not legally emancipated but whose parents or guardian are unaware of their whereabouts, the possibility that efforts would be made to obtain informed consent from parents could lead to absolute refusal on the part of the adolescent to participate. Researchers must make every effort to consider the importance of the research goals in relation to the need to maintain the dignity of the participants and the need to minimize the likelihood of potential harm.

Voluntary Participation

Participation in research is to be voluntary; yet, some individuals may be more susceptible to subtle pressure and coercion than others. The role of the researcher requires balancing successful recruiting and avoiding placing pressure on potential participants (Grisso et al., 1991). Protection for vulnerable populations, including children, has received considerable attention. Fisher (1991) identified families of high-risk infants and children as potentially more vulnerable, related in part to the families' distress over their child's high-risk status. Although instructed otherwise, parents recruited from social service agencies or medical settings may still feel that their treatment or quality of care will be threatened if they do not participate in the research. Maltreating parents may feel that their failure to participate in research could result in the loss of their child, jail sentence, or a failure to receive services.

Volunteerism is itself a biasing factor in research. Individuals agreeing to participate in research obviously differ from those who are approached but refuse, with the question remaining as to whether the volunteerism factor significantly biases findings on the variables of interest. To address this concern, some researchers have recommended the use of a semirandomized clinical trial design (Fisher, 1991). Potential participants who refuse to participate in the study because of the requirement that they be randomly assigned to a treatment or no treatment condition are included in the study, and are then provided treatment or no treatment as per their choice. Participants who agree to the random assignment procedures are similarly assigned to the treatment or no-treatment conditions, resulting in four groups. Although the design is no longer a true experimental design, the analyses do allow for estimating the effects of volunteerism.

Confidentiality and Anonymity

Information revealed by individuals through participation in research is to be safeguarded. Most institutions require that individuals be informed that any information that they disclose will be kept confidential, and also if there are any exceptions to confidentiality. In research with children, one of the most frequently encountered challenges to confidentiality occurs when the child or parent reveals past abuse or information that would suggest the possibility of future abuse of the child. Procedures for handling this situation will vary across studies and across states, depending on the circumstances of the disclosure (e.g., by an adult within the context of therapy) and the reporting requirements of the state. The quality of research data that are collected may vary with the degree to which the confidentiality of information is emphasized (Blanck, Bellack, Rosnow, Rotheram-Borus, & Schooler, 1992).

Information that is videotaped is regarded as particularly sensitive because it stores data that ordinarily would not be permanently recorded (Grisso et al., 1991) and because identities are difficult to mask. Most institutional review boards have policies about the storing and eventual erasing of videotaped information. Particular sensitivity must be exercised in handling videotaped data and in sharing it with other researchers.

Nonharmful Procedures

No research operations should be used that may harm the child either physically or psychologically. Whenever possible, the researcher also is obligated to use procedures that are the least stressful to the child and family. In some instances, psychological harm may be difficult to define, but, when in doubt, it is the researcher's responsibility to seek consultation from others. If harm seems inevitable, alternative methods must be found or the research must be abandoned. In cases where exposure of the child to stressful conditions may be necessary if therapeutic benefits associated with the research are to be realized, careful deliberation by an institutional review board is needed.

Other Ethical Concerns

Sensitivity to ethical concerns is especially important when the research involves potentially invasive procedures, possible entrapment, deception, the use of punishment procedures, the use of subject payment or other incentives, or possible coercion. Investigators must be particularly sensitive, and especially so in longitudinal research, to the occurrence of unexpected crises, unforeseen consequences of research, and issues surrounding the continuation of the research when findings suggest that some other course of action is required to ensure the child's well-being.

Some Pragmatic Issues

Many research problems that typically are addressed through standardized instructions and procedures, and through a reliance on the prior experiences and expectations of the participants, are compounded by children's generally limited experience and understanding of novel research tasks and by the particular characteristics of disturbed children and families. Children with ADHD, children with oppositional and conduct disorders, or children with limited intellectual functioning, learning difficulties, or language and sensory impairments may present special research challenges associated with establishing rapport, motivating the children, keeping within time limitations, ensuring that instructions are well understood, maintaining attention, and coping with possible boredom, distraction, and fatigue. Similarly, the families of children with problems often exhibit characteristics that may compromise their research participation and involvement. These include high levels of stress, marital discord, parental psychiatric disorders (e.g., anxiety and depression), substance use disorders, restricted resources or time for research, and limited verbal abilities.

SUMMARY

We have emphasized that research activities in child psychopathology are best conceptualized within a decision-making framework that is predicated on an understanding of the theoretical, methodological, and practical considerations that assist the researcher in making informed decisions about when certain research methods and strategies are appropriate, and when they are not. We have considered the kinds of questions that research in child psychopathology typically seeks to address, including those about the nature of childhood disorders, the determinants of childhood disorders, risk and protective factors, and treatment and prevention. Three fundamental issues in child psychopathology research are the relation between theory and research, the role of developmental factors, and the impact of the child's social context. We have described research in child psychopathology as a decision-making process and have highlighted issues that are relevant at various stages of this process. These include general approaches to research, sampling considerations, types of research designs, methods of measurement, and approaches to data analysis. Finally, we have discussed some of the special ethical and pragmatic issues that may be encountered in conducting research with disturbed children and families. It is believed that our understanding of child psychopathology can best be advanced through the use of a variety of research methods and strategies.

ACKNOWLEDGMENT

During the writing of this chapter, Eric Mash was partially supported by a Killam Foundation Grant from the University of Calgary Research Grants Committee.

REFERENCES

Abidin, R. R., Jenkins, C. L., & McGaughey, M. C. (1992). The relationship of early family variables to children's subsequent behavioral adjustment. *Journal of Clinical Child Psychology, 21,* 60–69.

Achenbach, T. M. (1978). *Research in developmental psychology: Concepts, strategies, methods.* New York: The Free Press.

Achenbach, T. M. (1982). *Developmental psychopathology* (2nd ed.). New York: Wiley.

Achenbach, T. M. (1985). *Assessment and taxonomy of child and adolescent psychopathology.* Beverly Hills, CA: Sage.

Achenbach, T. M. (1990). Conceptualization of developmental psychopathology. In M. Lewis & S. M. Miller (Eds.), *Handbook of developmental psychopathology* (pp. 3–14). New York: Plenum.

Achenbach, T. M. (1991). *Manual for the Child Behavior Checklist/4-18 and 1991 profile.* Burlington, VT: University of Vermont Department of Psychiatry.

Achenbach, T. M., Howell, C. T., Quay, H. C., & Conners, C. K. (1991). National survey of problems and competencies among four- to sixteen-year-olds: Parents' reports for normative and clinical samples. *Monographs of the Society for Research in Child Development, 56* (3, Serial No. 225).

Achenbach, T. M., McConaughy, S. H., & Howell, C. T. (1987). Child/adolescent behavioral and emotional problems: Implications of cross-informant correlations for situational specificity. *Psychological Bulletin, 101,* 213–232.

American Association on Mental Retardation. (1992). *Mental retardation: Definition, classification, and systems of supports.* Washington, DC: Author.

American Psychiatric Association. (1994). *Diagnostic and statistical manual of mental disorders* (4th ed.). Washington, DC: Author.

American Psychological Association Task Force on Psychological Intervention Guidelines. (1995). *Template for developing guidelines: Interventions for mental disorders and psycho-

logical aspects of physical disorders. Washington, DC: American Psychological Association.

Appelbaum, M., & McCall, R. B. (1983). Design and analysis in developmental psychology. In W. Kessen (Ed.), *Handbook of child psychology: Vol 1. History, theory, and methods* (4th ed. pp. 415–476). New York: Wiley.

Barkley, R. A. (1996). Attention-deficit/hyperactivity disorder. In E. J. Mash & R. A. Barkley (Eds.), *Child psychopathology* (pp. 63–112). New York: Guilford.

Barkley, R. A., Guevremont, D. C., Anastopoulos, A. D., & Fletcher, K. E. (1992). A comparison of three family therapy programs for treating family conflicts in adolescents with Attention-Deficit Hyperactivity Disorder. *Journal of Consulting and Clinical Psychology, 60,* 450–462.

Bellack, A. S., & Hersen, M. (Eds.). (1998). *Behavioral assessment: A practical handbook* (4th ed.). Needham Heights, MA: Allyn & Bacon.

Blanck, P. D., Bellack, A. S., Rosnow, R. L., Rotheram-Borus, M. J., & Schooler, N. R. (1992). Scientific rewards and conflicts of ethical choices in human subjects research. *American Psychologist, 47,* 959–965.

Blatt, S. J., Wein, S. J., Chevron, E. S., & Quinlan, D. M. (1979). Parental representation and depression in normal young adults. *Journal of Abnormal Psychology, 88,* 388–397.

Botvin, G. J. (1990). Preventing adolescent drug abuse through a multi-modal cognitive–behavioral approach: Results of a three year study. *Journal of Consulting and Clinical Psychology, 58,* 437–446.

Bowlby, J. A. (1988). *A secure base: Parent–child attachment and healthy human development.* New York: Basic Books.

Brady, E., & Kendall, P. C. (1992). Comorbidity of anxiety and depression in children and adolescents. *Psychological Bulletin, 3,* 244–255.

Browne, A., & Finkelhor, D. (1986). Impact of child sexual abuse: Review of the literature. *Psychological Bulletin, 99,* 66–77.

Caron, C., & Rutter, M. (1991). Comorbidity in child psychopathology: Concepts, issues and research strategies. *Journal of Child Psychology and Psychiatry, 32,* 1063–1080.

Cicchetti, D., & Cohen, D. J. (Eds.). (1995). *Developmental psychopathology; Vol. 1: Theory and methods.* New York: Wiley.

Cicchetti, D., & Serafica, F. C. (1981). Interplay among behavioral systems: Illustrations from the study of attachment, affiliation, and wariness in young children with Down Syndrome. *Developmental Psychology, 17,* 36–49.

Clarke, G. N., Hawkins, W., Murphy, M., Sheeber, L. B., Lewinsohn, P. M., & Seeley, J. R. (1995). Targeted prevention of unipolar depressive disorder in an at-risk sample of high-school adolescents: A randomized trial of a group cognitive intervention. *Journal of the American Academy of Child and Adolescent Psychiatry, 34,* 312–321.

Cohen, J. (1988). *Statistical power analysis for the behavioral sciences* (2nd ed.). Hillsdale, NJ: Lawrence Erlbaum Associates.

Collins, L. M., & Horn, J. L. (1991). *Best methods for the analysis of change: Recent advances, unanswered questions, future directions.* Washington, DC: American Psychological Association.

Costello, E. J. (1990). Child psychiatric epidemiology: Implications for clinical research and practice. In B. B. Lahey & A. E. Kazdin (Eds.), *Advances in clinical child psychology* (Vol. 13, (pp. 53–90). New York: Plenum.

Costello, E. J., & Angold, A. (1995). Developmental epidemiology. In D. Cicchetti & D. J. Cohen (Eds.), *Developmental psychopathology, Vol. 1. Theory and methods* (pp. 23–56). New York: Wiley.

Crockenberg, S., & Covey, S. L. (1991). Marital conflict and externalizing behavior in children. In D. Cicchetti & S. L. Toth (Eds.), *Rochester Symposium on Developmental Psychopathology: Vol. 3. Models and Integrations* (pp. 235–260). Rochester, NY: University of Rochester Press.

Danforth, J. S., Barkley, R. A., & Stokes, T. F. (1991). Observations of parent–child interactions with hyperactive children: Research and clinical implications. *Clinical Psychology Review, 11,* 703–727.

Denzin, N. K., & Lincoln, Y. S. (Eds.). (1994). *Handbook of qualitative research.* Thousand Oaks, CA: Sage.

Egeland, B. (1991). A longitudinal study of high-risk families: Issues and findings. In R. H. Starr, Jr. & D. A. Wolfe (Eds.), *The effects of child abuse and neglect: Issues and research* (pp. 33–56). New York: Guilford.

Farrington, D. P. (1991). Longitudinal research strategies: Advantages, problems, and prospects. *Journal of the American Academy of Child and Adolescent Psychiatry, 30,* 369–374.

Fincham, F. D., Grych, J. H., & Osborne, L. N. (1994). Does marital conflict cause child maladjustment? Directions and challenges for longitudinal research. *Journal of Family Psychology, 8,* 128–140.

Fisher, C. B. (1991). Ethical considerations for research on psychosocial intervention for high-risk infants and children. *Register Reporter, 17,* 9–12.

Foster, S. L., & Cone, J. D. (1986). Design and use of direct observation procedures. In A. R. Ciminero, K. S. Calhoun, & H. E. Adams (Eds.), *Handbook of behavioral assessment* (2nd ed., pp. 253–324). New York: Wiley.

Frick, P. J., Lahey, B. B., Loeber, R., Stouthamer-Loeber, M., Christ, M. A., & Hanson, K. (1992). Familial risk factors to oppositional defiant disorder and conduct disorder: Parental psychopathology and maternal parenting. *Journal of Consulting and Clinical Psychology, 60,* 49–55.

Gill, M., Daly, G., Heron, S., Hawi, Z., & Fitzgerald, M. (1997). Confirmation of a dissociation between attention deficit hyperactivity disorder and a dopamine transporter polymorphism. *Biological Psychiatry, 2,* 311–313.

Graham, J. W., Collins, L. M., Wugalter, S. E., Chung, N. K., & Hansen, W. B. (1991). Modeling transitions in latent stage-sequential processes: A substance use prevention example. *Journal of Consulting and Clinical Psychology, 59,* 48–57.

Greenberg, M. T., Speltz, M. L., Deklyen, M., & Endriga, M. C. (1991). Attachment security in preschoolers with and without externalizing behavior problems: A replication. *Development and Psychopathology, 3,* 413–430.

Greenspan, S. I., Harmon, R. J., Emde, R. N., Sameroff, A. J., & Wieder, S. (1991, December). *Emerging trends in the diagnosis of emotional problems in infants and toddlers.* Symposium conducted at the National Center for Clinical Infant Programs, Washington, DC.

Grisso, T., Baldwin, E., Blanck, P. D., Rotheram-Borus, M. J., Schooler, N. R., & Thompson, T. (1991). Standards in research: APA's mechanism for monitoring the challenges. *American Psychologist, 46,* 758–766.

Grossman, H. J. (Ed.). (1983). *Classification in mental retardation* (Rev. ed.). Washington, DC: American Association on Mental Deficiency.

Humphries, T., Kinsbourne, M., & Swanson, J. (1978). Stimulant effects on cooperation and social interaction between hyperactive children and their mothers. *Journal of Child Psychology and Psychiatry, 19,* 12–22.

Jacob, T., Krahn, G. L., & Leonard, K. (1991). Parent–child interactions in families with alcoholic fathers. *Journal of Consulting and Clinical Psychology, 59,* 176–181.

Jacobson, N. S., & Truax, P. (1991). Clinical significance: A statistical approach to defining meaningful change in psychotherapy research. *Journal of Consulting and Clinical Psychology, 59,* 12–19.

Kamphaus, R. W., & Frick, P. J. (1996). *Clinical assessment of child and adolescent personality and behavior.* Needham Heights, MA: Allyn & Bacon.

Kazdin, A. E. (1988). *Child psychotherapy: Developing and identifying effective treatments.* New York: Pergamon.

Kazdin, A. E. (1989). Developmental psychopathology: Current research, issues, and directions. *American Psychologist, 44,* 180–187.

Kazdin, A. E. (1998). *Research design in clinical psychology* (3rd ed.). Elmsford, NY: Allyn & Bacon.

Kazdin, A. E., & Kagan, J. (1994). Models of dysfunction in developmental psychopathology. *Clinical Psychology: Science and Practice, 1,* 35–52.

Kazdin, A. E., Siegel, T. C., & Bass, D. (1992). Cognitive problem-solving skills training and parent management training in the treatment of antisocial behavior in children. *Journal of Consulting and Clinical Psychology, 60,* 733–747.

Kazdin, A. E., & Weisz, J. R. (1998). Identifying and developing empirically supported child and adolescent treatments. *Journal of Consulting and Clinical Psychology, 66,* 19–36.

Kendall, P. C., Flannery-Schroeder, E., Panichelli-Mindel, S. M., Southam-Gerow, M., Henin, A., & Warman, M. (1997). Therapy for youths with anxiety disorders: A second randomized clinical trial. *Journal of Consulting and Clinical Psychology, 65,* 366–380.

Lahey, B. B., Loeber, R., Hart, E. L., Frick, P. J., Applegate, B., Zhang, Q., Green, S. M., & Russo, M. F. (1995). Four-year longitudinal study of conduct disorder in boys: Patterns and predictors of persistence. *Journal of Abnormal Psychology, 104,* 83–93.

Lavigne, J. V., & Faier-Routman, J. (1992). Psychological adjustment to pediatric physical disorders: A meta-analytic review. *Journal of Pediatric Psychology, 17,* 133–157.

Lochman, J. E. (1992). Cognitive–behavioral intervention with aggressive boys: Three-year follow-up and preventive effects. *Journal of Consulting and Clinical Psychology, 60,* 426–432.

Loeber, R. (1991). Questions and advances in the study of developmental pathways. In D. Cicchetti & S. L. Toth (Eds.), *Rochester Symposium on Developmental Psychopathology: Vol. 3. Models and Integrations* (pp. 97–116). Rochester, New York: University of Rochester Press.

MacMillan, D. L., Gresham, F. M., & Siperstein, G. N. (1993). Conceptual and psychometric concerns about the 1992 AAMR definition of mental retardation. *American Journal on Mental Retardation, 98,* 325–335.

Mash, E. J. (1991). Measurement of parent–child interaction in studies of child maltreatment. In R. Starr, Jr., & D. Wolfe (Eds.), *The effects of child abuse and neglect: Research issues* (pp. 203–256). New York: Guilford.

Mash, E. J., & Barkley, R. A. (Eds.). (1996). *Child psychopathology.* New York: Guilford.

Mash, E. J., & Dozois, D.J.A. (1996). Child psychopathology: A developmental-systems perspective. In E. J. Mash & R. A. Barkley (Eds.), *Child psychopathology* (pp. 3–60). New York: Guilford.

Mash, E. J., & Johnston, C. (1990). Determinants of parenting stress: Illustrations from families of hyperactive children and families of physically abused children. *Journal of Clinical Child Psychology, 19,* 313–328.

Mash, E. J., & Terdal, L. G. (1997a). Assessment of child and family disturbance: A behavioral-systems approach. In E. J. Mash & L. G. Terdal (Eds.), *Assessment of childhood disorders* (3rd ed., pp. 3–68). New York: Guilford.

Mash, E. J., & Terdal, L. G. (Eds.). (1997b). *Assessment of childhood disorders* (3rd ed.). New York: Guilford.

Mash, E. J., & Wolfe, D. A. (1991). Methodological issues in research on physical child abuse. *Criminal Justice and Behavior, 18,* 8–29.

McCubbin, H. I., & Patterson, J. (1983). The family stress process: The double ABCX model of adjustment and adaptation. *Marriage and Family Review, 8,* 7–37.

Mendelson, M. J. (1992, Fall). Let's teach case methods to developmental students. *SRCD Newsletter, 9,* 13.

Messick, S. (1983). Assessment of children. In W. Kessen (Ed.), *Handbook of child psychology: Vol 1. History, theory, and methods* (4th ed., pp. 477–526). New York: Wiley.

Miles, M. B., & Huberman, A. M. (1984). *Qualitative data analysis: A sourcebook of new methods.* Beverly Hills, CA: Sage.

Moffitt, T. E. (1993). Life-course persistent and adolescence-limited antisocial behavior. *Psychological Review, 100,* 674–701.

Morris, R. J., Bergan, J. R., & Fulginiti, J. V. (1991). Structural equation modeling in clinical assessment research with children. *Journal of Consulting and Clinical Psychology, 59,* 371–379.

Murphy, L. B. (1992). Sympathetic behavior in very young children. *Zero to Three, 12*(4), 1–5.

Newman, F. L., & Howard, K. I. (1991). Introduction to the special section on seeking new clinical research methods. *Journal of Consulting and Clinical Psychology, 59,* 8–11.

Overton, W. F., & Horowitz, H. A. (1991). Developmental psychopathology: Integrations and differentiations. In D. Cicchetti & S. L. Toth (Eds.), *Rochester Symposium on Developmental Psychopathology: Vol. 3. Models and integrations* (pp. 1–42). Rochester, NY: University of Rochester Press.

Patterson, G. R. (1982). *Coercive family process.* Eugene, OR: Castalia.

Patterson, G. R., Reid, J., & Dishion, T. (1992). *Antisocial boys.* Eugene, OR: Castalia.

Patton, M. Q. (1990). *Qualitative evaluation and research methods* (2nd ed.). Beverly Hills, CA: Sage.

Pisterman, S. J., McGrath, P., Firestone, P., Goodman, J. T., Webster, L., & Mallory, R. (1989). Outcome of parent-mediated treatment of pre-schoolers with attention-deficit disorder. *Journal of Consulting and Clinical Psychology, 57,* 628–635.

Ramey, C. T., Bryant, D. M., Wasik, B. H., Sparling, J. J., Fendt, K. H., & LaVange, L. M. (1992). Infant Health and Development Program for low birth weight, premature infants: Program elements, family participation, and child intelligence. *Pediatrics, 89,* 454–465.

Rauh, V. A., Achenbach, T. M., Nurcombe, B., Howell, C. T., & Teti, D. M. (1988). Minimizing adverse effects of low birthweight: Four-year results of an early intervention program. *Child Development, 59,* 544–553.

Reid, J. B., Patterson, G. R., Baldwin, D. V., & Dishion, T. J. (1988). Observations in the assessment of childhood disorders. In M. Rutter, A. H. Tuma, & I. Lann (Eds.), *Assessment and diagnosis in child psychopathology* (pp. 156–195). New York: Guilford.

Reid, W. J., & Crisafulli, A. (1990). Marital discord and child behavior problems: A meta-analysis. *Journal of Abnormal Child Psychology, 18,* 105–117.

Roosa, M., Gensheimer, L. K., Short, J. L., Ayers, T., & Shell, R. (1989). A preventative intervention for children in alcoholic families: Results of a pilot study. *Family Relations, 38,* 295–300.

Scarr, S., & Weinberg, R. A. (1983). The Minnesota Adoption Studies: Genetic differences and malleability. *Child Development, 54,* 260–267.

Schmidt, F. L. (1992). What do data really mean? Research findings, meta-analysis, and cumulative knowledge in psychology. *American Psychologist, 47,* 1173–1181.

Shonkoff, J., & Hauser-Cram, P. (1987). Early intervention for disabled infants and their families: A quantitative analysis. *Pediatrics, 80,* 650–658.

SRCD ethical standards for research with children. (1990, Winter). *SRCD Newsletter,* 5–7.

Steinberg, L. (1988). Reciprocal relation between parent–child distance and pubertal maturation. *Developmental Psychology, 24,* 122–128.

Stevenson, J., Batten, N., & Cherner, M. (1992). Fears and fearfulness in children and adolescents: A genetic analysis of twin data. *Journal of Child Psychology and Psychiatry, 33,* 977–985.

Stoneman, Z. (1989). Comparison groups in research on families with mentally retarded members: A methodological and conceptual review. *American Journal on Mental Retardation, 94,* 195–215.

Verhulst, F. C., & Koot, H. M. (1991). Longitudinal research in child and adolescent psychiatry. *Journal of the American Academy of Child and Adolescent Psychiatry, 30,* 361–368.

Verhulst, F. C., & Van der Ende, J. (1992). Agreements between parents' reports and adolescents' self-reports of problem behavior. *Journal of Child Psychology and Psychiatry, 33,* 1011–1023.

Wasserman, G. A., Shilansky, M., & Hahn, H. (1986). A matter of degree: Maternal interaction with infants of varying levels of retardation. *Child Study Journal, 16,* 241–253.

Weissman, M. M., Wickramaratne, P., Warner, V., John, K., Prusoff, B. A., Merikangas, K. R., & Gammon, G. D. (1987). Assessing psychiatric disorders in children. *Archives of General Psychiatry, 44,* 747–753.

Weisz, J. R. (1998). Empirically supported treatments for children and adolescents: Efficacy, problems, and prospects. In K. S. Dobson & K. D. Craig (Eds.) *Empirically supported therapies: Best practice in professional psychology* (pp. 66–92). Newbury Park, CA: Sage.

Weisz, J. R., Donenberg, G. R., Han, S. S., & Weiss, B. (1995). Bridging the gap between laboratory and clinic in child and adolescent psychotherapy. *Journal of Consulting and Clinical Psychology, 63,* 688–701.

Weisz, J. R., & Weiss, B. (1993). *Effects of psychotherapy with children and adolescents.* Newbury Park, CA: Sage.

Werner, E. E. (1995). Resilience in development. *Current Directions in Psychological Science, 4,* 81–85.

Wolfe, D. A., & Mosk, M. D. (1983). Behavioral comparisons of children from abusive and distressed families. *Journal of Consulting and Clinical Psychology, 51,* 702–708.

World Health Organization. (1992). *The ICD-10 classification of mental and behavioral disorders: Clinical descriptions and diagnostic guidelines.* Geneva, Switzerland: Author.

Yoder, P. J., & Feagans, L. (1988). Mothers' attributions of communication to prelinguistic behavior of developmentally delayed and mentally retarded infants. *American Journal on Mental Retardation, 93,* 36–43.

Zero to Three/National Center for Clinical Infant Programs. (1994). *Diagnostic classification of mental health and developmental disorders of infancy and early childhood (Diagnostic Classification: 0–3).* Washington, DC: Author.

Psychological Aspects
of Pediatric Disorders

Kenneth J. Tarnowski
Florida Gulf Coast University

Ronald T. Brown
Medical University of South Carolina

Few events are as distressing to parents as a child or adolescent who is seriously ill or injured. Virtually all children and their parents have experience with common childhood afflictions, such as acute viral infections, stomachaches, headaches, and minor injuries. Unfortunately, many children experience more threatening forms of acute or chronic illness and injury (e.g., cancer, burns). There is significant mortality associated with several of these conditions. In addition, many disorders are associated with marked medical (i.e., residual physical disability) and psychological (i.e., disruption of normal developmental processes) morbidity. Children and families experience negative psychological sequelae (e.g., depression) in response to a variety of specific pediatric conditions. Importantly, behavioral factors also have been demonstrated to be integral in determining onset, course, and prognosis of many disorders and injuries.

Even children suffering with benign and common conditions such as a cold may evidence behavioral changes (e.g., reduced cognitive efficiency, dysphoric mood); make specific causal attributions (e.g., I was out in the rain and now I am sick); and experience a variety of associated environmental responses (e.g., increased parental attention). It is apparent that psychological variables are relevant to discussion of any pediatric illness. For our purposes, we exemplify the role and diversity of psychological factors in childhood illness by considering two conditions: pediatric burn injuries and sickle cell disease (SCD).

Burn injuries were selected because they represent not a disease, but rather an acute injury that can pose serious long-term physical and psychological sequelae. Alternatively, sickle cell disease (SCD) is a chronic illness. Patients with SCD are frequently without symptoms yet may present with periodic sickling crises that are often of sudden onset and can be fatal. Although there are similarities in the psychosocial challenges both conditions pose for the child and family, there are also important differences that are highlighted in the case descriptions.

By way of background, we now turn to a brief overview of some general considerations in behavioral pediatrics. First, it is important to note that by age 18, approximately 10% to 15% of children and adolescents experience one or more chronic medical conditions. Chronic illnesses are those involving a protracted course that may be fatal or result in compromised mental or physical functioning and that often are characterized by acute exacerbations that may result in hospitalization or other forms of intensive treatment. A second point worthy of note is that the importance of psychological variables in understanding health and illness has become well established since the 1980s (Roberts, 1995; Routh, 1988; Russo & Varni, 1982). As infectious diseases have been eradicated and other serious pediatric disorders (e.g., acute lymphocytic leukemia) have yielded to improved medical treatment, more attention has been devoted to the role of psychosocial factors in health and illness. Currently, there is unequivocal support for the role of behavioral factors as major contributors to disease (and injury) onset and maintenance (e.g., smoking, lack of exercise, diet, treatment nonadherence, substance abuse; Brannon & Feist, 1997).

Given the number of children affected and the primacy of behavioral factors in understanding injury and illness, a major focus of recent work has been on increasing knowledge of health-related developmental variables (Roberts, 1995). Such variables are of central importance in behavioral pediatrics. A child's level of cognitive development influences his or her conceptualization of illness and injury, cooperation with specific care procedures, reaction to and understanding of life-threatening illness, and capacity to comprehend health-related communications. For example, it is apparent that a preschool child's understanding of cancer, death, and chemotherapy differs dramatically from those of an adolescent.

Developmental models of cognitive development, such as those developed by Piaget and Erickson, have been invoked frequently to conceptualize children's understanding of illness and health. Expanding on the work of Piaget, Bibace and Walsh (1980) categorized children's understanding of illness into various stages. The prelogical thinking of children aged 2 to 7 years was characterized by phenomenism and contagion. *Phenomenism* invokes an external concrete cause of illness that is spatially or temporally remote (e.g., How do people get colds? From the trees). *Contagion* locates the cause of illness in objects or individuals that are proximate to the child (e.g., How do people get colds? When someone gets near them). Concrete logical explanations of illness (ages 7 to 11 years) involve contamination and internalization types of explanation. *Contamination* involves coming into contact with a contaminant that can be a person, object, or "bad" behavior. *Internalization* is a more sophisticated explanation that locates illness inside the body even though the cause may be external. Formal logical explanations (after approximately 11 to 12 years of age) involve cause–effect relationships that are physiological (internal malfunction–nonfunctioning with separation of proximal and distal external causative factors). Psychophysiological explanations incorporate psychological causation in addition to physical factors (e.g., heart problem due, in part, to excessive life stress).

Children of a given age may differ considerably in their cognitive understanding of illness as a function of a variety of factors including experiential variables. Nonetheless, such models have proven invaluable in guiding communication, psychosocial policy (e.g., parental visitation guidelines), and the design of intervention methods. Although consideration of cognitive developmental variables is critical, attention must be given to other factors, as well (Ferrari, 1990). In many instances, reactions of children to specific illness or injury-related stressors (e.g., medical treatment) are contrasted with those of other children the same age. Although chronological age is a useful marker in outlining possible assessment and treatment endeavors, it should not be used in place of a careful consideration of salient developmental variables (e.g., cognitive developmental status). Mental age and maturation are variables that may be of particular relevance for the subset of patients who present with developmental disabilities (e.g., mental retardation).

The status of children's socioemotional development warrants special attention. Children who are seriously ill or injured often have to cope with extended hospitalization; separation from parents, siblings, and peers; and frequent painful medical procedures. Children's abilities to cope with the diverse challenges posed by chronic illness or injury may be severely taxed by such stressors. Under these circumstances, children's functioning may be characterized by negative affective responding (e.g., anxiety, overt distress, reduced ability to cope with pain, regressive behaviors, detachment, depression). Family functioning and support can provide a buffer from the deleterious short- and long-term effects of such stressors (Kazak, Segal-Andrews, & Johnson, 1995). However, child illness also can serve to erode family utilitarian (e.g., finances) and psychological (e.g., coping ability) resources (Wallander & Varni, 1992). A dysfunctional family environment serves as an additional risk factor that can function to potentiate socioemotional maladjustment. In general, the socioemotional status of seriously ill and injured children must be assessed and monitored carefully. Of course, the key issues in this domain of functioning are developmentally influenced. For example, for younger children, parental separation can be emotionally devastating. Disrupted peer relationships figure largely for older children, as is the case with adolescents who also may be attempting to cope with personal identity issues.

As noted previously, the environmental context of illness or injury is critical. Availability of basic resources (e.g., finances to secure appropriate treatment, medication, transportation) as well as psychological resources (e.g., parental support and caring) are important determinants of how well children function when challenged with compromised health. The behavioral contingencies that are in effect for an ill or injured child in the hospital, clinic, home, and school environments need careful assessment (Gross & Drabman, 1990; Kazak et al., 1995). For example, pediatric patients evidence behavioral reactions (e.g., crying, flailing, attempts to escape, seeking parental comfort, withdrawal, etc.) in response to certain aversive treatments that may be required as part of their health care (e.g., venipuncture) or in response to a particular disorder-related health symptom (e.g., arthritic pain). Although such responses are a function of biological differences (e.g., pain threshold) as well as developmental factors (e.g., a preschooler's understanding of the need for painful procedure), it is known that responses of others (parents, staff, peers) to specific child illness-related behavior (e.g., complaints of pain) critically influence and shape the topography (form of the behavior), intensity, and duration of child responding (Blount, Davis, Powers, & Roberts, (1991). Although it is imperative that parents and staff create a consistently supportive and caring environment for ill children, it is also important that behavioral contingencies that are operative in such environments promote developmentally appropriate coping, self-regulation, and self-care skills.

In summary, when considering the psychological aspects of pediatric disorders, it makes considerable sense to start with an assessment of basic developmental parameters. One then should ask how the nature of illness or injury, its cause, treatment, and associated side effects may serve to disrupt child developmental and family processes that are integral to optimal adjustment. The environments (e.g., family, hospital, clinic, school) in which ill children function should be carefully assessed. Utilitarian and psychological resources (e.g., supportive family, coping skills) should be identified. Health-related behavioral contingencies need to be carefully assessed to maximize adjustment and well-being.

We now exemplify the multiple challenges to children's coping and adjustment via discussion of an acute traumatic injury and childhood chronic disease.

PEDIATRIC BURN INJURIES

Clinical Description

The following description is based on studies reviewed by Tarnowski (1994), and the reader is referred to this source for detailed information concerning the etiology, epidemiology, assessment, medical aspects, psychological treatment, and prevention of pediatric burn injuries.

Children are a high-risk population for burn injuries. In the United States, approximately 1 million children sustain burn injuries that require medical attention each year. Approximately 50,000 of these injuries result in hospitalization for more intensive treatment. Each year, about 1,000 children die of these injuries. Children younger than 15 years of age account for about two thirds of all burn fatalities, with boys outnumbering girls by a ratio of greater than 2 to 1. Advances in the medical management of burns have resulted in an increased survival rate for burn victims.

Burns are typically described in terms of burn type (degree) and percentage of body surface area (BSA) affected. A first-degree burn involves injury that is restricted to the epidermis. Injuries to the dermis are labeled second-degree or partial thickness burns. Extensive injury involving multiple skin layers with possible damage of subcutaneous tissue and peripheral nerve fibers is known as full thickness or third-degree burns. Percentage of BSA is calculated using standard charts that display dorsal surface area. In children, partial thickness burns affecting up to 10% BSA or full thickness burns affecting less than 2% BSA (not including injuries to the face, eyes, ears, or genitals) are classified as minor. Full thickness burns of less than 10% BSA or partial thickness of 10% to 20% are considered moderate injuries. Full thickness burns greater than 10% BSA or partial thickness greater than 20% BSA or inhalation injuries or those affecting the face, eyes, ears, perineum, hands or feet are considered major, as are most burns that are electric or chemical in nature and those complicated by fracture or other major trauma.

Causes of the Problem

The causes of pediatric burn injuries are diverse. Burns typically are categorized as thermal, radiation, chemical, or electrical. Studies on such injuries reveal that the majority of burn victims are younger children (infants and toddlers; Tarnowski, 1994). Scalds account for the majority (approximately 50%) of burns and for about 80% of such injuries to younger victims. Most of these injuries involve accidents such as a child pulling a hot liquid off a table or stovetop. Flame burns account for more injuries as a function of increasing age. Such injuries account for approximately 20% of hospitalizations and 80% of burn injury mortality.

Although older children are less at risk for burn injuries, boys are at increased risk at any age. The ratio of male to female injuries is approximately 2 to 1. Concerning location of injury, the home is the most dangerous environment. Approximately 80% of children sustain their injuries in the home, with kitchens, bathrooms, and living rooms being the most probable sites of injury. It is also known that a subset of such injuries is the result of child abuse. In pediatric burn units, estimates of the incidence of children hospitalized for nonaccidental injuries range from 4% to 39%.

Course of the Disorder

In general, the course of burn patients consists of three overlapping phases: (a) emergency period, (b) acute phase, and (c) rehabilitation. Efforts during the emergency period are directed toward patient stabilization, including maintenance of fluid and electrolyte balance and ensuring cardiovascular and respiratory integrity. In the acute phase, infection (e.g., sepsis) and malnutrition are major concerns. Antibacterial therapy is instituted and total parenteral feedings may be needed. Pain is often severe at this time as damaged peripheral nerve endings regenerate and procedures are implemented to accomplish wound closure and healing. Typical procedures include skin grafting and debridement. Physiological ("live") dressings, composed of materials from cadavers, animals, or artificial skin, can be used to effect wound coverage. Because such dressings are not permanent and are biologically rejected, autografting procedures are often implemented. This procedure involves harvesting healthy skin from the patient for the purpose of transplanting it to the site of the burn injury. Debridement procedures are initiated at this time as well. This procedure is a major source of patient distress and typically involves daily "tankings" in which the patient is placed in a hydrotherapy tub and devitalized tissue is vigorously removed. Dressing changes, intravenous line placements, application of topical agents, and demands for increased fluid and food intake are routine. Physical therapy is often prescribed to promote function and preclude development of contractures. During the rehabilitation phase, patients are required to engage in specific self-care practices (e.g., physical therapy, wearing of customized elastic pressure garments). Multiple surgeries over an extended period may be required (e.g., reconstructive cosmetic surgery, release of contractures).

From a psychological perspective, children hospitalized for such injuries face multiple challenges including separation from family, restricted visitation, extended hospitalization, repeated exposure to painful medical procedures, observation of other seriously ill patients, reduced sensory stimulation in the pediatric burn care unit, compliance with painful physical therapy procedures, and coping with disfigurement (Tarnowski, Rasnake, Linscheid, & Mulick, 1989). A subset of children with severe biological derangement may evidence serious but transitory behavioral reactions such as hallucinations. More common acute behavioral reactions include anxiety and depression. Prolonged crying, clingingness, verbal and physical aggression toward medical treatment staff, sleep disturbances (e.g., nightmares, disrupted sleep–wake cycle), regressive behavior, compromised food intake, disrupted play, denial of the physical consequences of the burn, and suicidal ideation are commonly evidenced during the inpatient portion of treatment. In addition to hospitalization and the attendant medical treatment, a subset of pediatric burn victims also must cope with the loss of their home and belongings. Unfortunately, many children also face the tragic loss of parents and siblings.

On hospital discharge, some children experience a tumultuous transition back home, and the return to the school environment can be problem-ridden. Problems with self-esteem, dysfunctional peer relationships, disrupted body image development, modified school–career trajectories, coping with negative societal reactions to disfigurement, and increased family tensions are often seen in the posthospitalization period.

Children's responses to burn injuries depend, to a large extent, on their developmental status. Younger children may have extreme difficulty coping with separation from parents. Assuredly, they have a limited or incorrect conceptualization of what and why particular events are happening. Young children may view painful treatment procedures as a consequence or type of punishment for some misdeed that they believe they may have committed. Older children and adolescents may be devastated by the physical disfigurement and loss of function they currently experience. Coping strategies implemented by pediatric patients and the types of psychological treatments instituted by staff and family vary widely as a function of such developmental variables.

Deleterious long-term psychological sequelae have been reported for pediatric burn survivors. It is quite understandable that many would predict poor adjustment for most pediatric burn survivors given the devastating physical and psychological trauma imposed by such injuries. However, recent reviews of the empirical literature on this topic provided little support for the contention that the majority of burn victims exhibit severe poor postburn adjustment (Tarnowski & Brown, 1995; Tarnowski & Rasnake, 1994; Tarnowski, Rasnake, Gavaghan-Jones, & Smith, 1991). Adjustment outcome appears to be a complex function of several variables including patient injury parameters, course of hospitalization, premorbid adjustment, developmental status, family variables, and personal and social demographics (e.g., age, socioeconomic status). It also appears that such risk and resource variables combine in novel ways to produce differential clinical outcomes.

Familial Contributions

Family variables are critical in understanding pediatric burns. Family factors are relevant to understanding the context in which children are injured as well as an integral component of the treatment and recovery process.

As previously indicated, most children sustain burn injuries in the home setting. In considering circumstances under which children are injured, the interaction between specific setting factors and family variables becomes apparent. For example, the probability of a child sustaining a burn injury increases as one descends in socioeconomic status (SES). Several factors may be operative here. Economically disadvantaged families may not be able to afford quality housing. Substandard housing may pose specific risks of injury (e.g., faulty electrical systems). Lack of adequate basic resources also may lead parents to choose unsafe methods to meet their daily living needs (e.g., heating homes with makeshift stoves).

Another factor to consider is that rates of certain psychological disorders are highest in lower SES populations and the symptoms of such disorders may contribute to increased risk of childhood burn injury. For example, parental depression may result in a diminished ability to engage in the level of child monitoring required to prevent injuries. There is also reported evidence that the families of pediatric burn victims experience more geographic moves (Knudson-Cooper & Leuchtag, 1982). A subset of these families may be unstable. Alternatively, the attendant stressors of moving, coupled with the natural proclivity of young children to explore their new environments, may combine to increase risk.

The general stressors of daily living may function in the same manner (e.g., multiple stressors can erode psychological resources) such that a child can sustain injury during a momentary lapse of parental supervision. Multiple family stressors may also potentiate the likelihood of child abuse.

Finally, the issue of premorbid (preinjury) psychopathology is of relevance. Essentially, the issue here is that children may present with specific disturbances in behavior (e.g., excessive risk taking, conduct problems) that increase the likelihood of injury. Certain family factors (e.g., instability, abuse, lack of cohesion, lack of child supervision) contribute to emergence of specific childhood problems that may increase the risk of injury. It is also the case that poorer psychosocial outcome is associated with children who present with severe premorbid psychopathology and who reside in dysfunctional family environments. Given the severity of the psychological challenges posed by pediatric burn injuries, there is need to definitively engage families in the treatment and rehabilitation process. The absence of such family engagement can have devastating consequences for the child.

Psychophysiological and Genetic Influences

Genetic factors do not contribute directly to burn injuries. However, several lines of data (epidemiological, clinical) provide suggestive evidence that children with specific disorders (e.g., attention deficit hyperactivity disorder, or ADHD) may be disproportionately represented among young burn victims. Studies indicate that there is, in fact, a genetic component to this disorder (see chap. 6, this volume). Behavioral characteristics such as impulsive responding, high risk taking, and impaired attentional functioning may increase the risk for a variety of injuries including burns. Thus, for a subset of burn-injured children, a case can be made for the indirect influence of genetic factors.

Concerning psychophysiological factors, these may be relevant in understanding circumstances under which the burn injury occurred as well as in conceptualizing pediatric postinjury behavioral distress. As noted previously, high levels of psychophysiological arousal (e.g., stress) can lead to a variety of affective states that may increase probability of accidental injury.

Psychophysiological variables are also relevant in conceptualizing, assessing, and treating behavioral distress. Pediatric pain is a phenomenon that is a composite of several influences (e.g., sensory, affective, biological, motivational, behavioral). Physiological and biochemical manifestations of pain include increased respiration, muscular tension, diastolic and systolic blood pressure, pulse rate, skin resistance, and endogenous opiates. Monitoring of objective and subjective aspects of psychophysiological arousal is an integral component of the assessment and behavioral–pharmacological management of children's pain.

Current Treatments

The empirical literature on the psychological assessment and treatment of the pediatric burn victim is relatively limited (see comprehensive review by Tarnowski, 1994). However, recent advances have been reported in the treatment of procedure-related patient distress (e.g., debridement, physical therapy), consummatory behavior (e.g., nutritional intake), sleep-related problems, and self-excoriation (Tarnowski, Rasnake, & Drabman, 1987). Given the numerous challenges facing pediatric burn victims, it is apparent that the clinical child health psychologist has numerous opportunities from the time of initial hospitalization through extended postdischarge follow-up to influence the care of these patients and their families.

Experience indicates that one of the most frequently encountered consultation requests involves patient management of distress during debridement and dressing changes. Although analgesic medications are routinely used to mitigate procedure-related patient distress, other nonpharmacologic interventions are most often needed. Wound care can require 2 hours to complete and may be conducted twice daily. The following case presentation provides an overview of the approach to assessment and treatment adopted with a severely burned adolescent (Hurt & Tarnowski, 1990).

Keith was a 17-year-old male admitted to the burn unit following an auto accident in which he suffered second- and third-degree burns over 25% of his body. Psychology was consulted to assess and intervene with Keith's coping with daily burn care treatments. Initial assessment consisted of medical chart review, interviews with shift nurses, and direct behavioral observations of Keith during debridement and dressing changes. A comprehensive review of Keith's developmental, medical, and behavioral history was conducted with his mother and supplemented with an interview with Keith.

Integration of the interview and behavioral assessment data revealed the following: (a) A bright 17-year-old who had not evidenced significant premorbid psychosocial difficulties; (b) marked procedure-related distress characterized by verbal assaults and physical opposition and attempts to escape the treatment room; (c) distress inadequately controlled by analgesics; (d) Staff–patient interaction problems related to the fact that most patients on the unit were toddlers and children. Staff were unsure how to respond to Keith's specific questions concerning prognosis and treatment; (e) Keith's physical size made it difficult to manage his oppositional behavior. Physical restraint was not judged to be an option and cooperation was mandated for adequate wound treatment; (f) the inordinate amount of time needed for debridement and antibiotic application left little time for emotional recovery and restricted opportunities to engage in pleasant activities (e.g., television, listening to tapes, visitation, etc.); (g) The amount of time spent in daily wound care reinforced the notion that staff were there only to inflict pain. Medical staff essentially functioned as discriminative stimuli for pain; (h) Keith's affect was deteriorating as he believed he had lost control over any aspect of his current environment. Staff were informed of our assessment results and made aware of the range of interventions that might prove useful. Keith, his mother, and the medical and nursing staff agreed to our proposal to increase the predictability of his environment and to increase his coping skills via instruction in pain- and stress-management techniques.

An inservice training session was scheduled with staff to discuss issues involved in dealing with adolescent burn patients and the modifications of staff–patient interactions needed to promote adjustment. Nurses were advised to facilitate, as much as possible, Keith's participation in his treatment by removing bandages and engaging in self-debridement. This strategy has been shown to be effective in reducing the distress of pediatric burn victims (Tarnowski, McGrath, Calhoun, & Drabman, 1987).

Keith was provided with a variety of pain management strategies tailored to his developmental level. Use of multiple self-control techniques has been found to be useful in controlling procedure-related distress. Patients may use one method for a brief period to obtain relief. Relief may diminish quite rapidly, and patients are prompted to switch to an alternative pain management procedure. The program was modeled after the multicomponent stress inoculation program developed by Wernick (1983). Keith was taught passive relaxation procedures, breathing exercises, guided imagery, and calming self-talk strategies. Attention distraction techniques were presented and included a focus on: (a) aspects of the physical environment (e.g., counting tiles), (b) somatization (e.g., focusing on sensation in nonpainful areas), and (c) imaginative transformation (e.g., transferring pain to a smaller body part like a fingertip). Finally, Keith was taught to use these pain-management skills in the context of the four phase stress-inoculation procedure: (a) preparing for pain ("This is going to hurt, but I know how to deal with the pain"); (b) confronting the pain ("Relax, breathe deeply, I have made it through other debridement sessions, I'll make it through this one"); (c) coping with thoughts and feelings at critical moments ("Stay focused, I can switch to another strategy to stay in control"); and (d) positive self-statements ("I made it. Each time I get better at using the strategies. I feel more control").

To enhance predictability, arrangements were made for debridement and physical therapy to be conducted by the same staff at the same time each day. Medical chart and patient self-report data indicated that this procedure had marked impact on distress. The power struggle between Keith and the staff was essentially eliminated, and frequency and severity of observed and self-reported pain was diminished. Brief biweekly sessions were held with Keith's mother to provide support, enhance coping, provide feedback about the efficacy of the interventions, and provide suggestions on how she could contribute to Keith's recovery (e.g., verbally reinforce his daily accomplishments). Supportive psychological services were provided to address issues related to disfigurement, peer reactions, and physical disabilities. Effectiveness of the intervention package was evaluated on the basis of anecdotal reports of staff, patient, and parent, medical chart progress notes, and via direct behavioral observations of Keith by the psychology staff. These sources of data were consistent and indicated the stress inoculation treatment of procedural distress was marked and immediate. Collateral improvements in general affect were observed. He was followed intermittently on an outpatient basis for a period of 6 months.

Comments

The case presentation outlines the successful management of an adolescent who was exhibiting behavior that was interfering with and compromising the quality of his medical care. The case highlights an approach to assessment and treatment that was developmentally based and targeted multiple aspects of patient functioning. Our experience has impressed on us the importance of verifying (via behavioral observations) staff reports of problematic behavior. Often, such observations reveal that the optimal target of intervention is not with the patients but rather may be found at the level of the physical environment and/or staff. Specifically, we often have observed children who respond quite appropriately to the circumstance (i.e., exhibit normal behavior (crying and flailing) in the face of an abnormal circumstance, such as an invasive medical procedure). Although it is always worthwhile to determine if self-control strategies might ameliorate such distress, the goal of such interventions is not suppression of child's responses but rather enhancement of the child's coping skills. This case also illustrates that although providing instruction in self-control skills may be helpful, one needs also to consider whether simple environmental manipulations (e.g., scheduling to increase predictability) might be helpful. The need to adapt and tailor procedure to the patient's developmental level, cognitive status, and other behavioral characteristics (psychological resources and presenting symptomatology) is stressed. Finally, absence of premorbid psychopathology in this case proved to be a positive factor that was judged to be related to both positive inpatient response to treatment as well as minimization of postinjury psychological sequelae.

SICKLE CELL DISEASE

Clinical Description and Etiology of the Disorder

SCD is a group of genetic blood disorders (hematologic) that affect one of 400 African American babies born in this country (for a review, see Brown, Doepke, & Kaslow, 1993; Thompson & Gustafson, 1995). SCD results in normally round red blood cells assuming a rigid crescent or sickle shape. Because of their abnormal shape, these cells do not flow readily through the blood vessels but tangle and accumulate in the vessels, obstructing circulation and the delivery of adequate levels of oxygen to vital organs, tissues, and aerobic muscles. Those organs at greatest risk include the kidneys, spleen, bone marrow, eyes, and head of the femur (Brown, Doepke, & Kaslow, 1993). When adequate levels of oxygen are not delivered to these sites, pain, swelling, and fatigue often are experienced. The body attempts to avert this process in what is referred to as a vasoocclusive phenomenon or sickle cell crisis by rejecting and removing abnormally shaped cells. Because youth with SCD are unable to produce new red blood cells as quickly as the sickled cells are destroyed, anemia develops. Folic acid, a member of the vitamin B complex, is prescribed prophylactically to promote red blood cell production; for cases in which severe anemia occurs, transfusions may be indicated. As an iatrogenic effect of such transfusions, these youth frequently develop excess levels of iron, which are stored in the liver. Chelation therapy, a chemotherapy procedure for removing excess iron, is then required.

The numerous physiologic complications that may accompany SCD include painful events that are the result of ischemic injury to the tissues, delayed growth, delayed onset of puberty, splenic and gall bladder enlargement, osteomyelitis, pneumonococcal infections, meningitis, cerebral vascular accidents (strokes), skin ulcers, necrosis of the femoral head, and priapism (a persistent painful penile erection). As a result, youth with SCD typically have increased contact with medical personnel and decreased involvement in school and physical activities.

Course of the Disorder

Although advances in management of chronic complications associated with SCD have resulted in a more favorable prognosis, medical management is typically lifelong. These treatments are directed at minimizing dehydration, infection, and hypoxia and at managing pain with hydration and analgesia. Symptoms of SCD may appear as early as the first months of infancy, and may persist throughout the life span (Platt et al., 1994). Although symptoms are variable for each patient and often unpredictable, the most common manifestations of the disease are episodes of pain in the abdomen, back, extremities, or chest. In infants and toddlers, the earliest symptom may be painful swelling in the hands and feet (hand and foot syndrome, or "dactylitis") as well as splenic sequestration crisis (pooling of vast amounts of blood), where the hemoglobin level may drop suddenly, resulting in shock and sometimes death (Thompson & Gustafson, 1995). Pain is the most common reason children and adolescents seek medical attention for SCD. Frequency, intensity, and duration of pain crises vary considerably from person to person. For example, whereas some youth experience pain crises that require frequent medical intervention, including hospitalization, others may report no pain crises for several years. In a study of the natural history of SCD, Platt and associates (Platt et al., 1994; Platt, Thorington, & Brambilla, 1991) prospectively followed more than 3,500 patients, newborn to elderly. The degree of pain varied widely within these groups and also was found to be a function of both disease severity and psychosocial factors. Also, patients who were more than 20 years of age and had more frequent pain episodes tended to have earlier mortality rates than those with fewer pain episodes, suggesting that pain rate may be an important index of clinical severity. Each person's particular pain history naturally influences the choice of pain management techniques: pharmacotherapy (e.g., analgesics); behavioral medicine techniques, including relaxation and imagery; transfusions; and, more recently, bone marrow transplantation.

Psychological factors, including the ability to cope and perceived helplessness, have been demonstrated to be important predictors of pain management in both children and adults with SCD. Those who report less self-control over significant events, and who demonstrate thought patterns characterized by passive adherence and negative thinking have benefitted less from internal coping strategies (e.g., relaxation and imagery) when dealing with pain crises (Gil, Abrams, Phillips, & Keefe, 1989). Similar patterns have been seen in pediatric patients and their caregivers (Gil et al., 1993; Gil, Williams, Thompson, & Kinney, 1991). Although these coping strategies were unrelated to intensity or duration of pain, the children who employed active problem-solving coping strategies had fewer emergency room visits, whereas children who used passive–adherent coping had more emergency room visits and participated in fewer household chores and school activities. Psychological distress (i.e., internalizing problems of behavior), however, was associated with the frequency of pain episodes. Most importantly, children's pain coping strategies characterized by passive adherence and negative thoughts (i.e., catastrophizing and self-statements of fear and anger) were associated with a higher frequency of psychosocial adjustment difficulties and functional impairments. Stability of these pain coping strategies was found over a 9-month period for children, but less stability was found for adolescents (Gil et al., 1993).

Familial Contributions

Consistent with other pediatric chronic diseases, SCD produces numerous illness-related stressors that may place these children at risk for poor psychosocial adjustment (Brown, Doepke, & Kaslow, 1993). Nonetheless, any pediatric chronic illness involves the interaction between the child and the family system (for review, see Kazak et al., 1995). Studies that have been devoted to the impact of a child's SCD on other family members have suggested that levels of conflict and organization within these families are less adaptive than that reported by control families (Burlew, Evans, & Oler, 1989). The more educated the parents are about SCD and the more stable and available their social network, the better their coping and the higher their children's self-esteem (Burlew et al., 1989). Some evidence suggests less marital satisfaction in parents of children with SCD, a finding consistent with that in the general chronic illness literature (Burlew et al., 1989). Furthermore, an association has been found between family variables and the coping of adolescents who have increased family cohesion and organization, which seem to contribute to the resilience or coping competency of boys and of girls; family conflict negatively influenced the coping competency of girls only (Hurtig & Park, 1989).

Thompson, Gil, Burbach, Keith, and Kinney (1993), through their transactional model of stress and coping, specifically have focused on the psychological adaptation of mothers of children with SCD. Findings of this investigation indicate that compared with those mothers evidencing poor adjustment, mothers who endorsed fewer adjustment difficulties had significantly lower levels of daily stress, less use of palliative coping (the regulation of emotional states that are associated with, or result from, stress), and greater family support. In fact, when controlling for illness and demographic indexes, stress of daily hassles, coping, and family support accounted for nearly one half of the variance in maternal adaptation to their children's illness (Thompson et al., 1993). Thus, recent SCD research has paralleled pediatric psychology studies conducted from an ecological-systems theory perspective in delineating the adjustment to a chronic illness. Similar findings were obtained for children with congenital heart defects (Davis, Brown, Bakeman, & Campbell, 1998), with family support being associated with maternal adaptation to their child's illness after controlling for demographic and disease severity variables.

Consistent with other studies of the siblings of chronically ill children, siblings of SCD youth evidence symptoms of psychological distress and seem to have difficulties coping with negative life events (Treiber, Mabe, & Wilson, 1987). Healthy siblings may have more psychological adjustment difficulties and less adaptive responses to life events, and they may evidence greater psychological distress than their diseased siblings (Treiber et al., 1987). No other studies can be located that have examined the psychosocial adjustment of siblings of children with SCD. These results must be interpreted cautiously, however, as Drotar and Crawford (1985) have noted the variability of findings across studies of sibling adjustment.

Psychophysiological and Genetic Influences

SCD is a hemoglobin (Hb) disorder reflecting a basic deficit in the autosomal beta–globin gene. Healthy people have two A (normal) alleles of the beta–globin gene, one gene inherited from the parent. Children with SCD trait inherit one SS mutation allele (S) and one A allele from each parent. These children are therefore carriers of the disease, although sickle cell trait is not a disease. Typically, they are healthy and evidence few, if any, symptoms. Only when oxygen is less available (e.g., at high altitudes, during pregnancy) do their red blood cells take the form of sickled cells, which may result in pain crises or other complications.

There are three main forms of SCD: HbSS, HbSC, and HbS beta–thalassemia. HbSS, the homozygous and most severe condition, is caused by two abnormal S alleles of the beta–globin gene. Children with HbSS have inherited one S allele from each parent, each of whom have either the trait or the disease. In HbSC, a milder form of SCD in which the child has a compound heterozygous condition for hemoglobin S and hemoglobin C, an S allele has been inherited from only one parent. HbS beta–thalassemia, a more benign condition than either HbSS or HbSC, is inherited from one parent who has SCD trait (AS) while the other has no evidence of the disease or trait. HbS beta–thalassemia is distinguished from SCD trait only by the structure of the cells. Specifically, each HbS beta–thalassemia cell contains SS hemoglobin, fetal hemoglobin, and, possibly, adult hemoglobin; the cells in persons with sickle cell trait contain adult and sickle hemoglobin only. Fetal hemoglobin is produced during the prenatal period, remains in the blood stream in decreasing amounts throughout the life span, and has an ameliorating effect on pain, and ultimately may improve survival (Platt et al., 1991).

Particularly relevant to the prognosis for children with SCD are the frequently encountered physiologically based neurological impairments. As noted previously, SCD occludes blood vessels, possibly resulting in infarctions and pain. In the central nervous system (CNS), this may lead to major cerebral accidents (CVAs; strokes), microvascular infarcts, or, more rarely, cerebral hemorrhaging. CVAs are diagnosed in approximately 6% of children with SCD and occur more frequently in youth under the age of 15 than in older adolescents or adults. Incidence of microvascular infarctions is unknown because symptoms are not overt and rarely are identified on routine medical examinations. Notwithstanding, recent neuropsychologic research on brain structures that may be affected suggests that a significant percentage of youth with SCD may experience microvascular infarctions. It remains unclear whether these cognitive impairments may result from microvascular infarctions at critical developmental periods or from a series of progressive neurologic insults (Brown, Buchanan, Doepke, & Eckman, 1993; Brown, Doepke, & Kaslow, 1993).

In addition to the effects of CVAs and microvascular infarctions, chronic anemia (resulting in oxygen deprivation to the brain), nutritional deficiencies, and ischemia (tissue death) also may account for the neurocognitive deficits demonstrated in youth with SCD (for a review, see Brown, Doepke, & Kaslow, 1993). Furthermore, these cognitive impairments may be the result of a significantly altered metabolism, which has been observed in the frontal lobe area of the brain on positron emission tomography scans of adults with SCD. Taken together, these findings underscore the need for comprehensive neuropsychologic examinations to identify the more subtle CNS involvements. In an investigation of the neurocognitive functioning of youth with SCD, Brown, Buchanan, et al. (1993) compared the cognitive processing and the academic functioning of these youth and of their nondiseased siblings who were closest in age, socioeconomic status (SES), and gender. Children with SCD scored significantly lower than did nondiseased siblings on a reading decoding achievement test and a sustained attention task associated with frontal lobe functioning. More importantly, hemoglobin was found to be an important predictor of intellectual functioning, fine motor skills, and academic achievement, suggesting that chronic reduced oxygen delivery may be an etiologic factor in the neurological deficits. Should physiologic and cognitive variables be found to be related, children at risk for later neurologic deficits may be recognized before cognitive impairments are realized by cost-effective neuropsychologic assessments. Furthermore, appropriate medical (e.g., transfusions, bone marrow transplantation) and educational interventions (e.g., tutoring, special education) may be recommended for these children as a result of these assessments.

Current Treatments

Although some studies have focused on management of pain in adults with SCD, few studies have evaluated controlled trials of effective treatments for children. Although similarities in coping with SCD pain throughout life are likely, demands of SCD probably vary with age, requiring different coping resources at different stages of development.

In one of the few pediatric interventions with this population, Walco and Dampier (1987) developed individual treatment protocols aimed at reducing overreliance on the health care system by adolescent patients (e.g., emergency room visits, hospitalizations, and pain medication). The investigators established a series of behavioral contracts that included fixed schedules for tapering analgesic dosages, maximum days per hospitalization, minimal intervals between hospital admissions, maximum number of emergency room treatments during that interval, a maximum amount of outpatient analgesics, and finally, a structured program to promote a more adaptive lifestyle. Pain was presented to the children and their families as a lifelong problem, and patients were taught coping strategies and the regulation of pain perception as a means of mediating and tolerating the discomfort, rather than emphasizing the notion of curing the painful events. Walco and Dampier reported that each variable was modified over time to approximate successively the norm for matched peers. Although the strategy reduced the frequency and duration of hospitalizations and immediate dependency on the health care system, it did not promote a more adaptive lifestyle (that required significant psychotherapeutic and psychopharmacological interventions). Additional controlled trials will be needed to establish further the efficacy and durability of the program over time.

The limited research on the neurocognitive and psychosocial aspects of SCD provides at best a shaky foundation for practice (Brown, Doepke, & Kaslow, 1993). It has been suggested that only a small segment of the population with SCD is at risk for problems and that these children may be identified early and provided preventive intervention services, such as Head Start for preschool children, appropriate special education placement for school-age children, training in cognitive–behavioral approaches to coping for early adolescents, and education for all parents. However, prior to the initiation of global interventions, more research is needed on the incidence and unique sequelae of these children's problems as well as experimental validation of the correlational studies that have been conducted with this population.

A markedly more aggressive individualized assessment and intervention package needs to be developed. For some children with SCD, consequences of the disease can be quite severe. These high-risk children need to be identified quickly and provided with intervention services. Moreover, children who have sustained strokes need repeated, thorough neuropsychologic and academic evaluations, followed by close consultation with their school officials to develop optimal educational programs. Similarly, children without a diagnosed stroke but who nevertheless experience school difficulties should receive specialized neuropsychological evaluations and be provided with appropriate remedial education services. Children who miss an excessive number of school days because of pain episodes and associated problems should be targeted for assistance with pain management and strategies for coping. Finally, as is true with all pediatric chronic illnesses, children and adolescents who encounter difficulty with typical developmental transitions (e.g., between adolescence and adulthood) need special attention and programmatic support. The following case presentation provides an overview of a family psychoeducational treatment intervention that was developed for an adolescent with SCD who frequently had sought medical attention for chronic pain.

Latasha is a 14-year-old African American girl who had been admitted to the children's hospital on several occasions for pain crises. Psychology had been consulted at the last admission as Latasha appeared to be in some pain, although overt pain behaviors (i.e., grimacing, guarding, whimpering) were not present. Latasha reported her pain level to be "very bad," giving a pain rating of 9 on a scale of 1 to 10, yet she reported her mood to be "happy." Latasha reported having attempted various coping strategies prior to her arrival at the hospital: for example, "trying to think of other things," "trying to be busy/go out and do things," none of which was helpful in alleviating her pain. It is noteworthy that Latasha's pain crisis always occurred prior to major tests at school.

Mrs. J., Latasha's mother, reported that her daughter had a difficult time in school this past year, after the family recently had moved out of state. Latasha admitted that she intensely disliked the new school, did not inform the school officials or her classmates of her SCD, and encountered difficulty in making new friends. Latasha reported that the work was difficult and her teacher had little tolerance for Latasha's not understanding assignments. Psychological testing revealed specific learning disabilities in the areas of mathematics and reading comprehension, although no special education placement had yet been made due to Latasha's frequent absences from school.

Initially, Mrs. J. appeared very frustrated about having to respond to the questions presented at the interview and noted that she did not want to discuss Latasha's difficulties, stating that she was "tired of talking to psychologists, psychiatrists, and all of that, since Latasha is not crazy." Mrs. B. reported that she did not wish to bring Latasha to the hospital each time that Latasha experienced pain and that she well understood the repercussions of her daughter's reliance on the medical system and her inability to develop adaptive coping strategies. However, she indicated that Latasha's pain could be managed "if I had the right prescription." Mrs. J. also reported that Latasha received positive and special attention when she was hurting, especially from her father and grandmother. Mrs. J. further stated that it is difficult for her to manage Latasha's pain when she is continually informed by her family that she is a "bad mom who does not care about Latasha's problems." Moreover, Mrs. J. noted that she and Latasha feel "safe" when Latasha is in the hospital, as both she and Latasha expressed a great deal of fear about death and dying due to the premature death of a cousin from SCD. Mrs. J. and Latasha reside with her maternal grandmother, with Latasha's father coming in and out of her life but presenting no stable paternal influence.

In summary, factors that appear to promote Latasha's pain cycles are: (a) increased positive attention from her parents and family when she is in pain, (b) reprieve from a difficult school environment while she is in the hospital or in pain, (c) increased feelings of well-being and safety while she is in the hospital due to both her fear of death as well as that of her mother, (d) increased attention from hospital staff, (e) increased opportunity for socialization while in the hospital, (f) reprieve from negative home stressors, and (g) failure to obtain support from peers for Latasha's illness-related stressors.

Latasha and her entire family were enrolled in a 2-month treatment program for youth with SCD and their families that focused on the psychoeducational aspects of SCD, pain management, adaptive coping strategies, and peer support. The first session incorporated basic education about SCD and prevention of pain episodes. Latasha's family was educated about the facts of SCD, and information was provided about preventative health care strategies including eating healthy foods rich in iron, taking sufficient breaks when breathing hard from exercise, getting enough sleep, reducing stress, and avoiding extremes in temperature. The second session included application of preventative measures when Latasha experienced early warning signs that a pain crisis might occur. Pain-management techniques, including breathing, relaxation, and imagery also were taught during this session. The third session involved assisting Latasha and her family to articulate their feelings about the disease. Active listening techniques were taught to Latasha and her parents to promote parent–child communication. The primary goals of the fourth session were to enhance a mutual understanding among Latasha's family members that good family relationships facilitate effective coping with SCD and to motivate family members to develop active problem-solving strategies to handle difficulties pertaining to SCD. Latasha's parents also were assisted in obtaining a balance between being too restrictive and too permissive as to family rules and structure. The fifth session dealt with peer relationships, including assisting Latasha and her family members to explore the ways in which Latasha may seek support from peers at school regarding the limitations imposed by her illness. An examination of friendship patterns of children with SCD was discussed and included an analysis of involvement in peer activities, degree of isolation, and types of peers chosen. Helping Latasha develop more adaptive ways of explaining the causes of both good and bad events (e.g., "I am feeling some pain now and it is probably because I stayed in the cold too long") as well as assisting her family members in developing adaptive ways of explaining the causes of these events in her life and in her family (e.g., "SCD runs in my family and here is how we can help her") were the goals of the sixth session. The final session revolved around goal setting in which Latasha was taught how to set realistically attainable, flexible short- and long-term goals. Her family was encouraged to identify rewards for Latasha's goal attainment. Finally, family members were counseled regarding effective means of expressing their expectations and concerns about Latasha and her future.

Following this intervention program, emergency room visits and number of hospitalizations decreased, and school attendance increased. Although Latasha still experiences some pain episodes, albeit at a reduced frequency, these are managed well at home, with lower doses of analgesic pain medication than were utilized prior to this intervention. Latasha and her family still attend "booster" sessions on an as-needed basis.

Comments

The mortality rate associated with SCD has been reduced significantly as a result of medical advances over the past several decades. Unfortunately, many other aspects of the disease have yet to be addressed. This situation is particularly surprising, given the significant incidence of the disease compared with rates for other genetic diseases. In our clinical experience with children diagnosed with SCD, the dearth of identified intervention programs in the literature seems to reflect investigators' failure to ask pertinent questions, rather than the absence of problems. Available studies to date suggest that the impact of the disease does not seem to be universally negative; many children do well in school and are well adjusted. Thus, future research will need to focus both on the problems associated with the disease and the factors that mediate these problems so that appropriate intervention might take place. As is true of other pediatric chronic illnesses, the greatest clinical impact for children with SCD who have adjustment difficulties will come from what we learn from the children and families who develop adaptive strategies for coping.

SUMMARY

As the case examples presented previously illustrate, children, their families, and health care providers are all challenged by multiple stressors associated with serious injury and chronic illness. Reactions of children, families, staff, and society to such health problems are diverse and a complex function of many mediating variables, including the children's developmental level, SES, family utilitarian and personal resources, and operative environmental contingencies. Due to space limitations, we only are able to describe two disorders in detail. In the interest of expanding the scope of our discussion, Table 8.1 provides examples of some of the common psychological variables that often are relevant to other chronic pediatric health disorders.

We have learned that there is no one pattern of psychological response to a specific pediatric illness or injury. Children with the same health problem present with unique patterns of psychological strength and vulnerability. Alternatively, children with vastly different illnesses may evidence marked similarity in their behavioral responding (e.g., withdrawal, disrupted peer relations). Early research in the area of psychological aspects of pediatric disorders attempted to identify "personality" profiles or typical patterns of responding that would characterize children with specific disorders (e.g., asthmatic personality). These attempts were not fruitful. Subsequent research also has taught us that although specific illness and injury variables are important in understanding and conceptualizing a particular case, such variables by themselves often are of little predictive value, that is, although knowledge of specific illness parameters (e.g., severity, duration, age of onset) provides some guidance in predicting acute reaction and possible long-term sequelae, other variables (e.g., level of premorbid psychosocial functioning, family coping resources) often are of more clinical predictive value. Of course, it is often the interaction of health variables with other contextual (e.g., family), developmental, and environmental factors that are of central importance. For example, under typical circumstances, a small injury or time-limited illness may not pose a serious threat to a child's adjustment or well-being. However, in the context of a family environment that fails to provide adequate health care and monitoring, or alternatively functions to promote inappropriate responding, the extent of injury or illness severity provides limited guidance concerning management, course, and outcome.

Assisting children and their families in coping with the stressors induced by injury and chronic disease has necessitated joint working efforts of pediatric psychologists and pediatricians. Although such alliance represents a relatively new collaboration, it is one that has emerged strongly since the 1980s. The result has been a very productive and exciting working relationship that has spawned many innovative clinical and research programs designed to assist children in coping with the ongoing stressors of injury and disease and their associated treatments. Moreover, collaboration also has resulted in successful programs to mitigate the effects of chronic illness, including school-based programs (e.g., skin cancer prevention via reduced sun exposure, prevention of tobacco use). Furthermore, through family involvement and emphasis on patient education, the physical and psychosocial morbidity associated with serious childhood illnesses has been reduced significantly by enhancing compliance to treatment regimes. As treatment and the effective management of various pediatric chronic illnesses continues to advance, it is anticipated that the field of pediatric psychology will experience concomitant growth and progress requiring the additional training of psychologists for particular pediatric health subspecialties.

TABLE 8.1

Subset of Pediatric Disorders from Major Pediatric Subspecialty Populations With Examples of Relevant Psychological Aspects

Subspeciality	Condition	Representative Psychological Aspects
Trauma (Surgery)	Orthopedic trauma, burns	Coping with intense postinjury pain, adjustment to disfigurement, disability
	Head injury	Cognitive deficits
Cardiology	Congenital heart defects	Impaired cognitive function secondary to hypoxia, parental guilt about responsibility for anomaly
	Acquired heart defects	Restriction of activity secondary to blood trimer used in valve replacement
	Hypertension	Cognitive/mood effects of antihypertensive medication
Endocrinology	Diabetes melitus	Nonadherence with complex self-care regiment
	Short stature	Self-concept, peer relations
Gastroenterology	Encopresis	Coercive parent–child interactions around toileting, impaired child self-esteem
	Nonorganic recurrent abdominal pain	Reinforcement of child "sick" behavior, family dysfunction
	Ileitis (Crohn's disease)	Impaired self-esteem
Hematology	Sickle cell	Recurrent pain, cognitive changes
	Hemophilia	Chronic arthritic pain
Infectious Disease	AIDS	Cognitive deterioration, depression
	Meningitis	Cognitive changes
Neonatology	Brochopulmonary dysplasia	Feeding disorders, developmental delays
	Apnea	Sleep regulation
Nephrology	Renal failure	Treatment nonadherence, cognitive symptoms
	Cushing's syndrome	Muscle weakness, body composition changes
Neurology	Headaches	Stress
	Seizures	Medication-induced changes in cognitive functioning
Oncology	Leukemia	Coping with aversive medical diagnostic and treatment procedures
	Solid tumors	Pain, treatment-related cognitive changes, death, and dying issues

REFERENCES

Bibace, R., & Walsh, M. E. (1980). Development of children's concepts of illness. *Pediatrics, 66*, 912–917.

Blount, R. L., Davis, N., Powers, S., & Roberts, M. C. (1991). The influence of environmental factors and coping style on children's coping and distress. *Clinical Psychology Review, 11*, 93–116.

Brannon, L., & Feist, J. (1997). *Health psychology* (3rd ed.). Monterey, CA: Books/Cole.

Brown, R. T., Buchanan, I., Doepke, K. J., Eckman, J. R., Baldwin, K., Goonan, B., & Schoenherr, S. (1993). Cognitive and academic functioning in children with sickle cell disease. *Journal of Clinical Child Psychology, 22*, 207–218.

Brown, R. T., Doepke, K., & Kaslow, N. J. (1993). Risk-resistance adaptation model for pediatric chronic illness: Sickle cell syndrome as an example. *Clinical Psychology Review, 13*, 119–132.

Burlew, A. K., Evans, R., & Oler, C. (1989). The impact of a child with sickle cell disease on family dynamics. *Annals of the New York Academy of Sciences, 565*, 161–171.

Davis, C. C., Brown, R. T., Bakeman, R., & Campbell, R. (1998). Psychological adaptation and adjustment of children with congenital heart disease: The role of stress, coping, and family functioning. *Journal of Pediatric Psychology, 23*, 219–228.

Drotar, D., & Crawford, P. (1985). Psychological adaptation of siblings of chronically ill children: Research and practice implications. *Journal of Developmental and Behavioral Pediatrics, 6*, 355–362.

Ferrari, M. (1990). Developmental issues in behavioral pediatrics. In A. M. Gross & R. S. Drabman (Eds.), *Handbook of clinical behavioral pediatrics* (pp. 29–47). New York: Plenum.

Gil, K. M., Abrams, M. R., Phillips, G., & Keefe, F. J. (1989). Sickle cell disease pain: Relation of coping strategies to adjustment. *Journal of Consulting and Clinical Psychology, 57*, 725–731.

Gil, K. M., Thompson, R. J., Jr., Keith, B. R., Tota-Faucette, M., Noll, S., & Kinney, T. R. (1993). Sickle cell disease pain in children and adolescents: Change in pain frequency and coping strategies over time. *Journal of Pediatric Psychology, 18*, 621–637.

Gil, K. M., Williams, D. A., Thompson, R. J., & Kinney, T. R. (1991). Sickle cell disease in children and adolescents: The relation of parent and child pain coping strategies to adjustment. *Journal of Pediatric Psychology, 16*, 643–663.

Gross, A. M., & Drabman, R. S. (Eds.). (1990). *Handbook of clinical behavioral pediatrics*. New York: Plenum.

Hurt, F. J., & Tarnowski, K. J. (1990). Behavioral consultation in the management of pediatric burns. *Medical Psychotherapy, 3*, 117–124.

Hurtig, A. L., & Park, K. B. (1989). Adjustment and coping in adolescents with sickle cell disease. *Annals of the New York Academy of Sciences, 565*, 172–182.

Kazak, A. E., Segal-Andrews, A. M., & Johnson, K. (1995). Pediatric psychology research and practice: A Family/systems approach. In M. C. Roberts (Ed.), *Handbook of pediatric psychology* (2nd ed., pp. 84–104). New York: Guilford.

Knudson-Cooper, M. S., & Leuchtag, A. K. (1982). The stress of a family move as a precipitating factor in children's burn accidents. *Journal of Human Stress, 8*, 32–38.

Platt, O. S., Brambilla, D. J., Rosse, W. F., Milner, P. F., Castro, O., Steinberg, M. H., & Klue, P. P. (1994). Mortality in sickle cell disease: Life expectancy and risk factors for early death. *New England Journal of Medicine, 330*, 1639–1644.

Platt, O. S., Thorington, B. D., & Brambilla, D. J. (1991). Pain in sickle cell disease: Rates and risk factors. *New England Journal of Medicine, 325*, 11–16.

Roberts, M. C. (Ed.). (1995). *Handbook of pediatric psychology* (2nd ed.). New York: Guilford.

Routh, D. K. (Ed.). (1988). *Handbook of pediatric psychology*. New York: Guilford.

Russo, D. C., & Varni, J. W. (Eds.). (1982). *Behavioral pediatrics: Research and practice*. New York: Plenum.

Tarnowski, K. J. (Ed.). (1994). *Behavioral aspects of pediatric burns*. New York: Plenum.

Tarnowski, K. J., & Brown, R. T. (1995). Pediatric burns. In M. C. Roberts (Ed.), *Handbook of pediatric psychology* (2nd ed., pp. 446–462). New York: Guilford.

Tarnowski, K. J., McGrath, M. L., Calhoun, M. B., & Drabman, R. S. (1987). Pediatric burn injury: Self-versus therapist-mediated debridement. *Journal of Pediatric Psychology, 12*, 567–579.

Tarnowski, K. J., & Rasnake, L. K. (1994). Psychological sequelae of pediatric burns. In K. J. Tarnowski (Ed.), *Behavioral aspects of pediatric burns* (pp. 81–118). New York: Plenum.

Tarnowski, K. J., Rasnake, L. K., & Drabman, R. S. (1987). Behavioral assessment and treatment of pediatric burn injuries: A review. *Behavior Therapy, 18,* 417–441.

Tarnowski, K. J., Rasnake, L. K., Gavaghan-Jones, M. P., & Smith, L. (1991). Psychosocial sequelae of pediatric burn injuries: A review. *Clinical Psychology Review, 11,* 371–398.

Tarnowski, K. J., Rasnake, L. K., Linscheid, T. R., & Mulick, J. A. (1989). Ecobehavioral characteristics of a pediatric burn injury unit. *Journal of Applied Behavior Analysis, 22,* 101–109.

Thompson, R. J., Jr., Gil, K. M., Burbach, D. J., Keith, B. R., & Kinney, T. R. (1993). Role of child and maternal processes in the psychological adjustment of children with sickle cell disease. *Journal of Consulting and Clinical Psychology, 61,* 468–474.

Thompson, R. J., Jr., & Gustafson, K. E. (1995). *Adaptation to chronic childhood illness.* Washington: American Psychological Association.

Treiber, F., Mabe, A., & Wilson, G. (1987). Psychological adjustment of sickle cell children and their siblings. *Children's Health Care, 16,* 82–88.

Walco, G. A., & Dampier, C. D. (1987). Chronic pain in adolescent patients. *Journal of Pediatric Psychology, 12,* 215–225.

Wallander, J. L., & Varni, J. W. (1992). Adjustment in children with chronic physical disorders: Programmatic research on a disability–stress–coping model. In A. M. LaGreca, L. J. Siegel, J. L. Wallander, & C. E. Walker (Eds.), *Stress and coping in child health* (pp. 279–297). New York: Guilford.

Wernick, R. L. (1983). Stress inoculation in the management of clinical pain: Application to burn pain. In M. Meichenbaum & M. Jaremko (Eds.), *Stress reduction and prevention* (pp. 191–217). New York: Plenum.

Assessment and Treatment

Assessment always has been the hallmark of clinical psychology. From its earliest days, measurement and testing provided the foundation for examining abnormal behavior and have been the catalyst for the subsequent development of treatments. Assessment of intelligence, in particular, has been in the forefront of modern, empirically based approaches to measurement. More recently, as our definitions of what constitutes intelligence have broadened and our understanding of the antecedents of intelligence has deepened, measures of intellectual functioning have diversified to tap multiple cognitive domains and processes. Whereas the assessment of intelligence emanates from traditional psychometric approaches to test development, behavioral assessment focuses on measurement of overt, observable behaviors. Moreover, behavioral assessment is intricately linked with treatment, in that the behaviors measured become the direct focus of intervention.

Research on the treatment of abnormal behavior in children primarily has involved behavioral interventions in the last few decades. Such approaches emphasize assessment of target behaviors and manipulation of environmental contingencies in an effort to increase or decrease behavior. Behavioral interventions have become increasingly more sophisticated in the past decade, incorporating cognitive treatments and strategies that affect systems (e.g., family, classroom) where the child resides, plays, or works. As it has become increasingly evident that the etiologies of many child psychiatric disorders involve biological and environmental factors, pharmacological treatments also have emerged as important adjuncts to psychological interventions. Empirical research on the effectiveness of pharmacotherapy in children, however, is not as advanced as in adults. A third intervention approach that has gained considerable support in recent years in community prevention. In contrast to models of acute treatment, community preventions consists of identifying at-risk children and providing them with programs designed to forestall the future development of behavioral and emotional disorders. Such approaches are appealing given the ultimate savings in time and resources associated with successful early intervention.

The chapters in Part II cover assessment and treatment. In chapter 9, Kaufman, Kaufman, Lincoln, and Kaufman discuss intellectual and cognitive assessment. With a particular emphasis on traditional intelligence tests, the authors provide in-depth coverage of test development, administration, and interpretation of results. In addition to Wechsler's work and its revisions, the authors review the theoretical foundations and development of their alternatives to the traditional approach.

Beck (chap. 10) examines behavioral assessment. The A-S-O-R-K-C model is used to explain how most child behaviors are maintained by antecedent and consequent social–environmental events. Beck underscores that assessment strategies must account for cultural diversity in addition to evacuating economic costs involved in carrying out treatment interventions. In addition, he indicates that treatments should be developed on the basis of a careful evaluation of family functioning.

In chapter 11, LeBlanc, Le, and Carpenter show how most behavioral treatments combine several components across settings to maximize treatment efficacy and generalization. In describing such an approach, the chapter is organized into three areas: operant procedures, cognitive–behavioral therapies, and skill-building strategies. The most common principles and techniques are reviewed with respect to conduct disorders, anxiety disorders, depression, academic difficulties, and adjustment problems.

In chapter 12, McCleer and Wills argue that psychologists working with children and adolescents need to be knowledgeable about pharmacological strategies that have been empirically studied and applied in the treatment of child psychiatric disorders. Psychologists must be aware of which drugs are most often used and which may be used for specific disorders or symptoms. It is critical to be aware of the signs and symptoms of drug toxicity, side effects, and adverse reactions, because these problematic and potentially dangerous reactions may be noticed first by a psychologist treating or consulting on a case.

In the final chapter in Part II, Lorion writes on community prevention. The chapter invites the reader to consider community as both a locus and focus to prevent emotional disorder in children. The author critically reviews mechanisms through which context influences development, applying the evidence to conceptualize how interventions can prevent disorder and foster wellness in youth and families.

Intellectual and Cognitive Assessment

Alan S. Kaufman
James C. Kaufman
Yale University

Alan J. Lincoln
*California School of Professional Psychology, San Diego, CA
& Children's Hospital, San Diego, CA*

Jennie L. Kaufman
*PsychAssociates Group, New York
& Long Island Psychological Associates, Commack, NY*

The assessment of intelligence has long been controversial. Critics often have complained that IQ tests are biased and unfair, although today's critics are more likely to argue about what the IQ tests truly measure, how they should be interpreted, their relevance to intervention, and their scope. Despite the ongoing controversies, there is great interest and need for measurement of intelligence, especially in the educational, clinical, and neuropsychological contexts, to help anyone who is referred for a problem. Furthermore, these instruments remain a most technologically advanced and sophisticated tool of the profession for providing essential information to psychologists so they may best serve the needs of children, adolescents, and adults. When used in consideration of the American Psychological Association's Ethical Principles of Psychologists (American Psychological Association, 1990) Principle 2—competence, which encourages clinicians to recognize differences among people (age, gender, socioeconomic, and ethnic backgrounds) and to understand research-based limitations of their assessment tools—these tests have many benefits.

Indeed, standardized tests of intelligence routinely are administered as part of the clinical and psychoeducational assessment of children and adults. In addition to the ethical use of intelligence tests, the types of information derived from these instruments are most useful when interpreted by a psychologist in the context of a broader battery of psychological tests, the individual's personal history, and direct behavioral observations. Therefore, when discussing the contribution of intelligence tests, one must consider their significance as a component of a much more comprehensive approach toward assessment and diagnosis.

Most measures of intelligence that psychologists utilize for clinical and psychoeducational assessment have been standardized on large groups of individuals. The better measures have well-documented reliability and validity. The reliability and validity of such measures typically are found in the test manuals and through psychological, psychoeducational, or neuropsychological research studies examining diverse samples of individuals on dimensions of interest to the researcher.

However, in most instances of clinical and psychoeducational assessment, psychologists are not assessing large numbers of individuals. Rather, for the purpose of differential diagnosis, in either clinical or psychoeducational assessment, the psychologist generally is assessing a single person. The psychologist therefore is applying measures that have documented group reliability and validity to a single case. The potential problems associated with such an application of group data to a single case are, however, mitigated by utilizing a multimethod–multitrait approach for the clinical or psychoeducational assessment of the individual.

MULTIMETHOD–MULTITRAIT ASSESSMENT APPROACH

Multiple methods are applied by the psychologist in the assessment of the individual. These various methods can be conceptualized as individual databases, separate but complementary toward one another. The individual being assessed is, after all, the common denominator. These methods or databases include:

1. The presenting symptoms or problems.
2. The history of such symptoms.
3. The developmental, personal, and family history.
4. The school and work history.
5. The medical history.
6. A review of collateral information including aspects of history, previous test performance, medical history, and so forth.
7. Direct observations of behavior during the interview and testing session.
8. Performance on a range of specific psychological measures, neuropsychological measures, or both.
9. Feedback from additional evaluations (e.g., referral for hearing test, vision examination, neurological examination).
10. The literature known to be relevant to the ascertained history, test findings, and probable diagnosis.

Findings from an intelligence test are only one part of these more comprehensive methods for assessing and understanding the individual. Yet, these findings are only of optimal value if integrated with the other pertinent information about the individual, using an interpretive technique often referred to as *intelligent testing* (A. S. Kaufman, 1979, 1990a, 1994).

The Intelligent Testing Philosophy

The foundation of the intelligent testing philosophy is the notion that only highly trained scientist–practitioners are legally and ethically permitted to administer and interpret individual intelligence tests; first and foremost, the clinician must occupy a higher rung in the hierarchy than the test itself or the profile of scores it yields. Clinicians have accumulated vast stores of classroom and textbook knowledge about theories of learning, cognition, personality, development, and the like; they are familiar with a vast spectrum of results from empirical research investigations; and they have received real-life supervised clinical training with clients of all ages. This knowledge base and clinical training form the foundation of the interpretation of a person's test profile on any IQ test. Consequently, interpretation is unique for every individual tested—even if two people earn identical test scores. When interpreting a Wechsler test or similar scale, "Assessment is of the individual, by the individual, and for the individual" (A. S. Kaufman, 1994, p. 14).

Through research knowledge, theoretical understanding, and clinical insight, examiners must generate hypotheses about a person's strengths and weaknesses and then confirm or deny these hypotheses by exploring the multiple sources of evidence listed previously. Cross-validated hypotheses then need to be translated into meaningful recommendations for intervention, whenever possible. In addition, practitioner–scientists must possess an in-depth understanding of the state-of-the-art instruments that are available (including new and revised tests that are published subsequent to their formal training) and select tests that conform to the highest quality of psychometric standards. Nonetheless, sound judgment, knowledge of psychology and the literature, clinical training, and integration of multiple methods and multiple traits are more important than the specific instrument selected for an evaluation to move beyond the specific IQs and profile of subtest scores (A. S. Kaufman, 1990a, 1994; A. S. Kaufman & Lichtenberger, 1999). Each person who comes for an assessment has unique characteristics—his or her own way of approaching test items—and may be affected differently by the testing situation than the next child or adult. By using an integrated approach to interpretation, the various dimensions that influence an individual can become apparent.

More than any previous time in history, the current assessment scene offers an array of intelligence tests with superb psychometric properties, many of them (unlike Wechsler's popular scales) derived from theory. Just the past decade has produced two top-notch revisions of Wechsler's tests (Wechsler, 1991, 1997) and a handful of other excellent instruments, including the Woodcock–Johnson Psycho-Educational Battery–Revised Tests of Cognitive Ability (WJ–R; Woodcock & Johnson, 1989b); the Differential Abilities Scale (DAS; Elliott, 1990); the Kaufman Adolescent and Adult Intelligence Test (KAIT; A. S. Kaufman & Kaufman, 1993); and the Cognitive Assessment System (CAS; Naglieri & Das, 1997b). This chapter features the widely used Wechsler Intelligence Scale for Children–Third Edition (WISC–III; Wechsler, 1991) and Wechsler Adult Intelligence Scale–Third Edition (WAIS–III; Wechsler, 1997), the newest Wechsler test batteries. In addition, two of the newer, theory-based tests are introduced: the KAIT and the CAS.

Why Intelligence Tests are Used for Clinical Assessment

There are five primary reasons for including a measure of intelligence as part of the clinical assessment. First, there are several specific diagnoses of children and adults that require a standardized measure of general ability or intelligence. These include diagnoses of mental retardation, specific learning disabilities, and developmental language disorders in the *Diagnostic and Statistical Manual of Mental Disorders* (4th ed. [*DSM–IV*]; American Psychiatric Association, 1994).

Second, intelligence is perhaps the most predictive single measure of an individual's adaptive capabilities. This is why a measure of intelligence is employed to help ascertain the previous diagnoses and to help evaluate individual potential (e.g., for determining giftedness). Intelligence may also either increase vulnerability or provide protection with respect to development of specific psychiatric disorders (e.g., schizophrenia; Aylward, Walker, & Bettes, 1984).

Third, intelligence as a construct is important to individual personality assessment. David Wechsler was one of the foremost psychologists instrumental in developing both an understanding of the nature of human intelligence and methods by which it could be defined and measured operationally. Wechsler (1958) operationally defined *intelligence* as:

> the aggregate or global capacity of the individual to act purposefully, to think rationally and to deal effectively with environment. It is aggregate or global because it is composed of elements or abilities which, though not entirely independent, are qualitatively differentiable. … But intelligence is not identical with the mere sum of these abilities, however inclusive. There are three important reasons for this: 1) The ultimate products of intelligent behavior are a function not only of the number of abilities or their quality, but also the way in which they are combined. … 2) Factors other than intelligent ability, for example, drive and incentive, are involved in intellectual behavior. 3) Finally. … an excess of any given ability may add relatively little to the effectiveness of the behavior as a whole. (p. 7)

This operational definition of intelligence closely parallels the psychoanalytic, psychodynamic, and ego psychology attributes of functions of the ego. Wechsler (1958) believed that intelligence could no more be separated from "the total personality structure" (p. 5) than would the major theorists of the previous conceptual models separate the ego from the rest of human personality development. Indeed, Wechsler influenced the whole field of intellectual assessment, not just with his development of test batteries, but with his clinical approach to their interpretation. When the Stanford–Binet (Terman & Merrill, 1937) was the main instrument used for measuring IQ, during the 1930s through the 1950s, the approach to intellectual assessment was more psychometric than clinical. The leading text on Binet interpretation was written by Quinn McNemar (1942), a statistician, and the approach was decidedly statistical. When Wechsler's multiscore series of tests overtook the one-score Binet during the 1960s (in part because of the burgeoning learning disabilities movement that demanded a profile of scores to interpret), so too did Wechsler's clinical, personality-based approach to intellectual assessment supersede the more number-oriented approach.

The most widely used measures of intelligence in adults and children yield not only a single global IQ score, but, more importantly, they yield standard scores across multiple intellectual ability domains (Groth-Marnat, 1997; A. S. Kaufman, 1979, 1990a, 1994; Sattler, 1992). These ability domains are organized and integrated differently from person to person even when such persons have identical global IQ scores. This multiscore aspect of the tests allows flexibility in assessing individual differences.

Fourth, the methods used to assess the specific intellectual abilities tend to be relatively clearly defined and well-structured. This type of organization is in contrast to tests designed to maximize projection to assess personality functions and dynamic issues. Materials and questions used in intelligence tests tend to be fairly specific, easy to perceive, and call for certain correct responses. The format of the items and nature of the response process is also relatively familiar to the individual being tested. Less structured projective measures are designed to place a greater burden on the individual for both accurate perception and interpretation. With projective tests, there are no right or wrong responses; there are, however, responses that tend to conform to both the salient characteristics of the projective test stimuli and the instructions given the individual. The clinician is interested in the stability of perceptual accuracy and the ability to evoke a well-integrated response across levels of tests ranging from those that are well-structured and clearly defined (e.g., intelligence tests, achievement tests, and tests of visual–motor integration) to those tests that are less structured and clearly defined (projective tests). For example, perceiving the image of a familiar object or person is more easily accomplished than the identification of an incomplete drawing, as in the Gestalt Closure subtest of the Kaufman Assessment Battery for Children (K–ABC; A. S. Kaufman & Kaufman, 1983). Identification of the incomplete drawing is, in turn, a more clearly defined perceptual task than the task of identifying a percept from a Rorschach inkblot. Even within the so-called more structured tests, there are frequently subtests that can evoke a wider range of response and thus have the capacity to be somewhat projective.

A fifth reason for inclusion of an intelligence test in a psychological test battery is that it provides a sample of the individual's behavior in a fairly systematic manner. Individuals being tested are having their abilities sampled across a variety of domains, all of which contribute to their overall intellectual functioning. On the tests developed by Wechsler, such abilities include: verbal comprehension, attention, concentration, memory, abstract reasoning, knowledge of factual information, judgment, visual perception, visual–motor integration, planning, and cognitive flexibility. Each of these domains is not fully sampled by a single subtest; however, it is possible to acquire a great deal of information about an individual by what is sampled. Even a single response to a test item can provide significant information to the clinician. For example, an item from the Comprehension subtest from the WISC–III asks, "What should you do if you cut your finger?" A 9-year-old boy replies, "It bleeds, it is cut off … I scream … I'll bleed to death." In this single response, we learn that this child has difficulty thinking of the conventional response, "Wash it … put a band-aid on it," and instead becomes overly anxious and involved in the fantasy elicited by this test item. This child also personalizes the response in such a way that he seems to temporarily have difficulty differentiating a simple response to a test question from a real and threatening personal experience. In this example, the child does not receive credit for his response, and that has some effect on the score he achieves for the subtest. More importantly, however, this test item provided the clinician with a small sample of the child's behavior that, when evaluated in the context of the boy's history and symptoms, may provide insight into vulnerabilities that he experiences.

THE WECHSLER SCALES

The two most recently revised and restandardized versions of Wechsler's scales, spanning the ages of 6 to 89 years, are discussed here: the 1991 WISC–III, for elementary and high school children (ages 6 to 16); and the 1997 WAIS–III, for older adolescents through old age (16–89). The Wechsler Preschool and Primary Scale of Intelligence–Revised (WPPSR; Wechsler, 1989), for children aged 3 to 7 ¼, is not as popular as the other two Wechsler scales and has some practical flaws (A. S.

Kaufman, 1990b); it is excluded from this chapter. Following discussion of the WISC–III and WAIS–III, research on individuals diagnosed with exceptionalities, such as autism, is presented as an illustration of how Wechsler profiles are sometimes distinctive for clinical samples. That research summary includes the results of studies with a variety of versions of Wechsler's scales, past and present.

Theoretical Rationale

Despite Wechsler's comprehensive definition of intelligence, presented earlier, his tests were not predicated on his definition. Tasks did not emerge from research on concepts associated with his conception of intelligence; instead, virtually all of his tasks were adapted from other existing tests. Like Binet's (1903) and Terman's (1916) notions, Wechsler's definition of intelligence adheres to the notion of intelligence as an overall global entity ("g," or general ability factor). Wechsler believed that intelligence is not directly testable but must be inferred from an individual's thoughts, words, movements, and reactions to different stimuli. Wechsler did not value or hierarchize one task above another but believed that the global entity could be estimated by probing an individual with a wide array of cognitive tasks. Wechsler believed that tasks were not equally effective, but that each task was necessary for a thorough appraisal of intelligence. But despite Wechsler's (1950) lack of a theoretical framework, research on his tests has been instrumental in the development and elaboration of numerous theories, such as Sperry's (1968) distinction between the functions of the left and right cerebral hemispheres and Horn's (1989) elaboration of the different age-related patterns for fluid, crystallized, visualization, and other cognitive abilities.

Description and Basic Interpretive Approach

All of Wechsler's intelligence scales, from the Wechsler–Bellevue, Form I (Wechsler, 1939) to the WAIS–III (Wechsler, 1997) yield three IQs, each having a mean of 100 and standard deviation of 15: Verbal IQ (V–IQ), Performance IQ(P–IQ), and Full Scale IQ. In addition, Wechsler's scales are composed of separate subtests that yield scaled scores (for each: $M = 10$; $SD = 3$) that measure specific aspects of mental ability. Five or six Verbal subtests (e.g., defining words) are combined to yield a V–IQ, and five nonverbal, Performance subtests (e.g., arranging pictures in the right order to tell a story) are combined to yield a P–IQ. In addition, there are supplementary subtests on each scale, bringing the overall subtest total to 13 for the WISC–III and 14 for the WAIS–III. (Brief descriptions of these subtests are in the Appendix.). Unlike previous Wechsler scales, including the WPPSI–R (Wechsler, 1989), the WISC–III and WAIS–III each offers an additional set of four standard scores (like the IQs, $M = 100$, $SD = 15$) known as Factor Indexes. The Verbal subtests are subdivided into two factors, one that emphasizes solving verbal problems and expressing ideas in words (Verbal Comprehension) and the other that depends on short-term memory, sequential processing, attention, and concentration for success (known as Freedom from Distractibility on the WISC–III and Working Memory on the WAIS–III). Likewise, Performance subtests are subdivided into the factors Perceptual Organization (nonverbal reasoning and visual–motor coordination) and Processing Speed (visual–motor speed). Each factor is composed of two to four subtests.

The global or Full Scale IQ is examined for a general placement of the person on the continuum of intellectual ability. IQ tests were first developed to help determine whether an individual was mentally retarded. Tests such as the WISC–III and WAIS–III allow the evaluator to determine whether the individual's intellectual functioning falls anywhere from well below the first percentile to above the 99th percentile. The WISC–III and WAIS–III are sensitive to measuring moderate mental retardation (IQ between 40 and 54) and very superior intellectual ability (IQ $\geq$130). However, this global score provides only a small piece of the puzzle that merely summarizes—and often masks—the individual's complex array of strengths and weaknesses.

The first step in evaluating a person's assets and deficits is to examine his or her relative functioning on the V–IQ and P–IQ to determine whether there is a significant difference in the person's ability to express oneself via words and sentences versus manipulation of concrete materials. Some individuals score higher on the Verbal subtests, some score higher on the Performance subtests, and some score about evenly on both scales. It is possible to find evidence of uneven organization of intellectual abilities by comparing the magnitude of the V–IQs and P–IQs; typically, a difference of about 9 or 10 points is large enough to be meaningfully interpreted. In both children and adults, it has been found that individuals with receptive developmental language disorder have significantly lower V–IQs compared to their P–IQs (Lincoln, Courchesne, Harms, & Allen, 1993; Lincoln, Courchesne, Kilman, Elmasian, & Allen, 1988; Lincoln, Dickstein, Courchesne, Tallal, & Elmasian, 1992). In contrast, the opposite profile of High V–IQ–Low P–IQ occurs routinely for patients with damage to the right cerebral hemisphere, multiple sclerosis, or alcoholism (A. S. Kaufman, 1990a, chap. 9; Lezak, 1995).

Sometimes there is so much subtest variability within the Verbal Scale or Performance Scale that the global estimates of functioning become meaningless to interpret. In such cases, it is prudent to examine the pattern of standard scores on the four Factor Indexes and, perhaps, the pattern of scores making up the subtest profile. A hypothesis or inference is more valid when it is derived from converging scores of multiple subtests, each having added shared variance from their common domain, and when the hypothesis is supported with multiple pieces of evidence (Kamphaus, 1993), as noted previously. For example, one would have great confidence in the inference, "Billy has a relatively poor ability to evaluate verbal information," when that inference is supported by all of the subtests of the Verbal Comprehension factor converging into a low Factor Index, relative to notably higher factor scores on the three other factors. Furthermore, one would seek confirmation of the hypothesis from his scores on other verbal tasks, from observations of his spontaneous speech, from comments from those who referred him for evaluation, and so forth. In contrast, one would have less confidence in the inference of "poor ability to evaluate verbal information" if only the Vocabulary subtest score was low and not the other three subtests that also comprise the WISC–III Verbal Comprehension factor.

Because the WISC–III and WAIS–III each yield about 20 scores, it is important to investigate a person's profile systematically, working from the most global score (Full Scale IQ) to the least global (specific subtests). Additionally, because people are commonly evaluated for a suspected abnormality, the magnitude of discrepancies in the profile need to be examined to see if any are unusually or abnormally large. Systematic, step-by-step approaches for test interpretation are available for both the WISC–III (A. S. Kaufman, 1994) and WAIS–III (A. S. Kaufman & Lichtenberger, 1999).

WISC–III

The WISC–III (Wechsler, 1991), normed for children and adolescents from 6 years, 0 months through 16 years, 11 months, has the following lineage: Wechsler–Bellevue

Intelligence Scale, Form II (Wechsler, 1946), WISC (Wechsler, 1949), and WISC–R (Wechsler, 1974).

Psychometric Properties. The WISC–III was standardized on 2,200 children ranging in age from 6 through 16 years, meticulously stratified by age, gender, race–ethnicity, geographic region, and parent education. The average split-half reliability (consistency of the scores), across the age groups, for the IQs and Factor Indexes, are: .95 for the V–IQ, .91 for the P–IQ, .96 for the Full Scale IQ, .94 for the Verbal Comprehension Index, .90 for the Perceptual Organization Index, .87 for the Freedom from Distractibility Index, and .85 for the Processing Speed Index (Wechsler, 1991). These values denote excellent consistency. Exploratory and confirmatory factor analyses offer strong support for the psychological meaningfulness and construct validity of the four factors that underlie the WISC–III (Roid, Prifitera, & Weiss, 1993; Wechsler, 1991). Factor analyses conducted with a sample of children experiencing learning problems yielded mixed results. The four factors were identified in one study (Konold, Kush, & Canivez, 1997), but only the Verbal Comprehension and Perceptual Organization factors were given clear-cut support in a second study (Kush, 1996).

Psychometric and Clinical Critique. Some critics believe that the WISC–III reflects little progress in the assessment of intelligence, emphasizing that despite more than a half-century of theoretical advances and emerging cognitive constructs, the Wechsler philosophy of intelligence, stemming from the 1930s, remains the guiding principle of the WISC–III, and the test has changed little in content (Shaw, Swerdlik, & Laurent, 1993; Sternberg, 1993). In contrast to these fairly negative evaluations, A. S. Kaufman (1993) has praised the quality of the normative sample, and the sophisticated, state-of-the art approach to test development, validation, and interpretation. On the negative side, A. S. Kaufman (1993) was disappointed: (a) to see so much emphasis on speed of responding, noting that bonus points are awarded liberally for quick, perfect performance on many nonverbal items and on arithmetic items as well, placing too much stress on speed and too little on power; and (b) to see the elimination of many of the clinical items on the test (e. g., Picture Arrangement items involving violence), David Wechsler's favorite items in view of his perception that IQ tests are, first and foremost, clinical instruments intended to evoke emotional as well as cognitive responses.

WAIS–III

The newest addition to the Wechsler family of tests is the WAIS–III (Psychological Corporation, 1997; Wechsler, 1997), for adults aged 16 to 89 years. Its predecessors include the original Wechsler–Bellevue Intelligence Scale, Form I (Wechsler, 1939), WAIS (Wechsler, 1955), and WAIS–R (Wechsler, 1981). The WAIS–III is the first Wechsler adult scale to be normed with a carefully stratified sample above the age of 74.

Psychometric Properties. The WAIS–III was standardized carefully on 2,450 adult participants, selected according to 1995 U.S. Census data, and stratified according to age, gender, race–ethnicity, geographic region, and education level. Participants were divided into 13 age groups between 16 and 17 and 85 and 89, with each age group including 100 to 200 people (Psychological Corporation, 1997).

Average split-half reliability coefficients, across the 13 age groups, are as follows: .97 for V–IQ, .94 for P–IQ, and .98 for Full Scale IQ. The average value for Processing

Speed Index was .87 (a test–retest coefficient, because split-half is not applicable for highly speeded tasks), with the split-half coefficients averaging .93 to .96 for the other three indexes. These values denote superb reliability. The WAIS–III Technical Manual (Psychological Corporation, 1997) reports that numerous factor analytic studies (exploratory and confirmatory) supported the underlying four-factor structure of the WAIS–III for ages 16 to 74 years, thereby offering construct validity support for these ages. For ages 75 to 89, however, the Perceptual Organization factor was not distinct from the Processing Speed factor.

Psychometric and Clinical Critique.   Because the WAIS–III undoubtedly will succeed the WAIS–R as the leader in the field of adult assessment, the new norms and psychometric improvements of the WAIS–III are much welcomed by clinicians. The WAIS–III has strong reliability and validity for the V–IQ, P–IQ, and Full Scale IQ, as did the WAIS–R. The subtest with the lowest split-half reliability has been removed from the computation of the IQs (Object Assembly) and is not included on any factor. However, Picture Arrangement, with a reliability coefficient below .75 at several ages, remains part of the Performance IQ.

The WAIS–III standardization sample selection was done with precision, leading to a well-stratified sample. Several very easy items have been added on each subtest to improve the measurement of the abilities for lower functioning individuals; this represents an important improvement. However, as with the WAIS–R, individuals who are extremely gifted or severely retarded cannot be assessed adequately with the WAIS–III because the range of possible Full Scale IQs is only 45 to 155 (by contrast, the range for the WPPSI–R is 41 to 160, and the range for the WISC–III is 40 to 160). As on the WAIS–R, even if adults earn a raw score of zero on a subtest, they will receive 1 to 5 scaled-score points on that subtest (i.e., they are given a lot of credit for doing little or nothing).

The WAIS–III predecessors used a reference group (ages 20–34) to determine everyone's scaled scores, a practice that, fortunately, was dropped for the new test; scaled scores are computed for the WAIS–III for each individual based solely on his or her chronological age, the same procedure used for Wechsler's children's scales. The reference group technique was indefensible because use of this single reference group impaired profile interpretation below age 20 and above 34.

The failure to obtain construct validity evidence for all four factors for individuals aged 75 to 89 years is a problem for those who routinely evaluate elderly populations. The P–IQ seems to denote visual–motor speed rather than problem solving for this group, challenging the construct validity of the entire Performance Scale and Perceptual Organization Index as measures of cognitive ability for those aged 75 and above. In addition, A. S. Kaufman's (1998) analysis of age differences in test performance on the WAIS–III across its broad age span raises issues about the interpretation of the Working Memory Index for individuals in their 50s through 80s. Each of the three Working Memory subtests has a different relation to age: Arithmetic is an ability that is maintained across most of the life span, whereas Digit Span shows the age-related vulnerability that is characteristic of short-term memory tasks, and Letter–Number Sequencing demonstrates the dramatic decreases in old age that typify measures of fluid reasoning (see Horn, 1989, for a discussion of cognitive abilities that either are maintained through old age or vulnerable to the aging process).

In general, the WAIS–III has many outstanding features that make it an excellent clinical tool (see A. S. Kaufman & Lichtenberger, 1999, for a thorough discussion of the pros and cons of the WAIS–III).

Wechsler Profiles of Clinical Samples

Although it is not appropriate to diagnose a client based on an intelligence test profile (Kamphaus, 1993), some research has been conducted on various diagnoses that have found certain test profiles or subtest fluctuations in certain categories of children's disorders.

Attention Deficit Hyperactivity Disorder.   Many researchers have used the WISC, WISC–R, and WISC–III to determine consistent subtest patterns for children who have attention deficit hyperactivity disorder (ADHD; see Appendix). It is important to understand the cognitive functioning of children with ADHD because of the increased use of the diagnosis. Tests can be used along with behavioral observations to help identify these children (Sutter, Bishop, & Battin, 1987). These children frequently perform lower on the Freedom from Distractibility (FD) factor than do other groups of children, including children with other diagnoses and those who are in the normal population. This factor, comprised of the Digit Span, Arithmetic, and Coding subtests on the WISC–R (but only comprises Digit Span and Arithmetic on the WISC–III Factor Index), has been suggested to measure not merely attention but the ability to store information while performing other mental operations simultaneously. For example, one study found that children with ADHD performed significantly lower than emotionally disturbed and normal control children on the Arithmetic and Coding subtests (Lufi, Cohen, & Parish-Plass, 1990). Sutter et al. (1987) found that children with ADHD tend to have trouble understanding and remembering spoken words, numbers, and sentences, especially when they are distracted. They found auditory tasks to be the most discriminating, and the WISC–R's Arithmetic subtest best discriminated between ADHD children and other groups of children. Another study found that children with ADHD had a larger difference between the FD factor and the Verbal Comprehension (VC) factor (VC > FD) than did children in special education or regular education (Zarski, Cook, West, & O'Keefe, 1987). The fact that children with ADHD tend to perform lower on this factor could mean that they have deficits in executive functioning and short-term memory (Wielkiewicz, 1990).

Research with the WISC–III supports the previous results of subtest patterns for ADHD children and adolescents. In one study, a sample of 65 individuals aged 7 to 16 years with the diagnosis of ADHD earned their lowest mean scores on Coding and Digit Span and had significantly depressed factor scores on both the FD and Processing Speed (PS) factors (Prifitera & Dersh, 1993). In a second investigation, 45 ADHD children (aged 8 to 11 years) earned their poorest subtest scores on Coding and Arithmetic and also scored significantly lower on the FD and PS factors than on the VC and Perceptual Organization (PO) factors (Schwean, Saklofske, Yackulic, & Quinn, 1993). A third sample of 40 clinic-referred ADHD children (Anastopopolous, Spisto, & Maher, 1994) obtained a depressed FD Index, but the authors did not report a PS Index for the sample. With the WISC–R, deficits on the FD factor were consistently associated with ADHD; with the WISC–III, it appears that low PS score provides an additional diagnostic clue when assessing children or adolescents suspected of ADHD (A. S. Kaufman, 1994). (For a thorough treatment of WISC–III assessment of children with ADHD, consult Schwean and Saklofske, 1998.)

Conduct Disorder.   Over the years, many researchers have studied the cognitive profiles of juvenile delinquents. Many of these delinquents could be diagnosed as having Conduct Disorder as described by the *DSM–IV.* Although Wechsler predicted that children with antisocial acting-out patterns would have a P–IQ greater than V–IQ profile, there has been conflicting evidence of this pattern in the literature for the past 50 years. Quay (1987) said that no unique subtest pattern has been found for delinquents, with the exception of the controversial P–IQ > V–IQ general pattern. He felt that the difference that has been observed is not a large difference and that this phenomenon is generally due to the lower performance of the delinquents on tasks that measure verbal skills such as word knowledge, verbally coded information, and verbal reasoning. Quay also reasoned that having lower intellect in the verbal sphere compared to children in the normal population may contribute to these children's ability to fit into a school environment, and it may interact with other variables like poor parenting in producing the behavioral acting out seen in juvenile delinquents.

Hogan and Quay (1984) suggested that the reason there may not be a clear intellectual pattern for delinquents is because they are such a heterogeneous group that it is hard to find one pattern that fits all children in this category. By placing delinquents into subgroups, the chances of finding an intellectual pattern might increase. Some studies have found that IQ can be related to the severity of delinquent behaviors and, in some cases, early age of onset of delinquent behaviors.

Culbertson, Feral, and Gabby (1989) divided delinquent boys into subgroups and found a pattern of high and low subtests for this population. Culbertson et al. found that 70% of delinquent boys had the P–IQ > V–IQ pattern. They examined the group as a whole, and separated out subgroups of boys who had a P–IQ > V–IQ of less than 13 points (Group 1), 13 points and higher (Group 2), and 15 points and higher (Group 3). They found that for the boys with the larger P–IQ > V–IQ split, as well as the group as a whole, the highest subtests were Object Assembly, Picture Completion, and Picture Arrangement. This finding is consistent with this population's strength in the visual–motor area. The lowest subtests for the whole group were Information, Vocabulary, and Coding. The lowest subtests for Groups 2 and 3 were Information, Vocabulary, and Comprehension. This triad of low scores for the subgroups would indicate that the more severe juvenile delinquents are lower on school-related skills, verbal expression, and concept formation, in addition to poor social judgment and reasoning.

Children dually diagnosed with both ADHD and conduct disorder scored significantly lower on the WISC–R Verbal Comprehension factor than either children diagnosed with just ADHD or a clinic control sample of children with internalizing disorders; the latter two groups did not differ from each other (Semrud-Clikeman, Hynd, Lorys, & Lahey, 1993). Semrud-Clikeman et al. noted the importance of this finding in view of the high comorbidity of the two diagnoses (about 30%-50%) in epidemiological studies. This finding is consistent with the relatively low verbal abilities reported previously for delinquents.

Autism. In the past 2 decades, there have been numerous studies that have evaluated the intellectual abilities of people with autism on the Wechsler scales. These studies demonstrate that many individuals with autism have a distinct pattern of intellectual ability (Bartak, Rutter, & Cox, 1975; Freeman, Lucas, Forness, & Ritvo, 1985; Kuck, Lincoln, & Heaton, 1998; Lincoln et al., 1988; Lockyer & Rutter, 1970; Ohta, 1987; Rumsey & Hamburger, 1990). Most, but not all (e.g., Siegel, Minshew, & Goldstein, 1996), studies report higher P–IQ than V–IQ in samples of persons with autism. However, even though some studies do not show the characteristic P–IQ > V–IQ pattern, virtually all samples of autistic individuals display better nonverbal than verbal ability when "purer" measures of these constructs are compared—that is, groups of autistic individuals invariably evidence higher scores on the Perceptual Organization than Verbal Comprehension factors, even when the more global indicators (V–IQ and P–IQ) do not denote the expected pattern. The high nonverbal–low verbal pattern that consistently emerges when factor scores are examined is congruent with a verbal comprehension deficit in persons with autism compared to their more effective visual–motor and visual perception abilities. Patterns observed for autistic individuals in the United States have been cross-validated in several other countries as well, such as Japan (Ishisaka, Murasawa, Muramatsu, Kamio, & Toichi, 1997).

Lincoln et al. (1988) reported how autistic individuals demonstrate even more profound differences among selected subtests derived from the Verbal Comprehension factor (Vocabulary and Comprehension) relative to selected subtests derived from the Perceptual Organization factor (Block Design and Object Assembly). Vocabulary and Comprehension scaled scores were reported as being quite impaired compared to Block Design and Object Assembly scaled scores in almost all of the studies of autistic individuals. For example, in a recent investigation of 34 children and 27 adults with autism, Kuck et al. (1998) reported the following mean scaled scores on Block Design and Object Assembly versus the means on Vocabulary and Comprehension: 10.6 versus 2.2 for the children on the WISC–R; and 9.3 versus 4.1 for the adults on the WAIS–R. It is clear from these results and the findings from numerous other studies that the more specific comparison of Vocabulary and Comprehension versus Block Design and Object Assembly more sensitively demonstrates the significant unevenness in these individuals' verbal and visual–motor cognitive abilities.

It is noteworthy that both Block Design and Object Assembly are generally considered good measures of fluid intellectual ability (in concert with visualization ability), whereas Vocabulary and Comprehension are good measures of crystallized ability (see A. S. Kaufman, 1990a, 1994, for a review). Fluid intellectual ability is believed to relate closely to neurological development and is not a function of specific training or acculturation. Crystallized ability is influenced to a significant degree by environmental experience, learning, and culture. Furthermore, the ability to develop intellectual abilities based on environmental experience and learning is dependent on the efficacy of the fluid intellectual functions. Thus, early poor performance on measures sensitive to fluid ability may be more predictive of subsequent global intellectual deficits. The converse, however, may not be true. Adequate fluid ability may not necessarily facilitate crystallized intellectual functions.

In addition to relatively poor performance on measures of crystallized ability, autistic individuals usually have scored low on Digit Symbol and Coding, probably because these measures of psychomotor speed are extremely sensitive to brain impairment in general (Reitan, 1985).

Learning Disabilities. A fundamental component of the evaluation of children, adolescents, or adults with learning disabilities (LDs) requires the use of a measure of intelligence (*DSM–IV*; see Appendix, "Learning Disabilities"). To determine whether there is significant impairment of an academic skill, it is necessary to evaluate the level of that academic skill relative to the individual's general ability level. IQ tests are the best psychometric measures to evaluate an individual's general ability level. Thus, an LD diagnosis requires that the achievement measure be significantly discrepant and below the measure of intelligence.

There are, however, not clearly agreed-on criteria for how great that discrepancy should be nor how low the academic ability must be to make the diagnosis of an LD. Furthermore, there is no agreed-on measure of academic achievement or intelligence on which such evaluations should be based. Such criteria and selection of tests are presently left to the discretion of clinicians, schools, researchers, or government agencies.

IQ tests also may prove useful in helping to evaluate characteristics of the LD in a particular child. Rose, Lincoln, and Allen (1992) identified a group of children who all had global problems in reading, spelling, and arithmetic. These children were compared to a group of children who all had a history of developmental receptive language disorder and also currently demonstrated equally impaired reading, spelling, and arithmetic skill. Thus, academically, both groups of children showed similar impairment on standardized achievement tests. However, Rose et al. demonstrated that the children with developmental language disorder had significantly depressed V–IQ scores relative to their P–IQ scores on the WISC–R, whereas the LD children without the history of language disorder demonstrated a more even relationship between V–IQ and P–IQ.

Furthermore, typical subtest correlations among WISC–R Verbal subtests were not found for the group of children with developmental language problems but were maintained for the other group of LD children. Thus, it was possible to have the same magnitude of learning disability as measured by reading, spelling, and arithmetic achievement tests with very different language histories and current language abilities.

Examination of subtest patterns on Wechsler's scales has shown in a wide variety of research investigations that children diagnosed with reading and learning disabilities have scored low on four subtests, known as the ACID profile: Arithmetic, Coding (or Digit Symbol), Information, and Digit Span (A. S. Kaufman, 1979). WISC–III research has suggested that individuals diagnosed with reading or learning disabilities, or ADHD, score relatively low on the four subtests that together compose the PS and FD factors (the A, C, and D subtests from the ACID profile plus Symbol Search), relative to their performance on the PO factor; A. S. Kaufman (1994) has referred to this area of deficient performance as the SCAD profile. Indeed, data provided by Prifitera and Dersh (1993) indicate that 54% of 164 children diagnosed with ADHD or learning disabilities scored significantly higher on the PO factor than on the SCAD profile; for normal children in the standardization sample, the comparable value is 16% (A. S. Kaufman, 1994). Nonetheless, a body of research warns that neither the ACID profile nor the SCAD profile has demonstrated utility for the differential diagnosis of learning disabilities (e.g., Ward, Ward, Hatt, Young, & Mollner, 1995; Watkins, Kush, & Glutting, 1997).

TWO NEW THEORY-BASED TESTS: THE KAIT AND CAS

Although Wechsler's scales for children and adults remain the most widely used instruments in clinical practice, a variety of new, well-constructed, and well-normed tests for children and adults is now available. Several of these tests are developed directly from theory, something that is lacking in Wechsler's scales, yet is a highly desirable attribute for any test that purports to measure the construct of intelligence (Sternberg & J. C. Kaufman, 1996, 1998). In this section, two of the newer tests, the KAIT and the DAS, are discussed.

Kaufman Adolescent and Adult Intelligence Test (KAIT)

The KAIT (A. S. Kaufman, & Kaufman, 1993) is an individually administered intelligence test for individuals between the ages of 11 and more than 85 years. It provides Fluid, Crystallized, and Composite IQs, each a standard score with a mean of 100 and a standard deviation of 15. It includes a Core Battery of six subtests (three Fluid and three Crystallized) and an Expanded Battery that also includes alternate Fluid and Crystallized subtests plus measures of delayed recall of information learned earlier in the evaluation during two of the Core subtests. Each subtest (except a supplementary Mental Status task) yields age-based scaled scores with a mean of 10 and a standard deviation of 3. Subtests were designed to be realistic, when feasible; for example, Auditory Comprehension is a mock news broadcast on cassette. In addition, actual "learning" tasks were included in the KAIT, for example, Rebus Learning, which teaches the examinee to "read" a new language by learning various pictures (rebuses) that correspond to words and language concepts.

Fluid-crystallized theory (Horn & Cattell, 1966) forms the foundation of the KAIT and defines the constructs believed to be measured by the separate IQs. However, other theories guided the construction of the subtests–namely, Piaget's (1972) notion of formal operations and Luria's (1980) concept of planning ability, thereby ensuring that tasks would be high-level, involving decision making. Luria's notion of planning ability involves decision making, evaluation of hypotheses, and flexibility, and "represents the highest levels of development of the mammalian brain" (Golden, 1981, p. 285). Piaget's formal operations depicts a hypothetical–deductive abstract reasoning system that features the generation and evaluation of hypotheses and the testing of propositions. The prefrontal areas of the brain associated with planning ability mature at about ages 11 to 12 years (Golden, 1981), the age of onset of formal operational thought (Piaget, 1972). The convergence of the Luria and Piaget theories regarding the ability to deal with abstractions is remarkable and provides a rationale for having age 11 as the lower bound of the KAIT (A. S. Kaufman & Kaufman, 1993).

Horn and Cattell (1966) postulated a model of intelligence that separates Fluid from Crystallized intelligence, described previously in the discussion of individuals with autism. Within the KAIT framework (A. S. Kaufman & Kaufman, 1993), Crystallized intelligence "measures the acquisition of facts and problem solving ability using stimuli that are dependent on formal schooling, cultural experiences, and verbal conceptual development" (p.7). Fluid intelligence "measures a person's adaptability and flexibility when faced with new problems, using both verbal and nonverbal stimuli" (A. S. Kaufman & Kaufman, 1993, p. 7). Importantly, this Crystallized–Fluid construct split is not the same as Wechsler's Verbal–Performance split, a contention given empirical support from factor analysis; Wechsler's Performance subtests form a factor that is entirely separate from a factor composed of the KAIT Fluid subtests (A. S. Kaufman & Kaufman, 1993). Unlike Wechsler's Performance tasks, the KAIT Fluid subtests stress reasoning rather than visual–spatial ability, include verbal comprehension or expression as key aspects of some tasks, and minimize the role played by visual–motor speed for correct responding.

The KAIT scales measure what Horn (1989) refers to as broad fluid and broad crystallized abilities, rather than the purer and more specific skill areas (numbering about 8 to 10) that define Horn's expansion and elaboration of the original Horn–Cattell theory. The decision to use broad definitions of the constructs was based on clinical as well as theoretical considerations. Wechsler believed that the constructs measured by IQ tests should be complex (rather than laboratory pure) because intelligence is so complex; he also believed that IQ tests should be based on a small number of broad constructs in view of the practicalities involved in assessing intelligence in a relatively short time (about 60 to 90 minutes). A. S. Kaufman and Kaufman (1993) were influenced by Wechsler's clinical approach to assessing intelligence when they selected the use of broad constructs. In addition, research on aging and IQ across the life span has shown that the broad fluid-crystallized distinction was the most pertinent theoretical model for explaining observed patterns of growth and decline across the age span covered by the KAIT (A. S. Kaufman, 1990a, chap. 7). A large body of research indicates that crystallized abilities are mostly maintained throughout the adult life span, whereas fluid abilities peak in the late teens and early 20s before declining steadily throughout the aging process. This theoretical finding also supported the KAIT's focus on the two broad constructs.

The KAIT normative sample, composed of 2,000 adolescents and adults between the ages of 11 and 94 years, was stratified on the variables of gender, racial–ethnic group, geographic region, and socioeconomic status (A. S. Kaufman & Kaufman, 1993). Mean split-half reliability coefficients for the total normative sample were .95 for Crystallized IQ, .95 for Fluid IQ, and .97 for Composite IQ (A. S. Kaufman & Kaufman, 1993). Factor analysis, both exploratory and confirmatory, gave strong construct validity support for the Fluid and Crystallized Scales, and for the placement of each subtest on its designated scale. Correlational analyses with Wechsler's scales produced high coefficients (.82–.85) between KAIT Composite IQ and Wechsler's Full Scale IQ (A. S. Kaufman & Kaufman, 1993). Evaluation of changes in fluid and crystallized intelligence on the KAIT across the 17- to 94-year age range provided evidence of the scales' validity in terms of Horn's (1989) theory (A. S. Kaufman & Horn, 1996). A recent study of the WAIS–R and KAIT, using a sample of 60 college students (30 with LDs, 30 without), led the authors to conclude that the KAIT is a suitable choice for assessing the intelligence of the two groups of college students, and offered reasons why the KAIT may be a preferred method for students with LDs (Morgan, Sullivan, Darden, & Gregg, 1997). In another recent investigation, 50 preadolescents and adolescents (33 with scholastic concerns and 17 with central nervous system disorders) were administered the WISC–III and the KAIT Fluid subtests (Wodrich & Kush, 1998). The authors concluded that, "The KAIT Fluid measures appeared to have greater sensitivity to neurological problems than the WISC–III" (p. 220); also, more students with severe IQ and achievement discrepancies were identified by the KAIT (58%) than by the WISC–III (30%). In another neuropsychological study, the KAIT was used to better understand the relation between Fluid–Crystallized intelligence and evoked brain potentials at different sites of the cerebral cortex (J. L. Kaufman, 1995).

Anastasi and Urbina (1997) stated,

> In terms of its technical qualities, the KAIT appears to meet psychometric standards as well as any of the current generation of major intelligence scales. … Nevertheless, what really distinguishes the KAIT from other adult intelligence scales is the care taken to develop and try out its original pool of more than 2,500 items. The items were designed to appeal to adult test takers. … As a result, most of them are unusual and interesting. (p. 225)

Cognitive Assessment System (CAS)

The CAS (Naglieri & Das, 1997b), for ages 5 to 17 years, is based on the Planning, Attention, Simultaneous, and Successive (PASS) theory of intelligence—a multidimensional view of ability that is the result of the merging of contemporary theoretical and applied psychology (see summaries by Das, Naglieri, & Kirby, 1994; Naglieri & Das, 1997a, 1997b). Naglieri and Das (1997a) linked the work of Luria (1980) with the field of intelligence when they suggested that PASS processes are the essential elements of human cognitive functioning. This theory proposes that human cognitive functioning is based on four essential activities that employ and alter an individual's knowledge base: Planning processes that provide cognitive control, utilization of processes and knowledge, intentionality, and self-regulation to achieve a desired goal; attentional processes that provide focused, selective cognitive activity over time; and simultaneous and successive information processes that are the two forms of operating on information (Naglieri & Das, 1997b).

Planning processing provides the means to solve problems for which no solution is apparent. It applies to tasks that may involve attention, simultaneous and successive processes as well as acquired knowledge. Success on planning tests should require the child to develop a plan of action or strategy, evaluate the value of the method, monitor its effectiveness, revise or reject an old plan as the task demands change, and control the impulse to act without careful consideration. Successful performance on an *attention* task requires effort to be focused, selective, sustained, and effortful. Attention tests should present children with competing demands on their attention and require sustained focus over time.

The essence of *simultaneous processing* is that it allows for the interrelation of elements into a conceptual whole; it has strong spatial components in nonverbal tasks and in language tasks involving logical–grammatical relationships. Successive processing is involved when parts must follow each other in a specific order such that each element is only related to those that precede it. Successive processing is most important in tasks with serial and syntactic components. The serial aspect involves both the perception of stimuli in sequence and the formation of sounds and movements in order; the syntactic aspect allows for the comprehension of the meaning of narrative speech.

The CAS was designed to mirror the PASS theory, with subtests organized into four scales to provide an effective measure of each of the PASS cognitive processes. Planning subtests require the child to devise, select, and use efficient plans of action to solve the test problems, regulate the effectiveness of the plans, and self-correct when necessary. Attention subtests require the child to selectively attend to a particular stimulus and inhibit attending to distracting stimuli. Simultaneous processing subtests require the child to integrate stimuli into groups to form an interrelated whole, and successive processing subtests require the child to integrate stimuli in their specific serial order or appreciate the linearity of stimuli with little opportunity for interrelating the parts.

The CAS yields standard scores with a mean of 100 and standard deviation of 15 for the Planning, Attention, Simultaneous, Successive, and Full Scales. All subtests are set at a normative mean of 10 and standard deviation of 3. Interpretation of CAS also follows closely from the PASS theory, with emphasis on the scale rather than subtest-level analyses.

The CAS was standardized on 2,200 children ranging in age from 5 through 17 years stratified by age, gender, race, ethnicity, geographic region, educational placement, and parent education according to recent U.S. Census reports and closely matches the U.S. population characteristics on the variables used. In addition to administration of the CAS, a representative sample of 1,600 included in the standardization sample also completed achievement tests from the WJ–R Tests of Achievement (Woodcock & Johnson, 1989a). Finally, 872 children from special populations, including attention deficit, mentally retarded, and learning disabled, for example, were tested for validity and reliability studies.

The internal consistency reliability estimates for the CAS Full Scale are comparable with other tests of its type. The CAS Standard Battery (12 subtests) average scale reliability coefficients for the entire standardization sample of children aged 5 to 17 years are as follows: Full Scale = .96; Planning = .88; Simultaneous = .93; Attention = .88; and Successive = .93. Confirmatory factor analysis supports the construct validity of the four PASS components. Criterion-related validity was shown by the strong relations between CAS scores and WJ–R achievement tests, correlations with achievement for special populations, and PASS profiles for children with ADHD, traumatic brain injury, and reading disability. Additionally, the utility of the PASS scores for treatment and educational planning is demonstrated (Naglieri & Das, 1997a).

Anastasi and Urbina (1997) stated,

> Because of its sound theoretical and empirical bases and the careful, large-scale standardization it has undergone, the completion of the CAS has been eagerly anticipated by many test users. … Based on the preliminary evidence that is available regarding the validity of the CAS, it appears that this test will become an important, as well as innovative, tool for the assessment of cognitive status. (p. 233).

SUMMARY

The evaluation of intelligence has played an important role in the clinical and psychoeducational assessment of children, adolescents, and adults. As part of a comprehensive multimethod–multitrait evaluation process, and within the "intelligent testing" framework, the measurement of intelligence provides important quantitative and qualitative diagnostic information. For some specific diagnoses, a measure of intelligence provides an important reference on which other academic or adaptive deficits can be best understood. Intelligence is an inherently complex psychological construct with a foundation of theory deeply rooted in essential and basic human abilities. Personality is integrated with intellectual ability and style. An individual's intelligence cannot be separated from the rest of his or her personality or character makeup.

The clinician can use intelligence tests to evaluate abilities in a context where the demands on the individual are clearly defined and the emergence of conflict-based associations or responses are minimized. In addition, intelligence tests allow the clinician in a relatively brief period of time to observe direct samples of behavior across a variety of intellectual domains.

Intelligence tests have been used in the evaluation of many types of psychological disorders. Such tests have helped improve our understanding of disorders, for example, autism and LDs. Intelligence tests can provide important clinical and psychoeducational information about the organization of an individual's abilities and how such abilities might be affected in the context of a psychological disorder. The strong research and clinical heritage of the Wechsler scales for the past half-century render the latest versions, the WISC–III and WAIS–III, invaluable assessment tools. At the same time, the careful development and theoretical foundations of new tests, such as the KAIT and CAS, make it wise for clinicians to consider alternatives to the traditional Wechsler approach when choosing a cognitive test for a comprehensive test battery.

APPENDIX

WISC–III and WAIS–III

Verbal Subtests

Influenced by Verbal Comprehension and Expression

Information: Questions assess basic factual knowledge. Performance is influenced by cultural opportunities at home, outside reading, and school learning.

Similarities: Compare two verbal concepts and state how they are alike. Performance is influenced by reasoning ability, ability to distinguish essential from nonessential details, verbal expression, and abstract thinking.

Vocabulary: Define words. Performance is influenced by outside reading, school learning, verbal expression, and language development.

Comprehension: Assess social judgment by questions that tap development of moral sense, knowledge of practical information, and evaluation and use of past experiences.

Influenced by Attention, Concentration, Working Memory, and Sequential Processing Arithmetic: Mental arithmetic computation. Performance is influenced by attention span, anxiety, and concentration as well as sequencing ability, numerical facility, and school learning.

Digit Span: Repeat sequences of numbers, read by the examiner, forward and backward. Influenced by attention span, anxiety, distractibility, and short-term auditory memory.

Letter–Number Sequencing (WAIS–III only): Attend to an oral sequence of alternating letters and numbers, and then say the numbers in numerical order, from low to high, and then say the letters in alphabetic sequence. Influenced by attention span, anxiety, distractibility, working memory, flexibility, and visualization.

Performance Subtests

Influenced by Visual–Spatial Abilities, Nonverbal Reasoning, and Visual–Motor Coordination

Picture Completion: Pick out the important missing element from incomplete picture. Influenced by visual perception of meaningful stimuli, distinguishing essential from nonessential detail, and long-term visual memory.

Picture Arrangement: Quickly place scrambled pictures into a sequence that makes sense. Influenced by creativity, anticipation of consequences, and sequencing ability.

Block Design: Quickly place blocks together to imitate a pictured pattern. Influenced by visual–spatial ability, analysis of whole into component parts, and nonverbal concept formation.

Matrix Reasoning (WAIS–III only): Select the multiple-choice option that best completes a complex abstract analogy. Influenced by reasoning ability, fluid thinking, visual–spatial ability, and attention to visual detail.

Object Assembly: Arrange puzzle pieces into complete objects. Influenced by visual–motor coordination and ability to benefit from sensory–motor feedback, anticipation of relation among parts, and flexibility.

Mazes (WISC–III only): Influenced by planning ability, reasoning, and experience solving mazes. A. S. Kaufman (1994) recommends not administering this subtest because of its poor reliability and validity.

Influenced by Rapid Visual–Motor Processing Speed Coding (Digit Symbol/Coding on WAIS–III): Quickly write symbols that are paired with numbers in the appropriately coded boxes. Influenced by paper-and-pencil skill, working under time pressure, sequencing ability, anxiety, distractibility, and psychomotor speed.

Symbol Search: Rapidly scanning visual stimuli to determine whether or not one or two "target" symbols are included in an array of symbols. Influenced by anxiety, distractibility, visual processing speed, visual memory, and working under time pressure.

Attention Deficit Hyperactivity Disorder (ADHD)

As currently defined by the *Diagnostic and Statistical Manual of Mental Disorders* (4th ed. [*DSM–IV*]), ADHD requires children to display either six of nine symptoms of inattention or four of six symptoms of hyperactivity–impulsivity. These children have the most difficulty in situations where they are required to sustain their attention, such as at school. However, to be diagnosed with ADHD, they must manifest symptoms in at least two or more situations (e.g., school, home, sporting activities). Six to nine times more boys are diagnosed with the disorder than girls. Symptoms generally start to appear by age 4, but the disorder is frequently not diagnosed until the child begins school. Learning disabilities and conduct disorder frequently are also diagnosed in children who have ADHD. Treatments usually involve prescribing stimulant medications for the child, such as Ritalin. Drug therapies augmented with behavior modification and parent training are especially helpful.

Conduct Disorder

According to the *DSM–IV* (American Psychiatric Association, 1994), conduct disorder is a consistent way of behaving such that the basic rights of others as well as normal social rules are violated. Children with conduct disorder manifest behaviors such as stealing, lying, running away, truancy from school, physical cruelty, and forcing someone into a sexual activity. Children are generally diagnosed with this disorder between prepuberty and age 17. Many juvenile delinquents are diagnosed with this disorder.

Autism

Autism is a pervasive developmental disorder that severely impacts social, language, and adaptive development. Individuals are generally diagnosed with autism prior to their fourth year of life. About four males to each female have the disorder and about three quarters of afflicted individuals also have mental retardation. Although early theories of autism suggested that it was etiologically due to severe psychological stress experienced in infancy, it is now believed to be due to abnormalities of the central nervous system.

Learning Disabilities

Learning disabilities are a heterogeneous group of neurologically based developmental disorders that result in impaired academic functioning. They are not due to specific sensory loss such as hearing impairment or visual impairment or due to general intellectual delay. Learning disabilities can involve single academic domains such as reading (dyslexia) or multiple academic domains such as reading, spelling, and arithmetic. Children, adolescents, and adults with learning disabilities most frequently require special academic assistance in order to develop their impaired academic ability

REFERENCES

American Psychiatric Association. (1994). *Diagnostic and statistical manual of mental disorders* (4th ed.). Washington, DC: Author.

American Psychological Association. (1990). *Standards for educational and psychological tests and manuals.* Washington, DC: Author.

Anastasi, A., & Urbina, S. (1997). *Psychological testing* (7th ed.). Englewood Cliffs, NJ: Prentice-Hall.

Anastopopolous, A. D., Spisto, M. A., & Maher, M. C. (1994). The WISC–III Freedom from Distractibility factor: Its utility in identifying children with attention deficit hyperactivity disorder. *Psychological Assessment, 6,* 368–371.

Aylward, E., Walker, E., & Bettes, B. (1984). Intelligence in schizophrenia: Meta-analysis of the research. *Schizophrenia Bulletin, 10,* 430–459.

Bartak, L., Rutter, M., & Cox, A. (1975). A comparative study of infantile autism and specific developmental receptive language disorders. *British Journal of Psychiatry, 126,* 127–145.

Binet, A. (1903). L'etude experimentale de l'intelligence [The experimental study of intelligence]. Paris: Schleicher.

Culberton, F. M., Feral, C. H., & Gabby, S. (1989). Pattern analysis of Wechsler Intelligence Scale for Children–Revised profiles of delinquent boys. *Journal of Clinical Psychology, 45,* 651–660.

Das, J. P., Naglieri, J. A., & Kirby, J. R. (1994). *Assessment of cognitive processes: The PASS theory of intelligence.* Boston: Allyn & Bacon.

Elliott, C. D. (1990). *Differential Ability Scales (DAS) administration and scoring manual.* New York: Psychological Corporation.

Freeman, B. J., Lucas, J. C., Forness, S. R., & Ritvo, E. R. (1985). Cognitive processing of high functioning autistic children: Comparing the K–ABC and the WISC–R. *Journal of Psychoeducational Assessment, 4,* 357–362.

Golden, C. J. (1981). *The Luria-Nebraska Children's Battery: Theory and formulation.* In G. W. Hynd, & J. E. Obrzut (Eds.), Neuropsychological assessment of the school-age child. New York: Grune & Stratton.

Groth-Marnat, G. (1997). *Handbook of psychological assessment* (3rd ed.). New York: Wiley.

Hogan, A. E., & Quay, H. C. (1984). Cognition in child and adolescent behavior disorders. *Advances in Clinical Child Psychology, 7,* 1–34.

Horn, J. L. (1989). Cognitive diversity: A framework of learning. In P. L. Ackerman, R. J. Sternberg, & R. Glaser (Eds.), *Learning and individual differences* (pp.61–116). San Francisco: Freeman.

Horn, J. L., & Cattell, R. B. (1966). Refinement and test of the theory of fluid and crystallized intelligence. *Journal of Educational Psychology, 57,* 253–270.

Ishisaka, Y., Murasawa, T., Muramatsu, Y., Kamio, Y., & Toichi, M. (1997). Cognitive deficits of autism based on results of three psychological tests. *Japanese Journal of Child & Adolescent Psychiatry, 38,* 230–246.

Kamphaus, R. W. (1993). *Clinical assessment of children's intelligence.* Boston: Allyn & Bacon.

Kaufman, A. S. (1979). *Intelligent testing with the WISC–R.* New York: Wiley.

Kaufman, A. S. (1990a). *Assessing adolescent and adult intelligence.* Boston: Allyn & Bacon.

Kaufman, A. S. (1990b). The WPPSI–R: You can't judge a test by its colors. *Journal of School Psychology, 28,* 387–394.

Kaufman, A. S. (1993). King WISC the third assumes the throne. *Journal of School Psychology, 31,* 345–354.

Kaufman, A. S. (1994). *Intelligent testing with the WISC–III.* New York: Wiley.

Kaufman, A. S. (1998, August). *What happens to our WAIS–III scores as we age from 16 to 89 years and what do these changes mean for theory and clinical practice?* Invited Division 16 award address presented at the meeting of the American Psychological Association, San Francisco.

Kaufman, A. S., & Horn, J. L. (1996). Age changes on tests of fluid and crystallized intelligence for females and males on the Kaufman Adolescent and Adult Intelligence Test (KAIT) at ages 17 to 94 years. *Archives of Clinical Neuropsychology, 11,* 97–121.

Kaufman, A. S., & Kaufman, N. L. (1983). *Kaufman Assessment Battery for Children: Interpretive manual.* Circle Pines, MN: American Guidance Service.

Kaufman, A. S., & Kaufman, N. L. (1993). *Manual for Kaufman Adolescent & Adult Intelligence Test (KAIT).* Circle Pines, MN: American Guidance Service.

Kaufman, A. S., & Lichtenberger, E. O. (1999). *Essentials of WAIS–III assessment.* New York: Wiley.

Kaufman, J. L. (1995). *Visual and auditory evoked brain potentials, the Hendricksons' pulse train hypothesis, and the fluid and crystallized theory of intelligence.* Unpublished doctoral dissertation, California School of Professional Psychology, San Diego, CA.

Konold, T. R., Kush, J. C., Canivez, G. L. (1997). Factor replication of the WISC–III in three independent samples of children receiving special education. *Journal of Psychoeducational Assessment, 15,* 123–137.

Kuck, J., Lincoln, A., & Heaton, R. K. (1998). *Age related changes in intellectual ability among individuals with autistic disorder.* Manuscript submitted for publication.

Kush, J. C. (1996) Factor structure of the WISC–III for students with learning disabilities. *Journal of Psychoeducational Assessment, 14,* 32–40.

Lezak, M. D. (1995). *Neuropsychological assessment* (3rd ed.). New York: Oxford University Press.

Lincoln, A. J., Courchesne, E., Harms, L., & Allen, M. (1993). Contextual probability evaluation in autistic, receptive developmental language disorder, and control children: Eventrelated brain potential evidence. *Journal of Autism and Developmental Disorders, 23*(l), 37–58.

Lincoln, A. J., Courchesne, E., Kilman, B. A., Elmasian, R., & Allen, M. H. (1988). A study of intellectual abilities in people with autism. *Journal of Autism and Developmental Disorders, 18* (4), 505–524.

Lincoln, A. J., Dickstein, P., Courchesne, E., Tallal, P., & Elmasian, R. (1992). Auditory processing abilities in nonretarded adolescents and young adults with developmental language disorder and autism. *Brain and Language, 43,* 613–622.

Lockyer, L., & Rutter, M. (1970). A 5 to 15 year follow-up study of infantile psychosis: IV. Patterns of cognitive ability. *British Journal of Social and Clinical Psychology, 9,* 152–163.

Lufi, D., Cohen, A., & Parish Plass, J. (1990). Identifying attention deficit hyperactive disorder with the WISC–R and the Stroop Color and Word Test. *Psychology in the Schools, 27,* 28–34.

Luria, A. R. (1980). *Higher cortical functions in man* (2nd ed.). New York: Basic.

McNemar, Q. (1942). *The revision of the Stanford–Binet Scale.* Boston: Houghton Mifflin.

Morgan, A. W., Sullivan, S. A., Darden, C., & Gregg, N. (1997). Measuring the intelligence of college students with learning disabilities: A comparison of results obtained on the WAIS–R and the KAIT. *Journal of Learning Disabilities, 30,* 560–565.

Naglieri, J. A., & Das, J. P. (1997a). *Cognitive Assessment System interpretive handbook*. Chicago: Riverside.

Naglieri, J. A., & Das, J. P. (1997b). *Das Naglieri Cognitive Assessment System*. Chicago: Riverside.

Ohta, M. (1987) Cognitive disorders of infantile autism: A study employing the WISC, spatial relationship, conceptualization and gesture imitations. *Journal of Autism and Developmental Disorders, 17*(l), 45–62.

Piaget, J. (1972). Intellectual evolution from adolescence to adulthood. *Human Development, 15,* 1–12.

Prifitera, A., & Dersh, J. (1993). Base rates of WISC–III diagnostic subtest patterns among normal, learningdisabled, and ADHD samples. In B. A. Bracken & R. S. McCullum (Eds.), *Journal of Psychoeducational Assessment Monograph Series: Advances in Psychoeducational Assessment. Wechsler Intelligence Scale for Children–Third edition* (pp. 43–55). Germantown, TN: Psychoeducational Corporation.

Psychological Corporation. (1997). *WAIS–III and WMS–III technical manual*. New York: Psychological Corporation.

Quay, H. C. (1987). Intelligence. In H. C. Quay (Ed.), *Handbook of juvenile delinquency* (pp. 106–117). New York: Wiley.

Reitan, R. (1985). Relationships between measures of brain function and general intelligence. *Journal of Clinical Psychology, 41,* 245–253.

Roid, G. H., Prifitera, A., & Weiss, L. G. (1993). Replication of the WISC–III factor structure in an independent sample. In B. A. Bracken & R. S. McCallum (Eds.), *Journal of Psychoeducational Assessment monograph series, advances in psychoeducational assessment: Wechsler Intelligence Scale for Children–Third edition* (pp. 6–21). Germantown, TN: Psychoeducational Corporation.

Rose, J., Lincoln, A. J., & Allen, M. (1992). Ability profiles in language impaired and reading disabled children: A comparative analysis. *Developmental Neuropsychology, 8,* 413–426.

Rumsey, J., & Hamburger, S. (1990). Neuropsychological divergence in highlevel autism and severe dyslexia. *Journal of Autism and Developmental Disorders, 20*(2), 155–168.

Sattler, J. M. (1992). *Assessment of children: WISC–III and WPPSI–R supplement*. San Diego: Sattler.

Schwean, V. L., & Saklofske, D. H. (1998). WISC–III assessment of children with attention deficit/hyperactivity disorder (ADHD). In A. Prifitera & D. H. Saklofske (Eds.), *WISC–III: Clinical use and interpretation* (pp. 91–118). New York: Academic Press.

Schwean, V. L., Saklofske, D. H., Yackulic, R. A., & Quinn, D. (1993). WISC–III performance of ADHD children. In B. A. Bracken & R. S. McCallum (Eds.), *Journal of Psychoeducational Assessment monograph series. Advances in psychoeducational assessment Wechsler Intelligence Scale for Children–Third edition* (pp. 56–70). Germantown, TN: Psychoeducational Corporation.

Semrud-Clikeman, M., Hynd, G. W., Lorys, A. R., & Lahey, B. B. (1993). Differential diagnosis of children with ADHD and ADHD/with co-occurring conduct disorder. *School Psychology International, 14,* 361–370.

Shaw, S. R., Swerdlik, M. E., & Laurent, J. (1993). Review of the WISC–III. In B. A. Bracken & R. S. McCallum (Eds.), *Journal of Psychoeducational Assessment monograph series: Advances in psychoeducational assessment: Wechsler Intelligence Scale for Children–Third Edition* (pp. 151–160). Germantown, TN: The Psychoeducational Corporation.

Siegel, D. J., Minshew, N. J., & Goldstein, G. (1996). Wechsler IQ profiles in diagnosis of high-functioning autism. *Journal of Autism & Developmental Disorders, 26,* 389–406.

Sperry, R. W. (1968). Hemisphere deconnection and unity in conscious awareness. *American Psychologist, 23,* 723-733.

Sternberg, R. J. (1993). Rocky's back again: A review of the WISC–III. In B. A. Bracken, & R. S. McCallum (Eds.), *Journal of Psychoeducational Assessment Monograph Series, Advances in psychoeducational assessment. Wechsler Intelligence Scale for Children–Third Edition* (pp. 161–164). Germantown, TN: Psychoeducational Corporation.

Sternberg, R. J., & Kaufman, J. C. (1996). Innovation and intelligence tests: The curious case of the dog that didn't bark. *European Journal of Psychological Assessment, 12,* 167–174.

Sternberg, R. J., & Kaufman, J. C. (1998). Human abilities. *Annual Review of Psychology, 49,* 479–502.

Sutter, E., Bishop, P., & Battin, R. R. (1987). Psychometric screening for attention deficit disorder in a clinical setting. *Journal of Psychoeducational Assessment, 3,* 227–235.

Terman, L. M. (1916). *The measurement of intelligence.* Boston: Houghton Mifflin.

Terman, L. M., & Merrill, M. A. (1937). *Measuring intelligence.* Boston: Houghton Mifflin.

Ward, S. B., Ward, T. J., Jr., Hatt, C. V., Young, D. L., & Mollner, N. R. (1995). The incidence and utility of the ACID, ACIDS, and SCAD profiles in a referred population. *Psychology in the Schools, 32,* 267–276.

Watkins, M. W., Kush, J. C., & Glutting, J. J. (1997). Prevalence and diagnostic utility of the WISC–III SCAD profile among children with disabilities. *School Psychology Quarterly, 12,* 235–248.

Wechsler, D. (1939). *Measurement of adult intelligence.* Baltimore: Williams & Wilkins.

Wechsler, D. (1946). *Manual for the Wechsler–Bellevue Intelligence Scale, Form II.* New York: Psychological Corporation.

Wechsler D. (1949). *Manual for the Wechsler Intelligence Scale for Children (WISC).* New York: Psychological Corporation.

Wechsler D. (1950). Cognitive, conative, and non-intellective intelligence. *American Psychologist, 5,* 78–83.

Wechsler, D. (1955). *Manual for the Wechsler Adult Intelligence Scale (WAIS).* New York: Psychological Corporation.

Wechsler, D. (1958). *The measurement and appraisal of adult intelligence.* Baltimore: Williams & Wilkins.

Wechsler, D. (1974). *Manual for the Wechsler Intelligence Scale for Children—Revised (WISC–R).* New York: Psychological Corporation.

Wechsler, D. (1981). *Manual for the Wechsler Adult Intelligence Scale—Revised (WAIS–R).* New York: Psychological Corporation.

Wechsler, D. (1989). *Manual for the Wechsler Preschool and Primary Scale of Intelligence–Revised (WPPSI–R).* New York: Psychological Corporation.

Wechsler, D. (1991). *Manual for the Wechsler Intelligence Scale for Children: Third edition.* New York: Psychological Corporation.

Wechsler, D. (1997). *Manual for the Wechsler Adult Intelligence Scale: 3rd ed.* New York: The Psychological Corporation.

Wielkiewicz, R. M. (1990). Interpreting low scores on the *WISC–R* third factor: It's more than distractibility. *Journal of Consulting and Clinical Psychology, 2*(1), 91–97.

Wodrich, D. L., & Kush, J. C. (1998). Kaufman Adolescent and Adult intelligence Test (KAIT): Concurrent validity of fluid ability for preadolescents and adolescents with central nervous system disorders and scholastic concerns. *Journal of Psychoeducational Assessment, 16,* 215–225.

Woodcock, R. W., & Johnson, M. B. (1989a). *Woodcock–Johnson Revised, Tests of Achievement: Standard and supplemental batteries.* Chicago: Riverside.

Woodcock, R. W., & Johnson, M. B. (1989b). *Woodcock–Johnson Revised, Tests of Cognitive Ability: Standard and supplemental batteries.* Chicago: Riverside.

Zarski, J. J., Cook, R., West, J., & O'Keefe, S. (1987). Attention deficit disorder: Identification and assessment issues. *American Mental Health Counselors Association Journal, 9*(1), 5–13.

Behavioral Assessment

Steven J. Beck
Ohio State University

Behavioral assessment was first introduced in the clinical literature in the 1960s, derived from the dissatisfaction with the underlying assumptions, conceptual foundations, and methods of psychological assessment prevailing at the time. At that time traditional assessment paradigms, which primarily included medical and psychodynamic traditions, were lumped together, and behavioral assessment was promulgated more for its "difference" and contrasts from those more familiar assessment paradigms. Now, more than 30 years later, the distinction between traditional approaches of assessment and behavioral assessment have become blurred. The 1990s has witnessed a decline in behavioral assessment stridently being declared as a distinct enterprise, and a growing assimilation of its principles and methods are now found in contemporary assessment with children and their families (Mash & Terdal, 1997).

To indicate the impact that behavioral assessment has had on mainstream psychology, two assessment methods associated primarily with behavioral assessment—behavioral observations and self-monitoring—have been used in significant proportions of articles published in the *Journal of Consulting and Clinical Psychology*, considered the premier empirical journal in the field of clinical psychology (Haynes, 1998). A survey of four general purpose journals published in 1993 indicates that approximately one quarter of the articles published in the *Journal of Consulting and Clinical Psychology, Clinical Psychology Review, Psychological Assessment*, and *Journal of Abnormal Psychology*, all well-respected journals, had articles focusing on either behavior therapy procedures, conceptual issues related to behavior therapy, or issues in behavioral assessment (Haynes, 1996). In addition, a survey of doctoral training programs indicates that behavioral assessment is taught in approximately one half of the programs and program directors expected an increase in the teaching of behavioral assessment in the future (Piotrowski & Zalewski, 1993). In short, behavioral assessment is now well integrated into clinical assessment procedures. Hence, although it may no longer serve the same historical utility to highlight "differences" between behavioral assessment and more general psychological assessments because there are now many commonalities, for the purpose of this chapter it is still necessary to articulate distinguishing, core features synonymous with behavioral assessment and underlying assumptions regarding behavior, its determinants, and focus of inquiry.

CORE FEATURES OF BEHAVIORAL ASSESSMENT

First and foremost, the primary goal of behavioral assessment continues to be the identification and measurement of specific problem behaviors (i.e., as opposed to primarily determining a "diagnosis"). The second task involves identifying the functional relation with multiple person or environmental variables that initiate or maintain the identified behavioral problems. Behavioral assessment continues to focus on current (as opposed to historical) behaviors, situations, and environmental factors. Behavioral assessment emphasizes collecting data on multiple modes of behavior, including motoric, verbal, cognitive, and physiological responses, and using multiple informants. As an example, for children, this can include obtaining information from parents, teachers, child-care personnel, and the child. Methods of assessment can include direct observation in naturalistic or analog settings, diverse methods of observational strategies, interviews, ratings by parents and teachers, self monitoring, and self-report measures to gather a composite picture of the target child. Another hallmark of behavioral assessment is that assessments are frequent and ongoing.

The task, then, for an assessor is to derive information from multiple assessment methods with the goal of identifying the controlling variables, the interacting antecedent and consequent events in a child's internal and external environment, that influence the child's problematic behaviors. The heuristic "S-O-R-K-C," originally discussed by Kanfer and Phillips (1970) almost 30 years ago, still serves as a convenient way of organizing relevant classes of assessment information into broad categories of antecedent and consequent events, any of which can be designated as potential targets for treatment.

"S" refers to prior events, or the stimuli or environments that have some functional relationship to the identified problem, such as attempting to discern similar stimulus characteristics across settings that appear relevant to targeted child behaviors. As an example, assessing that a child with a receptive language disorder has difficulty following certain adult requests because the instructions are difficult for the child to understand would serve as a relevant antecedent to the child's targeted behavior of not following instructions.

"O" refers to broad biological aspects of the child and to internal events that reflect representations of past experiences, affect, information-processing mechanisms, and so forth. For example, for a child who experiences a catastrophic event that is life-threatening, such as a hurricane, the catastrophic event typically is relived through play, dreams, or flashbacks. In addition, there are now numerous studies supporting the interaction between biological and social variables in determining child behaviors (e.g., Strayhorn, 1987). Information regarding physical status is also important with children, given the frequent and rapid physical changes that occur throughout childhood and adolescence. The blending of assessment information related to biological and social variables has increased dramatically, primarily due to the increase of behavioral interventions in child health settings (e.g., Johnson et al., 1992).

"R" refers to the responses, which in the early behavioral assessment literature primarily emphasized overt motor behavior. Now, they encompass motor behavior, as well as cognitive–verbal behavior and physiological–emotional behavior.

"K" refers to the contingency relations between behavior and its consequences. Schedules of reinforcement clearly influence responses emitted and constitute an important category of assessment information (Ferster & Skinner, 1953), particularly for children, who are dependent on responses from parents and teachers. For example, it has been suggested that under continuous–reward conditions, the performance of children with attention deficit hyperactivity disorder (ADHD) and that of non-ADHD children may not differ, whereas children with ADHD may display less responsiveness under conditions of partial rewards (Douglas & Parry, 1994).

"C" refers to the consequences of behavior that typically include a wide variety of social and nonsocial events that vary on their positive or negative valence. Consequences are usually embedded within natural social exchanges and have important affect components. For example, a whiny child experiences the consequences of adult attention, or a preschool child hits another child to acquire his favorite toy.

However, there are practical problems with implementing the core features of behavioral assessment. The tenets of collecting direct behavioral observations from multiple informants and assessing multiple channels of behaviors, and done on an ongoing basis, are timely and costly, particularly for practicing clinicians. Surveys with clinicians identified with behaviorally oriented associations (e.g., Association for the Advancement of Behavior Therapy) indicate that the clinical interview is the most frequently used assessment method (Piotrowski & Lubin, 1990). In another survey of clinicians, the interview was the primary assessment method used, regardless of the theoretical orientation of the assessor (Guevremont & Spiegler, 1990). In their survey, objective "personality" questionnaires and self-reported inventories were used by more than 50% of clinicians, regardless of orientation, whereas self-monitoring was used by half of behaviorally oriented clinicians, with direct behavioral observations in a structured or natural setting used by 15% to 25% of behaviorally orientated clinicians.

Although multiple methods and multiple informants are ideal when assessing a child and his or her family, the reality is that clinicians are pressed for time, have limited resources, and typically have to deal with managed care companies that will not reimburse for such comprehensive assessment. From personal experience, I am more likely to employ behavioral observations of a child at the child's school or even home when there are available resources (e.g., graduate students) than when I see similar children and their families in my private practice. On the other hand, implicit in criticisms concerning that failure to translate features of behavioral assessment into clinical practice has been the tendency to equate all behavioral assessment exclusively with direct behavioral observations. Yet, another recent survey suggests that cognitive–behavioral practitioners indeed use a wide variety of assessment procedures, and the use of direct behavioral observations and rating scales has increased with practitioners over the past 15 years (Elliott, Miltenberg, Kaster-Bundgaard & Lumley, 1996).

FUNCTIONAL ANALYSIS IN BEHAVIORAL ASSESSMENT

Although behavioral assessment is considered an objective attempt to identify and measure meaningful behavioral, cognitive, or physiological responses and their controlling variables, functional analysis refers to the testing or verifying of hypotheses about controlling variables (Cone, 1997). There appears to be some confusion and definitional disagreements about the term "functional analysis" and the necessity of the concept to be considered separately from the general concepts of behavioral assessment (see Haynes & O'Brien, 1990). For instance, the assessment methods used for conducting functional analysis are the same as those used in behavioral assessment. To add to the misunderstanding between behavioral assessment and functional analysis, several authors have used various terms to describe the process of identifying controlling variables for problem behaviors. Terms such as "case formulation" (Persons, 1989), "functional behavioral analysis" (Wince, 1982), "functional assessment" (Sisson & Taylor, 1993), and "behavioral analysis" (Schulte, 1992) are some of the diverse and confusing terms used to address the integration of assessment information into an individualized case conceptualization. The term functional analysis refers to the emphasis in the behavioral assessment paradigm on "identifying important, controllable functional relationships applicable to a set of target behaviors for an individual client" (Haynes & O'Brien, 1990, p. 654). Consequently, functional analysis plays a central role in the overarching goal of behavioral assessment.

For example, the difference between a functional analysis approach toward assessment compared to the more common structural approach is best highlighted when discussing the *Diagnostic and Statistical Manual of Mental Disorders–IV* (4th ed.[*DSM–IV*], American Psychiatric Association, 1994). The *DSM–IV* is a classification of behavior disorders (or syndromes) adhering to a structuralist (as opposed to a functional) approach. Symptoms in the *DSM–IV* are generally clustered according to topography covariation, which is taken as evidence that there is some common "underlying" variable that binds the behaviors together to form a distinct disorder. For example, in the *DSM–IV*, oppositional–defiant disorder (ODD) for children is characterized as a "recurrent pattern of negativistic, defiant, disobedient, and hostile behaviors toward authority figures" (p. 91). Four of the eight following similar topographic behaviors must be present for at least 6 months for a child to be diagnosed with ODD: losing his or her temper, arguing with grown-ups, actively defying or not complying with adults' rules or requests, deliberately annoying other people, blaming others for their mistakes, being touchy or easily annoyed by others, exhibiting anger and resentment, and showing spite or vindictiveness.

However, from a functional analysis standpoint, understanding that a child presents with sufficient behaviors to be classified as ODD does not necessarily assist the assessor in identifying which important, controlling variables initiate or maintain the specific behaviors. Behaviors that constitute a child to be classified as ODD can be produced by very different causes (McMahon, 1994). For this reason, classifying behaviors together on the basis of similar topographic characteristics is not likely to lead to a straightforward understanding of the causes of these behaviors. Let's say that a knowledgeable assessor–clinician assesses a child with the ODD topography of behaviors and identifies the most frequent behavior problem to target for treatment, for example, noncompliance to parents' requests. The assessor can take a "nomothetic" (i.e., understanding causal relations for a problem behavior across clients) causal model of ODD behaviors by positing that inept parental discipline and child coercion are key causal variables, based on the seminal work of Patterson (1982). However, a functional analysis is idiographic (i.e., addressing causal relationships for behavior problems of individual clients). As such, a thorough assessment may indicate that specific inept parenting may not be causal for this particular child when other important functions are identified, such as the parents' divorcing and consequently being unavailable to attend or respond to the child properly.

Despite the logical basis and intuitive appeal of a functional analysis approach, it is currently limited (Haynes, 1998). Specifically, methods for selecting the best assessment instruments to develop a functional analysis for a particular client have not yet been delineated. Although general parameters for clinical assessment are well established—such as sufficient psychometric properties of assessment instruments, the use of more than one assessment method, and the use of multiple informants—there are no clear procedures for selecting assessment methods and instruments to develop a functional analysis for a particular child and his or her family. Relatedly, guidelines for integrating and prioritizing assessment data from several assessment sources have yet to be developed.

In many ways, a functional analysis is an ideal toward which all assessment paradigms should strive. Although common childhood disorders have an array of assessment methods available to them (see Mash & Terdal, 1997), there is not yet a standardized procedure to guide the assessor to verify which controlling variables account for the multitude of childhood behavior problems. Sisson and Taylor (1993) and Persons and Fresco (1996) suggested a "multiple gating" or "funnel" approach, in which more precisely focused assessment instruments are then selected on the basis of less costly, broadly focused instruments.

CONCEPTUAL FOUNDATIONS

Behavioral assessment is based on a set of underlying assumptions regarding behavior, its determinants, and focus of inquiry. These assumptions help organize and guide the child behavioral assessor's thinking and planning, the type of assessment methods used, and the search for causal explanations of target behaviors and possible intervention strategies. The purpose of this section is to examine four interrelated behavioral assessment assumptions as they relate to children: (a) a causal model emphasizing social–environmental determinants of behavior, (b) reciprocal determinism, (c) the importance of temporal contiguity of behavior, and (d) a reductionist view of childhood behavior problems. These conceptual underpinnings are not meant to be exhaustive of assumptions that guide behavior assessment, and the interested reader is referred to Haynes (1991).

A Social–Environmental Causal Model

A primary assumption that strongly influences and shapes the methods and focus of behavioral assessment is the view that determinants of behavior are mostly accounted for by social–environmental events. The determinants of behavior include response contingencies, situational contexts, antecedent cues, and associative learning experiences. A fundamental premise of behavioral assessment is that it is possible to account for a significant proportion of variance in the occurrence and maintenance of childhood behavior problems by assessing antecedent and consequent social–environmental events, particularly within learning paradigms. Within a broad social learning framework that takes into account cognitive mediated variables and modeling, behavioral clinicians can assess situational contexts and antecedental cues that are presumed to overate by classical conditioning or operant conditioning paradigms. As an example, behavioral assessors can explain why a young child who previously had been frightened in a thunderstorm (a conditioned stimulus) would become fearful and agitated (a conditioned response) when he sees a severe thunderstorm warning flashing on his television screen. Similarly, an operate conditioning paradigm readily explains how a child is negatively reinforced for his whining when his mother gives him a command to put away his toys and the mother eventually withdraws the request because of her son's aversive response.

Reciprocal Determinism

Children are too often viewed as passive recipients of environmental stimuli. The premise of behavioral assessment is that children can be active arrangers and determiners of their environment. Children are viewed as both strongly influenced by and powerful shapers of their environment. This bidirectional child–environment interaction is exemplified by the New York Longitudinal Study (Thomas, Chess, & Birch, 1976). In this ongoing study, 136 children from middle- and upper-middle-income families have been assessed since birth. The investigators report that a sample of children from their study have been identified as "difficult temperament" children. These children, who comprise approximately 10% of the sample, present with characteristics since birth as strong emotional reactivity, a general negative mood, and difficulty adjusting to new situations. Thomas et al. reported that by the age of 10, the majority of difficult temperament children appear to present with psychological adjustment problems. This study illustrates that largely regardless of family contextual factors and parenting styles, these children apparently interact with their environment in such a way as to impact negatively on themselves. Obviously, the mechanisms through which person–environmental interaction operates are multiple and complex, yet the presumption of reciprocal determinism is that the manner in which a child interacts with his or her environment affects his or her environment, that in turn, affects how the child thinks, feels, and behaves.

Temporal Contiguity of Determinants

Behavioral assessment emphasized the importance of determinants in close temporal proximity to the targeted behavior. There is an assumption that a greater proportion of variance in a child's behavior can be accounted for by reference to current rather than historical social–environmental influences. The de-emphasis on distal determinants in understanding childhood psychopathology should not be construed that behavioral assessors minimize earlier, historical determinants. It is hard to argue that long-standing aversive antecedental conditions that infringe on a child, such as marital distress, poverty, parental unemployment, or parental psychopathology, do not, in significant proportions, account for childhood adjustment problems. However, the child behavior treatment literature is replete with studies that have demonstrated clinically meaningful child behavior changes by focusing exclusively on current, contemporaneous interactional processes, for example, between parents and the target child. In fact, most naturalistic and analogue observations discussed in the next section are employed to detect ongoing, current determinants of proximal social–environmental events that occur with the target child toward his family, peers, and classmates.

A Reductionist View of Childhood Behavior Problems

Closely related to the concept of temporal contiguity is the position that behavior assessment attempts to take a reductionistic approach in the search for causal models of childhood behavior problems. This approach searches for increasingly smaller and narrower explanations of causal chains in the child's social–environmental interactions. A potential problem with the reductionist approach is the mistaken position that the most obvious, observable, least inferential cause of an event is the ultimate cause of a child's problematic behavior. In a car collision, for example, one car causes damage to a second car immediately in front of it. It is obvious, however, that the movement of that car is caused by another car behind it, and back to the car that began the collision. Even the car that began the chain cannot necessarily be thought of as the ultimate cause of the accident, because excess speed, faulty brakes, bad weather, or a combination of factors could account for the real source of the car collision.

As mentioned earlier, the behavioral assessor would not disagree with the premise that distal events may be important, powerful influences of childhood psychopathology. Parental psychopathology, such as long-standing maternal depression or paternal alcohol abuse, may be an impetus for the "chain car collision" in explaining a child's behavior problems, yet the child behavior assessor tends not to focus as much on the disorganizing or deleterious effects of such broad, negative effects (except perhaps to strongly encourage such parents to seek their own treatment). Instead, the behavioral clinician attempts to focus on "the car that causes damage to the last car in the collision chain" by attempting to search for more immediate, precise, and observable behaviors (e.g., such as discrete parent–child interactions) that currently may be maintaining the child's behavior problems.

METHODS OF BEHAVIORAL ASSESSMENT

Although the boundaries of behavioral and traditional assessment methods are increasingly diffuse as psychologists become less rigid and more practical in the use of assessment methods, a useful distinction is found in understanding differences between indirect and direct assessment methods. Indirect assessment procedures collect information about relevant behaviors that are obtained at a time and place different from where the actual problematic behaviors occur. Clinical interviews, ratings, and checklists provide descriptions in which a significant person in the child's environment (parent or teacher) provides information about a child's behavior based on current or retrospective observations. Such assessment methods are considered indirect, in that the relevant child behaviors are neither observed nor recorded by the assessor, and others provide information regarding the child's behaviors based on immediate past or even historical observations. Children's self-report instruments generally involve a child's retrospective rating of attitudes, feelings, and behaviors and as such, are also considered indirect methods of assessment.

Direct assessment procedures typically allow for the assessment of clinically relevant behaviors at the actual time and place of occurrence. These assessment methods are naturalistic observations. A full discussion of the methodological issues surrounding these assessment methods is beyond the scope of this chapter. However, direct methods, although perhaps intuitively appearing more valid than indirect assessment methods, contain several sources of error, such as problems with observer bias, reactivity, and generalizability. As mentioned previously, direct assessment procedures are often difficult to implement due to time, cost, and practical constraints. Consequently, each assessment method, direct or indirect, should be viewed as complementary to each other method, with each providing slightly different and potentially valuable information.

DIRECT ASSESSMENT METHODS

Naturalistic Observations

The sine qua non of behavioral assessment is the direct observation of a child's behavior in his or her natural environment. Naturalistic observation is the systematic monitoring and recording of a representative sample of a child's behavior in the environment where the behaviors have been identified as being problematic. Direct observation of problem behaviors in natural settings (such as homes or schools) played an important role in the initial development of behavioral assessment (Foster & Cone, 1986). The greatest advantage of invivo observation is that problem behaviors can be observed in their customary situational context, leading directly to hypotheses about possible controlling variables. Examples of common naturalistic observations are observing a child's "on task" behavior in a classroom or observing a child's interaction with peers on a playground. The frequent use of naturalistic observations, whereby target behaviors are optionally defined and are observed by trained, impartial observers who are not part of the child's natural environment, reflects the emphasis on minimizing the inferential nature of more indirect assessment methods. Furthermore, because deviant child behaviors rarely occur in an environmental vacuum, naturalistic observations typically allow for the observation and recording of possible antecedent and consequent factors that may be maintaining the problematic behaviors.

Naturalistic observations can provide information on behavior frequencies as well as length of duration. There are a variety of techniques for recording behaviors, but the most often used procedure appears to involve time sampling, in which observation periods are divided into circumscribed time frames (e.g, five 10-minute intervals in the morning and afternoon to observe the frequency, duration, and antecedent conditions of a child's disruptive behavior in the classroom). Trained observers can then record the occurrence of preselected behaviors within each interval. Depending on the target behavior being recorded, target behaviors can be recorded in frequency tallies (e.g., the number of times the child interrupts the teacher or other children in the classroom), response chains (e.g., recording who the child is most often likely to interrupt and under which classroom conditions), or observer ratings (e.g., rating the child at the end of each time interval on a 1 to 5 scale, with 1 representing no disruptive behavior and 5 denoting extreme disruptive behavior). Naturalistic observations have been used with a wide range of target behaviors, populations, and settings. Naturalistic observations have been instrumental in understanding such well-known clinical phenomena as the coercive process that occurs between conduct disordered children and their families by directly observing parent–child interactions in the home of conduct disordered children (Patterson, 1982). Another example where naturalistic observations have made contributions to understanding childhood psychopathology is the systematic observation of the differing types of aggression displayed by rejected children toward their peers in the classroom and playground (e.g., Dodge, 1983).

Although naturalistic observations are the least inferential of all assessment methods, they should not necessarily be viewed as better than other methods of assessment. In fact, potential limitations of direct behavioral observation preclude its widespread use in clinical practice. One potential problem with observational methods is "reactivity" (Tryon, 1998): Individuals tend to behave differently when they know they are being observed. However, research indicates that reactivity can be minimized by decreasing the intrusiveness of the observers and allowing individuals a period of adaptation before recording behaviors. Another potential problem with naturalistic observations is a phenomenon called "observer drift" or "observer bias." In this phenomenon, trained observers gradually "drift" from recording the preselected target behaviors, thereby threatening the validity of the observations. Although ongoing training sessions can minimize this potential source of error, recruiting, training, and then retraining observer–coders for naturalistic observations is expensive, often cumbersome, and thus not always practical in day-to-day child clinic settings. The validity of observations, denoting that the observations measure what they are intended to measure, can be influenced by many factors, including the comprehensiveness of the coding system, the number of observations conducted, and the extent to which different situations relevant to the problem behaviors are adequately sampled (Tyron, 1998). Hence, the most practical difficulty with direct observation is that it is expensive and time-consuming, which consequently prevents this method from often being used in day-to-day clinical practice.

Analogue Observations

Analogue observations involve the direct evaluation of children's behavior in settings that are structured to increase the occurrence of specific target behaviors. Typical analogue observations involve requesting a child to role-play a behavior (e.g., attempting to join in a basketball game on the playground) or a parent–child interaction in a structured setting in which specific instructions are given (e.g., having a parent request the child to clean up the playroom). Analogue observations are particularly efficient and useful when the target behavior is of low frequency or the assessor wants to standardize or better control the situation to elicit relevant target behaviors relative to other children or families. Similar to naturalistic observations, the measurement method most often employed in analogue situations involves short time samples and the identification of specific, predetermined behaviors recorded within those intervals by trained observers or taped for later observation and recording.

Analogue observations have been instrumental in deriving clinically rich findings related to child behavior problems. For example, Dodge, McClaskey, and Feldman (1985) developed an empirically based taxonomy of social situations that has successfully differentiated children identified by teachers as "socially competent" from children identified as "socially incompetent" based on children's analogue performance on five social situations: entry into a peer group, responding to peer provocation, responding to a school failure or school success, conforming to social expectations, and responding to teacher expectations. Similarly, based on analogue observations of child–mother semistructured interactions, Forehand and his colleagues (Griest et al., 1982) identified parental behaviors that increase the probability of noncompliant child behaviors. Subsequently, Forehand and McMahon (1981) developed a parent training program that reduces child oppositionality and increases positive parent–child interactions as well as parent satisfaction of childrearing.

The two greatest threats to the validity of analogue observations are the reactive nature of the observational process and the issue of external validity. It is well known that the presence of an observer affects behavior and that several observational sessions may be required before reactive effects are reduced. In addition, child behavioral assessors assume that analogue situations closely mimic the relevant behaviors in the target child's more natural environment. However, concurrent validity, or the degree of correspondence between contrived stimuli and real-life problems they represent, may not be great and has rarely been tested. For this reason, analogue methods have been used sparingly.

Participant Observations

An excellent alternative to when a target child may be reactive to external observers is participant observation. Participant observation involves an observer who is normally a part of the child's everyday environment, such as a parent, teacher, or even another child, such as a sibling, who monitors and records selected behaviors exhibited by the target child. Participant observation has certain advantages over naturalistic observations. It is an inexpensive method of collecting assessment data, particularly with the recording of low-rate behavior, such as stealing. Participant observation also has the obvious advantage over analogue observations of being recorded in the child's natural environment. Although this assessment method may appear to be promising, participant observation is subject to the sources of potential error found in naturalistic and analogue observations that can limit its utility. For example, participant observations may be particularly susceptible to observer bias and observer inaccuracy. The presumed sensitivity of this assessment method accounts for the fact that participant observations have been used in research on children's behavior problems as a secondary rather than primary outcome measure.

Self-Observations

Self-observation is another direct method of assessment that requires a child to observe his or her own behaviors in the natural environment and then record their occurrence. Self-observation has the clear advantages of being cost-efficient and portable (the child can record his or her behaviors anywhere). Self-observation also can reduce the measured error associated with retrospective self-report methods. Thus, although this method has the unique advantage of having a child record his or her behavior without having to rely on observations of others, this fact also raises important validity issues. For example, for self-observation to be valid, the child must be aware of and discriminate between the presence or absence of specific target behaviors. Second, the occurrence of the response must be recorded systematically, which has been done with various types of recording devices such as record books, checklist forms, counters, and so forth. With children, successful self-monitoring is facilitated through the use of uncomplicated recording procedures for simple, well-defined behaviors (such as fighting with siblings or using profanity). Reinforcement contingencies for accurate self-observation tend to increase the overall accuracy of the method. Specific methods of self-observation reported in the literature have varied considerably, depending on the characteristics of the child, the types of target behavior recorded, and aspects of the setting in which the observation takes place. As an example, academic settings, and in particular classroom behavior and performance, frequently have used self-observation as an assessment method. Self-observation is another hallmark of the behavioral assessment, and, as such, a significant amount of research has been conducted with this assessment method (see Shapiro & Cole, 1993, for a review). Studies generally suggest that children as young as 8 or 9 years of age can be reliable and accurate recorders of their own behavior, but that self-monitoring may result in behavior change due to the self-observation process itself and not necessarily due to treatment interventions. In short, self-monitoring has been found useful, although basically as a secondary assessment method, for a wide range of child behavior problems. In summary, even though problems related to their validity exist, behavioral observations are highly useful strategies and represent the hallmark of child behavioral assessment.

INDIRECT METHODS

The clinical interview is the most frequently used and the primary source of information about an identified child's problem (Guevremeont & Spiegler, 1990), yet it is the least frequently researched assessment method. The behavioral interview is a semistructured interaction between clients and the assessor for the purpose of ascertaining a preliminary model of controlling factors related to target behaviors, to select settings and methods of further assessment, and to implement treatments and evaluations of treatment success (Haynes, 1996). The following goals are part of a behavioral interview:

1. Establish good rapport with the target child or adolescent and his or her parents.
2. Gather adequate information about parental and the target child's concerns, expectations, and goals.
3. Gather sufficient evidence about the child's presenting problems.
4. Assess parental perceptions and feelings about the child or adolescent's problems.
5. Elicit relevant historical information.
6. Assess cognitive–mediational potential.
7. Identify reinforcers for the target child or adolescent.
8. Educate the parents and child with respect to the nature of the target behavior problems.
9. Obtain informed consent.
10. Communicate clearly about the procedure and goals of the assessment and ensuing treatment.

The behavioral interview, compared to the more traditional assessment interview, is more likely to focus on current behavior and its determinants and current child–environment interactions. Although the interview often may be supplemented by other assessment methods, it is generally considered the indispensable part of the assessment strategy.

The behavioral interview has several unique advantages over other assessment methods. The flexibility of the interview allows the psychologist to collect either broad-based information (e.g., asking a couple how they believe their marital relationship affects their child's problematic behaviors) or very narrow, specific information (e.g., asking a mother how she "grounds" her adolescent when he or she comes home late from his or her curfew). The interpersonal, social interaction inherent in an interview process may make parents or the target child more likely to divulge relevant information. The flexibility inherent in the interview allows the clinician to build a relationship with the child and his or her family and to obtain information that otherwise might not be revealed. Finally, the interview allows the assessor an opportunity to observe directly a parent and child's social behavior, although such observations are more similar to analogue observations.

Like all assessment methods, behavioral interviews have sources of error. Major threats to the validity of information derived from an interview format include the veracy of the participants retrospective information, the susceptibility to participants bias, and the demand by the interviewee to respond in a socially desirable (but erroneous) manner.

One of the recent major advances in assessment has been the development of structured interviews for the purpose of providing differential diagnosis of children's presenting problems and to assess the severity of symptoms associated with diagnostic categories (Morrison, 1988). An example of a better known structured clinical interview pertaining to children is the Diagnostic Interview for Children and Adolescents–Revised (DICA; Welner, Reich, Herjanic, Jung, & Amado, 1987). The DICA involves separate interviews for the child and his or her parents pertaining to the duration, content, course, and severity of specific child symptoms displayed by the child.

Structured interviews have advantages over more unstructured clinical interviews. For example, they have shown to be more reliable than unstructured interviews, and thorough information is gathered about the presence or absence of specific symptoms presented by the targeted child or adolescent (Morrison, 1988). However, they have important disadvantages as well, particularly for behaviorally oriented clinicians, such as not providing information about contextual factors related to problem behaviors. The use of structured interviews typically is confined to clinical situations where a precise diagnosis is required, such as in treatment studies of children experiencing similar psychological disorders.

Ratings and Checklists

Ratings and checklists are probably the second-most frequently used behavioral assessment method for identifying children's behavior problems. These paper-and-pencil measures usually are completed by an adult, are easy to administer, and can encompass a wide range of items quickly. Paper-and-pencil measures are generally perceived as providing information that is more global than other assessment methods. Other methods, such as interviews or naturalistic or analogue observations, allow for more flexibility and more subjective impressions compared to rating scales and checklists. Yet, ratings and checklists are ideal for identifying broad areas of child behavior problems and can ensure that significant areas not always covered in interview or observational methods are sampled. Another advantage of paper-and-pencil measures is that they often contain norms and traditionally have made attempts to emphasize psychometric properties, such as reliability and validity.

Cone (1998) stated that four types of validity should be demonstrated in acceptable checklists and rating scales. First, an instrument should demonstrate predictive validity (sometimes referred to as "criterion-related validity") which reflects the degree to which scores on an instrument accurately predict future performance on some relevant outcome or criterion measure. The second type of validity, concurrent validity, is the degree of relation between scores on an instrument compared to similar paper-or-pencil or other assessment methods at approximately the same time. The third type of validity is content validity, that measures how well items on the rating and checklists adequately represent what the investigator intends to measure. The fourth type of validity, and the most elusive, is construct validity, which is the extent to which an instrument measures a theoretical construct or trait (e.g., anxiety). Construct validity is established by correlating test scores derived from a particular paper-and-pencil measure with similar and dissimilar ratings and checklists and other assessment methods.

Two well-known and frequently used rating scales and checklists for children are the Child Behavior Checklist (CBCL; Achenbach, 1991) and the Conners Teacher Rating Scale (CTRS; Conners, 1990). The CBCL records in a standardized format the behavioral problems and competencies of children aged 4 to 18, as reported by a child's parent or teacher. The CBCL is unique because it reflects adaptive competencies, such as peer relationships and completing household chores, as well as behavior problems. The CBCL contains 113 items and uses a weighted scoring system with a three-step response (e.g., not true, somewhat or sometimes true, and very often true for each item). The CBCL is preferred by many child clinicians because it has separate norms for boys and girls at three developmental stages, ages 4 to 5, 6 to 11, and 12 to 18.

The CTRS has been widely used for both research and clinical purposes in the child clinical literature. The CTRS is completed by the child's teacher and consists of 39 items, a shorter form consists of 28 items. The CTRS also provides age and gender norms. The CTRS was specifically developed to aid in the identification of children with hyperactive characteristics and to evaluate drug treatment interventions. However, the CTRS is also recognized as being able to identify social and behavior problems in the classroom setting.

Self-Report Instruments

Of the various behavioral assessment methods, children's self-report has received the least attention and empirical support. The primary reason for the underutilization of children's self-report measures is that children are not viewed as being capable of accurately reporting their psychological state. Self-report measures often have been eschewed because of the apparent lack of correspondence between self-report measures and observable behaviors. However, it is now recognized that a child's perception of his or her problems can be a valuable complement to other assessment methods. Furthermore, the lack of agreement between child self-report measures and other assessment methods does not necessarily suggest that one method is more accurate than the other; instead, it suggests that each method taps a different dimension of multifaceted problems.

Two popular child self-report measures are the Children's Depression Inventory (CDI; Kovacs, 1992) and the Perceived Competence Scale (PCS; Harter, 1982). Within the last decade, no other area in child clinical psychology has received more attention than depression in children. The CDI is the standardized child self-report measure of dysphoria. The CDI is a 27-item severity measure of depression based on the well-known Beck Depression Inventory used with adults. Each of the 27 items consists of three sentences designed to range from mild to fairly severe and clinically significant depression. Kovacs reported that the instrument is suitable for children and adolescents from age 8 to 17, but research has been done with the CDI with first- and second-grade children when items are read aloud. Overall, the CDI has been shown to be reliable, valid, and a clinically useful instrument for children and adolescents.

The PCS is a self-report measure that assesses children's perceived competence across cognitive, social, and physical domains. Unlike other self-esteem measures that just derive a global measure of self-worth, the PCS provides information on three skill subscales, as well as a fourth independent subscale, general self-worth. The PCS is a 28-question format presented in such a manner to offset the tendency of children to respond in socially desirable responses. The PCS can be used for children aged 8 to 14, although the measure typically needs to be read to 8- to-10-year-old children who are poor readers. The PCS also presents with acceptable psychometric properties, and, although more frequently used for research purposes, this instrument can be valuable clinically because it assesses multifactorial dimensions of children's self-concept.

In summary, a variety of child self-report measures is available. Self-reports should be used with appropriate caution but can be used as an index of change following treatment.

SPECIAL CONSIDERATIONS OF BEHAVIOR ASSESSMENT OF CHILDREN

Developing children represent a unique population to assess. The most distinguishing characteristic of children is developmental change. The child clinician's task is made even more difficult because the most noteworthy characteristic of children's change is that it is often rapid and uneven. The task for a child psychologist is to assess children's level of functioning within different developmental domains (e.g., emotional, cognitive, social, physical) and their patterns of coping in relation to major developmental tasks (e.g., academic mastery, autonomy, self-control; Mash & Terdal, 1997). In fact, children are identified as needing psychological intervention in relation to their successes or failures in negotiating normative developmental expectations and demands.

The pervasiveness of developmental change and growth in children also suggests the future need to assess patterns of behavior over time. One of the tasks of behavioral assessment is to determine which aspect of a child's functioning is unique to specific contexts and which are cross-situational. For example, does a child who is assessed as being withdrawn and lacking friends in school present in a similar manner in the neighborhood or when he is playing on an organized baseball team?

Furthermore, from a diagnostic perspective exemplified by the DSM–IV nosology, childhood disorders are viewed as residing in the child rather than in the ongoing and reciprocal relationship between the child and the larger social system in which the child functions. Most assessment procedures focus on the individual child. Historically, the assessment of children has underappreciated the sensitivity of contextual factors and the give-and-take-behavior of a growing child. Children function in home, school, in afterschool programs, and in more formal (e.g., Cub Scouts, the soccer team) and informal (e.g., with neighborhood children) peer groups. These global settings are understudied and rarely targeted for assessment. For example, assessment information about sibling relationships, school or classroom environments, and even in the classification of families that may have important treatment implications, to name a few, is lacking in the child assessment literature.

Another important consideration when assessing children is the fact that children and usually adolescents are not self-referred; they typically are referred to child clinicians by parents, often based on recommendations made by teachers or physicians. As such, the child behavioral clinician may find it necessary to obtain descriptions from a variety of adults about the child's difficulties. Besides the parents being the primary informer, it is not uncommon for behavioral clinicians to collect information in interview format or to recruit as participant observers teachers, school principals, probation officers, pediatricians, and siblings. The inclusion of these additional sources is time-consuming and complicates the assessment process but is an indispensable part of the child behavior assessment process.

FUTURE DIRECTIONS

The introduction of technological advances, including computers, the Internet, and the World Wide Web, during both data-gathering and decision-making phases of assessment holds enormous promise and seems appropriate for discussion under the reading of future directions. Computer-aided interviews and questionnaires can facilitate the acquisition of client self-report data. More important for the goals and focus of behavioral assessment, computers can simplify the collection and analysis of behavioral observations and self-monitoring data (Farrell, 1991). Another core feature of behavioral assessment, ongoing or time-series assessments, lends itself readily to such technological advances as hand-held computers. Hand-held computers can enhance the clinical applicability of self-monitoring. For example, one study taught a fifth-grade boy to use a desk-top computer to monitor his out-of-seat behavior (Tombari, Fitzpatrick, and Childress, 1985). Since behavioral assessment emphasizes the use of minimally inferential assessment methods, direct measurement of a client's behavior is preferred to retrospective reports. Tyron (1991) has described instrument-assisted data collection that can facilitate the measurement of responses in the natural environment. As an example, actometers can provide an aggregated measure of motor activity and be useful in the clinical assessment of children diagnosed with ADHD, where motor activity is an important dependent variable.

As mentioned earlier when discussing functional analysis, there are potentially numerous variables and interactions that could be assessed with clinic-referred children or within disturbed family systems. However, child behavior assessors have not yet developed empirically validated decision rules to determine what factors should be assessed by what methods. Similarly, the area of child behavior assessment needs to develop assessment strategies, not as endpoints solely for the purpose of assessing the child or adolescent, but rather as prerequisites for designing and evaluating effective and efficient services for children, adolescents, and their families. As an example, multisystemic therapy (MST) is a package of different interventions based on a family systems approach for conduct-disordered adolescents and their families (Henggeler & Borduin, 1990). Treatment procedures are used "as needed" to address either the adolescent, the parent, the entire family, and even more broad-based community concerns, such as providing part-time employment for the identified adolescent or supervised activities at a community recreation center after school or in evenings when the adolescent may likely be unsupervised. Multiple assessments are made in MST recognizing that the identified adolescent is embedded in multiple systems, including the family (immediate and extended family members), peers, schools, and the surrounding neighborhood. Future treatment studies need to develop similar heuristic assessment procedures that lend themselves to the multiple settings in which children and adolescents and their families operate.

Even more rarely considered in the child behavioral assessment literature is the family perspective of child interventions. Consumer satisfaction, quality of life, and overall family functioning outcomes are lacking in the clinical child literature. For example, long standing notions of what is therapeutic (and what is not) guide our often too narrow conceptualizations of psychological treatment for children and their families. When asked to identify the most helpful aspect of treatment, families receiving various interventions describe "respite care" for the identified child as the single most valued component of treatment (Jensen, Hibbs, & Pilkonis, 1996). Ignoring such important feedback risks rendering psychological treatment approaches as unappreciated or not relevant. More globally, child behavior assessment also needs to address economic factors associated with treatments as critical outcome factors. In the era of managed care, reduced funding, and limited resources, there is a need to develop interventions that are flexible, sensible, cost-efficient, and palatable to families. Just how cost-effective is it to develop current assessment and treatment programs identifying at-risk 5-year-old preschool children and their families compared to future costs associated with specialized schools or additional interventions for these children and their families when the children are 12 years old? It is now imperative that studies compare the actual cost in dollars of children who receive such early interventions and similar at-risk children who do not. Child and educational specialists may be surprised to find that such costly "early intervention" programs do not necessarily defray additional "costs" that are required for specific children and their families in future years. Yet, even such seemingly discouraging findings inevitably would yield rich assessment information that would provide needed information about implementing better or more cost-efficient future intervention programs in the future.

Finally, child behavioral assessment, with few exceptions (e.g., Forehand & Kotchick,1996), have not considered ethnicity or cultural customs as critical factors in evaluating children and families. According to recent Census data, approximately 25% of the U.S. population belongs to ethnic minority groups. (U.S. Bureau of the Census, 1992a). Projections into the next century estimate the population of the non-Hispanic White population in the United States will drop from 76% in 1990 to 53% in 2050 (U.S. Bureau of the Census, 1992b). Clearly, as ethnic minority groups continue to represent larger percentages of the U.S. population, it becomes increasingly likely that child behavior therapists will encounter someone from an ethnic culture different from their own as clients. Moreover, the likelihood is increased by the fact that ethnic minorities are more likely to be over represented in the lower socioeconomic strata (Aponte & Crouch, 1995), placing children at higher risk for the development of externalizing behavior problems, which is the most common referral to child clinics (McGuire & Earls, 1991). There currently is a dearth of assessment information on child and parent behaviors in ethnic minority families. For example, are well-known instruments appropriate or relevant to various cultural groups? Are wording changes needed? Forehand and Kotchick (1996) addressed possible parent training issues with Latino or Chinese families that are counter to standard, well-researched, and accepted practices for White families. The research issues are undoubtedly complex, but without empirical research to assist assessors and clinicians in understanding how cultural differences affect child and family behavior, we do a disservice to a growing segment of our population.

SUMMARY

The distinction between child behavioral assessment and traditional child assessment has become blurred in recent years. Behavioral assessment procedures have become a part of mainstream child clinical psychology. Yet, the goals of child behavioral assessment continue to be the identification of specific behavior problems and understanding how current causal variables may initiate or maintain children's motoric, verbal, cognitive, or physiological responses. This task is accomplished by using multiple informants and an array of direct and indirect assessment methods. A S-O-R-K-C model is used to explain that the majority of problem child behaviors are maintained by antecedent and consequent social–environmental events and that children are not just influenced but shape their environment. It is also assumed in behavioral assessment that behavior change is more likely to occur by focusing on current, specific, and observable behaviors. Problems of child behavior assessment have been addressed, namely, practical limitations in using specific assessment methods, and the lack of empirically validated decision rules to guide a clinician in determining which assessment methods may best examine critical variables related to specific childhood behavior problems. In this context, the purpose of a functional analysis as an ideal to strive for in the assessment of children and their families was articulated.

The task of a child clinician is to capture children's and adolescent's ever-changing emotional, cognitive, social, and physical development in relation to major developmental imperatives, such as mastering academic material, developing autonomy and peer relationships, and developing self-control, to name a few. Children and adolescents are identified as requiring assessment and treatment when normative developmental expectations or demands are not successfully negotiated. It was acknowledged that there is a dearth of assessment information pertaining to children in relation to the larger context or social systems in which they reside. In addition, there is a need to develop assessment strategies that not only narrowly suggest treatments but more broadly assess overall family satisfaction and functioning, as well as economic costs associated with specific earlier child interventions. Finally, the need to expand assessment methods that take into account different ethnic or cultural customs is necessary now and into the next century as minority groups grow exponentially in the United States.

REFERENCES

Achenbach, T. M. (1991). *Manual for the Child Behavior Checklist/4–18 and 1991 Profile.* Burlington, VT: Author.

American Psychiatric Association. (1994). *Diagnostic and statistical manual of mental disorders.* (4th ed). Washington, DC: Author.

Aponte, J. F., & Crouch, L. T. (1995). The changing ethnic profile of the United States. In J. F. Aponte, L. Y. Rivers, & J. Wohl (Eds.), *Psychological interventions and cultural diversity* (pp. 1–18). Boston: Allyn & Bacon.

Cone, J. D. (1997). Issues in functional analysis in behavioral assessment. *Behaviour Research and Therapy, 35,* 259–275.

Cone, J. D. (1998). Psychometric considerations: Concepts, contents, and methods. In A. S. Bullock & M. Hersen (Eds.) *Behavioral assessment: A practical handbook* (4th ed., pp. 22–46). Boston: Allyn & Bacon.

Conners, C. K. (1990). *The Conners Rating Scales.* Toronto, Ontario, Canada: Multi-Health Systems, Inc.

Dodge, K. A. (1983). Behavioral antecedents of peer social status. *Child Development, 54,* 1386–1399.

Dodge, K. A., McClaskey, C. L., & Feldman, E. (1985). A situational approach to the assessment of social competence in children. *Journal of Consulting and Clinical Psychology, 53,* 344–353.

Douglas, V. I., & Parry, P. A. (1994). Effects of reward and nonreward on frustration and attention in attention deficit disorder. *Journal of Abnormal Child Psychology, 22,* 281–302.

Elliott, R. J., Miltenberg, R. G., Kaster-Bundgaard, J., & Lumley, V. (1996). A national survey of assessment and therapy techniques used by behavior therapy. *Cognitive and Behavioral Practice, 3,* 107–125.

Farrell, A. D. (1991). Computers and behavioral assessment: Curved applications, future possibilities, and obstacles to routine use. *Behavioral Assessment, 13,* 159–179.

Ferster, C. B., & Skinner, B. F. (1953). *Schedules of new reinforcement.* New York: Appleton Century-Crotko.

Forehand, L., & Kotchick, B. A. (1996). Cultural diversity: A wake-up call for parent training. *Behavior Therapy, 27*, 187–206.

Forehand, R., & McMahon, R. J. (1981). *Helping the noncompliant child: A clinician's guide to parent training*. New York: Guilford.

Foster, S. L., & Cone, J. D. (1986). Design and use of direct observation. In A. R, Ciminaro, K. S. Calhoun, & H. E. Adams (Eds.), *Handbook of behavioral assessment* (2nd ed., pp. 253–324). New York: Wiley.

Griest, D. L., Forehand, R., Rogers, T., Breiner, J., Furey, W., William, C. A. (1982). Effects of parent training enhancement therapy on the treatment outcome and generalization of a parent training program. *Behavior Research and Therapy, 20,* 429–536.

Guevremont, D. C., & Spiegler, M. D. (1990, November). *What do behavior therapists really do? A survey of the clinical practice of AABT members.* Paper presented at the 24th annual convention of the Association for Advancement of Behavior Therapy, San Francisco.

Harter, S. (1982). The perceived competence scale for children. *Child Development, 53,* 87–97.

Haynes, S. N. (1996). *Principles of behavioral assessment.* Manuscript submitted for publication.

Haynes, S. N. (1991). Behavioral assessment. In M. Hersen, A. E. Kazdin & A. S. Bellack (Eds.), *The clinical psychology handbook* (2nd ed., pp. 430–464). Elmsford, NY: Pergamon.

Haynes, S. N. (1998). The changing nature of behavioral assessment. In A. S. Bellack & M. Hersen (Eds), *Behavioral assessment: A practical handbook* (4th ed., pp. 1–22). Boston: Allyn & Bacon.

Haynes, S. N., & O'Brien, W. H. (1990). Functional analysis in behavioral therapy. *Clinical Psychology Review, 10,* 649–668.

Henggeler, S. W., & Borduin, C. M. (1990). *Family therapy and beyond: A multisystemic approach to teaching the behavior problems of childhood and adolescents.* Monterey, CA: Brooks/Cole.

Jensen, P. S., Hibbs, E. P., & Pilkonis, P. A. (1996). From ivory tower to clinical practice: Future directions for child and adolescent psychotherapy research. In E. D. Erthymia & P. S. Jenkins (Eds.), *Psychosocial treatment of child and adolescent disorders: Empirically-based strategies for clinical practice* (pp. 701–711). Washington, DC.. American Psychological Association.

Johnson, S. B., Kelly, M., Henretta, J., Cunningham, W., Tomen, R., & Silverstein, J. (1992). A longitudental analysis of adherence and health status in childhood diabetes. *Journal of Pediatric Psychology, 17,* 537–553.

Kanfer, F. H., & Phillips, J. S. (1970). *Learning foundations of behavior therapy.* New York: Wiley.

Kovacs, M. (1992). *The Children's Depression Inventory (CDI) manual.* Toronto, Ontario, Canada: Multi-Health Systems, Inc.

Mash, E. J., & Terdal, L. G. (1997). *Assessment of childhood disorders* (3rd ed.). New York: Guilford.

McGuire, J., & Earls, F. (1991). Prevention of psychiatric disorders in early childhood. *Journal of Child Psychology and Psychiatry, 32,* 129–153.

McMahon, R. J. (1994). Diagnosis, assessment and treatment of externalizing problems in children: The role of longitudinal data. *Journal of Consulting and Clinical Psychology, 62,* 901–917.

Morrison, R. L. (1988). Structured interviews and rating sides. In A. S. Bellack & M. Hersen (Eds.), *Behavioral Assessment: A Practical handbook* (3rd ed., pp. 252–277). Elmsford, NY: Pergamon.

Patterson, G. R. (1982). *Coercive family process.* Eugene, OR: Castalia.

Persons, J. B. (1989). *Cognitive therapy in practice: A case formulation approach.* New York: Norton.

Persons, J. B., & Fresco, D. M. (1996). Assessment of depression. In A. S. Bellack & M. Hersen (Eds.), *Behavioral Assessment: A practical handbook* (4th ed., pp. 210–231). Boston: Allyn & Bacon.

Piotrowski, C., & Lubin, B. (1990). Assessment practices of health psychologists: Survey of APA division 38 clinicians. *Professional Psychology: Research and Practice, 21,* 99–106.

Piotrowski, C., & Zalewski, C. (1993). Training in psychodiagnostic testing in APA-approved PsyD and PhD clinical psychology programs. *Journal of Personality Assessment, 61,* 394–405.

Schulte, D. (1992). Criteria of treatment selection in behavior therapy. *European Journal of Psychological Assessment, 8,* 157–162.

Shapiro, E. S., & Cole, C. L. (1993). Self-monitoring. In T. A. Ollendick & M. Hersen (Eds.) *Handbook of child and adolescent assessment* (pp. 124–139). Needham Heights, MA: Allyn & Bacon.

Sisson, L. A., & Taylor, J. C. (1993). Parent training. In A. S. Bellack & M. Hersen (Eds.), *Handbook of behavior therapy in the psychiatric setting*. (pp. 555–574). New York: Plenum.

Strayhorn, J. M., Jr., (1987). Medical assessment of children with behavioral problems. In M. Hersen & V. B. Van Handelt (Eds.), *Behavior therapy with children and adolescents: A clinical approach* (pp. 50–74). New York: Wiley-Interscience.

Thomas, A., Chess, S., & Birch, H. G. (1976). *Temperament and behavior disorders in children*. New York: New York University Press.

Tombari, M. L., Fitzpatrick, S. J., & Childress, W. (1985). Using computers as contingency managers in self-monitoring interventions: A case study. *Computers in Human Behavior, 1,* 75–82.

Tyron, W. W. (1991). *Activity measurement in psychology and medicine*. New York: Plenum.

Tyron, W. W. (1998). Behavioral Observation. In A. S. Bellack & M. Hersen, (Eds.), *Behavioral Assessment: A practical handbook* (4th ed., pp. 79–103). Boston: Allyn & Bacon.

U. S. Bureau of the Census. (1992a). *Census of population 1990 CP–1–4, general population characteristics*. Washington, DC: U.S. Government Printing Office.

U. S. Bureau of the Census. (1992b). *Current population reports, P25–1092, Population projections of the United States by age, sex, race and Hispanic origin: 1992–2050*. Washington DC: U.S. Government Printing Office.

Welner, E., Reich, W., Herjanic B., Jung K., & Amado, H. (1987). Reliability, validity, and parent–child agreement studies of the Diagnostic Interview for Children and Adolescents (DICA) *Journal of the American Academy of Child and Adolescent Psychiatry, 26,* 649–653.

Wince, J. P. (1982). Assessment of sexual disorders. *Behavioral Assessment, 4,* 257–271.

Behavioral Treatment

Linda A. LeBlanc
Western Michigan University

Loc Le
Michael Carpenter
Claremont Graduate University

BEHAVIORAL TREATMENTS

The field of behavioral psychology has grown enormously over the last 30 years in breadth and in specificity (Risley & Wolf, 1997). Behavior therapy involves the application of known principles of behavior to human beings to create positive and therapeutic effects in their living environments. There are several general principles that guide the science and practice of behavior therapy.

First, behavior therapy does not presume that psychiatric status dictates intervention strategies or presume that diagnosis will be altered by the intervention. Instead, behavioral interventions target specific behaviors for change. For example, a behavior therapist will target many problem behaviors of a child with attention-deficit/hyperactivity disorder (ADHD) such as inattention or excessive motor activity, without assuming that the intervention will eliminate the child's diagnostic label. Conversely, a behavior therapist could appropriately target those same problem behaviors in a child with no diagnosis and still create a therapeutic impact.

Second, behavioral treatments should be implemented with the goal of consistent evaluation of treatment effectiveness and guided by the current experimental treatment literature. Recent advances, such as functional analysis procedures, are moving the field toward more prescriptive interventions, but all of these interventions are based on our basic knowledge of learning theory. In addition, behavioral treatments are usually the product of many experimental examinations indicating their treatment effectiveness with different populations.

Third, behavior therapy places a strong emphasis on learning history, current environmental events, and current skills and performance levels as mediators of functioning. In contrast, other therapies typically focus on events and milestones in the distant past as mediators or determiners of current functioning. For example, psychodynamic and humanistic theories focus on progress or difficulties in various psychosexual and psychosocial stages as explanations for current problems, such as anxiety (Simeonsson & Rosenthal, 1992). Behavioral interventions focus more on modifications to the immediate environment, manipulation of contingencies and skill-building to effect therapeutic change.

Finally, behavioral interventions typically are designed to be implemented by a variety of individuals within the child's natural environment. Thus, when a child or family participates in behavior therapy, they do not experience the intervention solely in the confines of a psychologist's office. Most behavioral interventions are designed to be implemented by parents, teachers, and children. Thus, behavior therapies typically involve a large component of parent, teacher, peer, and sibling training as well as evaluation of treatment effectiveness in natural settings such as homes and schools.

Because a brief chapter cannot possibly cover the general field of behavior therapy exhaustively, we have included seminal articles, general reviews, and specific treatment intervention studies to illustrate the application of the basic principles and techniques. In addition, the interested reader is referred to specific sources for more detailed information on several of the topics covered in the chapter. The chapter is organized into three areas: operant-based procedures, cognitive–behavioral therapies, and skill-building procedures. Within each of these areas, we describe the most common prinicples and techniques and review their use with several common childhood problems, such as conduct disorders, anxiety disorders, depression, academic difficulties, and adjustment problems.

OPERANT-BASED PROCEDURES

Operant learning theories delineate techniques for behavioral acceleration (e.g., reinforcement) and techniques for behavioral deceleration (e.g., response cost). These procedures typically are used in tandem to increase appropriate behaviors while decreasing or eliminating inappropriate or destructive behaviors. Each prinicple and the techniques based on that operant principle are reviewed. In addition, we present research targeting a variety of different childhood problems as evidence of the effectiveness of the procedure and as examples of how to implement the procedure as part of a comprehensive behavioral treatment.

Functional Assessment

Functional assessment procedures are designed to identify those operant variables that may be associated with problem behavior or directly responsible for maintaining problem behaviors (Carr, 1977). Functional assessment procedures identify the antecedent conditions and/or naturally occurring consequences for problem behaviors. Once this information is obtained, the therapist can use the information to dictate an operant-based intervention that alters either the antecedents or consequences for problem behavior (Taylor & Romanczyk, 1994). This methodology originally was designed to evaluate the maintaining variables for extreme behaviors, such as self-injurious behavior, but recently the theory and methodology have been modified to assess and treat a variety of other behaviors, such as school refusal, classroom disruptive behavior, cursing, tantrums and aggression, and even social skill deficits (Derby et al., 1992; Frea & Hughes, 1997; Iwata, Dorsey, Slifer, Bauman, & Richman, 1994; Pace, Ivancic, & Jefferson, 1994; Taylor & Romanczyk, 1994). The primary classes of motivators for behavior are positive reinforcement (e.g., social reinforcers) and negative reinforcement (escaping from difficult situations). The interested reader should see Iwata et al. (1994) and Derby et al. (1992) for additional information on specific functional assessment procedures. Functional analysis is discussed further in the following sections within the context of the specific consequences that have been altered to treat childhood behavior problems.

Reinforcement

Positive Reinforcement. Positive reinforcement, a basic principle of human behavior, occurs when a behavior is followed by the presentation of a stimulus that increases the probability of the behavior occurring in the future (Miltenberger, 1997). In other words, when a desired behavior is followed by something that the child prefers, we should expect to see more of that behavior in the future. Positive reinforcement is considered the most pervasive and most appropriately used type of treatment for a wide range of target behaviors, and it is recommended that all behavioral treatments include positive reinforcement as a component (Karoly & Harris, 1986). (For a more comprehensive review of the basic principles of positive reinforcement, see Catania, 1984; Lattal, 1991; Sidman, 1991.)

The first key to success with positive reinforcement is choosing the right target behavior. The challenge to the behavior therapist is to assess the child and his or her current situation appropriately and determine which key behaviors should be changed in order to effect therapeutic change for the child. The identification of appropriate target behaviors may or may not be related to the child's diagnosis, but should include behaviors that are (a) important to the child, family, or school personnel; and (b) lead to an improvement in the child's functioning in his or her current environment. For example, appropriate target behaviors for a child who is diagnosed with ADHD and having problems in school may include (a) homework completion, (b) consistent attendance at school, and (c) inititation of social interactions. However, for another child with the same diagnosis the therapist may target (a) aggression, (b) noncompliance, and (c) paying attention in class.

The second key to success with positive reinforcement is choosing the right stimulus to use as a reinforcer. Anything from verbal praise to money or access to special privileges (e.g., borrowing the car) may function as a reinforcer. For positive reinforcement to be effective, the presented stimulus must be appropriate and preferred by the child and must be presented only when the targeted behavior occurs (Sarafino, 1996). Therefore, a preference assessment should be conducted to determine the child's relative likes and dislikes (Pace, Ivancic, Edwards, Iwata, & Page, 1985). The therapist also should determine which items parents are willing to provide contingently as reinforcers for the target behavior. Because each individual has his or her own personal preferences, the range of potential reinforcers can be limitless. (See DeLeon & Iwata, 1996, Northup, Jones, Broussard, & George, 1995, Fisher et al., 1992, for a discussion of reinforcer and preference assessment procedures).

Several factors can influence the effectiveness of reinforcers including establishing operations, stimulus variation, and choice-making options (Grant & Evans, 1994; Neef, Mace, Shea, & Shade, 1992). In general, the behavior therapist should account for and maximize the effects of establishing operations such as deprivation, which occurs when a person has not had contact with the stimulus for a period of time and can increase the effectiveness of your reinforcer (Michael, 1993). A second factor that can influence the effectiveness of certain stimuli is reinforcer variety (Bowman, Piazza, Fisher, Hagopian, & Kogan, 1997). Egel (1981) examined the effects of reinforcer variation on the work habits of children with autism and found that offering a variety of items to choose from resulted in children working harder on their tasks and maintaining greater interest in the tasks. In addition, it has been noted that even when children have to engage in unpreferred activies such as homework, allowing the child a choice of which homework to do first may reduce problem behavior (Vaughn & Horner, 1997). Thus, the therapist is reminded to identify several potential reinforcers, vary the reinforcers, and restrict the child's access to those reinforcers that are used as part of a differential reinforcement treatment program.

Differential reinforcement is a procedure that applies the principles of reinforcement to increase the frequency of desirable behaviors and decrease the frequency of undesirable behaviors (Vollmer & Iwata, 1992). Differential reinforcement should be used to increase the rate of a desirable behavior that already is occurring at least occasionally, thus indicating that the child has the skill but currently is not using it enough (Miltenberger, 1997). In addition, when a functional assessment indicates that a given problem behavior is maintained by positive reinforcers in the form of access to social attention or preferred items, those items can be used as reinforcers for alternative appropriate behavior to increase the effectiveness of the differential reinforcement procedure (Vollmer & Iwata, 1992).

There are two main types of differential reinforcement: differential reinforcement of other behavior (DRO) and differential reinforcement of alternative behavior (DRA; Vollmer & Iwata, 1992). DRO has been used to treat a variety of different behaviors and populations effectively, including compliance, communication, social skills, and self-esteem (Ogier & Hornby, 1996; Whitaker, 1996). DRO involves providing reinforcers contingent on a preset amount of time without the occurrence of the problem behavior.

Rangasamy, Taylor, and Ziegler (1996) successfully used a DRO procedure to eliminate inappropriate classroom behavior in an adolescent with learning disabilities by providing reinforcement at various preset intervals when the student refrained from being out of his seat and disturbing other students in the classroom. Reinforcement was contingent on the student staying in his seat for 15 minutes in the first intervention phase, 30 minutes in the second phase, 45 minutes in the third phase, and for 1 hour in the last intervention phase.

Wagaman, Miltenberger, and Williams (1995) used DRO to treat successfully a cough and throat-clearing habit in a child diagnosed with chronic vocal tic disorder. During baseline, the child was coughing at a rate of 4.6 times per minute. After failure to achieve positive results with a habit reversal protocol, DRO was implemented. Treatment for the coughing involved providing reinforcement (i.e., 5 cents) if the child did not cough during a designated time period, which gradually was increased across sessions. After two treatment sessions, the coughing stopped, but an increase in the child's throat-clearing was noticed. Therefore, reinforcement then was made contingent on the absence of coughing and the absence of throat clearing within the specified amount of time. Results showed that the child's coughing and throat clearing were eliminated after four treatment sessions.

Lalli, Browder, Mace, and Brown (1993) used the second type of differential reinforcement, DRA, to decrease children's problem behaviors and increase play and on-task behavior in a classroom setting. After descriptive functional assessment indicated that the children's problem behavior (aggression) was maintained primarily by attention, Lalli et al. provided attention contingent on on-task responding during instructional situations and appropriate play during breaks. In addition, the children were taught to use other adaptive behaviors to request attention (e.g., presenting the teacher with a toy or touching the teacher's arm). Results showed that the DRA successfully reduced the children's problem behavior.

Negative Reinforcement. A small but growing literature exists on the use of negative reinforcement for treating children with behavioral difficulties (Iwata, 1987). *Negative reinforcement* is defined as removing some unpleasant stimulus, resulting in an increase in the future likelihood of a behavior (Catania, 1992). For example, the loud noise of my alarm is removed or terminated when I hit the off button on my alarm clock, and the likelihood of my hitting the off button tomorrow is increased because I successfully terminated the aversive event today. Negative reinforcement procedures have been used most effectively with children in school settings, which frequently become an aversive situation for a child when learning disabilities or attention problems make schoolwork extremely difficult.

When a functional assessment indicates that behavior is maintained by escape from challenging situations, treatments involving negative reinforcement in the form of a contingent or "earned" break have proven effective. Carr and Durand (1985) developed a model called functional communication training to treat problem behaviors in the classroom that were occasioned by having to complete difficult tasks. After determining that the children exhibited more problem behavior when faced with difficult assignments versus easier assignments, they taught three children to request help appropriately when they did not understand schoolwork (e.g., "I don't understand"). Differential reinforcement of this alternative communication response resulted in near elimination of problem behaviors. Piazza, Moes, and Fisher (1996) used a similar model involving differential reinforcement of compliance to treat a child's destructive behavior associated with academic demand situations. It also has been demonstrated that a combination of positive and negative reinforcement may produce better treatment results for individuals with problem behavior by enhancing the quality of the break as a reinforcer by providing structured enjoyable activities during the break (Piazza et al., 1997).

Punishment

Punishment procedures decrease the future probability of an undesirable behavior by one of two general methods. Positive punishment consists of presenting an unpleasant consequence contingent on the occurrence of the problem behavior (Karoly & Harris, 1986). Negative punishment involves removing access to some preferred item or activity (e.g., removing privileges) contingent on the problem behavior (Miltenberger, 1997). In addition, to increase the effectiveness of punishment, these procedures always should be used in conjunction with the positive reinforcement procedures described previously that target more appropriate behaviors (Axelrod, 1990).

Because of many popular misconceptions about punishment, there has been a great deal of controversy about ethical and practical issues concerning the use of punishment procedures (Repp & Singh, 1990). Some punishment procedures, however, may be more acceptable than others. For instance, giving students detention for their truancies may be more acceptable for many than administering an electric shock to these students but both procedures meet the definition of punishment. (For a more extensive, comprehensive review of punishment procedures and controversies over the use of aversives, see Coe & Matson, 1990; Karoly & Harris, 1986; Linscheid & Meinhold, 1990; Sandler, 1986; Singh, Osborne, & Huguenin, 1996.)

Timeout.   Timeout is defined as the removal of access to positive reinforcement for a preset time contingent on a specific problem behavior (Sulzer-Azaroff & Mayer, 1977). Typical timeout procedures involve immediately removing the individual from the environment (e.g., placing the individual in a corner or in another room) when he or she engages in an unwanted or maladaptive behavior. For timeout procedures to be effective, a number of conditions must apply. First, the original environment must be positive and enjoyable for the individual or the child may not regret having to leave the environment and may learn to use timeout as an escape from the situation (e.g., getting out of a difficult class by being sent to timeout). When a functional assessment indicates that problem behavior is maintained by escape from a certain situation, timeout is contraindicated because the timeout may provide the child with escape. Second, timeout must be used consistently and immediately and must be contingent on the target behavior, that is, after each and every occurrence of the target behavior, timeout must immediately be administered. Finally, the timeout environment must be unpleasant and unstimulating. The individual should not receive attention or have access to toys, music, conversation, or other types of reinforcement during timeout.

Three types of timeout procedures have been identified (Harris, 1985). Isolation timeout, the most intrusive type, involves total removal of the individual from the reinforcing environment (i.e., placing him or her in a separate room for a specified period of time). The most common form of timeout, exclusion timeout, involves removing the child from the area where the problem behavior occurred, but the child remains in the room without being able to participate or observe (e.g., the individual sits in a corner chair facing a wall). Nonexclusion timeout is the least intrusive form of timeout, and it involves three subtypes: contingent observation, removal of reinforcing stimulus conditions, and planned ignoring. In contingent observation, the individual is placed in another location of the room but is allowed to observe the ongoing activity. With removal of reinforcing stimulus conditions, reinforcers such as food and toys are withheld contingent on problem behavior. Planned ignoring is implemented by simply turning away from the individual when he or she engages in the target behavior.

Timeout has been used extensively with children, and research has shown that it has been effective in decreasing a number of different problem behaviors. For example, White and Bailey (1995) used a timeout procedure with typical fourth-grade students to reduce noncompliance, aggression, and throwing during their physical education class. A nonexclusionary timeout procedure, 3 minutes of contingent observation, or "sit and watch" as it was called, was used contingent on unwanted target behaviors. In addition, backup procedures in the form of lost privileges (computer and free time) were used in conjunction with timeout. Results showed that the timeout procedure was effective in that it reduced the disruptive behaviors by 93%.

Timeout has also been used with populations other than typical individuals. For example, Kennedy et al. (1990) investigated the use of timeout for children in a multidisciplinary psychiatric inpatient unit, which tended patients with behaviors ranging from conduct disorder to affective disorder. Timeout was contingent on a wide variety of unwanted behaviors, including not following rules, provoking others, and aggression. In addition, a "processing" approach was added to the timeout procedure in which the child had to identify the maladaptive behavior, connect it to the timeout, and identify an alternative appropriate behavior. Results showed that a low incidence of negative behavior was maintained following the timeout and "processing" procedures.

Although timeout seems to be an effective procedure for decreasing unwanted behavior, this procedure does have potential problems and criticisms. For one, there may be paradoxical effects associated with timeout. That is, timeout may act as a negative reinforcer or escape procedure if the "timein" environment is not reinforcing or is aversive to the individual (e.g., demands are being placed or the individual must perform a difficult task). Second, timeout procedures remove the individual from the learning environment (Costenbadder & Reading-Brown, 1995). The student's opportunity to learn, therefore, is lessened while he or she is sitting in timeout. One study, however, has shown that there is no relation between the amount of time spent in timeout and academic achievement (Skiba & Raison, 1990). These researchers found that truancy appeared to be a better predictor of academic achievement than timeout, and they suggested that students who wanted to escape from schoolwork would do so with truancy rather than with timeout. Finally, timeout has been criticized in that it fails to teach individuals more appropriate behaviors unless used in conjunction with procedures such as positive reinforcement, "processing," and specific skills training (Gast & Nelson, 1977).

Response Cost. *Response cost* is a form of negative punishment in which positive reinforcers or privileges are withdrawn contingent on an unwanted or maladaptive behavior (Karoly & Harris, 1986). Examples of response cost include losing television privileges for not completing homework or being fined for a traffic violation. For individuals to develop a clear relation between a problem behavior and its penalty, response cost typically is used within the context of a token economy, where individuals earn positive reinforcers for appropriate behavior and, conversely, lose these reinforcers contingent on unwanted behavior (Sandler, 1986). (For additional examples of the use of response cost with problem behaviors such as weight control, sleep problems, and encopresis, see Mavis & Stoffelmayr, 1994; Piazza & Fisher, 1991; and Reimers, 1996.)

Empirical evidence indicates that response cost is effective with a number of behaviors and populations. Reynolds and Kelley (1997) used a response cost-based treatment package to manage aggression in preschoolers. The procedure involved giving students a good behavior chart with five yellow smiley faces. Each time the student engaged in the maladaptive behavior, one smiley face was removed from the chart. At the end of the observation period, if the student had at least one smiley face left on the chart, then he or she received a reward (e.g., being teacher's helper or receiving a toy or snack). Results showed that the rate of aggression for all students in this study decreased substantially following the response cost treatment.

In another study evaluating response cost, Gordon, Thomason, Cooper, and Ivers (1990) used response cost to increase attentiveness and task persistence for ADHD children. A small, electronic module with a counter and red light, known as "Mr. Attention," was placed on each child's desk. An observer would award a point on the counter for each minute that the child was attending to the task. However, if the child was off task (i.e., eye contact or physical movement wandering away from task for more than 15 seconds), a point would be deducted. This system was effective for improving children's level of attention. However, once the training system was removed, off-task behaviors began to increase to baseline levels again. It was suggested that the training system be extended for longer than the 2-month period in this study for maintenance to occur.

Token Economy

Token economy programs originally were developed in the mid-1960s by Ayllon and Azrin to treat chronic psychiatric patients (Kazdin, 1982). Since then, token economy programs have become a widely accepted and standard part of many hospital treatment programs. In addition, these programs now are used with diverse populations, including individuals with oppositional disorder, conduct disorder, and children in classroom settings (e.g., Dulcan, Mannarino, & Borcherding, 1991; Robinson, Powers, Cleveland, & Thyer, 1990; Sullivan & O'Leary, 1990). A token economy allows a child to earn rewards and privileges based on designated appropriate behavior (reinforcement) and to lose access to these rewards and privileges based on undesireable behaviors (response cost). In general, token economies can teach children that consequences exist for their behavior and teach them to begin making "self-control" decisions—choosing the positive behavior that leads to good things down the road over the negative behavior that changes the situation immediately. In addition, token economies may help frustrated parents or teachers focus more effectively on positive behaviors or periods of "good" child behavior. (For a comprehensive review of the empirical literature on token economy programs, see Kazdin, 1982; Williams, Williams, & McLaughlin, 1989).

A token economy has three main components (a) tokens (used as conditioned reinforcers); (b) backup reinforcers (can be "purchased" with tokens); and (c) a schedule for reinforcement and token exchange. Some easily distributed representation of a reinforcer is chosen as a token, such as points or chips. This token is then paired with several desirable items or activites, and the trade system is explained to the child (e.g., cost of each item, removal of tokens). The tokens serve as conditioned reinforcers to be exchanged at a later time for backup reinforcers (e.g., food items or special privileges). Explicit rules for receiving and losing tokens are first discussed with the child. The type of token (preferably a practical, convenient, and controllable token) and potent backup reinforcers should be identified with the help of the child. A menu can be devised with specifications for the amount of tokens needed and the time and place for the exchange or token trade (Kazdin, 1982). Finally, there must be a set schedule of reinforcement and trading for the tokens. Tokens can be earned on an hourly, daily, or weekly basis depending on the age and cognitive abilities of the child.

An example of a token economy program may help to illustrate this type of treatment. Mark, an 8-year-old boy, was put on a token economy program after problem behaviors began to emerge at home. Every time his mother placed a demand on him, such as telling him to clean his room or to take a bath, Mark would become noncompliant and engage in a tantrum. The token economy program consisted of Mark receiving a token (in this case, a laminated picture of a football) if he was compliant within 10 seconds of the demand without making a fuss. Each time Mark complied, he received a token, and his parents were instructed to provide a minimum of three opportunities per day to earn tokens. Mark and his parents also established a reinforcer menu with the help of a therapist. The menu included items that could be purchased with few tokens (e.g., 5 tokens) and more "expensive" items (such as a trip to his favorite restaurant), which cost more tokens (e.g., 20). At the end of the week, Mark could exchange his tokens for special privileges from his menu, such as a candy bar or going to the movies. Mark had to be compliant for the entire week to earn more "expensive" items. Thus, this family used a token economy without a response cost component. If tokens had been removed for tantrumming or arguing after a demand, then the response cost component would have been in effect for this token economy program.

The empirical research on token economies has suggested that this treatment program is effective with many different populations and behaviors. For example, Robinson et al. (1990) used a token economy in conjunction with other procedures to treat clinically depressed children and adolescents, targeting such behaviors as academic performance, appropriate classroom comportment, social skills, and improving peer relationships. As a result, patients showed statistically significant improvement on standardized measures such as the Hopelessness Scale for Children (Kazdin, French, Unis, Esveldt-Dawson, & Sherick, 1983) and the Beck Depression Inventory (Beck, Ward, Mendelson, Mock, & Erbaugh, 1961) after treatment.

Dulcan et al., (1991) also used a token economy to treat children with oppositional behavior, attention deficit disorder, and conduct disorder. Positive and negative behaviors such as completing homework, doing chores, stealing, lying, and participating in therapy were targeted at home, at school and in a clinic setting. Results indicated that two thirds of the 25 cases had a successful or partially successful treatment outcome. It was suggested that the cause of the failure for the remaining cases was that both parents and children remained hostile and uncooperative during treatment.

COGNITIVE–BEHAVIORAL THERAPIES

Cognitive–behavioral therapies (CBT) are designed to increase self-control and appropriate behavior in children who either have behavioral excesses or behavioral deficits, such as impulsivity or negative automatic thoughts. Thus, children are taught to display age-appropriate behavior as well as adequate levels of self control. CBTs developed from traditional behavior therapies but emphasize shifting the control of the contingencies from external sources (e.g., teacher, parent) to the child. CBTs assume that the child learns how environmental contingencies relate to his or her behavior and that the development of the child's mental processes are central to the improvement in skill acquisition and maintenance (Abramowitz & O'Leary, 1991; Braswell & Kendall, 1988).

Using CBTs, children's maladaptive behavior is assumed to be the result of distorted cognitive processing. For example, children with ADHD display overactivity, impulsivity, and attentional deficits, which are thought to be the result of a lack of processing abilities that would allow the child to control his or her behavior (Braswell & Kendall, 1988). Alternatively, children with depression display distorted cognitive representations of external events. They misinterpret neutral events as having a negative connotation and display negative automatic thoughts that are hypothesized to be a result of a dysfunction at the information processing level (Kendall, Kortlander, Chansky, & Brady, 1992; Swallow & Segal, 1995).

Usually, a self-management package is developed for a child that contains a combination of interventions (e.g., self-monitoring and self-reinforcement). These procedures have become more popular in recent years due to their success in treating various behavior problems and their applicability for practitioners (DuPaul & Stoner, 1994). This section defines and provides examples of CBTs including self-management techniques such as self-monitoring, self-reinforcement, self-instruction, and goal-setting for children with behavioral problems (e.g., ADHD, depression, anxiety).

Self-Monitoring

Self-monitoring teaches a child to record observations of his or her own behaviors. A child is taught to observe his or her actions that pertain to target behaviors. A clear operational definition of the target behaviors is needed to ensure that the child and therapist agree on the behavior of concern and that the child clearly understands the problem behavior. For example, a child with ADHD may be taught to recognize when he or she is engaging in off-task behavior. Off-task could be defined as being out of seat or talking to peers without permission. The child is then taught to keep a record of these target behaviors. Initially, the child's self-monitoring is compared to a therapist or teacher's report to ensure accuracy in the child's self-monitoring skills (DuPaul & Stoner, 1994). Reinforcement for accurate data collection is provided regardless of behavior.

Self-monitoring is an important self-management intervention because of its use in the assessment process, intervention process, and because it is so frequently used in combination with other techniques such as self-reinforcement (Hoberman, 1990). A benefit of self-monitoring is a child's increased awareness and reactivity. A child who uses self-monitoring for a target behavior may influence the occurrence of that behavior (reactivity). With the use of self-monitoring, unwanted behaviors may decrease, and desired behaviors may increase (Rehm & Rokke, 1988).

Self-monitoring has been implemented successfully with children with ADHD (DuPaul & Stoner, 1994). An auditory or visual stimulus (e.g., beep, light) is used during a specific time period to signal the child to observe his or her own behavior. The child is then taught to record whether he or she was on-task during the interval on a grid sheet taped to the child's desk. Self-monitoring, especially when combined with self-reinforcement, has been found to increase attentive behaviors in ADHD children (Abramowitz & O'Leary, 1991; DuPaul & Stoner, 1994).

Similarly, self-monitoring has been used with children with depression, anxiety, or both (Kendall et al., 1992). Clients are asked to monitor the occurrences of pleasant and aversive events on a daily basis. The therapist and client typically generate an individualized list of events and activities for the child to monitor. Self-monitoring functions primarily to help the therapist and patient become aware of the pattern of covariance that typically exists between mood and the rates of pleasant and unpleasant activities (Hoberman, 1990). Children who are old enough may be taught to graph and are encouraged to interpret their self-monitoring record to learn the relation between unpleasant events and mood. Self-monitoring helps the child take a more active role in determining his or her relationship with the environment and resulting mood (Hoberman, 1990; Swallow & Segal, 1995). Although self-monitoring can be used with children with depression or with anxiety, different treatment approaches should be used. The child with depression is taught to self-monitor and to avoid "misattributions," whereas the child with anxiety is taught to identify physiological arousal associated with his anxiety, and anxiety related cognition and attributes (Kendall et al., 1992). The child with anxiety is taught to ask the question, "What might happen?" (Kendall et al., 1992). In addition, self-monitoring has been used successfully to treat enuresis in children (Ronen, Wozner, & Rahav, 1992). The processes of teaching self-monitoring as a form of self-control was more beneficial than token economies, bell-and-pad, and a no-intervention control group (Ronen et al., 1992).

Self-Reinforcement

Self-management packages using both self-monitoring and self-reinforcement have been effective in dealing with numerous behavior problems in children with ADHD (Abramowitz & O'Leary, 1991). Self-reinforcement teaches children to observe their own behavior (self-monitoring) and to evaluate and reinforce their behavior when appropriate (Abramowitz & O'Leary, 1991). When using self-reinforcement, the child is first taught to use self-monitoring to observe his or her behavior. Second, the child is taught to evaluate his or her behavior based on a well-defined target goal, such as an acceptable level of behavior (e.g., on-task behavior). Finally, the child is taught to reinforce his or her behavior based on his or her own evaluation and to self-praise (DuPaul & Stoner, 1994). External reinforcers such as privileges should be used if possible. Self-reinforcement typically is introduced after an adult-run program has been established for the target behavior. As the child displays competence at self-reinforcement, the adult-run program is faded (DuPaul & Stoner, 1994). The use of the adult-run program initially helps establish the behavior in the child's repertoire as well as serving as a check that the child is evaluating and reinforcing his or her behavior appropriately. Periodic checks should be made to ensure that the child is properly observing, evaluating, and reinforcing his or her behavior. Again, reinforcement is provided for implementing contingencies correctly (DuPaul & Stoner, 1994). Self-reinforcement has been extremely effective in dealing with some of the core problems of ADHD, such as academic, on-task, and social behavior (Abramowitz & O'Leary, 1991).

Children with depression tend to display low levels of activity, feel unworthy, and receive limited reinforcement from their environment (Hoberman, 1990). Self-reinforcement can be used to encourage children to increase activity levels. It also is used to identify activities that a child finds reinforcing, and to ensure reinforcement for the completion of goals. Self-reinforcement also can provide the depressive child a feeling of self-control over his or her behavior and enhance change in that behavior and thoughts (Swallow & Segal, 1994). Similarly, children with anxiety are taught how to identify anxious feelings, how to use a coping strategy, and how to self-reinforce (Kendall et al., 1992).

Self-Instruction

Self-instruction teaches children to complete a task using a series of steps (Abramowitz & O'Leary, 1991). The steps can include repeating instructions for the task, describing the task, deciding how to proceed during the task, creating and following written lists, and evaluating their own behavior at the completion of the task. First, the therapist models a systematic approach to completing a task while verbalizing each step in the presence of the child. Second, the therapist asks the child to complete the task while verbalizing the steps necessary for the completion of the task. Third, the child is taught to complete the task while whispering the steps. Finally, the child is taught to complete the task without verbalizing the steps but by covertly thinking through the task (Abramowitz & O'Leary, 1991; DuPaul & Stoner, 1994).

Self-instruction was highly regarded because of the belief that it would lead to increased self-control and normalized behavior in children (Abramowitz & O'Leary, 1991). Unfortunately, research on self-instruction has indicated mixed results. Abikoff (1985) found that self-instruction led to increased cognitive gains in comparison to academic gains. Self-instruction, when used alone, has limitations in the area of the new skill generalizing to other settings (e.g., classroom). Self-instruction may be successful because it teaches cognitive training or because of the motivational components associated with reinforcement from the task (DuPaul & Stoner, 1994).

Self-instruction has been used with ADHD children. Typically, self-instruction is used in conjunction with self-monitoring and self-reinforcement. Initially, a child receives praise and backup reinforcers for providing self-instruction. Gradually, the external reinforcers are faded, and the child learns to provide praise in a covert manner. The use of self-instruction in ADHD children has led to greater increases in attention and cognition rather than academic performance and classroom behavior (Abramowitz & O'Leary, 1991). Also, ADHD children have showed increased self-control and used more self-coping strategies than a no-intervention control group (Braswell & Kendall, 1988).

Self-instruction also is used to treat children with depression or anxiety. Self-instruction is used to help the child with depression manage aversive situations, engage in pleasant activities, and foster planning and decision making in these children (Hoberman, 1990). In children with anxiety, self-instruction plays a role in helping the child learn to mediate anxiety-arousing situations (Kendall et al., 1992). Similarly, self-instruction and tutoring were demonstrated to increase mathematics performance when compared either to a condition with tutoring only, and to a no-intervention control condition (Braswell & Kendall, 1988).

Goal-Setting

In promoting the development of new skills in children, goals are used as clear and specific targets for the children to help focus their attention and to increase motivation (DuPaul & Stoner, 1994; Swallow & Segal, 1995). The most important aspect of goal-setting is the use of clearly defined goals that the child can understand. Graded task assignments should be used as the target. The length and complexity of the child's tasks should be increased slowly. The use of graded assignments allows the child to build on skills or increase the duration of an activity by providing goals that are attainable (DuPaul & Stoner, 1994). In goal-setting, the emphasis should be placed on initially maximizing the likelihood of successful completion of the assignment, so the child can receive ample amounts of reinforcement for working on the task (e.g., completion of a worksheet, on-task behavior, cleaning their bedroom). Later goals can be more challenging, but initial success depends on the combination of (a) clearly defined tasks, (b) graded task assignments, and (c) reinforcement. These strategies promote skill development and task completion in ADHD children and in children with depression.

If a child with ADHD is being treated and behavior during work sessions is the target goal, then the goals should be based on academic performance such as workload completed and percent correct rather than attention or on-task behavior. The use of specific targets promotes teacher monitoring of the behavior, and it promotes attention to the completion of academic tasks (DuPaul & Stoner, 1994). In addition, when treating a child with depression, graded task assignments should focus on increasing pleasant activities and decreasing aversive events (Hoberman, 1990; Swallow & Segal, 1995).

SPECIFIC SKILLS TRAINING

Another approach to behavior therapy with children is based in the view that a child's problem may be due to a lack of many of the necessary skills for optimal functioning. Behavior therapy should target those skills to improve the child's functioning. Specific skills training typically involves three behavioral techniques: modeling, rehearsal, and feedback. These techniques are combined to target the relevant behaviors until the child can demonstrate competency in his or her newly acquired skill.

Modeling involves having another individual actively demonstrate the new skill either in person (in vivo) or via videotape (Charlop, Schreibman & Tryon, 1983; Dowrick, 1991). Modeling allows the individual to see the behavior performed correctly and result in a positive outcome. Modeling typically works best when the model is similar to the child (peer-modeling; Ihrig & Wolchik, 1988). Rehearsal is an integral component of skills-training procedures because it allows the learner the opportunity to practice his or her new skill and allows the instructor to evaluate the performance of the new skill. Rehearsal should continue until the new behavior occurs quickly, easily, and naturally.

Feedback comes in two forms: reinforcement for correct performance and corrective feedback for incorrect performance. Skills-training programs initially incorporate a dense schedule of reinforcement for correct responses and descriptive praise for correct responses. The schedule of reinforcement is then faded as the behavior becomes more automatic and natural reinforcers take over (e.g., social initiations result in positive social interactions). Corrective feedback involves clearly describing the correct response in detail when a mistake occurs. Corrective feedback should occur immediately and without negative overtones. These techniques have been used in combination to teach many kinds of skills, including social skills, problem-solving skills, and relaxation skills to children with a variety of disorders. We review the utility of each of these specific skill areas with different childhood problems.

Social Skills Training

Social skills deficits have been implicated in a variety of childhood disorders including ADHD, depression, conduct disorders and juvenile delinquency, learning disabilities, and developmental delays (Barkley, 1990; Gresham, 1992; Kazdin, 1990; LaGreca & Vaughn, 1992; LeBlanc & Matson, 1995). Social skills generally involve exhibiting behaviors that allow a child to adapt to his or her environment, to avoid interpersonal conflict, and to maintain a desirable level of positive social interactions with peers and adults (Matson & Sweizy, 1994).

Social skills training has been conducted using specific skills-training packages such as the "Skillstreaming" programs (Goldstein, Sprafkin, Gershaw, & Klein, 1980; McGinnis, Goldstein, Sprafkin, & Gershaw, 1984) and the ASSET and ACCEPTS programs (Hazel, Schumaker, Sherman, & Sheldon-Wildgen, 1981; Walker et al., 1983). These programs target broad categories of social behavior that typically are problematic and target social problem solving. However, these packaged programs may neglect other specific idiosyncratic skills deficits for a given child. Thus, these standard programs may be supported or supplemented with specifically tailored programs that are based on the results of either a standardized measure of social skills or on direct observation of the child in social situations (Gresham & Elliot, 1990). (For comprehensive reviews and training programs see Curran & Monti, 1982; Elliot & Gresham, 1991; Gresham, 1981; Hughes, 1986; L'Abate & Milan, 1985; Ladd, 1985; Ladd & Mize, 1983; Zaragoza, Vaughn, & McIntosh, 1991.)

The literature on social skills training is vast, and the reported outcome effectiveness varies greatly, with many studies indicating that social skills training is very effective and others indicating only modest effectiveness (Forness & Kavale, 1996; Tiffen & Spence, 1986). Several factors appear to mediate the effectiveness and generalizability of social skills interventions. First, Reed (1994) found that gender affected the utility of a structured social skills training program in alleviating the depression of adolescents. The Structured Learning Therapy program (Goldstein, 1981) appeared to target the specific skills and deficits that are key to effective social functioning and alleviation of depression for boys (social judgment, and self-mastery) rather than for girls (adjustment to physical appearance and sexual identity). Thus, standardized packages are typically better suited to remediation of the deficits of boys who exhibit depression or more externalizing problems such as aggression and disruptive behavior associated with ADHD, oppositional–defiant disorder, and conduct disorders, as opposed to depressed young girls.

Age of intervention also may be related to the effectiveness of social skills training, with early intervention efforts typically proving quite effective (Guralnick, 1990). This finding makes sense because long-standing social skills deficits may have become compounded as social interactions become more complex throughout the early life span. In addition, the socially unskilled adolescent may have quite a long history of negative and aversive social interactions leading to avoidance of social situations and increased social awkwardness (Reed, 1994).

Finally, parent and teacher involvement in the training process and specific training directed at increasing their involvement and support in the child's natural social environment have proven beneficial (Ladd & Golter, 1988; Lollis, Ross & Tate, 1992; Sheridan, Dee, Morgan, McCormick, & Walker, 1996; Storey, Smith, & Strain, 1993). Storey, Danko, Ashworth, and Strain (1994) found that interventions that directly targeted the mediational skills of aides in preschool classrooms resulted in greater generalization of new social skills for preschoolers. In addition, the aides found their token-based interventions easy to implement within the context of ongoing classroom activities.

Frankel, Myatt, Cantwell, and Feinberg (1997) demonstrated that parents could be incorporated into social skills training by having them participate as supervisors and organizers for their children's social activities.

Given the variability in the effectiveness of social skills training procedures, the following recommendations are made. First, any social skills training program should be preceded by an individualized assessment of specific social skills deficits in a natural context (Gresham, 1986). Second, the social validity and generalization of social skills interventions can be increased by targeting behaviors that parents and teachers view as important and incorporating these adults into training and maintenance procedures (LeBlanc & Matson, 1995; Storey et al., 1994). Third, given the changing nature of social skills throughout childhood, assessments and interventions should be age-appropriate and adjusted as children approach new developmental milestones.

Problem-Solving Skills Training

Problem-solving therapies developed out of clinical applications of prevention techniques that focused on developing social competence. A "problem" is defined as a situation in which a child needs to find a response to promote effective functioning (D'Zurilla, 1988). Problem-solving training involves teaching a child how to develop appropriate coping responses that serve as solutions to the initial problem (D'Zurilla, 1988). This section outlines the basic components of problem-solving training: (a) problem orientation, (b) problem definition, (c) generating alternative solutions, (d) decision making, and (e) solution implementation and verification (D'Zurilla, 1988; D'Zurilla & Goldfried, 1971). The overall goal is for the child to use greater reflective thinking to promote prosocial behavior (DuPaul & Stoner, 1994).

Problem orientation involves teaching the child to identify the problem and to focus on problem-solving activities rather than maladaptive behaviors such as feeling inadequate or unlucky (D'Zurilla, 1988). Often, the child is taught to use his or her emotional response as a cue for problem recognition as well as specific behavior checklists. The child is taught to recognize that the problem is not a threat, but a normal event, and that a solution can be found (D'Zurilla, 1988).

Once the child can recognize when a problem exists, the next step is to define the problem and formulate an initial goal. The child is taught to define the problem by gathering objective information about the problem, and avoiding cognitive distortions or initial emotional responses to the problem (D'Zurilla, 1988). The child is taught to define the problem in concrete terms and to view the situation as "what is" and to identify "what should be" by defining the problem or obstacle that is creating the discrepancy in the present situation (D'Zurilla, 1988). Also, the child is taught to state clearly defined goals that are realistic and attainable. D'Zurilla (1988) noted that there are two types of formulations for highly emotional problems. There are problem-focused formulations that focus on developing problem-solving goals to change the situation (remove or minimize the problem), whereas emotion-focused formulations focus on changing a person's reaction to an event to reduce stress of the situation. Emotion-focused goals are especially important in dealing with children with impulsivity problems because they often need to learn to deal with their initial emotional reaction to a problem (DuPaul & Stoner, 1994). If necessary, both problem-focused and emotion-focused goals should be developed to deal with the problem.

Sometimes the first solutions are not the best ones to deal with the problem. Therefore, the child is next taught to develop alternative solutions. All solutions that are generated must be relevant and specific to the problem at hand. The child should be taught to defer judgment so that alternatives can be developed for the situation. Developing a high quantity and variety of solutions should be emphasized to promote a greater quality of solutions (D'Zurilla, 1988). By deferring immediate action, the child can orient to and define the problem as well as develop a number of coping responses to remove or minimize the problem in the current situation.

The next step is for the child to evaluate the alternative solutions and to decide on the best solution to the problem. The child is taught to review his or her list of alternative solutions and to imagine the outcome if the solution is used. The child is taught to evaluate the solution based on its ability to solve or minimize the problem, the amount of time and effort that must be expended when implementing the solution, and his or her emotional well-being and overall well-being. If the problem cannot be solved or minimized effectively, the child is instructed to go back to the problem definition and formulation phase. If an appropriate solution is selected, the child is instructed to develop a specific solution plan that may involve one solution or the combination of solutions to deal with the problem (D'Zurilla, 1988).

The final phase of problem-solving training is to implement the solution. All of the previous phases have involved dealing with the problem symbolically. In this phase, the child is taught to implement the solution, self-evaluate the outcome of dealing with the problem, and to use self-reinforcement (e.g., self-praise, tangibles; D'Zurilla, 1988). Goodman, Gravitt, and Kaslow (1995) noted that children who were able to develop effective alternative solutions to negative life events showed lower levels of depression than in did children who were not able to problem solve for their negative life events. Thus, effective problem solving is an important mediator in dealing with life stress and the development of depression. Nezu and Perri (1989) found problem solving therapy to be effective in treatment for depression.

The five-step procedure outlined above has been effective in treating children with anxiety. Problem solving teaches the child how to resolve the anxiety-related problem and provides the ability to cope with the problem (Kendall et al., 1991). Furthermore, problem solving may be beneficial in reducing relapses. Problem solving in addition to treatment (in vivo exposure) for agoraphobia was effective in reducing relapses in comparison to treatment alone. Thus, problem solving may be an effective addition to other treatments to enhance the therapy outcome (Kendall et al., 1991). The behavior therapist is cautioned that other treatments such as relaxation training may be more beneficial to use immediately and that problem-solving training can be added later to enhance the effectiveness of the initial intervention (D'Zurilla, 1988).

Kazdin, Esveldt-Dawson, French, and Unis (1987) demonstrated the effectiveness of reducing antisocial behavior in children when using their Problem-Solving Skills Training (PSST). Further, Kazdin, Siegel, and Bass (1992) found that the combination of PSST and parent management training was more effective than either alternative alone, and these benefits were maintained at a 1-year follow-up. Thus, problem-solving therapies are again shown to be effective in treatment as well as in combination with other treatments to improve overall treatment gains.

ADHD children also can use problem-solving strategies to deal with their impulsive behavior. These strategies often involve dealing with controlling their anger. Using a variation of the steps outlined previously, the child would identify his or her internal cues associated with anger, use self-statements to inhibit an aggressive response, generate a plan to respond (e.g., telling a peer to stop), and a backup plan (e.g., leave) if the child becomes too angry to use the initial plan. Also, the child can keep a daily problem-solving log book to promote generalization (DuPaul & Stoner, 1994).

Problem solving has been effective as the sole therapy or in combination with other therapies to enhance overall treatment effects or maintain these behavioral improvements (Kazdin et al., 1992; Kendall et al., 1991). As indicated previously, problem-solving skill training uses several techniques such as modeling, role playing, and feedback during the training process. Problem-solving therapies are of growing interest due to their success in treating a variety of disorders as well as their effectiveness in combination with other treatments (DuPaul & Stoner, 1994; Kazdin et al., 1992).

Relaxation Training

Relaxation procedures have proven useful with childhood disorders such as depression but primarily have been used to treat children with anxiety disorders such as fears and phobias, school refusal, and generalized anxiety disorder (McBurnett, Hobbs & Lahey, 1989). Relaxation procedures typically are combined with exposure-based interventions such as systematic desensitization and cognitive or cognitive–behavioral interventions (Ollendick, 1986; Ollendick, Hagopian, & Huntzinger, 1991). These interventions generally have proven very successful in treating fears and phobias, obsessive–compulsive disorders, and school and social phobias, but this section focuses on the specific training procedures rather than a review of the treatment literature. (For reviews of specific intervention studies for anxiety disorders, see Last, 1989; Milby, Robinson, & Daniel, 1998; Morris & Kratochwill, 1998.)

The primary forms of relaxation training used with children are diaphragmatic breathing and behavioral relaxation training (Poppen, 1988). Although other procedures such a progressive muscle relaxation have proven very effective with adults, these two simpler procedures are generally preferred with children. Each of these relaxation techniques should be practiced in a safe, relaxed environment until the child is able to use them readily and easily. Only then should exposure-based interventions be attempted (Last, 1989).

Diaphagmatic breathing involves having the child practice slow, rhythmic, deep breathing using only the diaphragm when inhaling. This type of breathing creates a more relaxed pattern of breathing that is incompatible with the greater autonomic arousal and shallow rapid breathing typically associated with anxiety responses (Miltenberger, 1997). Behavioral relaxation training involves having the child practice relaxed behaviors or body postures while sitting in a comfortable chair. Typically, the child is guided through 10 relaxed behaviors focusing on different parts of the body (Poppen, 1988). Cautella and Groden (1978) presented strategies for simplifying these procedures even more for individuals with special needs and suggested incorporating assistive devices such as bubble pipes to teach children how to breath effectively. The therapist provides instructions and models appropriate use of the techniques throughout the training process. In addition, the therapist may want to help the child set up a schedule for practicing the relaxation techniques at home and incorporate parents into the treatment by having them prompt the practice sessions and praise the child for completion of the sessions.

SUMMARY

The growing literature on behavioral interventions indicates that behavioral treatments can be an important component in addressing the concerns of children with a variety of psychological disorders. The effectiveness of a given intervention typically depends on a comprehensive assessment that incorporates direct links to intervention such as functional assessment or direct assessement of social deficits in natural settings (Derby et al., 1992; Gresham, 1986). In addition, most behavioral treatments combine multiple components in multiple settings to maximize treatment effectiveness and generalization. One of the hallmarks of behavioral treatments is that they can be implemented by individuals directly involved in the child's life, including parents, teachers, siblings, and even by self-administration (Reynolds & Kelley, 1997; Storey et al., 1994). Thus, with proper training in many of the procedures described, behavioral interventions can represent a valuable and user-friendly tool in the treatment of childhood psychological disorders.

REFERENCES

Abikoff, H. (1985). Efficacy of cognitive training intervention in hyperactive children: A critical review. *Clinical Psychology Review, 5,* 479–512.

Abramowitz, A. J., & O'Leary, S. G. (1991). Behavioral interventions for the classroom: Implications for students with ADHD. *School Psychology Review, 20,* 220–234.

Axelrod, S. (1990). Myths that (mis)guide our profession. In A. C. Repp & N. N. Singh (Eds.), *Perspectives on the use of nonaversive and aversive interventions for persons with developmental disabilities* (pp. 59–72). Sycamore, IL: Sycamore.

Barkley, R. A. (1990). *Attention-deficit hyperactivity disorder.* New York: Guilford.

Beck, A. T., Ward, C. H., Mendelson, M., Mock, J., & Erbaugh, J. (1961). An inventory for measuring depression. *Archives of General Psychiatry, 4,* 561–571.

Bowman, L. G., Piazza, C. C., Fisher, W. W., Hagopian, L. P., & Kogan, J. S., (1997). Assessment of preference for varied versus constant reinforcers. *Journal of Applied Behavior Analysis, 30,* 451–458.

Braswell, L., & Kendall, P. C. (1988). Cognitive–behavioral methods with children. In K. S. Dobson (Ed.), *Handbook of cognitive–behavioral therapies* (pp. 167–213). New York: Guilford.

Carr, E. G. (1977). The motivation of self-injurious behavior: A review of some hypotheses. *Psychological Bulletin, 8,* 800–816.

Carr, E. G., & Durand, V. M. (1985). Reducing problem behavior problems through functional communication training. *Journal of Applied Behavior Analysis, 18,* 111–126.

Catania, A. C. (1984). *Learning* (2nd ed.). Englewood Cliffs: Prentice-Hall.

Cautela, J. R., & Groden, J. (1978). *Relaxation: A comprehensive manual for adults, children and children with special needs.* Champaign, IL: Research Press.

Charlop, M. H., Schreibman, L., & Tryon, A. S. (1983). Learning through observation: The effects of peer modeling on acquisition and generalization in autistic children. *Journal of Abnormal Child Psychology, 11,* 355–366.

Coe, D. A., & Matson, J. L. (1990). On the empirical basis for using aversive and nonaversive therapy. In A. C. Repp & N. N. Singh (Eds.), *Perspectives on the use of nonaversive and aversive interventions for persons with developmental disabilities* (pp. 465–475). Sycamore, IL: Sycamore.

Costenbadder, V., & Reading-Brown, M. (1995). Isolation timeout used with students with emotional disturbance. *Exceptional Children, 61,* 353–363.

Curran, J. P., & Monti, P. M. (Eds.), (1982). *Social skills training.* New York: Guilford.

DeLeon, I. G., & Iwata, B. A. (1996). Evaluation of a multiple-stimulus presentation format for assessing reinforcer preferences. *Journal of Applied Behavior Analysis, 29,* 519–534.

Derby, K. M., Wacker, D. P., Sasso, G., Steege, M., Northup, J., Cigrand, K., & Asmus, J. (1992). Brief functional assessment techniques to evaluate aberrant behavior in an outpatient setting: A summary of 79 cases. *Journal of Applied Behavior Analysis, 25,* 713–723.

Dowrick, P. W. (1991). *Practical guide to using video in the behavioral sciences.* New York: Wiley.

Dulcan, M. K., Mannarino, A. P., & Borcherding, B. G. (1991). Integration of a token economy into a child and adolescent psychiatry training clinic. *Academic Psychiatry, 15,* 208–217.

DuPaul, G. J., & Stoner, G. (1994). *ADHD in the schools: Assessment and intervention strategies.* New York: Guilford.

D'Zurilla, T. J. (1988). Problem-solving therapies. In K. S. Dobson (Ed.), *Handbook of cognitive behavioral therapies* (pp. 85–135). New York: Guilford.

D'Zurilla, T. J., & Goldfried, M. R. (1971). Problem-solving and behavior modification. *Journal of Abnormal Psychology, 78,* 107–126.

Egel, A. L. (1981). Reinforcer variation: Implications for motivating developmentally disabled children. *Journal of Applied Behavior Analysis, 14,* 345–350.

Elliot, S. N., & Gresham, F. M. (1991). *Social skills intervention guide.* Circle Pines, MN: American Guidance Service.

Fisher, W., Piazza, C. C., Bowman, L. G., Hagopian, L. P., Owens, J. C., & Slevin, I. (1992). A comparison of two approaches for identifying reinforcers for persons with severe and profound disabilities. *Journal of Applied Behavior Analysis, 25,* 491–498.

Forness, S. R., & Kavale, K. A. (1996). Treating social skill deficits in children with learning disabilities: A meta-analysis of the research. *Learning Disability Quarterly, 19,* 2–13.

Frankel, F., Myatt, R., Cantwell, D. P., & Feinberg, D. T. (1997). Parent-assisted transfer of children's social skills training: Effects on children with and without attention-deficit hyperactivity disorder. *Journal of the American Academy of Child and Adolescent Psychiatry, 36,* 1056–1064.

Frea, W. D., & Hughes, C. (1997). Functional analysis and treatment of social–communicative behavior of adolescents with developmental disabilities. *Journal of Applied Behavior Analysis, 30,* 701–704.

Gast, D. L., & Nelson, C. M. (1977). Legal and ethical considerations for the use of timeout in special education settings. *Journal of Special Education, 11,* 457–467.

Goldstein, A. P. (1981). *Psychological skill training: The structure learning technique.* Elmsford, NY: Pergamon.

Goldstein, A. P., Sprafkin, R. P., Gershaw, M. J., & Klein, P. (1980). *Skill streaming the adolescent: A structure learning approach to teaching pro-social skills.* Champaign, IL: Research Press.

Goodman, S. H., Gravitt, G. W., Jr., & Kaslow, N. J. (1995). Social problem solving: A moderator of the relation between negative life stress and depression symptoms in children. *Journal of Abnormal Child Psychology, 23,* 473–485.

Gordon, M., Thomason, D., Cooper, S., & Ivers, C. L. (1990). Nonmedical treatment of ADHD/Hyperactivity: The attention training system. *Journal of School Psychology, 29,* 151–159.

Grant, L., & Evans, A. (1994). *Principles of behavior analysis.* New York: HarperCollins College.

Gresham, F. M. (1981). Social skills training with handicapped children: A review. *Review of Educational Research, 51,* 139–176.

Gresham, F. M. (1986). Conceptual and definitional issues in the assessment of social skills: Implications for classification and training. *Journal of Clinical Child Psychology, 15,* 16–25.

Gresham, F. M. (1992). Social skills and learning disabilities: Causal, concomitant or correlational? *School Psychology Review, 21,* 348–360.

Gresham, F. M., & Elliot, S. N. (1990). *Social skills rating system: Manual.* Circle Pines, MN: American Guidance Service.

Guralnick, M. J. (1990). Major accomplishments and future directions in early childhood mainstreaming. *Topics in Early Childhood Special Education, 10,* 1–17.

Harris, K. R. (1985). Definitional, parametric, and procedural considerations in timeout interventions and research. *Exceptional Children, 51,* 279–288.

Hazel, J. S., Schumaker, J. B., Sherman, J. A., & Sheldon-Wildgen, J. (1981). *ASSET: A social skills program for adolescents.* Champaign, IL: Research Press.

Hoberman, H. M. (1990). Behavioral treatments for unipolar depression. In B. B. Wolman & G. Stricker (Eds.), *Depressive disorders* (pp. 310–342). New York: Wiley.

Hughes, J. N. (1986). Methods of skill selection in social skills training: A review. *Professional School Psychology, 1,* 235–248.

Ihrig, K., & Wolchik, S. A. (1988). Peer versus adult models and autistic children's learning: Acquisition, generalization, and maintenance. *Journal of Autism and Developmental Disorders, 18,* 67–79.

Iwata, B. A. (1987). Negative reinforcement in applied behavior analysis: An emerging technology. *Journal of Applied Behavior Analysis, 20,* 361–378.

Iwata, B. A., Dorsey, M. F., Slifer, K. J., Bauman, K. E., & Richman, G. S. (1994). Toward a functional analysis of self-injury. *Journal of Applied Behavior Analysis, 27,* 197–210.

Karoly, P. , & Harris, A. (1986). Operant methods. In F. H. Kanfer & A. P. Goldstein (Eds.), *Helping people change: A textbook of methods* (3rd ed., pp. 111–144). New York: Pergamon.

Kazdin, A. E. (1982). The token economy: A decade later. *Journal of Applied Behavior Analysis, 15,* 431–445.

Kazdin, A. E. (1990). Childhood depression. *Journal of Child Psychology and Psychiatry, 31,* 121–160.

Kazdin, A. E., Esveldt-Dawson, K., French, N. H., & Unis, A. S. (1987). Problem-solving skills training and relationship therapy in the treatment of antisocial child behavior. *Journal of Consulting and Clinical Psychology, 55,* 76–85.

Kazdin, A. E., French, N. H., Unis, A. S., Esveldt-Dawson, K., & Sherick, R. B. (1983). Hopelessness, depression and suicidal intent among psychiatrically disturbed inpatient children. *Journal of Consulting and Clinical Psychology, 51,* 504–510.

Kazdin, A. E., Siegel, T. C., & Bass, D. (1992). Cognitive problem-solving skills training and parent management training in the treatment of antisocial behavior in children. *Journal of Consulting and Clinical Psychology, 60,* 733–747.

Kendall, P. C., Chansky, T. E., Freidman, M., Kim, R., Kortlander, E., Sessa, F. M., & Siqueland, L. (1991). Treating anxiety disorders in children and adolescents. In P. C. Kendall (Ed.), *Child and adolescent therapy: Cognitive–behavioral procedures* (pp. 131–164). New York: Guilford.

Kendall, P. C., Korlander, E., Chansky, T. E., & Brady, E. U. (1992). Comorbidity of anxiety and depression in youth: Treatment implications. *Journal of Consulting and Clinical Psychology, 60,* 869–880.

Kennedy, P., Kupst, M. J., Westman, G., Zaar, C., Pines, R., & Schulman, J. L. (1990). Use of the timeout procedure in a child psychiatry inpatient milieu: Combining dynamic and behavioral approaches. *Child Psychiatry, 20,* 207–216.

L'Abate, L., & Milan, M. A. (Eds.), (1985). *Handbook of social skills training and research.* New York: Wiley.

Ladd, G. W. (1985). Documenting the effects of social skills training with children. In B. H. Schneider, K. H. Rubin, & J. E. Legingham (Eds.), *Children's peer relations: Issues in assessment and intervention* (pp. 243–269). New York: Springer.

Ladd, G. W., & Golter, B. S. (1988). Parents' management of preschoolers' peer relations: Is it related to children's social competence? *Developmental Psychology, 24,* 109–117.

Ladd, G. W., & Mize, J. (1983). A cognitive–social learning model of social skills training. *Psychological Review, 90,* 127–157.

LaGreca, A. M., & Vaughn, S. (1992). Social functioning of individuals with learning disabilities. *School Psychology Review, 21,* 340–347.

Lalli, J. S., Browder, D. M., Mace, F. C., & Brown, D. K. (1993). Teacher use of descriptive analysis data to implement interventions to decrease students' problem behaviors. *Journal of Applied Behavior Analysis, 26,* 227–238.

Last, C. G. (1989). Anxiety Disorders. In T. H. Ollendick and M. Hersen (Eds.), *Handbook of child psychopathology* (2nd ed., pp. 219–228). New York: Plenum.

Lattal, K. A. (1991). Scheduling positive reinforcers. In I. H. Iversen & K. A. Lattal (Eds.), *Experimental analysis of behavior, parts 1 and 2. Techniques in the behavioral and neural sciences* (Vol. 6, pp. 87–134). Amsterdam, Netherlands: Elsevier Science.

LeBlanc, L. A., & Matson, J. L. (1995). A social skills training program for preschoolers with developmental delays: Generalization and social validity. *Behavior Modification, 19,* 234–246.

Linscheid, T. R., & Meinhold, P. (1990). The controversy over aversives: Basic operant research and the side effects of punishment. In A. C. Repp & N. N. Singh (Eds.), *Perspectives on the use of nonaversive and aversive interventions for persons with developmental disabilities* (pp. 435–450). Sycamore, IL: Sycamore.

Lollis, S. P., Ross, H. S., & Tate, E. (1992). Parents' regulation of children's peer interactions: Direct influences. In R. D. Parke & G. W. Ladd (Eds.), *Family–peer relationships: Modes of linkage* (pp. 255–281). Hillsdale, NJ: Lawrence Erlbaum Associates.

Matson, J. L., & Sweizy, N. (1994). Social skills training in autistic children. In J. L. Matson (Ed.), *Autism in children and adults: Etiology, assessment and treatment.* (pp. 241–260). Monterey, CA: Brooks/Cole.

Mavis, B. E., & Stoffelmayr, B. E. (1994). Multidimensional evaluation of monetary incentive strategies for weight control. *Psychological Record, 44,* 239–252.

McBurnett, K., Hobbs, S. A., & Lahey, B. B. (1989). Behavioral Treatment. In T. H. Ollendick and M. Hersen (Eds.), *Handbook of Child Psychopathology, Second Edition.* New York: Plenum.

McGinnis, E., Goldstein, A., Sprafkin, R., & Gershaw, N. (1984). *Skill streaming the elementary school child: A guide for teaching prosocial skills.* Champaign, IL: Research Press.

Michael, J. (1993). Establishing operations. *The Behavior Analyst, 16,* 191–206.

Milby, J. B., Robinson, S. L., & Daniel, S. (1998). Obsessive compulsive disorder. In R. J. Morris and T. R. Kratochwill (Eds.), *The Practice of Child Therapy* (3rd ed., pp. 5–47). Boston: Allyn & Bacon.

Miltenberger, R. (1997). *Behavior modification: Principles and procedures.* Monterey, CA: Brookes/Cole.

Morris, R. J., & Kratochwill, T. R. (1998). Childhood fears and phobias. In R. J. Morris and T. R. Kratochwill (Eds.), *The practice of child therapy,* (3rd ed., pp. 91–131). Boston: Allyn & Bacon.

Neef, N. A., Mace, F. C., Shea, M. C., & Shade, D. (1992). Effects of reinforcer rate and reinforcer quality on time allocation: Extensions of matching theory to educational settings. *Journal of Applied Behavior Analysis, 25,* 691–700.

Nezu, A. M., & Perri, M. G. (1989). Social problem-solving therapy for unipolar depression: An initial dismantling investigation. *Journal of Consulting and Clinical Psychology, 57,* 408–413.

Northup, J., Jones, K., Broussard, C., & George, T. (1995). A preliminary comparison of reinforcer assessement methods for children with attention deficit hyperactivity disorder. *Journal of Applied Behavior Analysis, 28,* 99–102.

Ogier, R., & Hornby, G. (1996). Effects of differential reinforcement on the behavior and self-esteem of children with emotional and behavioral disorders. *Journal of Behavioral Education, 6,* 501–510.

Ollendick, T. H. (1986). Child and adolescent behavior therapy. In S. L. Garfield & A. E. Bergin (Eds.), *Handbook of psychotherapy and behavior change,* (3rd ed., pp. 456–464). New York: Wiley.

Ollendick, T. H., Hagopian, L. P., & Huntzinger, R. M. (1991). Cognitive behavior therapy with nighttime fearful children. *Journal of Behavior Therapy and Experimental Psychiatry, 22*, 112–121.

Pace, G. M., Ivancic, M. T., Edwards, G. L., Iwata, B. A., & Page, T. J. (1985). Assessment of stimulus preference in reinforcer value with profoundly retarded individuals. *Journal of Applied Behavior Analysis, 18*, 249–255.

Pace, G. M., Ivancic, M. T., & Jefferson, G. (1994). Stimulus fading as treatment for obscenity in a brain-injured adult. *Journal of Applied Behavior Analysis, 27*, 301–306.

Piazza, C. C., & Fisher, W. W. (1991). A faded bedtime with response cost protocol for treatment of multiple sleep problems in children. *Journal of Applied Behavior Analysis, 24*, 129–140.

Piazza, C. C., Fisher, W. W., Hanley, G. P., Remick, M. L., Contrucci, S. A., & Aitken, T. A. (1997). The use of positive and negative reinforcement in the treatment of escape-maintained destructive behavior. *Journal of Applied Behavior Analysis, 30*, 279–298.

Piazza, C. C., Moes, D. R., & Fisher, W. W. (1996). Differential reinforcement of alternative behavior and demand fading in the treatment of escape-maintained destructive behavior. *Journal of Applied Behavior Analysis, 29*, 569–572.

Poppen, R. (1988). *Behavioral relaxation training and assessment*. Elmsford, NY: Pergamon.

Rangasamy, R., Taylor, R. L., & Ziegler, E. W. (1996). Eliminating inappropriate classroom behavior using a DRO schedule: A preliminary study. *Psychological Reports, 78*, 753–754.

Reed, M. K. (1994). Social skills training to reduce depression in adolescents. *Adolescence, 29*, 293–302.

Rehm, L. P., & Rokke, P. (1988). Self-management therapies. In K. S. Dobson (Ed.), *Handbook of cognitive–behavioral therapies* (pp. 136–165). New York: Guilford.

Reimers, T. M. (1996). A biobehavioral approach toward managing encopresis. *Behavior Modification, 20*, 469–479.

Repp, A. C., & Singh, N. N. (1990). *Perspectives on the use of nonaversive and aversive interventions for persons with developmental disabilities*. Sycamore, IL: Sycamore.

Reynolds, L. K., & Kelley, M. L. (1997). The efficacy of a response cost-based treatment package for managing aggressive behavior in preschoolers. *Behavior Modification, 21*, 216–230.

Risley, T. R., & Wolf, M. M. (1997). The origin of the dimensions of applied behavior analysis. *Journal of Applied Behavior Analysis, 30*, 377–380.

Robinson, R. M., Powers, J. M., Cleveland, P. H., & Thyer, B. A. (1990). Inpatient psychiatric treatment for depressed children and adolescents: Preliminary evaluations. *The Psychiatric Hospital, 21*, 107–112.

Ronen, T., Wozner, Y., & Rahav, G. (1992). Cognitive interventions in enuresis. *Child and Family Behavior Therapy, 14*, 1–14.

Sandler, J. (1986). Aversion methods. In F. H. Kanfer & A. P. Goldstein (Eds.), *Helping people change: A textbook of methods* (3rd ed., pp. 111–144). Elmsford, NY: Pergamon.

Sarafino, E. P. (1996). *Principles of Behavior Change: Understanding Behavior Modification Techniques*. New York: Wiley.

Sheridan, S. M., Dee, C. C., Morgan, J. C., McCormick, M. E., & Walker, D. (1996). A multimethod intervention for social skills deficits in children with ADHD and their parents. *School Psychology Review, 25*, 57–76.

Sidman, M. (1991). Positive reinforcement in education. In W. Ishaq (Ed.), *Human behavior in today's world* (pp. 171–184). New York: Praeger.

Simeonsson, R. J., & Rosenthal, S. L. (1992). Developmental models and clinical practice. In C. E. Walker & M. C. Roberts (Eds.), *Handbook of clinical child psychology* (2nd ed., pp. 19–32). New York: Wiley.

Singh, N. N., Osborne, J. G., & Huguenin, N. H. (1996). Applied behavioral interventions. In J. W. Jacobson, & J. A. Mulick (Eds.), *Manual of diagnosis and professional practice in mental retardation* (pp. 341–353). Washington DC: American Psychological Association.

Skiba, R., & Raison, J. (1990). Relationship between the use of timeout and academic achievement. *Exceptional Children, 56*, 36–45.

Storey, K., Danko, C. D., Ashworth, R., & Strain, P. S. (1994). Generalization of social skills intervention for preschoolers with social delays. *Education and Treatment of Children, 17*, 29–51.

Storey, K., Smith, D. J., & Strain, P. S. (1993). Use of classroom assistants and peer-mediated intervention to increase integration in preschool settings. *Exceptionality, 4*, 1–16.

Sullivan, M. A., & O'Leary, S. G. (1990). Maintenance following reward and cost token programs. *Behavior Therapy, 21,* 139–149.

Sulzer-Azaroff, B., & Mayer, R. G. (1977). *Applying behavior analysis procedures with children
and youth.* New York: Holt, Rinehart & Winston.

Swallow, S. R., & Segal, Z. V. (1994). Cognitive–behavioral therapy for unipolar depression. In K.
D. Craig & K. S. Dobson (Eds.), *Anxiety and depression in adults and children* (pp. 209–229).
Thousand Oaks, CA: Sage.

Taylor, J. C., & Romanczyk, R. G. (1994). Generating hypotheses about the function of student
problem behavior by observing teacher behavior. *Journal of Applied Behavior Analysis, 27,*
251–266.

Tiffen, K., & Spence, S. H. (1986). Responsiveness of isolated and rejected children to social
skills training. *Journal of Child Psychology and Psychiatry, 27,* 343–355.

Vaughn, B. J., & Horner, R. H. (1997). Identifying instructional tasks that occasion problem behaviors and assessing the effects of student versus teacher choice among these tasks. *Journal of Applied Behavior Analysis, 30,* 299–312.

Vollmer, T. R., & Iwata, B. A. (1992). Differential reinforcement as treatment for behavior disorders: Procedural and functional variations. *Research in Developmental Disabilities, 13,*
393–417.

Wagaman, J. R., Miltenberger, R. G., & Williams, D. E. (1995). Treatment of a vocal tic by differential reinforcement. *Journal of Behavior Therapy & Experimental Psychiatry, 26,* 35–39.

Walker, H., McConnell, S., Holmes, D., Todis, B., Walker, J., & Golden, N. (1983). *The Walker social skills curriculum: The ACCEPTS program.* Austin, TX: Pro-Ed.

Whitaker, S. (1996). A review of DRO: The influence of the degree of intellectual disability and
the frequency of the target behavior. *Journal of Applied Research in Intellectual Disabilities,
9,* 61–79.

White, A. G., & Bailey, J. S. (1990). Reducing disruptive behaviors of elementary physical education students with sit and watch. *Journal of Applied Behavior Analysis, 23,* 353–359.

Williams, B. F., Williams, R. L., & McLaughlin, T. F. (1989). The use of token economies with individuals who have developmental disabilities. In E. Cipani (Ed.), *The treatment of severe
behavior disorders: Behavior analysis approaches* (Monographs of the American Association on Mental Retardation, No. 12, pp. 3–18). Washington DC: American Association on
Mental Retardation.

Zaragoza, N., Vaughn, S., & McIntosh, R. (1991). Social skills interventions and children with behavior problems: A review. *Behavioral Disorders, 16,* 260–275.

Psychopharmacological Treatment

Susan V. McLeer
Cheryl Wills
State University of New York at Buffalo

Psychologists, working with children and adolescents, need to be knowledgeable regarding the pharmacological strategies that have been studied and applied empirically in the treatment of psychiatric disorders found in children and adolescents. It is important to be aware of which drugs are most often used and which may be used for specific disorders or symptoms. It is critical to be aware of the signs and symptoms of drug toxicity, side effects and adverse reactions, because these problematic and potentially dangerous reactions first may be noticed by a psychologist treating or consulting on a case.

This chapter reviews how children's reactions to medications differ from those of adults. Regulatory issues affecting the use of psychotropic medications in children and adolescents are elucidated. Some of the changes in thinking about approaches to the pharmacotherapy of psychiatric disorders in children are reviewed, and, finally, medications used in the treatment of specific disorders are outlined with emphasis on (a) the empirical basis for use of a drug; (b) elements of an adequate therapeutic trial; and (c) side effects, adverse reactions, and symptoms of toxicity.

PHARMACOTHERAPY IN CHILDHOOD

Children are not "little adults." Consequently, extrapolating from what is known about adult psychopathology and its treatment in developing treatment protocols for children and adolescents can be problematic. In the *Diagnostic and Statistical Manual of Mental Disorders* (4th ed.[*DSM–IV*]; American Psychological Association, 1994), the diagnostic criteria for adult disorders almost always are extrapolated and applied to children, with occasional changes in the quality, number or duration of specific symptoms. Are psychiatric disorders truly the same in children as in adults? Do children with psychiatric disorders respond to pharmacotherapies in the same way as adults do? If there are differences in therapeutic response, are they accounted for by differences in how medications are absorbed, distributed, metabolized, and excreted in children, or are there basic developmental differences in manifestations of the psychiatric disorders themselves? These are critical questions that can and must be answered empirically. The opportunities for research are staggering when one considers the answerable but unanswered questions encountered in addressing the phenomenology of psychiatric disorders and psychopharmacotherpies for children and adolescents.

Risk–Benefit Assessment

Whenever medication is prescribed, a risk–benefit assessment is paramount. The therapeutic gain must be balanced against the risk of toxicity, side effects and potential adverse reactions. How do these three factors differ? *Toxicity* refers to a dose-dependent adverse reaction that lessens when medication is reduced. The manifestations of toxicity range from minor, (e.g., mild hand tremor), to potentially lethal outcomes, (e.g., failure of cardiac or respiratory function). *Side effects* are undesired changes in function that are found at therapeutic drug levels. These side effects may, or may not, be dose dependent and may, or may not, dissipate with time. *Adverse reactions* are less prevalent reactions found in some, but not most, individuals. Adverse reactions might not be dose dependent and can range from mild to moderate effects, e.g. slight elevations in liver enzymes to potential lethal consequences, e.g. agranulocytosis (failure of the bone marrow to make blood cells and platelets).

Pharmacokinetics and Pharmacodynamics

A risk–benefit assessment is dependent on the (a) route, dose size, and frequency of drug administration; (b) the pharmacokinetics; and (c) the pharmacodynamics of a drug. Generally, drugs administered orally are absorbed more slowly than those administered parentally (i.e., by injection), with those administered intravenously having the most rapid delivery. The *pharmacokinetics* of a drug refers to how a drug is delivered to its site of action, including factors affecting the concentration of the drug and its duration of action. *Pharmacodynamics* refers to the drug's effect at its targeted site of action and the resultant end response of the drug on the organism in toto.

Dose and absorption are relevant variables affecting delivery of the drug, with absorption being dependent on route of administration, drug characteristics (including molecular size, charge, lipid solubility, etc.), as well as other factors that might influence permeability. For oral medications, permeability can be affected by the presence of food or disease states affecting the stomach or intestine. Other factors come into play with medications that are administered by injection. Generally, water soluble drugs have a smaller volume of distribution throughout the body and, because of being water soluble, these agents can be directly excreted from the body by the kidney. Drugs with high lipid solubility tend to have a larger volume of distribution and must undergo chemical changes through metabolic processes in order to become water soluble and, hence, able to be excreted in the urine.

In addition to its degree of water or lipid solubility, distribution of a drug is affected by the potential volume of distribution in an individual and the extent of the drug's binding to plasma proteins. These two factors are particularly relevant in children, in that the smaller the child, the smaller the volume of distribution. In addition, children have a higher concentration of a plasma protein called alpha-1-acid glycoprotein than do adults and the concentration of this protein can be increased further in the presence of infection or physical stress. Alpha-1-acid glycoprotein increases protein binding for certain psychotropic drugs like haloperidol (Haldol®); (Schley, & Mulller-Oerlinghausen, 1983). Drugs that are bound to plasma proteins are not available as free active substances in the blood. Therefore, this increased plasma protein binding of certain drugs in children decreases the plasma concentration of free drug, the active component; hence, counter intuitively, this requires higher dosing of children than of adults with certain drugs, (e.g., haloperidol). On first reflection, one might assume that with a smaller volume of distribution, concentration of the drug at a particular dose is higher, counterbalancing, in part, the effect of increased protein binding. However, this is not the entire story.

When drugs are studied for use in humans, one pharmacokinetic variable that is essential to determine is the drug's half-life. *Half-life* refers to the amount of time it takes for 50% of the active component of the drug to be removed from circulation and irreversibly eliminated from the body. The clearance of the drug from the blood is inversely proportional to the volume of distribution. Therefore, the smaller the volume of distribution, the faster its clearance and the shorter its half-life, indicating, again, that for some agents, either higher dosing or more frequent dosing is required in children than in adults because of the smaller volume of distribution.

The *therapeutic index* of a drug refers to the ratio of the dose that produces a toxic effect, divided by the dose that produces a therapeutic effect. The larger the therapeutic index, the safer the pharmacological agent. Some psychotropic drugs have different therapeutic indexes in children than in adults. Consequently, some medications used with children are associated with toxic effects, including sudden death, at doses and concentrations that would be therapeutic in adults (e.g., tricyclic antidepressants, or TCAs). This effect with TCAs in children appears to be secondary to children's increased production of a cardiotoxic metabolite (Greenberg, Stiglin, Finkelstein, & Berndt, 1993). The complexity of administering medication to children does not end here. Drugs that have long half-lives in adults may have different half-lives in children. Furthermore, half-life differences are not categorical but change with the age of the child. For example, imipramine (Tofranil®) has a long half-life in adults. Its half-life in children aged 5–12 years ranges from 11 to 42 hours, whereas in children aged 13–16 years, the range is 14 to 89 hours. Such shifts in drug half-life require adjustment of the dosing schedule to insure adequacy of drug concentration. Dosing, however, must be considered in light of data regarding the therapeutic index of the drug in question, particularly when using the TCAs.

Metabolic biotransformation refers to the chemical changes in a drug that take place, usually in the liver, to transform the drug into a water-soluble compound that can be excreted by the kidney. Metabolic biotransformation is but one component affecting the clearance of active pharmacological agents from the blood. This process is highly variable, with a tenfold to hundredfold intersubject variation in metabolism during adulthood. Studies have indicated that this intersubject variance is at least as great in children as in adults, and, in some instances, metabolism in the pediatric aged patient differs considerably from that of adults (Rodman, 1994). Some of the intersubject variance is accounted for by genetic factors affecting metabolic structures involved in drug metabolism, such as the cytochrome P–450 system. Some cytochrome activity has been found to be uniformly distributed in the population (e.g., P–450–3A4; Breimer, Schulens, & Soons, 1989), whereas other activity is multimodally distributed, (e.g., P–450–2D6; Jacqzl, Hall, & Branch, 1986). This results in there being subpopulations of individuals that are deficient in the basic metabolic structures necessary for deactivating some psychotropic agents (Gough et al., 1990). In such cases, small doses of a drug will result in exceptionally high concentrations of the active drug in the plasma. Clinicians usually do not test for such genetic difference; hence, it becomes critical to monitor blood levels of drugs as well as monitor the child for any signs of toxicity.

Finally, psychoactive drugs usually affect neurotransmitter systems in the brain and periphery. Some studies have indicated that significant differences exist in comparing concentrations of certain neurotransmitters associated with psychopathology in adulthood and childhood (Vitiello, 1997). These differences are considerable and suggest that there may be developmental shifts in the concentration, activity, and effects of neurotransmitters throughout the life cycle. The interaction of such factors with psychotropic drugs is obviously relevant to treatment considerations. However, studies regarding these developmental differences are still very preliminary.

Diagnosis Versus Symptom-Driven Pharmacotherapy

With the advent of the *DSM–III* (APA, 1980), *DSM–III–R* (APA, 1987), and *DSM–IV* (APA, 1994) and the associated development of structured and semistructured interviews with moderate to high diagnostic interrater reliability, the focus on designing pharmacological efficacy studies using homogeneous diagnostic groupings intensified. Additionally, the embraced medical model has fueled development of a quest for specific treatments for specific diseases. This quest has not been all that successful. Not all patients in a specific diagnostic category have responded equally to specific pharmacological agents. Consequently, investigators started looking for subgroups of patients, subgroups encompassed by a specific psychiatric diagnosis but subclassified on the basis of symptom cluster, treatment response, or other biological parameters. This approach has been partially successful; however, with the advent of pharmacological agents that target specific neurotransmitter systems—for example, the selective serotonin reuptake inhibitors (SSRIs)—the research focus is beginning to shift again with increased emphasis on targeting symptoms that may cross diagnostic categories. For example, anxiety as a symptom appears in the anxiety disorders, but also can be found associated with schizophrenia. Once it was considered bad practice to use benzodiazepines (antianxiety drugs) in treating schizophrenia, but now these agents may be used with antipsychotic medication in managing anxiety symptoms. In doing so, the dose of antipsychotics can be kept lower than previously and, hence, decrease side effects that interfere with treatment compliance. It is anticipated that more pharmacological research targeting symptoms that cross diagnostic lines will evolve over the next 5 to 10 years.

Comorbidity and the Use of Combined Pharmacotherapy

Polypharmacy has been considered a "dirty word" in medical circles. The term has been used in a derogatory manner to refer to the practice of "when one drug does not work sufficiently, add another and then another." Needless to say, the dangers of such practice are considerable because of drug interactions and the subsequent risk of toxicity, side effects, and adverse reactions. However, a shift in thinking is emerging. Although most agree that it is highly desirable to use one drug, not two or more, studies are demonstrating that, in some cases, there is less than satisfactory response to single pharmacological agents (Wilens, Spencer, Biederman, Wozniak, & Connor, 1995).

Researchers have found that some drugs, when used in combination, have a greater effect at lower doses than would be expected simply from an additive effect. An *additive effect* is that effect that would be expected based on the combined effect of each of two agents used independently. When the combined effect of two or more agents is greater than that expected from an additive effect, the resultant drug interaction is referred to as a *potentiated*, or enhanced treatment effect. Additionally, there now are considerable data from epidemiological studies indicating that many children and adolescents have not just one psychiatric disorder but two or more coexisting or comorbid disorders (Bird, Gould, & Staghezza, 1993). Each disorder might require a different pharmacological approach. Because of these factors, as well as the issue of targeting symptoms that cross diagnostic lines, researchers and scholars in the field are starting to use combined pharmacotherapies. When combined treatments are used, the need for the prescribing physician to be tremendously knowledgeable regarding drug interactions is considerable. Over the last decade, studies have demonstrated that many psychotropic drugs affect the cytochrome P–450 system in ways that reduce metabolism of other agents sufficiently that severe toxic levels of drug can accrue with major adverse consequences. As the scholarly and informed use of combined treatments increases, it will be difficult for the psychologist to determine if his or her client is being medically managed by a knowledgeable physician or a physician practicing the old and dangerous brand of polypharmacy.

Determining Efficacy

Given that pharmacotherapy requires a careful risk–benefit analysis, drugs that do not effect positive change have little benefit and still pose risk. Psychotropics need to be given an adequate therapeutic trial, which requires that sufficient medication be given for an appropriate period, the dose and duration being empirically derived. If a drug is still not of benefit following an adequate therapeutic trial, another agent should be considered, the diagnosis should be reconsidered, or both. At this time, there are numerous standardized rating scales available that allow systematic monitoring of symptoms. The importance of monitoring treatment response with standardized measures cannot be overemphasized.

Regulatory Issues in Pediatric Psychopharmacology

The role of the Food and Drug Administration (FDA) is frequently misunderstood. Laughren (1996) noted,

> The FDA does not regulate the practice of medicine, and consequently, physicians are free to prescribe approved drugs in the treatment of any illnesses for which they, in their medical judgement, consider those drugs appropriate, whether or not the illnesses in question are approved indications in the labeling for those products. (p. 1276)

When drugs are prescribed for disorders that have not been approved and specified in the labeling of the agent, the practice is referred to as "off–label use." With children and adolescents, the vast majority of psychotropics prescribed are off–label prescriptions (Vitiello, Conrad, Burkhart, Laughren, & Jensen, 1994). The reasons for this are complex. New drugs first are tested for safety in animal models and then in humans. Rigorous studies of efficacy follow the establishment of a reasonable standard of safety. Such studies are almost always done with adult participants and the laws and regulations pertaining to investigational new drugs and new drug applications do not address specifically the need to conduct studies with children and adolescents. In the absence of research with pediatric patients, labels and marketing literature must include a standard disclaimer: "Safety and effectiveness in children have not been established." If there is a desire to market the drug for use in the pediatric population, there are specific labeling regulations that must be followed to obtain FDA approval. Nonetheless, what is clear is that at this time, FDA approval of a drug for children and adolescents is a marketing issue, not a clinical research or practice issue. Most psychotropic drugs being used in pediatric pharmacotherapy are not approved by the FDA, such approval not being necessary for physician prescribing.

PSYCHOSIS IN CHILDREN AND ADOLESCENTS

Psychosis is a clinical condition characterized by impaired reality testing. The following disorders feature psychosis: schizophrenia; bipolar I disorder with psychotic features; schizoaffective disorder; brief reactive psychosis; major depressive disorder with psychotic features; delusional disorder; substance-induced psychosis, including psychosis induced by either prescribed or illicit drugs, and psychotic disorder due to a general medical condition. This section will focus on the pharmacological treatment of schizophrenia, a disorder that requires medication as well as specific psychosocial treatments. The pharmacological treatment of the other psychotic disorders also may require antipsychotic medications in addition to specific medication for the underlying affective or substance-induced disorder. Psychosis associated with medical conditions obviously requires medical management of the underlying etiology.

Schizophrenia rarely occurs in children, but the number of new cases approaches the adult incidence rate of 0.1% by late adolescence (McClellan & Werry, 1994). According to the *DSM–IV* (APA, 1994), the diagnostic criteria for schizophrenia require presence of at least two of the following five symptoms during a period of 1 month: (a) delusions, (b) hallucinations, (c) disorganized speech, (d) grossly disorganized or catatonic behavior, and e) negative symptoms (apathy, social withdrawal, poverty of speech, and affective flattening). Only one of five symptoms is required if the hallucination is a voice making a running commentary about the person's behavior or thinking, or if two or more voices are having a discussion. The disturbance must be present for at least 6 months and there must be evidence of deterioration in social, occupational, or daily care functioning.

Symptoms of schizophrenia are divided into two major categories: positive and negative symptoms. Positive symptoms appear to reflect an excess or distortion of normal functions such as inferential thinking (delusions), perception (hallucinations), language and communication (disorganized speech), or behavior (disorganized or catatonic behavior). Negative symptoms reflect a diminution or loss of normal functions, including the range and intensity of emotional expression (affective-flattening), fluency and productivity of thought and speech (alogia), and in the initiation of goal–directed behavior (avolition; *DSM–IV,* pp. 274–275). Antipsychotic medications are used to treat symptoms of schizophrenia and other psychotic illnesses. All antipsychotic medications reduce the severity of positive symptoms, and some of the newer antipsychotic medications (atypical antipsychotic medication) also improve negative symptoms. Antipsychotic medication should be prescribed as part of a multidisciplinary treatment plan, which may include specific psychosocial therapies and school interventions.

Traditional Antipsychotic Medications

These agents, also known as neuroleptics, block specific receptors in the brain known as dopamine receptors. These agents are effective in reducing positive symptoms of schizophrenia but are less successful in alleviating negative symptoms. Although efficacy of antipsychotics in schizophrenic adults has been demonstrated in more than 100 double-blind studies (Davis, Comaty, & Janicak, 1987), few studies have been completed in children and adolescents. Early drug trials were fraught with major methodological problems, the most significant being the lack of diagnostic homogeneity, with many children meeting criteria for pervasive developmental disorder or childhood autism (Rosenberg, Holttum, & Gershon, 1994). These early studies raised questions regarding the efficacy of antipsychotic medication in children who were prepubertal or younger. Case reports suggested that younger children did not demonstrate significant symptom remission when traditional antipsychotics were used (M. Campbell, Gonzolez, Ernst, Silva, & Werry, 1993). Hence, it was suggested that in younger children a trial of medication, should be instituted, and if symptoms did not lessen, the drug should be discontinued because lack of therapeutic benefit did not merit the risk of exposing the child to the drug's side effects and to the risk of developing tardive dyskinesia. More recent studies have suggested that both children and adolescents meeting *DSM–IV* criteria for schizophrenia respond much like adults to antipsychotic medication, providing adjustments are made for differences in pharmacodynamics and kinetics. Children require higher doses per kilogram than do adults to achieve comparable plasma drug levels (Wilens, Spencer, Biederman, & Linehan, 1998). However, because individual variability in metabolism is so great, dosing should start at low levels and be titrated on the basis of clinical response and side effect profiles (Teicher & Glod, 1990). Pool, Bloom, Roniger, and Gallant (1976), using a homogeneous group of subjects, found in a double-blind, placebo–controlled trial that loxapine (Loxitane®) had a small to modest effect in psychotic adolescents. Realmuto, Erickson, Yellin, Hopwood, and Greenberg (1984) showed a small to moderate response in a double-blind comparison study of thiothixene (Navane®) and thioridazine (Mellaril®). The preliminary results of E. K. Spencer, Kafantaris, Padron-Gayol, Rosenberg, and Cambell (1992), in their ongoing study of haloperidol (Haldol®) in psychotic adolescents, suggest that response to treatment with haloperidol is similar to that observed in adults. Definitive studies, sensitive to age of onset, have yet to be conducted.

Most traditional antipsychotics have a similar side effect profile, but the intensity of these side effects is related to the potency of the medication. This makes it possible to tailor the medication to a particular symptom profile. For example, low potency antipsychotics like chlorpromazine (Thorazine®) and thioridazine (Mellaril®) have higher rates of sedation. These medications may be beneficial to a youth who is having difficulty sleeping. A less sedating, more potent, antipsychotic medication, like haloperidol (Haldol®), may be a reasonable selection for a hypersomnolent child or adolescent. Higher potency antipsychotic medications are associated with extrapyramidal symptoms, such as acute dystonic reaction (muscle stiffness or immobility) and akathisia (subjective sense of motor restlessness). Mental dulling may occur in children who are prescribed higher doses. All antipsychotics should be prescribed at low doses initially; dose increases should occur slowly while monitoring the presence and severity of side effects. A medication trial takes 4 to 6 weeks at a therapeutic dose (McClellan & Werry, 1994). Side effects, poor supervision, and refusal of treatment may contribute to poor compliance with medication. Depot or long-acting antipsychotic medication, used with noncompliant adults, is problematic in adolescents because they have a higher incidence of side effects, especially dystonia. Rate of occurrence of dystonia is 20.9% to 50.4% (Gelenberg, 1987). Drooling may occur due to stiff facial muscles. Physical immobility, difficulty with ambulating, and breathing problems may occur. Patients with dystonic reactions may respond to a reduction in antipsychotic medication dose or to anticholinergic agents like benztropine (Cogentin®), trihexyphenidyl (Artane®), or diphenhydramine (Benadryl®).

Akathisia has an incidence rate of 20% to 30% (Perlmutter, 1995). It may contribute to sleep disturbance, hyperactivity, agitation, pacing, rocking, impulsivity, anxiety, and impaired judgment. Reducing the dose of antipsychotic medication may alleviate symptoms. Treatment with clonazepam (Klonopin®) or propanolol (Inderal®) may result in symptom improvement (Adler, Angrist, Reiter, & Rotrosen, 1989; Kutcher, Williamson, Mackenzie, Marton, & Murray, 1989; Lipinski, Zubenko, Cohen, & Barreira, 1984).

Parkinsonian symptoms mimic mental and motor changes observed in patients who have Parkinson's disease. These include tremor, slowed or masked facial expression, slowed body movements, slowed thinking, rigid muscles, drooling, cogwheeling, or racheting of muscles with activity and cognitive impairment. Parkinsonism may be treated with anticholinergic medication and medications used to treat Parkinson's disease (e.g., amantadine, or Symmetrel®).

Anticholinergic side effects may include: feeling faint or lightheaded, blurred vision, urinary retention, constipation, dry mouth, or mental confusion. These adverse sequelae commonly occur with the lower potency antipsychotic medications (chlorpromazine, thioridazine) and may improve with time. Antipsychotics have been associated with hormonally related side effects, including weight gain, increased appetite, irregular menses, breast tenderness and swelling, lactation, and changes in sexual desire or function. Thioridazine may cause delayed or retrograde ejaculation in male patients. These problems are less likely to be disclosed and may contribute to noncompliance in sexually active adolescents. Female patients prescribed antipsychotic medication should seek immediate medical attention if they become pregnant or plan to become pregnant (Cohen, Heller, & Rosenbaum, 1989).

Thioridazine (Mellaril®), at doses above 800 milligrams per day, has been associated with a potentially blinding visual disorder called pigmentary retinopathy. Sensitivity to sunlight and temperature changes has been described in patients who are prescribed antipsychotic medication, especially thioridazine and chlorpromazine. Pimozide (Orap®) sometimes causes a change in the heart activity, which may be detected and monitored by electrocardiogram (EKG). All antipsychotic medications may contribute to changes in liver enzyme functioning.

Potentially Irreversible or Fatal Adverse Drug Reactions

There are two potentially irreversible or life-threatening side effects to traditional antipsychotic medications: tardive dyskinesia and neuroleptic malignant syndrome. Tardive dyskinesia consists of persistent abnormal involuntary movements of the body musculature and is associated with the duration of antipsychotic treatment. Incidence of tardive dyskinesia is 3% to 4% (Gelenberg & Keith, 1997). It may be a permanent condition, although there have been no reports of unremitting tardive dyskinesia in children. The level of impairment varies and may be disabling. In severe cases, breathing may be interrupted due to spasms of the diaphragm muscle. Poor control of one's gait or posture may make the performance of everyday tasks an exhausting experience. Withdrawal dyskinesia is a transient condition that may occur when an antipsychotic medication is discontinued; it is not associated or predicative of tardive dyskinesia. Neuroleptic malignant syndrome is a rare but life-threatening condition of sudden onset. Body temperature, blood pressure, respiratory rate, and pulse destabilize. Mental confusion, agitation, muscle stiffness, and abnormal laboratory results occur. Patients with neuroleptic malignant syndrome require emergency medical attention.

Atypical Antipsychotic Medications

Atypical, or nontraditional, antipsychotic medications act not only on dopamine receptors but on other receptors as well. The efficacy and mechanisms of action of these agents have challenged basic theories regarding the neurobiology of schizophrenic symptoms. Their clinical effects represent an enormous advance in the field, improving both negative and positive symptoms of schizophrenia (APA, 1997). Thus far, none has been shown to cause tardive dyskinesia; however, use of these agents has been short-lived, and tardive dyskinesia may emerge with longer term usage.

Clozapine has FDA approval for treatment of psychosis that has not responded to other antipsychotic medications or for use in patients who have had severe side effects to traditional antipsychotic medication. It has fewer extrapyramidal symptoms (Kane, Honigfeld, Singen, & Meltzer, 1988). Kowatch, Suppes, Gilfillan, and Fuentes (1995), in a clinical case series of 10 treatment-resistant inpatients, ages 6 to 16 years, concluded that clozapine alleviates aggressive behavior, mood, and psychotic symptoms. Frazier et al. (1994), in an open trial of clozapine in 12 to 17-year-old youth, found clozapine to be well tolerated and effective. The most frequent untoward effects were sedation, hypersalivation, and weight gain. Rapid heart rate and feelings of lightheadedness occurred less frequently. Clozapine, at higher doses, has been associated with an increased incidence of seizures (Devinsky, Honigfeld, & Patin, 1991) and with agranulocytosis, a life-threatening blood disorder (Kane et al., 1988). If caught early, agranulocytosis is usually reversible. Weekly blood monitoring is required for the first 6 months of treatment, with biweekly monitoring thereafter. Medication is issued weekly to enhance compliance and to facilitate cessation of clozapine if a patient develops signs of agranulocytosis.

In double-blind placebo-controlled trials, risperidone has been as effective as haloperidol or perphenazine in treating acute adult-onset schizophrenia (Umbricht & Kane, 1995). Risperidone has been effective in improving negative symptoms in adults and has low rates of sedation (Gelenberg & Keith, 1997; Marder & Meibach, 1994). In an open pilot study of risperidone in 10 schizophrenic adolescents, a decrease in both positive and negative symptoms was found, untoward effects were not severe or disabling (Armenteros, Whitaker, Welikson, Stedge, & Gorman, 1997).

Olanzapine is a newer antipsychotic that has not been studied in children. It has been shown, in a double-blind placebo-controlled study, to have a greater effect than placebo or haloperidol on negative symptoms, especially affective-flattening and avolition–apathy. Olanzapine's side effect profile was less severe than that of haloperidol (Tollefson, Beasley, Tran, & Strut, 1997; Tran et al., 1997).

Quetiapine fumarate (Seroquel®) was approved in 1997 for treatment of psychotic disorders in adults. Ziprazidone soon may be approved for use in the United States. Sertindole (Serlect®) was withdrawn in January 1998 by the FDA due to concerns about its effect on cardiovascular functioning.

MOOD DISORDERS: BIPOLAR DISORDER

In bipolar disorder, an untreated manic episode may last for an average of 3 months, so pharmacotherapy is an essential part of treatment during the acute and latter stages of the illness. Additionally, some manic patients develop psychotic symptoms, such as delusions or hallucinations. Impaired judgment, paranoid or suicidal thoughts, and behavior increased the risk of lethal behaviors. Two medications (mood stabilizers) have FDA approval for the treatment of manic episodes: (a) Lithium has been approved by the FDA for treatment of acute mania and for prophylactic treatment of patients (12 years old and older) with recurrent bipolar I disorder and depression; (b) valproate (Depakote®) has been approved for treatment of adult mania and for prophylactic treatment of adult bipolar I disorder. Valproate and lithium have a delayed onset of action that may be as long as 3 weeks. Antipsychotic medication frequently is prescribed in addition to mood stabilizers during the early stages of the illness because antipsychotics have a more rapid onset of action. As the patient stabilizes on lithium carbonate or valproate, the antipsychotic medication may be tapered or discontinued. In adults, lithium has been used effectively to treat acute bipolar depressive episodes and to stabilize mood between major mood episodes Lithium has a positive effect on 80% of patients with either acute mania or depression, with mania improving within 2 weeks and depression requiring 6 to 8 weeks (Price & Heninger, 1994; Perry, Alexander, & Liskow, 1997). Studies involving children and adolescents are limited. Clinical reports suggest that the response of children and adolescents to lithium may be less robust because youth seem to have more frequent mixed bipolar episodes and more prominent psychotic symptoms than adults (Bowring & Kovacs, 1992).

Common side effects of lithium include tremor, acne, psoriasis, cognitive changes, transient muscle weakness, thirst, nausea, metallic taste, frequent urination, weight gain, skin irritation, and changes in cardiovascular functioning. Lithium has been associated with congenital heart abnormalities in the offspring of pregnant women who have been prescribed lithium. Lithium is excreted in breast milk. In high doses, lithium may become toxic to the heart and may be fatal in overdoses. Lithium also may induce hypothyroid in susceptible individuals. Active youth should drink water frequently because dehydration may elevate lithium to toxic levels.

In adults, valproate has been reported to be more effective than lithium in alleviating symptoms of atypical, psychotic and rapid cycling bipolar disorder as well as dysphoric mania (McElroy, Keck, Pope, & Hudson, 1992; McElroy & Keck, 1993; Janicak, Davis, Preskorn, & Ayd, 1997). West concluded, in their open-trial study, that adolescent mania was effectively treated with valproate. There are, however, no double-blind controlled studies comparing lithium with carbamazepine or valproate in children and adolescents (Janicak et al., 1995). Valproate may cause anorexia, indigestion, heartburn, nausea, sedation, confusion, and vomiting in more than 10% of patients. Fewer than 4% of patients complain of hair loss. Fatal liver toxicity is rare but may occur within the first 6 months of treatment. An increase in the frequency of neural tube defects in the offspring of valproate patients who continue therapy during pregnancy has been reported. Most of the side effects occur within the first 2 weeks of treatment.

Carbamazepine has not been approved by the FDA for treatment of bipolar I disorder but has been used for more than 25 years to treat affective illness (Ballenger & Post, 1978; Perry et al., 1997). Six double-blind studies of lithium refractory adults showed that more than half responded to carbamazepine (Ballenger, 1988;

Stromgren & Boller, 1985). Carbamazepine is thought to have a positive effect in patients who have not responded to lithium or who have an atypical pattern to their illness (e.g., rapid cycling or brain injury; double-blind studies have not been done). Nausea, vomiting, sedation, vertigo, and dizziness are the most common adverse side effects of carbamazepine therapy. Bone marrow suppression is a rare but dangerous side effect. A variety of dermatological side effects may occur, including life-threatening Stevens–Johnson syndrome; this condition necessitates immediate cessation of carbamazepine and prompt medical evaluation. Liver toxicity is a rare but dangerous side effect.

In a double-blind study, a benzodiazepine, clonazepam, was superior to placebo in reducing motor activity and excessive talking in manic patients but did not have a significant effect on mood elevation, insight, or rapidity of speech (Chouinard, Young, & Annable, 1983). Clonazepam has been used as an adjunct medication in adults who are manic. Two anticonvulsants, gabapentin (Neurontin®) and lamotrigine (Lamictal®), show promise as potential mood stabilizers, but further studies are needed.

MOOD DISORDERS: DEPRESSION

Tricyclic Antidepressants

Use of antidepressants in children and adolescents is controversial, at best, because many double-blind placebo-controlled studies have shown that TCAs, including desipramine, imipramine, and nortriptyline, were no better than placebo in reducing depressive symptoms (Hazell, O'Connell, Heathcote, Robertson, & Henry, 1995). Despite this finding, child psychiatrists continue to use TCAs in certain youth, depending on the severity of the illness, the family history of response to medication, and the overall need for treatment. A careful medical history and physical examination, including blood pressure, pulse, and EKG is necessary prior to starting medication. Medication should be increased gradually, with monitoring of plasma levels and EKG. The most serious adverse reaction attributed to TCAs is sudden cardiac death; seven cases have been reported (Varley & McClellan, 1997). Because of this risk, TCAs should not be used in prepubertal children with cardiac disease or with a family history of cardiac conduction defects, sudden death, or both. These agents should not be used during pregnancy, with anyone who has had a prior hypersensitivity reaction, or when someone is on a monamine oxidase inhibitor. TCAs can lower an individual's seizure threshold and can cause serious cardiac dysfunction (Mezzacappa, Steingard, Kindlon, Saul, & Earls, 1998). TCAs can cause hypertension and should be used with caution in youngsters with thyroid disease. TCAs can exacerbate psychotic disorders and precipitate onset of a manic episode in bipolar patients. Common side effects include those attributed to anticholinergic effects, (e.g,. dry mouth, constipation, blurred vision; other effects include tics, tremors, incoordination, confusion, insomnia, nightmares, increased anxiety, sexual dysfunction, rashes, and photosensitivity). Some of these lessen over time. Hard candy, gum, or special therapeutic mouthwashes may improve the discomfort associated with dry mouth. Bulk laxative and hydration may alleviate constipation. Lightheadedness may be lessened by increasing the dose slowly, by advising the patient not to stand rapidly, and by increasing fluid intake. Because overdosing with TCAs may be lethal, monitoring access to medication is essential in suicidal children and youths.

Monoamine Oxidase Inhibitors

MAOIs are a class of antidepressants with stimulant-like effects. Phenelzine (Nardil®) is FDA-approved for the treatment of atypical depression in adolescents and adults. Tranylcypromine (Parnate®) has been FDA-approved for treatment for nonmelancholic depression in adults. There are few studies of MAOIs in children and adolescents. Frommer (1967), in a double-blind placebo-controlled trial of MAOIs in 16 depressed youth and 15 school phobic youth, aged 9 to 15 years, found that the combination of phenelzine and chlordiazepoxide was superior to chlordiazepoxide alone or placebo in this mixed sample of depressed and anxious youth. Ryan et al. (1988) published a retrospective study of MAOIs in 25 TCA nonresponding adolescents diagnosed with major depressive disorder. Although 75% responded positively to MAOIs, only 57% of the sample complied with the tyramine-free diet.

MAOIs are dangerous in overdose, and patients must follow a diet free of tyramine-containing products, such as aged cheeses, yeast products, fermented meats, sausages, bologna, red wine, sherry, beer, caffeine, ginseng products, large amounts of chocolate, and other foods. Patients must also avoid certain cold and flu preparations. Failure to comply with the diet and medication plan may result in a life-threatening hypertensive crisis, which may include unstable blood pressure and pulse, headache, abnormal heart functioning, sweating, confusion, and agitation. Common side effects include insomnia, weight gain, dry mouth, agitation, lightheadedness, and transient increases in blood pressure and pulse. Anorgasmia and impotence are commonly reported sexual side effects. Rapid discontinuation of MAOIs has been associated with anxiety, nightmares and, on rare occasions, psychosis (Gelenberg & Bassuk, 1997; Joyce & Paykel, 1989). Although these medications may be used safely, concerns about side effects and dietary restrictions make MAOIs less likely to be prescribed as a first-choice treatment for depression. MAOIs are used as a therapeutic option in treatment of refractory and atypical depression.

Selective Serotonin Reuptake Inhibitors

The SSRIs include the following: fluoxetine (Prozac®), sertraline (Zoloft®), paroxtine (Paxil®), and fluvoxamine (Luvox®). Fluvoxamine has not been FDA-approved for use as an antidepressant but has been approved for treatment of obsessive–compulsive disorder in children and adults. Other SSRIs have FDA approval for treating depression in adults only. Although numerous clinical reports and open trials have been conducted suggesting the efficacy of SSRIs in depressed children and adolescents, controlled studies are still under way. A double-blind placebo-controlled study of 96 depressed youths found fluoxetine (Prozac®) more effective than placebo in reducing severe symptoms of depression, with a 56% rate of improvement. Complete symptom resolution was uncommon, and significant drug response did not occur until Week 5 of the study (Emslie, Rush, Weinberg, & Kowatch, 1997). These findings were in contrast to an earlier study which did not find significant difference between fluoxetine and placebo (Simeon, Dinicola, Ferguson, & Copping, 1990). However, that study had an unusually high placebo response rate and a small sample size.

The SSRIs' side effect profile is not as problematic as that of the TCAs. However, patients do occasionally report nausea, diarrhea, dyspepsia, dry mouth, weight loss, increased nervousness, insomnia, excess sweating, intensification of dreams, and motor restlessness. Fluoxetine, particularly, has been associated with sexual dysfunction. Because adolescents are not apt to volunteer information regarding their sexual functioning, one should inquire about this effect. All SSRIs may precipitate mania in bipolar patients. Abrupt discontinuation of medication therapy may lead to a withdrawal reaction that includes irritability, lightheadedness, nausea, and headaches. It should be noted that contrary to early popular press reports, fluoxetine (Prozac®) does not increase suicidal thoughts or behavior when compared with placebo. SSRIs should not be used during pregnancy or in individuals with hypersensitivity to this class of drugs. The SSRIs should not be used in patients who have been treated with MAOIs in the last 2 to 5 weeks (time period dependent on specific drug). These medications should be used with caution in the presence of liver disease. Because of their route of metabolism, there are many other medications that interact adversely with these drugs. Some interactions can be lethal; hence, requiring vigilance is needed in monitoring patient use of other medications. A serious condition, serotonin syndrome, may occur with an SSRI overdose or coadministration of an SSRI with an MAOI. Symptoms include tremor, confusion, restlessness or agitation, unstable blood pressure, sweating, and shivering. This condition can be life-threatening and requires immediate medical attention.

Other Antidepressant Medications

Nefazadone has demonstrated efficacy as an antidepressant in adults. Wilens, Spencer, Biederman, and Schleifer (1997) completed a chart review of 7 depressed, treatment–refractory youths with comorbid disorders, all meeting criteria for bipolar disorder or major depressive disorder. Fifty-seven percent responded positively to treatment with nefazadone, a response rate similar to that of TCAs. Although the sample size was small, the findings suggest that additional studies are warranted. Nefazadone's side effects include dry mouth, nausea, sedation, lightheadedness, headache, constipation, dizziness, confusion, and blurred vision. Due to concerns about rapid elevation of medication levels, nefazadone should not be used when the following medications are prescribed: astemizole (Hismanal®), cisapride (Propulsid®), triazolam (Halcion®), alprazolam (Xanax®), and terfenadine (Seldane®). A 2-week medication holiday should occur when changing from MAOIs to nefazadone or vice versa.

Bupropion (Wellbutrin®) has been demonstrated to be effective for depressed adults but it is contraindicated in patients with eating disorders and in patients with seizures. Side effects include agitation, insomnia, tremor, nausea, vomiting, rashes, headache, sleep disturbance, fatigue, appetite disturbance, constipation, dry mouth, blurred vision, weight loss, and seizures (when doses exceeded 450 milligrams per day). Bupropion usually does not cause sexual dysfunction in male patients. Systematic studies have not been conducted with children and adolescents, but trials are indicated. Amoxapine (Asendin®), maprotiline (Ludiomil®), trazodone (Desyrel®), venlafaxine, and mitirzapine have been used for treating adult depression, but no clinical reports have been published regarding their use in childhood. None is considered a first-line or even second-line treatment for depression in children and adolescents.

EATING DISORDERS

Anorexia Nervosa is a debilitating and potentially fatal illness frequently associated with comorbid disorders. As many as 21% to 91% of anorectics have depressive symptoms during the acute stages of illness (Kaye, 1997). Obsessive and compulsive symptoms occur in 11% to 83% (Rothenberg, 1988). Treatment of anorexia nervosa requires the immediate addressing of life-threatening complications of starvation, such as dehydration and heart failure. Refeeding (gradual dietary caloric increases to promote weight gain) is a critical part of treatment. Other treatment goals include helping the patient: (a) achieve and maintain a healthy body weight; (b) resume normal metabolic function; and (c) in females, commence or resume menstruation. Inpatient treatment of anorexia nervosa successfully restores weight in 85% of patients. The rate of relapse within the first year of treatment is high. Medication may be helpful to patients with this disorder. Kaye (1997) completed a double-blind placebo-controlled trial of fluoxetine in 35 adolescent and adult patients with restrictor-type anorexia nervosa. The participants were followed as outpatients for 52 weeks. Sixty-three percent of fluoxetine-treated patients as compared to 16% of those on placebo, completed the study, with patients in the fluoxetine group gaining weight. Fluoxetine-treated patients had significant reductions in obsessional thinking, compulsive behavior, eating disorder symptoms, depression, and anxiety. Amitriptyline (Elavil®), clomipramine (Anafranil®), lithium, and cyproheptadine (Periactin®, a gastrointestinal medication) may benefit anorectic patients, but placebo-controlled trials have not been completed.

Bulimia Nervosa

The medical complications of bulimia nervosa (menstrual dysfunction, electrolyte disturbance, dehydration, heart disease, dental problems, etc.) make treatment a priority. Psychosocial interventions, coupled with pharmacotherapies, have been demonstrated to be effective. Antidepressant medication consistently has been shown, in placebo-controlled trials, to be superior to placebo in improving early symptoms of bulimia nervosa, but clinical response does not seem to be related to the pretreatment level of depressive symptoms (Rothschild et al., 1994; Walsh & Devlin, 1995a; 1995b). Improved mood and a reduction in vomiting and binge eating frequencies occur with several classes and types of antidepressant medication, including: imipramine (Norpramin®), trazodone (Desyrel®), bupropion (Wellbutrin®), fluoxetine (Prozac®), amitriptyline (Elavil®), and lithium (Eskalith®); (Hsu et al., 1991; Rothschild, Clement, Santhouse, & Ju, 1994; Pope & Hudson, 1987). In a small double-blind study of bulimic patients with atypical depression, greater improvement was noted in patients taking the MAOI phenelzine (Nardil®) than with either imipramine (Norpramin®) or placebo (Rothschild et al., 1994). Antidepressants have not been shown to be effective in promoting long-term remission of bulimia. Patient compliance with antidepressants is limited by side effect profiles. Further studies are indicated with drugs with lower side effect profiles, such as the SSRIs.

Binge Eating Disorder

Many of the pharmacological treatment studies of binge eating are limited by small sample size. McCann and Agras (1990) concluded that although desipramine seemed to have a short-term effect on binge suppression in obese nonpurging bulimic women, most patients relapsed when the medication was discontinued. There was no significant change in weight despite the binge suppression. Alger, Schwalberg, Bigaouette, Michalek, and Howard (1991) treated obese binge eaters with naltrexone (opiate antagonist), imipramine, or placebo. Reduction in binge frequency for those on active medication was not statistically significant when compared with placebo. Marcus et al. (1990) found that fluoxetine and behavior modification led to a significant increase in weight loss at 1 year in obese binge eaters and obese nonbinge eaters when compared with placebo and behavior modification. Several studies have shown that fluoxetine may contribute to short-term weight loss, but the weight is usually regained at the end of 1 year even when medication therapy continues (Walsh & Devlin, 1995c). More research on the efficacy of combined psychosocial and pharmacotherapy therapy is indicated.

ANXIETY DISORDERS

The practice parameters for assessment and treatment of children and adolescents with anxiety disorders (American Academy of Child and Adolescent Psychiatry [AACAP], 1997) are clear: "Pharmacotherapy should not be used as the sole intervention but as an adjunct to behavioral or psychotherapeutic interventions. Interventions that help promote active mastery are important to prevent symptom return after discontinuation of medication" (p. 75S). There are three classes of medications that are indicated for the treatment of anxiety disorders in childhood and adolescence: (a) TCAs, (b) SSRIs, and (c) anxiolytics. Other drugs have been prescribed for anxiety but without specific indications for use. Antihistamines, particularly diphenhydramine (Benadryl®) and hydroxyzine (Atarax® or Vistaril®), have been extensively used by clinicians in treating symptoms of anxiety; however, no systematic studies of efficacy have been done and clinical effects appear to be related to general sedation. No data, in adults or children, indicate a specific antianxiety effect of the antihistamine class of drugs.

Other drugs that have been extensively but inappropriately used for nonspecific anxiety or anxiety disorders are the antipsychotic medications. For years, use of anxiolytic medications was discouraged out of fear that tolerance, dependence, or addiction would develop. Clinicians, instead, recommended the use of low doses of neuroleptic drugs, such as thioridazine (Mellaril®), chlorpromazine (Thorazine®), or haloperidol (Haldol®). None of these drugs produced a sense of well-being or carried risk of addiction. Hence, they were considered safer than the anxiolytics. However, all caused impairment of cognitive function and increased risk for the development of tardive dyskinesia (see section on psychotic disorders). Because of both risks and the lack of specificity in reducing anxiety symptoms, antipsychotic drugs are no longer recommended for the treatment of anxiety disorders and should not be prescribed (AACAP, 1997, p.77S).

SEPARATION ANXIETY DISORDERS

Tricyclic Antidepressants

Gittelman-Klein and Klein (1971, 1973), treated 35 children with separation anxiety disorder with 100 to 200 mg/day of imipramine (Tofranil®) and found that more treated children (81%) returned to school than did those on placebo (47%). However, in a more recent study, Klein, Koplewicz, and Kanner (1992) failed to replicate these findings, with no difference being found between those treated with imipramine when compared to placebo. Recruitment of participants differed between studies, with the latter having been recruited from children who "failed behavior therapy." Hence, participants may have been a highly selected subgroup who were more treatment resistant than those in the first study. Other investigators have reported inconsistent results in treating children with separation anxiety. Bernstein, Garkinkel, and

Borchardt (1990) compared imipramine (Tofranil®), alprazolam (Xanax®, a benzo-diazepine) and placebo in 24 children and adolescents with school refusal. Although a trend was noted in symptom reduction among those on imipramine and alprazolam, no significant differences were found between groups on standardized rating scales. However, symptom severity was not controlled between groups in this study and may well have confounded findings. Some children with separation anxiety disorder appear to meet criteria for panic disorder (Black & Robbins, 1990; Vitiello et al., 1990). Case reports have been published indicating that TCAs are effective in treating panic disorder in children and adolescents (Ballenger, Carek, Steele, & Cornish-McTighe, 1989; Black & Robbins, 1990; Garland & Smith, 1990); however, significance of these findings needs to be considered in light of the fact that children have a consistently higher placebo effect in drug studies than do adults (Simeon et al., 1990). If TCAs are used in children and adolescents for treating separation or panic disorders, dosage guidelines for use with major depressive disorders should be followed. Therapeutic effects may not be seen for 2 to 3 weeks after reaching therapeutic plasma levels of the drug. A trial of 6 to 8 weeks at therapeutic levels is necessary to determine efficacy. Side effects and adverse reactions are significant and have been reviewed in the section on depression. These, combined with the cardiotoxicity of TCAs in prepubertal children (Greenberg et al., 1993), provide strong indication for increased research on the efficacy of some of the newer non-TCA agents.

Selective Serotonin Reuptake Inhibitors

These drugs are marketed as antidepressants with a lower side effect profile and relative safety with overdosing (Doogan, 1991; Riddle et al., 1989). Preliminary data suggest use in treating childhood anxiety disorders. One study of a mixed diagnostic group of children and adolescents (social phobia, overanxious, or separation anxiety disorders) found that 81% of those on fluoxetine demonstrated marked improvement on the Global Impression Scale (Birmaher et al., 1994). No other clinical trials with youths have been reported. Findings from studies of adults with panic disorder and agoraphobia, however, are more robust (Coplan et al., 1997; DenBoer & Westenberg, 1990; Gorman et al., 1987). Effective dosage for treating separation anxiety and panic disorders in children has not been established. As with TCAs, therapeutic effect may not be seen for 2 to 3 weeks, with a necessity of a 6 to 8 week trial of medication to determine efficacy. (Treatment guidelines, as well as contraindications, side effects, and adverse reactions, were reviewed in the section on depression.)

Anxiolytics

Studies of the benzodiazepines have mostly been conducted for nonspecific anxiety. However, an early open clinical trial of chlordiazepoxide (Librium®) for school refusal in children, ages 8 to 11 years, was conducted by D'Amato (1962). He found that 8 out of 9 children in the medication group returned to school within 2 weeks, whereas only 2 of 11 children treated only with psychosocial interventions returned within that period of time. In a 4-week, double-blind placebo-controlled crossover study of the effects of clonazepam (Klonopin®) in 15 children with anxiety disorders (mostly separation anxiety), 9 demonstrated moderate to marked improvement on standardized rating scales, and 6 no longer met criteria for an anxiety disorder (Graae, Milner, Rizzotto, & Klein, 1994). In an open-label trial of alprazolam (Xanax®) in 18 children with separation anxiety disorder, improvement was reported in 82% to 89% when rated by mothers and psychiatrist, and 64% to 65% when rated by the children themselves or by teachers (unpublished data by Klein, cited in Kutcher, Reiter, Gardner, & Klein, 1992). A clinical case study has been published describing symptom improvement in 4 panic-disordered adolescents after 2 weeks of treatment with clonazepam (Kutcher & MacKenzie, 1988). Benzodiazepines have been used for treatment of nonspecific anxiety and anticipatory anxiety associated with separation anxiety disorders. Because of the risk for developing tolerance or dependence, these medications should be used only as adjunctive therapies and for short periods of time. Some children and adolescents have had disinhibitory reactions when on benzodiazepines, resulting in increased aggression and impulsivity (Petti, Fish, Shapiro, Cohen, & Campbell, 1982). These agents should not be used when there is a history of benzodiazepine dependence or abuse. Benzodiazepines should be used with caution, and sometimes not at all, in patients with liver disease or with HIV/AIDS being treated with zidovudine. Sedation is a common side effect, as is decreased psychomotor and cognitive performance. When taken with alcohol or other sedative nonprescribed drugs, effects are potentiated and potentially life-threatening, depending on toxicity levels.

Buspirone (BuSpar®), an anxiolytic that is not a benzodiazepine, has not been systematically studied in children with separation anxiety or panic disorders. This drug does not appear to have abuse potential. It can produce sedation, although less than the benzodiazepines. Gastrointestinal upset, headache, fatigue, anxiety, irritability, and excitement have been reported in association with the use of buspirone. Further research is indicated.

Generalized Anxiety Disorder With Childhood Onset

Little is known regarding the pharmacotherapy of generalized anxiety disorder with childhood onset. In a double-blind study of 30 children, diagnostically mixed between avoidant and overanxious, no differences were found between those treated with alprazolam and placebo (Simeon et al., 1992). In an open trial of fluoxetine in 21 children with overanxious disorder and other coexisting anxiety disorders (not panic or obsessive–compulsive disorders), 17 demonstrated moderate to marked improvement on the Clinical Global Impression Scale (Birmaher et al., 1994). Buspirone, in an open-label trial, was reported to result in significant decreases in the Hamilton Anxiety Scale (Kutcher et al., 1992). These preliminary studies suggest that further research evaluating the efficacy of buspirone and the SSRIs is merited.

Childhood Onset Social Phobia

As with general anxiety disorders, few studies have been conducted on the efficacy of drugs in treating childhood onset social phobia. No studies have evaluated the use of TCAs. The study by Birmaher et al. (1994) included some children with social phobia, and in this mixed diagnostic group, 81% were moderately to markedly improved on the Global Impression Scale. Dummit, Klein, Tancer, Asche, and Martin (1996) demonstrated in an open clinical trial that fluoxetine was associated with significant improvement for 21 children with selective mutism. In a 12-week, double-blind placebo-controlled study of fluoxetine, 15 children with selective mutism demonstrated improvement, as indicated by both global impression and parental ratings (Black & Uhde, 1994). More research is clearly indicated.

OBSESSIVE–COMPULSIVE DISORDER

Tricyclic Antidepressants

Clomipramine (Anafranil®) is the only TCA that has been demonstrated in double-blind studies to be efficacious when compared to placebo (DeVeaugh-Geiss et al., 1992; Flament et al., 1985) and to desipramine (Norpramine®), (Leonard et al., 1989). While on clomipramine, improvements were maintained; however, when children were blindly switched to desipramine for 2 months, 90% relapsed (Leonard et al., 1991), indicating the need for continued treatment. Although sudden death has not been reported among children on clomipramine, the same precautions need to be exercised in prescribing this tricyclic compound. Monitoring of EKG is essential, and the maximum daily dose should not exceed 5 mg/kg, or 250 mg per day. Treatment at a therapeutic dose should be maintained for 6 to 8 weeks before determining ineffectiveness. Clomipramine may be used with an SSRI in the treatment of obsessive–compulsive disorder (OCD). When used in combination the daily dose of clomipramine may be reduced; however, the combination frequently increases the side effect profile for the SSRI.

Selective Serotonin Reuptake Inhibitors

SSRIs have been demonstrated to be efficacious in treating OCD in adults (Chouinard et al., 1990; Greist, Chauinard, et al., 1995; Greist, Jefferson, et al., 1995). The low side effect profile of SSRIs, coupled with the cardiotoxic metabolites of TCAs in children (Greenberg et al., 1993) indicate that, if effective, these agents would be a more desirable alternative for treating OCD in children and adolescents. Fluvoxamine (Luvox®) is the only drug that has FDA marketing approval for use in the treatment of OCD in children and adolescents. Studies with children are still in their infancy, but results are promising. Efficacy for OCD was suggested in a small fixed-dose, double-blind crossover trial of fluoxetine (Riddle et al., 1992), with a 44% decrease, as compared to a 27% decrease for placebo on the Children's Yale–Brown Obsessive–Compulsive Scale (CY–BOCS), a not significant difference. Significant differences were found on the Global Impression Scale. In a larger double-blind placebo-controlled study of 120 children, 6 to 17 years old, efficacy was demonstrated for fluvoxamine using the CY–BOCS as an outcome variable. Four participants dropped out of the study secondary to side effects, none being serious. Common side effects included insomnia, agitation, hyperkinesis, somnolence, and dyspepsia (Riddle, 1996). The pharmacokinetics, tolerability, and efficacy of sertraline has been studied in an open clinical trial involving 61 participants, ages 6 to 17 years of age (Alderman, Walker, Chung, & Johnston, 1998). Results show that the pharmacokinetic profiles of sertraline and its major metabolites is similar in children to those found in adults. Moreover, the drug appears to be safe and likely to be efficacious. Additional double-blind crossover studies are needed to determine efficacy when compared to placebo or to established treatments such as clomipramine. Clearly, the side effect profile for SSRIs is of less concern than with TCAs. The most serious considerations in using these compounds are drug–drug interactions, which can be considerable and dangerous. (Common side effects are reviewed in the section on depression.)

POSTTRAUMATIC STRESS DISORDER

Only one systematic study has been published on the use of medication for treating Posttraumatic Stress Disorder (PTSD) in children and adolescents. Famularo et al (1988) treated 11 children with PTSD secondary to child abuse using propranolol (Inderal®) in an open-trial, off–on–off design over a 2-week period. Three children could not tolerate the maximum dose of propranolol; all children had fewer PTSD symptoms. A clinical report was published on the use of clonidine (Catapres®) in 7 preschool children with PTSD (Harmon & Riggs, 1996). This report suggested that clonidine was helpful in reducing symptoms; however, sample size was small, standardized rating scales were not used to monitor outcome, and there were no comparison groups in the study. Use of psychotropic medications in preschoolers is even less studied than in school-age children and adolescents. Caution is recommended, particularly when medications are being used that have potentially adverse effects. Adult studies have found that TCAs, MAOIs, SSRIs, propranolol, clonidine, benzodiazepines, and buspirone have been useful in reducing symptoms of PTSD (Davidson & van der Kolk, 1996). Again, because of the low side effect profile and lack of addictive potential, the SSRIs are promising. Clinical trials are needed to determine if such medications would be helpful adjuncts in children as well as adults.

Attention Deficit Hyperactivity Disorder

Attention deficit hyperactivity disorder (ADHD) is one of the most prevalent psychiatric disorders of childhood and adolescence. The practice parameters of the American Academy of Child and Adolescent Psychiatry indicate that "The decision to medicate is based on the presence of a diagnosis of ADHD and persistent target symptoms that are sufficiently severe to cause functional impairment at school and usually also at home and with peers" (AACAP, 1997, p. 91S). As with other disorders, pharmacotherapy should be part of a comprehensive and individualized treatment plan. It should not be considered a sufficient intervention on its own. The stimulant drugs are the first line for pharmacological treatment of ADHD. These include methylphenidate (Ritalin®), dextroamphetamine (Dexadrine®), and pemoline (Cylert®). More is known about these medications and their effects than about any other psychotropic drugs used with children and adolescents. The literature is voluminous, and research and clinical trials have been ongoing for almost 60 years (Greenhill, 1995; Greenhill & Osman, 1991). Nonetheless, use of these drugs is still controversial in the popular press, mainly because of concerns about potential abuse. Although studies have indicated that children and adolescents with ADHD have a twofold to fourfold increased risk for substance abuse, data do not demonstrate an association between the use of prescribed stimulants and the abuse of substances (Barkley, 1990; Dulcan, 1990). Use of stimulants in treating ADHD should be based on targeting specific symptoms interfering with function, and efficacy should be monitoring using standardized rating scales, such as the IOWA Connors Parent and Teacher Rating Scale (Barkley, 1990). Side effects can be monitored with the Stimulant Side Effects Checklist (Gadow, Nolan, Paolicelli, & Sprafkin, 1991). Although there is considerable variability of response between individuals (Rapport, Denney, DuPaul, & Gardner, 1994), studies have indicated that between 75% (Dulcan, 1990) and 96% (Elia, Borcherding, Rapoport, & Keysor, 1991) of ADHD children demonstrated improved behavior, attentiveness, and short-term memory in response to one or another stimulant. Response to stimulant medication is not diagnostic of

ADHD; normal children have cognitive and behavioral responses to the psychostimulants that are similar to ADHD children (Donnelly & Rapoport, 1985). Studies also have indicated that stimulants are as effective with ADHD children with co-existing aggressive behavior as they are with ADHD without comorbidity (Hinshaw, 1991). There is some question as to efficacy with children with comorbid anxiety disorders, with some studies indicating less response (Pliszka, 1989; DuPaul, Barkley, & McMurray, 1994) than in children without comorbid anxiety. This finding has not been universal (Gadow, Sverd, Sprafkin, Nolan, & Ezor, 1995; Livingston, Dykman, & Ackerman, 1992).

No markers have been identified that are helpful in determining which stimulant will be best. It does appear that if a child does not respond to one medication, a trail with the other is useful. In a study by Elia et al. (1991), 80% of nonresponders to methylphenidate responded to dextroamphetamine; 60% of nonresponders to dextroamphetamine responded to methylphenidate. Duration of action, dosing schedules, cost, and availability are also considerations in determining which stimulant to use. Methylphenidate is most frequently used but requires frequent dosing every 4 hours; dextroamphetamine costs less and has a longer duration of action but is frequently not included in drug formularies because of its higher potential for abuse by the child's peer group and family members. Long-acting preparations of stimulants are available, including Ritalin–SR (methylphenidate), Dexedrine Spansule (dextroamphetamine), and Cylert (pemoline).

Of these agents, pemoline has the strongest adverse reaction and side effect profile, the most serious adverse reaction is that of chemical hepatitis leading to fulminant liver failure (Berkovitch; Pope, Phillips, & Koren, 1995). Parents should be instructed to call the physician immediately if symptoms of nausea, vomiting, lethargy, malaise, or jaundice appear. Abdominal discomfort persisting more than 2 weeks also should be evaluated in light of the potential effects of pemoline on liver function. Routine monitoring of liver enzymes is not useful, because onset of hepatitis is unpredictable. Children on pemoline are also at risk for the development of movement disorders and insomnia.

Stimulants have been associated with growth retardation. Dexamphetamine's effect is greater than that of methylphenidate and pemoline. The primary effect is on weight gain, with a small but significant effect. Height does not appear to be significantly affected by stimulants (Greenhill, 1981; Zeiner, 1995). All stimulants may be associated with irritability, headaches, abdominal pain, and loss of appetite initially. Giving medication after meals reduces the drug effect on appetite. Starting medication with a low dose and increasing the dose weekly or even slower depending on side effects minimizes the side effect profile, with most of the unpleasant effects dissipating after a few weeks of use. Stimulants may increase blood pressure and heart rate in subpopulations of children, specifically hypertensive Black adolescents and children with comorbid anxiety disorders (Brown & Sexson, 1989; Tannock, Ickowicz, & Schachor, 1995). Clinicians have reported rebound effects, that is, increased excitability, activity, irritability, and insomnia as the drug levels decrease in children (Zahn, Rapoport, & Thompson, 1980). This effect has not been empirically demonstrated, however (Johnston, Pelham, Hoza, & Sturges, 1988). Use of stimulants may exacerbate tics or Tourette's disorder (Castellanos et al., 1997; T. Spencer et al., 1996) and therefore should be used with caution in children with pre-existing tics or with a family history of tics. Tics should be monitored systematically before the start of medication and throughout the course. Stimulants should not be used in children with overt psychosis or thought disorder.

Should a child be a nonresponder to the stimulant drugs or have an adverse response, two other classes of drug have been used as a second line of treatment: TCAs and bupropion. TCAs may be useful not only in nonresponders but may have increased efficacy in children with comorbid anxiety or depression (Kutcher et al., 1992; T. Spencer et al., 1996). Cognitive effects appear not as great with the TCAs as with stimulants, and the side effect profile, as noted in the section on depression disorders, is considerable, with increased risk of serious cardiac effects, overdose, and other adverse reactions. Bupropion has demonstrated efficacy with ADHD children (Barrickman et al., 1995; Conners et al., 1996; Simeon, Gerguson, & Fleet, 1986), but has potentially problematic side effects, including reduction of the seizure threshold and exacerbation of tics (Spencer, Biederman, Steingard, & Wilens 1993). Risk of these effects appears greater with doses above 450 mg/day. Efficacy has been suggested, but, to date, data are still limited for use of the SSRIs. Use of guanfacine hydrochloride is currently under investigation (Chappell et al., 1995; Horrigan & Barnhill, 1995; Hunt, Arnsten, & Asbell, 1995), as is buspirone (Malhotra & Santosh, 1998). Buspirone may be useful for ADHD children with comorbid Tourette's disorder, but no placebo-controlled studies have been reported yet. The use of clonidine in treating ADHD is controversial and potentially dangerous because of it's cardiovascular effects (Cantwell, Swanson, & Connor, 1997). Clonidine should not be used in children with a history of syncope. Clonidine has been used to treat tics or ADHD children with tics. However, cognitive functioning is not improved with this drug, and its sedative effects can be problematic. Sudden discontinuation of this medication can result in a serious withdrawal syndrome, consisting of increased motoric activity, headache, agitation, and, most seriously, high blood pressure. Blood pressure elevations can be considerable. The combined use of methylphenidate and clonidine has been associated with four sudden deaths (Fenichel, 1995; Popper, 1995; Swanson et al., 1995). Although causal relations have not been established, extreme caution is nonetheless advised.

CONDUCT DISORDER

No pharmacological treatment is available for conduct disorder. Treatment requires a comprehensive assessment and multimodal approach (Borduin et al., 1995). Pharmacological management of the disorder tends to be directed toward treating targeted symptoms and comorbid disorders, such as attention deficit hyperactivity, mood, psychotic and anxiety disorders (Abikoff & Klein, 1992; Ben-Amos, 1992; Loeber, Keenan, Lahey, Green, & Thomas, 1994; Marriage, Fine, Moretti, & Haley, 1986; Munir & Boulifard, 1995). Recent studies have indicated comorbidity with bipolar disorder (Beiderman et al., 1997). Conduct disordered children and adolescents are at heightened risk for the development of a substance use disorder which may require aggressive management (Huizinga et al., 1994). Comorbid learning disorders and neurodevelopmental disorders are common (Hinshaw, 1992; Aronowitz, Liebowitz, Hollander, & Fazzini, 1994). In cases where aggressive behaviors are impulsive in nature, pharmacological approaches may be indicated (M. Campbell, 1992); however, drug treatment is not efficacious in managing predatory aggression.

Various approaches have been taken in the pharmacological management of impulsive aggressive behavior; however, few have been supported by adequately designed studies. Neuroleptics have been used for controlling aggression in children and adolescents, but sedation and cognitive impairment are serious side effects (M. Campbell, 1992; M. Campbell & Cueva, 1995). Long-term use of neuroleptics is associated with tardive dyskinesia (Armenteros, Adams, Campbell, & Eisenberg, 1995).

Based on adverse side effects and potential risk of tardive dyskinesia, neuroleptics are no longer recommended in treating aggressive behavior. Mood stabilizers such as lithium and carbamazepine have been used; only lithium has been demonstrated to be efficacious (M. Campbell & Cueva, 1995). Carbamazepine (Tegretol®), although frequently used for managing aggression (Evan, Clay, & Gualfieri, 1987), has not been demonstrated to be superior to placebo in double-blind placebo-controlled studies (Cueva et al., 1996). Propranolol (Inderal®) has been used for managing aggression and rage attacks, but to date no definite, well designed studies of efficacy have been conducted (Kuperman & Stewart, 1987; Williams, Mehl, Yudofsky, Adams, & Roseman, 1982). Because of the association between low levels of serotonin and behavioral impulsivity, the SSRIs hold promise for treating impulse disorders, including impulsive aggression.

SUBSTANCE ABUSE

The diagnosis of substance abuse requires evidence of a maladaptive pattern of substance use that causes significant impairment in various domains, including physiological, cognitive, behavioral, emotional, and social functioning. Again, as with conduct disorder, treatment is multimodal, and the pharmacological aspects should be but one of many treatment approaches. Abstinence is the primary goal of treatment. Pharmacotherapy for children and adolescents who abuse substances is targeted toward (a) detoxification, (b) treatment of withdrawal, (c) substitution of a similar drug for prolonged withdrawal or maintenance, (e) counteracting the physiological and subjective effects of abused substances, and (f) the treatment of comorbid psychiatric disorders (AACAP, 1997, p. 148S). The latter poses particular problems in differential diagnosis because the prevalence of comorbid psychiatric disorders is considerable (Bukstein, Brent, & Kaminer, 1989; Demilio, 1989) and the difficulties in untangling primary psychiatric disorders from drug toxicity or withdrawal effects are significant.

There are marked differences between children and adolescents who abuse substances and adults. For example, clinically significant withdrawal symptoms are rare (Martin, Kaczynski, Maisto, Bukstein, & Moss, 1995). Medications to counteract the effects of withdrawal should not be prescribed routinely, but administered only after careful physiological monitoring for the emergence of withdrawal symptoms. With minors, prescribing drugs used for prolonged withdrawal, such as methadone, may be prohibited by law depending on the jurisdiction, and such medication is seldom needed. Increased research has been directed toward the use of pharmacological agents that counteract the pleasurable and reinforcing effects of abused substances in adult populations such as naltrexone and methadone; however, no systematic work has been done with children and adolescents. Use of aversive agents, such as disulfiram (Antabuse®), is not recommended because safety has not been established among children under the age of 18 years (Myers, Donahue, & Glodstein, 1994).

Substance Intoxication

Managing acute substance intoxication may involve treatment with a medication that reduces the toxicity of the drug. There are no medications approved for treatment of alcohol or cocaine intoxication. Severe alcohol intoxication may be life-threatening and should be treated in a hospital. Naloxone may be used to treat heroin or opiate intoxication, while monitoring the patient for respiratory depression in a closely super-vised medical environment. "Bad trips" due to LSD intoxication may be treated with antipsychotic medication, benzodiazepines, supportive care, and a low-stimulus en-vironment.

Substance Withdrawal

Several medications may be used to treat alcohol withdrawal, but none has been stud-ied extensively in children or adolescents. Benzodiazepines (diazepam/Valium®; oxazepam/Serax®) have been used and are associated with dose-related confusion, sedation, abuse, dependence, and slowed breathing. Clonidine (Catapres®), propanolol (Inderal®), and atenolol (Tenormin®) are heart and blood pressure medica-tions that have been used successfully to treat alcohol withdrawal, although neither is FDA-approved for this purpose. These increase the patient'level of comfort by reducing anxiety, tension, sweating, and nervousness. Side effects include sedation, low blood pressure, depressed mood, and low blood sugar. Carbamazepine (Tegretol®)has shown promise as a treatment for alcohol withdrawal. In addition to methadone, clonidine has been shown, in controlled and uncontrolled adult trials, to be an effective treatment of opiate withdrawal. It reduces yawning, sweating, and nausea. Clonidine stabilizes blood pressure, but it does not alleviate subjective complaints such as anxi-ety, insomnia, irritability, muscle discomfort, and irritability (Fishbain, Rosomoff, & Cuther, 1993). Clonazepam (Klonopin®) and the anticonvulsant carbamazepine (Tegretol®) also have been used to treat benzodiazepine withdrawal. In a double-blind study, carbamazepine successfully managed benzodiazepine withdrawal in more than 90% of adult patients who were started on carbamazepine 4 weeks before the 2-week benzodiazepine taper began (Rickels, Case, Schweizer, Garcia-Espana, & Fridman, 1990). Again, there are no studies with children and adolescents. No medications have been approved for treatment of cocaine withdrawal. However, cocaine withdrawal may be treated with bromocryptine, amantadine, desipramine, or carbamazepine. Valproate (Depakote®) also has shown promise in managing cocaine withdrawal (Halikas, 1993).

Although management of nicotine withdrawal in adolescents has not been de-scribed in the literature, nicotine replacement or substitution therapy may be used with motivated youth who are dependent on nicotine products. Use of nicotine sub-stitution products should be carefully supervised (AACAP, 1997, p.149S). Bupropion (Wellbutrin®) has shown promise as a possible treatment for nicotine dependence in adults; additional studies are needed.

Substitution Therapy/Drug Maintenance Therapy

Heroin withdrawal has been treated with methadone and naltrexone substitution therapy, which reduces drug-craving and drug-seeking behavior (Gelenberg & Bassuk, 1997). One study suggests that clonidine reduces symptoms and signs of opi-ate withdrawal in adults (Gold, Redmond & Kleber 1978). Desipramine has been shown, in double-blind parallel–group comparison, to reduce cocaine craving and improve abstinence after a several-week delay in adults (Oliveto, Kosten, Schottenfeld, Falcooni, & Ziedonis, 1995), but at least one study has not reproduced this finding (J. L. Campbell, Thomas, Gabrielli, Liskow, & Powell, 1994), suggesting that additional studies and larger sample sizes are needed. A case study of use of desipramine in adolescent cocaine dependence has been reported in the literature (Kaminer, 1992).

Naltrexone (ReVia®) is the first nonaversive medication to be approved by the FDA for treatment of alcohol dependence in adults. No studies have included children or adolescents. Naltrexone is relatively safe and has few adverse side effects. Nausea, abdominal discomfort, vomiting, and headaches are common side effects. Disulfiram (Antabuse®) is a form of aversion therapy that causes a person who ingests alcohol to have a noxious reaction that may include nausea, vomiting, flushing, sweating, rapid heart rate, chest pain, and blurred vision. Disulfiram is approved by the FDA for adult relapse prevention of alcohol consumption. Disulfiram has not consistently been found to be more effective than placebo in relapse prevention (Perlmutter, 1995). There have been case reports but no controlled trials of Disulfiram in children or adolescents. In view of safety and compliance concerns, Disulfiram and other aversive therapies should be limited to older highly motivated adolescents with alcohol dependence (AACAP, 1997, p. 149S).

Benzodiazepines such as lorazepam (Ativan®), oxazepam (Serax®), and diazepam (Valium®) are generally not suitable for use in alcohol substitution therapy because they have a potential for abuse and dependence. Citralopam and zimelidine have shown promise, in short-term double-blind placebo-controlled studies, as medications that may prolong abstinence in patients with alcohol use disorders (Perlmutter, 1995). None of these agents has been studied systematically in a double-blind placebo-controlled trial in adolescents or children.

Comorbidity of psychiatric and substance use disorders is fairly common. Clients may use substances to "medicate" or lessen the intensity of their psychiatric symptoms. The task of the treating clinician is to distinguish between self-medicating and a substance use disorder. A person who is self-medicating psychiatric symptoms with drugs may not require treatment for a substance use problem, beyond basic education about treatment of mental illness and the dangers of using substances to "treat" symptoms. A client who has a substance use disorder and a substance-induced transient psychiatric disorder (depression, anxiety, psychosis) may not require treatment for the psychiatric disorder after the substance use disorder is treated. Youth with psychiatric diagnoses and substance use problems must receive extensive treatment for both disorders. Treatment of comorbid disorders is dependent on degree of impairment and patterns of use of the abused substance. For disorders that are serious and potentially life-threatening, (e.g., severe mood disorders and psychosis), the patient should be observed carefully in an inpatient or partial hospitalization setting and treated with the appropriate medications for the specific comorbid disorder once it has been established that symptoms are not secondary to toxic effects of the abused substance. Factors that support use of medication in treating comorbid conditions include symptomatology that predates substance use–abuse and family history of the comorbid disorder. When possible, psychosocial interventions should be used as the first line of treatment. If such interventions are not effective, medication with empirically demonstrated efficacy, coupled with a low-abuse potential, should be selected for treating the targeted comorbid conditions. Medication for severely impairing psychiatric disorders—such as psychotic disorders, major depressive disorder, and bipolar disorders—should not be withheld simply because the patient has abused substances. These disorders do not tend to remit spontaneously and need to be treated appropriately. For individuals with these disorders, substance use and abuse may well reflect misguided efforts at self-medication.

SUMMARY

The pharmacological treatment of psychiatric disorders in children and adolescents is almost never indicated in isolation. The combined use of psychosocial interventions and even multimodal treatments with medication is paramount. Children do not necessarily respond to psychotropic medication in the same way as adults do. Therefore, it is critical that the prescribing clinician be knowledgeable regarding the empirical studies in the field as well as differences in pharmacodynamics and kinetics to choose the most effective agents with the lowest side effect profile. The psychologist and psychiatrist must work synergistically if children and youths with significant psychiatric disorders are to receive optimal treatment.

REFERENCES

Abikoff, H., & Klein, R. (1992). Attention-deficit hyperactivity and conduct disorder: Comorbidity and implications for treatment. *Journal of Consulting and Clinical Psychology, 60,* 881–892.

Adler, L., Angrist, B., Reiter, S., & Rotrosen, J. (1989). Neuroleptic-induced akathisia: a review. *Psychopharmacology., 97,* 1–11.

Alderman, J., Wolkow, R., Chung, M., & Johnston, H. F. (1998). Sertraline treatment of children and adolescents with obsessive–compulsive disorder or depression: Pharmacokinetics, tolerability and efficacy. *Journal of American Academy of Child and Adolescent Psychiatry, 37,* 386–394.

Alger, S. A., Schwalberg, M. D., Bigaouette, J. M., Michalek, A. V., & Howard, L. J. (1991). Effect of a tricyclic antidepressant and opiate antagonist on binge-eating in normal weight bulimic and obese, binge-eating subjects. *American Journal of Clinical Nutrition, 53,* 865–871.

American Academy of Child and Adolescent Psychiatry. (1997). Practice Parameters. *Supplement to the Journal of the American Academy of Child and Adolescent Psychiatry, 36*(Suppl. 10), 1405–1565.

American Psychiatric Association. (1980). *Diagnostic and statistical manual of mental disorders* (3rd ed.). Washington, DC: Author.

American Psychiatric Association. (1987). *Diagnostic and statistical manual of mental disorders* (3rd ed., rev.). Washington, DC: Author.

American Psychiatric Association. (1994). *Diagnostic and statistical manual of mental disorders* (4th ed.). Washington, DC: Author.

American Psychiatric Association. (1997). Practice guidelines for treatment of patients with schizophrenia. *Supplement to the American Journal of Psychiatry, 154*: 17–23.

Armenteros, J. L., Adams, P. B., Campbell, M., Eisenberg, A. W. (1995). Haloperidol related dyskinesias and pre- and perinatal complications in autistic children. *Psychopharmacological Bulletin, 31,* 363–369.

Armenteros, J. L., Whitaker, A. H., Welikson, M., Stedge, D. J., & Gorman, J. (1997). Risperidone in adolescents with schizophrenia: an open pilot study. *Journal of the American Academy of Child and Adolescent Psychiatry, 36,* 694–700.

Aronowitz, B., Liebowitz, M., Hollander, E., & Fazzini, E. (1994). Neuropsychiatric and neuropsychological findings in conduct disorder and attention-deficit hyperactivity disorder. *Journal of Neuropsychiatry and Clinical Neurosciences, 6,* 245–249.

Ballenger, J. C. (1988). The clinical use of carbamazepine in affective disorders. *Journal of Clinical Psychiatry, 49*(Suppl. 4), 13–19.

Ballenger, J. C., Carek, D. J., Steele, J. J., Cornish-McTighe, D. (1989). Three cases of panic disorder with agoraphobia in children. *American Journal of Psychiatry, 146,* 922–924.

Ballenger, J. C., & Post, R. M. (1978). Therapeutic effects of carbamazepine in affective illness: A preliminary report. *Communications in Psychopharmacology, 2*(2), 159–175.

Barkley, R. (1990). *Hyperactive children: A handbook for diagnosis and treatment.* New York: Guilford.

Barrickman, L. L., Perry, P. J., Allen, A. J., Kuperman, S., Arndt, S. V., Herrmann, K. J., & Schumacher, E. (1995). Bupropion versus methylphenidate in the treatment of attention deficit hyperactivity disorder. *Journal of the American Academy of Child and Adolescent Psychiatry, 35,* 649–657.

Ben-Amos, B. (1992). Depression and conduct disorders in children and adolescents: A review of the literature. *Bulletin of the Menninger Clinic, 56,* 188–208.

Berkovitch, M., Pope, E., Phillips, J., & Koren, G. (1995). Pemoline-associated fulminant liver failure: Testing the evidence for causation. *Clinical Pharmacology and Therapeutics, 57,* 696–698.

Bernstein, G. A., Garkinkel, B. D., & Borchardt, C. M. (1990). Comparative studies of pharmacotherapy for school refusal. *Journal of the American Academy of Child and Adolescent Psychiatry, 29,* 773–781.

Biederman, J., Faraone, S., Hatch, M., Mennin, D., Taylor, A., & George, P. (1997). Conduct disorder with and without mania in ADHD children. *Scientific Proceedings, 44th annual meeting of the American Academy of Child and Adolescent Psychiatry.* (Eds.). Schwab-Stone, & Mahone), Abstract: S–47a, p. 82.

Bird, H. R., Gould, M. S., & Staghezza, B. M. (1993). Patterns of psychiatric comorbidity in a community sample of children aged 9 through 16 years. *Journal of the American Academy of Child and Adolescent Psychiatry, 32,* 361–368.

Birmaher, B., Waterman, G. S., Ryan, N. et al. (1994). Fluoxetine for childhood anxiety disorders. *Journal of the American Academy of Child and Adolescent Psychiatry, 33,* 993–999.

Black, B., & Robbins, D. R. (1990). Panic disorder in children and adolescents. *Journal of the American Academy of Child and Adolescent Psychiatry, 29,* 36–44.

Black, B., & Uhde, T. W. (1994). Treatment of elective mutism with fluoxetine: A double-blind, placebo-controlled study. *Journal of the American Academy of Child and Adolescent Psychiatry, 33,* 1000–1006.

Borduin, C., Mann, B., Cone, L., Henggeler, S. W., Fucci, B. R., Blaske, D. M., & Williams, R. A. (1995). Multisystemic treatment of serious juvenile offenders: Long-term prevention of criminality and violence. *Journal of Consulting Clinical Psychology, 63,* 569–578.

Bowring, M. A., & Kovacs, M. (1992). Difficulties in diagnosing manic disorders in children and adolescents. *Journal of the American Academy of Child and Adolescent Psychiatry 31,* 611–614.

Breimer, D. D., Schellens, J.H.M., & Soons, P. A. (1989). Nifedipine: Variability in its kinetics in man. *Pharmacology and Therapeutics, 44,* 445–454.

Brown, R. T., & Sexson, S. B. (1989). Effects of methylphenidate on cardiovascular responses in attention deficit hyperactivity disordered adolescents. *Journal of Adolescent Health Care, 10,* 179–183.

Bukstein, O. E., Brent, D. A., & Kaminer, Y. (1989). Comorbidity of substance abuse and other psychiatric disorders in adolescents. *American Journal of Psychiatry, 146,* 1131–1141.

Campbell, J. L., Thomas, H. M., Gabrielli, W., Liskow, B. I., & Powell, B. J. (1994). Impact of desipramine or carbamazepine on patient retention in outpatient cocaine treatment: Preliminary findings. *Journal of Addictive Diseases, 13(4),* 191–199.

Campbell, M. (1992). The pharmacological treatment of conduct disorders and rage outbursts. *Psychiatric Clinics of North America, 15,* 69–85.

Campbell, M., & Cueva, J. E. (1995). Psychopharmacology in child and adolescent psychiatry: A review of the past seven years. Part II. *Journal of the American Academy of Child and Adolescent Psychiatry, 34,* 1262–1272.

Campbell, M., Gonzalez, N. M., Ernst, M., Silva, R. R., & Werry, J. S. (1993). Antipsychotics. In: J. S. Werry & M. G. Aman (Eds.), *Practitioner's Guide to Psychoactive Drugs for Children and Adolescents* (pp. 269–296). New York: Plenum.

Cantwell, D. P., Swanson, J., & Connor D. F. (1997). Case study: Adverse response to clonidine. *Journal of the American Academy of Child and Adolescent Psychiatry, 36,* 539–544.

Castellanos, F. X., Giedd, J. N., Elia, J., Marsh, W. L., Ritchie, G. F., Hamburger, S. D., & Rapoport, J. L. (1997). Controlled stimulant treatment of ADHD and comorbid Tourette's syndrome: Effects of stimulant and dose. *Journal of the American Academy of Child and Adolescent Psychiatry, 36,* 589–596.

Chappell, P. B., Riddle, M. A., Scahill, L., Lynch, K. A., Schultz, R., Amstein, A. Leckman, J. F., & Cohen, D. J. (1995). Guanfacine treatment of comorbid attention-deficit hyperactivity disorder and Tourette's syndrome: Preliminary clinical experience. *Journal of the American Academy of Child and Adolescent Psychiatry, 34,* 1140–1146.

Chouinard, G., Goodman, W., Greist, J., Jenike, M., Rasmussen, S., White, K., Hackett, E., Gaffney, M., & Bick, P. A. (1990). Results of a double-blind placebo controlled trial of a new serotonin uptake inhibitor, sertraline, in the treatment of obsessive–compulsive disorder. *Psychopharmacology Bulletin, 26,* 279–284.

Chouinard, G., Young, S. N., & Annable, L. (1983). Antimanic effect of clonazepam. *Biological Psychiatry, 18*, 451–466.

Cohen, L. S., Heller V. L., & Rosenbaum, J. F. (1989). Treatment guidelines for psychotropic drug use in pregnancy. *Psychosomatics, 30*(1), 25–33.

Connors, C. K., Casat, C. D., Gualtieri, C. T., Weller, E., Reader, M., Reiss, A., Weller, R. A., Khayrallah, M., & Ascher, J. (1996). Bupropion hydrochloride in attention deficit disorder with hyperactivity. *Journal of the American Academy of Child and Adolescent Psychiatry, 35*, 1314–1321.

Coplan, J. D., Papp, L. S., Pine, D., Martinez, J., Cooper, T., Rownblum, L. A., Klein, D. F., & Gorman, J. M. (1997). Clinical improvement with fluoxetine therapy and noradrenergic function in patients with panic disorder. *Archives of General Psychiatry, 54*, 643–648.

Cueva, J. E., Overall, J. E., Small, A. M., Armenteros, J. L., Perry R., & Campbell, M. (1996). Carbamazepine in aggressive children with conduct disorder: A double-blind and placebo-controlled study. *Journal of the American Academy of Child and Adolescent Psychiatry, 35*, 480–490.

D'Amato, G. (1962). Chlordiazepoxide in management of school phobia. *Diseases of the Nervous System, 23*, 292–295.

Davidson, J.R.T., & van der Kolk, B. A. (1996). The psychopharmacological treatment of posttraumatic stress disorder. In B. A. van der Kolk, A. C. McFarlane & L. Weisaeth (Eds.). In *Traumatic stress* (pp. 510–524). New York: Guilford.

Davis, J. M., Comaty, J. E., & Janicak, P. G. (1987). *Schizophrenia: Recent biosocial developments.* New York: Human Sciences.

Demilio, L. (1989). Psychiatric syndromes in adolescent substance abusers. *American Journal of Psychiatry, 146*, 1212–1214.

Den Boer, J. A., & Westenberg, H. G. (1990). Serotonin function in panic disorder: a double blind placebo controlled study with fluvoxamine and ritanserin. *Psychopharmacology, 102*, 85–94.

DeVeaugh-Geiss J., Moroz, G., Biederman, J., Cantwell, D. Fontaine, R., Griest, J. A., Reichter, R., Katz, R., & Landau, P. (1992). Clomipramine hydrochloride in childhood and adolescent obsessive–compulsive disorder: A multicenter trial. *Journal of the American Academy of Child and Adolescent Psychiatry, 31*, 45–49.

Devinsky, O., Honigfeld, G., & Patin, J. (1991). Clozapine-related seizures. *Neurology, 41*, 369–371.

Donnelly, M., & Rapoport, J. L. (1985). Attention deficit disorders. In J. M. Weiner (Ed.), *Diagnosis and psychopharmacology of childhood and adolescent disorders* (pp. 178–197). New York: Wiley.

Doogan, D. P. (1991). Toleration and safety of sertraline: Experience world-wide. *International Clinical Psychopharmacology, 6*(Suppl. 2), 47–56.

Dulcan, M. (1990). Using psychostimulants to treat behavioral disorders of children and adolescents. *Child and Adolescent Psychopharmacology, 1*, 7–22.

Dummit, S. E., Klein, R. G., Tancer, N. K., Asche, B., & Martin, J. (1996). Fluoxitine treatment children with selective mutism: An open trial. *Journal of the American Academy of Child and Adolescent Psychiatry, 35*, 615–621.

DuPaul, G. J., Barkley, R. A., & McMurray, M. B. (1994). Response of children with ADHD to methylphenidate: Interaction with internalizing symptoms. *Journal of the American Academy of Child and Adolescent Psychiatry, 33*, 894–903.

Elia, J., Borcherding, B. G., Rapoport, J. L., & Keysor, C. S. (1991). Methylphenidate and dextroamphetamine treatments of hyperactivity: Are there true non-responders? *Psychiatry Research, 36*, 141–155.

Emslie, G. J., Rush, A. J., Weinberg W. A., & Kowatch, R. A. (1997). A double-blind randomized, placebo-controlled trial of fluoxetine in children and adolescents with depression. *Archives of General Psychiatry, 54*, 1031–1037.

Evans, R. W., Clay, T. H., & Gualtieri, C. T. (1987). Carbamazepine in pediatric psychiatry. *Journal of the American Academy of Child and Adolescent Psychiatry, 26*, 2–8.

Famularo, T., Kinscherff, R., & Fenton, R. (1988). Propranolol treatment for childhood posttraumatic stress disorder, acute type: A pilot study. *American Journal of Diseases of Children, 142*, 1244–1247.

Fenichel, R. R. (1995). Combining methylphenidate and clonidine: The role of post-marketing surveillance. *Journal of Child and Adolescent Psychopharmacology, 5*, 155–156.

Fishbain, D. A., Rosomoff, H. L., & Cutler, R. (1993). Opiate detoxification protocols: A clinical manual. *Annals of Clinical Psychiatry, 5*, 53–65.

Flamant, M. F., Rapoport, J. L., & Berg, C. J., Sceery, W., Kilts, C., Mellstom, B., & Linnoila, M. (1985). Clomipramine treatment of childhood obsessive–compulsive disorder: A double-blind controlled study. *Archives of General Psychiatry, 42,* 977–983.

Frazier, J. A., Gordon, C. T., McKenna, K., Lenane, M. C., Jih, D., & Rapoport, J. L. (1994). An open trial of clozapine in 11 adolescents with childhood-onset schizophrenia. *Journal of the American Academy of Child and Adolescent Psychiatry, 33,* 658–663.

Frommer, E. A. (1967). Treatment of childhood depression with antidepressant drugs. *British Medical Journal, 1,* 729–732.

Gadow, K. D., Nolan, E. E., Paolicelli, L. M., & Sprafkin, J. (1991). A procedure for assessing the effects of methylphenidate on hyperactive children in public school settings. *Journal of Clinical Child Psychology, 20,* 268–276.

Gadow, K. D., Sverd, J., Sprafkin, J., Nolan, E. E., & Ezor, S. M. (1995). Efficacy of methylphenidate for attention-deficit hyperactivity disorder in children with tic disorder. *Archives of General Psychiatry, 51,* 444–455.

Garland, E. J., & Smith, D. H. (1990). Case study: Panic disorder on a child psychiatric consultation service. *Journal of the American Academy of Child and Adolescent Psychiatry, 29,* 785–788.

Gelenberg, A. J. (1987). Treating extrapyramidal reactions: some current issues. *Journal of Clinical Psychiatry, 48*(Suppl. 9), 24–27.

Gelenberg, A. J., & Bassuk, E. L. (Eds.). (1997). *The Practitioner's Guide to Psychoactive Drugs.* (4th ed.). New York: Plenum.

Gelenberg, A. J. & Keith, S. (1997). *Psychoses.* In A. J. Gelenberg & S. Keith (Eds.). The practitioner's guide to psychiatric drugs (4th ed., pp. 153–212). New York: Plenum.

Gittelman-Klein, R., & Klein, D. F. (1971). Controlled imipramine treatment of school phobia. *Archives of General Psychiatry, 25,* 204–207.

Gittelman-Klein, R., & Klein, D. F. (1973). School phobia: Diagnostic considerations in light of imipramine effects. *Journal of Nervous and Mental Disease, 156,* 199–215.

Gold, M. E., Redmond, D. C., & Kleber, H. D. (1978). Clonidine blocks acute opiate-withdrawal symptoms. *Lancet, 2,* 599–602.

Gorman, J. M., Liebovitz, M. R., & Fyer, A. J., Goetz, D., Campeas, R. B., Fyer, M. R., Davies, S. O., & Klein, D. F. (1987). An open trial of flouxetine in the treatment of panic attacks. *Journal of Clinical Psychopharmacology, 7,* 329–332.

Gough, A. C., Miles, J. S., Spurr, N. K., Moss, J. E., Gaedigk, A., Eichelbaum, M., Wolf, C. R. (1990). Identification of the primary gene defect at the cytochrome P–450 CYP2D locus. *Nature, 347,* 773–776.

Graae, F., Milner, J., Rizzotto, L., & Klein, R. G. (1994). Clonazepam in childhood anxiety disorders. *Journal of the American Academy of Child and Adolescent Psychiatry, 33,* 372–376.

Greenberg, P. E., Stiglin, L. E., Finkelstein, S. N., & Berndt, E. R. (1993). Depression: A neglected major illness. *Journal of Clinical Psychiatry, 54,* 419–424.

Greenhill, L. I. (1981). Stimulant-related growth inhibition in children: A review. In: M. Gittleman (Ed.), *Strategic interventions for hyperactive children* (pp. 39–63). New York: Sharp.

Greenhill, L. I. (1995). Attention deficit hyperactivity disorder: The stimulants. *Child and Adolescent Psychiatric Clinics of North America, 4,* 123–168.

Greenhill, L. I., & Osman, B. B. (1991). *Ritalin: Theory and patient management.* New York: Mary Ann Liebert.

Greist, J., Chouinard, G., & DuBoff, E., Halaris, A., Kim, S. W., Koran, L., Liebowitz, M., Lyland, R. B., Rasmussen, S., & White, K. (1995). Double-blind parallel comparison of sertraline and placebo in outpatients with obsessive compulsive disorder. *Archives of General Psychiatry, 52,* 289–295.

Greist, J., Jefferson, J. W., Kobak, K. A. et al. (1995). A 1-year double-blind placebo-controlled fixed dose study of sertraline in the treatment of obsessive compulsive disorder. *International Clinical Psychopharmacology, 10,* 57–65.

Halikas, J. A. (1993). Treatment of drug abuse syndromes. *Psychiatric Clinics of North America, 16,* 693–702.

Harmon, R. J., & Riggs, P. D. (1996). Clonidine for posttraumatic stress disorder in preschool children. *Journal of the American Academy of Child and Adolescent Psychiatry, 35,* 1247–1249.

Hazell, P., O'Connell, D., Heathcote D., Robertson, J., & Henry, D. (1995). Efficacy of tricyclic drugs on treating child and adolescent depression: A meta-analysis. *British Medical Journal, 310,* 897–901.

Hinshaw, S. P. (1991). Stimulant medication in the treatment of aggression in children with attentional deficits. *Journal of Clinical and Child Psychology, 12,* 301–312.

Hinshaw, S. (1992). Academic underachievement, attention deficits and aggression: Comorbidity and implications. *Journal of Consulting and Clinical Psychology, 60,* 264–271.

Horrigan, J. P,. & Barnhill, L. J. (1995). Guanfacine for treatment of attention-deficit hyperactivity disorder in boys. *Journal of Child and Adolescent Psychopharmacology, 5,* 215–223.

Hsu, L. K. G., Clement L., Santhouse, R., & Ju, W.S.Y. (1991). Treatment of bulimia nervosa with lithium carbonate: A controlled study. *Journal of Nervous and Mental Disease, 179,* 351–355.

Huizinga, D., Loeber, R., & Thornberry, T. (1994). *Urban delinquency and substance abuse.* (Research summary). Washington, DC: Office of Juvenile Justice and Delinquency Prevention.

Jacqz, E., Hall, S., & Branch, R. A. (1986). Genetically determined polymorphisms in oxidative drug metabolism. *Hepatology, 6,* 1020–1032.

Janicak, P. G., Davis, J. M., & Ayd, F. J. (1997). Treatment with mood stabilizers: Alternative treatment Strategies. In *Principles and practice of psychopharmacology* (2nd ed., pp. 441–460). Baltimore: Williams & Wilkins.

Johnston, C., Pelham, W. E., Hoza, J., & Sturges, J. (1988). Psychostimulant rebound in attention deficit disordered boys. *Journal of the American Academy of Child and Adolescent Psychiatry, 27,* 806–810.

Joyce, P. R., & Paykel, E. S. (1989). Predictors of drug response in depression. *Archives of General Psychiatry, 46*(1), 89–99.

Kaminer, Y. (1992). Desipramine facilitation of cocaine abstinence in an adolescent. *Journal of the American Academy of Child and Adolescent Psychiatry, 31,* 312–317.

Kane, J. M., Honigfield, G., & Singer, J., & Meltzer, H. (1988). Clozapine for the treatment-resistant schizophrenic: A double blind-comparison with chlorpromazine. *Archives of General Psychiatry, 45,* 786–789.

Kaye, W. H. (1997). Anorexia nervosa, obsessional behavior and serotonin. *Psychopharmacology Bulletin, 33,* 335–344.

Klein, R. G., Koplewicz, H. S., & Kanner, A. (1992). Imipramine treatment of children with separation anxiety disorder. *Journal of the American Academy of Child and Adolescent Psychiatry, 31,* 21–28.

Kowatch, R. A., Suppes, T., Gilfillan, S. K., & Fuentes, R. M. (1995). Clozapine treatment of children and adolescents with bipolar disorder and schizophrenia: A clinical case series. *Journal of Child and Adolescent Psychopharmacology, 5,* 241–253.

Kuperman, S., & Stewart, M. A. (1987). Use of propranolol to decrease aggressive outbursts in younger patients. *Psychosomatics, 28,* 315–319.

Kutcher, S. P., Reiter, S., Gardner, D. M., & Klein, R. G. (1992). The pharmacotherapy of anxiety disorders in children and adolescents. *Psychiatric Clinics of North America, 15,* 41–67.

Kutcher, S. P., & Mackenzie, S. (1988). Successful clonazepam treatment of adolescents with panic disorder. *Journal of Clinical Psychopharmacology, 8,* 299–301.

Kutcher, S., Williamson, P., MacKenzie, S., Marton, P., & Murray, E. (1989). Successful clonazepam treatment of neuroleptic-induced akathisia in older adolescents and young adults: A double-blind placebo-controlled study. *Journal of Clinical Psychopharmacology, 9,* 403–406.

Laughren, T. P. (1996). Regulating issues in pediatric psychopharmacology. *Journal of the American Academy for Child and Adolescent Psychiatry, 35,* 1276–1282.

Leonard, H. L., Swedo, S. E., Lenan, & M. C., Rettew, D. C., Cheslow, D. L., Hamburger, S. D., & Rapoport, J. L. (1991). A double-blind desipramine substitution during long-term clomipramine treatment in children and adolescents with obsessive–compulsive disorder. *Archives of General Psychiatry, 48,* 922–927.

Leonard, H. L., Swedo, S. E., Rapoport, J. L., Koby, E. V., Lenane, M. C., Cheslow, D. L., & Hamburger, S. D. (1989). Treatment of obsessive–compulsive disorder with clomipramine and desipramine in children and adolescents. A double-blind crossover comparison. *Archives of General Psychiatry, 46,* 1088–1092.

Lipinski, J.F.J., Zubenko, G. S., Cohen, B. M., & Barreira, P. J. (1984). Propanolol in the treatment of neuroleptic induced akathisia. *American Journal of Psychiatry, 141,* 412–415.

Livingston, R. L., Dykman, R. A. & Ackerman, P. T. (1992). Psychiatric comorbidity and response to two doses of methylphenidate in children with attention deficit disorder. *Journal of Child and Adolescent Psychopharmacology, 2,* 115–122.

Loeber, R., Keenan, K., Lahey, B., Green, S., & Thomas, C. (1994). Interaction between conduct disorder and its comorbid conditions: Effects of age and gender. *Clinical Psychological Review, 14,* 497–523.

Malhotra, S., & Santosh, J. (1998). An Open Clinical Trial of buspirone in Children with Attention-deficit/hyperactivity disorder. *Journal of the American Academy of Child and Adolescent Psychiatry, 37,* 364–371.

Marcus, M. D., Wing, R. R., Ewing, L., Kern, E., McDermott, M., & Gooding, W. (1990). A double-blind, placebo-controlled trial of fluoxetine plus behavior modification in the treatment of obese binge eaters and non-binge-eaters. *American Journal of Psychiatry, 147,* 876–881.

Marder, S. R., & Meibach, R. C. (1994). Risperidone in the treatment of schizophrenia. *American Journal of Psychiatry, 151,* 825–835.

Marriage, K., Fine, S., Moretti, M., & Haley, G. (1986). Relationship between depression and conduct disorder in children and adolescents. *Journal of the American Academy of Child Psychiatry, 25,* 687–691.

Martin, C. S., Kaczynski, N. A., Maisto, S. A., Bukstein, O. G., & Moss, H. B. (1995). Patterns of alcohol abuse and dependence symptoms in adolescent drinkers. *Journal of Studies on Alcohol, 56,* 672–680.

McCann, U. D., & Agras, W. S. (1990). Successful treatment of nonpurging bulimia nervosa with desipramine: A double-blind, placebo-controlled study. *American Journal of Psychiatry, 147,* 1509–1513.

McClellan, J., & Werry, J. (1994). Practice parameters for the assessment and treatment of children and adolescents with schizophrenia. *Journal of the American Academy of Child and Adolescent Psychiatry, 33,* 616–635.

McElroy, S. L., & Keck, P. E. (1993). Treatment guidelines for valproate in bipolar and schizoaffective disorders. *Canadian Journal of Psychiatry, 38*(Suppl. 2), 62–66.

McElroy, S. L., Keck, P. E., Pope H. G., Jr., & Hudson, J. I. (1992). Valproate in the treatment of bipolar disorder: Literature review and clinical guidelines. *Journal of Clinical Psychopharmacology, 12*(Suppl. 1), 42S–52S.

Mezzacappa, E., Steingard, R., Kindlon, D., Saul, J. P., & Earls, F. (1998). Tricyclic antidepressants and cardiac autonomic control in children and adolescents. *Journal of the American Academy of Child and Adolescent Psychiatry, 37,* 52–59.

Munir, K., & Boulifard, D. (1995). Comorbidity. In G. Sholevar (Ed.), *Conduct disorders in children and adolescents* (pp. 59–80). Washington, DC: American Psychiatric Association.

Myers, W. C., Donahue, J. E., & Goldstein, M. R. (1994). Disulfiram for alcohol use disorders in adolescence. *Journal of the American Academy of Child and Adolescent Psychiatry, 33,* 484–489.

Oliveto, A., Kosten, T. R., Schottenfeld, R., Falconi, J., & Ziedonis, D. (1995). Desipramine, amantadine, or fluoxetine in buprenorphine-maintained cocaine users. *Journal of Substance Abuse Treatment, 12,* 423–428.

Perlmutter, S. J. (1995). Pharmacologic treatment of substance abuse. *Child and Adolescent Psychiatric Clinics of North America, 4,* 435–452.

Perry, P. J., Alexander, B., & Liskow, B. I. (1997). *Psychotropic drug handbook* (7th ed.). Washington, DC: American Psychiatric Association.

Petti, T. A., Fish, B., Shapiro, T., Cohen, I. L., & Campbell, M.. (1982). Effects of chlordiazepoxide in disturbed children: A pilot study. *Journal of Clinical Psychopharmacology 2,* 270–273.

Pliszka, S. R. (1989). Effect of anxiety on cognition, behavior and stimulant response in ADHD. *Journal of the American Academy of Child and Adolescent Psychiatry, 28,* 882–887.

Pool D., Bloom, W., & Miekle D. H., Roniger, J. J., & Gallant, D. M. (1976). A controlled evaluation of loxitane in seventy five adolescent schizophrenia patients. *Current Therapeutic Research Clinics Excerpta Medica, 19,* 99–104.

Pope, H.G.J., & Hudson, J. (1987). Antidepressant medication in the treatment of bulimia nervosa. *Psychopathology, 20*(Suppl. 1), 123–129.

Popper, C. W. (1990). Child and adolescent psychopharmacology. In Michels et al. (Eds), *Psychiatry* (Rev. Ed., Vol. 2). Philadelphia: Lippincott.

Popper, C. W. (1995). Combining methylphenidate and clonidine: Pharmacologic questions and news reports about sudden death. *Journal of Child and Adolescent Psychopharmacology, 5,* 157–166.

Price, L. H., & Heninger, G. R. (1994). Lithium in the treatment of mood disorders. *New England Journal of Medicine, 33,* 591–598.

Rapport, M. D., Denney, C., DuPaul, G., & Gardner, J. J. (1994). Attention deficit disorder and methylphenidate: Normalization rates, clinical effectiveness and response prediction in 76 children. *Journal of the American Academy of Child and Adolescent Psychiatry, 33*, 882–893.

Realmuto, G. M., Erikson, W. D., Yellin, A. M., Hopwood, H, & Greenburg, L. M.. (1984). Clinical comparison of thiothixene and thioridazine in schizophrenic adolescents. *American Journal of Psychiatry, 141*, 440–442.

Rickels, K., Case, W. G., Schweizer, E., Garaa-Espana, F. & Fridman, R. (1990). Benzodiazepine dependence: Management of discontinuation. *Psychopharmacology Bulletin, 26*, 63–68.

Riddle, M. A. (1996, May). *Fluvoxamine in the treatment of OCD in children and adolescents: A multicenter, double-blind, placebo controlled trial*. Presented at the Annual Meeting of the American Psychiatric Association, San Diego, CA.

Riddle, M. A., Brown, N., Dzubinski, D., Jetmalani, A. N., Law, Y., & Woolston, J. L. (1989). Case study: Fluoxetine overdose in an adolescent. *Journal of the American Academy of Child and Adolescent Psychiatry, 28*, 587–588.

Riddle, M. A., Scahill, L., & King, R. A., Hardin, M. T., Anderson, G. M., Ort, S. I., Smith, J. C., Leckman, J. F., & Cohen, D. J. (1992). Double-blind, crossover trial of fluoxetine and placebo in children and adolescents with obsessive compulsive disorder. *Journal of the American Academy of Child and Adolescent Psychiatry, 31*, 1062–1069.

Rodman, J. H. (1994). Pharmacokinetic variability in the adolescent: Implications of body size and organ function for dosage regimen design. *Journal of Adolescent Health, 15*, 654–662.

Rosenberg, D. R., Holttum, J., & Gershon, S. (1994). *Textbook of pharmacotherapy for child and adolescent psychiatric disorders*. New York: Brunner/Mazel.

Rothenberg, A. (1988). Differential diagnosis of anorexia nervosa and depressive illness: A review of 11 studies. *Comprehensive Psychiatry, 29*, 427–432.

Rothschild, R., Quitkin, H. M., Quitkin, F. M., Stewart, J. W., Ocepek-Welikson, K., McGrath, P. J., & Tricamo, E. (1994). A double-blind placebo-controlled comparison of phenelzine and imipramine in the treatment of bulimia in atypical depressives. *International Journal of Eating Disorders, 15*, 1–9.

Ryan, N. D., Puig-Antich, J., & Rabinovich, H., Fried, J., Ambrosini, P., Meyer, V., Torres, D., Dachille, S., & Mazzie, D. (1988). MAOIs in adolescent major depression unresponsive to tricyclic antidepressants. *Journal of the American Academy of Child and Adolescent Psychiatry, 27*, 755–758.

Schley, J., & Muller-Oerlinghausen, B. (1983). The binding of chemically different psychotropic drugs to alpha–1–acid glycoprotein. *Pharmacopsychiatria, 11*, 82–85.

Simeon, J., Dinacola, V. F., Ferguson, H. B., Copping, W. (1990). Adolescent depression: A placebo-controlled fluoxetine treatment study and follow-up. *Progress in Neuropsychopharmacological and Biological Psychiatry, 14*, 791–795.

Simeon, J. G., Ferguson, H. B., & Knott, V., Roberts, N., Guathier, B., Dubois, C., & Wiggins, D. (1992). Clinical, cognitive and neurophysiological effects of alprazolam in children and adolescents with overanxious and avoidant disorders. *Journal of the American Academy of Child and Adolescent Psychiatry, 31*, 29–33.

Simeon, J. G., Gerguson, H. B., & Fleet, J.V.W. (1986). Bupropion effects in attention deficit and conduct disorders. *Canadian Journal of Psychiatry, 31*, 581–585.

Spencer, E. K., Kafantaris, V., Padron-Gayol, M. V., Rosenberg, C., & Campbell, M. (1992). Haloperidol in schizophrenic children: Early findings from a study in progress. *Psychopharmacology Bulletin, 28*, 183–186.

Spencer, T., Biederman, J., Steingard, R., & Wilens, T. (1993). Bupropion exacerbates tics in children with attention-deficit hyperactivity disorder and Tourette's syndrome. *Journal of the American Academy of Child and Adolescent Psychiatry, 32*, 211–214.

Spencer, T., Biederman, J., Wilens, T., Harding, M., O'Donnel, D., & Giffin, S. (1996). Pharmacotherapy of attention-deficit hyperactivity disorder across the life cycle. *Journal of the American Academy of Child and Adolescent Psychiatry, 35*, 409–432.

Stromgren, L. S., & Boller, S. (1985). Carbamazepine in treatment and prophyaxis of manic-depressive disorder. *Psychiatric Developments, 3*, 349–367.

Swanson, J. M., Flockhart, D., Udrea, D., Cantwell, D., Connor, D., & Williams, L. (1995). Clonidine in the treatment of ADHD: Questions about safety and efficacy (letter to the editor). *Journal of Child and Adolescent Psychopharmacology, 5*, 301–304.

Tannock, R., Ickowicz., A., & Schachar, R. (1995). Differential effects of methylphenidate on working memory in ADHD children with and without comorbid anxiety. *Journal of the American Academy of Child and Adolescent Psychiatry, 7,* 886–896.

Teicher, M. D., & Glod, C. A. (1990). Neuroleptic drugs: Indications and guidelines for their rational use in children and adolescents. *Journal of Child and Adolescent Psychopharmacology 1,* 33–56.

Tollefson, G. D., Beasley, C.M.J., Tran, P. V., & Street, J. S. (1997). Olanzapine versus haloperidol in the treatment of schizophrenia and schizoaffective and schizophreniform disorders: Results of an international collaborative trial. *American Journal of Psychiatry, 154,* 457–465.

Tran, P. V., Dellva, M. A., Tollefson, G. D., Beasley, C.M.J., Potvin, J. H., & Kiesler, G. M. (1997). Extrapyramidal symptoms and tolerability of olanzapine versus haloperidol in the acute treatment of schizophrenia. *Journal of Clinical Psychiatry, 58,* 205–211.

Umbricht, D., & Kane, J. (1995). Risperidone: Efficacy and safety. *Schizophrenia Bulletin, 21,* 593–606.

Varley, C. K., & McClellan, J. (1997). Case study: Two additional sudden deaths with tricyclic antidepressants. *Journal of the American Academy of Child and Adolescent Psychiatry, 36,* 390–394.

Vitiello, B. (1997). Developmental aspects of child psychopharmacology, *Scientific Proceedings, 44th Annual Meeting of the American Academy of Child and Adolescent Psychiatry* (Eds. Schwab-Stone & Mahone), Abstract: S–40d, p.75.

Vitiello, B., Behar, D., Wolfson, S., & McLeer, S. V. (1990). Case study: Diagnosis of panic disorder in prepubertal children. *Journal of the American Academy of Child and Adolescent Psychiatry, 29,* 782–784.

Vitiello, B., Conrad, T., Burkhart, G. Laughren, T., & Jensen, P. (1994). *Survey on the use of psychotropic medications in children and adolescents* [Abstract]. Presented at the 19th congress of the Collegium Internationale Neuro-Psychopharmacologicum (CINP), Washington, DC.

Walsh, B. T., & Devlin, M. (1995a). Eating disorders. *Child and Adolescent Psychiatric Clinics of North America, 4,* 343–355.

Walsh, B. T., & Devlin, M. (1995b). Pharmacotherapy of bulimia nervosa and binge eating disorder. *Addictive Behaviors, 20,* 757–764.

Walsh, B. T., & Devlin, M. J. (1995c). Psychopharmacology of anorexia nervosa, bulimia nervosa, and binge eating. In K. D. Bloom (Ed.), *Psychopharmacology: The fourth generation of progress* (pp. 1581–1589). New York: Raven.

West S. A., Keck, P. E., Jr., & McElroy, S. L. (1994). Open trial of valproate in the treatment of adolescent mania. *Journal of Child and Adolescent Psychopharmacology, 4,* 263–267.

Wilens, T., Spencer, T. J., Biederman, J., & Schleifer, D. (1997). Case study: Nefazodone for juvenile mood disorders. *Journal of the American Academy of Child and Adolescent Psychiatry, 36,* 481–485.

Wilens, T. E., Spencer, T., Biederman, J., Wozniak, J., & Connor, D. (1995). Combined pharmacotherapy: An emerging trend in pediatric psychopharmacology. *Journal of the American Academy of Child and Adolescent Psychiatry, 34,* 110–112.

Williams, D. T., Mehl, K., Yudofsky, S., Adams, D., & Roseman, B. (1982). The effects of propranolol on uncontrolled rage outbursts in children and adolescents with organic dysfunction. *Journal of the American Academy of Child and Adolescent Psychiatry, 21,* 129–135.

Zahn, T. P., Rapoport, J. L., & Thompson, C. L. (1980). Autonomic and behavioral effects of dextroamphetamine and placebo in normal and hyperactive prepubertal boys. *Journal of Abnormal Child Psychology, 8,* 145–160.

Zeiner, P. (1995). Body growth and cardiovascular function after extended treatment (1.75 years) with methylphenidate in boys with attention-deficit hyperactivity disorder. *Journal of Child and Adolescent Psychopharmacology, 5,* 129–138.

Community, Prevention, and Wellness

Raymond P. Lorion
Ohio University

In its original form (Lorion, Brodsky, Flaherty, & Holland, 1995), this chapter invited readers to think about community both as a locus and as a focus for efforts to prevent emotional and behavioral disorders in children and adolescents. Relevant to community as focus, conduct disorders in girls and affective disorders in boys were offered as counterintuitive examples of how contextual factors contribute to the etiology, maintenance, and remediation of psychological problems in youth. Relevant to community as locus, the value of incorporating preventive interventions within and across the natural settings and systems in which children live, learn, play, and relate to others was made clear.

Extending these prior themes, this chapter examines some mechanisms by which context influences development, critically reviews evidence of such influence and applies that evidence to the conceptualization of interventions to prevent disorder and promote wellness in youth and families. Effective preventive interventions offer strategies for reducing risks factors, righting existing wrongs, and, most importantly, actively shaping the future of youth. Targeted early in the life span, preventive interventions can have long-term positive social impacts by maximizing individual productivity and satisfaction (Haggerty & Mrazek, 1994; National Institute of Mental Health, 1996).

Avoidance of pathology should not be the only route taken by developmental scientists and practitioners to serve the needs of youth. Estimates obtained over nearly 3 decades indicate that approximately one quarter of youth suffer from an identifiable emotional or behavioral disorder prior to reaching adulthood (Glidewell & Swallow, 1967; Mrazek & Haggerty, 1994). The needs of these children must be addressed with the most effective preventive and early treatment strategies available. Attention, however, also must be paid to the remaining 75%. For these children, the challenge for parents, educators, and service providers is not to avoid pathology but to optimize development. Increasingly, this goal—the achievement and maintenance of wellness—is gaining the attention of health and mental health service providers (e.g., Cowen, 1991, 1994; Mrazek & Haggerty, 1994). For that reason, health and wellness promotion also is considered within this chapter. By appreciating the relative merits of, and combining, treatment, prevention, and health promotion efforts, providers of services to children gain access to a comprehensive strategy in support of children and adolescents.

Like its predecessor, this chapter has the dual focuses of prevention and community. The importance of contextual factors is not diminished with the addition of health promotion efforts. Effective preventive and health promotive interventions, we believe, must be based on an understanding of pathogenic and health-promotive processes inherent in the everyday settings in which children live, learn, play, and interact (Lorion, 1991,1998a, 1998b, in press-b). If carefully designed, implemented, evaluated, and disseminated, the array of available interventions can increase the resistance of children and adolescents to psychologically toxic elements in their environments and even may reduce the toxic quality of those settings (Lorion, Brodsky, & Cooley-Quille, 1998; Wandersman & Hess, 1985). Including a focus on wellness increases the chances to enhance youths' natural capacities to exploit positive elements of their everyday environments.

ISSUES OF HEALTH AND DISORDER

To design and implement for youth programs to promote health and prevent disorder, one must assume that established links among genetic, familial, and environmental circumstance and impaired development and problematic lives are malleable (Sroufe, 1997). Those who design such interventions have typically rejected the determinism of dynamic theories (e.g., Freud, 1964) and instead adopted the flexibility and hope of contemporary transactional developmental models (e.g., Hobbs, 1982; Lorion, Price, & Eaton, 1989; Mrazek & Haggerty, 1994; Sameroff & Fiese, 1989). Prevention and promotion advocates assume that proactive interventions can influence present experience in ways that increase the future likelihood of health enhancement and the avoidance of pathology (Albee, 1982, 1986; Cowen, 1986, 1991, 1994).

To achieve intervention goals described in this chapter depends on reaching agreement about definitions of health and pathology. In explaining disorder as "harmful dysfunction," Wakefield (1992, 1997) contributed substantively to such agreement by emphasizing two elements: "dysfunction" and "harm."

Wakefield (1992) noted:

> The focus is on *disorder* rather than *mental* because questions about the concept of disorder cause the most heated disputes in the mental health field. I argue that disorder lies on the boundary between the given natural world and the constructed social world: A disorder exists when the failure of a person's internal mechanisms to perform their functions as designed by nature impinges harmfully on the person's well-being as defined by social values and meanings. The order that is disturbed when one has a disorder is thus simultaneously biological and social; neither alone is sufficient to justify the label *disorder*. (p. 373)

Wakefield's harmful dysfunction hypothesis respects the seemingly competing views that, to be scientific, disorder must be defined according to the absolute presence or absence of specific signs and symptoms, and, to be ecologically valid, it must be defined relative to context. Wakefield (1997) explained:

> The harmful dysfunction analysis takes the position that disorder is an intrinsically hybrid term: A disorder judgment requires *both* a value judgment that there is harm *and* a scientific judgment that there is dysfunction (as defined by failure of a naturally selected function). " (pp. 279–280)

As applied to youth, disorder exists when an impairment in cognitive, emotional, or behavioral functioning interferes with expectations of the settings and people with whom the youth interacts. Wakefield (1997) provided criteria for assessing the need for intervention and its effectiveness regardless of intent (i.e., treatment, prevention, health promotion). When functioning is defective or potentially compromised, its actual or potential harm can be assessed and strategies implemented to reduce the harm. Attention to issues of health and wellness shifts the mental health disciplines' focus from their traditional attention to pathology and dysfunction to concerns about and involvement with normal human functioning.

The need for such a shift was foreseen more than 3 decades ago. In examining implications of the Community Mental Health Center movement for the mental health disciplines, the founders of community psychology recognized that interventions would need to move out of the clinic and into everyday settings. (Bennett et al 1966). A decade later, Kelly (1974) echoed the need for such a shift:

> The work of psychologists is moving from an emphasis on the troubles, the anxieties, the sickness of people, to an interest in how we develop, how we acquire positive qualities, and how social influences contribute to perceptions of well being, personal effectiveness, and even joy. There are signs that in the future, psychologists less and less will be viewing us as having diseases. Instead the psychological view will be one of persons in process over time and as participants in social settings. (p. 1)

Shortly thereafter, U.S. Surgeon General Julius Richmond (1979) released his seminal report, *Healthy People*, as a conceptual and political rationale for federal and state health and mental health care systems based on the identification, pursuit, and achievement of specific objectives (Public Health Service, 1979). That rationale and its subsequent strategic blueprints for the 1980s (U.S. Department of Health and Human Services, 1980, 1986) and the 1990s (U.S. Department of Health and Human Services, 1991) emphasize that treatment, prevention, and health promotion are necessary components of comprehensive health care. As Richmond explained:

> The linked concepts of disease prevention and health promotion are certainly not novel. Ancient Chinese texts discussed ways of life to maintain good health—and in classical Greece, the followers of the gods of medicine associated the healing arts not only with the god Aesculapius but with his two daughters, Panacea and Hygeia. While Panacea was involved with medication of the sick, her sister Hygeia was concerned with living wisely and preserving health. (Richmond, 1979, p. 6)

Further in the report, Richmond was even more explicit about the interconnections among these elements of health care:

> Medical care begins with the sick and seeks to keep them alive, make them well, or minimize disability. … Disease prevention begins with a threat to health—a disease or environmental hazard—and seeks to protect as many people as possible from the harmful consequences of that threat.

> Health promotion begins with people who are basically healthy and seeks the development of community and individual measures which can help them to develop lifestyles that can maintain and enhance the state of well being … Clearly, the three are comple-

mentary, and any effective national health strategy must encompass and give due emphasis to all of them. (Richmond, 1979, p. 119)

His perspective seems to leave little room for doubt about the social and scientific value of vigorously pursuing ways to assess, maintain, and enhance health. To date, however, relatively limited effort has gone into the development of health promotion efforts. Among the few venturing into this uncharted territory is Cowen (1994), for whom psychological wellness represents

one end of a hypothetical continuum, anchored at the other end by an opposing term such as pathology (sickness). The preceding sentence seeks to highlight two points: (a) wellness should indeed be seen as an extreme point on a continuum, *not* as a category in a binary classification system; and (b) wellness is something more than/other than the absence of disease, that is it is defined by the "extent of presence" of positive marker characteristics such as those cited above. And, for that reason, many people who fall well short of being glaring psychological casualties also fail to approach a predominant state of wellness. The two preceding points suggest that the ideal of wellness, and the goal of wellness enhancement, pertain to all people, not just to a limited or select portion of the population. (p. 153)

WELLNESS AS PROCESS

Elsewhere, I have argued that wellness refers not to a state but instead to a dynamic process of responding to the positive and negative events of everyday life (Lorion, in press-b). In my view, defining wellness as a level of functioning attained only by an unknown, but tiny, fraction of the population raises significant conceptual problems. What of those determined to be "less-than-well" because they occupy that intermediate state between the "wellness" end of a continuum and its pathological counterpart? May not the less-than-well acquire some of the stigmata heretofore associated with illness (Scheff, 1984; Levine & Perkins, 1997)? Would there not develop well-intended efforts to make the less-than-well better? Such efforts are likely bound by Sarason's (1978) maxim's concerning the nature of social problems. To the extent that wellness, like poverty, intelligence and academic readiness, represents a relative rather than absolute state, such interventions would have temporary effects which pass as the bar defining wellness rises.

In contrast, wellness is offered herein as the outcome of normative developmental processes, in effect as the default option. It is argued that a majority of individuals, under normative as well as high-risk circumstances, adapt and cope (Lorion, in press-b). Just as canalization accounts for how genetic processes emerge within species (Turkheimer & Gottesman, 1996), an analogous process may explain the human capacity to adapt to varying settings and circumstances and to cope with seemingly debilitating and pathogenic stressors. Support for this position may be found in epidemiological estimates of psychopathology in the general population (Rouse, 1995) and segments thereof, including the economically disadvantaged, adult survivors of childhood physical and sexual abuse, children of separated and divorced parents, and youth who experiment with alcohol and other drugs. Across these and other known risk conditions, one consistently discovers that the majority of those exposed survive and achieve a reasonable state of functioning.

As noted previously, Richmond (Public Health Service, 1979) explained that "Hygeia was concerned with living wisely and preserving health" (p. 6). Thus, health or wellness represents an active quality of individuals. Early on, preventive efforts were likened to rescuing those trapped in a river (i.e., the treatment seekers) either earlier (via secondary prevention) or in time to avoid their entering the river (via primary prevention). When I related this analogy to a psychoanalytic supervisor, his only response was to inquire "And how do they learn to swim?" From his perspective, life occurred in the river and not on the riverbank. Wellness, therefore, defined an individual's capacity to swim and to remain afloat in spite of turbulence and the river's debris. As an active process, therefore, wellness would be studied from a developmental rather than a pathological perspective.

In his 1974 address, Kelly cited Audy (1971): "Health is a continuing property, potentially measurable by the individual's ability to rally from insults, whether chemical, physical, infectious, psychological or social." (p. 142). To this perspective, Kelly (1974) added, "A psychology of healthiness emphasizes that knowledge derives from varied expressions of real life conditions" (p. 3). In effect, wellness refers to the psychological capacity to cope with the demands arising across time, circumstance, and setting. Describing health as *"lieben und arbeiten"* (i.e., the capacity to love and to work), for example, Freud portrayed psychological maturity as resulting from controlling socially unacceptable impulses (Freud, 1964). He failed, however, to acknowledge that a majority of the population somehow do so. Similarly, contemporary theorists tend to discuss "resilience" as the exceptional rather than normative avoidance of pathology (Brodsky, 1997).

WELLNESS AS OUTCOME

Focusing initially on pathology narrows one's assumptive bases. Unlike Freud, for example, Hartmann (1958) explained everyday behavior in terms of the operation of the "conflict-free ego spheres" (e.g., memory, concentration, sensation). These functions enabled individuals to handle normal and challenging encounters with the physical, social, and experiential world. Consistent with Wakefield's (1997) harmful dysfunction position, Hartmann (1958) underscored the normative quality of coping and adaptation. Echoing this perspective, Erikson (1951) viewed development as a succession of encounters between a growing individual and age-determined aspects of the social environment. These encounters define Erikson's classic "eight ages of man" as opportunities for the incremental development of adaptive capabilities. This framework reflected two primary assumptions:

> that the human personality in principle develops according to steps predetermined in the growing person's readiness to be driven toward, to be aware of, and to interact with, a widening social radius; and ... that society, in principle, tends to be so constituted as to meet and invite this succession of potentialities for interaction and attempts to safeguard and to encourage the proper rate and the proper sequence of their enfolding. This is the "maintenance of the human world. (Erikson, 1963, p. 270)

The first assumption echoes the position that an inherent human drive is the functional adaptation to environmental demands. Whether conceptualized as the psychological equivalent of the genetic process of canalization, of the philosophical explanation of teleology, or of the Piagetian principles of organization and adaptation (involving the complementary processes of assimilation and accommodation) to achieve equilibrium with the environment, people are assumed to engage actively with their environment. This assumption has important implications for defining wellness as an inherent human characteristic. As noted previously, were the existence of that characteristic and of its positive consequence for adjustment taken as a given, wellness would be viewed as the expected quality or default condition of individuals.

Erikson's (1963) second assumption implies that individuals have within themselves the capacity to adapt, to face adversity, and to succeed in that confrontation. This same optimistic and dynamic perspective of growth and adjustment to the demands encountered in the environment is found in Piaget's theory of cognitive development (Ginsburg & Opper,1969), Sroufe's (1997) analysis of the coherence of human development, Bronfenbrenner's (1979) conception of bio-psycho-social development, Sameroff's transactional theory (Sameroff & Chandler, 1979; Sameroff & Fiese, 1989) and Kellam's Life Course–Social Fields theory (Kellam, Branch, Agrawal, & Ensminger, 1975).

Respectively, these developmental theorists describe growth as involving social, biological, and psychological processes. Their theories depict coping and adjusting with life's demands as natural processes that occur through a series of active encounters with the physical and social environment. If valid, their shared view casts wellness as the expected state of individuals across the life span. Insofar as pathological states are qualitatively and quantitatively distinct from normative functioning, their avoidance, reduction, or resolution should not be defining markers for wellness. Rather, programs to enhance wellness will have qualities distinct from those to prevent disorder. Each, however, is made possible by an expanded, ecologically based developmental psychology. Appreciation of a contextual perspective expands our capacity to optimize development through comprehensive prevention and promotion efforts.

BASIC ISSUES IN ECOLOGICAL SCIENCE

Shifting perspective from individuals to individuals-in-contexts makes evident the following:

> Psychology is one of the few sciences that has no branch devoted to the observation of phenomena in their natural states. Psychology leaped from the armchair to the laboratory, omitting the study of people in natural settings. Because of this leap, psychology's concepts are concerned with "inside" properties of organisms and treat the outside as alien. (Levine & Perkins, 1997, p. 114)

This gap is evidenced by our tradition of studying, diagnosing, and even intervening in behavior without considering or involving the settings, circumstances, and conditions under which the disorders develop, intensify, and dissipate (Barker, 1968). Kelly's (1966) ecological principles provide a valuable foundation for recognizing the environment's dynamism and can inform the design of effective preventive interventions for youth, whether the salient environment is the family, school, neighborhood, or larger community (Trickett, Watts, & Birman, 1993).

The first of Kelly's (1966) principles, *interdependence,* refers to the mutual influence among components or systems within the environment. A change in one component inevitably ripples through other elements of the environment. Seeing the interdependence among community components, for example, alerts one to the potential to structure settings and, in response, to have that structure altered by countervailing forces. Interdependence argues for rooting interventions deeply within and across salient systems. Doing so should both accelerate the rate of change and insulate the intended impact from other influences.

Kelly's second ecological principle focuses on the *cycling of resources*. Given the interdependence of elements across family, school, or neighborhood, it is assumed that any intervention alters existing resource exchanges within and across systems. This principle also leads one to appreciate that the likely success of an intervention depends, in part, on knowledge of how a community distributes and uses its resources, adds to its available resources, and responds to shortages of resources. Interventions to prevent disorder and promote health will influence each of these aspects. Thus, understanding the nature of systems and their tributaries is essential before attempting to use, change, or replace them. Such information clarifies: (a) linkages between the behaviors and contexts to be modified; (b) the ecological fit of the "adaptive behaviors" to be promoted; and (c) the functions to be preserved, the harm to be mitigated, and the consequent "pathology" to be avoided.

Kelly's (1996) third ecological principle is *adaptation*. As change occurs within a community, resources increase or decrease, behavioral expectations and options vary, and individuals respond accordingly. Effective preventive interventions targeted to preschoolers, for example, can catalyze changes in primary grade curricula. Altering the parent–teacher relationship can increase expectations on each for further communication, involvement, and so forth. Facilitating mothers' access to day care can increase their demand for vocational training, secondary education, and jobs. This principle acknowledges that those affected by change will adapt their behavior accordingly, with rippling consequences for those with whom they relate.

Kelly's final principle involves the concept of *succession*. As Levine and Perkins (1997) noted, environments are not static entities. Change processes initiate subsequent changes. This principle highlights the temporal nature of community interventions. Like the ripples in a pond or the dominoes in a series, impacts of interventions move from their immediate point of contact to other components of the environment. The rate at which the sequence proceeds depends on intensity and, we believe, diversity (i.e., across multiple contextual elements) of the intervention. Not all ripples will be in the intended direction. Not infrequently, forces within a community will respond counter to the intervention. Rather than facilitate change, systemic elements will seek to maintain the status quo. This interplay between forces of change and forces of continuity exemplifies the dynamism integral to the transactional perspective.

Bronfenbrenner (1977) models the environment within which these principles occur as a system of concentric elements. For him, development represents the reciprocal interactions ("transactions" in Sameroff & Fiese's term) between the child and this multilayered environment. Most immediate is the child's microsystem, that is, the immediate interpersonal interactions, roles, activities, and settings in which he or she operates. The mesosystem comprises interrelations among two or more microsystems (e.g., the home and school; the church and local recreational facilities). These systems, in turn, operate within the exosystem or community systems (e.g., the school board or health department). Although not directly involved with a particular child, the exosystem nevertheless affects her or him. Finally, the macrosystem refers to the subculture or culture, including belief systems and values that affect all other levels.

Jasnoski's (1984) ecosystemic view of human development offers a similar multilayered model. The individual is central within an ecosystem of concentric influences expanding from the interpersonal, to the family, the peer group or friendship network, the community, and even the culture. Consistent with Sameroff's model, the reciprocal interactions within and across levels must be considered temporally to understand the process of development across the life span.

Incorporation of the ecological perspective within the design of preventive and health promotive interventions directed to youth addresses several important concerns. Key among these is recognition that successfully disseminated and adopted preventive interventions must fit the settings in which they are delivered (Lorion, 1990; 1998b; in press-b; Munoz, Snowden, & Kelly, 1979; Price & Lorion, 1989). The importance of such a fit is reflected in use of "ecological validity" as a critical yardstick for evaluating an intervention. This concept emerged from Bronfenbrenner's (1977) appreciation of the methodological significance of naturalistic, descriptive research to understanding how developmental processes actually evolve.

Ignoring the match between actual experience and the proposed intervention components is, in Bronfenbrenner's (1977) view, unlikely to produce findings that work in the real world (Lorion, 1991b). Kelly's (1966) ecological model and the concept of ecological validity shape strategies for prevention and health promotion programs and identify alternative target populations. Combining the contributions of Sameroff, Bronfenbrenner, and Jasnowski provides a solid theoretical foundation from which can arise interventions that are multilayered; contextually sensitive; and informed by an understanding of relevant pathogenic, and health-promotive processes.

CONTEXTUAL INFLUENCES

In a series of articles (Lorion, 1998a, in press-a; Lorion et al., 1998; Lorion & Saltzman, 1993), the author has examined exposure to pervasive community violence (PCV) to illustrate how contextual factors can shape emotional and behavioral functioning. Given a growing body of evidence of the negative consequences of such exposure, it seems legitimate to conceptualize PCV as an environmental toxin. Its behavioral implications can be understood in terms of Lewin's (1935) concept of "psychological ecology" as a perspective for the inclusion of setting and individual characteristics into predictions of human behavior. Building on Lewin's base, Barker (1968) demonstrated that setting characteristics were better predictors of children's behavior than were individual characteristics. He concluded that children acted more like each other within a given setting than like themselves across settings. Barker's concept of "behavior-setting" describes how setting characteristics influence behaviors. Wicker (1979) explained this process:

> *Behavior settings are self-regulating, active systems.* They impose their program of activities on the persons and objects within them. Essential persons and materials are drawn into settings, and disruptive components are modified or ejected. It's as if behavior settings were living systems intent on remaining alive and healthy, even at the expense of their individual components.

> To summarize some of the essential features of behavior settings. Most of them can be presented in a single sentence: *A behavior setting is a bounded, self-regulated and ordered system composed of replaceable human and nonhuman components that interact in a synchronized fashion to carry out an ordered sequence of events called the setting program.* (p. 12)

Although the heuristic potential of Barker's (1968) work on setting characteristics has yet to be aggressively mined (the potential richness of this vein is described in Levine & Perkins, 1997; Moos & Insel, 1974; Wandersman & Hess, 1985), it offers a heuristic avenue for understanding and responding to setting influences. It explains the need to understand "setting programs" in terms of the cognitive, emotional, and behavioral outcomes being "pulled for" and those factors that support or interfere with that program. Inhabitants of settings characterized by high PCV, for example, presumably would interpret interpersonal ambiguity as threatening and respond aggressively and defensively. Systematic studies must determine how contextual influences are sufficient to alter and shape ultimately individual predispositions.

It also must be determined whether all who inhabit a setting are potentially (or equally) responsive to contextual factors. It seems reasonable to assume, however, that some youth as well as some parents, caregivers (e.g., teachers), and other adults residing and working in intervention settings are differentially influenced by setting characteristics. Such information is critical, for example, if teachers or parents are to deliver the prevention or health promotion intervention. Depending on the context, it first may be necessary to mitigate environmental effects on parents' and teachers' functioning. Thus, the question confronting designers of prevention and health promotion interventions is how to create alternative setting programs that reduce the harmful costs of dysfunction and promote effectively coping with contextual expectations and demands.

CONCEPTS OF PREVENTION

Space does not allow for a comprehensive review of the history or record of preventive interventions in mental health. Interested readers are referred to Kessler and Goldston (1986), Kazdin (1993), Mrazek and Haggerty (1994), Lorion (Lorion,1990, 1998b; Lorion, Myers, Bartels, & Dennis, 1994), and the National Institute of Mental Health (1996) for such information. Prevention scientists recognize Caplan's (1964) *The Principles of Preventive Psychiatry* as an early, seminal catalyst for the emergence of prevention in the mental health sciences. He argued for applying basic public health principles to emotional and behavioral disorders. He reminded all of the public health truism that no major disease had ever been controlled by treatment but only by preventive efforts.

Caplan introduced the mental health disciplines to the triad of elements (i.e., the "host," the "agent," and the"environment") that public health applies to understanding occurrence and spread of disease. This triad effectively explained the etiology of physical disorders with an identifiable cause (i.e., the agent) that affects an individual (i.e., the host) under specific circumstances (i.e., the environment). Preventive interventions target one or more of these elements. Application of the triad model has effectively served public health efforts to prevent diverse physical disorders (Lilienfeld & Lilienfeld, 1980). Within the model, interventions can be introduced at any point during the genesis of disorder. Efforts prior to meeting diagnostic criteria (i.e., *primary prevention*) are designed to interrupt the pathogenic process early enough to avoid disorder. Success is defined as in reductions in the incidence (i.e., the number of new cases of the targeted disorder).

Alternatively, interventions may be introduced soon after confirmation of a diagnosis. Such *secondary prevention* efforts require psychometrically sound procedures for early case-finding. Identified cases are treated to interrupt ongoing pathogenic processes and thereby avoid further disorder and limit its duration. Traditionally, public health's preventive options included strategies to minimize the secondary consequences of an established disorder, that is, *tertiary prevention*. Such strategies included effective treatment and rehabilitation strategies. Successful tertiary efforts limited or precluded the long-term disabilities that can accompany serious disorder and also reduced the likelihood of recurrence of disorder.

The public health triad has been used effectively to control infectious diseases. Applied to childhood disorders such as polio, measles, smallpox, and phenylketonuria, preventive interventions have reduced markedly the incidence and prevalence of these threats to youth's health and welfare. The model's intervention categories (i.e., primary, secondary, and tertiary), however, apply less well to emotional and behavioral disorders. For these problems, distinguishing the agent and the environment has been hampered given their apparent overlap and interactive, even transactional, relation. Moreover, unlike many physical disorders, emotional and behavioral disorders rarely have an identifiable onset and continuity in their progression.

Appreciating the etiological complexity of behavioral disorders, Gordon (1983) offered an alternative categorical approach that considers the risks assumed recipients. Universal interventions, for example, are targeted broadly to the population. Efforts such as public service announcements, national campaigns (e.g., "Just Say No"), and educational curricula exemplify such approaches. These interventions typically are delivered at relatively little cost per contact and designed so that their effects, at worse, are neutral. With little possibility of selecting or influencing who receives how much of such an intervention, assessment of its impact on the prevalence of disorders is very difficult.

By contrast, *selective interventions* are targeted to segments of the population whose heightened risk for disorder has been epidemiologically confirmed. Such interventions are targeted to groups at risk for specific disorders. Although the potential for iatrogenic effects (i.e., unanticipated negative side effects) is heightened with selective interventions, this factor is balanced by the increased risk of those targeted. Evaluating the outcomes of selective interventions tends to be less methodologically challenging than their universal counterparts.

Finally, *indicated interventions* are targeted to specific individuals demonstrating early signs of disorder. The intensity of such interventions is typically greater than that of either universal or selective, again balancing the relative risk of disorder faced by their recipients. Understandably, that increased intensity includes an increased potential for iatrogenic consequences. Consequently, screening and problem assessment procedures used to select participants must be carefully designed, psychometrically sound, and systematically applied. If these conditions are met, however, indicated programs can be efficient and cost-effective approaches to reducing the prevalence of mental health disorders (Gordon, 1987; Lorion, 1998b; Lorion et al., 1989).

LINKING PREVENTION, PROMOTION, AND DEVELOPMENT

The design and implementation of preventive and health-promotive interventions inform and are informed by the developmental sciences in multiple ways. By definition, health promotion efforts support normal developmental processes. As such, they assist individuals to develop successful coping and adaptation techniques. In a complementary manner, effective preventive interventions protect youth from the direct and indirect effects of emotional and behavioral disorders. As these interventions are disseminated, the disruptive impact of risky settings and circumstances on normal development of youth and families lessens. Conceptually, health promotion and preventive interventions offer valuable opportunities for identifying and confirming etiological pathways (Lorion, 1990b; 1991b). Each can examine causal links among developmental mechanisms, risk and protective factors, and normative and pathological outcomes. If ineffective but systematically researched, preventive and health promotive interventions can extend our understanding of disorder and (dys)function and the design of appropriate strategies (Kellam et al., 1991; Lorion et al., 1994, 1995).

Moreover, inclusion of health promotion and preventive interventions among the human services can have far-reaching implications for professional roles and definitions (Price, 1983). Emergence of these interventions has redefined and will continue to redefine the childcare, pediatric, mental health, and other developmental professions. Gradually, service providers and researchers will shift their emphases from repair, treatment, and rehabilitation to the design and implementation of strategies to prevent pathology, optimize development, and promote growth. Inevitably, such activities will involve both person-oriented and system-oriented initiatives (Cowen, 1994, 1996). Over time, a portion of their efforts can be focused increasingly on the creation of risk-reducing and health-promotive environments (Lorion, 1998b). Thus, gradually, the human development disciplines will apply their skills and knowledge less frequently in professional settings and designated childcare facilities and more frequently in homes, schools, playgrounds, and other sites where daily life occurs.

Locating prevention programs within community settings maximizes their long-term impact. Such interventions seek to enable recipients to respond effectively to the demands of everyday settings. When participants confront, resolve, or avoid entirely problems under normal conditions, they gain capabilities that enhance adaptation and health. For that very reason, everyday community settings and circumstances must be the "where" of effective preventive and health-promotive interventions.

Admittedly, some settings (e.g., a child's home, school, or neighborhood) themselves are pathogenic and present seemingly unavoidable risks. In such cases, interventions must not only be located within the community, but they must modify characteristics of the settings in which they are located. In effect, an intervention may require transformation of the setting's pathogenic characteristics by: (a) weakening or reducing its level to fit within the residents' coping capacities, (b) neutralizing those characteristics so they no longer impact on the residents, or (c) modifying settings such that their encounter actually represents a health-promotive interaction for the residents.

Thus, this chapter urges recognition of community settings and characteristics of everyday environments as one of the "hows" of effective preventive interventions. Relevant to PCV, for example, interventions may be introduced that alter adults' acceptance of gang-related activity. Parents may cooperate in monitoring children in playgrounds; increased police surveillance, which reduces aggressive activities by adolescents. Prompt and consistent enforcement of parental rules may provide youth with clear expectations regarding the acceptability and response to behaviors. Thus, aspects of the community environment become the focus as well as the locus of the preventive processes. Within this perspective and consistent with Wakefield's (1997) position, disorder is viewed as a social and community as well as individual phenomenon. Interventions, therefore, may target individual children and families or neighborhoods and systems (e.g., schools or recreational programs) that affect youth. The former approaches benefit individual units; the latter have the capacity for broad and continuing impact.

Healthy as well as disordered emotional or behavioral outcomes (e.g., conduct problems) result from diverse sets of antecedents. Conversely, specific risk factors (e.g., ranging from parental divorce to early childhood abuse) and child-rearing circumstances which reflect different interactions between hosts and environments and can be linked to a variety of developmental outcomes (Lorion et al, 1989; Sroufe, 1997; Sroufe & Rutter, 1984). To that complexity must be added Bell's (1986) recognition of the developmental nature of risk and protective factors. In his work, Bell argued that presumed risks (e.g., parental conflict) and resources (e.g., parental competence) vary in their pathogenic and health-promotive quality across contextual factors and situations. Risk factors change over time. As the parental environment varies, for example, or other influences come and go in a child' life (e.g., a supportive grandparent or teacher), the potency of familial tension will wax and wane (e.g., Sandler, Wolchik, Braver, & Braver, 1991). Thus, the riskiness of individual, agent, or environmental factors rises and falls over time and across circumstances (Bell, 1986).

The discontinuous, "multiple–paths–multiple outcomes," quality of emotional disorders underlines the importance of examining environmental factors for etiological processes and intervention opportunities (Lorion, 1998b). Appreciation of the developmental processes of equifinality (i.e., multiple antecedents leading to a common outcome) and equipotentiality (i.e., common antecedents leading to multiple outcomes) argues strongly for designing interventions targeted to the broadest array of setting conditions, especially those linked to the greatest number of desired positive or targeted negative outcomes (Cicchetti & Rogosch, 1996). It also argues for recognition of how promotion of coping and adaptive skills early in life may have protective value in later years. At the very least, it is evident that extending the period without disorder has long-term benefit when subsequently confronted with significant demands (Turkheimer & Gottesman, 1996). Combining prevention and health promotion strategies appears to represent multiple stitches in time.

SUMMARY

In its various forms, community prevention may be offered as the ultimate "right stuff" of mental health intervention. Unquestionably, there needs to be continuing acceptance and refinement of this multidimensional approach to understanding and responding to the needs of children and adolescents. Interventions that prevent disorder and promote health are important tools for the mental health professions to acquire and apply. They are not, however, either the only tools or risk-free. As we and others have noted (Levin, Trickett, & Hess, 1990; Lorion,1987; Weithorn, 1987), preventive interventions are as vulnerable to iatrogenic consequences are as other forms of human service. Stating this fact should add caution to, but not reduce, continuing enthusiasm for the development of this challenging scientific and professional focus.

Included within that caution should be an appreciation of the unique complications associated with community-level interventions. Who, for example, should provide informed consent in school-based interventions—school administrators, teachers, parents, or students? Can parents overrule system administrators? Can teachers overrule parents? How can confidentiality be maintained? In this complicated milieu, how can we adequately assess risks of planned interventions so that individuals at each of the affected levels can be monitored and, if necessary, alerted? In fact, who exactly is the client or subject? Might not certain interventions promote health in some children but increase risk for disorder in others?

Conceptualization of preventive and health promotion interventions as contextually based strategies that impact across the multiple levels of influence on child and adolescent development is admittedly challenging. Problem analysis and intervention development must be carried out with populations of concern ranging from a single individual to the children, families, and residents of entire communities. Obviously, the fundamental theory and techniques of community-based prevention require the collaboration of developmental scientists, child-clinicians, educators, urban planners, and systems planners, but especially of the families, adults, and children living within those communities. A complex and challenging field, such as community prevention, cannot hope to achieve its potential unless it reflects the very contextual, multilevel quality of the phenomena on which it focuses.

REFERENCES

Albee, G. W. (1982). Preventing psychopathology and promoting human potential. *American Psychologist, 37*, 1043–1050.

Albee, G. W. (1986). Advocates and adversaries of prevention. In M. Kessler & S. E. Goldston (Eds.) *A decade of progress in primary prevention* (pp. 309–332). Hanover, NH: University Press of New England.

Audy, J. R. (1971). Measurement and diagnosis of health. In P. Shepart & D. McKinley (Eds.), Environmental essays on the planet as home (pp. 140–162). Boston: Houghton Mifflin.

Barker, R. G. (1968). *Ecological psychology: Concepts and methods for studying the environment.* Stanford, CA: Stanford University Press.

Bell, R. Q. (1986). Age specific manifestations in changing psychosocial risk. In D. C. Farran & J. D. McKinney (Eds.), *The concept of risk in intellectual and psychosocial development.* (pp. 169–185). New York: Academic Press.

Bennett, C. C., Anderson, L. S., Cooper, S., Hassol, L. Klein, D. C., & Rosenblum, G. (Eds.). (1996). *Community psychology: A report of the Boston conference on the education of psychologists for community mental health.* Boston: Boston University Press.

Brodsky, A. E. (1996). Resilient single mothers in risky neighborhoods: Negative psychological sense of community. *Journal of Community Psychology, 24*, 347–364.

Bronfenbrenner, U. (1977). Toward an experimental ecology of human development. *American psychologist, 32*, 513–531.

Bronfenbrenner, U. (1979). *The ecology of human development.* Cambridge, MA: Harvard University Press.

Caplan, G. (1964). *The principles of preventive psychiatry.* New York: Basic Books.

Cichetti, D., & Rogosch, F. A. (1996). *Equifinality and multifinality in developmental psychopathology, 8,* 597–600.

Cowen, E. L. (1986). Primary prevention in mental health: Ten years of retrospect and ten years of prospect. In M. Kessler & S. E. Goldston (Eds.), *A decade of progress in primary prevention* (pp. 3–46). Hanover, NH: University Press of New England.

Cowen, E. L. (1991). In pursuit of wellness. *American Psychologist, 46*, 404–408.

Cowen, E. L. (1994). The enhancement of psychological wellness: Challenges and opportunities. *American Journal of Community Psychology, 22,* 149–180.

Cowen, E. L. (1996). The ontogenesis of primary prevention: Lengthy strides and stubbed toes. *American Journal of Community Psychology, 24,* 235–250.

Erikson, E. (1963). *Childhood and society.* New York: Norton.

Freud, S. (1964). *A general introduction to psychoanalysis.* New York: Herald Square Press.

Ginsburg. H., & Opper, S. (1969). *Piaget's theory of intellectual development.* Englewood Cliffs, NJ: Prentice-Hall.

Glidewell, J. C., & Swallow, C. S. (1996). *The prevalence of maladjustment in elementary schools: A report prepared for the Joint Commission on the Mental Health of Children.* Chicago: University of Chicago Press.

Gordon, R. S. (1983). An operational classification of disease prevention. *Public Health Reports, 98,* 107–109.

Gordon, R. S. (1987). An operational classification of disease prevention. In J. A. Steinberg & M. M. Silverman (Eds.), *Preventing mental disorders: A research perspective* (DHHS Publication No. ADM 87–1492, pp. 20–26). Washington, DC: U.S. Government Printing Office.

Hartmann, H., (1958). *Ego psychology and the problem of adaptation.* New York: International Universities Press.

Hobbs, N. (1982). *The troubled and troubling child: Reeducation in mental health, education and human services programs for children and youth.* San Francisco: Jossey-Bass.

Jasnoski, M. (1984). The ecosystemic perspective in clinical assessment and intervention. In W. O'Connor & B. Lubin (Eds.). *Ecological approaches to clinical and community psychology.* New York: Wiley.

Kazdin, A. E. (1993). Adolescent mental health: Prevention and treatment. *American Psychologist, 48,* 127–142.

Kellam, S. G., Branch, J. D., Agrawal, K. C., & Ensminger, M. E. (1975). *Mental health and going to school: The Woodlawn Program of Assessment, Early Intervention, and Evaluation*. Chicago: University of Chicago Press.

Kellam, S. G., Werthamer-Larsson, L., Dolan, L. J., Brown, C. H., Mayer, L. S., Rebok, G. W., Anthony, J. C., Laudoff, J., Edelsohn, G., & Wheeler, L. (1991). Developmental epidemiologically based preventive trials: Baseline modeling of early target behaviors and depressive symptoms. *American Journal of Community Psychology, 19,* 563–584.

Kelly, J. G. (1966). Ecological constraints on mental health services. *American Psychologist, 21,* 535–539.

Kelly, J. G. (1968). Towards an ecological conception of preventive interventions. In J. W. Carter, Jr. (Ed.) *Research contributions from psychology to community mental health*. New York: Behavioral Publications.

Kelly, J. G. (1986). Content and process: An ecological view of the interdependence of practice and research. *American Journal of Community Psychology, 14,* 581–589.

Kelly, J. G. (1974, May). *Toward a psychology of healthiness*. Invited address as the Ichabod Spencer Lecture, Union College, Schenectady, NY.

Kessler, M., & Goldston, S. E. (Eds.). (1986). *A decade of progress in primary prevention.* Hanover, NH: University Press of New England.

Levin, G. B., Trickett, E. J., & Hess, R. E. (Eds.). (1990). *Ethical implications of primary prevention.* Binghampton, NY: Haworth.

Levine, M., & Perkins, D. V. (1997). *Principles of community psychology: Perspectives and applications* (2nd ed.). New York: Oxford University Press.

Lilienfeld, A. M., & Lilienfeld, D. E. (1980). *Foundations of epidemiology* (2nd ed.). New York: Oxford University Press.

Lorion, R. P. (1985). Environmental approaches and prevention: The dangers of imprecision. In A. Wandersman & R. Hess (Eds.), *Beyond the individual: Environmental approaches and prevention.* (pp. 193–205). Binghampton, NY: Haworth.

Lorion, R. P. (1987). The other side of the coin: The potential for negative consequences of prevention interventions. In J. A. Steinberg & M. M. Silverman (Eds.), *Preventing mental disorders: A research perspective* (DHHS Publication No. ADM 87-1492, pp. 243–250). Washington, DC: U.S. Government Printing Office.

Lorion, R. P. (Ed.), (1990). *Protecting the children: Strategies for optimizing emotional and behavioral development.* Binghampton, NY: Haworth.

Lorion, R. P. (1991). Targeting preventive interventions: Enhancing risk estimates through theory. *American Journal of Community Psychology, 19,* 859–866.

Lorion, R. P. (1998a). Exposure to urban violence: Contamination of the school environment. In D. S. Elliot, K. Williams, & B. Hamburg (Eds.), *Violence in American schools* (pp. 293–311). New York: Cambridge University Press.

Lorion, R. P. (1998b). Prevention goals and indirect/consultation strategies: Meeting current needs through a recommitment to underused means and ends. In A. S. Bellack & M. Hersen (Eds.), *Comprehensive clinical psychology* (Vol. 6, pp. 277–300). Elmsford, NY: Pergamon.

Lorion, R. P. (in press-a). Exposure to urban violence: Shifting from an individual to an ecological perspective. In N. Scheiderman, H. Tomes, J. Gentry, & J. Silva (Eds.), *Integrating behavioral and social sciences with public health*. Washington, DC: American Psychological Association.

Lorion, R. P. (in press-b) Theoretical and evaluation issues in the promotion of wellness and the protection of "well enough." In D. Cicchetti, J. Rappaport, I. Sandler, & R. Weissberg (Eds.), *The promotion of wellness in children and adolescents.* Thousand Oaks, CA: Sage.

Lorion, R. P., Brodsky, A. E., & Cooley-Quille, M. (1998). Exposure to pervasive community violence: Resisting the contaminating effects of risky settings. In D. E. Biegel & A. Blum (Eds.), *Innovations in practice and service delivery across the life span.* New York: Oxford University Press.

Lorion, R. P., Brodsky, A. E., Flaherty, M. J., & Holland, C. C. (1995). Community and prevention: Focus for change—vehicle for growth. In M. Hersen & R. T. Ammerman (Eds.), *Advanced abnormal child psychology* (pp. 213–234). Hillsdale, NJ: Lawrence Erlbaum Associates.

Lorion, R. P., Myers, T. G., Bartels, C., & Dennis, A. (1994). Preventive intervention research: Pathways for extending knowledge of child/adolescent health and pathology. In T. Ollendick & R. Prinz (Eds.), *Advances in clinical child psychology* (pp. 109–140). New York: Plenum.

Lorion, R. P., Price, R. H., & Eaton, W. W. (1989). The prevention of child and adolescent disorders: From theory to research. In D. Shaffer, I. Philips, & N. B. Enzer (Eds.), *Prevention of mental disorders, alcohol and other drug use in children and adolescents* (OSAP Prevention Monograph–2, DHHS Publication No. ADM 89–1646, pp. 55–96). Washington, DC: U.S. Government Printing Office.

Lorion, R. P., & Saltzman, W. (1993). Children's exposure to community violence in Maryland: Following a path from concern to research to action. *Psychiatry, 56,* 55–65.

Moos, R., & Insel, P. M. (1974). *Issues in social psychology: Human milieus.* Palo Alto, CA: National Press.

Mrazek, P. J., & Haggerty, R. J. (1994). *Reducing risks for mental disorders: Frontiers for preventive intervention.* Washington, DC: National Academy Press.

Munoz, R. F., Snowden, L. R., & Kelly, J. G. (Eds.). (1979). *Social and psychological research in community settings: Designing and conducting programs for social and personal well-being.* San Francisco: Jossey-Bass.

National Institute of Mental Health. (1986). *Fifth national conference on prevention research.* Rockville, MD: National Institutes of Health.

Price, R. H., & Lorion, R. P. (1989). Prevention programming as organizational reinvention: From research to implementation. In D. Shaffer, I. Philips, & N. B. Enzer (Eds.), *Prevention of mental disorders, alcohol and other drug use in children and adolescents* (OSAP Prevention Monograph–2, DHHS Publication No. ADM 89–1646, pp. 97–123). Washington, DC: U.S. Government Printing Office.

Public Health Service. (1979). *Healthy people: The Surgeon Generals report on health promotion and disease prevention* (DHEW [PHS] Publication No. 79–55071). Washington, DC: U.S. Government Printing Office.

Rouse, B. A. (Ed.). (1995). *Substance abuse and mental health statistics sourcebook* (DHHS Publication No. SMA 95–3064). Washington, DC: U.S. Government Printing Office.

Sameroff, A. J., & Chandler, M. J. (1975). Reproductive risk and the continuum of caretaking casualty. In F. D. Horowitz, M. Hetherington, S. Scarr-Salapatek & G. Siegel (Eds.), *Review of Child Development Research* (Vol. 4, pp. 187–244). Chicago: University of Chicago Press.

Sameroff, A. J., & Fiese, B. H. (1989). Conceptual issues in prevention. In D. Shaffer, I. Philips & N. B. Enzer (Eds.), *Prevention of mental disorders, alcohol and other drug use in children and adolescents* (OSAP Prevention Monograph–2, DHHS Publication No. ADM 89–1646 (pp. 23–53). Washington, DC: U.S. Government Printing Office.

Sandler, I., Wolchik, S. Braver, S., & Braver, B. (1991). Stability and quality of life events and psychological symptomatology in children of divorce. *American Journal of Community Psychology, 19,* 501–520.

Sarason, S. B. (1971). The nature of problem solving in social action. *American Psychologist, 33,* 370–380.

Scheff, T. J. (1978). *Being mentally ill: A sociological theory.* Chicago: Aldine-Atherton.

Sroufe, L. A. (1997). Psychopathology as an outcome of development. *Development and Psychopathology, 9,* 251–268.

Sroufe, L. A., & Rutter, M. (1984). The domain of developmental psychopathology. *Child Development, 55,* 17–29.

Trickett, E. J., Watts, R., & Birman, D. (1993). Human diversity and community psychology: Still hazy after all these years. *Journal of Community Psychology, 21,* 264–279.

Turkheimer, E., & Gottesman, I. I. (1996). Simulating the dynamics of genes and environment in development. *Development and Psychopathology, 8,* 667–678.

U.S. Department of Health and Human Services. (1980). *Promoting health/preventing disease: Objectives for the nation.* Washington, DC: U.S. Government Printing Office.

U.S. Department of Health and Human Services. (1986). *The 1990 health objectives for the nation: A midcourse review.* Washington, DC: U.S. Government Printing Office.

U.S. Department of Health and Human Services. (1991). *Healthy people 2000: National health promotion and disease prevention objectives.* Washington, DC: U.S. Government Printing Office.

Wakefield, J. C. (1992). The concept of mental disorder: On the boundary between biological facts and social values. *American Psychologist, 47,* 373–388.

Wakefield, J. C. (1997). When is development disordered? Developmental psychopathology and the harmful dysfunction analysis of mental disorder. *Development and Psychopathology, 9,* 269–290.

Wandersman, A., & Hess, R. (1985). *Beyond the individual: Environmental approaches and prevention.* Binghampton, NY: Haworth.

Weithorn, L. A. (1987). Informed consent for prevention research involving children: Legal and ethical issues. In J. A. Steinberg & M. M. Silverman (Eds.), *Preventing mental disorders: A research perspective* (DHHS Publication No. ADM 87–1492, pp. 226–242). Washington, DC: U.S. Government Printing Office.

Wicker, A. W. (1979). *An introduction to ecological psychology.* Monterey, CA: Brooks/Cole.

Description of the Disorders

Until relatively recently, it would have been impossible to organize a textbook of ab-normal behavior in children based on specific disorders. Prior to *DSM–III* and *DSM–III–R*, the diversity of children's behavioral and emotional disorders was not so clearly delineated. However, in the past 25 years, a considerable body of research has enhanced our understanding of previously neglected conditions, such as anxiety dis-orders, affective disorders, and eating disorders. Moreover, new and distinct areas have emerged, including pediatric psychology and substance use and abuse in chil-dren and adolescents.

As an increasingly sophisticated body of well-controlled research has been amasses, several general observations can be made regarding the etiology, assess-ment, and treatment of child and adolescent psychopathology. First, disorders must be understood within the context of the child's family and social environment. Fac-tors such as dysfunctional family system, poverty, and neighborhood violence, to name but a few, can contribute to the etiology and maintenance of the disorder and may impede treatment. Second, most disorders occur as a function of the interaction between biological and environmental risk factors. Treatment, therefore, must derive from an assessment of psychological, environmental, and psychophysiological sys-tems. Third, in order to maximize successful outcome, treatment should target the multiple settings (e.g., family, school) that ultimately affect the child's behavior. Finally, the chronic course of several disorders (e.g., mental retardation, pervasive developmental disorders) necessitates long-term treatment and frequent follow-ups.

The nine chapters in this section examine specific disorders of childhood and ado-lescence. In chapter 14, Rabian and Silverman point out that, whereas *DSM–III–R* contained three disorders under the broad heading of "Anxiety Disorders of Child-hood and Adolescence" (i.e., separation anxiety disorder, avoidant disorder, and overanxious disorder), the *DSM–IV* contains only separation anxiety, now under the category "Other Disorders on Infancy, Childhood, or Adolescence." The *DSM–III–R*'s diagnosis of overanxious disorder has been subsumed under generalized anxiety dis-order in *DSM–IV,* and avoidant disorder has been eliminated altogether. As in *DSM–III–R, DSM–IV* allows for additional "adult" anxiety diagnoses to be used with children. Of these, specific phobia and social phobia are the most common in youth. With respect to treatment, the most widely used approaches for childhood phobic and anxiety disorders are behavioral, psychodynamic, and pharmacological.

Stark, Bronik, Wong, Wells, and Ostrander (chapter 15) note that the study of depressive disorders during childhood is at an early stage. It is apparent that depressive disorders negatively affect a child's emotional, cognitive, motivational, and physical functioning. Diagnostic criteria for depressive disorders in children are similar to those for adults. General models of depressive disorders have been proposed, but it would appear that none of these models adequately explains the etiology of depressive disorders during childhood, nor do they adequately take into account the developmental nature of childhood problems. The bulk of evidence for use of treatment strategies, derived from use with adults, is based on nonclinical populations from school settings. In general, results suggest that a multicomponent and multimodal intervention that combines psychosocial, individual, and family intervention, along with pharmacological intervention, is most likely to be effective. However, much additional research is needed in this area.

Mental retardation is reviewed by Baumeister and Baumeister in chapter 16. By definition, mental retardation emerges in childhood and is characterized by low IQ and deficits in functional ability. Although there are a number of possible causes of mental retardation, broad distinctions are typically made between cultural–familial retardation, characterized by mild impairment in response to environmental deprivation, and organic retardation, involving more severe impairment and emanating from organic pathology or genetic factors. Mental retardation is chronic, and early intervention is needed to maximize developmental and cognitive potential. The authors note that there is no "cure" for mental retardation, although in certain instances some associated conditions can be treated. They argue that in the vast majority, treatment consists of providing supportive environments during the entire life span.

Harris in chapter 17 points out that pervasive developmental disorders are relatively rare, but that they are very serious disorders that begin in infancy or early childhood and require early, intensive intervention for maximum treatment benefits. Symptoms of these disorders include pervasive problems of social behavior and emotional expression, communication deficits, and disruptive behaviors, including stereotyped behaviors, self-injury, and resistance to change. Although once believed to be the result of poor parenting, these disorders are now know to be related to a variety of biologically based disorders. There appear to be genetic patterns for some of the disorders, and other neurological and neurochemical bases are being explored for these disorders. Applied behavior analysis is the most common treatment, and there exists an extensive database to document benefits of behavioral procedures for treating social, communication, and behavioral problems exhibited by these children.

Learning, motor, and communication disorders are described by Johnson and Slomka (chapter 18). These comprise a group of disorders characterized by significant deficiencies in development of skills related to academic, language, and motor abilities. It appears likely that causes of specific developmental disorders are multiple. Currently, associations between various environmental factors and genetic predispositions have been determined, but much more is to be learned about the etiology of these disorders. Treatment approaches that are commonly utilized include behavioral interventions, cognitive–behavioral treatments, information-processing and psychoeducational interventions, and pharmacological therapy.

In chapter 19, Webster-Stratton shows how conduct disorder is highly prevalent in our society and has an impact on school, community, family, and peer relationships. Children with conduct disorders are characterized by a "complex" pattern of behaviors, including lying, cheating, stealing, hitting, and noncompliance to parental requests. Multiple influences, including child-, parent-, and school-related factors, contribute to development and maintenance of child conduct disorder. The association between conduct disorder and psychophysiological or genetic influence is inconclusive. Rather, studies affirm that genetics and child biological factors, in conjunction with environmental factors, are influential in the development and maintenance of the disorder.

In chapter 20, Rapport and Chung argue that ADHD is a complex and chronic disorder of brain, behavior, and development whose behavioral and cognitive consequences affect multiple areas of functioning. Mounting evidence suggests that the disorder is significantly more common in certain families and probably is inherited through some yet unknown mechanism, with resulting underactivity of the prefrontal–striatal–limbic regions of the brain. Differences in the neurophysicolgical functioning of the brain, particularly executive and regulatory functioning, may help explain why these children experience profound difficulties in maintaining attention, regulating their arousal, inhibiting themselves in accordance with environmental demands, and getting along with others–yet only at specific times and under certain conditions. Behavioral and pharmacological interventions, both alone and in combination, represent the most efficacious treatments currently available for children with ADHD.

In chapter 21, Mizes and Miller illustrate how anorexia nervosa, bulimia nervosa, and the recently described binge eating disorder are fascinating psychological problems that have received much media attention. Eating disorders are multidetermined, with societal, psychological, and biological risk factors. Recent research suggests a much stronger role for a genetic predisposition to eating disorders than previously thought. Risk factors that appear to be related to eating disorders include negative life events, dieting and body dissatisfactions, and psychological distress. Developmental factors, such as early puberty and early dating, may increase the risk for eating disorders. Teasing about appearance, which may be influenced by early puberty, is also a risk factor. Sexual abuse appears to be a risk factor for bulimia, but not for anorexia nervosa. There is a debate as to whether sexual abuse is a general risk factor for psychological problems (including bulimia), or if it is a specific risk factor for bulimia nervosa. Also, treatments for bulimia nervosa and binge eating disorder have yielded promising results.

In chapter 22, Newcomb and Richardson indicate that use and abuse of mood-altering drugs by children and adolescents are related to a wide array of various risk factors. Even though very few children experiment to any extent with abusable substances prior to the sixth grade, such drug involvement by these children and older teenagers is of grave concern given the serious risks that such behaviors represent. Most adolescents experiment with alcohol prior to age 18; nearly half also experiment with at least one illicit drug by this age. National surveys indicate that most types of drug use have decreased since the early 1980s, and even rates of cocaine use have decreased consistently since the mid-1980s, although there is significant concern that these patterns may not reflect all segments of the population (inner-city youth, school dropouts, gang members).

Anxiety Disorders

Brian Rabian
University of Southern Mississippi

Wendy K. Silverman
Florida International University

CLINICAL DESCRIPTION

In the chapter we wrote on anxiety disorders for the first edition of this volume, we noted the increased research attention that had been directed to the anxiety disorders of childhood since publication of the third edition of the *Diagnostic and Statistical Manual of Mental Disorders* (*DSM–III*; American Psychiatric Association [APA], 1980). Additionally, we noted the significant changes that *DSM–IV* (APA, 1994) would bring to the classification of anxiety disorders in children. Specifically, *DSM–III* subsumed Overanxious Disorder (AOD) under the newly created subheading of *Anxiety Disorders of Childhood and Adolescence*, along with Separation Anxiety Disorder (described in detail later) and Avoidant Disorder. This recognition of three distinct anxiety subcategories was retained in the revision to *DSM–III*, published in 1987 (*DSM–III–R*; APA, 1987).

In addition to the *Anxiety Disorders of Childhood and Adolescence, DSM–III* and *DSM–III–R* contained several other categories of anxiety disorders, that were not classified specifically as "child disorders." These additional anxiety disorder categories included generalized anxiety disorder (GAD), panic disorder, obsessive–compulsive disorder, posttraumatic stress disorder, and phobic disorder (consisting of simple phobia, social phobia, and agoraphobia). Thus, anxiety conditions in children could be diagnosed under 10 possible categories.

The most recent revision of *DSM*, namely *DSM–IV* (APA, 1994) brought substantive changes in the categorization of childhood anxiety. Specifically, the broad category *Anxiety Disorders of Childhood and Adolescence* was not retained, and the diagnosis "separation anxiety disorder" was subsumed under the category *Other Disorders of*

Childhood and Adolescence (APA, 1994). Because of problems with the OAD category, this disorder was subsumed under the adult category of generalized anxiety disorder. Reasons for the latter change included the following: First, research found the reliability of OAD to vary considerably across studies. Second, high prevalence of OAD in epidemiological studies suggested that the threshold (i.e., the number of symptoms required to be present to receive the diagnosis) was low. Third, probably because of the nonspecific nature of its symptoms, OAD was found to be highly comorbid with other disorders, most notably social phobia. For these reasons, and also because OAD already shared a number of features with GAD, the decision was made to eliminate the subcategory of OAD in *DSM–IV* and to subsume it under the previous "adult" category of GAD (APA, 1994). More thorough reviews of the issues surrounding OAD can be found elsewhere (e.g., Silverman, 1992; Werry, 1991). Additionally, avoidant disorder was eliminated altogether from *DSM–IV*, like OAD. This was due in large part to its nonspecific criteria. Among the "adult" anxiety diagnostic categories, simple phobia is now referred to as *specific phobia*, and social phobia is referred to as *social anxiety*, that is, social phobia (social anxiety disorder).

Thus, childhood anxiety holds the distinction of being one of the few areas in *DSM–IV* where the movement was toward reduction rather than expansion. In large part, this movement reflects an ongoing *Zeitgeist* in the field of child psychopathology, in particular with respect to anxiety and depression, which calls for a broad rather than narrow classification of problems. In general, many questions remain about the validity of the *DSM* childhood diagnostic categories, in general, and the anxiety categories, in particular (see Silverman, 1992, 1993). That is, questions remain about the extent to which anxiety disorders in children are clearly distinct disorders. For example, although significant differences have been found among anxiety disorder diagnoses in children along such as factors as age at time of referral, gender, and socioeconomic status, thereby lending support to distinctiveness (e.g., Last, Strauss, & Francis, 1987), absence of differences among the subcategories in terms of family history, scores on questionnaire measures, and course, weakens support for distinctiveness (e.g., Cantwell & Baker, 1989; Last, Hersen, Kazdin, Orvaschel, & Perrin, 1991; Rabian, Peterson, Richters, & Jensen, 1993). This has led several investigators to question the subtyping of anxiety disorders in children; and that perhaps it would be wiser to have just one amalgamate category (e.g., Cantwell & Baker, 1989; Werry, Reeves, & Elkind, 1987), similar to what had existed with *DSM–II*. On the other hand, this approach was also viewed as problematic, and thus the changes that appeared in *DSM–III*.

In addition to the increased attention given to broad band categories, most of the issues relating to classification of anxiety disorders in children raised in the previous edition of this chapter remain relevant today. For example, there is the problem of comorbidity: that is, the common finding that children frequently display multiple problems, and thus, receive multiple diagnoses. With respect to anxiety disorders in children, depression has frequently been found to be a concurrent diagnosis (see Brady & Kendall, 1992). Externalizing behavior problems, such as attention deficit hyperactivity disorder (ADHD) and conduct disorder (CD) also have been found to frequently co-occur with anxiety disorders in children (e.g., Walker et al., 1991; Woolston et al., 1989). In general, it is important to keep in mind that comorbidity is the rule—not the exception in abnormal child psychology. However, the implications of comorbidity are not yet well understood, especially when it come to treatment planning, although attempts to delineate possible treatment strategies for work with anxious or depressed youth have recently been undertaken (Kendall, Kortlander,

Chansky, & Brady, 1992). Clearly, this is an avenue of research that is wide open and deserving of attention.

Separation Anxiety Disorder

Separation anxiety disorder is characterized by excessive anxiety or distress on separation or on threat of separation from a major attachment figure (usually the parent) or from home. According to *DSM–IV*, the child must meet three of eight criteria to receive this diagnosis. These criteria are presented in Table 14.1.

Although *DSM–IV* specifies that the individual must be "younger than 18 years old" to be diagnosed with separation anxiety disorder, the precise age range is not indicated. Specification of age would seem important, however, given that anxiety about separation is a common developmental occurrence in all young children. For instance, for an 18-month-old child who is displaying "normal" distress on separation from his or her caretaker, it would be inappropriate to view the child as suffering from separation anxiety disorder. It would be appropriate, however, if the child was 12 years of age. Thus, diagnosis of separation anxiety disorder is appropriate only to those cases where

TABLE 14.1
Criteria for *DSM–IV* Diagnosis of Separation Anxiety Disorder

A. Developmentally inappropriate and excessive anxiety concerning separation from home or from those to whom the child is attached, as evidenced by at least three of the following:

1. Recurrent excessive distress when separation from home or major attachment figures occurs or is anticipated

2. Persistent and excessive worry about losing, or about possible harm befalling, major attachment figures

3. Persistent and excessive worry that an untoward event will lead to separation from a major attachment figure

4. Persistent reluctance or refusal to go to school or elsewhere because of fear of separation

5. Persistently and excessively fearful or reluctant to be alone or without major attachment figures at home or without significant adults in other settings

6. Persistent reluctance or refusal to go to sleep without being near a major attachment figure or to sleep away from home

7. Repeated nightmares involving the theme of separation

8. Repeated complaints of physical symptoms (e.g., headaches, stomach aches, nausea, or vomiting) when separation from major attachment figures is anticipated or involved

B. Duration of disturbance of at least 4 weeks

C. Onset before the age of 18

D. The disturbance causes clinically significant distress or impairment in social, academic (occupational), or other important areas of functioning

E. Occurrence not exclusively during the course of a Pervasive Developmental Disorder, Schizophrenia, or any other psychotic disorder

Note. From *DSM–IV (APA, 1994).*

observed distress surrounding separation is extremely severe and is beyond what one would expect, given the particular developmental level of that child.

In a mental health setting, separation anxiety is a problem that can be readily ascertained in a child—at times, even immediately on his or her presentation. The child with separation anxiety disorder is one who is clinging to his or her parent, or who refuses to meet with the clinician, unless the parent can also be present. The child may also cry or beg the parent not to leave him or her when the parent is asked to meet with the clinician alone.

Outside the clinic setting, the child's separation difficulties may be observed in a variety of other circumstances that require separation from loved ones or anticipation of separation. These include attending school, being left with a babysitter, or sleeping at night by oneself. Somatic complaints (e.g., stomachaches, headaches) also are common among these children.

Although separation anxiety disorder is present in both children and adolescents, the disorder is more common among preadolescent children; and, in general, younger and older children appear to differ in the symptoms that are most frequently reported (Francis, Last, & Strauss, 1987). In older children (ages 12 to 16) with separation anxiety disorder, the presenting problem is often that they cannot sleep away from home overnight, for example, at a friend's house or at a camp. Another problem may be that their reluctance to go to school on most days. In younger children (ages 5 to 11), the presenting problem is often excessive worry about harm befalling parents on separation and reported nightmares with separation themes.

Generalized Anxiety Disorder
(Including Overanxious Disorder)

In *DSM–IV*, to receive a diagnosis of GAD, a child must experience excessive anxiety and worry about a number of events (such as school), where the worry is associated with at least three of six symptoms. A full listing of the criteria for GAD is contained in Table 14.2.

Although developmental differences in the expression of the *DSM–IV* category of GAD have not yet been examined, developmental differences in the manifestation of the *DSM–III–R* subcategory of OAD have been observed. Specifically, an examination of OAD symptom-expression differences was reported by Strauss, Lease, Last, and Francis (1988), who divided a sample of 55 children and adolescents with OAD into two age groups: those younger than 12 years of age ($n = 32$) and those 12 years of age and older ($n = 32$). Compared to the younger children, the older children endorsed a greater number of symptoms, with "worry about future events" endorsed as the most common symptom.

Specific Phobia and Social Phobia
(Social Anxiety Disorder)

A specific phobia is a "marked and persistent fear that is excessive or unreasonable, cued by the presence or anticipation of a specific object or situation," such that the object or event is avoided whenever possible, or is endured only with intense anxiety (APA, 1994). Typically, the intensity of the fear is severe enough to lead to interference in the child's functioning—in school, home, or social relations.

TABLE 14.2

Criteria for *DSM–IV* Diagnosis of Generalized Anxiety Disorder

A. Excessive anxiety and worry (apprehensive expectation), occurring more days than not for at least 6 months, about a number of events or activities (such as work or school performance):

B. The person finds it difficult to control the worry

C. The anxiety and worry are associated with at least three of the following six symptoms:

    1. Restlessness or feeling keyed up or on edge

    2. Being easily fatigued

    3. Difficulty concentrating or mind going blank

    4. Irritability

    5. Muscle tension

    6. Sleep disturbance (difficulty falling or staying asleep, or restless, unsatisfying sleep)

D. The focus of anxiety and worry is not confined to features of an Axis I disorder

E. The anxiety, worry, or physical symptoms cause clinically significant distress or impairment in social, occupational, or other important areas of functioning.

F. Not due to the direct effects of a substance or a general medical condition

Note. From *DSM–IV (APA, 1994).*

To properly differentiate specific phobia from other anxiety disorders, it is important to ensure that the child's fear is not related to other fears such as separation (as in separation anxiety), panic attacks (as in panic disorder), or social humiliation or embarrassment (as in social phobia/social anxiety; see later). Common specific phobias observed in children include small animals, such as dogs, darkness, thunder and lightning, and doctors and dentists.

Social phobia (social anxiety disorder), is a persistent fear of situations in which the child is exposed to possible scrutiny by others, and fears that he or she may act in a way that will be humiliating or embarrassing. This problem may be manifested in the school setting, where the child may avoid activities such as giving a speech in class or asking a question in class. Outside the school setting, a child with social phobia may avoid attending social gatherings such as birthday parties, or boy or girl scout meetings.

CAUSES OF THE DISORDERS

Causes of anxiety and phobias in children are still not well understood, but they appear to be multifaceted. The most theorizing about "cause" has centered on separation anxiety disorder and specific phobia. In terms of separation anxiety disorder, psychodynamic formulations emphasize the hostile wishes of the child toward the attachment figure, usually the mother. Fearing the possible fulfillment of these hostile wishes, the child avoids separation from the mother as a way to suppress such thoughts and to help ensure her safety. According to the psychodynamic formulation, the child's insistence to be with the mother serves to satisfy the dependency needs and internal conflicts of both the child and the mother. Unfortunately, little is said about the father's role in this process (Wicks-Nelson & Israel, 1991).

Evidence for the psychodynamic formulation of separation anxiety is based primarily on clinical case studies. Although the clinical case study can richly describe phenomena, the reliability and validity of such descriptions are weak. In terms of reliability, because the descriptions in a case study are based on the reporting of past events, accuracy and completeness of such retrospective data are often suspect. In terms of validity, when case studies go beyond descriptions to interpretations, there are few guidelines to judge their veracity (Wicks-Nelson & Israel, 1991).

A behavioral formulation of separation anxiety disorder points to a combination of both classical and operant learning factors. For example, a behavioral explanation of school avoidance as a symptom of separation anxiety presumes that the child has learned to stay away from school because of some association of the school with an intense fear of losing the mother or other attachment figure. Once avoidance behavior has occurred, it may be reinforced by attention and other rewards (e.g., watching television when at home) received by the child (Wicks-Nelson & Israel, 1991).

With respect to specific phobia of childhood, Freud's (1953) case of "Little Hans," serves as the prototype in psychodynamic theory. According to Freud's formulation, the experience or threat of helplessness (from physical or psychic danger) is key. For example, in the case of Little Hans, the child's phobia of horses was viewed as arising from desire for his mother and desire to do away with his father: the competitor. However, for Hans to act on such instinctual wishes would put him in conflict with his father. His father would then want to be rid of or harm him, and Hans would then be in a position of helplessness. According to Freud, flight or repression (from internal or instinctual danger) was the response to this threat of helplessness. Because Hans' repression was incomplete, unconscious anxiety was displaced onto some external object that in some way was related to or symbolic of the unconscious wish. For Hans, the horse was related to such things as playing "horsie" with his father, his father's appearance (the horse's muzzle symbolized his father's mustache), and castration (symbolized by the horse's biting). Displacement allowed Hans to avoid the phobic object—the horse—whereas he could not avoid his father.

As was true for the psychodynamic formulation of separation anxiety, the psychodynamic formulation of specific phobias is based primarily on clinical case studies. And thus, the reliability and validity of such descriptions may be questioned on scientific grounds.

Several behavioral theories, derived from principles of learning, have been proposed to explain the causes of phobias in children. According to Rachman (1977), simple (specific) phobias may develop either through direct acquisition (e.g., conditioning) or through indirect acquisition (e.g., vicarious exposure and/or the transmission of information or instruction). Support for these pathways in the development of childhood phobia has been provided by Ollendick, King, & Hamilton (1991). Specifically, these researchers administered a questionnaire, designed to assess the pathways for 10 highly prevalent fears (e.g., nuclear war, fire—getting burned, etc.), to 1,092 Australian and U.S. children (ages 9 to 14 years). Results indicated that vicarious and instructional factors were most influential (56% and 89%, respectively). However, these factors were frequently combined with direct conditioning experiences as well.

Although results of the Ollendick et al. (1991) study are based exclusively on retrospective reports of a nonclinical sample of children, the findings are consistent with what is frequently heard from clinical samples of phobic children and their parents. It is not unusual for many parents of children with phobias to indicate that they too share the same fear as their child. Moreover, the child is aware of or has observed parental fear behavior. Similarly, it is not unusual for parents of phobic children to report that they have told their child "to be careful" of certain aspects of a particular object or event. Thus, the influence of parental modeling, or what Rachman (1977) referred to as "vicarious exposure," as well as "transmission of information and instruction," is apparent in the etiology of childhood phobia, based on the anecdotal reports of clinical samples (Silverman & Rabian, 1994).

In addition to the pathways proposed by Rachman (1977), phobias may be acquired through operant conditioning. Specifically, the positive consequences that follow a fearful response (e.g., avoidance) may initiate and maintain that fearful response. For example, a youngster who exhibits avoidance behavior on encountering a certain object or event, such as swimming in a pool or lake, and whose parents attend to this avoidance behavior may be positively reinforcing that behavior.

The notion that phobias are acquired via classical conditioning (the pairing of a neutral stimulus with an aversive unconditioned stimulus produces the initial fear or anxiety) but are maintained via operant conditioning (the reduction of visceral arousal via avoidance) is the basic premise of the two-factor model (Mowrer, 1939). Because questions have been raised about the relation between avoidance to fear reduction, a revision of the two-factor model has been proposed (Delprato & McGlynn, 1984). Briefly, the revision emphasizes positive reinforcement that results from the relaxation and relief experienced following avoidance, rather than negative reinforcement (due to fear avoidance).

In addition to psychodynamic and learning theory, cognitive theories of etiology have been proposed (e.g., Beck & Emery, 1985). Cognitive models are generally based on the assumption that emotional and behavioral problems, including anxieties and phobias, are due to maladaptive thinking. For example, unlike their nonphobic counterparts, phobic children are viewed as being more likely to hold faulty cognitions about a specific stimulus (e.g., I'll get hit by lightening) and have difficulty in controlling these cognitions.

Another aspect of the cognitive model of anxiety disorders relates to the construct of anxiety sensitivity. Anxiety sensitivity refers to the tendency of individuals to make irrational interpretations about the significance of anxiety symptoms (e.g., rapid heart rate comes to mean that a heart attack is pending; racing thoughts are interpreted as "going crazy"). Anxiety sensitivity is thought to act as a possible risk factor for the development of anxiety because it increases the likelihood that fear will become conditioned to things that make one aroused. Although the bulk of research in this area has been with adults, there is growing evidence that anxiety sensitivity may serve as a risk factor for anxiety disorders in children as in adults (for a review, see Silverman & Weems, 1999).

Research on potential risk factors for anxiety has also pointed to several other factors that may play a role in anxiety's onset. One such set of risk factors is that of stressful life events. In this connection, investigators have found that stressful life events are associated with the manifestation of anxious symptoms (Kashani & Orvaschel, 1990; Manfro, Otto, McArdle, & Worthington, 1996). Costello (1989) found an association between parental stress and OAD, although McGee et al. (1990) found that stressful life events were no more characteristic of OAD than any other disorder. Recently, research has hinted at a link between the quality of early attachments and childhood anxiety (Manassis, Bradley, Goldberg, Hood, & Swinson, 1994). Certainly, the influence of stressful life events and other risk factors, such as low socioeconomic status, poor social support, and so on, in the development of anxiety and phobic disorders in children, requires further study (Velez, Johnson, & Cohen, 1989).

Finally, in addition to any nonspecific contribution they might make to creating a stressful environment, family and parental influences have also been studied for the direct contributions to anxiety in children. The results of recent research (Dadds, Barrett, Rapee, 1996) involving parent–child interaction patterns in families of children with anxiety disorders (including separation anxiety, specific phobia, social phobia, and OAD) indicate that parents may directly contribute to the selection of avoidance behaviors in anxious children forced to generate solutions to a series of hypothetical situations. For example, when asked to help children find ways to deal with an imaginary math test, parents of anxious children are more likely to suggest or to support solutions that involve avoiding the test.

COURSE

There are few data on the course of anxiety disorders in children. As a result, findings from available studies do not allow for a definitive conclusion about whether the course of anxiety disorders is chronic or transient. In one of the few longitudinal studies, Cantwell and Baker (1989) followed 151 children and adolescents over a 5-year period after an initial outpatient evaluation. At the time of the initial evaluation, 14 children were identified with a *DSM–III–R* diagnosis of avoidant disorder, 9 with separation anxiety, and 8 with OAD. At the 5-year follow-up, the majority of the children who initially presented with an anxiety disorder either showed spontaneous remission or now met criteria for a different disorder—usually another anxiety disorder. Of the anxiety disorders, avoidant disorder was the most stable at follow-up, with 29% of the children still meeting criteria for that disorder. This contrasts with separation anxiety disorder, where only one child still met criteria for this disorder five years later; and OAD, where only two children continued to meet criteria. Cantwell and Baker (1989) also reported that at the 5-year follow-up, 44% of the children with the original diagnosis of separation anxiety were completely recovered. This compares to 36% for the children with the diagnosis of OAD and 25% for the children with the diagnosis of avoidant disorder.

In a second study, published since the last edition of this chapter, Last, Perrin, Hersen, and Kazdin (1996) evaluated the course and outcome of *DSM–III–R* anxiety disorders in 84 clinically referred children over a 3- to 4-year period. The majority of anxious children (82%) were free of their intake anxiety disorders at the end of follow-up, and only 8% experienced a relapse of their disorder. These numbers compare quite favorably to children with ADHD. However, during follow-up, 30% of previously anxious children had developed new psychiatric disorders (in descending order of frequency: anxiety, depression, or a behavioral disorder). Thus, although anxious children displayed a low rate of relapse after remission of their original condition, the data suggest that they were still at considerable risk for new disorders, particularly anxiety disorders.

Several investigators have hypothesized that children with separation anxiety disorder grow up to be adults with agoraphobia or panic disorder (e.g., Gittelman & Klein, 1984; Zitrin & Ross, 1988). This view was noted in *DSM–III–R's* description of panic disorder, which stated that "separation anxiety disorder in childhood and sudden loss of social supports or disruption of important interpersonal relationships apparently predisposes to the development of" panic disorder (APA, 1987, p. 237). Research support for continuity between childhood separation anxiety disorder and adult agoraphobia or panic disorder is mixed, however. For example, although several studies, based on the retrospective reports of patients with agoraphobia, found that many patients (approximately 20%–35%) experienced separation anxiety disorder as children (e.g., Gittelman & Klein, 1985; Klein, Zitrin, Woerner, & Ross, 1983;

Zitrin, Klein, Woerner, & Ross, 1983), just as many studies failed to find such a relationship (e.g., Breier, Charney, & Heninger, 1986; Mendel & Klein, 1969; Thyer, Himle, & Fischer, 1988). To date, therefore, it is difficult to draw conclusions about the nature of the relationship, if any, between separation anxiety disorder in childhood and agoraphobia in adulthood. Moreover, due to limitations of patients' retrospective reports (e.g., memory loss, distortion, and bias)—which has been the primary method used in this type of research—it is necessary for future research to employ prospective, longitudinal designs.

With respect to phobic disorders in children, although evidence suggests that milder fears and phobias are relatively transient, some types of simple phobias appear to persist into adulthood, if untreated (Silverman & Rabian, 1994). In one of the few longitudinal studies on the natural history of phobia, Agras, Chapin, and Oliveau (1972) followed 30 phobic individuals (10 of whom were children) who reported a variety of fears over a 5-five year period. During this time, none received treatment. All of the children were viewed as "improved" after 5 years, compared to 43% of the adults. However, most of the children still exhibited symptoms at follow-up.

Although these results appear encouraging, especially for children with phobias, Ollendick (1979) pointed out that "improved" children in the Agras et al. study were not completely symptom free. In fact, the majority of children assessed at follow-up continued to exhibit symptoms of sufficient intensity to be rated between "no disability" and "maximum disability." Thus, Ollendick's (1979) reinterpretation of the Agras et al. (1972) data suggests that phobias, or at least some of the symptoms of phobias, persist over time for some children.

Studies that examine age of onset of phobias are yet another means by which their course may be evaluated (e.g., Ost, 1987; Sheehan, Sheehan, & Minichiello, 1981) Although these studies are limited as they are based on subjects' retrospective reports, some interesting trends can be gleaned from this work, nevertheless. For example, Ost (1987) reported that among a sample of adults with agoraphobia, social phobia, and simple phobia (mean age = 34 years old), their phobia problems developed, on average, between the ages of 7 and 28 years, with the simple phobias having the earliest age of onset. Thus, consistent with Ollendick's (1979 reinterpretation of the longitudinal study of Agras et al. (1972), these data suggest that simple phobias tend to persist into adulthood for some proportion of children.

FAMILIAL CONTRIBUTIONS

Although it continues to be an important area of research, research in the last several years has done little to advance the understanding of specific familial risks for childhood anxiety disorders. Researchers continue to uncover evidence that familial and parental stress plays a role in the development and maintenance of anxiety. However, this section addresses the issue of whether aggregation of anxiety disorders tends to occur within families. It is in this specific area that understanding remains much as it was in the previous edition of this text. Two types of studies in this area have been most common: those examining the offspring of adults with anxiety disorders (top–down), and those examining the first-degree relatives of children with anxiety disorders (bottom–up; Last, 1993).

In general, studies on adults diagnosed with anxiety disorders demonstrate an increased likelihood of anxiety disorders among their children (Silverman, Cerny, Nelles, & Burke, 1988). For example, Turner, Beidel, and Costello (1987), in a top–down study on the offspring of mothers with anxiety disorders (obsessive–compulsive disorder or agoraphobia), found that these children were seven times more likely to be diagnosed with an anxiety disorder as children of "normal" parents. Also, they were twice as likely to have an anxiety disorder as compared to children of depressed mothers (although the latter was not a significant difference).

Although findings such as these are tantalizing, what is not clear from such top–down studies is whether the increased risk observed among offspring is for a specific disorder or for psychopathology in general. Nor is it clear why some offspring whose parents suffer from severe anxiety symptoms appear to be unaffected by their parents' pathology. The mechanisms used by youngsters to help cope with parental problem behaviors are also not clear. Overall, the issue of resilience and coping among the offspring of parents with anxiety disorders is a critical area requiring future research attention.

In addition to top–down studies, several bottom–up studies have evaluated the first-degree relatives of children with anxiety disorders. Last, Phillips, and Statfeld (1987) examined prevalence of separation anxiety and OAD in the histories of mothers whose children had these disorders and in mothers whose children had a nonanxiety psychiatric disorder. Overall, results indicated that the rate of OAD was significantly higher in mothers of overanxious children than in mothers of children with separation anxiety or a nonanxiety disorder.

In another study, Last, Hersen, Kazdin, Francis, and Grubb (1987) evaluated rates of both past and current psychiatric disorders among mothers of children with an anxiety disorder (separation anxiety and OAD; $N = 58$) versus mothers of children with a nonanxiety disorder (e.g., CD or ADHD). Overall, mothers of children with anxiety disorders were significantly more likely to report a past history of some anxiety disorder, or to currently meet criteria for an anxiety disorder, relative to mothers of children in the comparison group. Specifically, more than 80% of the mothers of children with anxiety disorders reported a past history of anxiety disorder, and more than 50% were currently symptomatic.

Last and colleagues (1991) compared first- and second-degree relatives of children with anxiety disorders ($n = 94$) with relatives of children with ADHD ($n = 58$) and children with no history of psychopathology ($n = 87$). The findings of this study showed higher rates of anxiety disorders in the relatives of children with anxiety disorders compared to the relatives of either children with ADHD or children with no disorder.

All together, as was the case with top–down studies, evidence from bottom–up studies suggests that there is a familial contribution to the development of anxiety disorders in children. The evidence is mixed, however, as to whether this familial contribution is specific to anxiety disorders or to psychopathology in general. Thus, additional work is necessary to clarify this issue.

With respect to familial contributions to the development of phobias in children, to date, only a small number of studies have been conducted. For example, interviewing the first-degree relatives of adults with simple phobia, and those of "normal" adults Fyer et al. (1990) found that the relatives of simple phobics were more likely to exhibit simple phobia themselves (31%), as compared to the relatives of the "normal" group (11%). Moreover, the relatives of the adults with simple phobia were more likely to display simple phobia specifically, rather than any other anxiety or phobic disorder. Similarly, other investigators have found the first-degree relatives of adults with social phobia to be more at risk for social phobia than for another anxiety disorder (e.g., Reich & Yates, 1988).

In summary, results from top–down and bottom–up studies have yielded valuable information pertaining to the familial contribution to phobic and anxiety disorders in children. However, such studies do not allow for the disentanglement of the relative contributions of genetic and environmental factors. Rather, what family studies can provide is "negative proof." That is, "if a higher frequency of a disorder is not observed among biological relatives, then genetic factors cannot be involved" (Last, 1993; p. 109). To specifically answer questions about the genetic influences in anxiety disorders, it is necessary to examine evidence from twin and adoptive studies; such work is summarized in the next section.

GENETIC INFLUENCES

There are a number of methods to examine genetic influences on the development of anxiety in children. These include twin studies, adoptive studies, and "genetic linkage" studies. An excellent summary of each of these methods is provided by Torgersen (1993). Briefly, twin studies examine concordance rates between monozygotic twins (MZ), who share identical genes, and dizygotic twins (DZ), who are no more similar genetically than nontwin siblings. Evidence showing higher concordance rates for a disorder between MZ twins than between DZ twins would indicate the influence of genetics on the appearance of the disorder. Adoptive studies examine twins reared in separate homes, thereby eliminating the possibility that high concordance rates for a disorder between twins simply reflect the fact that they were raised in the same environment. Genetic linkage studies attempt to use genetic markers to pinpoint the chromosomal location of a gene that may carry a particular disorder.

To date, few studies using these methods have been conducted in the area of childhood anxiety and phobia. Those studies that have been conducted have largely focused on temperamental variables such as withdrawal or on now outdated diagnostic labels such as *anxiety neurosis* (Torgersen, 1985). Twin studies, using adult subjects, have focused on more diffuse concepts, such as neuroticism (Eysenck, 1959), or on fears and phobias.

In the body of research on temperamental variables, findings related to the construct of behavioral inhibition (Kagan, Resnick, & Snidman, 1987) are particularly exciting. Behavioral inhibition is a temperament style characterized by various behavioral and emotional markers that are reminiscent of anxiety, namely, avoidance, withdrawal, dependence on attachment figures, fearfulness, and arousability (see Silverman & Ginsburg, 1998). Relevant to this discussion, children whose parents present with anxiety are far more likely to display inhibition than children whose parents present with a nonanxious condition (Rosenbaum et al., 1988). Since the late 1980s, Jerome Kagan and his colleagues have reported findings from numerous studies that suggest that a behaviorally inhibited temperament in infancy acts as a risk factor for the development of anxiety disorders later in childhood. In one study, when compared to uninhibited and healthy controls, only inhibited children met criteria for four or more anxiety disorders at a later point in development (Biederman et al., 1990). This risk is not perfect, however, as a high percentage of children (70%) did not go on to develop problems with anxiety. Despite many questions that remain about the nature of the relation between behavioral inhibition and anxiety, there appears to be consensus among researchers in the field of childhood anxiety that additional study of this construct may lead to important insights into the onset of childhood anxiety.

Given the paucity of research, what conclusions can be drawn regarding genetic influences on the development of anxiety and phobias in children? Overall, research findings suggest that anxious or fearful characteristics, in general, may be at least partly influenced by genetic features, although there is little evidence that genetic transmission takes place for a specific disorder. That is, it appears that offspring of adults with anxiety or phobic disorders may inherit a tendency to anxiousness or fearfulness that may manifest itself in a number of ways, but not necessarily in the same specific way as that observed in the parent (Torgersen, 1993). This general conclusion holds true for most of the anxiety and phobic disorders; however, there is growing evidence that panic disorder is caused by dominant genetic factors (Torgersen, 1993).

CURRENT TREATMENTS

Although the literature focusing specifically on the treatment of anxiety disorders in children remains relatively meager, the past few years have seen the production of new and promising data, particularly in the area of behavioral and cognitive–behavioral approaches to anxiety. More importantly, these new data have been produced using well-controlled experimental designs, thus reducing our reliance on case studies in the support of treatments.

The most widely used treatment approaches for childhood phobic and anxiety disorders are the behavioral, psychodynamic, and pharmacological. Each of these is briefly described here.

Behavior Therapy

Behavioral strategies used to treat childhood anxiety and phobia include the following:

1. Contingency management: external agents (parents, therapists) rearrange the environment to ensure that positive consequences follow exposure tasks.
2. Systematic desensitization: involves gradually exposing the child to the fear-evoking situation while he or she engages in an activity incompatible with fear, usually some form of relaxation.
3. Implosion and flooding: involve prolonged exposure.
4. Modeling: involves observing a model—either live or symbolic—confront the feared stimulus.
5. Self-control, which involves teaching the child cognitive strategies that are to be applied when he or she experiences feelings of fear or anxiety, or is in a situation that elicits fear or anxiety. Although many questions remain as to which is the "best" behavioral strategy to use, there is general consensus in the field that exposure to the fearful or anxiety-provoking object or situation is essential for a successful fear- or anxiety-reduction program (Marks, 1975). With the exception of implosion and flooding procedures, when exposure has been used with children with anxiety disorders, it has been carried out in a gradual fashion. That is, the child is usually asked to conduct exposure exercises, either live or imagined, along the *steps of a fear hierarchy*. Use of the hierarchy provides an opportunity for the child to gradually gain confidence (and reduce fear or anxiety) when in the presence of the phobic or anxious stimulus, as he or she successful completes each "step" of the hierarchy.

An example of a fear hierarchy for a child with a phobia of dogs might be

1. Seeing pictures of dogs in magazines.
2. Going to a pet shop and looking at a dog through the window.

3. Going to a pet shop and petting a small puppy that is being held by somebody.
4. Petting a larger size dog that is on a leash.
5. Petting yet a larger dog that is not leashed (Silverman & Eisen, 1993).

Several recent, controlled clinical trials studies underscore the importance of exposure used in conjunction with cognitive–behavioral treatment in reducing or eliminating problems with anxiety. Kendall (1994) reported the results of such a 16-week intervention. Compared to children assigned to a wait-list control group, children receiving cognitive–behavioral treatment showed significantly greater improvement in their anxiety, as measured by self-report, parent report, and behavioral measures. Moreover, these gains were maintained more than 3 years later (Kendall, 1994). Barrett, Dadds, and Rapee (1996) made comparisons between a cognitive–behavioral treatment, a cognitive–behavioral treatment combined with family management, and a wait-list condition for children diagnosed with anxiety. Both the cognitive–behavioral and cognitive–behavioral–family management groups showed improvement in anxiety over the wait-list group (with almost 70% of children in the two treatment conditions no longer meeting criteria for a disorder), and maintained gains at follow-up. Additionally, the data suggest that for some children, behavioral treatment may be enhanced through the addition of family management.

Finally, Silverman and her colleagues have reported the results of two controlled clinical trials for treating anxiety and phobic disorders in children. The first study (Silverman et al., in press) compared the relative efficacy of contingency management and self-control in reducing children's phobias. The second study (Silverman et al., 1998) examined the efficacy of utilizing cognitive–behavioral therapy using a group format. Overall, the results of these two studies were very positive in that children's phobic and anxiety disorders were significantly reduced in both of them. These studies thereby provided further evidence that procedures that help facilitate child exposure to fearful objects and situations, as in behavioral (i.e., contingency management) and cognitive (i.e., self-control) therapies are effective (for a detailed summary, see Silverman & Ginsburg, 1998).

Although these studies are encouraging, further research is needed to examine how variables such as the child's developmental level, comorbidity, and familial factors (e.g., parental psychopathology, marital discord, etc.) influence treatment outcome.

Psychodynamic Therapy

Evidence for the efficacy of the psychodynamic approach in the treatment of childhood phobia and anxiety is based almost exclusively on reports from case studies. In general, psychodynamic therapies are based on the notion that the focus of the child's anxiety or fear is a symbolic manifestation of some underlying intrapsychic conflict. Psychodynamic therapy, therefore, addresses the child's emotional conflict. To pursue this aim, play therapy is frequently employed. In play therapy, the therapist uses the content and process of the child's play activities to provide interpretations about the perceived source of the conflict. In older children, psychodynamic therapy might also involve interpretations about the child's attitudes and behaviors toward the therapist. Lack of empirical study of psychodynamic therapy in the treatment of anxiety and phobic disorders in children renders it difficult to recommend its routine application.

Pharmacological Therapy

As with psychodynamic approaches, the literature on pharmacotherapy with anxious children consists largely of clinical reports, many with methodological limitations. As a result, it is difficult to draw conclusions from this work (Gittelman & Koplewicz, 1986). Antidepressants, such as imipramine and clomipramine, are the most frequently administered class of drugs. These medications have been tested in double-blind, placebo-controlled studies, examining their use for school refusal and associated symptoms of anxiety and depression (Bernstein & Borchardt, 1991). However, the findings have been mixed. Although antidepressants appear to be effective in helping separation anxious children return to school, some evidence suggests that they may be no more effective than placebos. Certainly, more work in this area is warranted before such agents with potential side effects are widely used with youngsters.

Case Study

Jerry is a 9-year-old boy who was referred to a childhood anxiety program by his school psychologist because of repeated absences from school. Jerry's parents reported that he is very fearful of school and cries almost every morning when preparing to leave for that setting. Jerry, an only child, complains to his parents about feeling uncomfortable around other children. Both in and out of school, Jerry has few friends and avoids participation in group activities whenever he can. Additionally, Jerry's parents indicated that he is a "worry wart," who is almost constantly seeking reassurance from others about his abilities and performance. Although Jerry had experienced these problems for some time, they became problematic (repeated absences from school) only recently.

Jerry and his parents were individually administered a structured interview. Results of the structured interviews indicated that Jerry met criteria for GAD and for social phobia. Although Jerry and his parents also reported some depressive symptoms, he did not meet sufficient criteria to warrant a diagnosis of affective disorder. Depression was seen as secondary to Jerry's difficulties in establishing social contacts with peers.

Jerry's mother indicated that she had experienced similar problems herself when in school, although she does not currently experience significant anxiety in social settings. Nevertheless, Jerry's parents considered themselves "homebodies," and reported that they did not engage in social activities outside of the home very often. Similarly, they had never encouraged Jerry to become involved in extracurricular activities. Apart from anxiety experienced by Jerry's mother during childhood, no other family history of anxiety was reported, although Jerry's parents were uncertain of the histories of many extended relatives.

Graduated in vivo exposure (where Jerry was required to confront his fear of interacting with other children at school) was conducted. Contingency contracting procedures were instituted to help him carry out these exposure tasks each week. Specifically, Jerry's parents were taught how to rearrange the environment to ensure that positive consequences followed each exposure task. To ensure that positive consequences followed each exposure, Jerry and his parents signed a written contract each week that stated that "if Jerry does (a specified exposure task) then (a specified reward) is provided by the parents." To assist Jerry in dealing with the social exposure tasks, he received coaching in social skills, such as making conversation, asking questions, and maintaining eye contact.

Additionally, because of Jerry's excessive worrying and need for reassurance, it appeared important to provide him with skills that would help him manage his feelings of anxiety on his own. Thus, self-control training was initiated. The focus of this training was on teaching Jerry specific thinking styles and on how to apply these styles when experiencing feelings of anxiety, fear, or worry.

After approximately seven sessions of treatment, Jerry reported that he felt less fearful about attending school and better able to control his anxiety during most interactions with peers at school. By session 10 (the final session), Jerry had accepted an invitation to a classmate's birthday party, and he expressed interest in joining a soccer team with a new friend from school. Most important, Jerry had not missed a day of school in the previous 5 weeks.

Following treatment, Jerry and his parents continued to work on their own in devising exposure exercises, so that he could continue to practice his newly acquired self-control skills. Follow-up visits, conducted at intervals of 3, 6, and 12 months revealed that treatment gains had been maintained. Jerry was attending school regularly, was involved in extracurricular activities both in and out of school, and reported feeling more comfortable interacting with peers. He now worried less than before initiation of treatment. Furthermore, he was no longer seeking constant reassurance from his parents. Overall, both Jerry and his parents indicated that much progress had occurred. An abbreviated version of the structured interview administered to the child and parents further indicated that Jerry no longer met diagnostic criteria for GAD or social phobia.

SUMMARY

Whereas *DSM–III–R* contained three disorders under the broad heading of *Anxiety Disorders of Childhood and Adolescence* (i.e., separation anxiety disorder, avoidant disorder, and OAD), *DSM–IV* maintains only separation anxiety, now under the category Other Disorders of Infancy, Childhood, or Adolescence. *DSM–III–R's* diagnosis of OAD has been subsumed under GAD in *DSM–IV*, and avoidant disorder has been eliminated altogether. As in *DSM–III–R*, *DSM–IV* allows for additional "adult" anxiety diagnoses to be used with children. Of these, specific phobia and social phobia are the most common in youth.

Questions remain about the validity of the *DSM* anxiety categories. Specifically, questions remain about the extent to which the disorders listed are distinct. There also is the problem of comorbidity: that is, the common finding that children with anxiety disorders tend to receive multiple diagnoses.

Separation anxiety disorder is characterized by excessive anxiety or distress on separation or on threat of separation from major attachment figures, such as parents. Because anxiety about separation is a common developmental occurrence in the young child, the diagnosis of separation anxiety is appropriate only to those cases where the child's distress is severe and is not typical of the current developmental level. The symptoms of this disorder, which are more common among preadolescent children, may be readily observed in a variety of settings, such as going to school, being left with a babysitter, and so on.

GAD (or OAD in *DSM–III–R*) is characterized by excessive worry and fearful behavior not focused on a specific object or situation, and not due to a recent stressor. Like separation anxiety disorder, there appear to be developmental differences in the manifestation of this disorder.

Specific phobia refers to a persistent fear of a circumscribed stimulus, usually leading to avoidance. Common phobias in children include small animals, darkness, thunder and lightning, and the doctor or dentist. Social phobia (anxiety) refers to a persistent fear of situations in which the person is exposed to possible scrutiny by others and fears that he or she may act in a way that will be humiliating or embarrassing.

At the present time, causes of anxiety and phobic disorders in childhood are not well understood and appear to be multifaceted. Although several models have been proposed to explain onset of these disorders, behavioral and cognitive–behavioral theories have gained the most attention and support in the research literature. Few conclusions, if any, can be drawn about the course of anxiety disorders in children. At the present time, evidence is mixed as to whether children with separation anxiety disorder grow up to become adults with agoraphobia. Also mixed is the evidence about whether children with generalized excessive worry (or with what was referred to as OAD) grow up to become adults with GAD. With regard to phobic disorders, evidence suggests that milder fears and phobias tend to be transient, while more severe fears and phobias persist into adulthood for some proportion of children.

Overall, findings from top–down and bottom–up studies indicate that there is a trend for anxiety and phobic disorders to aggregate in families. However, with the exception of the phobias, the findings suggest that what may be transmitted within families is a risk for developing some anxiety disorder, in general, rather than a specific anxiety disorder. Some studies suggest that genetics may play a part in this transmission. No definitive conclusions can be made, however, about the influence of genetics versus the environment until further work is conducted.

The most widely used treatment approaches for childhood phobic and anxiety disorders are behavioral, psychodynamic, and pharmacological. Currently, most of the treatment literature consists of case reports, although there is a growing body of controlled clinical trials that provide evidence for the efficacy of behavioral and cognitive–behavioral treatments that incorporate the child's gradual exposure to fear or anxiety-provoking stimuli. One topic of agreement in the field is that effective fear and anxiety reduction programs should include exposure to the fear or anxiety-provoking stimulus.

REFERENCES

Agras, W. S., Chapin, H. N., & Oliveau, D. C. (1972). The natural history of phobia. *Archives of General Psychiatry, 26*, 315–317.

American Psychiatric Association. (1980). *Diagnostic and statistical manual of mental disorders* (3rd ed.). Washington, DC: Author.

American Psychiatric Association. (1987). *Diagnostic and statistical manual of mental disorders* (3rd ed., rev.). Washington, DC: Author.

American Psychiatric Association. (1994). *Diagnostic and statistical manual of mental disorders* (4th ed.). Washington, DC: Author.

Barrett, P. M., Dadds, M. R., & Rapee, R. M. (1996). Family treatment of childhood anxiety: A controlled trial. *Journal of Consulting and Clinical Psychology, 64*, 333–342.

Beck, A. T., & Emery, G. (1985). *Anxiety and phobias: A cognitive perspective.* New York: Basic Books.

Bernstein, G. A., & Borchardt, C. M. (1991). Anxiety disorders of childhood and adolescence: A critical review. *Journal of the American Academy of Child and Adolescent Psychiatry, 30*, 519–532.

Biederman, J., Rosenbaum, J. F., Hirshfeld, D. R., Faraone, V., Bolduc, E., Gersten, M., Meminger, S., & Reznick, S. (1990). Psychiatric correlates of behavioral inhibition in young children of parents with and without psychiatric disorders. *Archives of General Psychiatry, 47,* 21–26.

Brady, U., & Kendall, P. C. (1992). Comorbidity of anxiety and depression in children and adolescents. *Psychological Bulletin, 111,* 244–255.

Breier, A., Charney, D. S., & Heninger, G. R. (1986). Agoraphobia with panic attacks: Developmental, diagnostic stability and course of illness. *Archives of General Psychiatry, 43,* 1029–1031.

Cantwell, D. P., & Baker, L. (1989). Stability and natural history of *DSM–III* childhood diagnoses. *Journal of the American Academy of Child and Adolescent Psychiatry, 29,* 691–700.

Costello, E. J. (1989). Developments in child psychiatric epidemiology. *Journal of the American Academy of Child and Adolescent Psychiatry, 28,* 836–841.

Dadds, M. R., Barrett, P. M., & Rapee, R. M. (1996). Family process and child anxiety and aggression: An observational analysis. *Journal of Abnormal Child Psychology, 24,* 715–734.

Delprato, D. J., & McGlynn, F. D. (1984). Behavioral theories of anxiety disorders. In S. M. Turner (Ed.), *Behavioral treatment of anxiety disorders.* New York: Plenum.

Eysenck, H. J. (1959). *Maudsley personality inventory.* London: University of London.

Francis, G., Last, C. G., & Strauss, C. C. (1987). Expression of separation anxiety disorder: The roles of age and gender. *Child Psychiatry and Human Development, 18,* 82–89.

Freud, S. (1953). Analysis of a phobia in a five-year-old boy (1909). *Standard edition* (Vol 10., Ed. and trans. J. Strachey). London: Hogarth.

Fyer, A. J., Mannuzza, S., Gallops, M. S., Martin, L. Y., Aaronson, C., Gorman, M., Liebowitz, M. R., & Klein, D. F. (1990). Familial transmission of simple phobias and fears: A preliminary report. *Archives of General Psychiatry, 47,* 252–256.

Gittelman, R., & Klein, D. F. (1984). Relationship between separation anxiety and panic and agoraphobic disorders. *Psychopathology, 17,* 56–65.

Gittelman, R., & Klein, D. F. (1985). Childhood separation anxiety and adult agoraphobia. In A. H. Tuman & J. Maser (Eds.), *Anxiety and the anxiety disorders* (pp. 389–402). Hillsdale, NJ: Lawrence Erlbaum Associates.

Gittelman, R., & Koplewicz, H. S. (1986). Pharmacotherapy of childhood anxiety disorders. In R. Gittelman (Ed.), *Anxiety disorders of childhood* (pp. 188–201). New York: Guilford.

Kagan, J., Reznick, J. S., & Snidman, N. (1987). The physiology and psychology of behavioral inhibition. *Child Development, 58,* 1459–1473.

Kashani, J. H., & Orvaschel, H. (1990). A community study of anxiety in children and adolescents. *American Journal of Psychiatry, 147,* 313–318.

Kendall, J. H. (1994). Treating anxiety disorders in children: Results of a randomized clinical trial. *Journal of Consulting and Clinical Psychology, 62,* 200–210.

Kendall, P. C., Kortlander, E., Chansky, T. E., & Brady, E. U. (1992). Comorbidity of anxiety and depression in youth: Treatment implications. *Journal of Consulting and Clinical Psychology, 60,* 869–880.

Klein, D. F., Zitrin, C. M., Woerner, M. G., & Ross, D. C. (1983). Treatment of phobias: 2. Behavior therapy and supportive psychotherapy: Are there any specific ingredients? *Archives of General Psychiatry, 40,* 139–145.

Last, C. G. (1993). Relationship between familial and childhood anxiety disorder. In C.G. Last (Ed.), *Anxiety across the lifespan: A developmental perspective* (pp. 94–112). New York: Springer.

Last, C. G., Hersen, M., Kazdin, A. E., Francis, G., & Grubb, H. J. (1987). Psychiatric illness in the mothers of anxious children. *American Journal of Psychiatry, 144,* 653–657.

Last, C. G., Hersen, M., Kazdin, A. E., Orvaschel, H., & Perrin, S. (1991). Anxiety disorders in children and their families. *Archives of General Psychiatry, 48,* 928–934.

Last, C. G., Perrin, S., Hersen, M., & Kazdin, A. E. (1996). A prospective study of childhood anxiety disorders. *Journal of the American Academy of Child and Adolescent Psychiatry, 35,* 1502–1510.

Last, C. G., Phillips, J. E., & Statfeld, A. (1987). Childhood anxiety disorders in mothers and their children. *Child Psychiatry and Human Development, 18,* 103–112.

Last, C. G., Strauss, C. C., & Francis, G. (1987). Comorbidity among childhood anxiety disorders. *Journal of Nervous and Mental Disease, 175,* 726–730.

Manassis, K., Bradley, S., Goldberg, S., Hood, J., & Swinson, R. P. (1994). Attachment in mothers with anxiety disorders and their children. *Journal of the American Academy of Child and Adolescent Psychiatry, 33,* 1106–1113.

Manfro, G. G., Otto, M. W., McArdle, E. T., Worthington, J. J. (1996). Relationship of antecedent stressful life events to childhood and family history of anxiety and the course of panic disorder. *Journal of Affective Disorders, 41,* 135–139.

Marks, I. M. (1975). Behavioral treatment of phobic and obsessive–compulsive disorders: A critical appraisal. In M. Hersen, R. M. Eisler, & P. M. Miller (Eds.), *Progress in behavior modification* (Vol 1). New York: Academic Press.

McGee, R., Feehan, M., Williams, S., Partridge, F., Silva, P. A., & Kelly, J. (1990). *DSM–III* disorders in a large sample of adolescents. *Journal of the American Academy of Child and Adolescent Psychiatry, 29,* 611–619.

Mendel, J., & Klein, D. F. (1969). Anxiety attacks and subsequent agoraphobia. *Comprehensive Psychiatry, 10,* 476–478.

Mowrer, O. H. (1939). A stimulus–response analysis of anxiety and its role as a reinforcing agent. *Psychological Review, 46,* 553–565.

Ollendick, T. H. (1979). Fear reduction techniques with children. In M. Hersen, R. M. Eisler, & P. M. Miller (Eds.), *Progress in behavior modification* (Vol 8, pp. 127–168). New York: Academic Press.

Ollendick, T. H., King., N. J., Hamilton, D. I. (1991). Origins of childhood fears: An evaluation of Rachman's theory of fear acquisition. *Behaviour Research and Therapy, 29,* 117–123.

Ost, L. (1987). Age of onset in different phobias. *Journal of Abnormal Psychology, 96,* 123–145.

Rabian, B., Peterson, R., Richters, J., & Jensen, P. R. (1993). Anxiety sensitivity among anxious children. *Journal of Child Clinical Psychology,*

Rachman, S. (1977). The conditioning theory of fear acquisition: a critical examination. *Behaviour Research and Therapy, 15,* 375–387.

Reich, J., & Yates, W. (1988). Family history of psychiatric disorders in social phobia. *Comprehensive Psychiatry, 29,* 72–75.

Rosenbaum, J. F., Biederman, J., Gersten, M., Hirshfeld, D. R., Meminger, S. R., Herman, J. B., Kagan, J., Reznick, J. S., & Snidman, N. (1988). Behavioral inhibition in children of parents with panic disorder and agoraphobia: A controlled study. *Archives of General Psychiatry, 45,* 463–470.

Sheehan, D. V., Sheehan, K. E., & Minichiello, W. E. (1981). Age of onset of phobic disorders: a reevaluation. *Comprehensive Psychiatry, 22,* 544–553.

Silverman, W. K. (1992). Taxonomy of anxiety disorders in children. In G. D. Burrows, M. Roth, & R. Noyes, Jr. (Eds.), *Handbook of Anxiety* (Vol 5): *Contemporary issues and prospects for research in anxiety disorders.* Amsterdam: Elsevier.

Silverman, W. K. (1993). DSM and classification of anxiety disorders in children and adults. In C. G. Last (Ed.), *Anxiety across the lifespan: A developmental perspective* (pp. 7–36). New York: Springer.

Silverman, W. K., Cerny, J. A., Nelles, W. B., & Burke, A. (1988). Behavior problems in children of parents with anxiety disorders. *Journal of the American Academy of Child and Adolescent Psychiatry, 27,* 779–784.

Silverman, W. K. & Eisen, A. E. (1993). Phobic disorders. In R. T. Ammerman, C. G. Last, & M. Hersen (Eds.), *Handbook of prescriptive treatments for children and adolescents.* New York: Pergamon.

Silverman, W. K., & Ginsburg, G. S. (1998). Anxiety disorders. In T. H. Ollendick & M. Hersen (Eds.), *Handbook of child psychopathology* (3rd ed., pp. 239–268). New York: Pergamon.

Silverman, W. K., Kurtines, W. M., Ginsburg, G. S., Weems, C. G., Lumpkin, P., & Carmichael, D. (1998). *Treating anxiety disorders in children with group-cognitive behavior therapy: A randomized clinical trial.* Manuscript submitted for publication.

Silverman, W. K., Kurtines, W. M., Ginsburg, G. S., Weems, C. F., Rabian, B., & Serafini, L. T. (in press) A randomized clinical trials investigation of childhood phobic disorders. *Journal of Consulting and Clinical Psychology.*

Silverman, W. K. & Rabian, B. (1994). Simple phobias. In T. H. Ollendick, N. J. King, & W. Yule (Eds.), *Handbook of phobic and anxiety disorders of children.* (87–109). New York: Plenum.

Silverman, W. K., & Weems, C. F. (1999). Anxiety sensitivity in children. In S. Taylor (Ed.), *Anxiety sensitivity: Theory, research, and treatment of the fear of anxiety.* Mahwah, NJ: Lawrence Erlbaum Associates.

Strauss, C. C., Lease, C. A., Last, C. G., & Francis, G. (1988). Overanxious disorder: An examination of developmental differences. *Journal of Abnormal Child Psychology, 16,* 433–443.

Thyer, B. A., Himle, J., & Fischer, D. (1988). Is parental death a selective precursor to either panic disorder or agoraphobia? A test of the separation anxiety hypothesis. *Journal of Anxiety Disorders, 2*, 333–338.

Torgersen, S. (1985). Hereditary differentiation of anxiety and affective neuroses. *British Journal of Psychiatry, 146*, 530–534.

Torgersen, S. (1993). Relationship between adult and childhood anxiety disorders: Genetic hypothesis. In C. G. Last (Ed.), *Anxiety across the lifespan: A developmental perspective* (pp. 113–127). New York: Springer.

Velez, C. N., Johnson, J., & Cohen, P. (1989). A longitudinal analysis of selected risk factors for childhood psychopathology. *Journal of the American Academy of Child and Adolescent Psychiatry, 28*, 861–864.

Walker, J. L., Lahey, B. B., Russo, M. F., Frick, P. J., Christ, M., McBurnett, K., Loeber, R., Stouthaser-Lober, M., & Green, S. B. (1991). Anxiety inhibition and conduct disorder in children: I. Relations to social impairment. *Journal of the American Academy of Child and Adolescent Psychiatry, 30*, 187–191.

Werry, J. S. (1991). Overanxious disorder: A review of taxonomic properties. *Journal of the American Academy of Child and Adolescent Psychiatry, 30*, 533–544.

Werry, J. S., Reeves, J. C., & Elkind, G. S. (1987). Attention deficit, conduct, oppositional, and anxiety disorders in children: I. A review of research on differentiating characteristics. *Journal of the American Academy of Child and Adolescent Psychiatry, 26*, 133–143.

Wicks-Nelson, R., & Israel, A. (1991). *Behavior disorders of childhood* (2nd ed.). Englewood Cliffs, NJ: Prentice-Hall.

Woolston, J. L., Rosenthal, S. L., Riddle, M. A., Sparrow, S. S., Cicchetti, D., Zimmerman, L. D. (1989). Childhood comorbidity of anxiety/affective disorders and behavior disorders. *Journal of the American Academy of Child and Adolescent Psychiatry, 28*, 707–713.

Zitrin, C. M., Klein, D. F., Woerner, M. G., & Ross, D. C. (1983). Treatment of phobias: 1. Comparison of imipramine hydrochloride and placebo. *Archives of General Psychiatry, 40*, 125–138.

Zitrin, C. M., & Ross, D. C. (1988). Early separation anxiety and adult agoraphobia. *Journal of Nervous and Mental Disease, 176*, 621–625.

Depressive Disorders

Kevin D. Stark
Michelle D. Bronik
Stephen Wong
Greggory Wells
University of Texas

Rick Ostrander
Georgetown University

CLINICAL DISCRIPTION

Although depressive disorders may be the most widely studied and best understood psychological disorders among adults, our empirical knowledge of depressive disorders in children just began to emerge in the 1980s. The field has made many strides during the past two decades, but it appears as though the existing research raises more new questions than it answers. Why has research on depressive disorders in youths lagged behind that for adults? Perhaps it is due to the widely held misbelief that childhood is a carefree, happy time; therefore, a youngster would not be depressed. Maybe it is due to the common misbelief that adolescence is a time of turmoil and distress; thus, signs of depression would be dismissed as something to be expected during this developmental period. On a professional level, prior to the 1980s, debates over the existence of depression in childhood dominated the literature, and it is very likely that these debates delayed relevant research. Psychodynamic theorists initially argued that children could not experience depression. According to psychodynamic theory, depression is a superego phenomenon, and, because children have undeveloped superegos, they cannot be depressed. Later, the debate centered around the idea of masked depression: Children were believed to experience a depressive disorder as an underlying pathological phenomenon that caused a variety of overtly expressed disturbances, including virtually all psychological disorders of childhood. The shortcomings of this view were realized (e.g., when was an emotional disturbance during childhood a disorder other than depression?), and this position was abandoned. Subsequently, it was argued that depressive disorders during childhood and adolescence were a normal developmental phenomenon that did not require clinical attention. Empirical research soon refuted this position. Depressive disorders during childhood and adolescence clearly are not the norm, and, although episodic, tend to be of long duration (Strober, Lampert, Schmidt, & Morrell, 1993), more severe than adult variants, and they tend to recur (Ambrosini, Bianchi, Rabinovich, & Elia, 1993).

During the 1980s, the third edition of the *Diagnostic and Statistical Manual of Mental Disorders* (APA, 1980) formally recognized the existence of depressive disorders during childhood, and the debate moved to the failure of *DSM–III* and its revision to recognize the developmental course of depressive symptoms. In the *DSM–III* and *DSM–III–R* (APA, 1987), adult criteria were used to diagnose depressive disorders in children and this approach continues with the *DSM–IV* (APA, 1994). However, the *DSM–IV* places a greater emphasis on the developmental course and expression of depressive disorders in children. Although the core characteristics of a depressive episode may be the same for children and adolescents, prominence of particular symptoms may change with age. For example, in children, somatic complaints, irritability, and social withdrawal tend to be common, whereas psychomotor retardation, sleep disturbances, and delusions may be more common in adolescence and adulthood.

There remains a paucity of research concerned with the treatment of depressive disorders during childhood, although emergence of programs that are designed to prevent the development of depressive disorders is an exciting new development. Based on our own research and clinical experience, it is evident that a multimodal approach to intervention that includes psychosocial as well as pharmacological interventions is most effective. Within the psychologist's realm, the most effective approach is for the child to receive individual treatment, but the youngster's parents should be involved in the treatment in a variety of capacities, ranging from serving as a cognitive–behavioral coach for the child to involvement in their own personal therapy as it relates to the child's problems, and through involvement in family therapy.

In this chapter, the clinical description and diagnostic categories used to describe childhood depressive symptomatology are presented. We have chosen to emphasize unipolar depressive disorders because they are more widely researched and more common among children. After describing the two major types of mood disorders (unipolar and bipolar), we no longer discuss the bipolar disorders (episodes of mania and depression). The interested reader is referred to Fristad, Weller, and Weller (1992) or Nottelmann (1995) for a discussion of bipolar disorders in children. In addition to describing the clinical picture and course of depressive disorders during childhood, the major psychological and physiological models of depression are briefly described. Research related to the potential influence of family variables, both psychosocial and genetic, on the development of depressive disorders during childhood is discussed. Finally, some treatment strategies that have been utilized with depressed children and adolescents are described.

When determining whether a child is experiencing a mood disorder, the clinician must consider the combination, severity, and duration of symptoms that the child is experiencing. Many of the symptoms associated with mood disorders, such as dysphoric mood, are commonly experienced by children who have no diagnoses as well as by children with other psychological disturbances. A mood disorder can best be conceptualized as a syndrome in which a group of symptoms reliably co-occur (Carlson & Cantwell, 1980). It has been argued that the essential symptoms of mood disorders, especially unipolar depressive disorders, are identical between youths and adults (e.g.,

Cantwell, 1982; Kaslow & Rehm, 1983). It appears as though the essential diagnostic criteria are the same across ages, but there are some additional symptoms that are unique to the individual's age and developmental stage (e.g., running away from home). These latter symptoms are referred to as age-specific associated features.

The principal feature of mood disorders is a disturbance in mood either excessively elevated (mania), dysphoric, irritable, or anhedonic (loss of interest or pleasure in most previously enjoyed activities) that occurs to a significant degree for a specified duration of time. A child with a mood disorder experiences a number of additional affective, cognitive, motivational, or physical disturbances (Kovacs & Beck, 1977). Dependent on the specific symptoms the child experiences, he or she receives a diagnosis of a unipolar depressive disorder (the child is experiencing a depressive episode and has no history of a manic episode) or a bipolar disorder (a disorder in which at least one manic episode has occurred).

In addition to dysphoric mood, children who are experiencing an episode of unipolar depression may experience additional affective symptoms including anhedonia, irritability, excessive weepiness, feeling unloved, a sense of worthlessness, self-pity, and self-deprecation. Included among the possible cognitive symptoms are negative self-evaluations, excessive guilt, hopelessness, difficulty concentrating, and indecisiveness. Possible motivational symptoms include suicidal ideation and behavior, social withdrawal, and impaired academic functioning. A depressed child may experience any of the following physical symptoms: fatigue, sleep disturbance, change in appetite or weight, psychomotor agitation and retardation, or somatic complaints.

Children who are experiencing a manic episode have a feeling of extreme elation. They also may experience a number of cognitive symptoms, including flight of ideas, racing thoughts, elevated self-esteem that may reach the point of grandiosity, distractibility, overoptimism, and creative or sharpened thinking. Motivational disturbances might include increased productivity, excessive involvement in activities with the potential for producing painful consequences, increased energy, and uninhibited people seeking. Among the possible physical symptoms are restlessness, talkativeness, and a decreased need for sleep.

Dependent on which of the symptoms are present, for how long, and to what level of severity, the child may receive a diagnosis of major depression or dysthymic disorder. The specific diagnostic criteria for each of these disorders is provided in the next section of this chapter. Briefly, a child who receives a diagnosis of major depression is experiencing a full-blown, severe episode of depression. The child who receives a diagnosis of dysthymic disorder is experiencing a less severe episode of depression that is of long duration.

More youths are affected by depressive disorders, and they are experiencing depressive disorders at an earlier age than in the past. It appears as though this increase is due to changes in the family and the broader society. Prevalence rates for major depression and dysthymic disorder combined for children in the general population range from 2% to 5%. Much higher rates are reported for children from psychiatric populations, children of depressed parents, medically ill youth, and children with educational and learning problems (for a review, see Stark, 1990). Prior to adolescence, an equal proportion of girls and boys suffer from depression. Following puberty, major depressive disorder is twice as common in adolescent girls. Higher rates are reported by African American (Garrison, Jackson, Marsteller, McKewon, & Addy, 1990) and Hispanic girls (Emslie, Weinberg, Rush, Adams, & Rintelmann, 1990) relative to White boys and girls.

Diagnostic Categories

The *DSM–IV* groups the mood disorders into two basic categories: bipolar and unipolar depressive disorders. Both types of disorders are characterized by depressive episodes. However, bipolar disorders include presence of a manic episode. Manic episodes can occur in isolation, but usually follow occurrence of a depressive episode. Each of the two categories of mood disorders is further divided into major syndromes (bipolar disorder and major depression) that are characterized by a full-blown disorder, minor syndromes that are less severe disorders of at least 1 year in duration (cyclothymic disorder and dysthymic disorder), and disorders not otherwise specified that have a disturbance in mood as their central characteristic but cannot be classified into one of the major or minor syndromes. The unipolar depressive disorders are divided into three diagnostic categories based on symptom expression, severity, and duration: major depressive disorder, dysthymic disorder, and depressive disorder not otherwise specified. Bipolar disorders are divided into four diagnostic categories, including bipolar I disorder, bipolar II disorder, cyclothymic disorder, and bipolar disorder not otherwise specified. For a list of the specific symptoms required for each of the previously mentioned diagnoses, the reader is referred to the *DSM–IV.* The fourth edition of the *DSM* includes important changes in the diagnostic criteria for depressive disorders. One is the addition of rule-out criteria for medical conditions that present as depressive disorders, such as withdrawal from substance abuse and hyperthyroidism. Another change is the delineation of a time frame for differentiating between a disorder and the natural grieving that follows the loss of a loved one. Depressive symptoms are not considered to be a reflection of a depressive disorder if they occur within 2 months of the loss of a loved one. In this case, they would be a reflection of the normal grieving process.

Some significant changes are evident in the diagnostic criteria for dysthymic disorder. In the *DSM–III–R,* the youngster had to demonstrate a mood disturbance plus two of six possible additional symptoms. In the *DSM–IV,* in addition to the mood disturbance, the individual must experience three of nine possible symptoms. The pool of additional symptoms has been both changed and expanded. Disturbances in eating and sleeping have been eliminated. The new symptoms include social withdrawal; anhedonia; excessive guilt; irritability or anger; and decreased activity, effectiveness, or productivity. The latter symptom would be especially evident in a youngster's behavior in school. Now that the diagnostic distinction between unipolar depressive disorders and bipolar disorder has been delineated, the remainder of this chapter discusses unipolar depressive disorders.

Issues in Differential Diagnosis

When initially attempting to diagnose a depressive disorder in a child, the clinician first determines whether the symptoms the child is experiencing are a result of depression or part of the normal grieving process that is a result of a significant loss, such as the death of a loved one. Such a reaction is considered appropriate and is termed *bereavement* (APA, 1994). A diagnosis of a depressive disorder is generally not made unless the symptoms are still present 2 months after the loss. Symptoms not characteristic of "normal" bereavement include marked functional impairment, preoccupation with worthlessness, suicidal ideation, psychotic symptoms, or psychomotor retardation, and they suggest that bereavement is complicated by a major depressive episode. If a depressive disorder is present, then it is important to look for symptoms that would suggest the presence or history of an episode of mania.

Although it appears that it would be very easy to determine whether a child is experiencing, or has experienced, an episode of mania, it is not that straightforward. The distinction is clouded by the fact that the hypomanic periods between depressive episodes in children with bipolar disorder may appear to the children or their parents to be periods in which the children are symptom-free. This stems from the fact that the child seems to be doing so much better that no one thinks that the child could be experiencing another disorder. Rather, it appears to be a return to normal functioning. Another factor that can create some diagnostic confusion is the fact that a relatively large proportion of children experiencing a depressive disorder are also experiencing an attention deficit hyperactivity disorder (ADHD). In some of these cases, it is difficult to distinguish this combination of disorders from cyclothymic disorder. It is important to note that a diagnosis of a bipolar disorder precludes a diagnosis of ADHD.

Research is revealing that children can experience *double depression*. Double depression consists of major depression superimposed on the chronic dysthymic disorder. This disorder is often misdiagnosed as major depression because of its more dramatic presentation. Recognition of the double depression diagnosis is important because this disorder has a different course than either disorder alone, and it is more detrimental.

One of the more common differential diagnoses the clinician faces is between a depressive disorder and an adjustment disorder that includes a mood disturbance, such as adjustment disorder with depressed mood and adjustment disorder with mixed emotional features. Children with either a mood disorder or adjustment disorder may report the same symptoms. However, the definitive characteristic is the presence of a psychosocial stressor (e.g., parents get a divorce) that has occurred in the previous 3 months and seems to have triggered the depressive symptoms. If a stressor is identified and could have accounted for the disturbance, then an adjustment disorder diagnosis would be most appropriate. However, if a stressor has been identified, but the depressive symptoms remain for more than 6 months and are sufficiently severe, the diagnosis would be major depression.

Given that the predominant mood in children and adolescents with a depressive disorder can be irritability that may be expressed through angry acting-out, there may be some confusion as to whether a child is actually depressed, experiencing a disruptive behavior disorder (e.g., conduct disorder or oppositional defiant disorder), or both. Further clouding this picture is the fact that many depressed children have a comorbid conduct disorder. Puig-Antich (1982) found that one third of a sample of preadolescent boys with a diagnosis of a depressive disorder also met criteria for conduct disorder. It is necessary, therefore, to consider the constellation of symptoms before making the decision about which of these disorders the child is e xperiencing.

Research has made it increasingly clear that most children who are depressed are also experiencing another psychological disorder. This phenomenon is referred to as *comorbidity*. Depressive disorders in children occur most frequently in conjunction with disruptive behavior disorders and anxiety disorders. In adolescents, depressive episodes are associated with many of these same disorders in addition to substance-related and eating disorders. It appears as though fewer than one third of children who are diagnosed as depressed are experiencing a pure depressive disorder. Due to the co-occurrence of depression with other disorders, the accurate identification and successful treatment of depressive disorders is a comple x task.

Probably the most common disorders that are comorbid with depression among children are anxiety disorders (Brady & Kendall, 1992). Frequency of co-occurring depressive and anxiety disorders has led some investigators to suggest that they are the same disorder expressed differently over the evolution of the disturbance, with anxiety disorders predating the depressive disorder (Kendall & Ingram, 1987; Kovacs, Gatsonis, Paulauskas, & Richards, 1989). The disorders share a number of symptoms, such as somatic complaints, crying, feelings of tension, social withdrawal, and sleep problems. Finch, Lipovsk, and Casat (1989) suggested that the symptoms of depression and anxiety represent a single unitary construct—negative affect—rather than two distinct disorders. However, positive affect is useful in distinguishing between the two disorders. Whereas both anxiety and depressive disorders involve high negative affect, low positive affect appears to be more characteristic of depressive disorders. Current research suggests that co-occurrence of an anxiety disorder increases the severity of depressive disorders (Mitchell, McCauley, Burke, Calderon, & Schloredt, 1989). When a child is suspected of experiencing a depressive disorder, it is important to also assess for presence of an anxiety disorder.

CAUSES OF THE DISORDERS

Overview

It is likely that there are multiple etiological pathways to the development of depressive disorders during childhood. In other words, any of a number of pathways may lead to development of a depressive disorder. The predominant etiological models are stress–diathesis ones, in which stress is hypothesized to interact with a vulnerability within the child (the etiological pathway) to produce a depressive disorder. Stressors may take any of many forms (chronic strains, daily hassles, major life events) and may be chronic or of an acute onset. The diathesis also varies across theories and probably across youngsters, and includes such variables as a deficit in the production of neurotransmitters (Schildkraut, 1965), depressogenic schema (Beck, 1967), an insidious attributional style and hopelessness (Abramson, Metalsky, & Alloy, 1989), social skill disturbances (Lewinsohn, 1975), or a lack of perceived competence (Cole & Turner, 1993), to name just some of the variables that have received empirical attention and support. It is our belief that a combination of biological, cognitive, behavioral, and familial–environmental variables reciprocally interact with each other and with stress to produce and maintain a depressive disorder (Stark, Laurent, Livingston, Boswell, & Swearer, in press). In the following sections, the predominant psychosocial and biological theories of depression and related research are discussed. Subsequently, an integrated model is proposed.

Psychosocial Models of Depression

Lewinsohn's Behavioral Model. Lewinsohn (1974) proposed a behavioral model of depression, which states that part of the depressive syndrome is caused by a prolonged lack of contingency between the emission of adaptive behavior and subsequent reinforcement that places the adaptive behavior on an extinction schedule. In addition, the individual is reinforced for not emitting adaptive behavior through attention. The low rate of response–contingent positive reinforcement leads to dysphoric mood, fatigue, and somatic complaints. A number of cognitive complaints, including decreased self-esteem, pessimism, and guilt, stem from the difficulty associated with labeling the feeling of dysphoria. The label the individual attaches to the feeling determines the nature of the symptom. For example, if the individual labels the sensation as "I am weak–inadequate" this would produce decreased self-esteem.

Lewinsohn (1974) stated that the amount of positive reinforcement a person receives is a function of three variables. Individuals who are prone to depression are assumed to have a restricted range of potentially reinforcing events due to biological or experiential differences. Another limiting factor is the availability of positive reinforcement in their environments. They either have few potential reinforcers in their environments, or they may have experienced a sudden reduction in the amount of reinforcement available in the environment due to the loss of a loved one, a financial crisis, or social isolation. The third and most important variable (Lewinsohn, 1974) for eliciting positive reinforcement from the environment is how socially skilled the individual is. In addition to possessing necessary social skills, the person must emit the socially skilled behaviors that elicit positive reinforcement. Thus, depressed individuals may not receive response–contingent positive reinforcement either because they do not have the skill to elicit it or because they have the skill in their repertoires but fail to perform the behavior. Consequently, they are unable to elicit positive reinforcement even when it is potentially available.

Once depressed people begin exhibiting depressive symptomatology, significant others in their social milieu inadvertently reinforce the depressive behavior by showing increased interest, concern, or sympathy. However, even this positive reinforcement is short-lived, because interactions with depressed people are aversive. Eventually, the significant others withdraw, resulting in a further reduction in the availability of reinforcement.

Rehm's Self-Control Model.   Rehm (1977) extended Kanfer's (1970) three stage (self-monitoring, self-evaluation, self-consequation) model of self-control, by adding an attributional dimension and applied it as a heuristic model for studying the symptoms, etiology, and treatment of depression. Within Rehm's self-control framework, depression is conceptualized as a failure to adjust to, or cope with, change or an undesirable outcome. Depressed individuals either disengage from the self-regulatory process early in the chain or they may suffer from a deficit in a self-regulatory skill.

Rehm identified two disturbances in the self-monitoring of depressed individuals. These individuals demonstrate a proclivity for attending to negative events to the exclusion of positive events, and they tend to attend selectively to immediate rather than the delayed outcomes of their behavior.

Depression may result from either of two forms of maladaptive self-evaluation, including setting excessively stringent criteria for positive self-evaluation or failure to make accurate internal attributions for causality. Self-evaluative standards may be stringent due to a high threshold requiring great quantitative or qualitative excellence for self-approval, low thresholds for negative self-evaluation (a minimal deficiency is considered to be a total failure), and a sense of excessive breadth (failure in one instance is taken as a failure in an entire class of behaviors).

The final disturbance in self-regulation is in the area of self-consequation. Depressed individuals self-administer relatively low rates of reinforcement and high rates of self-punishment. The self-punishment also produces an internal dialogue, which is dominated by negative self-statements.

The Reformulated Theory of Learned Helplessness.   The basic premise of Seligman's (1975) original learned helplessness model of depression was learning that outcomes are uncontrollable results in the motivational, cognitive, and emotional symptoms of depression. Due to identification of four basic shortcomings in the original model, Abramson, Seligman, and Teasdale (1978) reformulated the model within an attributional framework. The reformulated theory, like the original theory, holds the expectation of response–outcome independence to be the crucial determinant of learned helplessness. However, Abramson et al. (1978) hypothesized that mere exposure to noncontingency is not enough to produce helplessness. Rather, the individual must first perceive the noncontingency and then the causal attribution he or she makes for such lack of contingency determines the expectations the individual holds for the future, and these expectations in turn "determine the generality, chronicity, and type of his helplessness symptoms" (Abramson et al., 1978, p. 52).

To construct a comprehensive model, Abramson et al. (1978) refined attribution theory by hypothesizing the existence of three attributional dimensions: specificity (global–specific), stability (stable–unstable), and internality (internal–external). The first two dimensions predict when and where the expectations of helplessness will occur. An attribution to specific factors predicts that the expectation of helplessness will only occur in situations that are very similar to the original situation. An attribution to global factors predicts that the expectation of helplessness will recur across many situations. An attribution to stable factors predicts that the expectations of helplessness will become chronic. An attribution to unstable factors predicts that the expectation need not recur after a time lapse. The internality dimension determines whether the helplessness is experienced as personal or universal. Individuals who make external attributions for failure are universally helpless, whereas those who make internal attributions for failure are personally helpless. Individuals who make internal attributions for failure experience lower self-esteem.

Abramson et al. (1978) postulated that depressed individuals make internal, global, and stable attributions for failure. Thus, they will attribute the cause of their failure to themselves across many situations and over an extended period of time. In addition, when a depressed individual experiences success, it will be attributed to external sources, to the specific situation, and will not necessarily be expected to occur in the future.

Beck's Cognitive Model. Beck (1967) proposed a cognitive model of depression that is based on the premise that depression stems from negatively distorted information processing. Central to Beck's theory is the cognitive construct of *schema*. A schema is hypothesized to have both a structural and functional component. Structurally, a schema is an organized cluster of knowledge about aspects of the domain of interest that has been derived from lifetime experiences. Functionally, a schema is believed to act as a filter through which incoming stimuli are interpreted. When individuals encounter a situation, their conceptualization and evaluation of it is dependent on which of a vast array of stimuli are attended to. A schema serves as a filter and determines which stimuli are attended to and helps the individual derive meaning from the situation. The interpretation of a situation is dependent on which schemata are activated and the appropriateness of them. In the healthy individual, a schema that is relevant to the situation and enables accurate and adaptive information processing would be activated. Beck (1967) believed that depressed individuals distort their conceptualizations and evaluations of situations to "fit" prepotent dysfunctional schemata. The distortions are evident in errors in information processing such as selective abstraction, overgeneralization, and so forth. (Beck, Rush, Shaw, & Emery, 1979). Negative schema give rise to negative automatic thoughts and give rise to the distortions in information processing. Of particular relevance to depressive disorders is a constellation of depressive thoughts about the self, the world, and the future, which Beck refers to as the *depressive cognitive triad*. The negative thoughts are hypothesized to underlie and support the depressive symptoms.

In the next section, the natural course and recurrence of the depressive disorders are discussed. Subsequently, the familial contributions to depression are reviewed. Research on the psychosocial and genetic contributions to depressive disorders is reviewed. In a later section, the major psychosocial theories and related research, as well as the research on familial contributions are integrated into a multifaceted model of depression during childhood.

COURSE OF THE DISORDERS

Longitudinal research indicates that major depression and dysthymia follow different natural courses. The average duration of an episode of major depressive disorder is reported to be between 32 and 36 weeks (Kovacs et al, 1984). The rate of recovery tends to be slow, with the greatest improvement starting between the 24th and 36th week (Strober et al., 1993). Within 6 months of onset of an episode of major depressive disorder, the episode has remitted for 40% of the children. At 1 year, 80% of the children are no longer experiencing a depressive episode (McCauley et al., 1993). The natural course of dysthymic disorder is more protracted, with average length of an episode being 3 years (Kovacs et al., 1984). A chronic course is reported for a significant percentage of depressed children (McGee & Williams, 1988), although it is not clear whether these figures vary between the diagnostic groups (major depression and dysthymic disorder).

Longitudinal research also indicates that depressive disorders are recurrent. Kovacs et al. (1984) reported that 72% of their population of depressed youths experienced an additional depressive episode within 5 years. McCauley et al. (1993) reported that 54% of their sample of depressed youths experienced another depressive episode within a 3-year period. Thus, it appears as though depressed youngsters are at risk for experiencing additional depressive episodes during adolescence or later during early adulthood.

A few variables have been identified that appear to predict duration of a depressive episode. Age of onset may be a predictor, but results of this research are contradictory, as some investigators reported that an earlier age of onset was associated with a more protracted course (Kovacs et al., 1984; McGee & Williams, 1988). In contrast, Harrington, Fudge, Rutter, Pickles and Hill (1990) reported that a more problematic course was found for youngsters who reported a first depressive episode following puberty. Severity is a predictor of the duration of an episode (McCauley et al., 1993), with more severe episodes having a more protracted course. Another predictor, family dysfunction, is associated with a more protracted course (McCauley et al., 1993). Finally, gender has been associated with the overall severity and course of a depressive disorder, with females experiencing a more severe and protracted episode.

A substantial percentage of youngsters who are depressed will later develop bipolar disorder (Kovacs et al., 1984). Identification of variables that can be used to identify youngsters who will later develop bipolar disorder is critical because these youngsters may not respond to a psychosocial treatment program and may benefit from a pharmacological regimen that is different from that used with youngsters who have unipolar disorder. It appears as though an episode of psychotic depression

(Strober et al., 1993) or comorbid ADHD may be risk factors for the later occurrence of bipolar disorder (Carlson & Kashani, 1988).

FAMILIAL CONSIDERATIONS

The contribution of the family to the development and maintenance of depressive disorders during childhood remains an area in need of further empirical exploration. Overall, current research suggests that disturbances in family functioning may contribute to development and maintenance of unipolar depressive disorders during childhood. However, it is too simplistic to assume that a disturbance in family functioning is always found among depressed youths. Furthermore, when a disturbance in family functioning is found, it is a mistake to assume that the dysfunction led to development of the depressive disorder. It also is possible that the expression of the youngster's depressive symptoms significantly contributes to the disturbance in family functioning, a point that is discussed subsequently.

The nature of the disturbance in family functioning, when it exists, is not well defined or empirically established. Perhaps this reflects the possibility that any of a number of disturbances in the family milieu may create a stressful and unhealthy environment that breeds depression. The consistencies that have emerged from the literature are highlighted here. Family variables may have a direct or indirect effect on development of a depressive disorder. An example of a direct effect would be passing along a genetic predisposition toward depressive disorders. An example of a direct psychosocial effect would be a family in which a parent is allowed to chronically abuse or neglect a child. An indirect path would stem from a family environment that fails to teach a child the necessary coping skills to deal with stress. Consequently, when a stressor is present in the child's life, the youngster becomes overwhelmed and eventually depressed. Another possible indirect pathway would be a family environment in which the youngster has repeated learning experiences that produce cognitive disturbances that, in the presence of related stressors, lead to depression. Of critical importance in the study of child psychopathology is research that helps us understand mechanisms through which disturbances in family functioning might contribute to the maintenance and development of a youngster's depressive disorder. Some of our hypotheses about this question are noted in a later section of this chapter. However, we first review the relevant research.

Parenting Style

An emerging pattern within our clinical observations of families with a depressed youth is that the parents' method of managing their children's behavior is dominated by punitive and restrictive techniques that are enacted in a way that belittles or demeans the youngster and cuts the child off from external social, emotional, material, or activity rewards. In other instances, accompanying the aforementioned punishment is an angry attacking outburst in which the affect appears to dramatically magnify the negative impact on the child's sense of self-worth, which subsequently plummets. This atmosphere of heightened emotionality appears to leave a more lasting and damaging imprint. Other investigators have reported similar obser vations.

Arieti and Bemporad (1980) described a destructive parenting style in which one dominant and highly critical parent uses punitive and psychologically damaging methods, such as guilt, shame, and threats of abandonment to enforce rules and coerce compliance. Affection is expressed by these parents contingent on compliance with parental expectations. Poznanski and Zrull (1970) culled the hospital case notes of 14 children between the ages of 3 and 12 who were depressed. They reported a pattern in which the parents had frequent temper outbursts and employed severe, punitive disciplinary techniques. The children were rejected when they misbehaved or experienced difficulty mastering a situation. Similarly, in another study of the interactions of depressed children and their parents, Kashani, Venzke, and Millar (1981) reported that parents were excessively critical of their children and teased them in a mean-spirited fashion. Parental criticism is associated with childhood depression (Schwartz, Dorer, Beardslee, Lavori, & Keller, 1990; Stubbe, Zahner, Goldstein, & Leckman, 1993). Asarnow and colleagues (Asarnow, Tompson, Hamilton, Goldstein, & Guthrie, 1994) noted that excessive criticism from a parent may reinforce a depressed child's negative feelings of himself or herself and the future that, in turn, may result in continued depression.

In addition to the body of clinical reports of disturbances in parenting style, there are a handful of empirical reports that also suggest that disturbances in parenting style are associated with depression during childhood. Amanat and Butler (1984) reported that parents of depressed children exerted nearly total control over the decision making of their children and that their primary tool for exerting this control was oppression. Cole and Rehm (1986) found that parents, and mothers in particular, of depressed children set high standards for their children and only express affection contingent on achievement of these high standards. However, the authors noted that such constriction in the expression of affection may have been a product of the mothers' own depression. In one of our own investigations, Stark, Humphrey, Crook, and Lewis (1990) found that parenting style in families with a depressed child was characterized by less democracy, as the children had minimal say in decisions that were being made within the family. This took place within a more hostile and conflictual family environment. Puig-Antich et. al. (1985a) reported that the relationship between mothers and their depressed children was characterized as cold, hostile, and sometimes rejecting. Parents of depressed children reported using more severe forms of punishment. Radziszewska, Richardson, Dent, and Flay (1996) considered various types of parenting styles in relation to adolescent depressive symptoms. Results indicated that degree of warmth expressed by parents was inversely related to depressive symptoms. The lowest level of depressive symptoms was evident among youngsters of parents who were warm and exerted moderate levels of control. Relative to families with a nondepressed child, the parenting practices of families with a depressed child were characterized as more negative (Messer & Gross, 1995). Puig-Antich et al. (1985b) conducted a follow-up investigation in which they evaluated the same psychosocial variables 4 months after the youngster's depressive episode had remitted. Results indicated that the disturbances in child–parent interactions had lessened, and they concluded that the disturbances in parent–child interactions were a result of the youngster's depressive symptoms rather than vice versa.

Activity Level

Clinical experience working with families of depressed children indicates that some of the families engage in fewer pleasant activities relative to families with nondisturbed children. Once again, it is important to not view this as a unidirectional phenomenon in which the failure to engage in activities is something that the parents do that contributes to the child's depressive disorder. In some instances, families of depressed youths engage in fewer activities due to the depressed youngster refusing to leave the home and do anything enjoyable. In other instances, it is due to anger and explosiveness of the depressed youngster. The youngster's angry and explosive behavior in public situations embarrass the parents, so they stop doing things. In other cases, the parents do seem to be the source of the limitation. The family does not engage in pleasant activities as a group, and the parents restrict their children from engaging in recreational (Puig-Antich et al., 1985a), social, intellectual or cultural, and religious activities (Stark et al., 1990). The reasons for such failure to engage in pleasant activities is not clear. In some cases, it appears as though this is due to the parents' belief that recreational activities are of no value or a waste of time. In other families, it seems to stem from the fact that the parents' work schedule prevents them from engaging in such activities, or the parents believe that they cannot afford to engage in pleasant activities. In other cases it is due to the parents having to work into the evenings and on weekends and because they are not available to supervise their children, the youngsters are restricted from going out of the house. Another common theme in the families that restrict their children's access to pleasant activities is parental overconcern for their children's safety. The parents have a difficult time letting go of their children out of fear that something bad is going to happen to them.

Family Milieu

The family milieu of depressed youths has been examined in a few studies. Our own research (Stark et al., 1990) indicates that families with a depressed child are described by the children, and to a lesser degree by their mothers, as being more conflictual and hostile. Conflict within the family has been reported by a number of investigators (Forehand, McCombe, Long, Brody, & Fauber, 1988; Puig-Antich et al., 1985a) using a variety of methodologies, suggesting that this could be a significant contributor to the development of depressive disorders in children. In addition to being more conflictual, interactions of families of depressed youth are described as less positive (Messer & Gross, 1995). Family members engage in fewer positive behaviors with one another (i.e., smiling, approving, complementing), and they tend to engage in more solitary (i.e., sitting alone, reading, working) behavior. In fact, parents of depressed youths showed an inclination to react negatively to their child's positive behavior. Depressed children were less likely than nondepressed children to reciprocate positive family member behavior and less likely to respond prosocially to the families' neutral behavior (i.e., talking or attending); (Messer & Gross, 1995). Interactions within families of depressed children relative to nondepressed controls have been described as more rejecting, less expressive of affect, less supportive, and more abusive (Kaufman, 1991; McCauley & Myers, 1992).

Family Support

Social support, and family support in particular, has been associated with children's adjustment. For example, Kashani, Canfield, Borduin, Soltys, and Reid (1994) found that children who reported fewer supportive people in their lives were less attentive, more withdrawn, more harmful to others, more damaging to property, more uncooperative, and had higher levels of hopelessness. In addition, those who had a low level of satisfaction with their social support were less attentive and more withdrawn. Similarly, researchers have found that depression is negatively related to family support. In general, adolescents who reported low levels of family support were more depressed than those who reported high levels of family support (Barrera & Garrison-Jones,

1992; Cumsille & Epstein, 1994). Interestingly, degree of satisfaction with paternal support was a better predictor of depression than satisfaction with maternal support (Barrera & Garrison-Jones, 1992).

Abuse and Neglect

Results of a pair of case studies completed by Kashani and colleagues (Kashani & Carlson, 1987; Kashani, Ray, & Carlson, 1984) on depressed preschoolers clearly implicated extreme family chaos, parental psychopathology, abuse, neglect, and substance abuse in their families. Recent research also indicates a relation between abuse and elevated levels of depressive symptoms (Toth, Manly, & Cicchetti, 1992), and when abuse is combined with parental psychopathology, children are at an especially high risk for developing depressive symptoms. Although this more recent research implies a relation between child maltreatment and depressive disorders, it does not firmly implicate maltreatment as a cause.

Cicchetti (1995), using a developmental framework, reported findings from a number of studies examining the effects of child abuse and neglect. Among some of the more salient findings are that physically abused infants are more likely to demonstrate high levels of negative affect and a paucity of positive affect. Maltreated toddlers also were found to be more angry, frustrated, and noncompliant than were nonmaltreated children, and, as preschoolers, these children were rated as more hyperactive, distractible, and lacking in self-control. In kindergarten, maltreated children were rated as more inattentive, aggressive, and overactive by teachers. Studies also indicate that maltreated children experience heightened levels of physical and verbal aggression in peer interactions (Cicchetti, 1995). Across the investigations reviewed by Cicchetti (1995), physical abuse was linked with higher levels of childhood depressive symptomatology, as well as higher rates of ADHD, oppositional defiant disorder, and PTSD.

Marital Discord

At the core of some family systems theories of childhood psychopathology is the tenet that the child's disorder stems from a disturbance in the parents' marital relationship (Fine & Carlson, 1992). Empirical evaluations of this hypothesis have provided mixed and inconclusive results. In one investigation (Kashani et al., 1981), marital discord was found to be "intense" in families with a depressed child. In another, boys who experienced increases in marital conflict scored higher on measures of depression than did controls (MacKinnon-Lewis & Lofquist, 1996). The source and character of the marital discord is not clear. One possible source of the distress is evident in a study conducted by Forehand et al. (1988), who reported that parents of depressed youths experienced conflict over child rearing practices. However, disagreement over childrearing is a common source of friction between parents, and this is an even greater problem in families with a child who has special needs. In contrast to previous findings reported in nonempirically based case studies, Puig-Antich et al. (1985a) did not find marital discord to be a significant factor in families with a depressed child. These investigators did not find any evidence of elevations in irritability, hostility, complaining, or quarrels, nor did they find that the marital dyads engaged in fewer activities together. Families of depressed children also did not report less affection, satisfaction, warmth, problem-solving, or sharing of housework than families of non-depressed children.

Marital discord can lead to development and maintenance of a depressive disorder through a number of different avenues. However, it may depend on the way discord is expressed and duration of time to which the child is exposed to such discord. In addition, the parent's reaction to the discord and the eventual outcome for the family all enter into the formula. Marital discord could lead to bitterness between parents, which may be expressed through an angry, conflictual, negatively charged family environment in which a parent or both parents displace their anger for their spouse onto their children. This anger may be expressed through excessively punitive behavior (Arieti & Bemporad, 1980; Poznanski & Zrull, 1970) and rejection (Puig-Antich et al., 1985a) or personalized criticism (Kashani et al., 1981). If the parents do not enjoy each other's company, the family may engage in fewer enjoyable and social activities together (Stark et al., 1990), and the parents may drift apart physically as well as emotionally, which may leave a child with a sense of loss. The emotional loss also may be real as a parent becomes withdrawn and incapable of providing the child with adequate nurturance and support. Fincham, Grych, and Osborne (1994) provided support for this multifaceted view of the relation between marital discord and depression in children. They asserted that to better understand the influence of marital discord on children, researchers must examine how such conflict is related to other aspects of functioning within the family that also affect children. In other words, to reduce the effect of marital conflict to a single path of causation reflects a linear model of causation that is too simplistic. Researchers must begin to consider how multiple factors interact to affect children's adjustment.

Parental Psychopathology

Based on the belief that there is a strong genetic basis to depressive disorders, investigators began studying prevalence of depressive disorders in offspring of depressed parents. Results of this research and research on prevalence of depressive disorders among offspring of parents with other psychological disorders indicate that children of parents with psychological disorders, and depressive disorders in particular, are at risk for developing a depressive disorder. A very large body of research exists in this area, and a complete discussion is beyond the scope of this chapter. Therefore, the primary conclusions that can be drawn from this research are discussed. For more detailed reviews, see Beardslee, Bemporad, Keller, and Klerman (1983), Hammen (1991), Orvaschel, Weissman, and Kidd (1980), and Williamson (1995).

Results of early studies that were limited by a number of methodological shortcomings (see Hammen, 1991) indicate that children of unipolar depressed parents are at risk for disturbances in functioning including depressive symptoms (Orvaschel et al., 1980), depressive disorders, anxiety disorders, impulsivity, and ADHD (Beardslee, 1993). A number of well-designed studies indicate that children of depressed parents, relative to normal controls, are three times more likely to have a diagnosable disorder, with depressive disorders being the most common (Weissman et al., 1984; Williamson, 1995). Klein, Clark, Dansky, and Margolis (1988) report that one in six children of a unipolar depressed adult suffers from a low-grade chronic depressive disorder. They also are more likely to have a lifetime diagnosis of major depression, substance abuse disorder, multiple comorbid disorders, and to be hospitalized for a psychological disturbance. Furthermore, age of onset of a depressive disorder was much earlier for the offspring of depressed parents (Weissman et al., 1987).

The degree to which the youngster is at risk of developing a depressive disorder appears to be related to a number of parental variables. The offspring are at greater risk if the parent's depressive disorder had an early onset, has been recurrent (Orvaschel, Walsh-Allis, & Ye, 1988), and if the parent had been repeatedly hospitalized for the disorder (Hammen, 1991). In addition, as the number of relatives with an affective disorder increases, so does the risk for the offspring. Hammen (1991) also noted that the severity of the offspring's depressive disorder is related to their mothers experiencing more episodes of depression, and that the chronicity of the child's disorder is related to the number of relatives who have depressive disorders. Another variable that portends an unfavorable outcome is the loss of the child's father.

Children of parents who are experiencing a number of other disorders are at risk for developing a depressive disorder. Children of alcoholics are most likely to develop an externalizing disorder, but they also are at risk for developing a depressive disorder (West & Prinz, 1987). Bipolar disorder is another risk factor (Weintraub, 1987), especially if the mother is experiencing the bipolar disorder (Klein, Depue, & Slater, 1985). Children of parents with a personality disorder, especially if there is hostility in the home, are at risk for developing a depressive disorder (Rutter & Quinton, 1984).

Although research is consistent in demonstrating that offspring of depressed parents are at risk for developing depressive disorders, the underlying mechanism is unclear, and these results must be interpreted cautiously. Increased rates of depression in offspring of depressed parents could be attributed to genetics, shared family environment, the interaction of genes and environment, or a combination of these. However, a recent twin study provides further evidence for a genetic component in the tendency for depression to aggregate in families (Kendler, Neale, Kessler, Heath, & Eaves, 1992). Additional risk factors include assortative mating (the tendency of depressed individuals to marry a person with a psychological disorder), marital conflict, and parent–child conflict (Gotlib & Hammen, 1992).

Conclusions

From the previously cited research, it appears that family variables play an important role in the etiology of depressive disorders in many children. The emerging picture of the family of a depressed youth is one in which the child is given a genetic predisposition (see the next section) for a depressive disorder from a parent who has a psychological disturbance, most commonly a depressive disorder. The parent's own disturbance has a negative impact on the family and prevents the children from receiving support, affection, nurturance and a consistently healthy environment. The family environment of the depressed preschool-age child is likely to include substance abuse as well as child maltreatment. The family milieu of depressed school-age children is characterized by conflict and hostility that is exacerbated by the fact that family members are entrapped within this environment by a failure to engage in pleasant activities outside of the home. The parents often are controlling and make decisions that affect the children with a minimum of input. They rely on punitive, critical, and psychologically damaging means of coercing the youngsters into behaving in ways that are pleasing to the parent. Affection is not expressed in a consistent and supportive fashion. Rather, affection is withheld and is contingent on compliance with parental expectations. Research on the health of the marital relationship is equivocal with some studies reporting marital discord and other more well-controlled studies failing to report any disturbance. There is also evidence that disturbance in family functioning may stem from the expression of the youngster's depressive symptoms, as the disturbance in the depressed child–mother relationship improves after the youngster's depressive episode subsides (Puig-Antich et al., 1985b).

The mechanism through which the disturbances in family functioning lead to depressive symptoms is unclear. Garber and Hilsman (1992) asserted that parents may teach their children to "give up" during a difficult task and may not present positive methods for coping with negative feelings. Another hypothesis, based on an information processing perspective, suggests that it is possible that family conflict sends the child the message that he or she is not worthwhile, lovable, or acceptable. This, in turn, is internalized and structuralized into a negative self-schema. The child may develop a sense of hopelessness as he or she begins to believe that any action leads to conflict or punishment, so why bother to try? In one of our most recent investigations (Stark, Schmidt, & Joiner, 1996), we hypothesized that severity of a child's depressive symptoms would be related to their cognitive triad and that their thoughts about the self, world, and future would be related to the messages they receive from their mothers and fathers about the self, world, and future. Furthermore, we evaluated the relation between the parents' cognitive triad and the children's perceptions of their family environment on their own sense of self, world, and future. Using mediational analyses, we found that the children's perceptions of the messages they received from their mothers and fathers predicted their cognitive triad ratings, which, in turn, predicted severity of depressive symptoms. These results suggest that a possible mechanism for development of a youngster's depressive thinking is the messages that he or she receives about the self, world, and future within the family. These messages are communicated directly through verbalizations, such as "You are useless!" and "This sure is a crazy world you are growing up in, and it just seems to be getting worse!" and indirectly through actions such as excessive punishment and abusive behaviors. As the child repeatedly experiences these messages, they become structuralized as schemata and begin to drive the child's information processing. Once structuralized, due to the confirmatory bias (Turk & Salovey, 1985), the youngster seeks information that confirms his or her schemata, thus perpetuating the maladaptive schemata.

The affect within the home is angry and unpleasant; this combines with the youngster's negative cognitions to produce a mood disturbance. The impact of this conflict and hostility is heightened by the fact that the families seem to be insulated from the outside world by not engaging in an adequate number of activities (social, recreational, cultural, or religious) outside of the home that could provide family members with some respite from the hostility. In addition, failure to engage in enjoyable activities reduces the family's opportunities to spend pleasurable time together. This impedes their opportunity to develop positive relationships that are built on good feelings. This failure to engage in enjoyable activities stifles the building of appropriate positive relationships between family members and may lead the children to learn an aversive and hostile style of interacting. Furthermore, this pattern would be reciprocated by similarly hostile interactions and rejection, thereby confirming the child's sense of worthlessness and the belief that he or she is unlikeable. Depressed youths also rate their families as less supportive, which could stem from the conflict, and they perceive their families to be less desirable than their peer's families (Stark et al., 1990).

PSYCHOPHYSIOLOGICAL AND GENETIC INFLUENCES

Psychophysiology and Depression

In the past decade, depression has been viewed by researchers as the combination of psychological stress and biological vulnerability that impact the individual. Psychophysiological variables have been widely researched in depressed adults and are now being explored in depressed children (Burke & Puig-Antich, 1990). Researchers have delineated several psychophysiological variables that may be implicated in childhood depressive disorders (Burke & Puig-Antich, 1990; Kalat, 1992; Shelton, Hollon, Purdon, & Loosen, 1991) including neurotransmitter systems, neuroendocrine dysfunction, and biological rhythms. These variables are thought to underlie the expression of depressive symptomatology.

The monoamine neurotransmitter system model of depression implicates the central nervous system monoamine neurotransmitters—norepinephrine, serotonin, and dopamine—in the expression of depressive symptoms. This model is based on the fact that certain drugs that decrease norepinephrine and serotonin produce depression, and drugs that increase these neurotransmitters alleviate depressive symptoms.

When drugs that increase monoamines in the depressed individual are administered, a time delay of two to three weeks occurs before the individual experiences a relief from depressive symptoms. However, the biochemical effects of the drugs take only 2 to 3 hours. This temporal dilemma led researchers to realize that depression was affected not only by a deficit in neurotransmitters but also by a deficit in the number of binding sites for the neurotransmitters. A synapse, the space between neurons, responds to a neurotransmitter deficit by increasing the number of receptor sites on the postsynaptic neuron. The depressed individual may not only be suffering from a deficit in neurotransmitters but also from an abnormally high number of binding sites that have formed in response to the neurotransmitter deficit. This indicates that depression is more than a deficit (or excess) in neurotransmitters and that depression is a combination of irregularities in the neuroendocrine system and normal biological rhythms. Although monoamines do not appear to have a direct effect on mood regulation, they play a major modulatory role on other neurobiologic systems involved in the recovery from depression (Henninger, Delgado, & Charney, 1996). Kolb and Whishaw (1996) postulated that depression results from dysfunctions in multiple, specialized receptor sites within the monoamine system. Monoaminergic mechanisms play a critical role in the nervous system and affect sleep, arousal, and response to incoming stimuli. Thus, disruptions in this system seem to explain the symptomatic expression of depression (Shelton et al., 1991). Norepinephrine and serotonin are directly linked to functioning of the limbic system. The limbic system, consisting of the amygdala, hippocampus, and the hypothalamus, regulates the individual's drives, instincts, and emotion. The hypothalamus exerts control over the endocrine and autonomic nervous systems, which coordinate physiological and behavioral responses to stimuli. The noradrenergic neurotransmitter system illuminates the link between monoamines and the expression of depression. Carstens, Engelbrecht, Russell, van Zyl, and Talijaard (1987) found that elevated a 2-adrenoceptor and imipramine Kd values were found in children with a major depressive disorder and a suicide attempt. Carstens et al. propose that these elevated values may be biological markers for suicide attempts in children with major depressive disorder. This finding supports the presence of noradrenergic abnormality in depression, which also involves the neuroendocrine system (Siever & Davis, 1985).

The monoamine neurotransmitters and neuroendocrine systems are closely linked. Serotonin and norepinephrine are found in the limbic system, which elucidates the connection between behaviors controlled by the limbic system such as eating, sleeping, and emotion and depression. Two endocrine systems, the hypothalamic–pituitary–thyroid (HPA) axis and the hypothalamic–pituitary–adrenal (HPA) axis, are closely linked to depression. The dexamethasone suppression test (DST) has been used to assess dysregulation in the HPA axis. As a biological marker of depression, the DST has been used in adult studies of depression with mixed results. The DST is sensitive to the failure of dexamethasone to inhibit cortisol secretion after giving the individual the drug dexamethasone. This reaction assesses dysregulations in the HPA axis which modulates the individual's response to stress (Shelton et al., 1991). In children and adolescents, DST results are contradictory (Fristad, Weller, Weller, Teare, & Preskorn, 1988; Puig-Antich, 1986) and age is hypothesized to have an interactive effect with depression (Burke & Puig-Antich, 1990). Stress triggers the increase in levels of cortisol, a stress hormone, that has been linked to depressive disorders. Meanwhile, the stress response of individuals with depression may be abnormal. Dinan (1994) suggested that HPA overdrive is the essential feature of depression rather than monoamine abnormalities. From this perspective, chronic psychological stress may trigger changes in central monoamines within individuals prone to depression (Dinan, 1994). Stress also may account for differences in cortisol secretion studies among children and adolescents (Burke & Puig-Antich, 1990). Further research in this area is needed.

Neuroendocrine dysfunction and the role of both the HPA axis and the HPT axis in depressives have been examined in adults and children (Shelton et al., 1991). Mild hypothyroidism is seen in patients with clinical depression, and thyroid hormone replacement decreases depressive symptoms. This suggests that the HPT axis is implicated in depression. However, these responses to thyroid hormone replacement have not been found in prepubertal depressed children (Burke & Puig-Antich, 1990). Further research is needed in this area, as this response may be mediated by age.

Hormonal changes, particularly presence of estrogen in girls, also have been linked to depressive disorders. Estrogen accounts for some individual differences between boys and girls in growth hormone (GH) secretion, with girls secreting significantly more GH than boys (Burke & Puig-Antich, 1990). GH release during sleep in depressed prepubertal children was found to be significantly greater than in controls; however, this finding was not found in depressed adolescents (Burke & Puig-Antich, 1990). Burke and Puig-Antich hypothesize that age and puberty may interact in the control of GH release. The complex relation between hormones and the HPA and HPT axes, which are mutually regulated with the monoamine neurotransmitters, contribute to the complexity of biological explanations for depression.

Biological rhythms determine human functioning and involve natural circadian and ultradian rhythms. These physical processes provide another competing explanation for the biological basis of depression and focus on the mutual influences of the sleep–wake cycle, neuroendocrine activity, and body temperature that follow the daily light–dark cycle. Disruptions in these processes are potential links to the expression of depressive symptoms. Circadian activity rhythms were found to be abnormal in depressed children and adolescents. Furthermore, depressed adolescents were reported to have a significantly higher 12-hour hemicircadian rhythms, which may be related to diurnal mood variation (Teicher & Pahlavan, 1993). One of the most important rhythmic patterns in the body is sleep, and the association between sleep and depression has been widely studied. Sleep disturbances are implicated via electroencephalographic (EEG) studies in depressed patients. A shortened latency to onset of rapid eye movement (REM) sleep has been found in depressed adults and adolescents (Cowen & Wood, 1991; Shelton et al., 1991). However, before puberty, there are no changes in EEG sleep among depressed children (Burke & Puig-Antich, 1990). Both an underlying depressive trait or a past episode of depression have been hypothesized to be determined by a shortened first REM latency period. This effect seems to only implicate the individual after puberty. Therefore, EEG studies lead us to view depression as possibly having distinct stages at different points in life. It also points to the value of an integrated developmental model of depression across the life span that includes biological and psychological variables.

These biological models provide explanations for some depressive symptoms; however, they do not suffice as an all-inclusive explanation for depression in children and adolescents. There is a need to integrate biological and psychological phenomena to elucidate the depth and breadth of clinical manifestations of depression (Shelton et al., 1991), and it is likely that multiple biological and psychological precursors influence depression.

Age and puberty appear to affect most psychobiological markers of depressive disorders in children and adolescents (Burke & Puig-Antich, 1990; Puig-Antich, 1986). Similarly, Newman and Garfinkel (1992) postulated that different neurobiological systems and processes may be responsible for depression at different ages. Developmental differences and similarities in the neurochemistry of depression confound conclusions regarding age-related differences in the pathophysiology of depression (Koplewics, Klass, & Kafantaris, 1993). To date, there is no identified biological marker of depression that reliably separates depressed individuals from healthy or psychiatric controls (Cowen & Wood, 1991). Future research will continue to examine possible biological markers that are triggered via environmental stresses that influence the expression and progression of child and adolescent depression.

Genetic Influence

Several investigations have been conducted to determine whether there is a genetic basis to depressive disorders during childhood. Overall, evidence supporting such a link is compelling (Clarkin, Hass, & Glick, 1988). The data gathered in support of the genetic factor in depressive disorders are based on studies of twins, families, and adopted children.

Twin studies compare the concordance rates between monozygotic (MZ) and dizygotic (DZ) twins. Although results vary according to the research methodology employed in a particular study, these investigations find substantially higher concordance rates for depressive disorders among MZ twins relative to DZ twins (Tsuang & Farone, 1990). In fact, MZ twins are approximately three times more likely to develop a depressive disorder than DZ twins (Clarkin et al., 1988). Because twins share not only the same genes but also the same psychosocial environment, studies of twins reared together versus those reared in separate environments are important. Investigators have compared concordance rates of MZ twins reared apart and found a concordance rate of 67% for the development of depressive disorders. Results of these studies suggest that genetics play a significant role in who is at risk for development of a depressive disorder during childhood.

Family research also gives credence to the genetic link in depressive disorders. Family studies usually compare the rates of a disorder in first-degree relatives, consisting of parents, children, and siblings of participants sharing 50% of their genes, to second-degree relatives, consisting of grandparents, aunts, uncles, nieces, and nephews who have 25% of their genes in common. Family studies of depressive disorders have found a considerably higher rate of depressive disorders in first-degree relatives of depressed probands than in the general population (Gershon et al., 1982). First-degree relatives of adolescents with major depressive disorder (MDD) have an increased lifetime rate of MDD and other psychiatric disorders (Williamson, Ryan, Birmaher, & Dahl, 1995). In fact, children with a depressed parent have a 15% risk of developing a depressive disorder, which is six times greater than for children with nondepressed parents (Downey & Coyne, 1990). Furthermore, if both parents have a depressive disorder, the child's chances increase to 40% (Goodwin, 1982). Interestingly, children who have second-degree relatives with a depressive disorder are not at any greater risk for developing a depressive disorder than anyone else in the general population (Tsuang & Farone, 1990). Williamson et al. (1995) found that second-degree relatives of adolescents with MDD have higher lifetime rates of psychiatric disorders, but not depression. Although results of these studies provide support for the genetic link to depressive disorders in children, it is important to note that these studies are confounded by sharing of a common family environment in the studies of first-degree relatives. Once again, adoption studies can help us understand the contribution of genetic and environmental factors.

From a methodological standpoint, adoption studies suffer from fewer confounding variables when the children are adopted at birth rather than later in life, because the children have the genes of their biological parents but live in an environment that is different from that of their biological parents. Mendlewicz and Rainer (1977) conducted a study using individuals who were adopted as infants and who developed a depressive disorder. A depressive disorder was found in 31% of the participant's biological parents versus 12% in adoptive parents. Because the concordance rate is higher among biological compared to adoptive parents, the results once again suggest that there is a genetic link to depression. Although adoption studies have not led to unequivocal proof, these results do strengthen the case for involvement of genetic factors in the development of depressive disorders in children.

Taken together, these twin, family, and adoption studies provide compelling evidence for a genetic link in the etiology of childhood depressive disorders. Recent reviews regarding the genetics of depressive disorders suggest that depression is caused by multiple genes and that these genes predispose susceptible individuals to develop the disorder (Farmer, 1996). Studies that examine genetic and environmental factors in the same participants indicate that reactions to and self-selection into stressful life events also are mediated genetically (Farmer, 1996; Kendler & Karkowski-Shuman, 1997). A twin study conducted by Thapar and McGuffin (1996) suggested that environmental factors play a greater role in the transmission of depressive symptoms in childhood, and genetics largely influences depressive symptoms in adolescence. Recent evidence indicates that a complex relation exists between genetic and environmental factors in the etiology of depression.

AN INTEGRATED MODEL OF DEPRESSIVE DISORDERS DURING CHILDHOOD

Based on theory and research, it is hypothesized that multiple pathways lead to the development of depressive disorders. This hypothesis has a number of implications. First, research may reveal that there are a limited number of causal variables, but there will be variability across cases in terms of which one or ones are most relevant. Thus, the cause or causes of one child's depressive disorder may be different from that of another child. Another important implication is that, for any given child, there may be multiple causal variables that are interacting in an additive or simultaneous fashion. Furthermore, a disturbance in one area of functioning is likely to reciprocally interact with other domains. For example, a biochemical disturbance would affect mood, vegetative functioning, and information processing and leave the youngster more vulnerable to the effects of stress. The disturbance in mood and information processing would feedback to, and affect, the biochemical disturbance, and they would affect the youngster's behavior, which, in turn, affects relationships with others. The behaviors and reactions of significant others may be misperceived due to distortions in information processing, which lead to a confirmation of, or the activation of, dysfunctional schemata. Once activated, these dysfunctional schemata guide information processing.

The following example may clarify some of the major tenets of the model. A child may have a genetic predisposition toward depression that stems from having a depressed parent. This predisposition would place the child at risk for developing a neurochemical diathesis. The depressed parent would be a chronic stressor. Depressed mothers, for example, tend to perceive more misbehavior in their children than actually exists (Forehand et al., 1988). This increases the number of punitive interchanges and establishes a negative affective atmosphere in the home. The attachment behaviors would likely be characterized by an insecure style, and the internal working model would be one of contradictions. Sometimes the child is smothered with affection, and other times the mother is cold, distant, and hostile. The schema about relationships would be one that defines relationships as fraught with pain and unreturned love.

Children are active constructors of their environments both in terms of their actions and with respect to their perceptions of that environment. They try to make sense of, or derive meaning from, their interactions with the environment and especially from interactions with significant others. The message that they would perceive from repeated punitive interactions with the depressed mother would be "I'm bad." In addition, lack of emotional availability of the depressed parent, along with the negative interactions, would lead to the self-perception, "I'm unlovable". If these messages are communicated often enough, and they are accompanied by other learning experiences that communicate the same message, this self-view becomes internalized and structuralized as a core schema that guides information processing. The other schema that comprise the internal working model would become structuralized in a similar fashion and guide interpersonal behavior. The youngster would be unlikely to get close to others because he or she would expect to be hurt and rejected. Thus, the youngster's behavior would reinforce his or her internal working model and prevent the child from having schema inconsistent learning experiences. During times of stress, the youngster would not seek social support as he or she has a history of not receiving it. Thus, the youngster would not have access to interpersonal warmth and a sense of security that comes from social support during stressful times. In addition, the child would not have access to the consoling conversations with significant others that often produce a reframing of what is happening and how it is likely to affect one's life. Schemata serve as filters that eliminate schema-inconsistent information and process schema-consistent information, which further strengthens the developing sense of self and the internal working model. Furthermore, this negative style of thinking and other depressive symptoms, as well as the youngster's "stand-offish" behavior, may be aversive to peers, which could lead to further isolation, alienation, or rejection. Thus, in this example, biological (genetic predisposition), cognitive (self-schema, internal working model), behavioral (distant, aversive interpersonal behavior), and interpersonal–family (depressed parent, negative messages) disturbances reciprocally interact to produce and maintain a depressive disorder.

It has been hypothesized (e.g., Beck et al., 1979; Cole & Turner, 1993), and research (Stark et al., 1996) is emerging that supports the notion, that the core schemata are formed through early learning experiences and communications within the family.

We have referred to this as the *cognitive interpersonal pathway*. In the case of the depressed youngster, schemata that make the youngster vulnerable to stress may develop as a result of interactions that are characteristic of an insecure attachment, negative evaluative statements directed at the child from parents (Stark et al., 1996), from interactions that communicate rejection (Puig-Antich et al., 1985a), and an overreliance on punitive parenting procedures (Poznanski & Zrull, 1970), which once again communicate to the child that he or she is "bad" or "unlovable" and the world is an unpleasant place. It is important to note that the child, through genetic predispositions and temperament factors, plays a role in constructing this environment. Furthermore, the youngster's behaviors affect the environment in a fashion that supports the developing schemata.

It is within the family milieu that the child develops crucial attachment behaviors, interpersonal skills, and the expectations that guide interpersonal relationships. In the case of the depressive family milieu, the child learns a more impulsive and angry style of interacting and one in which rejection or a lack of support is expected (Stark et al., 1990). As the child develops, he or she begins to interact with others, and these interactions are shaped by and shape existing social skills as well as the youngster's schema about social situations (internal working model). The depressed youngster behaves in an impulsive and angry style, which leads to rejection. This rejection, in turn, leads to the development of a sense of self that is comprised of a poorly developed positive self-schema and a more active negative self-schema (Prieto, Cole, & Tageson, 1992), a negative world schema (Kaslow, Stark, Printz, Livingston, & Tsai, 1992), and negative schema about interpersonal relationships as well as the self within these relationships. In addition, rejection may lead to withdrawal (Kazdin, Esveldt-Dawson, Sherick, & Colbus, 1985), which insulates the youngster from corrective learning experiences. As the youngster matures and faces new stressors, he or she does not have the parental (Stark et al., 1990) or peer social support (e.g. Blechman, McEnroe, Carella, & Audette, 1986) necessary to help buffer their impact. The impact is further heightened through negative distortions in information processing (Kendall, Stark, & Adam, 1990) and a possible deficit in coping skills. Affect interacts with the previously mentioned variables in a reciprocal fashion. The youngster may experience dysphoria due to the perception of social or familial rejection, from the conflictual and punitive atmosphere within the family milieu (Forehand et al., 1988), or from biochemical imbalances. Similarly, the mood disturbance affects the youngster's information processing and behavior.

Once developed, schemata can be in either an active or latent state (although research has not consistently supported the notion of latent schemata). It is possible that they become active through a variety of means. A traumatic or stressful event that is related to the content of the schemata may occur and trigger the activation of the schemata. Once activated, schemata guide the information processing system that leads to depressed affect and the accompanying depressive symptoms. With time, these disturbances in cognition reciprocally affect brain chemistry, perhaps through a stress-like reaction.

What might be the link between stress, cognition and biochemical functioning? As noted previously, stress affects a child's neurochemical functioning. Stressful events have both a direct impact on biological functioning and an indirect effect through the individual's perceptions of stress and the potential harm that they may experience. The depression-prone individual, due to errors in information processing that are a reflection of early learning experiences, may believe that he or she does not possess the skills or abilities to effectively cope with stress. In addition, these individuals are more likely to perceive a wider variety of events as potentially harmful, which would lead to greater stress. Social support is a buffer for the effects of stress, but, due to the youngster's internal working model (core schema), he or she is less likely to seek social support or to receive it. Stress appears to affect the hypothalamic–adrenal system, causing the adrenal glands to oversecrete hydrocortisone or cortisol. When stressed, hypothalamic neurons, regulated by norepinephrine neurons in the locus coeruleus, secrete corticotropin-releasing hormone, which stimulates the production of adrenocorticotropin (ACTH) by the pituitary. ACTH then stimulates the adrenal glands to produce cortisol. Stress-related hormones and neurotransmitters influence many aspects of cerebral functioning (Kolb & Whishaw, 1996). This may lead to a disruption in the neurotransmitter system and produce many of the symptoms of depression.

As noted previously, this model also may have relevance to the phenomena of comorbidity. It is hypothesized that the interpersonal context is highly influential in the development of comorbid conditions. The depressed conduct-disordered youngster, for instance, would live in an environment that supports a negative self-schema or lack of a positive self-schema, and a conduct-disordered self-schema. The family environment would be characterized by the classic coercive family system. Acting-out behavior would reinforce the child's schema, either engage or disengage the parents, and may lead to a temporary improvement in mood, because as acting-out behaviors can be thrilling or chemically mood-enhancing. Acting-out can serve as a method for relating to other youths and it can provide the youngster with a peer group and a means of gaining social status. In the case of the oppositional defiant disordered youth, a coercive family system would exist, but the parents would be more observant of the youngster's behavior and punitive in a stifling fashion. The primary caregivers often are depressed themselves, and to the child they appear to spread their anger and distress. Similarly, the youngster is edgy and angers quickly as a method of controlling others' behavior and as a means of making other people feel what he or she is feeling. The depressed and anxious child possesses a negative sense of self and believes that the world is a dangerous and hurtful place.

CURRENT TREATMENTS

The psychosocial approaches for treating depressed children vary considerably, although they tend to be associated with a few approaches to therapy including psychodynamic, cognitive–behavioral, and family systems interventions. Unfortunately, research concerning the relative efficacy of these approaches with depressed children is limited. Before briefly describing each of these approaches to treating depressed youths, we highlight a few issues that complicate the treatment picture.

When discussing treatment of depressed youths, one needs to consider comorbidity and developmental and environmental issues. Although some depressed children may be viewed as exhibiting a "pure" or uncomplicated depressive disorder, this is more likely the exception rather than the rule. It appears that fewer than one third of all children diagnosed as depressed have no additional diagnoses (Anderson, Williams, McGee, & Silva, 1987; Bird et al., 1988).

Variations in the child's level of development are reflected by variations in the clinical presentation of depressive symptoms. For instance, adolescents present with more lethal suicide attempts and more anhedonia when compared to prepubertal children (Ryan et al., 1987). Similarly, developmental considerations also may influence treatment considerations. Some researchers would contend that the immature cognitive development of the prepubescent child limits treatment options; consequently, therapeutic approaches that attempt to change cognitive structures may be less effective for younger children (e.g., McCracken & Cantwell, 1992).

Most of the approaches to treatment recognize that childhood depression evolves within an environmental context. As a result, it is often crucial to recognize the most salient environmental factors that can influence the etiology and maintenance of mood disorders in young people. This should include not only the family but also encompass other environmental factors, such as peer interactions (Barrera and Garrison-Jones, 1992), the community and culture in which the child lives, and the school environment.

PSYCHOSOCIAL TREATMENTS FOR DEPRESSED YOUTHS

Interpersonal Therapy

Over the past few years, Mufson and colleagues have adapted Interpersonal Therapy (IPT) to the treatment of depressed adolescents (Mufson, Moreau, Weissman, & Klerman, 1993). The primary therapeutic goals of IPT are to decrease depressive symptoms and to improve interpersonal functioning. To accomplish these goals, the youngster and the therapist identify one or two problem areas from among the following: (a) grief, (b) interpersonal role disputes, (c) role transitions, (d) interpersonal deficits, and (e) single-parent families.

Treatment is divided into three phases, each of which consists of four sessions. During the initial phase, problem areas are identified, a rationale for treatment is provided, a formal therapeutic contract is written and signed, and the adolescent's role in therapy is defined. Some psychoeducation about the nature and impact of depression is provided to the youngster and his or her parents. The therapist works with the youngster and his or her parents to ensure that the child is socially engaged in the family, school, and with friends. Parents are asked to encourage their child to engage in as many normal activities as possible.

During the middle phase of treatment, the nature of each previously identified problem is clarified, effective strategies for attacking the problems are identified, and relevant plans are developed and implemented. When developing plans, an overarching goal is the desire to improve interpersonal functioning. Youngsters are taught to monitor the experience of depressive symptoms and their emotional experiences.

To achieve these therapeutic objectives, the therapist uses exploratory questioning, encouragement of affect, linking affect with events, clarification of conflicts, communication analysis, and behavior change techniques such as role playing. Throughout these sessions, the therapist provides the youngster with feedback about symptom change in an attempt to enhance "self-esteem." The therapist and youngster work as a team. Together, they assess the accuracy of the initial formulation of problem areas and evaluate the impact of ongoing events occurring outside of the sessions for their impact on depressive symptoms. The therapist evaluates the youngster's interpersonal style through their within-session interactions. With the youngster's informed permission, the family is encouraged to support the treatment goals.

The final phase of treatment, sessions 9 to 12, comprise the termination phase. The primary objectives of this phase are to prepare the youngster for termination and to establish a sense of personal competence for dealing with future problems. The youngster's feelings about termination are discussed, and feelings of competence are engendered.

Results of outcome studies on adolescents treated with IPT have been positive. Using an open clinical trial methodology, Mufson et al. (1994) investigated the effects of 12 weeks of IPT–A on 14 depressed adolescents. Participants were evaluated at 0, 2, 4, 8, and 12 weeks. Results indicated a significant decrease in the participants' depressive symptomatology, and symptoms of psychological and physical distress, and a significant improvement in functioning over the course of treatment. In a second investigation, Mufson and Fairbanks (1996) found that 10 adolescents with depression who were treated with IPT–A for three months reported few depressive symptoms and maintained improvements in their social functioning 1 year posttreatment.

Cognitive–Behavioral Approaches

Cognitive Therapy. Aaron Beck's cognitive therapy is perhaps the most widely cited cognitive–behavioral treatment for depression (Beck et al., 1979). The goals of therapy are to modify negative views about one's self, the world, and the future as well as systematic errors in information processing, including selective abstraction, overgeneralization, personalization, dichotomous thinking, and so forth.

Stark (1990) adapted Beck's approaches for children. To allow young people to better recognize and label a broad range of emotions, "affective education" provides the foundation for cognitive restructuring procedures that are used later in treatment. Affective education also serves as the initial means of linking thoughts with feelings and behaviors. Concepts are introduced through the use of cartoons and role playing. Techniques for children and adolescents also include a process whereby daily events, affects, and reactions are logged for later review (Stark & Kendall, 1996). Over time, maladaptive cognitions are identified and the linkages between distorted assumptions and depression are examined by both the therapist and the child. As this process evolves, the child and therapist begin to question systematically the validity of these assumptions, and more adaptive alternatives are proposed. Homework assignments also make the process of cognitive restructuring more personally relevant. Through repeated applications of logical analysis and cognitive restructuring, the child or adolescent becomes accustomed to rational evaluation and modification of his or her beliefs.

Several studies have incorporated aspects of Beck's therapy in treating depressed children and adolescents. However, there has been only one research effort that specifically examined the relative efficacy of cognitive restructuring. Butler, Miezitis, Friedman, and Cole (1980) found cognitive restructuring to be superior to waiting-list and attention-only controls; however, it proved no more effective than another active treatment (i.e., social problems solving). Subsequent studies (Kahn, Kehle, Jenson, & Clark 1990; Lewinsohn, Clarke, Hops, & Andrews, 1990; Reynolds & Coates, 1986; Stark, 1990; Stark, Reynolds, & Kaslow, 1987) have included cognitive restructuring as one component of their treatment program. In general, interventions that have included cognitive restructuring have been superior to nonspecific treatments, attention-only conditions or waiting-list controls. However, most studies failed to demonstrate much difference in the relative efficacy of approaches that include cognitive restructuring to other active treatments, such as relaxation training.

Rehm's Model of Treatment. The primary focus of Rehm's (1977) self-control treatment is on changing the deficits in self-regulation associated with depression. These deficits include disturbances in self-monitoring, negative self-evaluations, inadequate rates of reinforcement, and high rates of self-punishment (Kaslow & Rehm,

1983). Self-control therapy is a didactic treatment that is often conducted in a group setting. Intervention techniques stress the importance of homework assignments between therapy sessions.

The initial treatment is concerned with teaching the child or adolescent how depressed individuals tend to selectively ignore positive experiences while they focus unduly on negative experiences. Early homework assignments require the child to monitor pleasant events and daily mood. The child subsequently learns about the relation between mood and pleasant activities. This offers the child a concrete illustration of how high rates of pleasant events and elevated mood are related. The goal of therapy is then to increase the rate of pleasant events and to continue to monitor daily mood (Stark, 1990). The child or adolescent also can be encouraged to differentiate immediate versus long term consequences of behavior. As such, the child is taught how positive consequences may not result immediately from their behavior, but other consequences may be delayed and evolve over a longer period of time. As the child continues to monitor behavior and mood, he or she may be instructed to identify a delayed effect of behavior on a regular basis (Carey, 1993).

The tendency of depressed individuals to set unrealistic goals and also to define success in absolute terms is another target of the therapy (Stark, 1990). First, the client is taught to identify realistic goals. Once realistic goals are set, the client is taught to task-analyze the primary goal into subgoals; self-reinforcement is provided for obtainment of these subgoals. Teaching the principles of covert and overt self-praise and reinforcement is an important aspect of therapy. In order to increase the rate of self-reinforcement, it is incorporated into other components of therapy. For example, the individual is taught how to self-reward after completing homework assignments. Increasing the rate of self-reinforcement serves two functions. First, self-reinforcement may lead to an elevation in mood, and second, as the rate of self-reinforcement increases, the child has less opportunity to self-punish.

In two studies, Stark and colleagues (Stark, 1990; Stark et al., 1987) evaluated the efficacy of self-control techniques for the treatment of depressed children. Reynolds and Coates (1986) have used similar techniques for treating depressed adolescents. These studies provides general support for the efficacy of self-control techniques as one component of treatment of depressed youngsters. Results of these studies would indicate that treatment involving self-control techniques provide significant improvement in depressive symptoms relative to waiting-list controls. However, self-control approaches appear to be no more effective than other active treatments, such as relaxation training or behavioral therapy. It is also noteworthy that no study has examined the efficacy of self-control techniques with clinic-referred populations. To date, self-control approaches have been evaluated using nonreferred, school-based populations. As a result, further studies are needed to evaluate the efficacy of self-control techniques with clinic-referred populations.

Lewinsohn's Model of Treatment. Lewinsohn and associates (Clarke, Lewinsohn, & Hops, 1990) designed treatment approaches that focus on the relation between reinforcement and punishment rates, which are proposed to be the primary factors that contribute to depression (Lewinsohn & Hoberman, 1982). This treatment approach is designed for both adolescents and their parents. Treatment is in the form of a formal class, one attended by the adolescent and another class provided for the parent. The curriculum for these sessions involves introduction of a particular skill during the course of several sessions. Skill review and practice is individualized through the use of homework assignments. Specific skills include ways to control irrational maladaptive thoughts, strategies for increasing pleasant events, social skills training, in conjunction with communication and conflict resolution between parent and child (Lewinsohn et al., 1990).

In the only large-scale treatment study of cognitive–behavioral methods as applied to clinic populations, the Lewinsohn approach to treatment has resulted in both immediate and long-term improvement in the severity of depressive symptoms. Moreover, parent involvement appeared to heighten treatment effectiveness. It is noteworthy, however, that adolescents with a comorbid diagnosis were excluded from the study, that the study only included middle to late adolescents. Adolescents also were excluded from the study if they did not possess a seventh-grade reading level (Lewinsohn et al., 1990). These limitations make generalizations concerning clinically complicated, lower functioning, or younger populations tentative.

Conclusions

The various treatment programs noted share many of the same treatment components. In fact, elsewhere, we have suggested that interpersonal therapy and cognitive–behavioral therapies for depression are so similar that they do not represent distinct approaches to treatment (Stark et al., in press). For example, each model emphasizes the need to introduce specific skills during therapy and the need to apply those skills outside of the therapy session through the use of homework assignments. For the most part, the various approaches recognize the need to incorporate traditional behavioral procedures. Differences typically arise in the emphasis placed on one technique over another. For example, cognitive therapy and interpersonal therapy may focus on interpersonal relationships, but the cognitive therapist also targets the cognitions that foster the interpersonal difficulties. Intervention studies generally support the efficacy of cognitive–behavioral treatments; however, it is unclear which techniques, or set of techniques, represents the most parsimonious treatment approach. Most of the various studies have been confined to nonreferred samples of depressed children or adolescents; however, the findings of Lewinsohn and colleagues suggest that cognitive–behavioral therapy can be an effective treatment approach for clinically depressed adolescents, as well. Moreover, this study also provides qualified support for a strong family component to treatment.

Family Therapy

Despite the research that links parental psychopathology and other family considerations with childhood depression, there is little research that includes family-based interventions as a major component of treatment. The families of depressed children tend to be oppressive, conflictual, controlling, and less supportive than families of nondepressed young people. Moreover, parents of depressed children are often psychiatrically involved themselves. Parental psychopathology can, in turn, lead to parent–child interactions that are maladaptive.

Despite absence of empirical efforts that have addressed efficacy of treating depressed children through family-based interventions, several authors have indicated that the family should play an essential role in the treatment of the depressed child or adolescent (Lewinsohn, Hoberman & Clarke, 1989; McCracken & Cantwell, 1992; Stark, Rouse, & Livingston, 1991). Parental psychopathology often needs to be treated apart from the child-focused therapy. In many families, the goals of therapy can be to lower family conflict through behavior management or problem-solving techniques.

However, even in relatively healthy families, parental involvement is often essential to ensure homework assignments are completed and to help generalize skills beyond the confines of therapy.

One group study has included a significant family component in treatment (Lewinsohn et al., 1989). These researchers incorporated parent training as an adjunct component to individual treatment of adolescents with depression. Parent training provided an overview of the skills presented to the adolescent in addition to specific instruction concerning conflict resolution for managing parent–child difficulties. By including a significant parental component to treatment, the adolescent appeared to demonstrate a more pervasive and long-lasting improvement in depressive symptoms (Lewinsohn et al., 1989). We believe that both family therapy and parent training are necessary for the successful treatment of depressed youths.

Psychopharmacological Treatments

The "advent of antidepressants, and their effectiveness in the treatment of depression of adult patients, can be considered the greatest success in psychiatric treatment in the past four decades" (Campbell & Cueva, 1995; p. 1266). The same cannot be said about antidepressants for the treatment of depressive disorders during childhood and adolescence. In fact, Vitiello and Jensen (1995) stated that there "is still no proven superiority of antidepressant drugs over placebo in children or adolescents" (p. 75). Despite lack of empirical evidence for the efficacy of antidepressants, they are so commonly used with depressed youngsters that many consider them to be the standard of care (Dillon, Tsai, & Alessi, 1996).

Currently, there are four main classes of antidepressants that may be prescribed to youths, including the tricyclics, monoamine oxidase inhibitors, selective serotonin reuptake inhibitors (SSRIs), and second-generation antidepressants. The specific mechanisms of action of the antidepressants is on the monoamine neurotransmitter system, more specifically on the neurotransmitters including acetylcholine, norepinephrine, serotonin, and, to a lesser extent, dopamine. Antidepressant medications influence the metabolism or reuptake of the neurotransmitters, which results in increased levels of functionally available neurotransmitters, (Werry & Aman, 1993). Most of the antidepressants have a broad spectrum effect; in other words, they affect the metabolism and reuptake of acetylcholine, norepinephrine, serotonin, and dopamine. A few of them are more focused and influence specific brain monoamine systems. Desipramine, for example, mainly affects norepinephrine reuptake, fluoxetine affects serotonin, and buproprion affects dopamine.

Conclusions regarding the effectiveness of the tricyclic antidepressants is mixed for children. Initial controlled studies indicated no difference between imipramine and placebos. When the plasma level of imipramine is controlled for, treatment success rates have been high (Puig-Antich et al., 1987; Puig-Antich & Weston, 1983). There is no evidence that the tricyclics are effective with adolescents (Ambrosini et al., 1993; Dillon et al., 1996; Ryan, 1992; Strober, Freeman, & Rigali, 1990; Vitiello & Jensen, 1995). This outcome does not appear to vary depending on whether the youngsters are treated as inpatients or outpatients, nor whether the youngsters are experiencing an endogenous or exogenously based disorder (Ambrosini et al., 1993).

There is room for optimism concerning the effects of the SSRIs. This class of drugs currently is being evaluated by investigators who are using more sophisticated and methodologically elegant experimental designs, which eliminate those youngsters who respond to either the placebo or the drug within the first few days of treatment.

Another often-used strategy for the treatment of depressed youths involves polymedicating. Proponents of this approach believe that one medication may potentiate the effectiveness of the other medication. There is some literature that suggests that adolescents who are nonresponsive to an antidepressant may respond favorably to augmentation of the antidepressant with lithium (Strober, Freeman, Rigali, Schmidt, & Diamond, 1992). Other augmentation strategies include the use of thyroid supplements and stimulants (Dillon et al., 1996).

In a recent article, five preeminent psychiatrists were interviewed regarding their approach to treating depressed children and adolescents (Ambrosini et al., 1993). All five stated that they would first try an SSRI due to its efficacy, safety profile, and because it produces fewer side effects. Another rule that seemed to guide their choice of treatment was the presence and types of comorbid conditions. If the youngster also was experiencing a comorbid ADHD, then a tricyclic may be used or buproprion would be the first choice. If the youngster was experiencing comorbid obsessive–compulsive disorder, then fluoxetine would be the preferred choice. If the youngster was experiencing a comorbid anxiety disorder, then doxipin or amitriptyline was the preferred medication. Because there is no way to know with complete confidence whether a youngster is going to respond to an antidepressant, recommendations were offered regarding the duration that a medication would be tried before moving to an alternative one. The recommended length of a trial was 6 to 10 weeks. If the medication did not result in improvement during this time period, then an augmentation strategy would be initiated. If the medication regimen is successful, the recommended duration of treatment ranges from two months to two years

CASE STUDY

Bryan is a 10-year-old boy who manifests many of the signs of childhood depression. He expresses sadness, social withdrawal, and disinterest in sports, and increasing complaints of stomachaches. Over the past 10 weeks, Bryan has become increasingly disinterested in his studies. Although continuing to display excellent scores on standardized achievement tests, he has been receiving failing grades in many subject areas. His grades began deteriorating immediately after his father and mother separated. The separation resulted after a protracted period of conflict between his parents, which ultimately included both verbal and physical aggression. During the interval that immediately preceded the separation, the parents admit that they were preoccupied and had little inclination to interact with Bryan. Both parents have experienced depression in the past, and Bryan's mother currently is involved in therapy and receiving antidepressants. Bryan believes that he is at fault for his parents' separation and believes that there is little hope for a reconciliation between his parents. Although his father visits him on a weekly basis, Bryan is afraid that each visit is the last and that he will never see his father again.

Bryan's treatment included several cognitive–behavioral and family components. First, further investigation indicated that his mother was experiencing signs of depression. Consequently, she was encouraged to seek treatment. In addition to supportive psychotherapy, she was prescribed imipramine. Although his father refused to play an active role in treatment, Bryan's mother agreed to participate in Bryan's treatment. Within the context of cognitive–behavioral therapy, Bryan and his mother were taught how to enhance mood by increasing the rate of pleasant events. They also were instructed how maladaptive cognitions can affect mood and how to evaluate cognitions more realistically. To ensure these skills were practiced at home, his mother acted as cotherapist. Bryan's mother was encouraged to model more adaptive cognitions herself and to reinforce Bryan for completing homework assignments. Over the course of therapy, Bryan and his mother became quite adept at supporting each other for viewing the world more realistically. Bryan increasingly engaged in pleasant activities, both with his mother and independently. Over a 3-month period, Bryan's and his mother's depression gradually lifted. These positive results were maintained at a 1-year follow-up visit.

SUMMARY

The study of depressive disorders during childhood is at an early stage, in which many new questions about the disorder are arising. It is apparent that depressive disorders negatively affect a child's emotional, cognitive, motivational, and physical functioning. The diagnostic criteria for depressive disorders for children are similar to those for adults. Between 2% to 5% of children from the general population are experiencing either major depression or dysthymic disorder. Although depressive disorders are episodic, the episodes tend to be long-lasting and to recur. In most cases, the depressive disorder is accompanied by another psychological disorder. A number of models of depressive disorders have been proposed. Currently, it would appear as though none of these models adequately explains the etiology of depressive disorders during childhood, nor do they adequately take into account the developmental nature of childhood depressive disorders. It behooves theoreticians to consider the reciprocal interplay of cognitive, affective, physiological, and environmental variables in the construction of models that explain the development and maintenance of unipolar depressive disorders. It is apparent that each of these systems, along with stress, plays a crucial role in depressive disorders.

The family plays an important role in the development, maintenance, and prevention of depressive disorders during childhood. A pattern of family dysfunction appears to be emerging from the literature, in which the families are characterized by elevated levels of conflict, a less democratic style of management, and the use of coercive and psychologically destructive punitive techniques. These families are insulated from external sources of pleasure due to the fact that they engage in fewer pleasant activities of a social, recreational, or religious nature. There is strong evidence for a genetic basis to depressive disorders. It is highly likely that this genetic predisposition is activated in families that are characterized by the aforementioned family environment and parenting style.

A variety of adult treatment models has been used for the development of intervention programs for depressed youths. To date, the bulk of the evidence that supports their utility is based on nonclinic populations from school settings. In general, results suggest that a multicomponent and multimodal intervention that combines psychosocial, individual and family intervention, and pharmacological intervention is most likely to be effective. However, much additional research is needed in this area.

REFERENCES

Abramson, L. Y., Metalsky, G. I., & Alloy, L. B. (1989). Hopelessness depression: A theory-based subtype of depression. *Psychological Review, 96,* 358–372.

Abramson, L. Y., Seligman, M.E.P., & Teasdale, J. D. (1978). Learned helplessness in humans: Critique and reformulation. *Journal of Abnormal Psychology, 87,* 49–74.

Amanat, E., & Butler, C. (1984). Oppressive behaviors in the families of depressed children. *Family Therapy, 11,* 65–77.

Ambrosini, P. J., Bianchi, M. D., Rabinovich, H., & Elia, J. (1993). Antidepressant treatment in children and adolescents: I. Affective disorders. *Journal of the American Academy of Child and Adolescent Psychiatry, 32,* 1–6.

American Psychiatric Association. (1980). *Diagnostic and statistical manual of mental disorders* (3rd ed.). Washington, DC: American Psychiatric Association.

American Psychiatric Association. (1987). *Diagnostic and statistical manual of mental disorders* (3rd ed., rev.). Washington, DC: American Psychiatric Association.

American Psychiatric Association. (1994). *Diagnostic and statistical manual of mental disorders* (4th ed.). Washington, DC: American Psychiatric Association.

Anderson, J. C., Williams, S., McGee, R., & Silva, P. A. (1987). *DSM–III* disorders in pre-adolescent children. *Archives of General Psychiatry, 44,* 69–76.

Arieti, S., & Bemporad, J. R. (1980). The psychological organization of depression. *American Journal of Psychiatry, 137,* 1360–1365.

Asarnow, J. R., Tompson, M., Hamilton, E. B., Goldstein, M. J., & Guthrie, D. (1994). Family expressed emotion, childhood-onset depression, and childhood-onset schizophrenia spectrum disorders: Is expressed emotion a nonspecific correlate of child psychopathology or a specific risk factor for depression? *Journal of Abnormal Child Psychology, 22,* 129–146.

Barrera, M., & Garrison-Jones, C. (1992). Family and peer support as specific correlates of adolescent depressive symptoms. *Journal of Abnormal Child Psychology, 20,* 1–16.

Beardslee, W. R. (1993). The impact of parental affective disorder on depression in offspring: A longitudinal follow-up in a nonreferred sample. *Journal of the American Academy of Child and Adolescent Psychiatry, 32,* 723–731.

Beardslee, W. R., Bemporad, J., Keller, M. B., & Klerman, G. L. (1983). Children with parents with major affective disorder: A review. *American Journal of Psychiatry, 140,* 825–832.

Beck, A. T. (1967). *Depression: Clinical, experimental, and theoretical aspects.* New York: Harper & Row.

Beck, A. T., Rush, A. J., Shaw, B. F., & Emery, G. (1979). *Cognitive therapy of depression.* New York: Guilford.

Bird, H. R., Canino, G., Rubio-Stripes, Gould, M. S., Ribera, J., Sesman, M., Woodbury, M., Huertas-Goldman, S., Pagan, A., Sanchez-Lecay, A., & Moscaso, M. A. (1988). Estimates of prevalence of childhood maladjustment in a community survey in Puerto Rico. *Archives of General Psychiatry, 45,* 1120–1126.

Blechman, E. A., McEnroe, M. J., Carella, E. T., & Audette, D. P. (1986). Childhood competence and depression. *Journal of Abnormal Psychology, 95,* 223–227.

Brady, E. U., & Kendall, P. C. (1992). Comorbidity of anxiety and depression in children and adolescents. *Psychological Bulletin, 111,* 244–255.

Burke, P., & Puig-Antich, J. (1990). Psychobiology of childhood depression. In M. Lewis & S. M. Miller (Eds.), *Handbook of developmental psychopathology* (pp. 327–339). New York: Plenum.

Butler, L., Miezitis, S., Friedman, R., & Cole, E. (1980). The effects of two school-based intervention programs on depressed symptoms in preadolescents. *American Educational Research Journal, 17,* 111–119.

Campbell, M., & Cueva, J. E. (1995). Psychopharmacology in child and adolescent psychiatry: A review of the past seven years. Part II. *Journal of the American Academy of Child and Adolescent Psychiatry, 34,* 1262–1272.

Cantwell, D. P. (1982). Childhood depression: A review of current research. In B. B. Lahey & A. E. Kazdin (Eds.), *Advances in clinical child psychology* (Vol. 5, pp. 39–93) New York: Plenum.

Carey, M. P. (1993). Child and adolescent depression: Cognitive–behavioral strategies and interventions. In A. J. Finch, W. M. Nelson & E. S. Ott (Eds.), *Cognitive–behavioral procedures with children and adolescents.* Needham Heights, MA: Allyn & Bacon.

Carlson, G. A., & Cantwell, D. P. (1980). Unmasking masked depression in children and adolescents. *American Journal of Psychiatry, 137,* 445–449.

Carlson, G. A., & Kashani, J. H. (1988). Manic symptoms in a nonreferred adolescent population. *Journal of Affective Disorders, 15,* 219–226.

Carstens, M. E., Engelbrecht, A. H., Russell, V. A., van Zyl, A. M., & Talijaard, J. F. (1987). Biological markers in juvenile depression. *Psychiatry Research, 23,* 77–88.

Cicchetti, D. (1995). A developmental psychopathology perspective on child abuse and neglect. *Journal of the American Academy of Child and Adolescent Psychiatry, 34*, 541–566.

Clarke, G., Lewinsohn, P. M., & Hops, H. (1990). *Leader's manual for adolescent groups: Adolescent coping with depression course*. Eugene, OR: Castalia.

Clarkin, J. F., Haas, G. L., & Glick, I. D. (Eds.). (1988). *Affective disorders and the family: Assessment and treatment*. New York: Guilford.

Cole, D. A., & Rehm, L. P. (1986). Family interaction patterns and childhood depression. *Journal of Abnormal Child Psychology, 14*, 297–314.

Cole, D., & Turner, J., Jr. (1993). Models of cognitive mediation and moderation in child depression. *Journal of Abnormal Psychology, 102*, 271–281.

Cowen, P. J., & Wood, A. J. (1991). Biological markers of depression. *Psychological Medicine, 21*, 831–836.

Cumsille, P. E., & Epstein, N. (1994). Family cohesion, family adaptability, social support, and adolescent depressive symptoms in outpatient clinic families. *Journal of Family Psychology, 8*, 202–214.

Dillon, J. E., Tsai, L., & Alessi, N. E. (1996). Child and adolescent psychopharmacology: A decade of progress. In F. L. Mak & C. C. Nadelson (Eds.), *International Review of Psychiatry* (pp. 379–423). Washington, DC: American Psychiatric Association.

Dinan, T. G. (1994). Glucocorticoids and the genesis of depressive illness: A psychobiological model. *British Journal of Psychiatry, 164*, 365–371.

Downey, G., & Coyne, J. C. (1990). Children of depressed parents: An integrative review. *Psychological Bulletin, 108*, 50–76.

Emslie, G. J., Weinberg, W. A., Rush, A. J., Adams, R. M., & Rintelmann, J. W. (1990). Depressive symptoms by self-report in adolescence: Phase I of the development of a questionnaire for depression by self-report. *Journal of Child Neurology, 5*, 114–121.

Farmer, A. E. (1996). The genetics of depressive disorders. *International Review of Psychiatry, 8*, 369–372.

Finch, A. J., Lipovsky, J. A., & Casat, C. D. (1989). Anxiety and depression in children and adolescents: Negative affectivity or separate constructs. In D. Watson & P. C. Kendall (Eds.) *Anxiety and Depression* (pp. 171–202). New York: Academic Press.

Fincham, F. D., Grych, J. H., & Osborne, L. N. (1994). Does marital conflict cause child maladjustment? Directions and challenges for longitudinal research. *Journal of Family Psychology, 8*, 128–140.

Fine, M. J., & Carlson, C. (1992). *The handbook of family–school intervention: A systems perspective*. New York: Allyn & Bacon.

Forehand, R., McCombe, A., Long, N., Brody, G., & Fauber, R. (1988). Early adolescent adjustment to recent parental divorce: The role of interparental conflict and adolescent sex as mediating variables. *Journal of Consulting and Clinical Psychology, 56*, 624–627.

Fristad, M. A., Weller, E. B., & Weller, R. A. (1992). Bipolar disorder in children and adolescents. *Child and Adolescent Psychiatric Clinics of North America, 1*, 13–29.

Fristad, M. A., Weller, E. B., Weller, R. A., Teare, M., & Preskorn, S. H. (1988). Self-report vs. biological markers in assessment of childhood depression. *Journal of Affective Disorders, 15*, 339–345.

Garber, J., & Hilsman, R. (1992).Cognition, stress, and depression in children and adolescents. *Child & Adolescent Psychiatric Clinics of North America, 1*, 129–167.

Garrison, C. Z., Jackson, K. L., Marsteller, F., McKewon, R., & Addy, C. (1990). A longitudinal study of depressive symptomatology in young adolescents. *Journal of the American Academy of Adolescent Psychiatry, 29*, 580–585.

Gershon, E. S., Hamovit, J., Guroff, J. J., Dibble, E., Leckman, J. F., Sceery, W., Targum, S. D., Nurnberger, J. I., Goldin, L. R., & Bunney, W. E. (1982). A family study of schizoaffective, bipolar I, biopolar II, unipolar, and normal control probands. *Archives of General Psychiatry, 39*, 1157–1167.

Goodwin, F. (1982). *Depression and manic–depressive illness*. Bethesda, MD: National Institutes of Health.

Gotlib, I. H., & Hammen, C. L. (1992). *Psychological aspects of depression: Toward a cognitive–interpersonal integration*. New York: Wiley.

Hammen, C. (1991). *Depression runs in families*. New York: Springer-Verlag.

Harrington, R., Fudge, H., Rutter, M., Pickles, A., & Hill, J. (1991). Adult outcomes of childhood and adolescent depression: II. Links with antisocial disorders. *Journal of the American Academy of Child & Adolescent Psychiatry, 30*, 434–439.

Henninger, G. R., Delgado, P. L., & Charney, D. S. (1996). The revised monoamine theory of depression: A modulatory role for monoamines, based on new findings from monoamine depletion experiments in humans. *Pharmacopsychiatry, 29*, 2–11.

Kahn, J. S., Kehle, T. J., Jenson, W. R., & Clark, E. (1990). Comparison of cognitive–behavioral, relaxation, and self-modeling interventions for depression among middle-school students. *School Psychology Review, 19*, 196–211.

Kalat, J. W. (1992). *Biological psychology*. Belmont, CA: Wadsworth.

Kanfer, F. H. (1970). Self-regulation: Research, issues and speculations. In C. Neuringer & J. L. Michael (Eds.), *Behavioral modification in clinical psychology* (pp. 178–220). New York: Appleton-Century-Crofts.

Kashani, J. H., Canfield, L. A., Borduin, C. M., Soltys, S. M., & Reid, J. C. (1994). Perceived family and social support: Impact on children. *Journal of American Academy of Child Adolescent Psychiatry, 33*, 819–823.

Kashani, J. H., & Carlson, G. A. (1987). Seriously depressed preschoolers. *American Journal of Psychiatry, 144*, 348–350.

Kashani, J. H., Ray, J. S., & Carlson, G. A. (1984). Depression and depressive-like states in preschool-age children in a child development unit. *American Journal of Psychiatry, 141*, 1397–1402.

Kashani, J. H., Venzke, R., & Millar, E. A. (1981). Depression in children admitted to hospital for orthopaedic procedures. *British Journal of Psychiatry, 138*, 21–25.

Kaslow, N., & Rehm, L. (1983). Childhood depression. In R. J. Morris & T. R. Kratochwill (Eds.). *The practice of child therapy* (pp. 27–51). New York: Pergamon.

Kaslow, N. J., Stark, K. D., Printz, B., Livingston, R., & Tsai, S. (1992). Cognitive triad inventory for children: Development and relationship to depression and anxiety. *Journal of Clinical Child Psychology, 21*, 339–347.

Kaufman, J. (1991). Depressive disorders in maltreated child. *Journal of the American Academy of Child Abuse, 30*, 257–265.

Kazdin, A. E., Esveldt-Dawson, K., Sherick, R. B., & Colbus, D. (1985). Assessment of overt behavior and childhood depression among psychiatrically disturbed children. *Journal of Consulting and Clinical Psychology, 53*, 201–210.

Kendall, P. C., & Ingram, R. E. (1987). The future of the cognitive assessment of anxiety: Let's get specific. In L. Michelson & M. Ascher (Eds.), *Anxiety and stress disorders: Cognitive–behavioral assessment and treatment* (pp. 89–104). New York: Guilford.

Kendall, P. C., Stark, K. D., & Adam, T. (1990). Cognitive deficit of cognitive distortion in childhood depression? *Journal of Abnormal Child Psychology, 18*, 267–283.

Kendler, K. S., & Karkowski-Shuman, L. (1997). Stressful life events and genetic liability to major depression: Genetic control of exposure to the environment? *Psychological Medicine, 27*, 539–547.

Kendler, K. S., Neale, M. C., Kessler, R. C., Heath, A. C., & Eaves, L. J. (1992). A population-based twin study of major depression in women. The impact of varying definitions. *Archives of General Psychiatry, 49*, 257–266.

Klein, D. N., Clark, D. C., Dansky, L., & Margolis, E. T. (1988). Dysthymia in offspring of parents with primary unipolar affective disorder. *Journal of Abnormal Psychology, 97*, 265–274.

Klein, D. N., Depue, R. A., & Slater, J. F. (1985). Cyclothymia in the adolescent offspring of parents with bipolar affective disorder. *Journal of Abnormal Psychology, 94*, 115–127.

Kolb, B., & Whishaw, I. Q. (1996). *Fundamentals of human neuropsychology*. San Francisco: Freeman.

Kovacs, M., & Beck, A. T. (1977). An empirical clinical approach towards a definition of childhood depression. In J. G. Schulterbrandt & A. Raskin (Eds.), *Depression in childhood: Diagnosis, treatment, and conceptual models* (pp. 1–25). New York: Raven.

Kovacs, M., Feinberg, T. L., Crouse-Novak, M., Paulauskas, S. L., Pollack, M., & Finkelstein, R. (1984). Depressive disorders in childhood: I. A longitudinal prospective study of characteristics and recovery. *Archives of General Psychiatry, 41*, 643–649.

Koplewics, H. S., Klass, E., & Kafantaris, V. (1993). The psychopharmacology of childhood and adolescent depression. In H. S Koplewics & E. Klass (Eds.),

Kovacs, M., Gatsonis, C., Paulauskas, S., & Richards, C. (1989). Depressive disorders in child-hood: IV. A longitudinal study of comorbidity with and risk for anxiety disorders. *Archives of General Psychiatry, 46*, 776–782.

Lewinsohn, P. M. (1974). A behavioral approach to depression. In R. J. Friedman & M. M. Katz (Eds), *The psychology of depression: Contemporary theory and research* (pp. 50–87). New York, NY: Wiley.

Lewinsohn, P. M. (1975). The behavioral study and treatment of depression. In M. Hersen, R. M. Eisler & P. M. Miller (Eds.), *Progress in behavior modification* (Vol. 1, pp. 16–64). New York: Academic Press.

Lewinsohn, P. M., Clarke, G., Hops, H., & Andrews, J. (1990). Cognitive–behavioral treatment for depressed adolescents. *Behavioral Therapy, 21*, 385–401.

Lewinsohn, P. M., & Hoberman, H. M. (1982). Depression. In A. S. Bellack, M. Hershen & A. E. Kazdin (Eds.), *International handbook of behavior modification and therapy.* (pp. 397–432) New York: Plenum.

Lewinsohn, P. M., Hoberman, H. M., & Clarke, G. N. (1989). The Coping with Depression Course: Review and future directions. *Canadian Journal of Behavioral Science, 21*, 470–493.

MacKinnon-Lewis, C., & Lofquist, A. (1996). Antecedents and consequences of boys' depres-sion and aggression: Family and school linkages. *Journal of Family Psychology, 10*, 490–500.

McCauley, E., & Myers, K. (1992). Family interactions in mood disordered youth. *Child & Adoles-cent Psychiatric Clinics of North America, 1*, 111–127.

McCauley, E., Myers, K., Mitchell, J., Calderon, R., Schloredt, K., & Treder, R. (1993). Depression in young people: Initial presentation and clinical course. *Journal of the American Academy of Child and Adolescent Psychiatry, 32*, 714–722.

McCracken, J. T., & Cantwell, D. P. (1992). Management of Child and adolescent mood disor-ders. *Child and Adolescent Psychiatric Clinics of North America, 1*, 229–255.

McGee, R., & Williams, S. (1988). A longitudinal study of depression in nine year old children. *Journal of the American Academy of Child and Adolescent Psychiatry, 27*, 12–20.

Mendlewicz, J., & Rainer, J. D. (1977). Adoption study supporting genetic transmission in manic-depressive illness. *Nature, 268*, 327–329.

Messer, S. C., & Gross, A. M. (1995). Childhood depression and family interaction: A naturalistic observation study. *Journal of Clinical Child Psychology, 24*, 77–88.

Mitchell, J., McCauley, E., Burke, P., Calderon, R., & Schloredt, K. (1989). Psychopathology in parents of depressed children and adolescents. *Journal of the American Academy of Child and Adolescent Psychiatry, 28*, 352–357.

Mufson, L., & Fairbanks, J. (1996). Interpersonal psychotherapy for depressed adolescents: A one-year naturalistic follow-up study. *Journal of American Academy of Child and Adolescent Psychiatry, 35*, 1145–1155.

Mufson, L., Moreau, D., Weissman, M. M., & Klerman, G. L. (1993). *Interpersonal psychotherapy for depressed adolescents.* New York: Guilford.

Mufson, L., Moreau, D., Weissman, M., Wickramaratne, P., Marin, J., & Samoilov, A. (1994). Mod-ification of interpersonal psychotherapy with depressed adolescents (IPT): Phase I & II stud-ies. *Journal of the American Academy of Child and Adolescent Psychiatry, 33*, 695–705.

Nottelmann, E. D. (1995). Bipolar affective disorder in children and adolescents. *Journal of the American Academy of Child and Adolescent Psychiatry, 34*, 705–709.

Newman, J. P., & Garfinkel, B. D. (1992). Major depression in childhood and adolescence. In S. R. Hooper, G. W. Hynd & R. E. Mattison (Eds.), *Child psychopathology: Diagnosis criteria and clinical assessment* (pp. 65–106. Hillsdale, NJ: Lawrence Erlbaum Associates.

Orvaschel, H., Walsh-Allis, G., & Ye, W. (1988). Psychopathology in children of parents with re-current depression. *Journal of Abnormal Child Psychology, 16*, 17–28.

Orvaschel, H., Weissman, M. M., & Kidd, K. K. (1980). Children and depression. *Journal of Affec-tive Disorders, 2*, 1–16.

Poznanski, E. O., & Zrull, J. P. (1970). Childhood depression: Clinical characteristics of overtly depressed children. *Archives of General Psychiatry, 23*, 8–15.

Prieto, S. L., Cole, D. A., & Tageson, C. W. (1992). Depressive self-schemas in clinic and nonclinic children. *Cognitive Therapy and Research, 16*, 521–534.

Puig-Antich, J. (1982). Major depression and conduct disorder in prepuberty. *Journal of the American Academy of Child Psychiatry, 21*, 118–128.

Puig-Antich, J. (1986). Psychobiological markers: Effects of age and puberty. In M. Rutter, C. Izard, P. B. Read (Eds), *Depression in young people* (pp. 341–381). New York: Guilford.

Puig-Antich, J., Lukens, E., Davies, M., Goetz, D., Brennan-Quattrock, J., & Todak, G. (1985a). Psychosocial functioning in prepubertal major depressive disorders: I. Interpersonal relationships during the depressive episode. *Archives of General Psychiatry, 42*, 500–507.

Puig-Antich, J., Lukens, E., Davies, M., Goetz, D., Brennan-Quattrock, J., & Todak, G. (1985b). Psychosocial functioning in prepubertal major depressive disorders: II. Interpersonal relationships after sustained recovery from affective episode. *Archives of General Psychiatry, 42*, 511–517.

Puig-Antich, J., Perel, J. M., Lupatkin, W., Chambers, W. J., Tabrizi, M. A., King, J., Goetz, T., Davies, M., & Stiller, R. L. (1987). Imipramine in prepubertal major depression disorders. *Archives of General Psychiatry, 44*, 81–89.

Puig-Antich, J., & Weston, B. (1983). The diagnosis and treatment of major depressive disorder in childhood. *Annual Review of Medicine, 34*, 231–245.

Radziszewska, B., Richardson, J. L., Dent, C. W., & Flay, B. R. (1996) Parenting style and adolescent depressive symptoms, smoking, and academic achievement: Ethnic, gender, and SES differences. *Journal of Behavioral Medicine, 19*, 289–305.

Rehm, L. P. (1977). A self-control model of depression. *Behavior Therapy, 8*, 787–804.

Reynolds, W. M., & Coates, K. I. (1986). A comparison of cognitive–behavioral therapy and relaxation training for the treatment of depression. *Journal of Consulting and Clinical Psychology, 54*, 654–660.

Rutter, M., & Quinton, P. (1984). Parental psychiatric disorder: Effects on children. *Psychological Medicine, 14*, 853–880.

Ryan, N. D. (1992). Pharmacological treatment of major depression. In M. Shafii & S. L. Shafii (Eds.), *Clinical guide to depression in children and adolescents* (pp. 219–232). Washington, DC: American Psychiatric Association.

Schildkraut, J. (1965). The catecholamine hypothesis of affective disorders: A review of supporting evidence. *American Journal of Psychiatry, 122*, 508–522.

Schwartz, C. E., Dorer, D. J., Beardslee, W. R., Lavori, P. W., & Keller, M. B. (1990) Maternal expressed emotion and parental affective disorder: Risk for childhood depressive disorder, substance abuse, or conduct disorder. *Journal of Psychiatric Research, 24*, 231–250.

Seligman, M.E.P. (1975). *Helplessness.* San Francisco: Freeman.

Shelton, R. C., Hollon, S. D., Purdon, S. E., & Loosen, P. T. (1991). Biological and psychological aspects of depression. *Behavior Therapy, 22*, 201–228.

Siever, L. J., & Davis, K. L. (1985). Overview: Toward a dysregulation hypothesis of depression. *American Journal of Psychiatry, 142*, 1017–1031.

Stark, K. D. (1990). *Childhood depression: School-based intervention.* New York: Guilford.

Stark, K. D., Humphrey, L. L., Crook, K., & Lewis, K. (1990). Perceived family environments of depressed and anxious children. *Journal of Abnormal Child Psychology, 18*, 527–547.

Stark, K. D., & Kendall, P. C. (1996). *ACTION: Therapist's manual for treating depressed children.* Philadelphia: Workbook.

Stark, K. D., Laurent, J., Livingston, R., Boswell, J., & Swearer, S. (in press). Implications of research for the treatment of depression during childhood. *Journal of Applied and Preventive Psychology.*

Stark, K. D., Reynolds, W. M., & Kaslow, N. (1987). A comparison of the relative efficacy of self-control therapy and a behavioral problem solving therapy for depression in children. *Journal of Abnormal Child Psychology, 15*, 91–113.

Stark, K. D., Rouse, L. W., & Livingston, R. (1991). Treatment of depression during childhood and adolescence: Cognitive and behavioral procedures for the individual and family. In P. C. Kendall (Ed.), *Child and Adolescent Therapy: Cognitive–Behavioral Procedures* (pp. 165–206). New York: Guilford.

Stark, K. D., Schmidt, K., & Joiner, T. E. (1996). Depressive cognitive triad: Relationship to severity of depressive symptoms in children, parents' cognitive triad, and perceived parental messages about the child, him or herself, the world, and the future. *Journal of Abnormal Child Psychology, 24*, 615–625.

Strober, M., Freeman, R., & Rigali, J. (1990). The pharmacotherapy of depressive illness in adolescence: I. An open label trial of imipramine. *Psychopharmacology Bulletin, 26*, 80–84.

Strober, M., Freeman, R., Rigali, J., Schmidt, S., & Diamond, R. (1992). The pharmacotherapy of depressive illness in adolescence: II. Effects of lithium augmentation in nonresponders to imipramine. Special section: New developments in pediatric psychopharmacology. *Journal of the American Academy of Child and Adolescent Psychiatry, 31*, 16–20.

Strober, M., Lampert, C., Schmidt, S., & Morrell, W. (1993). The course of major depressive disorder in adolescents: I. Recovery and risk of manic switching in a follow-up of psychotic and nonpsychotic subtypes. *Journal of the American Academy of Child and Adolescent Psychiatry, 32*, 34–42.

Stubbe, D. E., Zahner, G. E., Goldstein, M. J., & Leckman, J. F. (1993) Diagnostic specificity of a brief measure of expressed emotion: A community study of children. *Journal of Child Psychology and Psychiatry and Allied Disciplines, 34,* 139–154.

Teicher, M. H., Glod, C. A., Harper, D. H., Magnus, E., Brasher, C., Wren, F., & Pahlavan, K. (1993). Locomotor activity in depressed children and adolescents: I. Circadian dysregulation. *Journal of the American Academy of Child and Adolescent Psychiatry, 32*, 760–769.

Thapar, A., & McGuffin, P. (1996). The genetic etiology of childhood depressive symptoms: A developmental perspective. *Development & Psychopathology, 8* , 751–760.

Toth, S., Manly, J. T., & Cicchetti, D. (1992). Child maltreatment and vulnerability to depression. *Development and Psychopathology, 4*, 97–112.

Tsuang, M. T., & Farone, S. V. (1990). *The genetics of mood disorders.* Baltimore: Johns Hopkins University Press.

Turk, D., & Salovey, P. (1985). Cognitive structures, cognitive processes, and cognitive–behavior modification: I. Client issues. *Cognitive Therapy and Research, 9*, 1–19.

Vitiello, B., & Jensen, P. S. (1995). Developing clinical trials in children and adolescents. *Psychopharmacology Bulletin, 31*, 75–81.

Weintraub, S. (1987). Risk factors in schizophrenia: The Stony Brook high-risk project. *Schizophrenia Bulletin, 13*, 439–450.

Weissman, M. M., Prusoff, B. A., Gammon, G. D., Merkangas, K. R., Leckman, J. F., & Kidd, K. K. (1984). Psychopathology in children (6–10) of depressed and normal parents. *Journal of the American Academy of Child Psychiatry, 23*, 78–84.

Werry, J. S., & Aman, M. G. (1993). *Practitioner's guide to psyhoactive drugs for children and adolescents.* New York: Plenum.

West, M. O., & Prinz, R. J. (1987). Parental alcoholism and childhood psychopathology. *Psychological Bulletin, 102*, 204–218.

Williamson, D. E. (1995). A case-control family history study of depression in adolescents. *Journal of the American Academy of Child and Adolescent Psychiatry, 34*, 1596–1608.

Williamson, D. E., Ryan, N. D., Birmaher, B., & Dahl, R. E. (1995). A case-control family history study of depression in adolescents. *Journal of the American Academy of Child and Adolescent Psychiatry, 34,* 1596–1607.

Mental Retardation: Causes and Effects

Alan A. Baumeister
Louisiana State University

Alfred A. Baumeister
Vanderbilt University

The most general description of mental retardation typically is presented in terms of an individual's failure to demonstrate skills that are age-, cultural-, and situational-appropriate. Mental retardation is a problem of human development, an expression of behavioral differences among people as reflected in speed and quality of adaptation and adjustment to changing demands of environments. Although adaptation can take many forms in different situations, the essence of this fundamental quality or attribute, for layman and professional alike, is inherent in the term commonly known as *intelligence*.

Despite obvious individual differences in many characteristics among people with mental retardation, they do, both by intuition and formal definition, share one common feature: diminished intelligence. Concepts of mental retardation and intelligence, by tradition and practice, are inextricably interwoven. An understanding of mental retardation demands a consideration of intelligence, notwithstanding the ageless and acrimonious debate as to the essential nature or meaning of "intelligence." Broadly conceived, intelligence refers to ability to solve problems regarded as important within a cultural milieu. Because of commonly accepted defining features that incorporate cultural standards, mental retardation is as much a sociological as a biological concept.

Linkage of mental retardation to the construct of intelligence, along with myriad other social implications concerning causes and consequences, has resulted in a history throughout which the concept of mental retardation has been buffeted about in divisive and frequently contradictory ways. Practical effects of value judgments are enormous because they determine who is included and excluded from health and education services and even which services are available. In fact, the concept of mental retardation is so heavily laden with sociopolitical ramifications that scientific and professional distinctions frequently become obscured or compromised with respect to such basic issues as definition, etiology, clinical description, epidemiology, treatment, and prognosis. Both professional practice and research, particularly in behavioral and educational domains, often tend to be reactive rather than proactive. For the individual who is affected, these are not trivial considerations.

In point of fact, the constellation of etiologies, symptoms, impairments, and outcomes that encompass mental retardation is enormous. Although a particular biological cause sometimes may be observed or inferred, in most instances, factors controlling an individual's fate are multiply determined. Of course, in some cases impairments are so profound that an individual would be handicapped in practically every setting, with little doubt about diagnosis, at least in a functional sense. Extreme intellectual deviation could be therefore considered absolute. More common, however, are instances where impairments are milder and more significant or apparent in one context than another—that is, *relative* retardation.

Basic and applied scientific considerations are, or course, vitally important to understanding mental retardation. Indeed, the only linear and predictable features of the knowledge base are to be found in research domains, particularly biological aspects. But where treatment, broadly construed, is concerned, the history of the field has been characterized by sharp ideological shifts between epochs of pessimism and optimism, fear and compassion, denial and acceptance, nature and nurture.

CLINICAL DESCRIPTION

Definition and Classification of Mental Retardation

Numerous systems of classification and terminology are currently used in the United States, although differences among them tend to be variations of degree rather than of kind. On the other hand, over the years a great deal of controversy, sometimes blatantly contentious, has surrounded problems of classification and terminology. Some of the major disputes include: (a) continued reliance on the construct of general intelligence as the principal defining feature; (b) relative importance and quality of measures of adaptive behavior; (c) malleability of intelligence, especially in the context of the nature–nurture wars; (d) social stigmatization, particularly for minority groups; (e) medical versus social explanatory models; (f) vested disciplinary interests; (g) implications for research; (h) precision of definition; (i) role of etiology and prognosis; and (j) arbitrariness as reflected in shifting values driven by consensus rather than science.

The American Association on Mental Retardation. The most widely employed definition, classification, and terminology system is that promulgated by the American Association on Mental Retardation (AAMR), formerly the American Association on Mental Deficiency (AAMD). The first AAMD manual on terminology was published in 1921. Updated and expanded editions have appeared in 1959, 1961, 1973, 1977, 1983, and 1992.

In many respects, the recent version represents the greatest departure from previous conceptions, particularly with respect to the issue of classification. The most significant change is that traditional classification according to IQ-defined levels of mental retardation has been abandoned in favor of classification based on the specific needs of the individual and levels and types of support required. Nevertheless, the three traditional operational characteristics remain: (a) subaverage intellectual functioning—an IQ of between 70 to 75 or below; (b) concurrent limitations in adaptive behavior or functioning (10 domains); and (c) existing before age 18.

The definition of mental retardation advocated by the AAMR in 1992 (Luckasson et al., 1992) eschews reference to measurement of IQ in terms of standard deviations—a curious departure from informed professional practice and conventional psychometric principles. The major standardized individual tests of intelligence (Wechsler Scales and the Stanford–Binet) have different standard deviations, meaning that the scores obtained from these instruments are not exactly equivalent. The practical effect of this change is to diagnose mental retardation by a low IQ score (75 to 70 or below), irrespective of the psychometric properties of the instrument.

As we observed, the major change reflected in the latest AAMR terminology system concerns classification. Traditionally the terms *mild, moderate, severe,* and *profound* have been used to classify people with mental retardation, usually on the basis of IQ scores. The new system advocates a multi-dimensional approach: (a) intellectual functioning and adaptive skills, (b) psychological and emotional considerations, (c) etiology considerations, and (d) environmental considerations. Purportedly, the intent is to avert categorical labels and to design flexible and individually determined services by focusing on multiple areas of functional limitations.

To say that the recent AAMR definition, terminology, and classification system has not come in for blistering attack would be a grievous understatement. At stake are numerous issues—clinical, programmatic, research—as summarized by MacMillan and Reschly (1997). The current AAMR definition is heavily invested in an egalitarian advocacy position. In particular, diagnosis, classification, and services are construed within an explicit inclusionary philosophy. According to Luckasson et al (1992), this orientation represents a "fundamental paradigm shift" (p. 135) that requires "significant changes in thinking" (p. 11) in order to "guide and shape future research and practice" (p. 11) that will, in turn, "demand a redirection of services" (p. 135). The heavy emphasis on inclusionary doctrine and consumerism that permeates the entire Manual is, as Baumeister (in press) argued, fundamentally at cross-purposes with objective scientific inquiry and research progress toward understanding, preventing, and treating mental retardation.

Furthermore, the financial implications are enormous. Consider the major defining feature: IQ between 70 and 75. From a statistical model that assumes a normal distribution of IQ scores ($m = 100, SD = 15$), about 2% of the population has an IQ below 70. But the percentage of people below 75 is about 5%, leaving 3% in that diagnostically ambiguous range. When these percentages are converted into numbers of people, eligibility for services is left in doubt for literally millions of people. In addition, when the standard error of measurement of the most commonly used intelligence tests is taken into account, the upper boundary becomes an IQ of about 80—including huge numbers of people. Clearly, this is an arbitrary definition designed, from an advocacy standpoint, to be inclusive as possible.

American Psychiatric Association. The *Diagnostic and Statistical Manual of Mental Disorders* (4th ed. [*DSM–IV*]; American Psychiatric Association, 1994) defines mental retardation exactly in the same manner as AAMR, (a) IQ of 75 to 70 or below, (b) significant limitations in at least two skill areas, and (c) onset below age 18 years. However, there are some differences. Although acknowledging the need for clinical assessment of adaptive behavior and recognizing contextual and social constraints in diagnosing mental retardation, the *DSM–IV* continues the tradition of describing levels of severity based on degree of measured intellectual impairment. These include (a) mild (IQ 50–55 to approximately 70), (b) moderate (IQ 35–40 to 50–55), (c) severe (IQ 20–25 to 35–40), and profound (IQ 20–25). In addition, when there is a strong presumption of mental retardation but, because of severe impairment or uncooperativeness, the individual cannot be assessed by conventional intelligence tests, a fifth category is employed: mental retardation, severity unspecified. This would be particularly applicable with infants.

American Psychological Association. The most recent entry into the definitional and terminology dispute is the American Psychological Association (Jacobson & Mulick, 1996). Again, the same basic criteria are employed: significant limitations in general intellectual functioning, impairments in adaptive functioning, and probable onset before age of 22 years. Note that in this case, age of onset is somewhat higher than in the other definitions described, but is consistent with precedents set forth in federal legislation such as the Developmental Disabilities Act (ADA, 1990, 42 U.S.C. 12101), and the Individuals with Disabilities Education Act of 1990 (IDEA), formerly the Education for All Handicapped Children Act (Public Law 94–142).

The American Psychological Association *Manual of Diagnosis and Professional Practice in Mental Retardation* is by far the most comprehensive and current exposition of assessment, diagnosis, treatment, legal considerations, prevention, advocacy, and classification concepts. Numerous topics are covered, both in historical context and within existing scientific foundations. In addition, attention is directed to the growth of antiscience sentiments and their effects on social role representations, a point emphasized in greater detail by Baumeister (in press).

Unlike the other organizations (AAMR and American Psychiatric Association), the *Manual* provides much more complete rationales for all decision rules. However, definition and classification are still primarily derived from psychometric rather than etiological distinctions. Classification (mild, moderate, severe, and profound) is based on IQ ranges and concurrent adaptive limitations. With regard to the former, IQ ranges are essentially the same as those suggested by the American Psychiatric Association, but include standard deviations. Both mild and moderate categories require adaptive limitations in two or more domains. For more serious cases, deficits are required in all realms of adaptive behavior.

Intelligence as the Primary Feature

As previously emphasized, the most prominent defining feature of mental retardation is low intelligence. The term "intelligence" has been and continues to be a rich source of acrimonious controversy. Few other human characteristics have been the subject of more speculation, interest, and polemics. Nevertheless, a century of debate and research has failed to produce a consensus as to the essential meaning of intelligence. There probably exists today a wider array of views and theories than ever.

In a pragmatic sense, we are dependent on a "stipulative nominal" definition of intelligence and, therefore, of mental retardation. A stipulative nominal definition refers to how a word is used as specified by the user. The eminent historian of psychology Edwin Boring, perhaps out of exasperation, concluded that "Intelligence is what intelligence tests measure" (Boring, 1923). Such caveats notwithstanding, the IQ is the most robust predictor of performance that psychology has ever produced—whether indexed by academic achievement, adaptive behavior, job success, income, social status, mental health, and so on (Gottfredson, 1997; Lubinski & Humphreys, 1997).

Nevertheless, reliance on the IQ conceals enormous heterogeneity with respect to etiology, disease pathogenesis, symptomatology, and outcome. Although intelligence tests typically serve administrative needs well, beyond initial diagnosis they are of limited value for purposes of intervention and treatment at the individual level. Results of intelligence testing yield little information pertaining to myriad causes and consequences of mental retardation. Indeed, there is generally greater intra- and interperson variability within groups of people designated as mentally retarded than among people considered to be within the normal range of ability.

When two individuals (one with Down syndrome and another with fetal alcohol syndrome) have IQs of 50, both may be diagnosed as mentally retarded—but very little else can be said about their comparability, especially with respect to cause, comorbidity, prevention, and prognosis. The only shared aspect, and not a very programmatically useful one at that, is moderate or "serious" retardation. Measured intelligence reveals nothing about how these deviations in development occur, whether they are endogenous or exogenous, whether they present differing medical and/or behavioral complications, whether the basic underlying condition is alterable, and how individual development will proceed. The fact is that different diagnostic entities often exhibit distinctive physical and behavioral profiles. Moreover, intelligence tests typically are regarded as measures of maximal rather than typical performance.

Adaptive Behavior

Functional limitations include deficits in adaptive skill areas such as communication, self-care, home living, social skills, community use, self-direction, health and safety, functional academics, leisure, and work. Collectively, these are the behavioral or coping skills that are typically displayed when the individual confronts environmental demands in daily experience (Widaman & McGrew, 1996). The most recent AAMR definition (Luckasson et al., 1992) requires demonstrable limitations in 2 or more of these 10 domains, impairments construed and evaluated in terms of what is typical for the individual's age group and cultural milieu.

The relatively high prevalence of mental retardation during the school years is undoubtedly due to the fact that academic skills, which can be readily and reliably measured, are salient indicators of adaptation. This is a circumstance that led to identification of the "6-hour retarded child"—that is, the child who displays relatively poor academic performance, but whose behavior outside of school is not notably deficient.

Measurement of adaptive skills in areas other than academic performance is not so clear-cut, nor is the failure to meet the standard of adequacy so unquestionably apparent. In fact, reliable clinical evaluation of functional deficits has proven to be an elusive goal. Although the 10 skill domains identified by the AAMR undoubtedly are important behavioral considerations that describe human adaptation at a general level, they do not lend themselves readily to valid and reliable measurement. Nor are there any empirical studies that demonstrate the independent existence of these domains (MacMillan, Gresham, & Siperstein, 1993). It is in this aspect of ascertainment where clinical judgment, notoriously unreliable, greatly influences the diagnostic process and, not incidentally, accounts for the greatest amount of disagreement among clinicians.

Objective measures of adaptive behavior may, in some situations, provide useful adjunctive information for diagnostic refinement, treatment, and education. But such indicators are not as central to definition and classification as is the intelligence quotient and etiology. Primarily for these reasons, along with other theoretical and psychometric considerations, some have argued that the IQ and etiology should be the only formal bases for identification of mental retardation (e.g., Clausen, 1967; Zigler, Balla, & Hodapp, 1984).

There are many adaptive behavior scales of varying quality. The AAMD Adaptive Behavior Scale (Nihira, Foster, Shellhaas, & Leland, 1975), the Vineland Social Maturity Scale (Sparrow, Balla, & Cicchetti, 1984), and the Scales of Independent Behavior (Bruninks, Woodcock, Weatherman, & Hill, 1984) are the most widely applied behavior assessment instruments, although only the last two are adequately normed on national samples. Measurements typically are obtained through interviews with informants, such as parents and teachers, who are presumed to be very familiar with the client. However, there are significant shortcomings. For example, standardized scales pay relatively little formal attention to the constraints and demands of the environment, and different environments define competence differently.

Although there can be little doubt that biological perturbations—mild or severe, endogenous or exogenous, localized or systemic—are implicated in all cases of mental retardation, severity of handicap only can be gauged against the ability of the individual to adapt to demands and constraints of particular environments. Adaptive behavior scales tap some aspects of some of these environments, but they are far from a systematic taxonomy. The quandary facing educators and clinicians is generally one of what particular individuals can do in the environment in which they must function—not of what they could do if environmental circumstances were ideal.

Another misleading feature of the standard conceptualization of mental retardation in terms of a twofold definitional system is that these dimensions are not orthogonal. Adaptive behavior scores can be predicted from IQ, although at higher functional levels, the correlation drops for some areas of adaptive behavior. Another problem is that standard measures of adaptive behavior do not generally meet acceptable criteria for reliability in psychometric terms. Moreover, the construct validity of these measures is not established.

Despite serious limitations in such interview-based scales, in all likelihood psychologists will continue to use them, for these measures may yield some information about specific behavioral deficits useful in program development. To the extent that adaptive behavior scales provide information about distinctive behavioral deficits, they are not necessarily redundant with general intelligence.

Etiological Classification

Classification is a necessary process for purposes of resource allocation, program development, prevention, treatment, and research. Clearly, different systems are more or less appropriate depending on the purpose. Of course, the problem with any system that purports to cluster people according to fairly broad and nondifferentiating characteristics is that relevant information will be sacrificed or obscured. Measures may be high in sensitivity (identifying all those who have a problem) but critically low in specificity (identifying those who do not have the problem). The wider the diagnostic net, the higher the sensitivity and the lower the specificity. The challenge is to devise classification taxonomies that are compatible and that, when used in tandem, provide a comprehensive, coherent, and useful model for understanding and managing the problem of mental retardation.

Several classification systems have been proposed, although those that empha-size functional rather than pathological processes still dominate. Nevertheless, medi-cal taxonomy is important from the standpoint of research, prevention, treatment, and prognosis. Since the late 1970s, there has been a virtual explosion of information regarding biological aspects of mental retardation, particularly in genetics.

The World Health Organization Classification (1978) of Diseases (ICD–9); is the most widely used because it is a comprehensive system for classifying medical con-ditions (although the World Health Organization also classifies mental retardation by grade of intellectual defect). In 1985, the U.S. Health Care Finance Administration is-sued regulations requiring use of ICD–9 codes for Medicaid and Medicare reimburse-ment. Given that huge sums of money are involved, it is not surprising that, of practical necessity, this ruling has had a significant influence on medical classification systems employed at the state level.

In addition to a revised definition of mental retardation, the AAMR has proposed a coding scheme (Dimension III) for purposes of classification based on etiology con-siderations (Luckasson et al., 1992). Most of these are biomedical conditions, but the system does include mental retardation resulting from psychosocial factors. Familial considerations, involving polygenic heritability are omitted from this system, un-like other versions of the *Manual*. The etiological organization moves from broad cat-egories, primarily based on timing of occurrence, to increasingly specific conditions. The major generic categories are presented in Table 16.1. It should be emphasized that many conditions, such as hydrocephalus, can be either inborn or acquired, or are secondary to other diseases.

Within this etiologic classification system literally hundreds of distinct conditions can be enumerated. Of course, not all inevitably result in mental retardation for every afflicted individual. Whether the causative agent is genetic or environmental, variabil-ity of phenotypic expression is the rule, not the exception. Gene effects are usually pleiotropic. Nevertheless, the risk for mental retardation is significantly elevated when a child presents with one or more of these diagnoses.

Classification based on etiology is constantly changing because of rapid growth of genetic and medical knowledge and burgeoning technology, especially in the fields of neurodiagnostic imaging, neurometabolic analysis, cytogenetics, and molecular genetics. Consider, for instance, that several hundred genetic diseases are associated with mental retardation (Wahlstrom, 1990). Increasingly, more conditions can be identified through sophisticated systems for analyzing organization of DNA. One obvi-ous consideration, having both theoretical and immediate practical implications, in-volves the problem of relying on the generic condition of "mental retardation" as a unitary and inclusive diagnostic entity, even for administrative purposes. The causes, outcomes, disease-course, and strategies for intervention and prevention are so di-verse that serious questions must be raised as to whether such a heterogeneous array of biological and behavioral manifestations can be meaningfully embraced under a common rubric. From etiologic, clinical, and scientific points of view, the general concept of mental retardation is no longer a particularly useful designation, except as a reference point for much more refined analysis that emphasizes causal consider-ations (Baumeister, 1997).

Etiological classification does present some problems. For one, costs of diagnostic assessments are frequently high. For another, even knowing the specific cause of mental retardation may not suggest alternative treatments for treatment or appropri-ate care. These problems notwithstanding, for an ever-increasing number of people, improved understanding of etiology increasingly will provide possibilities for treat-

TABLE 16.1

Examples of Disorders Resulting in Mental Retardation

1. Prenatal causes

    A. Chromosome disorders (e.g., Down syndrome and Fragile X)

    B. Syndrome disorders (e.g., neurofibromatosis)

    C. Inborn error of metabolism (e.g., phenylketonuria)

    D. Developmental disorders (e.g., neural tube defects such as spina bifida)

    E. Intrauterine malnutrition (e.g., fetal alcohol syndrome and other prenatal toxicants)

    F. Infection (e.g., toxoplasmosis)

    G. Maternal disease (diabetes mellitus)

    H. Trauma (e.g., ionizing radiation)

2. Perinatal causes

    A. Intrauterine disorders (e.g., prematurity)

    B. Neonatal disorders (e.g., intracranial hemorrhage and HIV)

3. Postnatal Causes

    A. Head injuries (e.g., cerebral concussion)

    B. Infections (e.g., pediatric HIV)

    C. Demyelinating disorders (e.g., Schilder disease)

    D. Denerative disorders (e.g., Rett syndrome)

    E. Seizure disorders (e.g., myoclonic epilepsy)

    F. Toxic-metabolic disorders (e.g., lead exposure)

    G. Malnutrition (e.g., protein caloric deficiency)

    H. Environmental deprivations (e.g., psychosocial disadvantage)

Note. This is an abbreviated adaptation of the classification system proposed by Luckasson et al. (1992).

ment and prevention. From a public health perspective, etiology, ranging from proximal to distal causes, is the most sensible alternative (Baumeister, Kupstas, & Woodley-Zanthos, 1993).

Educational Classification.   Another major and traditional classification model for mental retardation has evolved within educational settings to devise teaching methods and content according to ability to learn. Basically three categories have been commonly used, roughly corresponding to different IQ ranges: educable (50–75), trainable (25–55) and severe (< 25). Although such an educational model may, on the surface, appear to have predictive validity, it is clearly tautological. Lately, this system seems to be yielding to a more individualized education plan.

INCIDENCE AND PREVALENCE

There is great variability in empirical and statistical estimates of the number of persons with mental retardation in the United States. This uncertainty stems from definitional inconsistencies, inadequate or uneven ascertainment, regional and time differences in diagnostic procedures, situational determinants, and even confusion over the terms incidence and prevalence. *Incidence* is essentially a longitudinal measure of the number or rate of new cases appearing in a population during a certain time frame. *Prevalence* is assessed by determining a ratio of the number of people, relative to the population, who express the disorder at a specified or within a designated time. These measures have different meanings. One may decrease whereas the other may increase—as in the case of Down syndrome in some regions. Incidence, the number of new cases of a disease, is more useful for evaluating prevention initiatives; prevalence is more useful for resource allocation.

Estimates of rates of mild mental retardation range from 1% to 3% of the total population. When translated into numbers of people affected, the proportional discrepancy has enormous professional and policy implications, because service systems cannot effectively and flexibly provide for hundreds of thousands of people whose eligibility is questionable. In the United States; prevalence typically is gauged through statistical rather than epidemiological methods. This is another situation where an arbitrary and flexible IQ-based definition produces great mischief. Unlike serious or severe mental retardation, projections of rates of mild mental retardation vary much more widely, with a strong social class gradient (Durkin & Stein, 1996).

Data reported by the U. S. Department of Education suggests that, among schoolchildren, over the past 20 years there has been a dramatic decrease in prevalence of mild mental retardation. The bad news is that over the same time period there has been an epidemic of learning disabilities. These data, obtained from The Center for Educational Statistics, are shown in Fig. 16.1 (Smith, Young, Bae, Choy, & Alsalam, 1997).

These changes occurred despite more liberal definitions of mental retardation. Although it is possible that, through intensive early intervention programs, many chil-

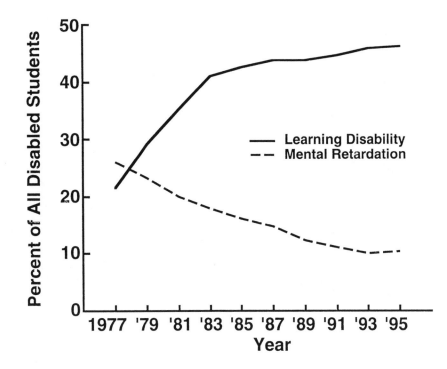

FIG. 16.1.   Percentages of children in public schools diagnosed as Learning Disabled or Mentally Retarded, 1977–1995.

dren were "cured" of their mental retardation, a far more compelling explanation is that shifting ideological sentiments and legal challenges are at the root. First, a diagnosis of "learning disabilities" may be more socially acceptable because it does not convey the sense of hopelessness and stigmatization that is usually imbued in the term "mild mental retardation". In addition, this has been and continues to be a period of class-action litigation alleging that minorities are over-represented in segregated programs for students with "educable" (i.e., mild) mental retardation—that is, determinations based on IQ are discriminatory.

These changes occurred despite more liberal definitions of mental retardation. Although it is possible that, through intensive early intervention programs, many children were "cured" of their mental retardation, a far more compelling explanation is that shifting ideological sentiments and legal challenges are at the root. First, a diagnosis of "learning disabilities" may be more socially acceptable because it does not convey the sense of hopelessness and stigmatization that is usually imbued in the term "mild mental retardation." In addition, this has been, and continues to be, a period of class-action litigation alleging that minorities are overrepresented in segregated programs for students with "educable" (i.e., mild) mental retardation—that is, determinations based on IQ are discriminatory.

Here is still another situation where courts intercede to define research and science and, thus, classification and service provision, to say nothing of liability (e.g., Angell, 1996). There can be no better illustration than the opinion of Judge Peckham (U.S. Federal District Court of the Northern District of California) in a decision banning intelligence tests for placement of Black children in classes for the educable mentally retarded in a California school district: "the history of the IQ test is not a history of neutral scientific discoveries ... but a history of racial prejudice, social Darwinism, and the use of scientific 'mystique' to legitimate such prejudices" (*Larry P. v. Riles*, 1972; 1979).

In light of such discordant views as to the nature of mild mental retardation, along with all concomitant social and legal implications, it is little wonder that many school administrators, educators, and psychologists have opted for a seemingly more neutral stance regarding classification, de-emphasizing mental retardation while promoting "inclusion." Not only is there state-to-state variation in definition, classification, and eligibility requirements, but there is even lack of uniformity between agencies within states (Lowitzer, Utley, & Baumeister, 1987; Utley, Lowitzer, & Baumeister, 1987). From scientific, professional, and clinical perspectives, the greatest inconsistencies arise in regard to higher functioning individuals.

For this reason, it is not entirely surprising that in some instances, where greater precision is required for establishing public health goals, the focus is on those whose level of retardation is more absolute. Recently, the U.S. Department of Health and Human Services placed the number of "serious" (IQ < 50) instances of mental retardation, including moderate, profound, and severe cases, at 2.7 per 1,000 (U.S. Department of Health and Human Services, 1990). Other researchers have reported figures that range from 3 to 4 per 1,000. Because of methodological weaknesses in many epidemiologic studies, some claim that even these are underestimates of the true prevalence of serious mental retardation (McLaren & Bryson, 1987).

The National Health Interview Survey (NHIS), despite some limitations, is one of the continuing barometers of the nation's health profile. Data obtained from this survey indicated that in 1988 there were approximately 2 million people identified with mental retardation or other developmental disabilities (LaPlante, 1989). Clearly, this figure is significantly below other estimates of prevalence, whether obtained from statistical models or extrapolated from samples with known characteristics. Because of the indirect methods of ascertainment employed in the NHIS, these data are likely to produce an underestimate of the true prevalence of mental retardation, especially the mild cases.

Economic costs associated with developmental disabilities are enormous. Among the chronic health conditions, mental retardation is associated with the highest rate (87.5%) of major activity limitations (Kraus, Stoddard, & Gilmartin, 1996). Data from the National Medical Care Utilization and Expenditure Survey revealed that, in 1988, children with chronic disabilities accounted for $4.4 billion in health care expenditures. This does not take into account costs for special education, social services, residential treatment, and lost productivity. The most recent and comprehensive cost analyses associated with 18 of the most common birth defects (many of which produce mental retardation) were reported by Waitzman, Scheffler, and Romano (1996). Using a discount rate of 5% (costs discounted back to year of birth), they calculated aggregate costs to be over $8 billion in 1992 dollars. Medical, special education, developmental service, and indirect expenditures for Down Syndrome alone were in excess of $1.8 billion. Prevention, both from economic and quality-of-life standpoints, is a good investment.

Associated Disorders

Many people diagnosed as mentally retarded present with other serious disabilities, a problem that has enormous service implications. The more serious the mental retardation, as indexed by IQ, the greater the variety of associated disabilities, both in number and severity. Cerebral palsy, epilepsy, behavior disturbances, sensory disorders, and other health problems are common and affect developmental course. Fortunately, these accompanying problems often can be treated or alleviated.

For some specific etiologies, associated disabilities are particularly frequent and of such serious nature as to command attention prior to dealing with the mental retardation per se. For instance, heart defects are a common and sometimes life-threatening consideration in children with Down syndrome or with maternal phenylketonuria (PKU). Children with a genetic disorder known as galactosemia are at risk for cataracts. Infants born with Lesch–Nyhan syndrome, an inborn error of metabolism, later experience extremely severe self-injurious behavior. Muscular–skeletal problems, often of a degenerative nature, are common with certain syndromes. Early death is inevitable for some, including children with Tay–Sachs disease or born infected with HIV.

A long-standing concern has been the connection between mental retardation and psychopathology. Contingent on how one defines affective disorder, persons with mental retardation are 3 to 10 times more likely to have a serious emotional disturbance. Various studies have shown that persons with mental retardation frequently experience disorders such as stereotyped movements, hyperactivity, self-injurious behavior, pica, aggression, and extreme noncompliance. Prevalence estimates of self-injurious behavior, the most serious form of behavioral comorbidity, range from 3.5% to 40%, depending on definition and group sampled (Winchel & Stanley, 1991). Intensity and frequency of these problems increases as IQ decreases, implicating pervasive or focal central nervous system damage. A considerable number of genetic and other biological risk factors for mental retardation are also associated with psychological disturbances, including childhood psychoses, attention deficits, conduct disorders, and neurosis.

CAUSES OF THE DISORDERS

Diagnostic and intervention strategies historically have been, and generally still are, couched within a dichotomous view of primary causes of mental retardation: organic versus psychosocial, exogenous versus endogenous, cultural versus biological. These are distinctions arising from clinical experience that repeatedly has shown that individuals with very low IQs (< 50) are much more likely to present some type of clear physical abnormality.

In fact, actual frequency distributions of intelligence test scores are known to be bimodal, with a substantial number of individuals concentrated at the lower end of the range, far greater than would be statistically predicted from the commonly accepted normal symmetrical distribution of scores. Dingman and Tarjan (1960) gathered IQ data from numerous sources and found considerable excess of cases in the range from zero to 50, forming its own distribution with an average IQ of 32 and a standard deviation of 16. This departure from the normal distribution has come to be known as the "bump of pathology" (Dingman & Tarjan, 1960).

Cultural–Familial Mental Retardation. A long-standing and widely accepted distinction has been made between mental retardation resulting from biologic perturbations (e.g. genetic mutations) and from cultural–familial factors. Persons in the latter category, which includes most cases of mild mental retardation, tend to show few gross physical stigmata, come from lower socioeconomic strata, and have close relatives who score in the subaverage intelligence range. In practice, the distinction between biologic and cultural–familial mental retardation is really one of exclusion, that is, the diagnosis of cultural–familial retardation is typically made merely because no known biologic causative agent is apparent.

It is widely believed that cultural–familial mental retardation is an expression of both polygenically inherited low intelligence that is within the normal range of human variability and environmental circumstances that are not conducive to optimal cognitive development. This view of cultural–familial mental retardation has been supported by its strong association with poverty; data from family studies; and by analyses of performance on cognitive tasks showing that for most children with retardation, differences are of degree, not of kind. With regard to family studies, heritability for IQ (i.e., differences in IQ explained by genetic variance) is much higher among those with mild mental retardation than among those with more serious forms where there is greater likelihood that a specific inherited biological perturbation is implicated. The term cultural–familial retardation is currently in disfavor in some quarters due to its ethnic and racial genetic connotations. Consequently, other terms have been used to describe this group, such as "psychosocial disadvantage" (Robinson & Robinson, 1976).

Given that cultural familial mental retardation results from complex biologic and environmental processes that act in concert to condition individual outcome, a multiple-risk approach is appropriate to gauge and measure predisposition for signs and symptoms. Baumeister et al., (1993) have described an elaborate model, termed the "New Morbidity," in which five classes of variables (predisposing, catalytic, resource, proximal, and outcome) interact to produce the general outcome of mental retardation and accompanying features, that is, the clinical description. The generalized model is presented in Fig.16.2.

A brief account of these variables follows:

1. *Predisposing variables* include demographic factors such as race, parental education, and socioeconomic status; behavioral influences such as personal habits; and genetic—biologic factors.
2. *Catalytic variables* involve acute and chronic poverty or other political, economic, and social conditions that act as catalysts to initiate or limit the operation of other factors, such as resources, that affect outcome.
3. *Resource variables* refer to the array of health, education, social support systems, programs, and services that are not universally or equitably available to all people.
4. *Proximal variables* include those events and circumstances, greatly influenced by the preceding variables, that are the most immediately relevant to the outcomes or symptomatology (e.g., medical complications in the pre- or perinatal period).
5. *Outcome variables* are the product of various combinations and interactions among the other classes of variables.

This model is not only designed to serve as a comprehensive clinical descriptive system for delivery of services, but also to provide a unified basis for truly effective prevention of mental retardation and other health problems of children. Within this conception, prevention of mental retardation must be considered within a hierarchical framework that recognizes that biological, behavioral, and social factors all may be connected with expression of disability. Prevention measures can be designed to interrupt the causal sequence at the point where the intervention is most cost-effective.

When one contemplates disease pathogenesis over time, implicating both immediate and more distal causes, it becomes clear that the dichotomous view of mental

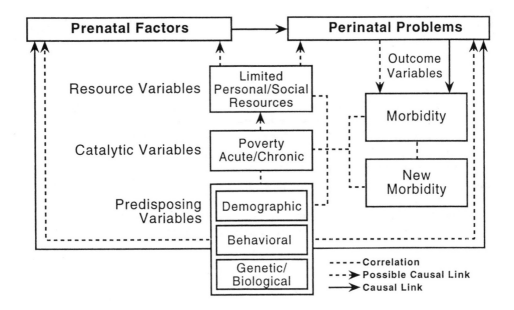

FIG. 16.2.   Generalized model of the new morbidity.

retardation as due to either a social or physical cause is generally a glaring oversimplification. For instance, a high-risk social behavior (unsafe sex practices) may lead to a biological risk (infected fetus), which may lead to behavior deficiency (school failure). Only when the complex multivariate causes and consequences of psychosocial mental retardation are identified, can we begin systematically to intervene and to employ preventive and intervention methods on a wide-scale basis.

Mental Retardation Due to Organic Pathology

Abnormalities in the nervous system (structural or chemical) comprise at least 25% of all cases of mental retardation. Mental retardation due to organic pathology, accounting for the vast majority of persons functioning in the severe and profound ranges (see Table 16.1), is more evenly distributed across social class than is cultural– familial mental retardation. Organic mental retardation can have either genetic or environmental causes. Furthermore, the interaction of genetic and environmental effects accounts for a significant portion of phenotypic expression.

Genetic Syndromes.   Genetic disorders associated with mental retardation can be caused by inheritance of defective genes or by chromosome abnormalities. Disorders attributable to inheritance of defective genes can be classified according to whether the defective genes are dominant or recessive and whether they are located on the autosomes or the X sex chromosome. Genetic problems due to inheritance of dominant genes are relatively rare and are characterized by incomplete penetrance (the gene is not expressed in some individuals) and variable expression (the severity and nature of the disorder are variable). The variable nature of such disorders is explained by the fact that genetic transmission of a dominant gene that consistently produced conditions that reduced reproductive fitness (e.g., profound mental retardation) would be diminished or precluded. If, on the other hand, some individuals who carry a defective dominant gene are only mildly affected, they can reproduce and transmit the gene to their offspring.

A group of diseases involving the skin and nervous system has a dominant autosomal mode of inheritance. Representative examples include neurofibromatosis, tuberous sclerosis, and Sturge–Weber syndrome. Mental retardation may occur in each of these diseases.

Autosomal disorders caused by the inheritance of two recessive genes are more common and less variable in expression than are dominant gene disorders. Included in this category are inborn errors of metabolism. This is a large group of disorders in which an inherited enzyme defect blocks biosynthesis in particular metabolic pathways. Representative diseases associated with mental retardation include PKU and Tay–Sachs disease.

The biochemical consequences of a metabolic block may include an accumulation of the enzyme substrate and its metabolites and a deficiency of the products of metabolism. Mental retardation often is associated with the former consequence and therefore, may, be prevented by reducing enzyme substrate in the body through dietary restrictions or other means. A classic example is PKU, which is caused by an inherited deficiency of phenylalanine hydroxylase, the enzyme that catalyzes the conversion of phenylalanine to tyrosine. If not treated by early dietary prophylaxis, PKU results in severe mental retardation. It was once thought that the low-phenylalanine diet could in some cases be discontinued without harmful consequence when the child reached school age. However, maintenance of the dietary restriction throughout life is now thought to be the better practice, although compliance becomes increasingly difficult to accomplish as the child becomes older.

It is particularly important that women with PKU be placed on low-phenylalanine diets prior to and during pregnancy. Due to the teratogenic effect of phenylalanine, there is an extremely high probability (in excess of 90%) of mental retardation, microcephaly, and heart defects in offspring who are not homozygous for PKU but who are born to mothers with elevated phenylalanine. In fact, early neonatal screening, lauded as a major breakthrough in prevention of mental retardation, has led to a new public health problem. Girls with untreated PKU were not likely to reproduce. With universal screening in the 1960s, these females are reproducing at a rate that will, in a single generation, completely offset the gains from early diagnosis and dietary prophylaxis (Kirkman, 1982).

An ongoing international clinical-trial study supported by the National Institute of Child Health and Human Development is designed to determine whether restriction of phenylalanine among PKU women will reduce the risk of maternal PKU. Preliminary results of this study reveal that if the mother is treated preconceptually or early in pregnancy, teratogenic risks can be lessened greatly.

The other major category of genetic disorders associated with mental retardation includes those caused by abnormalities in the number (aneuploidy) or structure of chromosomes. The most common form of aneuploidy associated with mental retardation is Down syndrome. Several distinct chromosomal abnormalities are recognized in Down syndrome, the most common (95%) being the presence of an extra chromosome number 21. This condition, called trisomy 21, results from nondysjunction of the chromosome during meiotic cell division. Other chromosome abnormalities that result in Down syndrome are translocation, in which extra material from chromosome 21 is attached to another chromosome, and mosaicism, in which both trisomic 21 and normal cell lines exist.

Down syndrome has a distinctive phenotype. Classic physical features include a flat facial profile, upward-slanting palpebral fissures, epicanthic folds, flat nasal bridge, thick protruding tongue, short broad neck, short stature, short stubby extremities, and distinct dermatoglyphic abnormalities. Mental retardation, usually severe to moderate, is a consistent feature of Down syndrome. Global developmental problems involve impaired gross and fine motor coordination and speech and language delays. Gross neuropathological findings include reduced brain size and simplification of the convolutional pattern of the cortex. In addition, numerous studies have shown that virtually all persons with Down syndrome who live beyond 35 years develop neuropathological changes characteristic of Alzheimer's disease, and a substantial proportion show clinical signs of dementia (Zigman, Schupf, Haveman, & Silverman, 1997).

Prevalence of Down syndrome in the general population is just under 1 in 1,000 live births, affecting about 350,000 people. The principal known risk factor for Down syndrome is maternal age. Risk increases dramatically as maternal age increases. In women at 30 years of age, the rate is about 1 in 900; the rate rises to about 1 in 30 at 45 years. This relationship between maternal age and risk is independent of earlier pregnancies. But lest there be confusion about the effects of maternal age on incidence, it should always be kept in mind that most children with Down Syndrome are born to mothers under 40. Down syndrome also appears to be related to paternal age.

Mental retardation also can be linked to abnormalities in the structure of the X sex chromosome. It has long been known that the population of persons with mental retardation has a preponderance of men and boys. This sex difference is attributable in large part to disorders that are caused by X-linked genes. An example of such a disorder is the Lesch–Nyhan syndrome, a metabolic disease that is caused by an inherited deficiency of a particular enzyme. An especially interesting aspect of this syndrome is the nearly invariable occurrence of severe self-injurious behavior.

The most common X-linked disorder is the fragile X syndrome, which is associated with a gap or break near the distal end of the long arm of the X chromosome. Prevalence of fragile X syndrome has been estimated to be approximately 1 in 830 in boys and 1 in 500 in girls (Simensen & Fisch, 1993). However, because of underascertainment, these figures appear to be too low (Baumeister & Woodley-Zanthos, 1996). Fragile X syndrome probably accounts for more cases of mental retardation than any other single genetic cause. Compared to other X-linked disorders, fragile X syndrome is unusual, in that the frequency of nonpenetrant males and the percentage of heterozygous females with phenotypic manifestations (approximately 30%) are relatively high. The physical phenotype in the male is variable, but typical findings include elongated face; enlarged ears, mandibles, and testes; and hyperextensible joints. Recently, a neuropsychiatric phenotype has been defined consisting of mental retardation (usually moderate to mild), social impairment, attentional deficits, stereotyped behavior, and a variety of cognitive deficits. The syndrome in females is less severe but qualitatively similar to the male syndrome. Most male heterozygotes are mentally retarded, whereas most females are not.

Environmental Syndromes.   Organic mental retardation also can be caused by environmental insults. Included in this category are infectious diseases, toxicant exposure, and trauma. These etiologic factors may be further categorized according to whether they occur prenatally, perinatally, or postnatally. The severity and nature of the abnormalities caused by environmental insults depends greatly on the developmental timing of the insult. Risks for significant neurological sequelae are often greatest during prenatal development due to a variety of factors such as heightened susceptibility of the nervous system and immaturity of protective systems such as the blood–brain barrier and immunological responses. Among the prenatal insults that have been associated with mental retardation are maternal malnutrition, anoxia, radiation, physical injury, intrauterine infections, mother–infant blood incompatibilities, and maternal exposure to toxicants.

Infections.   A variety of infectious diseases—such as cytomegalovirus, rubella, toxoplasmosis, syphilis, and HIV–AIDS—can be transmitted from the mother to the fetus, causing teratogenic effects, including congenital mental retardation. Many other infections that can produce irreversible damage to the brain occur postnatally. These include diseases that cause encephalitis (e.g., measles), meningitis (e.g., streptococcus pneumoniae), fungal infections, parasitic infestations (e.g., malaria), and slow viral infections (e.g., Mad Cow Disease).

Fortunately, vaccines are available for many in this group, including diphtheria, tetanus, pertussis, poliovirus, hemophilus influenza, measles, rubella, and mumps. On a national basis, vaccination coverage in 1995 for the full recommended levels among preschool-age children was 74% (Centers for Disease Control, 1997). But the range from state to state was considerable—64% to 87%. Local variations were even greater. Although herd immunity will protect many nonvaccinated children against some infectious diseases, approximately 1 million children are not fully immunized.

The most common infectious agent transmitted in utero is cytomegalovirus (CMV), a member of the herpesvirus group. Between 1% and 2% of infants are infected with CMV at birth. Teratogencity is relatively low, in that the majority of these infants (85% to 90%) are asymptomatic at birth. Among those clinically asymptomatic at birth, approximately 25% have nervous system involvement, and the vast majority of these children (approximately 90%) have mental retardation.

One of the most serious and long-range threats to children's health is the pandemic of symptomatic pediatric HIV. Virtually all infected children (almost always by transmission from mother to child pre- or perinatally) demonstrate prominent and devastating central nervous system damage along with other immune system disorders. It is not clear why some babies are infected through the mother and others are not, although maternal viral load is probably implicated. Estimates vary, but the risk of maternal–infant transmission is about 30%. Progression of HIV disease is much more rapid among children than adults. Although treatments with drugs such as azidothymidine and antibiotic agents can extend life for some children, most infected infants die within the first 2 years (Baumeister & Woodley-Zanthos, 1996).

An examination of epidemiologic data and disease transmission patterns confirms the alarming fact that HIV infection promises to become the primary infectious cause of developmental disabilities and neurologic impairment among children. However, recent findings indicate that risk of transmission from infected mother to child can be greatly reduced (up to two thirds) by antepartum and intrapartum administration of zidovudine to the mother and newborn (Connor et al., 1994). Obviously, this important scientific development poses the troubling question as to the public health desirability of more systematic prenatal screening among high-risk mothers. Therein lies a major sociopolitical dilemma, because high-risk mothers are much more likely to be found among minority groups. Infection rates are, respectively, about 1 per 1,700, 100, and 200 among White, Black, and Hispanic women in their late 20s and early 30s (Rosenberg, 1995).

In addition to HIV, there are many other sexually transmitted diseases (STDs) that produce developmental abnormalities, ranging from very mild to devastating. These include gonorrhea, chlamydia trachomatous, human papilloma virus, herpes simplex, and syphilis. Women at risk for one tend to be at risk for another. In principle, they are all preventable.

Perhaps the most devastating STD throughout history has been syphilis. Although historically congenital syphilis has been a common cause of mental retardation, with the advent of premarital and prenatal screening, along with antibiotic treatment, this disease has been greatly reduced. However, a resurgence of primary and congenital syphilis in the United States since 1985 has raised new concerns (Baumeister, Kupstas, & Woodley-Zanthos, 1993).

Congenital rubella (German measles) was once a significant cause of birth defects in the United States. Among the sequelae of congenital rubella are heart defects, visual and auditory impairment, microcephaly, and mental retardation. The nature and severity of the defects produced by congenital rubella depend on the gestational timing of the disease. Exposure during the first trimester is especially critical. An epidemic in 1963 to 1965 produced about 25,000 cases of congenital rubella syndrome—leading the U.S. Public Health Service to produce a vaccine. The development of effective vaccines for rubella, combined with compulsory vaccination of school-age children, nearly eradicated congenital rubella in the United States, with only six cases reported in 1995.

Toxoplasmosis is caused by a protozoan parasite which may be acquired by exposure to cat feces or ingestion of raw meat. Approximately 40% of offspring of infected mothers will have the infection at birth, though most are asymptomatic at this time. Among those infected 10% to 15% will develop severe symptoms, usually months or years after birth, which include growth retardation, seizures, microcephaly, hydrocephaly, and mental retardation.

Historically, the most important recurring infectious cause of mental retardation is the bacterium Hemophilus Influenza type b (Hib). Until recently, there were about 20,000 cases annually—most likely to occur between 4 months and 4 years of age. One in 10 infected children died, and one in three of the survivors was mentally retarded. Hib was responsible for approximately 80% of cases of childhood meningitis after the neonatal period. Vaccines that are effective against Hib have been recently developed. Since introduction of the first Hib conjugate vaccine in 1988, incidence of the disease has dropped dramatically, to fewer than 100 cases in the United States per year (Robbins, Schneerson, Anderson, & Smith, 1996).

Toxins.   Another significant cause of mental retardation is prenatal exposure to toxic agents. The most significant of these agents is alcohol. Alcohol is a small water-soluble molecule that is readily distributed to the fetus. Consumed in sufficient quantities during pregnancy, alcohol is associated with a variety of abnormalities referred to as fetal alcohol syndrome (FAS). Characteristics of FAS include growth retardation, facial abnormalities, microcephaly, motor dysfunction, and mental retardation. The literature concerning prevalence of FAS reveals great inconsistencies, depending on the population studied, the definition employed, the method of ascertainment, and reporting bias. Nevertheless, a recent review conducted by the Institute of Medicine suggests that FAS may be the most common known nongenetic cause of mental retardation (Stratton, Howe, & Battaglia, 1996). We believe this is probally an exaggeration, but there is no doubt that FAS ia an important cause of mental retardation, especially among certain subgroups. Generally, reported rate ranges between 0.6 to 3 births per 1,000 in most populations, although among Native Americans and Canadians, rates appear to be much higher. For children of alcoholic mothers, prevalence may be as high as 1 in 3.

The dose of alcohol required to cause deleterious effects is the subject of considerable debate. It generally is accepted that consumption of between 2 to 3 ounces of alcohol per day during pregnancy results in FAS. However, alcohol consumption in lower doses may produce more subtle behavioral and cognitive abnormalities in the absence of any clear physical teratogenic effect. Thus, there may be no level of alcohol exposure during pregnancy that is entirely safe. Alcohol also enters breast milk which can be a source of intoxication in newborns.

Mental retardation also can be a sequela of postnatal encephalopathies, such as that produced by lead. Lead from flaking paint, gasoline emissions, leaded and lead-soldered pipes, pottery, and industrial sources is ubiquitous in the environment. Lead exposure is one of the most common chronic environmental health problems in the United States. According to some estimates, about 1.7 million children from 1 to 5 years of age experience exposure to lead sufficient to significantly affect intellectual development (Centers for Disease Control, 1994). Children, who have a propensity for putting inedible substances in their mouths, may acquire lead poisoning by ingesting paint chips, dust, or dirt contaminated with lead. Exposure to high levels of lead produces widespread cerebral damage and neurologic signs such as ataxia, convulsions, and coma. In these cases, nervous system damage is irreversible, and children who survive direct lead encephalopathy often have mental retardation. Exposure to moderate or subclinical levels of lead may produce more subtle but enduring behavioral and cognitive deficits. If the damage is not too severe, these effects are sometimes reversible by chelation—flushing the metal from the blood stream.

To understand the epidemiology of lead intoxication and to devise effective prevention and treatment measures, it is necessary to consider socioeconomic and geographic variables. Only about 7% of children from medium- and high-income families are exposed to excessive lead levels. But the rate accelerates to 25% and 55% for poor white and black children, respectively—especially those concentrated in urban areas (Baumeister, Kupstas, & Woodley-Zanthos, 1993). Although removal of contamination is costly (about $10 billion over the past decade), progress has been made: Mean blood levels for all age groups have decreased almost fourfold over the past 20 years—due in large part to regulations that prohibit lead additives in gasoline (Centers for Disease Control, 1994). Nevertheless, exposure to lead remains a major threat to the behavioral development of many children.

A variety of other biological disorders resulting from known and unknown prenatal influences are also associated with mental retardation. Included in this group of disorders are primary microcephaly, craniostenosis, hydrocephaly, and anencephaly. These are structural defects that can result from both genetic problems and environmental sources.

COURSE OF THE DISORDERS

As previously mentioned, there are literally hundreds of known causes of mental retardation, ranging from specific genetic defects, through myriad acquired diseases and exogenous hazards, to complex psychosocial factors. Even within one specific disorder, say, neurofibromatosis, differences in symptomatology and ultimate outcome can be enormous. Taken across conditions, it is very difficult to offer anything other than general statements concerning the course of the disorder of mental retardation. When one speaks of the "abnormal psychology" associated with mental retardation, that is at best a very broad characterization. Indeed, there are very few disorders that produce identical behavior attributes. The most that can be said, even about a specific condition giving rise to mental retardation, is that there is increased relative risk or probability that similarly exposed individuals will display certain behavioral abnormalities.

Some conditions always lead to early death, such as Tay–Sachs disease or pediatric AIDS, whereas others are severely debilitating and life is so compromised the affected child is said to exist in a "vegetative state," such as in the case of severe anencephaly ("without brain"). Yet, many conditions produce much more subtle signs detected, for instance, only when the child does poorly in school, such as in the case of low level of lead exposure. Given that fewer than 50% of diagnosed cases of mental retardation can be traced to identifiable causes in which some sort of prognostic statement is possible, our ability to make definitive statements about the course of the mental retardation disorder is seriously compromised.

Another factor to be considered has to do with treatment and intervention. Mental retardation per se is essentially incurable. Nevertheless, prevention or amelioration is possible for some disorders that, if left unattended, would produce severe and profound mental retardation. Examples are congenital hypothyroidism, maternal–fetal blood type incompatibilities, lead encephalopathy, certain infectious diseases, and some inborn errors of metabolism. There are a number of other conditions that yield to medical, dietary, or behavior intervention, significantly influencing course of development. On the other hand, the generalization can be made that mental retardation associated with organic brain disease, with exceptions as noted, presents relatively poor prognosis compared with mental retardation stemming from psychosocial factors. When there is explicit brain damage, serious intellectual deficits are usually seen early, are more severe, are not as amenable to education interventions, and are much more likely to be chronic and progressive.

Secondary problems, such as heart defects, cerebral palsy, epilepsy, blood disorders, skeletal contractions, speech defects, behavior disturbances, social acceptability and the like obviously must be considered in an evaluation of the course of development of children with mental retardation. Certainly many related health and behavior problems complicate primary treatment of mental retardation. Children with mental retardation are at relatively high risk for multiple handicapping conditions. As unfair as it may seem, adversity begets adversity.

FAMILIAL CONTRIBUTIONS

As we previously noted, mental retardation, both with respect to cause and course, is best regarded within a multivariate framework, expressed along continua that include risk exposure, vulnerability, presentation of symptomatology, and causality. There is no doubt that familial factors weigh heavily in all these respects. In evaluating the impact of familial contributions, a number of general considerations must be taken into account. The first is that there are many specific single gene effects, both dominant and recessive, that produce conditions linked to mental retardation. In some of these instances, almost all affected individuals are phenotypically mentally impaired. However, there is also usually variability in the degree of handicap. This may be due to operation of other genetic influences, environmental influences, or both. In certain cases, nevertheless, single gene effects are usually very profound, universal, and irreversible.

Perhaps in half the cases of mental retardation, a specific cause can be identified. Even this estimate is misleading, however, because frequently, medical diagnosis, although having the appearance of precision, is apt to fall within a poorly defined, general, and vacuous category such as "of prenatal origin, cause unknown." As previously noted, in those instances of mild mental retardation where cognitive disability cannot be attributed to a specific etiology or circumstance, the prevailing theory is that the observed IQ deficit is an expression of normal human variability, mediated by polygenic factors in combination with environmental influences.

No other field of inquiry can match that of intelligence theory for acrimonious confrontation when it comes to a consideration of the relative influence of nature versus nurture. Although the basic arguments have persisted from the writings of the ancient Greeks to the present, the relative contributions of genome and environment to intelligence remain unresolved and hotly debated. High-volume and vitriolic public controversy has been engendered by publication of *The Bell Curve: Intelligence and Class Structure in American Life* by Herrnstein and Murray (1994). At the core of their argument is the conclusion that individual differences in intelligence—differences that have a large hereditary component—are a major determinant of educational outcome, occupational success, and other aspects of social life.

Much of the debate has evolved from the problem of mental retardation and societal responsibility to deal with that problem. Early in this century, many of our social ills were attributed to the prolific breeding of people who were themselves from "weak and poor stock." Thus, the eugenics movement gained prominence because it promised to cast out the weak, infirm, and "depraved." Immigration laws were enacted to control entry of people into the United States who, in reproducing, might mix bad seed into good. Many states passed sterilization laws to control the fecundity of the "mental deficient." In 1927, the U.S. Supreme Court upheld the sterilization law of Virginia in the case of Carrie Buck (Buck v. Bell, 1925), who had been diagnosed as "feebleminded," as had been her mother and her illegitimate child. The mood of much of the country was reflected in the opinion handed down by Justice Oliver Wendell Holmes:

> It is better for all the world, if instead of waiting to execute degenerate offspring for crime, or to let them starve for their imbecility, society can prevent those who are manifestly unfit from continuing their kind. The principle that sustains compulsory vaccination is broad enough to cover the cutting of fallopian tubes. Three generations of imbeciles are enough.

Holmes was speaking of that group of persons with mental retardation who have variously been described as "imbecile," "moron," "feebleminded," "educable mentally retarded," "mildly mentally retarded," "psychosocially mentally retarded," and "cultural–familial mentally retarded" (although the terms do not always overlap precisely). And this, the largest subgroup (psychosocial or cultural–familial) in the population of people with mental retardation, is the group whose etiology is least understood.

During the height of the "eugenics alarm," researchers such as Ivan Pavlov and Vladimir Bechterev in Russia and John B. Watson in the United States were refining a school of thought that came to be known as behaviorism—a conceptual model concerned with behavior and its relation to environmental stimulation. Only 1 year before Holmes delivered the Supreme Court ruling in the case of Carrie Buck, Watson (1926) said, in what has become one of the most famous statements in the history of Psychology:

> Give me a dozen healthy infants, well-formed, and my own specified world to bring them up in and I'll guarantee to take any one at random and train him to become any type of specialist I might select—a doctor, lawyer, artist, merchant-chief and, yes, even into beggarman and thief, regardless of his talents, penchants, tendencies, abilities, vocations and race of his ancestors. (p. 10)

In any discussion of the nature versus nurture controversy, it is important to distinguish between the phenotype and the genotype. The *phenotype* represents the visible properties of an organism, the combination of our experience and our genotype. The *genotype* is our genetic composition and, until fairly recently, generally has been inferred from classical family studies. Current developments in cytogenetics and molecular genetics are enabling a more direct examination of the genetic makeup of the individual.

There is evidence to support both sides partially, and, ironically, it is sometimes the same evidence. For example, Higgins, Reed, and Reed (1962) reported the results of a study that indicated that children born to two normal parents have an average IQ of 107, children born to one retarded and one normal parent have an average IQ of 90, and children born to two retarded parents have an average IQ of 74. But, whereas the nature proponents point to this study as strong evidence in support of the heritability notion, the nurture faction interprets the findings as important environmental evidence, assuming that retarded parents provide an impoverished intellectual environment for their children.

An elementary point usually lost in the nature–nurture debate is that heritability refers to and only to differences between people within a specified population. In other words, one may infer that a great deal of the variation in IQs, say 50%, is attributable to genetic differences within a well-defined population. But it is inappropriate to say that 50% of an individual's IQ is due to genetic influences. Generalizing from the aggregate to the individual is the "ecological fallacy." It is also wrong to assume that the reasons for variations in intelligence within a population are the same reasons for variations between populations.

PSYCHOPHYSIOLOGICAL AND GENETIC INFLUENCES

Psychophysiological and genetic influences in mental retardation are discussed in detail in other sections. As we previously emphasized, diagnosis, treatment, and prognosis of mental retardation involves an almost bewildering constellation of psychological, social, biological, and even political influences. These factors are interactive and synergistic in conditioning individual outcomes, both immediate and long-term. Uncertainties about etiology, symptomatology, and intervention are not likely to be resolved by unidimensional explanatory models because specific causative factors rarely act in isolation. Understanding, prevention, and treatment of mental retardation must be approached from a multiple-risk perspective.

CURRENT TREATMENTS

As we repeatedly have observed, "mental retardation" is a very general and inclusive categorical term that conceals all manner of variability with respect to causation, behavioral, and medical sequelae, course of development, and amenability to treatment. In addition, mental retardation has been the object of vigorous political and legal advocacy, especially in the last 3 decades. As an example, the principle of "normalization" has been widely adopted as integral to treatment goals and methods. Taken together, all these considerations have a profound effect on treatment strategies, whether medical, behavioral, educational, or sociological.

In addition, the advocacy movement has raised serious questions about whether certain procedures (e.g., contingent electric shock to suppress self-injurious responding) should ever be applied, regardless of efficacy. The basic argument is rooted in an appeal to ethical dogma, stating that people with mental retardation, because of their limited ability to participate in their own treatment, should not be subjected to atypical, aversive, or dehumanizing procedures. Of course, just about everyone agrees with this general premise, but there is considerable controversy as to what the term "normalized" means, especially in regard to people who are behaving in decidedly abnormal or destructive ways and who will not respond to less intrusive interventions.

The concept of "treatment" with respect to mental retardation covers a wide range of activities, some of which are circumscribed and fairly well defined and others that involve consideration of the entire milieu. The latter category includes highly publicized early intervention programs designed to reduce risks associated with psychosocial disadvantage.

The most clinically and educationally salient feature of the mental retardation picture is diminished capacity to learn, retain information, and transfer learning to new situations. Children with mental retardation have relatively great difficulty in acquiring language and academic skills. Problems with higher level functioning, such as maintenance, transfer and generalization, and concept formation have long been an educational challenge with respect to persons with mental retardation.

In fact, the first formal intelligence tests, developed by Binet and his collaborator Simon in the early part of this century, were constructed on the premise that cognitive processes could be modified and the intellect could be trained. The tests were intended to identify children in the public schools who would profit from special training toward this end. Although the trend recently has been to equate intellectual deficiency with higher level cognitive impairment, the notion of educability of higher order functions has not always been the predominant assumption, and dispute continues today over the viability of the concept.

At the heart of the debate is the question of whether "control processes" (i.e., essentially modifiable characteristics) or "structural features" (i.e., fixed limitations) are the essence of retarded behavior. Baumeister (1984) invoked the "reaction range" concept (well known in genetics) in which intrinsic biological factors, or structural features, establish a limit beyond which control processes exert little influence on adaptive behavior. Rather heated arguments have been aroused by the distinction between control processes and structural features because of exceedingly significant theoretical, practical, and even legal implications.

Another aspect of mental retardation that is often the focus of treatment is aberrant behavior. Aggression, self-injury, and stereotyped behavior (repetitive movements such as body rocking), for example, are common problems among mentally retarded persons, especially those with severe functional and intellectual impairments. Such behaviors are often given high priority in habilitation plans because they may be physically harmful or they may interfere with socialization and efforts to develop cognitive skills and adaptive behavior. The two most widely used approaches to dealing with problem behaviors are behavior modification and pharmacology.

Behavior Modification

Behavior modification refers to a technology for behavior change that is based on the principles of instrumental conditioning. This technology is widely applied in efforts to educate and habilitate persons with mental retardation. The emphasis in behavior modification programs with mentally retarded persons is to shape and strengthen desirable behavior through the contingent application of appetitive stimuli (i.e., positive reinforcement).

Appetitive procedures are also employed in efforts to reduce problem behavior. For example, behavior may be reduced by reinforcing low rates of the behavior or by reinforcing competing responses—techniques respectively referred to as differential reinforcement of low rates (DRL) and differential reinforcement of other behavior (DRO). Undesirable behavior also may be reduced by contingent withdrawal of appetitive stimuli (i.e., response cost) or contingent application of aversive stimuli (i.e., punishment). The latter technique is only used for severe problem behavior (e.g., self-injurious behavior) and then only after nonaversive techniques have been tried without success. However, as previously mentioned, there are some who believe that no circumstance justifies the use of aversive techniques.

In any event, recent meta-analyses of published research reports indicate that some excessive claims may have been made in support of behavior analytical interventions, especially in regard to difficult behavior problems. For example, despite widely held assumptions to the contrary, in approximately 40% to 50% of published studies on this topic, the interventions have been ineffective or have had questionable effectiveness (Scotti, Evans, Meyer, & Walker, 1991).

Psychotropic Treatment

Psychotropic medications are widely used to control aberrant behavior in persons with mental retardation. Approximately 55% of mentally retarded persons who reside in institutions and 40% of those residing in community settings receive such medications (Baumeister, Todd, & Sevin, 1993). Antipsychotics (e.g., chlorpromazine, thioridazine, and haloperidol), antidepressants (e.g., fluoxetine), and anticonvulsants (e.g., carbamazipine) are the medications most frequently prescribed. The extent and manner in which antipsychotic medications are used in this population borders on abuse. Approximately one in three residents of state institutions receives such medication. In the vast majority of these cases, the drug is administered to control aberrant behavior, not to treat psychotic disorders.

To a degree, the high rates of administration of anticonvulsants represent the high frequency of seizure disorders in this population. However, these medications are also widely used to control behavior, though the rationale for this use is not well developed.

Although antipsychotic drugs appear to be somewhat effective in controlling aberrant behavior, they have a number of serious side effects. For example, these drugs tend to suppress behavior generally and may therefore interfere with adaptive behavior. In addition, chronic treatment with most antipsychotics produces a potentially irreversible movement disorder called "tardive dyskinesia." Other drugs with more selective actions and fewer side effects are also used. For example, naltrexone, an opioid antagonist, may be effective in reducing self-injurious behavior in some cases. Methylphenidate (Ritalin) has long been described as very effective in treating attention deficit hyperactivity disorder (ADHD), especially among mildly mentally retarded persons. However, use of stimulants, such as Ritalin, is controversial. Over the short term, stimulant treatment of children with ADHD appears to be beneficial. On long-term follow-up, there does not appear to be an enduring effect on consequential measures such as occupational success, intelligence, and educational achievement (Weiss & Hechtman, 1993).

Etiology Based

Relatively few treatments for aberrant responding are based on an appreciation of the underlying disease pathology. However, there are some notable exceptions, particularly the inborn errors of metabolism. Dietary control is an effective treatment of severe behavior problems often associated with hyperphenylalaninemia (Baumeister & Baumeister, 1998). Other diseases, such as Down and fragile X syndromes, present different psychological profiles and developmental trajectories—etiological considerations that may prove useful in designing targeted behavioral inter vention.

Early Intervention

Perhaps the most widely employed general treatment or prevention strategy is early intervention. The literature on the effects of early intervention on children who are developmentally disabled or at risk is enormous, diverse, and continues to grow. The best known of these programs, of course, is Head Start. But there are many others focusing on children with Down syndrome, low-birth-weight babies, children with sensory disorders, and those at risk owing to socioeconomic disadvantage. Effectiveness of early intervention and special education is often characterized by excessive claims in the professional literature and in the popular media (Baumeister & Bacharach, 1996; Detterman & Thompson, 1997; Spitz, 1986). In their review of special instructional methods, Detterman and Thompson concluded that these educational methods have not changed over the past 2,500 years and that "There is nothing special about special education" (p. 1082).

There have been many efforts, over the past century and longer, to "cure" or prevent mental retardation through pedagogical means. By and large, these have been failures, as shown by Spitz (1986) through his detailed and scholarly review of the best-known projects in the past and in the present. In fact, Spitz concluded that exorbitant and unsubstantiated claims concerning early education intervention are an "embarrassment" to the "entire field of psychology" (p. 218). Others have shared similar sentiments concerning efficacy of early compensatory pedagogical interventions. Clarke and Clarke (1989) summed up their review of this research with the observation that "The lack of enduring benefits on cognitive skills from preschool programs has been documented so many times that it scarcely needs repeating" (pp. 291–292).

Long-term gains, if any, resulting from early intervention programs are not clearly delineated. Nevertheless, comprehensive early childhood educational interventions often are reported to produce a number of direct and indirect positive effects for children and their families. Among the alleged benefits are: facilitating intellectual gains, enhancing interactions between children and their families, instructing parents to become effective teachers, enhancing socialization, improving motivation, and increased family awareness of other social programs. It should be emphasized that early intervention efforts must be grounded in and address the child's broader life contexts, not just IQs. Although early interventions typically yield short-term intellectual gains, these are small and transient. One-size-fits-all educational and psychological interventions are not inoculations that provide enduring positive effects (Baumeister & Bacharach, 1996). Hodapp (1997) also argued that interventions should be etiologically based, that is, tailored to individuals on the basis of their unique behavioral phenotypes. For instance, certain genetic diseases such as fragile X, Down syndrome, and Prader–Willi Syndrome present different behavioral profiles (Dykens & Kasari, 1997).

CASE ILLUSTRATION

Emma dropped out of school when she became pregnant in the 10th grade. There was no discussion of marriage between Emma and the father of the child, nor was adoption or abortion considered as an option. Emma neither sought nor received prenatal care until early in the third trimester of the pregnancy when she experienced abdominal cramping and a small amount of vaginal bleeding. Two weeks after she began experiencing these symptoms and 1 week after her first prenatal visit, Emma's grandmother took her to the emergency room of a local public hospital where Emma gave birth to a son whom she named Derek. At his birth, Derek weighed slightly under 1,400 g (about 3 lbs.). He was sent to the hospital's neonatal intensive care unit (NICU) where his progress was monitored and he was treated for a number of problems common to low-birth-weight infants.

After 6 weeks, Derek was discharged to his mother, who had agreed to participate in a long-term study of low-birth-weight children. When Derek was tested at 1 year, his developmental score fell within the normal range. At 2 years, however, developmental tests indicated that Derek's progress had failed to keep pace with that of the comparison group, a decline that was even more pronounced at the 4-year testing. Midway through Derek's first year in school, his teacher recommended that he be tested by a school psychometrist to determine if he was eligible for special educational placement. On the Wechsler Intelligence Scale for Children–Revised (WISC–R; [Wechsler, 1974]) Derek scored 73 on the performance section of the test and 61 on the verbal section, yielding a full-scale IQ of 68. Derek was labeled educable mentally retarded (EMR) by the school system and placed in a special class for those so labeled. Derek, now in the sixth grade, has remained in special education classes. He reads on the first-grade level and has mastered some addition, subtraction, and multiplication facts.

The results of the study in which Derek was a participant indicate that Derek's low birth weight, by itself, probably had little influence on his later academic performance. Low-birth-weight children whose mothers had some college education, were married, and were from a higher income group than Derek's mother, performed no differently academically than normal-birth-weight children of similar circumstances.

Is Derek mentally retarded? Derek's case is representative of millions of school-age children in the United States whose "borderline" status makes it difficult for epidemiologists to agree on the prevalence of persons with mental retardation in this country.

What "caused" Derek's low IQ and learning difficulties? Sociodemographic factors, income level, maternal intelligence, and maternal level of education, followed by mother's marital status and age at the child's time of birth, are the most potent predictors of outcomes such as that of Derek. By no means, however, do these factors provide a clear-cut answer to the roles played by biologic and environmental factors in mild mental retardation.

SUMMARY

Mental retardation is defined primarily by two criteria: (a) subaverage intellectual development, and (b) deficiencies in adaptive behavior. The former refers to intelligence test scores below the range of 70 to 75, and the latter to a number of domains of adaptations that are age- and culturally appropriate. Mental retardation is also a developmental concept, in that, by most definitions, the onset must be during childhood, and diagnosis is made in terms of age–graded standards.

There are many known causes of mental retardation, numbering in the hundreds. The largest category, sometimes referred to as "cultural–familial" or "psychosocial" mental retardation, is comprised mostly of individuals with mild impairments who lack obvious signs of nervous system pathology and who fall in low socioeconomic strata. This type of mental retardation is thought to be caused by a complex interaction between inherited low "normal" intelligence and environmental deprivation that precludes optimal intellectual development. In other cases, mental retardation is clearly the result of organic pathology caused by genetic factors (e.g., inheritance of defective genes or chromosome abnormalities) or environmental insults (e.g., congenital syphilis or prenatal toxicant exposure). Mental retardation associated with clear signs of organicity tends to be more severe, more evenly distributed across social class, and far less common than cultural–familial mental retardation. In most cases, however, the precise etiology of mental retardation is unknown.

Incidence and prevalence estimates are not very precise. But in the United States, there are several million cases of mental retardation. Most of these are in the mild category, although there are many individuals whose disabilities are so severe that they are in constant need of care. Costs for health care, social services, special education, and other needs run into the billions of dollars annually. For some individuals, certain disorders that cause mental retardation can be prevented. There is no "cure" for mental retardation, although in certain instances some associated conditions can be treated. For the vast majority, treatment consists of providing supportive environments during the entire life span.

REFERENCES

American Psychiatric Association. (1994). *Diagnostic and statistical manual of mental disorders* (4th ed.). Washington, DC: Author.

Angell, M. (1996). *Science on trial: The clash of medical evidence and the law in the breast implant case*. New York: Norton.

Baumeister, A. A. (1984). Some conceptual and methodological issues in the study of cognitive processes. In P. Brooks, R. Sperber, & C. McCauley (Eds.), *Learning and cognition in the mentally retarded* (pp. 1–38). Hillsdale, NJ: Lawrence Erlbaum Associates.

Baumeister, A. A. (1997). Behavioral research: Boom or bust? In W. E. MacLean, Jr. (Ed.), *Ellis' handbook of mental deficiency, psychological theory and research* (3rd ed., pp. 3–45). Mahwah, NJ: Lawrence Erlbaum Associates.

Baumeister, A. A. (in press). The meaning of mental retardation: Sentiment versus science. In S. Greenspan & H. Switzky (Eds.), *What is mental retardation? Ideas for the new century*. Washington, DC: American Association on Mental Retardation.

Baumeister, A. A., & Bacharach, V. R. (1996). A critical analysis of the Infant Health and Development Program. *Intelligence, 23,* 79–104.

Baumeister, A. A., & Baumeister, A. A. (1998). Dietary treatment of destructive behavior associated with hyperphenylalaninemia. *Clinical Neuropharmacology*.

Baumeister, A. A., Kupstas, F. D., & Woodley-Zanthos, P. (1993). *The new morbidity: Recommendations for action and up-dated guide to state planning for the prevention of mental retardation and related conditions associated with socioeconomic conditions*. Washington, DC: President's Committee on Mental Retardation.

Baumeister, A. A., Todd, M. E., & Sevin, J. A. (1993). Efficacy and specificity of pharmacological therapies for behavioral disorders in persons with mental retardation. *Clinical Neuropharmacology, 16,* 271–294.

Baumeister, A. A., & Woodley-Zanthos, P. (1996). Prevention: Biological factors. In J. W. Jacobson & J. A. Mulick (Eds.), *Manual of diagnosis and professional practice in mental retardation* (pp. 229–242). Washington, DC: American Psychological Association.

Boring, E. G. (1923). Intelligence as the tests test it. *New Republic, 35,* 35–37.

Bruninks, R., Woodcock, R., Weatherman, R., & Hill, B. (1984). *Scales of independent behavior*. Park Allen, TX: DLM Teaching Resources.

Buck v. Bell. (1925). (143 Va. 301, 130 S. E. 516, 51 A.L.R. 855; affirmed, 274 U.S. 200, 71 L. Ed. 663, Sup. Ct., 584)

Centers for Disease Control. (1994). Blood lead levels—United States, 1988–1991. *Morbidity and Mortality Weekly Report, 43,* 545–548.

Centers for Disease Control. (1997). National, state, and urban area vaccination coverage levels among children aged 19–35 months—United States, January–December 1995. *Morbidity and Mortality Weekly Report, 46,* 176–182.

Clarke, A. M., & Clarke, A.D.B. (1989). The latter cognitive effects of early intervention. *Intelligence, 13,* 289–297.

Clausen, J. A. (1967). Mental deficiency: Development of a concept. *American Journal of Mental Deficiency, 71,* 727–745.

Connor, E. M., Sperling, R. S., Gelber, R., Kiselev, P., Scott, G., O'Sullivan, M. J., VanDyke, R., Bey, M., Shearer, W., Jacobson, R. L., Jimenez, E., O'Neill, E., Bazin, B., Delfraissy, J. F., Culnana, M., Coombs, R., Stratton, P., & Balsley, J. (1994). Reduction of maternal–infant transmission of human immunodeficiency virus type 1 with zidovudine treatment. *New England Journal of Medicine, 331,* 1173–1180.

Detterman, D. K., & Thompson, L. A. (1997). What is special about special education? *American Psychologist, 52,* 1082–1090.

Dingman, H. F., & Tarjan, G. (1960). Mental retardation and the normal distribution curve. *American Journal of Mental Deficiency, 64,* 991–994.

Durkin, M. S., & Stein, Z. A. (1996). Classification of mental retardation. In J. W. Jacobson & J. A. Mulick (Eds.), Manual of diagnosis and professional practice in mental retardation. Washington, DC: American Psychological Association.

Dykens, E. M., & Kasari, C. (1997). Maladaptive behavior in children with Prader–Willi Syndrome, Down syndrome, and nonspecific mental retardation. *American Journal on Mental Retardation, 102,* 228–237.

Gottfredson, L. S. (1997). Why *g* matters: The complexity of everyday life. *Intelligence, 24,* 79–132.

Herrnstein, R. J., & Murray, C. (1994). *The bell curve: Intelligence and class structure in American life.* New York: The Free Press.

Higgins, J. V., Reed, E., & Reed, G. C. (1962). Intelligence and family size: A paradox resolved. *Eugenics Quarterly, 9,* 84–90.

Hodapp, R. M. (1997). Direct and indirect behavioral effects of different genetic disorders of mental retardation. *American Journal on Mental Retardation, 102,* 67–79.

Jacobson, J. W., & Mulick, J. A. (Eds.). (1996). *Manual of diagnosis and professional practice in mental retardation.* Washington, DC: American Psychological Association.

Kirkman, H. N. (1982). Projections of a rebound in frequency of mental retardation from phenylketonuria. *Applied Research in Mental Retardation, 3,* 319–328.

Kraus, L. E., Stoddard, S., & Gilmartin, D. (1996). *Chartbook on disability in the United States, 1996.* Washington, DC: U.S. National Institute on Disability and Rehabilitation Research.

LaPlante, M. P. (1989). *Disability in basic life activities across the life span* (Disability Statistics Report I). San Francisco: University of California, Institute for Health and Aging.

Larry P. v. Riles. (343 F. Supp. 306, 1972; 495 F. Supp. 926, 1979).

Lowitzer, A. C., Utley, C. A., & Baumeister, A. A. (1987). AAMD's 1983 Classification in Mental Retardation as utilized by state mental retardation/developmental disabilities agencies. *Mental Retardation, 25,* 287–291.

Lubinski, D., & Humphreys, L. G. (1997). Incorporating general intelligence into epidemiology and the social sciences. *Intelligence, 24,* 159–201.

Luckasson, R. R., Coulter, D. L., Polloway, E. A., Reiss, S., Schalock, R. L., Snell, M. E., Spitalnik, D. M., & Stark, J. A. (1992). *Mental retardation: Definition, classification, and systems of supports* (9th ed.). Washington, DC: American Association on Mental Retardation.

MacMillan, D. L., Gresham, F. M., & Siperstein, G. N. (1993). Conceptual and psychometric concerns over the 1992 AAMR definition of mental retardation. *American Journal on Mental Retardation, 98,* 325–335.

MacMillan, D. L., & Reschly, D. J. (1997). Issues of definition and classification. In W. E. MacLean, Jr. (Ed.), *Ellis' handbook of mental deficiency, psychological theory and research* (3rd ed., pp. 47–74). Mahwah, NJ: Lawrence Erlbaum Associates.

McLaren, J., & Bryson, S. E. (1987). Review of recent epidemiological studies of mental retardation: Prevalence, associated disorders, and etiology. *American Journal of Mental Retardation, 92,* 243–254.

Nihira, K., Foster, R., Shellhaas, M., & Leland, H. (1975). *AAMD Adaptive Behavior Scale* (Rev.). Washington, DC: American Association on Mental Deficiency.

Robbins, J. B., Schneerson, R., Anderson, P., & Smith, D. H. (1996). Prevention of systemic infections, especially meningitis, caused by *Haemophilus influenza* type b: Impact on public health and implications for other polysaccharide-based vaccines. *Journal of the American Medical Association, 276,* 1181–1185.

Robinson, N. M. & Robinson, H. B. (1976). The mentally retarded child (2nd ed.). New York: McGraw-Hill.

Rosenberg, P. S. (1995). Scope of the AIDS epidemic in the United States. Science, 270, 1372–1375.

Scotti, J. R., Evans, I. M., Meyer, L. H., & Walker, P. (1991). A meta-analysis of intervention research with problem behavior: Treatment validity and standards of practice. American Journal on Mental Retardation, 96, 233–256.

Simensen, R. J., & Fisch, G. S. (1993). Fragile X syndrome. Psychology in Mental Retardation and Developmental Disabilities, 19, 3–5.

Sparrow, S. S., Balla, D. A., & Cicchetti, D. (1984). Vineland Adaptive Behavior Scales. Circle Pines, MN: American Guidance Service.

U.S. Department of Education, National Center for Education Statistics, The condition of education 1997, NCES 97–388, by Smith, T. M., Young, B. A., Bae Y., Choy S. P., & Alsalam, N. Washington, DC: U.S. Government Printing Office, 1997.

Spitz, H. H. (1986). The raising of intelligence: A selected history of attempts to raise intelligence. Hillsdale, NJ: Lawrence Erlbaum Associates.

Stratton, K., Howe, C., & Battaglia (Eds.). (1996). Fetal alcohol syndrome: Diagnosis, epidemiology, prevention, and treatment (Institute of Medicine). Washington, DC: National Academy Press.

U.S. Department of Health and Human Services. (1990). Healthy people 2000: National health promotion and disease prevention objectives. Washington, DC: Public Health Services.

Utley, C. A., Lowitzer, A. C., & Baumeister, A. A. (1987). A comparison of the AAMD's definition, eligibility criteria, and classification schemes with state departments of education guidelines. Education and Training in Mental Retardation, 22, 35–43.

Wahlstrom, J. (1990). Gene map of mental retardation. Journal of Mental Deficiency Research, 34, 11–27.

Waitzman, N. J., Scheffler, R. M., & Romano, P. S. (1996). The costs of birth defects: Estimates of the value of prevention. Lanham, MD: University Press of America.

Watson, J. B. (1926). What the nursery has to say about instincts. In C. Murchison (Ed.), Psychologies of 1925. Worcester, MA: Clark University Press.

Wechsler, D. (1974). Wechsler Intelligence Scale for Children–Revised. New York: Psychological Corporation.

Weiss, G., & Hechtman, L. T. (1993). Hyperactive children grown up: ADHD in children, adolescents, and adults (2nd ed.). New York: Guilford.

Widaman, K. F., & McGrew, K. S. (1996). The structure of adaptive behavior (pp 97–110). In J. W. Jacobson & J. A. Mulick (Eds.), Manual of diagnosis and professional practice in mental retardation. Washington, DC: American Psychological Association.

Winchel, R. M., & Stanley, M. (1991). Self-injurious behavior: A review of the behavior and biology of self-mutilation. American Journal of Psychiatry, 148, 306–317.

World Health Organization. (1978). International classification of diseases (9th ed.) Geneva: Author.

Zigler, E., Balla, D., & Hodapp, R. (1984). On the definition and classification of mental retardation. American Journal of Mental Deficiency, 89, 215–230.

Zigman, W., Schupf, N., Haveman, M., & Silverman, W. (1997). The epidemiology of Alzheimer disease in intellectual disability: Results and recommendations from an international conference. Journal of Intellectual Disability Research, 41, 76–80.

Pervasive Developmental Disorders: The Spectrum of Autism

Sandra L. Harris
Rutgers, The State University

CLINICAL DESCRIPTION

Children with pervasive developmental disorders (PDD) are hard to overlook. Their profound aloneness, bizarre rituals, and lack of language have caused great pain to their families and been the object of concern and study for several generations of scientists, educators, and clinicians.

The best-known type of PDD is autistic disorder (variously called autism or infantile autism). Although first identified by Leo Kanner in the early 1940s (Kanner, 1943), autism did not become an official part of psychiatric nomenclature for 40 years, until publication of the *Diagnostic and Statistical Manual of Mental Disorders* (3rd ed. [*DSM–III*]; American Psychiatric Association [APA], 1980). The definition of autism and other pervasive developmental disorders has gone through several refinements with each revision of the Diagnostic Manual, including the most recent edition (4th ed. [*DSM–IV*]; APA, 1994). This latest version identifies several diagnostic categories under the broad heading of PDD (see Table 17.1).

Included as PDDs are autistic disorder, Rett's disorder, childhood disintegrative disorder, Asperger's disorder, and pervasive developmental disorder not otherwise specified (PDDNOS). Although each of these conditions has its own symptom pattern, there are common threads that bind them together under the PDD heading. Their basic symptoms fall under three broad headings: social, communication, and behavior (see Table 17.2). The focus of this chapter is on describing autistic disorder, the most common of the PDDs. Other conditions will be mentioned briefly to show how they contrast with autistic disorder.

TABLE 17.1

Pervasive Developmental Disorders

Autistic disorder

Rette's disorder

Childhood disintegrative disorder

Asperger's disorder

Pervasive developmental disorder not otherwise specified

TABLE 17.2

Symptom Categories in the Pervasive Developmental Disorders

Social	Impairment of interpersonal relatedness, impaired capacity for empathy, lack of interest in others
Communication	Deficits in language, abnormalities of form, and/or content of language, deficits in nonverbal communication
Behavior	Stereotyped behavior, need for constancy in the environment, resistance to change

Impaired Social Behavior

Persons with autistic disorder exhibit major deficits in their ability to relate to others. The child with autistic disorder often appears content to dwell in a separate world, showing little empathic interest in parents or siblings. Unlike the normally developing baby, the child with autistic disorder may not raise his arms to be picked up or may stiffen in protest when his parents try to cuddle him. The children's lack of social interest may make some of these babies seem like "easy babies" because they do not seek parental attention, and appear content to remain in their cribs, watching a mobile or staring at their hands. As they get older, such lack of demandingness is recognized for the relative indifference it actually reflects.

The child with autistic disorder may not seek others for comfort when she is hurt or upset, finding little consolation in the gentle words and hugs that are so important to other children. Not only do the children not ask for comfort, they typically are quite indifferent to other people's distress and do not seem to share their joy. A sibling's tears or a parent's happiness may elicit no response from the child with autistic disorder.

Children with autistic disorder show little interest in the domestic imitation that most children enjoy. For example, unlike the normally developing child, the child with autistic disorder usually does not use his miniature mower to cut the grass like mommy or pretend to shave while he watches daddy. This lack of interest in imitation interferes with one of the primary channels for learning by young children: their ability to model adult behaviors and master them through role play.

Social play is one of the primary activities of childhood. A few simple toys can create the backdrop for long hours of companionship. The child with autistic disorder does not know how to join this kind of play, sometimes completely ignoring other children, or perhaps standing on the sidelines, not comprehending how to become part of the group. Not surprisingly, given the range of social deficits they exhibit, children with autistic disorder are very impaired in their ability to make childhood friends.

As a person with autistic disorder grows older, the nature and intensity of her social deficits may change. Many parents report that as the child gets older, she begins to show a differential attachment to them and to develop at least a rudimentary awareness of other people's needs. However, these changes are of a relative nature, and when compared to their normally developing peers, the young person with autistic disorder is sadly deficient in the ability to form intimate relationships.

Impaired Communication

Children with autistic disorder are impaired in verbal and nonverbal communication. For the very young child, this may mean a lack of communicative babbling, and substantial delays in the onset of rudimentary speech. Early nonverbal communication may be similarly deficient, with a failure to use eye-to-face gaze for communication and a lack of facial expression.

For those children who do develop speech, there typically are abnormalities in production, including problems with volume, rate, and intonation. Some children with autistic disorder are said to sound like "robots" because they do not appear to be aware of the importance of variation in inflection and pace as part of the process of communication.

Children with autistic disorder also demonstrate abnormalities in the content of speech itself; for example, rotely repeating back what others have said, a behavior called *echolalia*. Echolalia can occur in immediate response to a question or at a later time. An example of immediate echolalia would be the child who, being asked, "What do you want for dinner?" responds, "want for dinner." In the case of delayed echolalia, the child might repeat something heard days or even years before. Children with autistic disorder may recite an entire dialogue from videotape or a television show. Another abnormality of speech exhibited by some children with autistic disorder is called *pronominal reversal*. This refers to a tendency to reverse pronouns, often confusing "I" and "you." For example, when asked, "Do you want a cookie?" the child might answer "Yes, you want cookie." Both echolalia and pronominal reversal are sometimes seen in very young normally developing children, but they rapidly outgrow those behaviors, whereas for the child with autistic disorder these behaviors may be more enduring and pervasive.

Older, intelligent persons with autistic disorder may have complex speech but be unable to sustain a conversation because they are insensitive to their audience. For example, one young man is preoccupied with air conditioning units including brand names, cooling capacity, and so forth, but he fails to recognize that, for most people, that topic holds very limited appeal.

Abnormalities of Routine and Behavior

Children with autistic disorder often show repetitive, stereotyped body movements such as rocking, hand waving, or head banging. They may become quite absorbed in these movements, often to the exclusion of awareness of other events going on around them. For example, a person with autistic disorder may hold her hands up to the light and wave her fingers back and forth, staring at the pattern created as her fingers wave before her eyes. Under these conditions, she may not hear her mother calling her to dinner or notice that her younger brother has come into the room and turned on the television.

Seemingly trivial changes in their environment may trigger emotional responses in some children with autistic disorder, who insist that things remain constant. For example, a child with autistic disorder may spend long periods of time day after day setting toy cars in a row, with each one having a precise relationship to the others, and then engage in a tantrum if his mother moves one of the cars out of line.

Changes in routine also may be upsetting to the child with autistic disorder. For example, if she wears pink flannel pajamas to bed every night of the winter, she may shriek in protest when spring arrives and her parents attempt to dress her in a lightweight blue cotton nightgown. At the more advanced level of development, this ritualistic behavior may manifest itself in a narrow range of interest in specific topics, such as train schedules or bus routes.

Although none of these symptoms is unique to autistic disorder and may be seen in some form in children who are developing normally, as well as children with other disorders such as mental retardation, it is the grouping or constellation of symptoms that enables us to distinguish autistic disorder from other, related disorders.

The Other Pervasive Developmental Disorders

The other forms of PDD may best be understood in how they contrast with autistic disorder. For example, critical features of Rett's disorder, found only in girls, include normal development through the age of 5 months, followed by a decreased rate of growth of the head, a loss of previously mastered purposeful hand movements, and a decline in social interest (Perry, 1991). The pattern of symptoms changes over time, with the most autistic symptoms occurring from about 12 to 36 months. As the children get older, their social behaviors improve, but their motor skills decline.

Childhood disintegrative disorder is a rare disorder that differs from autistic disorder because the child has at least 2 years of seemingly normal development and then a major loss of skills in at least two of the following areas: language, social skills, bowel or bladder control, play, or motor skills. Symptoms usually appear between 3 and 4 years of age. This condition differs from Rett's disorder, because in childhood disintegrative disorder the child's loss of skills follows at least 2 years of normal development, whereas in Rett's disorder, this normal phase lasts only a few months.

Asperger's disorder is distinguished from the other PDDs by the lack of a significant delay in the onset of speech. Typically, these children have average to above average intelligence, whereas in the other forms of PDD, there is often mental retardation. Deficits in social skills may be most unusual behavior in a child with Aspereger's disorder. These children may be able to keep up academically with their peers but have a difficult time adjusting to the social world of childhood. Like the person with autistic disorder, they may exhibit a preoccupation with a circumscribed topic or interest.

Finally, the category of PDDNOS is used to encompass those people who exhibit some but not all of the symptoms of autistic disorder or another form of PDD. These children would have fewer symptoms or milder symptoms than other children with a PDD diagnosis.

CAUSES OF THE PERVASIVE DEVELOPMENTAL DISORDERS

Until the mid-1960s, most people believed that autism (as autistic disorder was known then) was the result of poor parenting. The best-known advocate of this now largely discredited view, Bruno Bettelheim (1967), argued that these children recognized the incapacity of their parents to be loving and withdrew from that harsh reality. Scientific research failed to provide support for this view, and since the 1970s, there has been accumulating evidence to support the notion that the PDDs are biologically based disorders.

Although *DSM–IV* has subdivided the PDDs more finely than the official nomenclature of the past, that there are even more disorders grouped under the various categories such as autistic disorder or childhood disintegrative disorder. We gradually are uncovering a variety of different biologically based disorders that are known to be linked to the symptoms of the PDDs (see Table 17.3). For example, one of the first known infectious diseases associated with autism was identified when it was noted that disproportionate numbers of babies whose mothers had German measles during pregnancy demonstrated autistic behaviors (Chess, 1977).

Symptoms of PDDs have been traced to some chromosomal defects. One of the most common of these is called Fragile X syndrome. This disorder was long known to be a cause of mental retardation but now has been linked to PDDs, as well (Gillberg, 1992). PDDs similarly have been found to be associated with seizure disorders, tuberous sclerosis, and phenylketonuria (PKU; Gillberg, 1992).

Continuing research will doubtless gradually disentangle the many separate disorders that are subsumed under the heading of PDD and enable the prevention or treatment of some of these disorders. Later in the chapter, some of the current research on the biological bases of PDDs is discussed in greater depth.

COURSE OF THE PERVASIVE DEVELOPMENTAL DISORDERS

For most children, the PDDs last a lifetime. Although early intervention for many young children with autistic disorder, Aspereger's disorder, and PDDNOS has produced major developmental changes (Lovaas, 1987), the technology has not yet reached the point where the majority of children make the degree of change that allows them to blend imperceptibly into their peer group. As a result, although most children with PDD benefit in important ways from treatment, many still become adults with PDD or some significant residuals of PDD. It is therefore important to understand how symptoms of PDDs manifest themselves across the life span.

This section focuses on the developmental changes seen in people with autistic disorder because that is the most widely studied of the PDDs. The symptoms of autistic disorder typically increase gradually through the child's second year, reach a peak between 2 and 4 years of age, and then show some improvement. Young children with greater cognitive ability who receive very early intensive intervention may show dramatic improvement at this age, whereas those who are more impaired will make more modest changes.

TABLE 17.3
Some Disorders Known to Be Linked to Pervasive Developmental Disorders

Maternal rubella (German measles)

Fragile X syndrome

Seizure disorders

Phenylketonuria

In general, even if untreated, the troubling behaviors of children with autistic disorder tend to improve somewhat as the child grows older. However, some children experience a temporary or permanent worsening of symptoms when they enter adolescence, including onset of seizures, a decrease in cognitive skills, an increase in activity level, aggression, destruction, and increased resistance to change (Gillberg, 1991). An increase in aggression or self-injury is especially troubling in an adolescent or adult because the person's physical size makes it difficult to keep him or her safe. Fortunately, for most young people with autistic disorder, behavior tends to remain stable or improve rather than decline with age. It is realistic to expect most people with autistic disorder to improve self-help skills, to show improvement in language and social skills, and to develop prevocational and vocational skills.

In Rett's disorder, the clinical picture changes several times over a girl's lifetime. After a few months of normal development, there follows a period when the child's symptoms include a decline in muscle tone and a decrease in interest in the environment. Between 12 and 36 months, the girl's behaviors resemble those of a person with autistic disorder. Between 2 years and 10 years, her social aloofness decreases, and her motor problems increase. Beyond the age of 10, there are increasing motor problems and continued improvement in social relatedness (Perry, 1991).

The long-term course of development for children with childhood disintegrative disorder is problematic. These children tend to have a poor prognosis, with a lower IQ, greater likelihood of muteness, and greater chance of residential placement than children with autistic disorder (Volkmar & Rutter, 1995).

Although people with Aspereger's Disorder may continue to have serious social problems into adulthood, their good verbal skills and strong cognitive abilities often enable them to hold competitive jobs in the community and, in many respects, to blend in with their peers. They may, however, need continuing social support.

FAMILIAL CONTRIBUTIONS

Although it was once believed that poor parenting was the cause of autism, research over the years has revealed few if any differences between parents of children with PDDs and other parents. Today, there is an understanding that parents of children with PDDs are "ordinary people" to whom an extraordinary thing has happened. Although there is a greater than chance probability that a family with one child with a PDD will have a second child with PDD, these family patterns seem more closely linked to genetic factors than to environmental variables.

PHYSIOLOGICAL AND GENETIC INFLUENCES

We do not know the details of what causes PDDs. However, our understanding of some of these conditions is increasing due to recent research on the genetic, neurological, neurochemical, and biochemical factors that appear to underlie these conditions. This research is not seeking a single explanation for PDDs but working to identify the multiple causes that may be involved. In that respect, PDDs are similar to mental retardation, where we know that different conditions such as microcephaly and Down syndrome have different causes, although they share the common symptom of cognitive deficits.

Genetic Factors

There appears to be a genetic contribution to at least some kinds of autistic disorder. For example, Fragile X syndrome is a chromosomal disorder than long has been linked to mental retardation and more recently has been shown to be related to autistic disorder. This disorder gets its name from a narrowing near the end of the long arm of the X chromosome that sometimes makes the tip fragile. Fragile X syndrome shows an X-linked (sex gene-linked) recessive pattern of inheritance. As a result, this disorder typically is transmitted to boys by their mothers. Fragile X syndrome accounts for a small but significant number of boys diagnosed with autistic disorder (Gillberg, 1992). Similarly, tuberous sclerosis and PKU are hereditary disorders usually accompanied by mental retardation, which have been identified in some people with autistic disorder (Gillberg, 1992).

If one identical twin has autism, the odds are very great that the second will, as well. Ritvo, Freeman, Mason-Brothers, Mo, and Ritvo (1985) found a 95.7% concordance rate for autism in identical twins and only 23.5% in fraternal twins. The familial factor in autistic disorder also may be seen in the siblings of these youngsters, who exhibit a greater than chance frequency of problems with general intelligence, reading, and language (Folstein & Rutter, 1987). For example, August, Stewart, and Tsai (1981) found that 15% of the siblings of children with autism had cognitive abnormalities such as mental retardation, whereas only 3% of the siblings of children with Down syndrome exhibited similar problems.

Physiological Factors

General support for the notion that the symptoms of autistic disorder reflect underlying physiological dysfunction comes from research showing that autistic disorder occurs more often than would be predicted by chance among children whose mothers had German measles during pregnancy (Chess, 1977), that these children experienced a higher than expected rate of problems during pregnancy or birth (Schreibman, 1988), and that they are at greater risk for seizures than other children (Gillberg, 1992). Findings such as these raise important questions about where in the brain abnormalities may occur and how these neurochemical, biochemical, or neurological factors may be linked specifically to the development of the language, social, affective, and behavioral symptoms that characterize autistic disorder and the other PDDs.

The neurological approach to PDDs searches for those portions of the brain that are specifically involved. Much of this research is based on comparing what we know about the behaviors of persons who are known to have suffered damage in specific areas of the brain (Reichler & Lee, 1987). Although a few of these studies have been done on post mortem examination of people with PDDs who died from other causes (e.g., Bauman, 1996), the development of noninvasive methods for studying brain structure and function in living persons is enabling us to look more closely at the brains of people with PDDs than was possible in the past.

Two commonly used methods of studying brain structure and function are computerized tomographic (CT) scans and magnetic resonance imaging (MRI). CT scans involve passing multiple X-ray beams through the brain in a stepwise or circular pattern and measuring the intensity of these beams as they exit the head. These measurements are analyzed by computer and displayed as a picture of the brain on a cathode ray tube (Brahme, 1982). Brain lesions show a different density on the CT scan than does healthy tissue, thus making it possible to see abnormalities in brain structure. The MRI procedure takes this technology one step further than the CT scan because it does not use X-ray beams, and thereby reduces the risk to the patient. Rather than X-rays, the MRI measures the magnetic properties of hydrogen and phosphorus in the brain, and, with the use of computer, converts these into pictures of the living brain, a measure that often is more detailed than the CT scan (Elliott & Ciaranello, 1987).

Bauman (1996) and Filipek (1996), in reviews of research on brain structure and function in PDDs, concluded that a high proportion of these children have a recognizable neurological dysfunction. Nonetheless, the specific locations of these lesions is quite variable, and we have not yet identified the relations between these observed brain abnormalities and the specific behaviors of the PDDs.

In addition to CT scans and MRIs to inspect brain structure, another noninvasive way of studying brain function is to measure the electrical activity of the brain. This is done by placing electrodes on the surface of the scalp that record the minute electrical impulses constantly emitted by the living brain. We know, for example, that epilepsy is characterized by specific abnormalities of brain electrical activity as measured by an electroencephalogram (EEG). Similar abnormalities may occur with some of the PDDs. Courchesne (1987) measured highly localized brain responses called event-related potentials (ERPs) in people with autistic disorder by placing electrodes on the scalp and then presenting a specific stimulus event. This measurement differs from an EEG in that the ERP allows for a direct link between a specific response and a specific stimulus. The results of his work are consistent with the notion that there is abnormal brain processing in the person with autistic disorder, which interferes with attending and awareness. He speculated that these abnormalities of brain function are analogous to, although perhaps different from, epilepsy.

In addition to looking for specific lesions or areas of anatomical abnormality in the brains of persons with PDDs, it is also possible to examine the neurotransmitters in the brain to determine whether there are abnormalities in brain chemistry. Neurotransmitters are the chemicals that enable information to be transferred from one neuron to another. Because these chemicals control sleep, arousal, affect, motor coordination, and so forth, they are major targets of investigation of the etiology of any psychiatric disorder (Yuwiler & Freedman, 1987). For example, one neurotransmitter called dopamine has been linked to the development of movement disorders in Parkinsonism and schizophrenia. Similarly, norepinephrine has been implicated in bipolar affective disorder.

Both dopamine and serotonin have been implicated in PDDs. For example, Gillberg (1992) noted that babies born to mothers addicted to "crack" cocaine sometimes show symptoms consistent with autistic disorder. It is known that crack influences dopamine in the brain. Although not a conclusive argument, this hypothesis draws a potentially useful parallel between symptoms of PDD in children where the etiology of their disorder is known and other children for whom we do not have an etiology.

The neurotransmitter serotonin thus far has been the brain chemical most closely examined as a possible cause of autism. Serotonin is found in the blood as well as the brain, and research typically has focused on this indirect measure of the chemical's presence. Recent research has reported elevated levels of serotonin in the blood platelets of children with autistic disorder (Cook, 1996). However, we have not yet identified any consistent relation between specific autistic behaviors and blood serotonin levels. Important research is being done using a scanning technology called positron emission tomography to study cerebral metabolism (Cook, 1996). This work may ultimately enable us to learn how the brain of a person with PDD differs in the metabolism of serotonin or other neurotransmitters as compared to the metabolism in the brain of the person who functions normally.

In general, research on the role of brain anatomy, biochemistry, and neurotransmitters in PDDs has not yet provided sufficient information to allow us to draw definitive conclusions about the role of these factors in PDDs. Inconsistency of diagnosis from one study to another, the use of small samples, variability in diagnosis, and the technological limits of the tools available to study brain function all have impeded progress (see Table 17.4). However, the research is growing in technical sophistication, and, as we gain a greater database, it becomes possible to ask increasingly precise questions, which doubtless will yield important answers about the specific biological etiologies of PDDs.

CURRENT TREATMENTS

The best documented approach to the treatment of people with PDD is a form of behavior therapy called applied behavior analysis. Since the mid-1960s,when Ivar Lovaas and his colleagues (Lovaas, Berberich, Perloff, & Schaeffer, 1966) demonstrated that children with autism responded to carefully planned applied behavior analytic techniques, there has been extensive research on the use of these methods to treat the PDDs, especially for autistic disorder, Asperger's disorder, and PDDNOS. Three decades of research have contributed to the development of a substantial array of specific behavioral treatment techniques and of documentation to support the efficacy of these methods in treatment of PDDs. This research also has demonstrated the essential role that parents can play in the treatment of their children by providing consistency of intervention between home and school (Harris, 1994), or even in some cases as the child's primary therapist.

Traditionally, applied behavior analytic procedures have relied on a technique called the "discrete trial format" to convey small units of information to the child with PDD. In this format, the teacher first gains the child's attention, gives a brief command (e.g., "Point to cup"), waits for the child's response, and reinforces a correct response with praise and perhaps a small treat. The teacher then records whether the child's response was correct and goes on to the next trial. In the event that the child fails to respond or makes an error, a correct response would be prompted. Hundreds of discrete trials might be necessary to teach a child a skill such as zipping a jacket or discriminating a circle from a square. This discrete trial format is important in educating children with PDDs, but, in recent years, there also has been an emphasis on teaching in a naturalistic context that resembles the setting in which the child lives. For example, if one were teaching a child to name colors, it might be done during the course of choosing crayons to color a picture, or selecting a ball to play catch.

TABLE 17.4

Commons Flaws of Research on the Etiology of the Pervasive Developmental Disorders

1. Small sample size

2. Heterogeneous sample

3. Inconsistency of diagnosis

4. Lack of appropriate control group

When they first enter treatment, many children with PDDs have little if any motivation to do the things their parents and teachers wish they would do. Paying attention to an adult's instructions, talking, zipping a jacket, or interacting with another child have little if any interest for many children with PDDs. As a result, it is sometimes necessary to offer artificial reinforcers at the early stages of treatment. For example, a child who remains in a chair for a few moments might receive a taste of pudding. Gradually, these artificial inducements are replaced by the more natural reinforcements that occur between children and adults.

Social Skills

Children with PDDs often have to be taught in considerable detail all of the complexities of how to play a game with another child, how to express affection, how to wait one's turn, how to empathize with another child's distress, or how to initiate social play. Normally developing peers can be invaluable in helping the child with PDD learn these skills, because the peers offer age-appropriate models of behavior and can learn to encourage the first tentative social gestures of the child with PDD (Harris & Handleman, 1997). Twenty-five years of research have documented the feasibility of teaching many discrete social skills to the child with PDD, although mastery of all of these individual behaviors does not necessarily result in the child's being able to hold his or her own in the spontaneous rough and tumble of daily childhood living.

In one study, adolescents learned how to offer assistance to an adult who was having difficulty with a task (Harris, Handleman, & Alessandri, 1990). For example, for 14-year-old Rick, a baseline observation period was conducted during which it was noted that he essentially ignored other people who were struggling to do such tasks as putting a key in a lock, tearing off a piece of tape, or buttoning a jacket. Then, Rick was taught to say, "Can I help you?" when another person was having trouble with a task. When Rick made his offer of assistance, the second person would say, "Thanks a lot, could you please button my jacket?" Rick was then praised for his helpful behavior. Under these conditions, his offers of assistance increased to an average of 88% of the opportunities, and he began to offer help at home as well as at school.

Treatment for the child with PDD can be helpful for the rest of the family, as well. Celiberti and Harris (1993) taught siblings of children with autistic disorder how to play with their brother or sister. In one family, Jack, a 4-year-old boy with autistic disorder, was a source of distress to his 8-year-old sister Alice. She would have liked nothing better than to play with her little brother, but her efforts were ignored or actively rebuffed by his tantrums. This was vividly clear during a baseline assessment, when Jack ignored Alice's efforts to get him to play, and she, in turn, was quickly discouraged and withdrew from her brother. During the training program, Alice learned the behavioral skills necessary to get her brother's attention, to invite him to play with attractive toys, to prompt his play appropriately, and to reinforce his play behaviors. By following these steps, she transformed their play time into an experience enjoyable to both children, and their parents were delighted to see the youngsters share good times.

Speech and Language

The earliest behavioral research in the area of speech and language focused on using operant conditioning to teach basic grammatical forms such as nouns and verbs. There were serious limitations to these preliminary studies, because the children tended to become dependent on the specific cues of the instructional setting and to have problems transferring their language skills to the natural environment. As a result, later research focused on techniques for increasing spontaneous speech and the generalized use of communication skills in many settings. This has been done, in part, by creating a more richly varied instructional setting, by encouraging the child to take the lead in initiating communication, and by trying to ensure that language is met by rich and varied natural reinforcers (Harris, 1995). An example of such work by Koegel, O'Dell, and Koegel (1987) documented the value of learning speech as an integral aspect of the natural interactions that occur between an adult and a child.

Disruptive Behaviors

One of the areas in which major advances have been made in the treatment of persons with PDDs is the management of disruptive or dangerous behaviors such as self-injury, stereotyped behavior, and aggression. We have learned there is often a link between environmental events and disruptive behaviors. Much of this research on what is called "functional assessment" has focused on behaviors that have an escape function or that are attention-seeking (e.g., Durand, 1990). If the function of the behavior can be determined, then it is often possible to teach a substitute behavior that will create the desired outcome without being disruptive. For example, the child who engages in a tantrum to avoid work can be taught to ask for a break from work. Similarly, the youngster who throws toys to seek adult attention can be taught to raise her hand and ask the teacher to look at her work.

Determining which variables are functional for a client may require a highly sophisticated behavioral assessment, including detailed recording of such data as the nature of the disruptive behavior, the day, time, physical location, persons present, specific antecedent and consequent events, and so forth. Careful inspection of these data often reveals patterns of responding that can be verified through the use of analogue assessments, in which variables of interest such as attention or escape factors are deliberately manipulated to assess their impact on behavior.

Although substituting a new, adaptive response for an old, disruptive behavior is often effective in reducing unwanted behaviors, sometimes it may be necessary to suppress the disruptive behavior, as well. The use of physical exercise, brief restraint, or time out from a reinforcing situation are among the range of mildly aversive techniques that are available to help persons with PDD learn to control their disruptive behaviors (Harris, 1995). Sometimes, when less aversive alternatives fail, and the behavior is of a life-threatening nature such as severe self-injury, it may be necessary to use a more potent aversive technique including very brief but not physically dangerous electrical shock. Such methods are only used as a last resort, and must be done by persons well trained in their application in order to avoid the risk of abuse (Harris, 1995). Many facilities have special student rights advocates who would review these methods to ensure they are necessary; informed parental consent also would be required.

Most often, disruptive behavior can be treated without resorting to powerful aversive procedures. For example, in one study, physical exercise was used to help Mark, a 7-year-old boy with autistic disorder, learn to control his disruptive, out-of-seat behavior (Gordon, Handleman, & Harris, 1986). During a 5-day baseline before treatment, it was determined that Mark was jumping out of his seat an average of 77 times during the school day. An exercise period was introduced that required him to jog with his teacher each time he got out of his chair without permission. Using this procedure, the frequency of his out-of-seat behavior quickly declined to an average of four times a day.

Medication

Drugs may be a useful adjunct treatment for the problem behaviors of some children with PDDs. Medication is most likely to be considered for students who are aggressive or self-injurious and do not respond to behavioral techniques. Among the drugs used are clonodine, fluoxetine, haloperidol, and naloxone (Lewis, 1996). Because of the wide range of individual responses to medication, these and other drugs must be closely monitored for physical side effects, and careful behavioral measures should be taken to demonstrate efficacy.

Early Intervention—A Case Report

Pauline M. was admitted to the Douglass Developmental Disabilities Center at 4 years, 2 moths of age. The intake report notes that she was a cute little girl with lovely smile, who left her parents to go with the examiner without a backward glance for reassurance. She had little interpersonal eye contact, was aloof, noncompliant, and several times pinched the examiner. Pauline had a number of behaviors consistent with the diagnosis of autistic disorder, including smelling objects, putting her hands over her ears, lining up crayons in a precise row, and making a variety of odd noises. She also used immediate and delayed echolalia.

According to Mrs. M, the pregnancy was full-term and uneventful. Pauline's motor milestones, including sitting up, standing, and walking, were all on time. However, her language development was very slow, with a few words emerging around 12 months and very little speech after that time. At the age of 4 years, Pauline had a number of single words and a few two-word combinations.

At home, Pauline engaged in a great deal of stereotyped behavior including rocking, spinning in circles, and posturing her fingers. She engaged in a tantrum when someone disrupted the pattern of objects she had arranged or when she was otherwise frustrated. She also liked to lick and sniff objects. She was an emotionally removed child who seemed to be in "her own world."

Pauline's behavior fit the criteria for a diagnosis of autistic disorder. Because of her limited speech and her tantrums, we admitted her to the Center's specialized class for young children who needed one-to-one instruction.

Within the framework of intensive, behavioral intervention, Pauline made impressive progress during her first year at the Center. Her tested IQ on the Stanford–Binet IV (Thorndike, Hagen, & Sattler, 1986) went from 37 at the time of admission to 63, a very impressive 26-point gain at the end of the school year. On the Preschool Language Scale (Zimmerman, Steiner, & Pond, 1979), her language quotient showed a similarly substantial gain, from 55 at the time of admission to 83 at the end of the year.

Pauline's progress on these objective tests was paralleled by her gains in instructional programming. At the end of the first quarter, her progress report showed that she had mastered 41% of her instructional goals for that period. In the second period, this rose to 56%, in the third period 63%, and in the final period of the year she mastered 73% of an ever-growing pool of programs. Her progress was evident in domains including behavior management, speech and language, cognitive skills, fine and gross motor coordination, and self-help skills. Her most impressive progress was in the area of cognitive skills where she mastered 33 out of 35 programs by the end of the year. This included activities such as naming colors, counting objects, naming shapes, matching numerals, and telling time by the hour. She also had stopped using tantrums and learned to ask for what she wanted when frustrated. Socially, she showed an increased awareness of the presence of other people and an interest in being with them.

Pauline's developmental progress at school was paralleled at home, where her parents instituted a number of behavior management, self-help, speech, and socialization programs to ensure the transfer of school-based activities to the home. After a 2 more years at the Center, she was ultimately able to move into a regular first grade in the public schools.

SUMMARY

PDDs are relatively rare, but they are very serious disorders that begin in infancy or early childhood and require early, intensive intervention for maximum treatment benefits. Symptoms of these disorders include pervasive problems of social behavior and emotional expression, communication deficits, and disruptive behaviors, including stereotyped behavior, self-injury, and resistance to change.

Although once believed to be the result of poor parenting, PDDs are now known to be related to a variety of biologically based disorders. There appear to be genetic patterns for some PDDs, and other neurological and neurochemical bases are being explored for these disorders.

Applied behavior analysis is the most common treatment for PDDs, and there exists an extensive database to document the benefits of behavioral procedures for treating the social, communication, and behavior problems exhibited by these children.

REFERENCES

American Psychiatric Association. (1980). *Diagnostic and statistical manual of mental disorders* (3rd ed.). Washington, DC: Author.

American Psychiatric Association. (1994). *Diagnostic and statistical manual of mental disorders* (4th ed.). Washington, DC: Author.

August, G. J., Stewart, M. A., & Tsai, L. (1981). The incidence of cognitive disabilities in the siblings of autistic children. *British Journal of Psychiatry, 138,* 416–422.

Bauman, M. L. (1996). Brief report: Neuroanatomic observations of the brain in pervasive developmental disorders. *Journal of Autism and Developmental Disorders, 26,* 199–203.

Bettelheim, B. (1967). *The empty fortress.* New York: The Free Press.

Brahme, F. J. (1982). Neuroradiology. In W. C. Wiederholt (Ed.), *Neurology for the non-neurologist* (pp. 107–142). New York: Academic Press.

Celiberti, D. A., & Harris, S. L. (1993). Behavioral intervention for siblings of children with autism: A focus on skills to enhance play. *Behavior Therapy, 24,* 573–599.

Chess, S. (1977). Follow-up report on autism in congenital rubella. *Journal of Autism and Childhood Schizophrenia, 7,* 69–81.

Cook, E. H. (1996). Brief report: Pathophysiology of autism: Neurochemistry. *Journal of Autism and Developmental Disorders, 26,* 221–225.

Courchesne, E. (1987). A neurophysiological view of autism. In E. Schopler & G. B. Mesibov (Eds.), *Neurobiological issues in autism* (pp. 285–324). New York: Plenum.

Durand, V. M. (1990). *Severe behavior problems. A functional communication training approach.* New York: Guilford.

Elliott, G. R., & Ciaranello, R. D. (1987). Neurochemical hypotheses of childhood psychoses. In E. Schopler & G. B. Mesibov (Eds.), *Neurobiological issues in autism* (pp. 245–261). New York: Plenum.

Filipek, P. A. (1996). Brief report: Neuroimaging in autism: The state of the science 1995. *Journal of Autism and Developmental Disorders, 26,* 211–215.

Folstein, S. E., & Rutter, M. L. (1987). Autism: Familial aggregation and genetic implications. In E. Schopler & G. B. Mesibov (Eds.), *Neurobiological issues in autism* (pp. 83–105). New York: Plenum.

Gillberg, C. (1991). Outcome in autism and autistic-like conditions. *Journal of the American Academy of Child and Adolescent Psychiatry, 30,* 375–382.

Gillberg, C. (1992). Autism and autistic-like conditions. In J. Aicardi (Ed.), *Diseases of the nervous system in childhood* (pp. 1295–1320). New York: Cambridge University Press.

Gordon, R., Handleman, J. S., & Harris, S. L. (1986). The effects of contingent versus non-contingent running on the out-of-seat behavior of an autistic boy. *Child and Family Behavior Therapy, 8,* 337–344.

Harris, S. L. (1994). Treatment of family problems in autism. In E. Schopler & G. B. Mesibov (Eds.), *Behavioral issues in autism* (pp. 161–175). New York: Plenum.

Harris, S. L.(1995). Educational strategies in autism. In E. Schopler & G. B. Mesibov (Eds.), *Learning and cognition in autism* (pp. 293–309). New York: Plenum.

Harris, S. L., & Handleman, J. S. (1997). Helping children with autism enter the mainstream. In D. Cohen & F. Volkmar (Eds.), *Autism and the pervasive developmental disorders* (pp. 665–675). New York: Wiley.

Harris, S. L., Handleman, J. S., & Alessandri, M. (1990). Teaching youths with autism to offer assistance. *Journal of Applied Behavior Analysis, 23,* 297–305.

Kanner, L. (1943). Autistic disturbances of affective contact. *Nervous Child, 2,* 217–240.

Koegel, R. L., O'Dell, M. C., & Koegel, L. K. (1987). A natural language teaching paradigm for nonverbal autistic children. *Journal of Autism and Developmental Disorders, 17,* 187–200.

Lewis, M. H. (1996). Brief report: Psychopharmacology of autism spectrum disorders. *Journal of Autism and Developmental Disorders, 26,* 231–235.

Lovaas, O. I. (1987). Behavioral treatment and normal educational and intellectual functioning in young autistic children. *Journal of Consulting and Clinical Psychology, 55,* 3–9.

Lovaas, O. I., Berberich, J. P., Perloff, B. F., & Schaeffer, B. (1966). Acquisition of imitative speech by schizophrenic children. *Science, 151,* 705–707.

Perry, A. (1991). Rett syndrome: A comprehensive review of the literature. *American Journal on Mental Retardation, 96,* 275–290.

Reichler, R. J., & Lee, E.M.C. (1987). Overview of biomedical issues in autism. In E. Schopler & G. B. Mesibov (Eds.), *Neurobiological issues in autism* (pp. 13–41). New York: Plenum.

Ritvo, E. R., Freeman, B. J., Mason-Brothers, A., Mo, A., & Ritvo, A. M. (1985). Concordance for the syndrome of autism in 40 pairs of afflicted twins. *American Journal of Psychiatry, 142,* 74–77.

Schreibman, L. (1988). *Autism.* Newbury Park, CA: Sage.

Thorndike, R. L., Hagen, E. R., & Sattler, J. M. (1986). *The Stanford–Binet scale* (4th ed.) Chicago: Riverside.

Volkmar, F. R., & Rutter, M. (1995). Childhood disintegrative disorder: Results of the *DSM–IV* autism field trial. *Journal of the American Academy of Child and Adolescent Psychiatry, 34,* 1092–1095.

Yuwiler, A., & Freedman, D. X. (1987). Neurotransmitter research in autism. In E. Schopler & G. B. Mesibov (Eds.), *Neurobiological issues in autism* (pp. 263–284). New York: Plenum.

Zimmerman, I. L., Steiner, V. G., & Pond, R. E. (1979). *Preschool language scale.* Columbus, OH: Charles Merrill.

Learning, Motor,
and Communication Disorders

Cynthia R. Johnson
Gregory Slomka
Western Psychiatric Institute and Clinic
University of Pittsburgh School of Medicine

Learning, motor, and communication disorders refer to a group of disorders in the *Diagnostic and Statistical Manual of Mental Disorders* (4th ed. [*DSM–IV*]; American Psychiatric Association [APA], 1994) characterized by severe deficiencies in the development of skills in the academic, language, and motor domains. These disorders were previously referred to as specific developmental disorders in the third revised edition of the *DSM* (*DSM–III–R*; APA, 1987). The learning disorders are further divided into reading disorder, mathematics disorder, and disorder of written expression. There is also a learning disorder not otherwise specified diagnosis. Under motor skills disorder is developmental coordination disorder. Included in the communications disorders are expressive language disorder, mixed receptive–expressive language disorder, phonological disorder, and stuttering. As with learning disorders, there is also a communication disorder not otherwise specified diagnosis.

Although these are the psychiatric diagnostic labels used in the *DSM–IV* nomenclature, these disorders are subsumed under various labels by other classification systems to include learning disability, learning disorder, specific learning disability, language impairment, and communication disorder. Historically, many terms also have been used to describe learning and communication disorders. Earlier labels commonly applied included minimal brain dysfunction, congenital word blindness, dyslexia, developmental aphasia, and congenital aphasia (Baker & Cantwell, 1989; Silver & Hagin, 1990). According to Silver (1991), children with significant learning difficulties were considered mentally retarded before the 1940s. Since that time, the possibility of other influences has been considered.

Within the educational system, learning and communication disorders are encompassed under the terms "learning disability" and "speech and language impairment." According to Public Law 94–142, Education for Handicapped Children (1976), *learning disability* is defined as:

> a disorder in one or more of the more basic psychological processes involved in understanding or in using language, spoken or written, which may manifest itself in an imperfect ability to listen think, speak, read, write, spell, or to do mathematical calculations. The term includes such conditions as perceptual handicaps, brain injury, minimal brain dysfunction, dyslexia, and developmental aphasia. The term does not include children who have learning problems primarily the result of visual, hearing, or motor handicaps or mental retardation, or emotional disturbance, or of environmental, cultural, or economic disadvantage. (p. 46977).

Communication disorders are defined in the educational category of speech and language impairment. This category is narrowly defined as impairments in language, voice, fluency, or articulation that are not a result of sensory impairment or developmental delay. It should be underscored here that the definitions of learning, motor, and communication disorders in the *DSM–IV* (1994), as well as those of learning disability and speech and language disorders in the education system, are problematic in that the degree of deficits in skill development is not specified or standardized. Most commonly, a discrepancy model, meaning an unexpected discrepant between intellect or aptitude and learning achievement, has been applied. However, the formulas used to determine a discrepancy, as well as the varying assessment procedures, have been hotly debated over the past 25 years (see Shaw, Cullen, McGuire, & Brinckerhoff, 1995, for a review). Differing definitions and lack of precision have led to inconsistent criteria applied to diagnosing these disorders, thus resulting in a heterogeneous group. This is further complicated by the accepted view that learning disabilities present on a continuum from mild to severe impairment in skill development.

CLINICAL DESCRIPTION

Learning Disorders

Central to the diagnosis of the three disorders falling under this domain is more impairment in skill development than expected based on intellectual ability. In the educational system, the three disorders here are subsumed under the learning disabilities classification. The learning disability classification is the most prevalent of the educational handicapping conditions identified. Although the prevalence of learning disabilities is unclear, of the 20% of children who present with academic difficulties, 3% to 7% have some learning disability.

Reading Disorder. The critical feature of this learning disorder is significant impairment in skill development related to reading, such as word recognition, decoding skills, and comprehension. Again, the diagnosis is made when a discrepancy exists between intellectual ability and reading achievement levels and when mental retardation, sensory impairment, and environmental factors have been excluded as causes. The prevalence of reading disorder has been estimated to be 4% of school-age children (APA, 1994). Boys represent 60% to 80% of those individuals diagnosed with a reading disorder. Converging lines of research (Fletcher et al., 1994; Shaywitz, Fletcher, & Shaywitz, 1996) identify phonological processing deficits as a core vulnerability in impaired readers (i.e., deficits in sound–symbol associative skills). Deficiencies in naming and verbal fluency, limited vocabulary sophistication, auditory sequential memory, sentence recall, and problems with comprehending more complex grammatical structures constitute other higher level language processing inefficiencies that may be associated with impaired readers (Mann, 1994). As such, it is common that children who meet the diagnostic criteria for a reading disorder also will express deficits in other academic and language areas, possibly warranting other learning or communication disorder diagnoses. The specificity of language dysfunction (any deficiencies in the processing of the sound patterns of language) and risk for language-related learning disability is exemplified by Tallal, Dukelte, & Curtiss's (1989) finding that 85% of children exhibiting language disorders as preschoolers subsequently develop learning problems.

Mathematics Disorder. According to the *DSM–IV* (1994), the primary characteristic for mathematics disorder is marked impairment in arithmetic skills that is not attributable to mental retardation, school issues, or sensory impairment such as blindness or deafness. The level of significance must be such that impairment hinders achievement or living skills requiring arithmetic skills. A diagnosis typically is made when a severe discrepancy between overall cognitive ability and arithmetic achievement level is determined from the administration of standardized measures. These measures may be administered after the child has experienced difficulty in the school setting. Specific areas of impairment may include deficits in understanding math terminology, concepts, and operations; problems with the recognition of symbols; attention difficulties; and math problems requiring multiple skills. These deficiencies have been found to covary, with a wide range of deficits in higher cognitive functioning (see Keller & Sutton, 1991, for review). According to the *DSM–IV*, the prevalence of mathematics disorder is difficult to determine, but it is estimated to be found in 1% of school children.

Disorder of Written Expression. The main facet of this disorder is severe impairment in the development of expressive writing abilities. These include spelling, grammatical and punctuation skills, and poor paragraph organization. Manifestations of only spelling or legibility problems do not result in diagnosis of this disorder. The presence of this disorder, if severe, may become evident in the first couple of years of school. The disorder, however, may not become evident until later elementary levels if there is only mild impairment. Reading and language disorders very often are associated with this diagnosis. This condition is unfortunately often overshadowed by the severity of these disorders. As with the other learning disorders, a diagnosis is made with the help of standardized measures of ability and writing achievement.

Motor Skills

Developmental Coordination Disorder. This diagnostic category is reserved for significantly impaired coordination given chronological age and intellectual ability. The motor coordination must interfere with achievement or daily living activities including physical activities typical for age. An estimated 6% of young children are suspected to meet criteria for this diagnosis (Arnold, 1990). However, very little is reported about this category in comparison to other learning disorders.

Communication Disorders

Expressive Language Disorder. This diagnostic label implies significant deficiencies in the development of expressive language that may not be explained by other causes. A range of 3% to 10% of children are reported to be affected with expressive language disorder (APA, 1994; Arnold, 1990). Areas of difficulty may include a limited (small) vocabulary, limited sentence structure, omissions in spoken sentences, delayed speech development, and idiosyncratic word ordering. Other language disorders may coexist in an individual, particularly phonological disorder. A diagnosis usually depends on the demonstration of an expressive language score on a standardized test that is well below assessed intellectual ability and interferes with daily or academic functioning.

Mixed Expressive–Receptive Language Disorder. The hallmark characteristic for this diagnostic label is inadequacy in the development of both receptive and expressive language skills. The prevalence of this disorder is thought to be around 3% of school-age children. As with the other disorders, a continuum exists from mild impairment to severe impairment in the capability to understand words. Impairment is usually noticed in the toddler or preschool years depending on the severity level. Standardized language measures assessing receptive and expressive skills in comparison to assessed intellectual functioning are used to make a diagnosis.

Phonological Disorder. The essential clinical manifestation of this disorder is the failure to develop expected speech sounds given age and dialect of the individual's environment. *DSM–IV* (1994) reports 2% to 3% of elementary school-age children evidence moderate to severe phonological disorder. A higher prevalence rate of 5% to 10% of young children has been reported by Arnold (1990). Other learning and communication difficulties often are present in the same individual with a Phonological Disorder.

Stuttering. Disturbance of fluency and time patterning are the hallmarks of this disorder. Characteristic errors include repetitions of sounds, syllables, words, broken words, and production of words with excessive tension. The prevalence of stuttering in children is 1%, with a male to female ratio estimated at 3 to 1 (APA, 1994).

CAUSES OF THE DISORDERS

It is accepted that the causes of the these disorders are multiple. A general underlying assumption regarding the etiology is the presence of cerebral dysfunction, which may be of unknown origin (Obrzut & Boliek, 1991). Although in many cases, the particular reasons of a child's learning or language difficulty may be unclear, commonly cited etiologic factors include perinatal and neonatal insult. There is a correlation between disorders in this area and factors such as low birth weight, maternal smoking and alcohol consumption during pregnancy, and exposure to other toxins (Silver, 1991). Fifty percent of children with an elevated lead level have a reading disorder (Needleman, Schell, Bellinger, Leviton, & Allred, 1990). Additionally, specific infections such as a particular type of meningitis (Silver & Hagin, 1990) also have been related to later learning difficulties.

Although research findings have been equivocal, recurrent otitis media has been implicated in at least placing a child at risk for learning communication disorder

(Bishop & Edmundson, 1986). This is suggested as particularly the case when other perinatal risks are also present. Other causative or at least contributing risk factors involve early deprivation and malnutrition (Arnold, 1990). These is also speculation that a relation exists between learning and language disorders and seizure disorders (Klein, 1991; Silver & Hagin, 1990).

COURSE OF DISORDERS

Learning Disorders

The three disorders in this category—reading disorder, mathematics disorder, and disorder of written expression— progress in similar courses across time. These three disorders are most commonly identified during the early elementary school years, although the types of academic difficulty depend on the tasks required in each grade-level. Depending on the degree of impairment, improvement in the development of skills may be realized over time or, conversely, the impairment may interfere more as the child moves through school and academic tasks become increasingly challenging. Recent investigations of adults with learning disabilities add further support for this mixed prognosis.

Although some young adults with learning disabilities experience minimal difficulty in securing and maintaining satisfying employment, other persons with learning disabilities may have difficulty finding employment and may be quite dissatisfied with their attainments (Spreen, 1988). Currently, 5% to 10% of vocational rehabilitation caseloads consist of adults exhibiting learning disabilities. Variables likely influencing the prognosis include the level of impairment, early educational experiences, vocational track demands, and the coexistence of any other disabilities or illnesses.

There has been much speculation about the psychosocial adjustment of children with learning disabilities. More recently, findings have refuted the notion that all children with learning disabilities are socially and emotionally disturbed (Rourke, 1991), although it generally is held that among the learning disorder group are a disproportionate number who also experience psychosocial problems. Of particular interest is recent work suggesting that one proposed subtype of learning disability (i.e., better arithmetic skills than reading skills) places children more at risk for socioemotional and psychiatric problems (Rourke & Fuerst, 1991). Students labeled as learning disabled have been found to have lower status among their peers and are thought to be deficient in social skills or social competency (Bryan & Lee, 1990). There is a significant overlap of children with both a learning disorder and attention deficit hyperactivity disorder (ADHD). However, it is important to note that many children with learning disabilities experience no psychosocial difficulties (Pearl, 1992).

Communication Disorders

Among the communication disorders, a mild phonological disorder is the most likely to be resolved. Because this disorder is likely to be identified during the preschool years, early detection and intervention lead to a positive treatment outcome. However, children with severe phonological problems may need continued intensive treatment throughout childhood. In contrast, the prognosis of both expressive and mixed expressive–receptive language disorders is more variable and depends on the severity of the impairment, but difficulty is more likely to be experienced through childhood and adulthood. For expressive communication disorder, 50% of children are thought eventually to "outgrow" the disorder whereas the other half continue to experience difficulties, some subtle, in this domain (APA, 1994). A similar course has been noted for developmental receptive language disorder. Not surprisingly, the course of language disorders is closely tied to the demands placed on the individual. A person with a language disorder who remains in a line of employment where language skills are not critical may be very minimally affected. Conversely, the young adult who enters a vocational area where language skills are in demand is more likely to continue to be hindered by a language disorder.

Children with communication disorders are at increased risk for behavior and other psychiatric problems (Beitchman, Nair, Clegg, Ferguson, & Patel, 1986). In an extensive study conducted by Cantwell and Baker (1991), children with language and speech disorders had increased rates of psychiatric disorders when compared with the general population. Within this context, children with language comprehension deficits have the highest rates of social–emotional problems. Furthermore, the magnitude of undiagnosed language disorders in clinically referred groups of children remains substantial. Cohen (1996) found 34% of children referred for treatment of a primary psychiatric disorder revealing undiagnosed language disorder features. As with the learning disorder group, there is significant overlap between language disorder and ADHD.

Motor Coordination Disorder

As mentioned previously, developmental coordination disorder has received little investigative attention. It is thought that the course of this disorder is variable, with lack of coordination continuing through adulthood (APA, 1994). The impact of the disorder has not been clearly elucidated.

In summary, there is significant overlap or comorbidity of learning or academic skill disorders, language disorders, and other psychiatric disorders. From a theoretical standpoint, it is logical to assume that children who experience difficulty in comprehending and mastering academic demands, and who encounter failure repeatedly are more likely to develop behavioral or emotional problems. In this case, psychiatric and behavior problems are secondary to the learning or communication disorder. It has been suggested as well that the underlying mechanisms for the different disorders are similar, thus, if one disorder emerges, there is an increased likelihood that another will develop (Rourke & Fuerst, 1991). For example, the cerebral dysfunction assumed to be present in learning disorders also may be present in other disorders.

FAMILIAL CONTRIBUTIONS

As with most childhood disorders, socioeconomic and familial variables play a significant role in the development and prognosis of learning disorders. The putative effects of neglect and abuse, for example, on the development of children in general has been clearly documented (Garbarino, 1982). Ironically, this contributory cause of delay also places the child more at risk for future neglect and abuse. Although little has been noted particularly about learning, motor, and communication disorders, the presence of developmental and physical disabilities has been demonstrated to put children at increased risk for abuse (see Ammerman, Van Hasselt, & Hersen, 1988).

Not surprisingly, functioning of the family affects the prognosis of a child with learning problems. Ziegler and Holden (1988) described the different family characteristics that may influence the outcome and intervention needs of a child with a learning disability. They found that a "healthy" family may cope adequately in parenting a child with a learning disorder, whereas families described as "disorganized" and "blaming" have more difficulty responding to the child's needs and providing appropriate support and intervention.

PSYCHOPHYSIOLOGICAL INFLUENCES

Neurologic Contributions to Developmental Disorders

Neurobiologic foundations of learning and language disabilities have been investigated from three perspectives: electrophysiological, postmortem–cytoarchitectonic studies and structural brain imaging. Electroencephalographic (EEG) investigations of children with learning and language disorders have attempted to uncover a specific brain abnormality. Although no conclusive evidence has been obtained, there has been some noted differences in EEG findings in children with and without a reading disorder (Willis, Hooper, & Stone, 1992). However, no common EEG pattern typical of learning and language problems has been determined. Another electrophysiological indicator is the event-related potential (ERP) which is the average of electrical response to a stimulus that purportedly requires cognitive processing. Differences in waveforms have been shown on this measure between reading-disordered participants and a control group (Willis et al., 1992).

Neuroanatomical variations identified in reading-disabled participants include left cerebral hemisphere abnormalities in cortical laminar structure, small size of magnocellar thalamic nuclei, and asymmetry in the planum temporale. These abnormalities correlate with presumptive deficiencies in aspects of language mediation. Other abnormalities have been identified, including symmetry or reversed asymmetry in parieto–occipital regions, rightward asymmetry in prefrontal regions, and abnormalities in the structure of the corpus collosum. More recently, functional brain imaging has heralded a new epoch in neuroanatomical correlation. Basic processes underlying language mediation now are being elucidated via this technique (refer to Bookheimer & Dapretto, 1996).

Currently, neuroradiologic and neurometric techniques are not diagnostic of these conditions. From a research perspective, however, they offer important linkages to neural systems subserving language and other higher cognitive functions.

Assessment

The remarkable heterogeneity expressed in individuals with learning and developmental disorders, the frequency of co-occurring disorders, and the risk for associated behavior and adjustment disorders necessitate use of comprehensive assessment methodologies. Regardless of definitional criteria utilized (i.e., *DSM–IV*, federal, state, and local), commonalities identifiable within these classificatory systems include (a) failure to develop within a domain of functioning (academic, language, or motor); (b) documentation of a severe discrepancy between aptitude and objective measures of domain-specific functioning; (c) documentation of associated psychological process disorders; and (d) exclusion of other conditions that could adversely affect development (i.e., sensory–perceptual dysfunction, medical–neurological conditions, psychiatric conditions, or other environmental or psychosocial factors). Clinical history taking targeted at identification of maturational variance, description of the functional correlates of the disorder, and the delineation of any comorbid or exclusionary conditions begin the assessment process. Traditional psychoeducational assessment would follow if sufficient risk factors are identified. Utilization of intelligence testing establishes a "level of performance" or criterion against which performances on standardized tests of academic, language, or motor functioning can be contrasted. At this stage, the criterion of aptitude–performance discrepancy is accepted or rejected. Frequently, assessment is curtailed at this categorical level. To satisfy full criteria for differential diagnosis, specification of underlying or associated "psychological process disorder" features (cognitive, memory, sensory–motor, language, etc.) is required. Use of neuropsychological batteries aids in specifying such vulnerabilities.

The major contribution of neuropsychology as a discipline to the investigation of developmental disorders has been the application of empirical methods that permit the mapping of the underlying cognitive processing deficits constituting these disorders. Such methodologies have contributed to the (a) development of subtyping schemes to further specify variance within the major diagnostic clusters, (b) specification of unique patterns of strength and weakness to direct intervention planning, (c) development of multivariate baseline data that can be used to examine the interaction of maturation and treatment effects, and (d) outcome studies.

A variety of "fixed" (Halstead–Reitan; Reitan & Wolfson, 1993; or Luria Nebraska; Golden, Purisch, & Hammeke, 1985) and "flexible" test battery approaches has yielded demonstrated efficacy in supporting the differential diagnosis of developmental disabilities. Regardless of the strategy used, the breadth of coverage afforded in these batteries offers an opportunity for enhanced description of a disorder. In addition to psychological and neuropsychological evaluations, further behavioral assessment is used to aid in the exclusion of any primary or secondary psychopathology. The assessment process also may involve consultation from other disciplines to include audiology, speech pathology, occupational therapy, physical therapy, psychiatry, or neurology. With the integration of these data within a model driven by a neurodevelopmental framework—encompassing developmental, neurocognitive, behavioral, and psychosocial factors—an opportunity exists not only to describe a child from a categorical criterion (the "diagnosis"), but asks to provide the foundation for the implementation of remedial–accommodative inter ventions.

Genetic Contributions

There is mounting evidence that at least some of the disorders falling under the rubric of learning, motor, and communication disorders are significantly influenced by genetics. Reading and communication disorders have received the most attention with respect to genetic contributions. Support of the heritability of these disorders is provided by findings that there is a higher rate of these disorders in biological relatives than would be expected in general (APA, 1987, 1994; Arnold, 1990; Pennington & Smith, 1983). Twin studies have offered further evidence of a genetic predisposition for certain learning and language problems, with monozygotic (identical) twins showing a higher concordance of reading disorders than dizygotic (fraternal) twins. Converging evidence suggests that, although heterogeneity is expressed in the transmission of reading disability, a primary feature linked to heritibility is phonological coding problems (Olson, Wise, Conness, Rack, & Fulkner, 1989). Chromosomal studies suggest that some sex chromosome abnormalities are correlated with learning disorders. For example, boys with 47XXY have been shown to have poor reading skills (Bender, Puck, Salenblatt, & Robinson, 1986), and both 47XXX and 47XXY karotypes are correlated with language and motor skill delays (Bender et al., 1983). Much attention has been devoted to the relation of Fragile X syndrome, an abnormality of the X chromosome, and learning and language disabilities. The implication of chromosome number 6 and also has been recently uncovered as playing a role in learning and communication disorders (Caron et al., 1994). Learning and communication disorders also have been associated with low-incidence, genetically transmitted syndromes. The learning or communication impairment may be a primary or secondary feature of the syndrome. Examples include syndromes resulting in cleft palate, some lyssomal storage diseases, and some craniofacial syndromes (Shprintzen & Goldberg, 1986).

Overall, evidence from genetic research and investigations indicate that the genetic transmission of learning and communication disorders is likely to be heterogeneous with multiple paths of transmission (Pennington & Smith, 1983). There are likely many genetic mechanisms that produce the same phenotype. Furthermore, the expression of this genetic transmission is likely to be highly variable and at this point is not fully understood.

CURRENT TREATMENTS

Educational Placement and Services Models

Within the education system where children with learning and language disorders are served, several service options typically are considered. Service delivery options most typically have included regular classroom placement with and without consultation services, itinerant services, resource room services, self-contained classrooms, and separate special schools. An estimated 16% of children labeled as learning disabled are served in regular classrooms (Silver & Hagin, 1990). An advantage of educating such children in the regular classroom is the hope of removing the stigma of a special placement. However, the disadvantage is that the child with special learning needs may be in a large classroom with a regular education teacher who is not equipped to instruct such a student. Consultation services may be provided to the classroom teacher with special methods of instruction and curricula. Typical itinerant models involve a special education teacher with training in instructional methods for children with learning and language disorders to provide services to a child within the regular classroom setting. A majority of children classified as learning disabled are served in a resource room where educational intervention efforts are undertaken in the particular area of weaknesses; the child spends the remainder of the day in a regular classroom. An estimated 21% of children classified as learning disabled are enrolled in a self-contained classroom (Silver & Hagin, 1990), where they spend all or most of the day for academic instruction. Lastly, a small percentage of children with learning disabilities attend a special school. In keeping with the "least restrictive environment" mandate of P. L. 94–142 and IDEA, children classified as learning disabled or speech or language impaired are to be placed in the educational service that is least restrictive within this continuum of service options. Thus, this latter option is rarely used.

Specific modes of intervention that might be applied within any of these educational settings are described subsequently. Intervention strategies taken for specific developmental disorders rest in the assumptions made about the etiology of the disorder and the deficits targeted for treatment.

Behavioral Interventions

Within this framework, assumptions are made that the probability of a behavior occurring is a function of environmental antecedents and consequences of that particular behavior. The focus is on observable behavior and not on underlying inferred processes. Application of behavioral theory and principles have been widely implemented in educational settings and have had significant influence on instructional strategies for both learning disorders and communication disorders. Specific behavioral procedures may be divided into consequence strategies or stimulus control strategies.

Consequence strategies or approaches refer to the presentation of a reinforcer or punisher contingent on an observer behavior. Examples include the implementation of token or tangible reinforcement contingent on the observation of a prespecified target behavior. As a consequence, error correction methods, such as feedback, feedback with rehearsal, and positive practice, also have been demonstrated to promote academic progress (Singh, Deitz, & Singh, 1992).

Stimulus control strategies that have included modeling, stimulus fading, prompting, and delayed prompting. With *modeling* procedures, the correct response may first be modeled for the students by the teacher. This is often used in teaching sight words (Singh et al., 1991). *Stimulus fading* refers to a technique by which difficult discriminations are taught by slowly moving from an easy discrimination to the more difficult but target discrimination skill needed. For example, to teach a discrimination between the letters "N" and "M," the first letter might be presented initially as much larger than the second. As the student consistently identifies the letters appropriately, the sizes of the letters are systematically changed until the child is able to discriminate the letters when presented in equal sizes. *Prompting* refers to the addition of an addition cue or discriminative stimulus to respond in a particular manner. The presentation of a picture of a written word is used in teaching sight words, for example, showing a picture of a ball when presenting the word "ball." *Delayed prompting* refers to simply delaying the presentation of the cue or prompt with the goal of systematically fading out the need to have the prompt presented. Although presented separately here, it is often the case that a combination of behavioral approaches is implemented to ameliorate academic deficits. Published educational curricula incorporate these behavioral techniques in their programs. One example is the *Corrective Reading Program* (Englemann et al., 1978), which incorporates modeling, behavioral rehearsal, immediate corrective feedback, and frequent delivery of reinforcement from the teacher.

CASE ILLUSTRATION 1—READING DISORDER

Bobby, an 11-year-old boy, was the product of a breach delivery, with palsy noted in his right arm immediately after birth, but he recovered soon afterwards. Major developmental milestones were achieved at appropriate ages. On standardized intelligence testing, Bobby obtained above-average scores. Extensive academic testing indicated Bobby was 3 years below his grade level in reading, having no difficulty in math, and was approximately a year below grade level in language skills. Specific reading skill deficits involved decoding skills and comprehension of passages. Based on these findings, Bobby was placed in a resource room, where he participated in the corrective reading program. This highly structured program—which facilitates increased student attention—incorporates modeling, behavioral rehearsal, immediate corrective feedback, and high levels of reinforcement. The program involves a decoding strand and comprehension strand. Additionally, a home–school token program for students in this reading program was implemented. Students could earn a token in the form of play money for every 10 minutes of correct responding and participation. The "money" earned was used to purchase special privileges at home at the end of the school week, such as a later bedtime, renting a video, and choosing the menu for a meal. After1 year in this remedial program, Bobby was tested to be on grade level in reading. Hence, although he no longer needed the intensive remedial services in the resource room, during the subsequent school year, the resource room teacher provided consultation to the regular classroom teacher to facilitate ongoing academic adjustment.

Cognitive–Behavioral Interventions

A primary assumption made with cognitive–behavioral interventions is that thoughts and "cognitions" as well as environmental consequences influence overt behavior. This model further posits a reciprocal interaction between overt behavior and cognitions or feelings. It has been suggested that children with specific learning disorders are deficit in their ability to regulate, organize, and execute cognitive functions in an efficient, organized manner. Furthermore, it has been proposed that some children may lack verbal mediation skills or use verbal mediation in an ineffective manner (Meichenbaum & Genest, 1980). Based on these premises, goals of cognitive–behavioral interventions are to teach self-control and self-regulation. Commonly employed techniques include the use of self-assessment, self-monitoring, self-recording, and self-reinforcing techniques. Likewise, application of problem-solving or self-instructional strategies are often chosen for treatment. In the educational arena, these strategies are often collectively referred to as "learning strategies." Instruction in specific learning strategies involves teaching and providing practice in using the strategy tied to the academic material. Learning strategies are often incorporated as a component of the curriculum.

Psychoeducational, Neuropsychological, and Information Processing Interventions

The assumption in the psychoeducational model is that academic problems result from inability to perceive and integrate information received accurately. The goal within this framework is to assess strengths and weaknesses and then teach according to these assessed abilities. This is often referred to as "teaching to the modality" of strength or preference. The efficacy of this approach has yet to be proven; little academic gain has been noted in implementing this approach (Lyon & Moats, 1988).

   Similar to the psychoeducational approach are the information processing and neuropsychological approaches. As in the psychoeducational model, these models hold the assumption that the underpinning of learning disorders are deficits in how information is processed. Neuropsychological models posit that these processing deficits are manifestations of specific brain regions deficits or dysfunction. The processes are inferred from observed behaviors and are the target of remediation, not specific academic skills as with behavioral and cognitive–behavioral interventions.

Pharmacological Intervention

No medication is specifically recognized by the Federal Drug Administration as a treatment for learning disorder (Gadow, 1991). Although the use of pharmacological interventions for specific learning disorders remains controversial, there is evidence to suggest that a high percentage of children with diagnosed learning disorders receive medication. One estimate has been that 10% to 20% of children enrolled in special education services for learning disabilities are prescribed psychoactive medication (Gadow, 1991). The primary class of medication has been cerebral stimulants (Aman & Rojahn, 1991). This group includes methylphenidate (Ritalin), dextroamphetamine (Dexedrine), and pemoline (Cylert). The efficacy of these medication in the management of ADHD children has been well established. Given the significant overlap between ADHD and specific developmental disorders, it is not surprising that this class of medication has been used. In a recent review of numerous studies investigating the effects of stimulants on specific learning disorders, improvement on perceptual–cognitive and academic tasks was realized in approximately 30% to 40% of the measures, with medication having a larger impact on the perceptual–cognitive tasks (Aman & Rojahn, 1992).

Furthermore, the effects of stimulant therapy have been suggested to be more short-term in nature with questionable long-term effects (Aman & Rojahn, 1992). Similarly, Gadow (1991) concluded that although immediate academic productivity and efficacy increases, long-term gains on academic tests have not been demonstrated.

Other medications that have received some attention with regard to their effects on learning problems have included antianxiety agents, antidepressants, and neuroleptics or major tranquilizers. Although the number of studies evaluating the effects of these classes of medication on learning performance has been minimal, it is generally thought that unless the medication is indicated for other behavioral or psychiatric reasons, they are not appropriate to treat learning disorders. The use of vitamin therapy for treatment of learning disorders has similarly met with the same conclusion. Although the use of megavitamins, mineral supplements, and specific dietary regimens quickly gained popularity, findings have been equivocal and nonconclusive with regard to learning and behavior improvements. Hence, in way of summary, the current state of affairs suggests only minimal support for pharmacological intervention for specific developmental disorders. Medication is most likely to be indicated and effective if comorbid disorders are present that respond to a particular medication. Moreover, Aman and Rojahn (1991) warned that, in fact, adverse effects on learning may result from medication, and psychoactive medications should be prescribed with care.

CASE ILLUSTRATION 2—READING DISORDER; MATHEMATICS DISORDER; DEVELOPMENTAL EXPRESSIVE LANGUAGE DISORDER; DEVELOPMENTAL RECEPTIVE LANGUAGE DISORDER; ATTENTION DEFICIT HYPERACTIVITY DISORDER (ADHD)

Danny was an 8-year-old boy with a history of recurrent otitis media. In school, he was described as a cooperative student who tried very hard to please others. Academically, Danny had made no progress in the past year. He also was observed to be off task often and was easily distracted when doing independent seat work. He was assessed to have academic skills at the kindergarten level. The lack of academic gains were alarming in view of his average to high average intellectual potential.

According to guidelines, Danny qualified for services for students labeled learning disabled. This was based on the significant discrepancy between his ability level and current academic functioning. Danny was placed in a self-contained classroom for students with learning disabilities. In this classroom, the curriculum employed was the Direct Instructional System for Teaching Arithmetic and Reading (DISTAR) program (Engelmann & Bruner, 1974) and the DISTAR Language Program (Englemann & Osborn, 1976). As with the corrective reading program for older students, the DISTAR curriculum is highly structured and incorporates modeling, behavioral rehearsal at a fast pace, prompting and delayed prompting, corrective feedback, and immediate reinforcement. Additionally, Danny's attention difficulty and distractibility were treated with pharmacological therapy and cognitive–behavioral intervention. First, although Danny was prescribed Ritalin, this proved unsuccessful. An antidepressant was then prescribed. In combination, Danny was taught to self-monitor and self-record his on-task behavior. At the signal of a random bell, Danny was instructed to record whether he was paying attention with a plus or minus sign on an index card taped to his desk. Initially, Danny was rewarded for all self-monitoring efforts but was later rewarded only when he was in agreement with the teacher's recording of his on-task behavior. The combination of medication and self-monitoring increased Danny's attention, as indicated on the results from the Conners Teacher Rating Scale Hyperactivity Index (Connors, 1969). In the long-term, the specialized curriculum, cognitive–behavioral intervention, and pharmacological therapy are hoped to remediate skill deficits associated with the specific developmental disabilities.

SUMMARY

Specific developmental disorders comprise a group of disorders characterized by significant deficiencies in the development of skills related to academic, language, and motor abilities. Similarly, for all the specific developmental disorders, the delay in development must seriously interfere with the individual's function for a diagnosis to be made. A discrepancy between expected level of development based on current development in the specific domain is also a critical criterion for a specific developmental disorder diagnosis. This discrepancy typically is determined by the administration of standardized tests of cognitive or intellectual potential and achievement in academic, language, or motor skills.

It is likely that the causes of specific developmental disorders are multiple. Currently, associations between various environmental factors and genetic predispositions have been determined, but much more is to be learned about the etiology of these disorders. Psychophysiological measures have been used to investigate differences in these disorders and likely will provide more clues in the future to the understanding of the causes and mechanism of specific developmental disorders.

Treatment approaches that commonly are used include behavioral interventions, cognitive–behavioral treatments, information processing and psychoeducational interventions, and pharmacological therapy. There are many educational services for children classified as learning disabled, ranging in levels of restrictiveness from services in the regular classroom to special school placements. Although current treatment approaches have met with some degree of success, much more investigative efforts are necessary for a fuller understanding of these developmental disorders.

REFERENCES

Aman, M. G., & Rojahn, J. (1992). Pharmacological intervention. In N. N. Singh & I. L. Beale (Eds.), *Current perspectives in learning disabilities: Nature, theory, and treatment* (pp. 478–525). New York: Springer-Verlag.

American Psychiatric Association. (1987). *Diagnostic and statistical manual of mental disorders* (3rd ed.). Washington, DC: Author.

American Psychiatric Association. (1987). *Diagnostic and statistical manual of mental disorders* (3rd ed.). Washington, DC: Author.

American Psychiatric Association. (1994). *Diagnostic and statistical manual of mental disorders* (4th ed.). Washington, DC: Author.

Ammerman, R. T., Van Hassett, V. B., & Hersen, M. (1988). Maltreatment of handicapped children: A critical review. *Journal of Family Violence, 3,* 53–72.

Arnold, L. E. (1990). Learning disorders. In B. D. Garfinkel, G. A. Carlson, & E. B. Weller (Eds.), *Psychiatric disorders in children and adolescents* (pp. 237–256). Philadelphia: Saunders.

Baker, L., & Cantwell, D. P. (1989). Specific language and learning disorders. In T. H. Ollendick & M. Hersen (Eds.), *Handbook of child psychopathology* (2nd ed., pp. 93–104). New York: Plenum.

Beitchman, J. H., Nair, R., Clegg, M. A., Ferguson, B., & Patel, P. G. (1986). Prevalence of psychiatric disorders in children with speech and language disorders. *Journal of the American Academy of Child Psychiatry, 25,* 528–535.

Bender, B., Fry, E., Pennington, B., Puck, M., Salenblatt. J., & Robinson, A. (1983). Speech and language development in 41 children with sex chromosome anomalies. *Pediatrics, 71,* 262–267.

Bender, B., Puck, M., Salenblatt, J., & Robinson, A. (1986). Cognitive development of children with sex chromosome abnormalities. In S. D. Smith (Ed.), *Genetics and learning disabilities* (pp. 175–201). San Diego, CA: College-Hill.

Bishop, D.V.M., & Edmundson, A. (1986). Is otitis media a major cause of specific language disorders? *British Journal of Disorders of Communication, 21,* 321–338.

Bookheimer, S. Y., & Dappetto, M. (1996). Functional neuroimaging of language in children: Current directions and future challenges. In R. W. Thatcher, G. R. Lyon, & K. Krasnegor (Eds.), *Developmental neuroimaging: Mapping the development of brain and behavior* (pp. 143–153). New York: Academic Press.

Bryan, T., & Lee, J. (1990). Social skills training with learning disabled children and adolescents: The state of the art. In T. E. Scruggs & B.Y.L. Wong (Eds.), *Intervention research in learning disabilities* (pp. 263–278). New York: Springer-Verlag.

Cantwell, D. P., & Baker, L. (1991). *Psychiatric and developmental disorders in children with communication disorder.* Washington, DC: American Psychiatric Associates.

Caron, L. R., Smith, S. D., Fulker, D. W., Kimberling, W. J., Pennington, B. F., & DeFries, J. C. (1994). Quantitative trait locus for reading disability on chromosome 6. *Science, 266,* 276–279.

Cohen, N. J. (1996). Unsuspected language impairment in psychiatrically disturbed children: Developmental issues and associated conditions. In J. H. Beitchman, N. J. Cohen, M. M. Konstantareas & R. Tannock (Eds.), *Language, learning, and behavior disorders: Developmental, biological and clinical perspectives* (pp. 105–127). Cambridge, England: Cambridge University Press.

Conners, C. K. (1969). A teacher rating scale for use in drug studies with children. *American Journal of Psychiatry, 126,* 884–888.

Education of handicapped children and incentive grants program, 41 Fed. Reg. 46977 (1976).

Englemann, S., & Bruner, E. (1974). *DISTAR: An instructional system.* Chicago: Science Research Associates.

Englemann, S., Johnson, G., Hanner, S., Carnine, L., Meyers, L., Osborn, S., Haddox, P., Becker, W., Osborn, W., & Becker, J. (1978). *Corrective reading program.* Chicago: Science Research Associates.

Engelman, S., & Osborn, J. (1976). *DISTAR: An instructional system.* Chicago: Science Research Associates.

Fletcher, J. M., Shaywitz, S. E., Shankweiler, D. P., Katz, L., Liberman, I. Y., Stuebing, K. K., Francis, D. J., Fowler, A. E., & Shaywitz, D. A. (1994). Cognitive profiles of reading disability: Comparisons of discrepancy and low achievement definitions. *Journal of Educational Psychology, 86,* 6–23.

Gadow, K. (1991). Psychopharmacological assessment and intervention. In H. L. Swanson (Ed.), *Handbook on the assessment of learning disabilities* (pp. 351–372). Austin, TX: Pro-Ed.

Golden, C. J., Pourisch, A. D., & Hammeke, T. A. (1985). *Luria-Nebraska Neuropsychological Battery: Form I and II.* Los Angeles: Western Psychological Services.

Klein, S. K. (1991). Cognitive factors and learning disabilities in children with epilepsy. In O. Devinsky & W. H. Theodore (Eds.), *Epilepsy and behavior* (pp. 171–179). New York: Wiley.

Lyon, G. R., & Moats, L. C. (1988). Critical issues in the instruction of the learning disabled. *Journal of Consulting and Clinical Psychology, 56*, 830–835.

Mann, V. (1994). Phonological skills and the prediction of early reading problems. In N. C. Jordan & J. Goldsmith-Phillips (Eds.), *Learning disabilities: New direction for assessment and intervention* (pp. 67–87). Boston: Allyn & Bacon.

Meichenbaum, D., & Genest, M. (1980). Cognitive behavior modification: An integration of cognitive and behavioral methods. In F. H. Kanfer & A. P. Goldstein (Eds.), *Helping people change* (2nd ed., pp. 390–422). Elmsford, NY: Plenum.

Needleman, H. L., Schell, A., Bellinger, D., Leviton, A., & Allred, E. (1990). The long-term effects of exposure to low doses of lead in childhood. *New England Journal of Medicine, 322*, 83–88.

Obrzut, J. E., & Boliek, C. A. (1991). Neuropsychological assessment of childhood learning disorders. In H. L. Swanson (Ed.), *Handbook on the assessment of learning disabilities* (pp. 121–145). Austin, TX: Pro-Ed.

Olson, R., Wise, B., Conness, F., Rack, J., & Fulker, D. (1989). Specific deficits in component reading and language skills: Genetic and environmental influences. *Journal of Learning Disabilities, 22*, 339–348.

Pearl, R. (1992). Psychosocial characteristics of learning disabled students. In N. N. Singh & I. E. Beale (Eds.), *Current perspectives in learning disabilities: Nature, theory, and treatment* (pp. 96–125). New York: Springer-Verlag.

Pennington, B., & Smith, S. D. (1983). Genetic influences on learning disabilities and speech and language disorders. *Child Development, 54*, 369–387.

Reitan, R. M., & Wolfson, D. (1993). *The Halstead Reitan Neuropsychological Test Battery: Therapy & Interpretation.* Tuscon, AZ: Neuropsychology Press.

Rourke, B., & Fuerst, D. R. (1991). *Learning disabilities and psychosocial functioning.* New York: Guilford.

Shaw, S. F., Cullen, J. P., McGuire, J. M., & Brinckerhoff, L. C. (1995). Operationalizing a definition of learning disabilities. *Journal of Learning Disabilities, 28*, 586–597.

Shaywitz, S. E., Fletcher, J. M., & Shaywitz, B. A. (1996). A conceptual model and definition of dyslexia: Findings emerging from the Connecticut Longitudinal Study. In J. H. Beitchman, N. J. Cohen, M. M. Konstantareas, & R. Tannock (Eds.), *Language, learning and behavior disorders: Developmental, biological and clinical perspectives* (pp. 199–223). Cambridge, England: Cambridge University Press.

Shprintzen, R. J., & Goldberg, R. B. (1986). Multiple anomoly syndromes and learning disabilities. In S. D. Smith (Ed.), *Genetics and learning disabilities* (pp. 153–174). San Diego, CA: College-Hill.

Silver, L. B. (1991). Developmental learning disorders. In M. Lewis (Ed.), *Child and adolescent psychiatry: A comprehensive textbook* (pp. 522–528). Baltimore: Williams & Wilkins.

Silver, L. B., & Hagin, R. A. (1990). *Disorders of learning in childhood.* New York: Wiley.

Singh, N. N., Deitz, D. E., & Singh, J. (1992). Behavioral approaches. In N. N. Singh & I. E. Beale (Eds.), *Current perspectives in learning disabilities: Nature, theory, and treatment* (pp. 375–414). New York: Springer-Verlag.

Tallal, P., Dukette, D., & Curtiss, S. (1989). Behavior/emotional profiles of preschool language-impaired children. *Neuropsychologia, 27*, 987– 988.

Willis, W. G., Hooper, S. R., & Stone, B. H. (1992). Neuropsychological theories of learning disabilities. In N. N. Singh & I. E. Beale (Eds.), *Current perspectives in learning disabilities: Nature, theory, and treatment* (pp. 201–245). New York: Springer-Verlag.

Ziegler, P., & Holden, L. (1988). Family therapy for learning disabled and attention-deficit disordered children. *American Journal of Orthopsychiatry, 58*, 196–219.

Oppositional–Defiant and Conduct-Disordered Children

Carolyn Webster-Stratton
University of Washington

Clinicians working with families typically encounter children who exhibit persistent and frequent patterns of aggressive behavior resulting in significant impairment in everyday functioning at home, at school, or both. Such children are considered unmanageable by parents and teachers and are frequently rejected by their peer group. The term *externalizing* is used in this chapter to summarize a set of negativistic behaviors that commonly co-occur during childhood. These include noncompliance, aggression, tantrums, and oppositional–defiant behaviors in the preschool years; classroom and authority violations, such as lying and cheating, in school years; and violations of community, such as shoplifting in adolescence. The labels of oppositional–defiant disorder (ODD) and conduct disorder (CD) are used when we specifically characterize children according to the diagnostic criteria of the *Diagnostic and Statistical Manual of Mental Disorders* (4th ed., [*DSM–IV*]; American Psychiatric Association [APA], 1994).

Results of epidemiological studies have indicated that the percentage of children meeting the criteria for the clinical diagnoses of ODD and CD ranges from 7% to 25%, with the prevalence varying according to the population surveyed (Campbell, 1995; Earls, 1980; Jenkins, 1980; Landy & Peters, 1991; Richman & Graham, 1975; Richman, Stevenson, & Graham, 1982). The referral of children to clinicians for treatment of ODD and CD comprises one third to one half of all child and adolescent clinic referrals. These children and their families use multiple social and educational services provided to manage such children on a daily basis. Moreover, the prevalence of these behavioral disorders is increasing, creating a need for services that far exceeds available resources and personnel. Recent projections suggest that fewer than 10% of children with conduct problems ever receive mental health treatment (Hobbs, 1982). Fewer still receive treatment that has some empirical validation.

387

Although most parents at one time or another have problems with children's lying, cheating, stealing, hitting, and noncompliance to parental requests, it is the degree of destruction and disturbance, the occurrence of the behaviors in more than one setting (e.g., at home and at school), and the persistence of these behaviors over time beginning at an early age that causes concern for families and clinicians alike.

The following case description illustrates the type and severity of problems represented by the child with externalizing problems. Eric is an 8-year-old boy living at home with his father, mother, younger brother and an infant sister. He was referred to our clinic because of excessive aggressive behavior. Eric made a recent attempt to stab his younger brother, and makes frequent threats of violence toward both younger siblings. Eric's history reveals an escalation in aggressive activity including the initiation of physical fights with his peers, destruction of household property, and refusal to do what his parents request. Eric's parents express exasperation and exhaustion in dealing with Eric and talk about placing him in a boarding school. They have experienced difficulties managing his behavior since he was a toddler, and although initially they were told by professionals he would "outgrow" these problems, they found he became increasingly aggressive and defiant. He was kicked out of four preschools before he started grade school. The parents reported that they had tried every discipline strategy they could think of—such as time-out, yelling, hitting and spanking, taking away privileges, and grounding him. They felt none of these approaches worked. The parents reported feeling isolated and stigmatized by other parents with more "normal" children and felt teachers blamed them for his misbehaviors.

An evaluation of his behavior in Grade 3 reveals inattentiveness and distractibility in the classroom, aggression towards his peers—particularly during recess—and frequent reports of teacher calls to his mother to take him home from school because of misbehavior. His intellectual performance is within the normal range (WISC–R Full Scale IQ = 105; Wechsler, 1974) and his academic performance is barely passing. His school absences and physical fights have resulted in frequent contact with his parents and threats of expulsion.

Eric's home life includes the following characteristics: a mother with moderate depression and a father who drinks heavily. The father becomes abusive when he drinks, and often the children as well as the mother are targets of the abuse. Less than a year ago, the mother had another child, which has increased the stress in the family in that the mother had difficulty attending to the care and supervision of the older children.

DIAGNOSIS AND CATEGORIZATION

DSM–IV Criteria

According to the *DSM–IV* criteria (APA, 1994), externalizing behavior problems are referred to collectively as "Disruptive Behavior Disorders and Attention Deficit Disorders." There are three subgroups related to this larger category: ODD, attention deficit hyperactivity disorder (ADHD), and CD. As CD is rarely diagnosed before age 6, most young children with externalizing symptoms fit the criteria for ODD, ADHD, or a combination of the two disorders. The primary features of CD are conduct disturbance lasting at least 6 months, the number of conduct problems, and violation of the rights of others. A diagnosis of CD requires a disturbance lasting for at least 6 months during which three of the following symptoms are present: often bullies, threatens, or intimidates others; often initiates physical fights; has used a weapon that can cause serious physical harm; has stolen with confrontation with a victim; has been physically cruel to people; has been physically cruel to animals; has forced someone into sexual activity; often lies or breaks promises; often stays out at night despite parental prohibitions, beginning before age 13; has stolen items of nontrivial value; has deliberately engaged in fire setting; has deliberately destroyed another's property; has run away from home overnight at least twice while living in parental home; often truant from school beginning before age 13; and has broken into someone else's house, building, or car.

The *DSM–IV* criteria (APA, 1994) mention three subtypes of CD: childhood onset type, which consists of at least one conduct problem occurring before age 10, and the adolescent onset type, where there are no conduct problems prior to age 10. Also, severity is rated from mild to moderate to severe.

The diagnosis of ODD requires a pattern of negativistic, hostile, and defiant behavior lasting 6 months, during which four of the following are present: often loses temper; often argues with adults; often actively defies or refuses to comply with adults' rules; often deliberately does things that annoy other people; often blames others for his or her mistakes; is often touchy or easily annoyed; is often angry and resentful; and is often vindictive.

Other Classifications

Another method for classifying CD is through empirically derived syndromes. Two distinct syndromes that consistently emerge from the literature are undersocialized–aggressive and socialized–aggressive (Quay, 1986). The undersocialized–aggressive syndrome includes behaviors such as fighting, disobedience, temper tantrums, destructiveness, uncooperativeness, and impertinence. The socialized–aggressive syndrome includes truancy from school, absence from the home, stealing with peers, loyalty to delinquent friends, and gang involvement (Quay, 1986). It is important to remember that conduct disorder, although relatively stable, is manifested by different patterns of behavior in different age and gender children. For example, for young girls, the behavior pattern reflects similar verbal aggression and oppositional behavior as for young boys, but less overt physical aggression (Webster-Stratton, 1996). This difference in physical aggression may account for the fact that three times as many young boys are referred to clinics for this problem as girls.

Another method of categorization is known as the *salient symptom approach*. This method suggests subcategorizing CD based on the specific behaviors displayed by the child. The dimensions of the subcategorization are the overt dimension (e.g., physical aggression, disobedience, destruction of property) and the covert dimension (e.g., lying, stealing, truancy). The overt–covert dimensions are supported by evidence that certain behaviors tend to cluster together, and that the two dimensions differ in their response to treatment.

Comorbidity

There seems to be considerable diagnostic ambiguity between CD, ODD, and ADHD in the young pre-school age group as well as true comorbidity (i.e., hyperactive, impulsive, inattentive children have externalizing problems). Current reports suggest that as many as 75% of children who are identified as having ADHD are also identified as conduct-disordered (Safer & Allen, 1976). It has been proposed that hyperactivity may influence the emergence of CD. Loeber and Schmaling (1985) suggested that hyperactivity is inherent in conduct-disordered children. However, careful assessment of the child may reveal that the child actually meets the criteria for one and not the other. The criteria for ADHD and conduct disorder, although similar, are not identical, and it is important that ODD and ADHD be differentiated for both clinical and empirical reasons. Furthermore, those children who display concurrent ODD and ADHD appear to be at higher risk for development of severe antisocial behavior than children with either single-disorder category (Walker, Lahey, Hynd, & Frame, 1987).

CAUSES OF THE DISORDER

It is widely accepted that multiple risk factors that often are interrelated contribute to the development and maintenance of child CD (Caspi & Moffitt, 1995). It is important to review briefly the major categories influencing the establishment of CD. These include child biological factors, school-related factors, and parent psychological factors.

Child Biological Factors

The "child deficit" hypothesis argues that some abnormal aspect of the child's internal organization at the physiological, neurological, or neuropsychological level—which may be genetically transmitted—are at least partially responsible for the development of CDs. The most overt evidence for a biological component for children with ODD/CD includes the disproportion of boys to girls and the apparent heritability of antisocial traits, based on the high number of criminals in some families (Hutchings & Mednick, 1977). Although psychobiological research in young children with ODD and/or CD has lagged behind the family research, the last decade has seen substantial evidence that supports the inclusion of biological factors in etiologic models of development of CDs.

Temperament has perhaps been researched the most in regard to conduct problems. *Temperament* refers to aspects of the personality that show consistency over time and across situations and are identified as constitutional in nature. These personality characteristics include activity of the child, emotional responsiveness, quality of mood, and social adaptability (Thomas & Chess, 1977). It appears that there is support for the mother's objective rating of child temperament and independent observations of the child, and that these objective components are not overwhelmed by subjective components. Research has indicated that there are links between specific temperament scales and specific behavior problem scales. For example, studies have shown strong correlations between early assessments of temperamental characteristics (e.g., infant unadaptability, irritability, inattentiveness, impulsivity) and later externalizing problems (Bates, 1990; Campbell, Ewing, Breaux, & Szumowski, 1986; Lillenfield & Waldman, 1990). Frequent and intensive negative child affect also consistently predicts behavior problems (Bates, 1990). In one longitudinal study, mother reports of infant difficultness (at 6 months) and infant resistance to control (at 1 year) showed significant predictions to maternal report of externalizing problems at ages 6 and 8 years (Bates, Bayles, Bennett, Ridge, & Brown, 1991).

Although studies have shown that early assessments of temperament predict later behavior problems, the amount of variance accounted for in the outcome is relatively small. Factors such as family conflict or support and quality of parent management strategies appear to interact with temperament to influence outcome. Several recent studies have shown that extreme (difficult) infant temperament in the context of favorable family conditions is not likely to increase the risk of disruptive behavior disorder at age 4 (Maziade, Cote, Bernier, Boutin, & Thivierge, 1989). In general, the findings on temperament clearly support the notion of Thomas and Chess (1977) that "no temperamental pattern confers an immunity to behavior disorder, nor is it fated to create psychopathology" (p. 4).

In addition to temperament, other factors related to cognition have been implicated. The seminal work of Dodge and his colleagues has been extraordinarily helpful in suggesting that aggressive children may have cognitive deficits in their ability to process and encode their social experiences (Crick & Dodge, 1994). A series of studies has revealed that aggressive children display deficits in social problem-solving skills (Asarnov & Callan, 1985), define problems in hostile ways, seek less information, generate fewer alternative solutions to social problems, and anticipate fewer consequences for aggression (Richard & Dodge, 1982; Rubin & Krasnor, 1986; Slaby & Guerra, 1988; Webster-Stratton & Lindsay Woolley, 1997).Aggressive behavior in children is correlated with their low empathy for others across a wide age range (Feshbach, 1989). It also has been suggested that children with CDs distort social cues during peer interactions (Milich & Dodge, 1984), including attributing hostile intent to neutral situations. Aggressive children search for fewer cues or facts (i.e., they underutilize cues) when determining another's intentions (Dodge & Newman, 1981) and focus more on aggressive cues (Goutz, 1981). There is also a suggestion in the literature that attributional distortions and underutilization of cues pertain specifically to the subgroup of aggressive children with comorbid ADHD (Milich & Dodge, 1984).

It is theorized that the impulsive cognitive style of these children limits their scanning of pertinent social cues before responding, so that they have difficulty perceiving or understanding another person's point of view and are unable to interpret interpersonal situations accurately. This would explain both their lack of social competence and their antisocial behavior. Negative exchanges with peers or with parents and teachers then contribute to rejection, further negative responses, and further negative attributions.

School-Related Factors

Academic performance has been implicated in child CD. Low academic achievement and learning disabilities often manifest themselves in conduct-disordered children early on during the elementary grades and continue through high school (Kazdin, 1987). Reading disabilities in particular are associated with CD (Sturge, 1982). One study indicated that conduct disordered children exhibited reading deficits, defined as a 28-month lag in reading ability, compared with the reading ability of normal children (Rutter, Tizard, Yule, Graham, & Whitmore, 1976). The relation between academic performance and CD is not merely unidirectional but is considered a bidirectional relation. It is unclear whether disruptive behavior problems precede or follow the learning disabilities, language delay, or neuropsychological deficits. However, there is some evidence that cognitive and linguistic problems may precede disruptive behavior problems (Schonfeld, Shaffer, O'Connor, & Portnoy, 1988).

The school setting has been studied as a risk factor contributing to CDs. Rutter et al. (1976) found that characteristics such as emphases on academic work, teacher time on lessons, teacher use of praise, emphasis on individual responsibility, teacher availability, school working conditions (e.g., physical condition, size), and teacher–student ratio were related to delinquency rates and academic performance.

Parent Psychological Factors

Parent psychopathology places the child at increased risk for CD. Specifically, depression in the mother, alcoholism and substance abuse in the father, and antisocial behavior in either parent have been implicated in increasing the child's risk for CD (Faraone, Biederman, Keenan, & Tsuang, 1991; Frick, Kuper, Silverthorn, & Cotter, 1995). Maternal depression is associated with misperception of a child's behavior. For example, mothers who are depressed perceive their child's behavior as maladjusted or inappropriate. Depression also influences the parenting behavior directed toward a child's misbehavior. For example, depressed mothers often increase the number of commands and criticisms they give their children. The child, in response to the increase in parent commands, displays an increase in noncompliance and deviant child behavior (McMahon & Forehand, 1988; Webster-Stratton & Hammond, 1988). Therefore, it is hypothesized that maternal depression and irritability indirectly leads to behavior problems as a result of negative attention reinforcing inappropriate child behaviors, inconsistent limit-setting, and emotional unavailability. A community study found that maternal depression, when evident when the child was 5 years old, was related to parent and teacher reports of behavior problems at age 7 (Williams, Anderson, McGee, & Silva, 1990). However, it is also important to recognize that depression is associated with other stressors, such as poverty, marital distress, and negative life events, making it difficult to determine what effects are attributable to depression per se.

As might be expected, the presence of antisocial or criminal behavior in either parent places the child at greater risk for CDs. In particular, criminal behavior and drug abuse in the father are consistently demonstrated as parental factors increasing the child's risk. Grandparents of conduct-disordered children are also more likely to show antisocial behavior compared to grandparents of children who are not antisocial. An association also has been found between children's aggression and their parents' aggression at the same age (Huesmann, Eron, Lefkowitz, & Walder, 1984). In a recent prospective study of 171 clinically referred boys, parental antisocial personality disorder (ADP) was a significant correlate of conduct problems, but the interaction of parental ADP and boys' verbal intelligence predicted the persistence of conduct problems over time (Lahey, Loeber, Hart, & Frick, 1995).

COURSE OF THE DISORDER

A number of theorists have shown high continuity between disruptive and externalizing problems in the preschool years and conduct disorders in the school-age and adolescent period (Campbell, 1995; Egeland, Kalkoske, Gottesman, & Erickson, 1990; Loeber, 1990; Rutter, 1985). Richman et al. (1982) found that 67% of children with externalizing problems at age 3 continued to be aggressive at age 8. Other studies have reported stability correlations between .5 and .7 for externalizing scores (Rose, Rose, & Feldman, 1989). Campbell's (1991) review of a series of longitudinal studies of hard-to-manage preschoolers revealed a surprising convergence of findings. At least 50% of preschool children with moderate to severe externalizing problems continued to show some degree of disturbance at school age, with boys doing more poorly than girls. Of those with continuing behavior problems, 67% met diagnostic criteria for ADHD, ODD, or CD at age 9. Moreover, Loeber (1991) contended that these estimates of stability may actually be higher because manifestations of the problems are episodic, situational, and change in nature (e.g., from tantrums to stealing). Additionally, the more dysfunctional families are often lost to follow-up.

Early onset of ODD also appears to be related to antisocial behavior and the development of severe problems in later life (e.g., alcoholism, drug abuse, juvenile delinquency, adult crime, marital disruption, interpersonal problems, and poor physical health; Campbell, 1991; Kazdin, 1987). However, not all children with ODD–CD incur a poor prognosis as adults. Data suggest that fewer than 50% of the most severe conduct-disordered children become antisocial adults; this represents an unusually high percentage.

Developmental theorists have suggested that there may be two developmental pathways related to conduct disorders: the "early starter" versus "late starter" model (Patterson, DeBaryshe, & Ramsey, 1989). The hypothesized early onset pathway begins formally with the emergence of oppositional disorders (ODD) in early preschool years and progresses to aggressive and nonaggressive symptoms of CDs in middle childhood, and then to the most serious symptoms by adolescence (Lahey, Loeber, Quay, Frick, & Grimm, 1992). In addition, there is an expansion of settings in which the problem behaviors occur, from home to daycare or preschool, then to school, and finally to the broader community. For adolescents who develop CDs later in their adolescent years, the prognosis seems more favorable than for the adolescents who have a chronic history of CDs stemming from their preschool years. Adolescents who are most likely to be chronically antisocial are those who first evidenced symptoms of ODD in the preschool years (White, Moffit, Earls, & Robins, 1990). Thus, the primary developmental pathway for serious conduct disorders in adolescence and adulthood appears to be set in the preschool period. ODD is a sensitive predictor of subsequent CD, in that nearly all CD youths have shown previous ODD.

Although not all ODD children become CD, and not all conduct-disordered children become antisocial adults, certain risk factors contribute to the continuation of the disorder: (a) early age of onset (preschool years); (b) breadth of deviance (across multiple settings such as home and school); (c) frequency and intensity of antisocial behavior; (d) diversity of antisocial behavior (several versus few) and covert behaviors at early ages (stealing, lying, fire-setting); and (e) family and parent characteristics (Kazdin, 1987). Different types of family adversity, psychological distress, and insularity are likely to co-occur, making it difficult to isolate the individual contribution of any of these factors to the development of CDs. It is most likely the additive or synergistic effects of a number of risk factors that predicts chronic CDs.

FAMILY CONSIDERATIONS

Divorce, Marital Distress, and Violence

Specific family characteristics have been found that contribute to the development and maintenance of child CD. Interparental conflict leading to and surrounding divorce are associated with, but are not strong predictors of, child CD (Kazdin, 1987).

In particular, boys appear to be more apt to show significant increases in antisocial behaviors following divorce. However, some single parents and their children appear to do relatively well over time postseparation, whereas others are chronically depressed and report increased stress levels. One explanation might be that for some single parents, the stress of divorce sets in motion a series of stages of increased depression and increased irritability. This increased irritability leads to a loss of friendships and social support, placing the mothers at increased risk for more irritable behaviors, ineffective discipline, and poor problem-solving outcomes. The poor problem-solving of these parents, in turn, results in increased depression and stress, completing the spiraling negative cycle. This irritability simultaneously sets in motion a process whereby the child also becomes increasingly antisocial (Forgatch, 1989).

Once researchers began to differentiate between parental divorce, separation, and discord, they began to understand that it was not the divorce per se that was the critical factor in the child's behavior, but rather the amount and intensity of parental conflict and violence (Grych & Fincham, 1990; O'Leary & Emery, 1982; Porter & O'Leary, 1980), spousal physical aggression (Jouriles et al., 1991; Jouriles, Murphy, & O'Leary, 1989), and child-rearing disagreements (Dadds, Schwartz, & Sanders, 1987). For example, children whose parents divorced but whose homes were conflict-free were less likely to have problems than children whose parents stayed together but experienced a great deal of conflict; children whose parents divorced and continued to have conflict had more conduct problems than did children whose parents experienced conflict-free divorce. In Webster-Stratton's (1997b) studies of over 600 families with conduct problem children, 75% of the parents reported having been divorced at least once described their current marriage as distressed, or both; half of the married couples reported experiences with spouse abuse and violence. These findings highlight the role of parents' marital conflict and spousal aggression as key factors influencing children's behavior problems. This is corroborated by the earlier work of Rutter et al. (1974), who reported that marriages characterized by tension and hostility were more closely associated with children's behavior disturbances than were marriages characterized as apathetic and indifferent. In a recent study (Webster-Stratton & Hammond, 1999), it was reported that observations of marital interactions characterized as high in negative affect, uninvolved, and with ineffectual conflict management skills were significantly correlated with children's peer interactions characterized as noncollaborative, aggressive, and high in negative conflict management skills.

Marital conflict is associated with more negative perceptions of the child's adjustment, inconsistent parenting, the use of increased punitiveness and decreased reasoning, and fewer rewards with children (Stonemen, Brody, & Burke, 1988). Conflictual, unhappy marriages that display aggressive behavior are more likely to incite the formation of CD. It is consistently demonstrated that, if aggressive behavior is present in the marital relationship, the likelihood of CD is greater than if verbal conflict is present alone. The explanation is that the aggressive parent may serve as a model to the child.

Frick, Lahey, Hartdagen, and Hynd (1989) have proposed two models to account for the correlation between marital distress and child CDs. One model proposes a direct and an indirect path from marital satisfaction to child CDs. The other model predicts that the significant correlations between marital satisfaction and child conduct problems are more an artifact of the common effects of maternal antisocial personality and social class. They found the relation between marital satisfaction and child conduct problems was based primarily on the common association with maternal antisocial personality, but that social class did not play an important role as a third variable. These findings seem to argue the importance of the parents' psychological adjustment as a primary determinant of the effects of marital stress on parent–child interactions.

Family Adversity.   Research suggests that life stressors, such as poverty, unemployment, crowded living conditions, and illness, have deleterious effects on parenting and are related to a variety of forms of child psychopathology, including CDs (Kazdin, 1985; Rutter & Giller, 1983). Families with conduct-disordered children report the incidence of major stressors two to four times greater than in nonclinic families (Webster-Stratton, 1990c). Parents of conduct-disordered children indicate that they experience more day-to-day hassles as well as major crises than do nonclinic families. An accumulation of minor day-to-day chronic life hassles is related to more aversive maternal interactions, including higher rates of coercive behavior and irritability in the mother's interactions with their children. Reports also have shown maternal stress to be associated with inept discipline practices, such as explosive discipline and "nattering" with children (Forgatch, Patterson, & Skinner, 1988; Webster-Stratton, 1990c).

The link between social class and child CD is confounded by variables such as overcrowding, poor supervision, single-parenthood, community violence, and other related risk factors (Kazdin, 1987). When control is obtained for these risk factors, social status shows little relation to CD. Social class as a summary label that includes multiple risk factors can influence child CD.

Family Insularity. Maternal insularity is another parental factor implicated in child CD. *Insularity* is defined as "a specific pattern of social contacts within the community that are characterized by a high level of negatively perceived social interchanges with relatives and/or helping agency representatives and by a low level of positively perceived supported interchanges with friends" (Wahler & Dumas, 1984, p. 387). This definition is important because it appears that rather than the number or the amount of social contacts, it is the individual's perception of whether the social contact is supportive or helpful that makes the social contact advantageous. Mothers characterized as insular are more aversive and use more aversive consequences with their children than noninsular mothers (Wahler & Dumas, 1986).

Insularity and lack of support also have been reported to be significant predictors of a family's relapse or failure to maintain treatment effects (Webster-Stratton, 1985d; Webster-Stratton & Hammond, 1990)

Parent–Child Interactions. Parenting interactions are clearly the most well researched and most important proximal cause of CDs. Research has indicated that parents of conduct-disordered children lack certain fundamental parenting skills. For example, parents of such children have been reported to exhibit fewer positive behaviors; to be more violent and critical in their use of discipline; to be more permissive, erratic, and inconsistent; to be more likely to fail to monitor their children's behaviors; to be less likely to be involved in their child's schooling; and to be more likely to reinforce inappropriate behaviors and to ignore or punish prosocial behaviors (Patterson & Stouthamer-Loeber, 1984; Webster-Stratton, 1985a, 1985c). Patterson and his colleagues have called this the *coercive process* (Patterson, 1982), whereby children learn to escape or avoid parental criticism by escalating their negative behaviors, which in turn leads to increasingly aversive parent interactions. These negative responses, in turn, directly reinforce the child's deviant behaviors. In addition, it is important to note the affective nature of the parent–child relationship. There is considerable evidence that a warm, positive bond between parent and child leads to a more socially competent child (Baumrind, 1971).

Research on family socialization related to aggression increasingly recognizes the bidirectionality of child and parent behavior (Lytton, 1990). It is conceivable that negative parenting behavior is, in part, a reaction to difficult, oppositional, aggressive child behavior. Certainly, research has indicated that conduct-disordered children engage in higher rates of deviant behaviors and noncompliance with parental commands than do nonconduct-disordered children. When interacting with their mothers, conduct-disordered children exhibit fewer positive verbal and nonverbal behaviors (smiles, laughs, enthusiasm, praise) than nonconduct disordered children. In addition, conduct-disordered children exhibit more negative nonverbal gestures, expressions, and tones of voice in interactions with both mothers and fathers. These children have less positive affect, seem depressed, and are less reinforcing to their parents, thus setting in motion the cycle of aversive interactions for mothers as well as fathers (Webster-Stratton & Lindsay Woolley, 1997).

Other Family Characteristics.   Other family characteristics contributing to the formation of CD include birth order (delinquency and antisocial behaviors are found more often in middle children; Wadsworth, 1979) and family size (increased family size is associated with higher rates of delinquency, but only when there is a greater number of male children; Offord, 1982).

PSYCHOPHYSIOLOGICAL, NEUROPSYCHOLOGICAL AND GENETIC INFLUENCES

Neurological abnormalities are inconsistently correlated with CD. An association exists more generally with childhood dysfunction than with CD, in particular (Kazdin, 1987). There is some evidence and much speculation that deficits in verbal functioning, language comprehension, impulsivity, and emotional regulation may be related to the left frontal lobe and its relation to the limbic system in aggressive children (Gorensten & Newman, 1980). However, it is important to note that conduct-disordered children have an increased likelihood of abuse and subsequent head and facial injuries, resulting in neurological abnormalities (e.g., soft signs, EEG aberrations, seizure disorders).

Other psychophysiological variables have been implicated in child CD. Quay (1993) and McBurnett and Lahey (1994) provided detailed interpretations of theories related to key constructs of arousal and reactivity. In particular, Quay provides a framework for interpreting findings regarding aggressive CDs by integrating Jeffrey Gray's (1987) neurobiological and neuroanatomical theories with current research, focusing on a behavioral activation (or reward) system, a behavioral inhibition system, and a generalized arousal (fight–flight) system, each comprised of distinct neuroanatomical regions and neurotransmitter pathways. Children with early-onset CD (aggressive-type) appear to differ from normal children by having lower psychophysiological or cortical arousal and low autonomic reactivity on a variety of indexes (e.g., lower heart rate and lower skin conductance; Mednick, 1977; Quay, 1993; Quay, Routh, & Shapiro, 1987; Raine, Venables, & Williams, 1990; Wadsworth, 1976). Furthermore, children with ODD—CD in combination with ADHD have been reported to be the lowest on autonomic measures (Quay, 1993). Underarousal has been thought to be a component of the failure of conduct problem children to learn to inhibit impulsive behavioral responses. Moreover, underarousal lessens the emotional impact of punishment: The child is less responsive to normal parental social sanctions for negative behavior and appears relatively indifferent to negative behavioral feedback (from parents, teachers, and peers). Because negative consequences are not as salient for these children, attempts by parents and teachers to extinguish misbehavior may fail to generalize to the next occasion. The assumption is that low arousal and low reactivity diminish avoidance conditioning—the effects of socialization stimuli—fueling a poor response to punishment. Underarousal also may contribute to sensation-seeking behavior. This pattern of underarousal appears different for children with late-onset CD, who display arousal and reactivity responses that are elevated above those of early-onset children as well as normal comparison samples (McBurnett & Lahey, 1994).

Findings with neurotransmitter metabolites have been interpreted in terms of an imbalance favoring the behavioral activation—reward system over the behavioral inhibition system in young children (e.g., Daugherty & Quay, 1991; Quay, 1993). Research on hormonal influences, particularly cortisol levels, is less conclusive. Cortisol secretion may be related to comorbid anxiety disorders in CD samples (McBurnett & Lahey, 1994). There is incomplete evidence for a relation between testosterone and aggression (McBurnett & Lahey, 1994). A controversial but more complex model presents children with CD as indexed by two systems: an underactive inhibitory system (characterized by lower noradrenergic activity and autonomic response) combined with an overactive dopanergic system, thought to reflect a reward-seeking behavioral motivation (Fowles, 1988; Raine et al., 1990; Scerbo et al., 1990). Cumulative evidence comparing children with ADHD and children with CD on measures of sympathetic response- and reward-seeking responses (Raine & Jones, 1987; Raine et al., 1990) suggests that children with conduct problems rate lower than normal on inhibitory responses and high on noveltyseeking, whereas children with ADHD rate lower than normal on inhibitory responses only. However, although there is substantial biological evidence for an underactive inhibitor system, most evidence thus far for an overactive reward system has been behavioral rather than biological.

With regard to neuropsychological variables, Moffitt and Lynam (1994) have contended, in a controversial perspective, that youth with early-onset CD have an IQ deficit that is an indicator of broad-based neuropsychological dysfunction. Furthermore, they argued that deficits in verbal reasoning and "executive" functioning (thought to measure planning, inhibition of impulses, internalization of language, and working memory) characterize the profiles of early-onset, aggressive, antisocial youngsters who are comorbid for ADHD. Such deficits in language have implications for the regulation and inhibition of behavior. For example, verbal deficits may make it more difficult for children to comprehend rules and instructions, as well as to utilize self-talk to modulate and inhibit their own responses. Findings regarding verbal deficits are supported by other research that finds an increased prevalence of reading disabilities in children with conduct problems (Sturge, 1982).

Biological explanations for antisocial behavior need not imply that an antisocial personality is biologically predetermined. Instead, biology is subject to environmental impact. Biology in itself is only suggestive of a vulnerability to other risk factors (e.g., parental socialization influences) for antisocial behaviors. Furthermore, biological markers of antisocial behavior thus far have been isolated only for subsets of children with more extreme deficits, such as undersocialized aggressive CD, who are often doubly impaired with ADHD. We do not know what, if anything, biology has to contribute to our understanding of milder deficits. Lahey, Hart, Pliszka, Applegate, and McBurnett (1993) stated clearly that investigation of biological variables such as neurotransmitters, brain imaging techniques, skin conductance, or hormonal influences does not imply that psychosocial factors have no role in the maintenance of childhood conduct problems. On the contrary, Lahey et al. (1993) postulated "that a socioenvironmental event (e.g., abnormal infant experience) could be one of the causes of aggression, but that the effect of this experience on aggression is mediated by alterations in neurotransmitter activity" (p. 142). Indeed, as noted earlier, the amount of variance accounted for by biological factors appears to be relatively small. Factors such as family support, quality of parent management strategies and SES appear to interact with the child's biology or temperament to influence outcome, again suggesting the mediating role of the child's microsystems.

These findings have implications for how biological deficits may be amplified over time and for how parenting can exacerbate or minimize inherent deficits. For example, children with these biological deficits are not as responsive to their parents' normal efforts to praise, reward, set limits, and impose negative consequences; they even may appear to their parents to be indifferent to their discipline attempts. This lack of responsiveness on the part of the child not only makes the child less reinforcing to the parent but leads parents to feel the effects of their parenting approaches are unpredictable. As parents continue to experience a lack of success in parenting, they develop a low sense of self-efficacy and become more inconsistent in their parenting responses and sometimes resort to increased use of spanking and harsh punishment.

Finally, there is little direct evidence regarding genetic contributions to child CD. However, twin studies have shown greater concordance of antisocial behavior among monozygotic rather than dizygotic twins (see Kazdin, 1987). Adoption studies that assess children separated from biological parents indicate that offspring show a greater increase in antisocial behavior. The increased risk due to antisocial behavior in the biological parent establishes some credence for the inclusion of genetics in accounting for a portion of the variance in CD (Rende & Plomin, 1993). Yet, it also has been established that genetic factors alone do not account for the emergence of the disorder. Rather, these studies affirm the effect of genetic influences in conjunction with environmental factors, such as adverse conditions in the home (e.g., marital discord, psychiatric dysfunction), and ineffective family problem-solving and coping techniques (Cadoret & Cain, 1981).

CURRENT TREATMENTS

A variety of interventions have been proposed to decrease the prevalence (i.e., the number of existing cases at a given point in time) and incidence (i.e., the number of new cases) of ODD and CDs. The former are directed toward treatment, and the latter towards prevention. Treatment and prevention are not separate entities. Prevention is implemented when the child has not yet manifested the disorder, and treatment consists of reducing or eliminating the severity, duration, and manifestation of the disorder.

Child Training

Several prominent strategies are emphasized as a means of preventing child conduct problems. One view that has received particular attention is training children to be more socially competent. *Social competence* refers to

> the ability of the child to negotiate the course of development including effective interactions with others, successful (adaptive) completion of developmental tasks and contacts with the environment (e.g., school performance), and use of approaches that increase adaptive functioning (e.g., problem-solving). (Kazdin, 1990)

However, the development of social competence has rarely been applied to conduct-disordered children. Rather, it has been found to be useful in protecting the child against risk factors that can lead to maladjustment and psychopathology (Kazdin, 1990).

Treatment interventions for children have been aimed toward altering the child's cognitive processes (e.g., problem-solving and self-control skills and positive self-statements) and developing prosocial rather than antisocial behaviors (e.g., play skills, friendship and conversational skills). The first type of intervention is based on a hypothesized skills relationship. Such programs coach children in positive social skills, such as LaGreca and Santogrossi's (1980) program that targets nine behaviors (including smiling, greeting, joining, inviting, conversing, sharing, cooperating, complimenting, and grooming). The second type of intervention relies on verbal instructions and discussions, opportunities to practice the skill with peers, role-playing, games, stories, and therapist or teacher feedback and reinforcement. Most of these programs have not specifically focused on children with CDs (Spivak, Platt, & Shure, 1976). Those that do specify this population have tended to intervene with older school-age children and adolescents (rather than preschool and early school-age children; Lochman, Lampron, Gemmer, Harris, & Wyckoff, 1989).

Evaluations of these innovative child training programs are somewhat encouraging, but with certain caveats. First, there is a lack of evidence to indicate that these programs are effective in reducing conduct problems per se (Denham & Almeida, 1987); their effectiveness has been demonstrated primarily in terms of improved social skills—and only for older children, and only at school (e.g., Kazdin, Esveldt, French, & Unis, 1987; Kendall & Braswell, 1985; Lochman & Dunn, 1993; Spivak et al., 1976). Younger or less mature children, as well as more aggressive children, have been relatively unaffected by social skills and problem-solving interventions (Coie, 1990). Other limitations of existing child training interventions include a failure to show generalization of skills. Improvements in social and cognitive skills demonstrated in the laboratory, in inpatient settings, or at school do not readily generalize to other settings. Nor are short-term treatment effects consistently maintained over time (for review, see Beelmann, Pfingste, & Losel, 1994; Prinz, Blechman, & Dumas, 1994). The absence of generalization and maintenance of acquired skills appears to hold regardless of the child's age.

In a study with young children (ages 4 to 7 years) with conduct problems, it was reported that a child training program that is multifaceted, involving affective, behavioral, and cognitive components, was effective in promoting more positive peer interactions, more successful problem-solving strategies, and fewer conduct problems—results that were maintained 1 year later (Webster-Stratton, 1997). It appears that child programs such as this one that involve videotape modeling, practice activities, games, home activities with parents and coordination with teachers will be more likely to be effective and to generalize across sections (Webster-Stratton, 1997).

Parent–Family Interventions

In many parent–family interventions, the objective has been to reduce or eliminate the severity, duration, and manifestation of conduct problems. The modification of problematic parenting skills can serve as the primary mechanism for change in child CD. The rationale for this approach is supplied by research indicating that parents of conduct-disordered children have an underlying deficit in certain fundamental parenting skills.

One of the most highly influential parent training programs was developed by Patterson, Reid, and their colleagues at the Oregon Social Learning Center (Patterson, Chamberlain, & Reid, 1982). The parent training program originally was developed for children ages 3 to 12 years who are engaged in overt CDs. Program content also has been modified for use with adolescents. Parents begin by reading a programmed text, either *Living with Children* (Patterson, 1976) or *Families* (Patterson, 1975). They then participate in learning five family management practices, which include pinpointing and tackling problem behaviors, social tangible reinforcement techniques, discipline procedures, monitoring or supervision of the children, and problem-solving and negotiation strategies.

A second important parent training program was designed to treat noncompliance in young children, ages 3 to 8 years. Originally developed by Hanf (1970), the program was later modified and evaluated extensively by McMahon and Forehand (1984). Phase 1 of the program teaches parents how to use "descriptive commenting" with appropriate behaviors—that is, to describe their children's behavior when they are acting in appropriate, positive ways—and to praise those behaviors. Parental attention reinforces and thus promotes positive behaviors that replace negative behaviors. Phase 2 of the program includes teaching parents ways to give direct, concise, and effective commands and how to use 3-minute time-outs for noncompliance.

Eyberg (1988) developed "parent–child interaction therapy" (Hembree-Kigin & McNeil, 1995). Although the emphasis on behavior management is maintained, the skills for child-directed play are elaborated in great detail, composed of "DRIP skills:" describe, reflect, imitate, praise. Eyberg (1988) presented this program as an integration of traditional play skill values and current behavioral thinking about child management (Eyberg & Boggs, 1989). It is believed that parents' nondirective play with their children improves children's frustration tolerance, helps reduce the anger level of oppositional children, and offers more opportunities for the occurrence of prosocial behavior (Hembree-Kigin & McNeil, 1995). Moreover, engaging in play with their children helps parents recognize their children's positive qualities. As parents learn nondirective play skills, they learn how to respond in a sensitive and genuine manner, how to relate to their child's level of development, and how to stimulate their learning. The primary goal of this intervention is to strengthen attachment and establish a warm, loving relationship between the parent and child.

A fourth example of a parent training program for young conduct-disordered children is a parenting program developed by Webster-Stratton (1981, 1982a, 1982b, 1984). The method of the BASIC program utilizes a series of 10 videotapes (250 vignettes) to model parenting skills and was designed for parents with children ages 3 to 8 years. The content includes components of Hanf and Kling (1973) and Eyberg, Boggs and Algina's (1995) "child-directed play" approaches, as well as the strategic use of differential–attention and effective use of commands. The content incorporates Patterson's (1982) discipline components concerning time-out, logical and natural consequences, and monitoring. In addition, teaching parents problem-solving and communication strategies with their children is emphasized (D'Zurilla & Nezu, 1982; Spivak & Shure, 1985). The training content is embedded in a relational framework including parent group support, mutual problem-solving, self-management, and a collaborative relationship with the therapist. This treatment approach is designed to promote parental self-efficacy and engagement with the program and reduce parental resistance and dropout (Webster-Stratton & Hancock, 1998). Cognitive aspects of the program include teaching parents how to examine and alter irrational thinking, which interferes with implementation of effective parenting practices.

A fifth family-based intervention, called "Functional Family Therapy" (Alexander & Parsons, 1982; Barton & Alexander, 1981), was developed for delinquent adolescents. This approach integrates family systems, behavioral, and cognitive perspectives. The program consists of several components. The first component is identifying and modifying (through relabeling) family members' blaming attributions and inappropriate expectations. The next component involves teaching behavioral management strategies, such as communication skills, behavioral contracting, and contingency management. During the final component, therapists help parents generalize and maintain their new skills.

The use of parent training as an intervention for child conduct problems has been extensively researched, and there are a number of excellent reviews (Henggler, Borduin, & Mann, 1993; Kazdin, 1987; Miller & Prinz, 1990; Patterson, Dishion, & Chamberlain, 1993). Programs have reported high parental ratings of acceptability and consumer satisfaction (Cross Calvert & McMahon, 1987; McMahon & Forehand, 1984; Webster-Stratton, 1989). The success of short-term treatment outcome has been verified by significant changes in parents' and children's behavior, and in parental perceptions of child adjustment in comparison to waiting-list control families. Home observations have indicated that parents are successful in reducing children's levels of aggression by 20% to 60%. Generalization of behavior improvements from the clinic setting to the home over reasonable follow-up periods (1 to 4 years) and to untreated child behaviors also has been demonstrated (e.g., McMahon & Forehand, 1984; Patterson et al., 1982; Webster-Stratton, 1984; Webster-Stratton, Kolpacoff, & Hollinsworth, 1988). Although the majority of studies have been conducted with White mothers, there is some beginning evidence that parent training is also effective with fathers (Webster-Stratton, 1985b; Webster-Stratton, 1990b), and with ethnic minorities (Strayhorn & Weidman, 1989; Webster-Stratton, 1998b).

Nonetheless, for about one third of families with conduct-disordered children, these parent management strategies are insufficient. Parent and family characteristics such as marital distress, spouse abuse, lack of a supportive partner, maternal depression, poor problem-solving skills, and high life stress are associated with fewer treatment gains (Forehand, Furey, & McMahon, 1984; Forgatch, 1989).

A more comprehensive approach, which encompasses parents' cognitive, psychological, marital, and social adjustment, would seem to be more appropriate given the number of issues faced by at least one third to one half of these families. Several programs have instituted expansions to their standard parent training treatment. Dadds et al. (1987) have incorporated Partner Support Training to their Child Management Training program. A "parent enhancement therapy" designed by Griest, Forehand, Wells, and McMahon (1980) augments general family functioning, marital adjustment, parent personal adjustment, and the parents' extrafamilial relationships. The advanced videotape program (ADVANCE) developed by Webster-Stratton (1990a) and colleagues focuses on personal parent issues other than parent skills and cognitive perspectives such as anger management, how to cope with depression, effective communication skills, problem-solving and conflict resolution skills, ways to give and get support, how to teach children to problem-solve and manage their anger, and, finally, how to support children's education (Webster-Stratton, 1994). These and other expanded programs have resulted in improvements in intervention outcomes (Dadds & McHugh, 1992; Wahler, Cartor, Fleischman, & Lambert, 1993; Webster-Stratton, 1994). In a randomized study, it was found that in families who completed the expanded parent training (ADVANCE plus BASIC) for parents and a 22-week social skills and problem-solving training program (for children), there was a significant increase in positive social skills in children when interacting with peers than in the children whose parents only received the parenting intervention (without the child training; Webster-Stratton, 1997).

School and Community Interventions

Several preventive interventions relevant to CD have focused on the school and the community. The High/Scope Perry Preschool Program was designed to aid children who are considered at risk for school failure. The parents of families involved in this program were low-income, living in stressful environments, and had low levels of education. The children began the program at age 3 and participated for a 2-year period (Schweinhart & Weikart, 1988). The program addressed children's intellectual, social, and physical needs necessary for the adequate development of decision-making and cognitive processes.

Another strategy aimed at preventing CD emphasizes the development of conventional values and behaviors as a way of protecting the child against deviance. Social bonding refers to the integration of commitment, attachment, and adherence to the values of the family, school, and peers (Hawkins & Lam, 1987; Hawkins & Weiss, 1985). There are several components to this approach. The classroom component addresses issues of deportment, interactive teaching, and cooperative (peer-involved) learning techniques. The family component consists of parent management training and assists family members in conflict resolution. Peer social-skills training and community-focused career education and counseling are also included. The multiple contexts of family, school, and peers may increase the bonding necessary to reduce the onset of antisocial behavior (Kazdin, 1990).

The School Transitional Environmental Program (STEP; Felner & Adan, 1988) was designed to help children through the normal process of entering a new school (e.g., middle to high school). Transitions are associated with decreased academic performance, and psychological problems, including antisocial behavior. The STEP attempts to reduce the negative effects of school transitions and increase the child's coping responses.

In addition to prevention programs, efforts also have focused on populations where CD is evident. One school-based program was designed to prevent further adjustment problems among children who evinced signs of low academic motivation, family problems, and a record of disciplinary referrals (Bry & George, 1980). The program included meetings with students where rewards were given for appropriate classroom behavior, punctuality, and a reduction in the amount of disciplinary action. Meetings also were scheduled with teachers and parents to focus on specific problems with individual children.

In another school-based approach, Webster-Stratton (1998a, 1998b) adapted the BASIC parenting program for use as a prevention program with Head Start parents who were considered at risk for having children with conduct problems because of their increased number of risk factors associated with poverty. The program was offered to all parents enrolled in Head Start either in the schools, housing units, or church settings near where the parents were living. The focus of the intervention was on parenting and promoting stronger parent bonds with teachers and schools.

Another school-based approach targeted adolescent anger control (Lochman, Lampron, Gemmer, & Harris, 1987). Content includes teaching adolescents interpersonal problem-solving skills, strategies for increasing physiological awareness, and learning to use self-talk and self-control during problem situations. Another example for older school-age children with CDs is the Problem-Solving Skills Training (PSST) program (Kazdin, Esveldt-Dawson, French, & Unis, 1987), which was based on the programs developed by Kendall and Braswell (1985). The PSST focuses on cognitive processes (perceptions, self-statements, attributions, expectations, and problem-solving skills) that presumably underlie maladaptive behavior. The primary focus of treatment is on the thought processes rather than on the behavioral acts that result and teaches children a step-by-step approach to solving problems. Shure and Spivak (1982) also developed an interpersonal problem-solving training program that has been used with a variety of populations to train children to be socially competent. Finally, Webster-Stratton (1990a) developed a videotape-based training curriculum for young children ages 3 to 8 years that focuses on teaching children to understand feelings, to problem-solve, to manage anger, how to be friendly, how to talk to friends, and how to succeed in school. This program uses life-size puppets, real (nonacted) videotape examples of children at home and in school situations, cartoons, and practice assignments that can be used by both parents and teachers (Webster-Stratton, 1997).

Community-based interventions address prevention (for those youth at risk for antisocial behavior) and treatment (those youth identified with signs of antisocial behavior). One extensive program targeted a housing project with over 400 children from poverty-stricken families (ages 5–15) considered to be at risk for antisocial behavior (Offord & Jones, 1983). Youths were involved in activity programs and trained in specific skill areas (e.g., swimming, hockey, dancing, and musical instruments). Children were evaluated on their progress in the programs, and rewards were provided for attendance and participation.

Another program was designed for youth who were identified as delinquent. The intervention assigned the youth to a college student volunteer who worked with the youth 6 to 8 hours per week in the community (Davidson & Basta, 1988). Weekly supervision for the volunteers was provided by a juvenile court staff member and supervision took place in the court worker's office (Wicks-Nelson & Israel, 1991).

Community-based interventions also have addressed both prevention and treatment. One program used existing community facilities to intervene with delinquent youth and youth who had no history of prior arrests (Fo & O'Donnell, 1975; O'Donnell, Lygate, & Fo, 1979). Adults were recruited from the community and trained to conduct behavior modification programs with youth. They also involved youth in various activities (e.g., arts and crafts, fishing, and camping). Individualized reward programs focused on such behaviors as home activity, fishing, and truancy (Kazdin, 1990).

The parent and child programs reviewed here are not an exhaustive review but rather they are examples of programs that provided some evidence to indicate that early preventive interventions can reduce risk factors that place children at risk for CDs and can reduce the onset of antisocial behavior.

Case Illustrations

Mr. and Mrs. W came into the Parenting Clinic with their 7-year-old son Doug. Mrs. W describes Doug's behavior as unmanageable at home. Her concerns include (a) hitting and other aggressive behaviors, especially when Doug does not get what he wants; (b) noncompliance with his mother's requests; and (c) intense negative exchanges between Doug and her.

When the parents were asked how they usually discipline Doug, they reported that they put him in "time-out for a couple of minutes" or take away a privilege. They also yell frequently and use threats and spankings. Mrs. W, however, expresses concern that none of the discipline techniques has really achieved any success, and she reports feelings of helplessness and discouragement. Mr. W quickly established himself as a management expert and claimed that it is his wife who lacks the ability to deal with Doug. He feels that she is not a "tough enough" disciplinarian.

Mr. and Mrs. W stated that his problems hitting other children began in preschool, and that he always has had difficulties in making transitions from one activity to the next. Doug's previous teacher reported frequent conflicts between Doug and his peers. Both parents talk about long months during which they waited for Doug to get older, in the expectation that things would get easier for them. However, they agree that things have not changed with time, and instead their child has become increasingly defiant and noncompliant.

Mrs. W is working full-time and is pregnant with her second child. Mrs. W states that she has not had any recent psychological treatment, but says she has dealt with depression several times and has taken antidepressants on one occasion. However, she is not taking medication now and states that at this time she is not depressed. Mrs. W also admits that she receives very little support from friends with similar-aged children and fears rejection from other parents if they "knew what my child really was like."

Mrs. W also has no support from her own family. She states that her mother is an alcoholic and is verbally abusive toward her. Also, several years ago, Mrs. W and her mother had a major break in communication, although currently she continues to have contact with her mother once or twice a week. According to Mrs. W, her father is a very capable and responsible man.

Mr. W's mother was recently hospitalized and is quite ill. Mr. W's father is an alcoholic and continues to drink moderately. Mr. W described his mother as caring and very giving. He states that his father "didn't have much in the way of parenting skills" and punished excessively. Mr. W is completing a graduate degree and is in the process of interviewing for a job that will lead to a family move in the near future.

Recent stressors that have occurred in this family include attending graduate school, potential move to a new residence, and responsibility for one difficult child during a second pregnancy. Positive indicators include a supportive marriage, no alcohol or drug use, and no indication of child or spousal abuse.

Assessment of both the parents and child indicate that parent training would be appropriate for this family, and plans are made for Mr. and Mrs. W to attend the 12-week group training sessions. As they participate in the videotape training program the attitude of Mr. and Mrs. W at first oscillates between despair and guilt concerning their previous parenting approaches to Doug's problems and the unrealistic hope that they will have a "quick fix" to his problems before the new baby arrives.

As Mr. and Mrs. W participate in the parent training program and learn new parenting strategies such as play skills, effective reinforcement, and nonviolent discipline approaches, they come to realize that different children require different degrees of parental supervision and different parenting skills in order to be successfully socialized. They begin to blame themselves less, and focus more constructively on which parenting techniques will work to enhance Doug's prosocial behavior and personality strengths, as well as decrease his noncompliance and aggression. Initially, they experience some immediate success with Doug using the play and praise strategies.

As the program progresses, Mrs. W notices that Mr. W appears to become increasingly critical of the program. Mr. W believes strongly that spanking is the optimal discipline strategy for Doug, and that it works to manage his behaviors. He has difficulty with the use of strategies such as sticker charts, ignoring, logical consequences, and problem-solving. This resistance to the program and conflict with his wife's viewpoint results in marital stress. Also, Doug's behavior begins to regress in spite of the parents' initial hard work. Mrs. W's reaction is depression and anger as she experiences setbacks and states that she is having difficulty motivating herself to complete program assignments. Both parents experience feelings of resignation as the therapist collaborates with them and helps them realize the chronic nature of Doug's problems, which require them to agree on strategies that will be used consistently by both of them over the "long haul." Mr. W is helped to understand that many of his attitudes toward discipline come from his father's approach, which he readily admits was an approach that led to alienation and resentment in their relationship. Working toward the long-term benefits of nonviolent discipline rather than the short-term benefits of spanking becomes an objective to which they both agree.

In learning to cope more effectively with Doug's problems, Mr. and Mrs. W work with the therapist to apply concepts and practices shown in the standardized videotapes. Mrs. W acknowledges difficulty generalizing certain parenting techniques to various problem behaviors. However, the parent group sharing and problem-solving provides a variety of different examples for Mrs. W and helps her understand how to generalize the skills she has learned to new situations and problems.

During the final weeks of treatment, Mr. and Mrs. W are supportive of each others' efforts and begin to discover they can cope successfully with the daily hassles of having a conduct-disordered child. They have gained confidence in themselves and their ability to cope with future problems. Both parents indicate that they also have gained an acceptance and understanding of Doug's temperament and needs and are better able to empathize with his feelings and perspectives. Mrs. W was particularly encouraged because the parent group provided support and a safe place where she could be honest and vulnerable about her feelings and difficulties with Doug. She felt that the parent group provided a tremendous sense of connection with other parents who had experienced similar problems and thereby reduced her feelings of isolation and loneliness.

SUMMARY

Conduct disorder is highly prevalent in our society, and has an impact on the school, community, family, and peer relationships. Children with CDs are characterized by a "complex" pattern of behaviors, including lying, cheating, stealing, hitting, and noncompliance to parental requests.

Multiple influences, including child, parent, and school-related factors, contribute to the development and maintenance of child CD. The association between CD and psychophysiological or genetic influence is inconclusive. Rather, studies affirm that genetics and child biological factors, in conjunction with environmental factors, are influential in the development and maintenance of the disorder.

The course of the disorder indicates that early oppositional and conduct problems often persist into adulthood and appear to be related to aggressive and antisocial behavior later in life. The primary factors contributing to the continuation of CD include age of onset; deviant behavior across multiple settings; several versus few behaviors; and number and type of child, family, and school risk factors.

Current treatments have been proposed to decrease the prevalence and incidence of conduct disorder. Intervention measures have been proposed on various levels—community, school, family, peer, and child—and have achieved varying success. The importance of developing prevention and treatment programs designed to arrest or curtail child CD cannot be overemphasized. An integrated and comprehensive approach treating both the child and the family, in the home and in broader social contexts (including tender training in school), will produce better results than if multiple factors are not included. Program design also must consider that CD is often a chronic problem transmitted across generations. Therefore, successful intervention necessitates periodic training and support offered at critical stages throughout the child's and family's development and within a variety of settings (home and school).

REFERENCES

Alexander, J. F., & Parsons, B. V. (1982). *Functional family therapy*. Monterey, CA: Brooks/Cole.

American Psychiatric Association. (1994). *Diagnostic and statistical manual of mental disorders* (4th ed.). Washington, DC: Author.

Asarnov, J. R., & Callan, J. W. (1985). Boys with peer adjustment problems: Social cognitive processes. *Journal of Consulting and Clinical Psychology, 53,* 80–87.

Barton, C., & Alexander, J. F. (1981). Functional family therapy. In A. S. Gurman & D. P. Kniskern (Eds.), *Handbook of family therapy* (pp. 403–443). New York: Brunner/Mazel.

Bates, J. (1990). Conceptual and empirical linkages between temperament and behavior problems: A commentary on the Sanson, Prior and Kyrios study. *Merrill-Palmer Quarterly, 36,* 193–199.

Bates, J. E., Bayles, K., Bennett, D. S., Ridge, B., & Brown, M. M. (1991). Origins of externalizing behavior problems at eight years of age. In D. J. Pepler & K. H. Rubin (Eds.), *The development and treatment of childhood aggression* (pp. 93–120). Hillsdale, NJ: Lawrence Erlbaum Associates.

Baumrind, D. (1971). Current patterns of parental authority. *Psychology Monographs, 1,* 1–102.

Beelmann, A., Pfingste, U., & Losel, F. (1994). Effects of training social competence in children: A meta-analysis of recent evaluation studies. *Journal of Abnormal Child Psychology, 5,* 265–275.

Bry, B., & George, F. (1980). The preventive effects of early intervention on the attendance and grades of urban adolescents. *Professional Psychology, 11,* 252–260.

Cadoret, R., & Cain, C. (1981). Environmental and genetic factors in predicting adolescent antisocial behavior. *Journal of the University of Ottawa, 6,* 220–225.

Campbell, S. B. (1991). Longitudinal studies of active and aggressive preschoolers: Individual differences in early behavior and outcome. In D. Cicchetti & S. L. Toth (Eds.), *Internalizing and externalizing expressions of dysfunction: Rochester Symposium on Developmental Psychopathology* (pp. 57–90). Hillsdale, NJ: Lawrence Erlbaum Associates.

Campbell, S. B. (1995). Behavior problems in preschool children: A review of recent research. *Journal of Child Psychology and Psychiatry and Allied Disciplines, 36,* 113–149.

Campbell, S. B., Ewing, L. J., Breaux, A. M., & Szumowski, E. K. (1986). Parent-referred problem three-year-olds: Follow-up at school entry. *Journal of Child Psychology and Psychiatry, 27,* 473–488.

Caspi, A., & Moffitt, T. E. (1995). The continuity of maladaptive behavior: From description to understanding in the study of antisocial behavior. In D. Cicchetti & D. J. Cohen (Eds.), *Developmental psychopathology* (Vol. 2, pp. 472–511). New York: Wiley.

Coie, J. D. (1990). Toward a theory of peer rejection. In S. R. Asher & J. D. Coie (Eds.), *Peer rejection in childhood* (pp. 365–398). Cambridge, England: Cambridge University Press.

Crick, N. R., & Dodge, K. A. (1994). A review and reformulation of social information processing mechanisms in children's social adjustment. *Psychological Bulletin, 115,* 74–101.

Cross Calvert, S., & McMahon, R. J. (1987). The treatment acceptability of a behavioral parent training program and its components. *Behavior Therapy, 18,* 165–179.

Dadds, M. R., & McHugh, T. (1992). Social support and treatment outcome in behavioral family therapy for child conduct problems. *Journal of Consulting and Clinical Psychology, 60,* 252–259.

Dadds, M. R., Schwartz, M. R., & Sanders, M. R. (1987). Marital discord and treatment outcome in behavioral treatment of child conduct disorders. *Journal of Consulting and Clinical Psychology, 16,* 192–203.

Daugherty, T. K., & Quay, H. C. (1991). Response perseveration and delayed responding in childhood behavior disorders. *Journal of Child Psychology and Psychiatry,* 453–461.

Davidson, W., & Basta, J. (1988). Diversion from the juvenile justice system: Research evidence and a discussion of issues. In B. B. Lahey & A. E. Kazdin (Eds.), *Advances in clinical child psychology* (Vol. 9, pp. 375–379). New York: Plenum.

Denham, S. A., & Almeida, M. C. (1987). Children's social problem solving skills, behavioral adjustment, and interventions: A meta-analysis evaluating theory and practice. *Journal of Applied Developmental Psychology, 8*, 391–409.

Dodge, K. A., & Newman, J. P. (1981). Biased decision-making processes in aggressive boys. *Journal of Abnormal Psychology, 90*, 375–379.

D'Zurilla, T. J., & Nezu, A. (1982). Social problem-solving in adults. In P. C. Kendall (Ed.), *Advances in cognitive behavioral research and therapy* (Vol. 1,). New York: Academic Press.

Earls, F. (1980). The prevalence of behavior problems in 3-year-old children. *Archives of General Psychiatry, 37*, 1153–1159.

Egeland, B., Kalkoske, M., Gottesman, N., & Erickson, M. F. (1990). Preschool behavior problems: Stability and factors accounting for change. *Journal of Child Psychology and Psychiatry, 31*, 891–909.

Eyberg, S., & Boggs, S. R. (1989). Parent training for oppositional–defiant preschoolers. In C. E. Schaeffer & J. M. Brienmeister (Eds.), *Handbook of parent training* (pp. 105–132). New York: Wiley.

Eyberg, S. M., Boggs, S., & Algina, J. (1995). Parent–child interaction therapy: A psychosocial model for the treatment of young children with conduct problem behavior and their families. *Psychopharmacology Bulletin, 31*, 83–91.

Eyberg, S. M. (1988). Parent–child interaction therapy: Integration of traditional and behavioral concerns. *Child and Family Behavior Therapy, 10*, 33–46.

Faraone, S. V., Biederman, J., Keenan, K., & Tsuang, M. T. (1991). Separation of *DSM–III* attention deficit disorder and conduct disorder: Evidence from a family genetic study of American child psychiatry patients. *Psychological Medicine, 21*, 1091–1121.

Felner, R., & Adan, A. (1988). The school transitional environmental project: An ecological intervention and evaluation. In R. H. Price, E. L. Cowen, R. P. Lorion, & J. Ramos-McKay (Eds.), *13 ounces of prevention: A casebook for practitioners* (pp. 111–122). Washington, DC: American Psychological Association.

Feshbach, N. (1989). The construct of empathy and the phenomenon of physical maltreatment of children. In D. Cicchetti & V. Carlson (Eds.), *Child maltreatment: Theory and research on the causes and consequences of child abuse and neglect* (pp. 349–373). Cambridge, England: Cambridge University Press.

Fo, W., & O'Donnell, C. (1975). The buddy system: Effect of community intervention on delinquent offenses. *Behavior Therapy, 6*, 522–524.

Forehand, R., Furey, W. M., & McMahon, R. J. (1984). The role of maternal distress in a parent training program to modify child noncompliance. *Behavioral Psychotherapy, 12*, 93–108.

Forgatch, M. (1989). Patterns and outcome in family problem solving: The disrupting effect of negative emotion. *Journal of Marriage and the Family, 5*, 115–124.

Forgatch, M., Patterson, G., & Skinner, M. (1988). A mediational model for the effect of divorce in antisocial behavior in boys. In E. M. Hetherington & J. D. Arasteh (Eds.), *The impact of divorce, single parenting and stepparenting on children* (pp. 135–154). Hillsdale, NJ: Lawrence Erlbaum Associates.

Fowles, D. C. (1988). Psychophysiological and psychopathy: A motivational approach. *Psychophysiology, 25*, 373–391.

Frick, P. J., Kuper, K., Silverthorn, P., & Cotter, M. (1995). Antisocial behavior, somatization, and sensation-seeking behavior in mothers of clinic-referred children. *Journal of American Academy of Child and Adolescent Psychiatry, 34*, 805–812.

Frick, P., Lahey, B., Hartdagen, S., & Hynd, G. (1989). Conduct problems in boys: Relations to maternal personality, marital satisfaction, and socioeconomic status. *Journal of Clinical Child Psychology, 18*, 114–120.

Gorensten, E. E., & Newman, J. P. (1980). Disinhibitory psychopathology: A new perspective and model for research. *Psychological Review, 87*, 301–315.

Goutz, K. (1981). Children's initial aggression level and the effectiveness of intervention strategies in moderating television effects on aggression. In K. R. Goutz (Ed.), *Attention and social problem-solving as correlates of aggression in preschool males* (pp. 181–197).

Gray, J. A. (1987). Perspectives on anxiety and impulsiveness: A commentary. *Journal of Research and Personality, 21*, 493–509.

Griest, D. L., Forehand, R., Wells, K. C., & McMahon, R. J., (1980). An examination of differences between nonclinic and behavior-problem clinic-referred children and their mothers. *Journal of Abnormal Psychology, 89*, 497–500.

Grych, J. H., & Finchman, F. D. (1990). Marital conflict and children's adjustment: A cognitive contextual framework. *Psychological Bulletin, 108,* 267–290.

Hanf, C. (1970). *Shaping mothers to shape their children's behavior.* Unpublished manuscript, Portland, OR: University of Oregon Medical School.

Hanf, E., & Kling, J. (1973). *Facilitating parent–child interactions: A two-stage training model.* University of Oregon Medical School, Portland, OR.

Hawkins, J., & Lam, T. (1987). Teacher practices, social development and delinquency. In J. D. Burchard & S. N. Burchard (Eds.), *Prevention of delinquent behavior* (pp. 241–274). Newbury Park, CA: Sage.

Hawkins, J. D., & Weiss, J. G. (1985). The social developmental model: An integrated approach to delinquency prevention. *Journal of Primary Prevention, 6,* 73–95.

Hembree-Kigin, T. L., & McNeil, C. B. (1995). *Parent–child interaction therapy.* New York: Plenum.

Henggler, S. W., Borduin, C. M., & Mann, B. J. (1993). Advances in family therapy: Empirical foundations. *Advances in Clinical Child Psychology, 15,* 207–241.

Hobbs, N. (1982). *The troubled and troubling child.* San Francisco: Jossey-Bass.

Huesmann, L. R., Eron, L. D., Lefkowitz, M. M., & Walder, L. O. (1984). Stability of aggression over time and generations. *Developmental Psychology, 20,* 1120–1134.

Hutchings, B., & Mednick, S. A. (1977). Criminality in adoptees and their adoptive and biological parents: A pilot study. In S. A. Mednick & K. O. Christiansen (Eds.), *Biosocial bases of criminal behavior* (pp. 127–141). New York: Gardner.

Jenkins, S. (1980). Behavior problems in preschool children. *Journal of Child Psychology and Psychiatry, 21,* 5–18.

Jouriles, E. N., Murphy, C. M., Farris, A. M., Smith, D. A., Richters, J. E., & Waters, E. (1991). Marital adjustment, parental disagreements about child rearing, and behavior problems in boys: Increasing the specificity of the marital assessment. *Child Development, 62,* 1424–1433.

Jouriles, E. N., Murphy, C. M., & O'Leary, K. D. (1989). Interspousal aggression, marital discord, and child problems. *Journal of Consulting and Clinical Psychology, 57,* 453–455.

Kazdin, A. (1985). *Treatment of antisocial behavior in children and adolescents.* New York: Dorsey.

Kazdin, A. E. (1987). Treatment of antisocial behavior in children: Current status and future directions. *Psychological Bulletin, 102,* 187–203.

Kazdin, A. (1990, February). *Prevention of conduct disorder.* Paper presented at the National Conference on Prevention Research, National Institute of Mental Health, Bethesda, MD.

Kazdin, A. E., Esveldt, D. K., French, N. H., & Unis, A. S. (1987). Problem-solving skills training and relationship therapy in the treatment of antisocial child behavior. *Journal of Consulting and Clinical Psychology, 55,* 76–85.

Kazdin, A. E., Esveldt-Dawson, K., French, N. H., & Unis, A. S. (1987). Problem-solving skills training and relationship therapy in the treatment of antisocial child behavior. *Journal of Consulting and Clinical Psychology, 55,* 76–85.

Kendall, P. C., & Braswell, L. (1985). *Cognitive–behavioral therapy for impulsive children.* New York: Guilford.

LaGreca, A. M., & Santogrossi, D. A. (1980). Social skills training with elementary school students: A behavioral group approach. *Journal of Consulting and Clinical Psychology, 48,* 220–227.

Lahey, B. B., Hart, E. L., Pliszka, S., Applegate, B., & McBurnett, K. (1993). Neurophysiological correlates of conduct disorder: A rationale and review of current research. *Journal of Clinical Child Psychology, 22,* 141–153.

Lahey, B. B., Loeber, R., Hart, E., & Frick, P. J. (1995). Four-year longitudinal study of conduct disorder in boys: Patterns and predictors of persistence. *Journal of Abnormal Psychology, 104,* 83–89.

Lahey, B. B., Loeber, R. L., Quay, H. C., Frick, P. J., & Grimm, J. (1992). Oppositional defiant and conduct disorders: Issue to be resolved for *DSM–IV. Journal of the American Academy of Child and Adolescent Psychiatry, 31,* 539–546.

Landy, S., & Peters, R. D. (1991, February). Understanding and treating the hyperaggressive toddler. *Zero to Three,* 22–31.

Lillenfield, S. O., & Waldman, I. D. (1990). The relation between childhood attention-deficit hyperactivity disorders and adult antisocial behavior reexamined: The problem of heterogeneity. *Clinical Psychology Review, 10,* 669–725.

Lochman, J. E., & Dunn, S. E. (1993). An intervention and consultation model from a social cognitive perspective: A description of the anger coping program. *School Psychology Review*, *22*, 458–471.

Lochman, J., Lampron, L., Gemmer, T., & Harris, S. (1987). Anger coping intervention with aggressive children: A guide to implementation in school settings. In P. A. Keller & S. R. Heyman (Eds.), *Innovations in clinical practice: A sourcebook* (Vol. 6, pp. 339–356). Sarasota, FL: Professional Resource Exchange.

Lochman, J. E., Lampron, L. B., Gemmer, T. C., Harris, S. R., & Wyckoff, G. M. (1989). Teacher consultation and cognitive–behavioral interventions with aggressive boys. *Psychology in the Schools*, *26*, 179–188.

Loeber, R. (1990). Development and risk factors of juvenile antisocial behavior and delinquency. *Clinical Psychology Review*, *10*, 1–41.

Loeber, R. (1991). Antisocial behavior: More enduring than changeable? *Journal of the American Academy of Child and Adolescent Psychiatry*, *30*, 393–397.

Loeber, R., & Schmaling, K. B. (1985). The utility of differentiating between mixed and pure forms of antisocial child behavior. *Journal of Abnormal Child Psychology*, *13*, 315–335.

Lytton, H. (1990). Child and parent effects in boys' conduct disorder: A reinterpretation. *Developmental Psychology*, *26*, 683–697.

Maziade, M., Cote, R., Bernier, H., Boutin, P., & Thivierge, J. (1989). Significance of extreme temperament infancy for clinical status in pre-school years II. *British Journal of Psychiatry*, *14*, 544–551.

McBurnett, K., & Lahey, B. B. (1994). Neuropsychological and neuroendorcrine correlates of conduct disorder and antisocial behavior in children and adolescents. In D. C. Fowles, P. Sutker, & S. H. Goodman (Eds.), *Progress in experimental personality and psychopathology research* (pp. 199–231). New York: Springer.

McMahon, R. J., & Forehand, R. (1984). Parent training for the noncompliant child: Treatment outcome, generalization, and adjunctive therapy procedures. In R. F. Dangel & R. A. Polster (Eds.), *Parent training: Foundations of research and practice* (pp. 298–328). New York: Guilford.

McMahon, R., & Forehand, R. (1988). Behavioral assessment of childhood disorders. In E. J. Mash & L. G. Terdal (Eds.), *Behavioral assessment of childhood disorders* (105–153). New York: Guilford.

Mednick, S. A. (1977). A bio-social theory of the learning of law-abiding behavior. In S. Mednick & K. Christiansen (Eds.), *Biosocial bases of criminal behavior* (1–8). New York: Gardner.

Milich, R., & Dodge, K. A. (1984). Social information processing in child psychiatric populations. *Journal of Abnormal Child Psychology*, *12*, 471–489.

Miller, G. E., & Prinz, R. J. (1990). Enhancement of social learning family interventions for childhood conduct disorder. *Psychological Bulletin*, *108*, 291–307.

Moffitt, T. E., & Lynam, D. (1994). The neuropsychology of conduct disorder and delinquency: Implications for understanding antisocial behavior. In D. C. Fowles, P. Sutker, & S. H. Goodman (Eds.), *Progress in experimental personality and psychopathology research* (pp. 233–262). New York: Springer.

O'Donnell, C., Lygate, T., & Fo, W. (1979). The buddy system: Review and follow-up. *Child Behavior Therapy*, *1*, 161–169.

Offord, D. (1982). Family backgrounds of male and female delinquents. In J. Gunn & D. P. Farrington (Eds.), *Abnormal offenders: Delinquency and the criminal justice system*. New York: Wiley.

Offord, D., & Jones, M. (1983). Skill development: A community intervention program for the prevention of antisocial behavior. In S. B. Guze, F. J. Earls, & J. E. Barrett (Eds.), *Childhood psychopathology and development* (pp. 165–188). New York: Raven.

O'Leary, K. D., & Emery, R. E. (1982). Marital discord and child behavior problems. In M. D. Levine & P. Satz (Eds.), *Middle childhood: Developmental variation and dysfunction* (pp. 345–364). New York: Academic Press.

Patterson, G. R. (1975). *Families: Applications of social learning to family life*. Champaign, IL: Research Press.

Patterson, G. R. (1976). *Living with children: New methods for parents and teachers*. Champaign, IL: Research Press.

Patterson, G. R. (1982). *Coercive family process*. Eugene, OR: Castalia.

Patterson, G. R., Chamberlain, P., & Reid, J. B. (1982). A comparative evaluation of a parent training program. *Behavior Therapy, 13*, 638–650.

Patterson, G. R., DeBaryshe, B. D., & Ramsey, E. (1989). A developmental perspective on antisocial behavior. *American Psychologist, 44*, 329–335.

Patterson, G. R., Dishion, T. J., & Chamberlain, P. (1993). *Outcomes and methodological issues relating to the treatment of antisocial children*. New York: Plenum.

Patterson, G. R., & Stouthamer-Loeber, M. (1984). The correlation of family management practices and delinquency. *Child Development, 55*, 1299–1307.

Prinz, R. J., Blechman, E. A., & Dumas, J. E. (1994). An evaluation of peer coping skills training for childhood aggression. *Journal of Clinical Child Psychology, 23*, 193–203.

Porter, B., & O'Leary, K. D. (1980). Marital discord and childhood behavior problems. *Journal of Abnormal Psychology, 16*, 97–109.

Quay, H. C. (1986). Conduct disorders. In H. C. Quay & J. S. Werry (Eds.), *Psychopathological disorders of childhood* (pp. 35–72). New York: Wiley.

Quay, H. C. (1993). The psychopathology of undersocialized aggressive conduct disorder: A theoretical perspective. *Development and Psychopathology, 5*, 165–180.

Quay, H. C., Routh, D. K., & Shapiro, S. K. (1987). Psychopathology of childhood: From description to validation. *Annual Review of Psychology, 38*, 491–532.

Raine, A., & Jones, F. (1987). Attention, autonomic arousal, and personality in behaviorally disordered children. *Journal of Abnormal Child Psychology, 15*, 583–599.

Raine, A., Venables, P. H., & Williams, M. A. (1990). Autonomic orienting responses in 15-year-old male subjects and criminal behavior at age 24. *American Journal of Psychiatry, 147*, 933–937.

Rende, R., & Plomin, R. (1993). Families at risk for psychopathology: Who becomes affected and why? *Development and Psychopathology, 5*, 529–540.

Richard, B. A., & Dodge, K. A. (1982). Social maladjustment and problem solving in school-aged children. *Journal of Consulting and Clinical Psychology, 50*, 226–233.

Richman, N., & Graham, P. (1975). A behavioral screening questionnaire for use with three-year old children: Preliminary findings. *Journal of Child Psychology and Psychiatry, 16*, 277–287.

Richman, N., Stevenson, L., & Graham, P. J. (1982). *Pre-school to school: A behavioural study*. London: Academic Press.

Rose, S. L., Rose, S. A., & Feldman, J. (1989). Stability of behavior problems in very young children. *Development and Psychopathology, 1*, 5–20.

Rubin, K. H., & Krasnor, L. R. (1986). Social–cognitive and social behavioral perspectives on problem-solving. In M. Perlmutter (Ed.), *The Minnesota Symposia on Child Psychology: Vol. 18. Cognitive perspectives on children's social and behavioral development* (pp. 1–68). Hillsdale, NJ: Lawrence Erlbaum Associates.

Rutter, M. (1985). Resilience in the face of adversity: Protective factors and resistance to psychiatric disorder. *British Journal of Psychiatry, 147*, 598–611.

Rutter, M., & Giller, H. (1983). *Juvenile delinquency: Trends and perspectives*. New York: Penguin.

Rutter, M., Tizard, J., Yule, W., Graham, P., & Whitmore, K. (1976). Research report: Isle of Wight studies. *Psychological Medicine, 6*, 313–332.

Rutter, M., Yule, B., Quinton, D., Rowlands, O., Yule, W., & Berger, M. (1974). Attainment and adjustment in two geographic areas: Some factors accounting for area differences. *British Journal of Psychiatry, 126*, 520–533.

Safer, D., & Allen, R. (1976). *Hyperactive children: Diagnosis and management*. Baltimore: University Park Press.

Scerbo, A., Raine, A., O'Brien, M., Chan, C. J., Rhea, C., & Smiley, N. (1990). Reward dominance and passive avoidance learning in adolescent psychopaths. *Journal of Abnormal Child Psychology, 18*, 451–464.

Schonfeld, I. S., Shaffer, D., O'Connor, P., & Portnoy, S. (1988). Conduct disorder and cognitive functioning: Testing three causal hypotheses. *Child Development, 59*, 993–1007.

Schweinhart, L., & Weikart, D. (1988). The High/scope Perry preschool program. In R. H. Price, R. P. Cowen, R. P. Lorion, & J. Ramos-McKay (Eds.), *13 ounces of prevention: A casebook for practitioners* (pp. 53–56). Washington, DC: American Psychological Association.

Shure, M. B., & Spivak, G. (1982). Interpersonal problem-solving in young children: A cognitive approach to prevention. *American Journal of Community Psychology, 10*, 341–356.

Slaby, R., & Guerra, N. (1988). Cognitive mediators of aggression in adolescent offenders: 1. Assessment. *Development Psychology, 24*, 580–588.

Spivak, G., Platt, J. J., & Shure, M. B. (1976). *The problem solving approach to adjustment*. San Francisco: Jossey-Bass.

Spivak, G., & Shure, M. B. (1985). ICPS and beyond: Centripetal and centrifugal forces. *American Journal of Community Psychology, 13*, 226–243.

Stonemen, Z., Brody, G., & Burke, M. (1988). Marital quality, depression, and inconsistent parenting: Relationship with observed mother–child conflict. *American Journal of Orthopsychiatry, 59*, 105–117.

Strayhorn, J. M., & Weidman, C. S. (1989). Reduction of attention deficit and internalizing symptoms in preschoolers through parent–child interaction training. *Journal of the American Academy of Child and Adolescent Psychiatry, 28*, 888–896.

Sturge, C. (1982). Reading retardation and antisocial behavior. *Journal of Child Psychology and Psychiatry, 23*, 21–23.

Thomas, A., & Chess, S. (1977). *Temperament and development*. New York: Brunner/Mazel.

Wadsworth, M. E. (1976). Delinquency, pulse rates and early emotional deprivation. *British Journal of Criminology, 16*, 245–255.

Wadsworth, M. (1979). *Roots of delinquency: Infancy adolescence and crime*. New York: Barnes & Noble.

Wahler, R. G., Cartor, P. G., Fleischman, J., & Lambert, W. (1993). The impact of synthesis teaching and parent training with mothers of conduct disordered children. *Journal of Abnormal Child Psychology, 12*, 425–440.

Wahler, R. G., & Dumas, J. E. (1984). Changing the observational coding styles of insular and noninsular mothers: A step toward maintenance of parent training effects. In R. F. Dangel & R. A. Polster (Eds.), *Parent training: Foundations of research and practice* (pp. 379–416). New York: Guilford.

Wahler, R. G., & Dumas, J. E. (1986). Maintenance factors in coercive mother–child interactions: The compliance and predictability hypotheses. *Journal of Applied Behavioral Analyses, 19*, 13–22.

Walker, J. L., Lahey, B. B., Hynd, G. W., & Frame, C. L. (1987). Comparison of specific patterns of antisocial behavior in children with conduct disorder with or without coexisting hyperactivity. *Journal of Consulting and Clinical Psychology, 55*, 910–913.

Webster-Stratton, C. (1981). Modification of mothers' behaviors and attitudes through videotape modeling group discussion program. *Behavior Therapy, 12*, 634–642.

Webster-Stratton, C. (1982a). The long term effects of a videotape modeling parent training program: Comparison of immediate and 1-year followup results. *Behavior Therapy, 13*, 702–714.

Webster-Stratton, C. (1982b). Teaching mothers through videotape modeling to change their children's behaviors. *Journal of Pediatric Psychology, 7*, 279–294.

Webster-Stratton, C. (1984). Randomized trial of two parent-training programs for families with conduct disordered children. *Journal of Consulting and Clinical Psychology, 52*, 666–678.

Webster-Stratton, C. (1985a). Comparison of abusive and nonabusive families with conduct disordered children. *American Journal of Orthopsychiatry, 55*, 59–69.

Webster-Stratton, C. (1985b). The effects of father involvement in parent training for conduct problem children. *Journal of Child Psychology and Psychiatry, 26*, 801–810.

Webster-Stratton, C. (1985c). Mother perceptions and mother–child interactions: Comparison of a clinic-referred and a non-clinic group. *Journal of Clinical Child Psychology, 14*, 334–339.

Webster-Stratton, C. (1985d). Predictors of treatment outcome in parent training for conduct disordered children. *Behavior Therapy, 16*, 223–243.

Webster-Stratton, C. (1989). Systematic comparison of consumer satisfaction of three cost-effective parent training programs for conduct problem children. *Behavior Therapy, 20*, 103–115.

Webster-Stratton, C. (1990a). The incredible years parent training leader Manual: Effective communication, anger management and problem solving (ADVANCE). 1411 8th Avenue west, Seattle, WA 98119.

Webster-Stratton, C. (1990b). Long-term follow-up of families with young conduct problem children: From preschool to grade school. *Journal of Clinical Child Psychology, 19*, 144–149.

Webster-Stratton, C. (1990c). Stress: A potential disruptor of parent perceptions and family interactions. *Journal of Clinical Child Psychology, 19*, 302–312.

Webster-Stratton, C. (1994). Advancing Videotape Parent Training: A Comparison Study. *Journal of Consulting and Clinical Psychology, 62*, 583–593.

Webster-Stratton, C. (1996). Early onset conduct problems: Does gender make a difference? *Journal of Consulting and Clinical Psychology, 64*, 540–551.

Webster-Stratton, C. (1997). Treating children with early-onset conduct problems: A comparison of child and parent training interventions. *Journal of Consulting and Clinical Psychology, 65*, 93–109.

Webster-Stratton, C. (1998a). Parent training with low-income clients: Promoting parental engagement through a collaborative approach. In J. R. Lutzker (Ed.), *Handbook of child abuse research and treatment* (pp. 183–210). New York: Plenum.

Webster-Stratton, C. (1998b). Preventing conduct problems in Head Start children: Strengthening competencies. *Journal of Consulting and Clinical Psychology, 66*, 715–730.

Webster-Stratton, C., & Hammond, M. (1988). Maternal depression and its relationship to life stress, perceptions of child behavior problems, parenting behaviors and child conduct problems. *Journal of Abnormal Child Psychology, 16*, 299–315.

Webster-Stratton, C., & Hammond, M. (1990). Predictors of treatment outcome in parent training for families with conduct problem children. *Behavior Therapy, 21*, 319–337.

Webster-Stratton, C., & Hammond, M. (1999). Marital conflict management skills, parenting style, and early-onset conduct problems: Processes and pathways. *Journal of Child Psychology and Psychiatry, 40*, 6.

Webster-Stratton, C., & Hancock, L. (1998). Parent training: Content, Methods and Processes. In C. E. Schaefer & J. M. Briesmeister (Eds.), *Handbook of parent training* (pp. 98–152). New York: Wiley.

Webster-Stratton, C., Kolpacoff, M., & Hollinsworth, T. (1988). Self-administered videotape therapy for families with conduct-problem children: Comparison with two cost-effective treatments and a control group. *Journal of Consulting and Clinical Psychology, 56*, 558–566.

Webster-Stratton, C., & Lindsay Woolley, D. (1997). *Social competence and early-onset conduct problems: Issues in assessment.* Unpublished manuscript, University of Washington, Seattle.

Wechsler, D. (1974). *Wechsler intelligent scale for children—revised.* New York: Psychological Corp.

White, J., Moffit, T., Earls, F., & Robins, L. (1990). Preschool predictors of persistent conduct disorder and delinquency. *Criminology, 28*, 443–454.

Williams, S., Anderson, J., McGee, R., & Silva, P. A. (1990). Risk factors for behavioral and emotional disorder in preadolescent children. *Journal of the American Academy of Child and Adolescent Psychiatry, 29*, 413–419.

Attention Deficit Hyperactivity Disorder

Mark D. Rapport
Kyong-Mee Chung
University of Hawaii

CLINICAL DESCRIPTION

Attention deficit hyperactivity disorder (ADHD) is estimated to affect literally millions of children throughout the world (i.e., between 3% and 5% of the childhood population, or approximately one child in every classroom). It accounts for an estimated 30% to 60% of clinical caseloads in child psychiatry and mental health outpatient clinics in the United States. Currently, there is no known cure. As a result, ADHD is considered one of the most serious and perplexing clinical disorders of childhood.

Historical Overview

While reading through the clinical description section of this chapter, the reader will discover that he or she probably knew several classmates affected by ADHD—however, the name of the disorder was different. Historically, children with ADHD were referred to as having "minimal brain damage" (1947 to the early 1950s). The association between brain damage and behavioral deviance was a logical one and introduced following the 1918 encephalitis epidemics. Many of the postencephalitic children were observed to be motorically overactive, inattentive, and aggressive, in addition to displaying a wide variety of emotional and learning difficulties. Subsequent attempts to validate the concept of minimal brain damage, however, were unsuccessful. Neither "soft neurological signs"—objective physical evidence that is perceptible to the examining physician as opposed to the subjective sensations or symptoms of the patient—nor a positive history of brain damage or birth difficulties was evidenced in a majority of children with a history of behavioral problems.

413

The concept of a clinical disorder resulting from brain damage was gradually discarded and replaced with the subtler but nebulous concept "minimal brain dysfunction," (MBD; late 1950s to mid-1960s). The distinction between brain damage and brain dysfunction was an important one. It implied a hypothesis of brain dysfunction resulting from manifestations of central nervous system dysfunction, as opposed to brain damage as an assumed fact in affected children. It also suggested that a wide range of learning and behavioral disabilities could accompany the hypothesized deviations of the central nervous system (CNS). These symptoms could be inferred from various combinations of impairment in attention, impulse control, gross motor activity, perception, language, and memory, among others.

The concept of minimal brain dysfunction was eventually replaced with the moniker "hyperkinetic reaction of childhood," in the American Psychiatric Association's second edition of its *Diagnostic and Statistical Manual of Mental Disorders* (2nd ed. [*DSM–II*]; American Psychiatric Association, 1968). The change in diagnostic labels reflected a general dissatisfaction with the untestable notion of brain dysfunction and concomitantly suggested that an excessive degree of and difficulties in regulating gross motor activity best represented the core symptoms of the disorder. The term "reaction" reflected prevailing psychoanalytic influences concerning causes of mental disorders during the 1960s.

The concept of an independent syndrome of *hyperactivity* prevailed between 1968 and 1979, during which time considerable effort was spent trying to validate the notion of a hyperactive child syndrome. An upsurge in child psychopathology research directly affected the evolution of thinking over this time period and resulted in a focus on *attentional difficulties* or deficits as the core disturbance of the disorder. Excessive gross motor activity was subsequently relegated to an associative feature in defining the disorder, which, in turn, was considered to be neither sufficient nor necessary to establish a formal diagnosis. This rather dramatic shift in diagnostic emphasis was reflected in the *Diagnostic and Statistical Manual of Mental Disorders* (3rd ed. [*DSM–III*]; American Psychiatric Association, 1980), wherein the disorder was renamed "attention deficit disorder" (ADD) and could occur with hyperactivity (ADDH) or without hyperactivity (ADD).

A second important change in the *DSM–III* nomenclature involved the conceptualization of the disorder itself. Earlier diagnostic conceptualizations of the disorder required, among other clinical criteria, that a child meet a specified number of symptoms from a prepared list to qualify for a diagnosis (e.g., any eight criteria on the list). This type of diagnostic conceptualization, in which no single behavioral characteristic is essential or sufficient for group membership, and in which members having a number of shared characteristics or clinical features are grouped together, is referred to as a *polythetic* schema. The *DSM–III* nomenclature, however, incorporated a *monothetic* schema for the first time, wherein an individual was now required to present with a specified number of symptoms from each of three independent behavioral categories for a diagnosis to be established: inattention, impulsivity, and overactivity. The difference may appear subtle, but it has important implications for diagnostic categorization and defining what constitutes a particular clinical disorder. In the case of ADDH, for example, it would be much more difficult to meet multiple criteria in three distinct behavioral domains (versus from a single list of symptoms), which, in turn, would have the effect of refining the disorder to a more homogeneous (similar) grouping of children.

As a consequence of this conceptual shift, researchers began focusing their efforts on establishing whether inattention, impulsivity, and hyperactivity were, in fact, independent behavioral domains—primarily by conducting factor analytic studies on child behavior rating scales obtained from classroom teachers. In factor analytic studies, researchers use statistical techniques to discern whether certain rating scale items or descriptions of specific types of behavior covary or "go together" to form one or more independent domains of behavior. If all items correlate highly with one another (i.e., they are significantly related to one another), then a single factor (such as "inattention") is thought to account for the different rating scale items. A two-factor solution suggests that some items or behavioral descriptions of behavior covary with one another but not with the remaining behavioral descriptions entered into the equation. These remaining items might subsequently be found to covary or go together in a statistical sense to form a second behavioral domain, such as "impulsivity."

What emerged from factor analytic studies was a mixed and often confusing picture. Most studies failed to find evidence of independent factors or behavioral domains to support the three dimensions associated with ADDH. Several of the studies found evidence for a separate "attentional disturbance" domain, whereas impulsivity and hyperactivity loaded together on a second factor, that is, items making up these latter two domains were frequently inseparable from one another, suggesting that impulsivity and hyperactivity were probably different but related behaviors of a single dimension of behavior.

The evolution from the *DSM–III* to the revised third edition (*DSM–III–R;* American Psychiatric Association, 1987) was much quicker than had been the case with earlier evolutions. In fact, many researchers were displeased with the rapidity of the change. Information was still being collected and analyzed concerning critical questions having a direct bearing on the independence of factors or behavioral dimensions assumed to be integral components of ADDH. Furthermore, insufficient evidence was available concerning whether ADD represented a special subtype of the disorder that could occur without the hyperactivity component.

Nevertheless, the disorder was renamed in the *DSM–III*, with hyperactivity re-emerging as a central feature of the disorder. Several other important changes were adopted in the revised 1987 nomenclature. The modified monothetic classification schema that required the presence of behavior problems in three different dimensions (inattention, impulsivity, and hyperactivity) was discarded. Furthermore, the new classification schema reverted back to a polythetic dimensional approach: A diagnosis now required that 8 out of 14 behaviors from a single list be present in a child for a minimum of 6 months' duration, with onset of difficulties occurring prior to age 7. ADD without hyperactivity was abandoned as a distinct subtype of the disorder, and a secondary category termed "undifferentiated attention deficit disorder" was added to subsume those children with attentional problems occurring without hyperactivity. Finally, the "residual ADDH" category, which was used in the earlier edition to describe older individuals (usually adolescents) who no longer presented with the full complement of ADDH symptoms, was discarded.

The most recent version of the *Diagnostic and Statistical Manual* (4th ed., [*DSM–IV*]; 1994) constitutes a modified classification schema, wherein three distinct subtypes of ADHD are possible. Diagnosis requires that a minimum of 6 symptoms be present for at least 6 months to a degree that is maladaptive and inconsistent with the child's developmental level in accord with two sets of criteria. Children meeting only the inattention criteria are thought to have a predominantly inattentive type of ADHD. Those meeting only the hyperactivity–impulsivity criteria are referred to as having a predominantly hyperactive–impulsive type of ADHD. Finally, those meeting both sets of criteria are considered a combined type of ADHD.

Description and Distinguishing Features

The first distinction that should be noted in understanding children with ADHD is that it is not the type or kind of behavior they exhibit that is particularly deviant, but the quantity or degree and intensity of their behavior, that is, they tend to exhibit higher rates of behavior and frequently with greater intensity in situations that demand lower rates or more subtle kinds of behavior (e.g., becoming disruptive and behaving inappropriately in school or while interacting with others). Lower rates of behavior are exhibited at other times when higher rates are demanded (e.g., not paying attention and completing academic assignments in the classroom). Overall, they appear to be out of sync with environmental demands and expectations, particularly in situations that require careful sustained attention and protracted effort at tasks that are not particularly interesting or stimulating to the child.

Children's behavior also must be viewed in an appropriate developmental context. For example, younger children typically are more active, cannot pay attention to a particular task for as long a time interval, and tend to spend less time in making decisions or analyzing problems compared to older children. Other factors, such as gender and cultural differences, also may play a defining role in determining what constitutes normality, and it is only when a child's behavior consistently and significantly exceeds these expectations that it is considered deviant.

In ADHD, the developmental behavioral pattern typically observed is associated with an early onset, a gradual worsening of symptoms over time, and an unrelenting clinical course until late adolescence, when the child is no longer in school. Most children with ADHD continue to exhibit symptoms of the disorder as adults, the severity of which depends on a number of factors. As noted later in the chapter, many believe that the disorder is inherited and thus present from birth.

A third feature characteristic of children with ADHD is that their behavioral difficulties tend to be pervasive across situations and settings. Most people have been "hyper" at one time or another, have experienced difficulty concentrating, and have acted impulsively in particular situations. These occurrences tend to be isolated events, and one usually can point to particular environmental circumstances, situations, or contingencies as responsible for or contributing factors associated with the behavior (e.g., feeling ill or having to study for a particularly uninteresting class). Children with ADHD, on the other hand, exhibit this pattern of behavior in most situations and settings, day after day, year after year. A gradual worsening of behavioral and academic difficulties is usually evident as the child grows older. This is because the environment demands that one be able to pay attention, sit still, and control one's impulses for longer periods of time with increasing age. Difficulties are especially conspicuous on entry into the fourth and seventh grades, when classroom demands and academic assignments become increasingly more complex, take a longer time to complete, and rely heavily on one's ability to work independently.

Children with ADHD are also known for their "consistently inconsistent" behavior, that is, they tend to behave rather erratically both within and across days, even when their home and school environments are relatively stable. Teachers frequently report, for example, that the child appears relatively settled and able to pay attention and complete academic assignments on some days, although most days are characterized by disruptiveness, inattention, and low work completion rates. Parents report a similar phenomenon at home, even among those who are highly skilled in managing their child's behavior. The reasons for the ADHD child's inconsistent pattern of behavior are varied and may be related to a complex interaction between brain regulation mechanisms and prevailing environmental stimulation and contingencies.

Primary Symptoms and Diagnostic Criteria

The primary symptoms or clinical features of ADHD are developmentally inappropriate degrees of inattention, impulsivity, and gross motor overactivity. Presented in Table 20.1. are the current *Diagnostic and Statistical Manual* (4th ed., [DSM–IV]; American Psychiatric Association, 1994) diagnostic criteria for ADHD. The diagnosis requires a child to exhibit a minimum of six symptoms (or problem behaviors) listed under the A(1) criteria (attention-deficit/ hyperactivity disorder, predominantly inattention type) but fewer than six symptoms from the "hyperactivity–impulsivity" list; a minimum of six symptoms listed under the A(2) criteria (attention-deficit/hyperactivity disorder, predominantly hyperactive–impulsive type) but fewer than six symptoms from the "inattentive" list; or a minimum of six symptoms from both lists (attention-deficit/hyperactivity disorder, combined type). It should be noted, however, that the *DSM* field trials contained large numbers of preschool children. These children would likely meet criteria for the hyperactivity–impulsive subtype because it is too early to discern whether prominent difficulties with attention will emerge. Follow-up studies of these children after they enter primary grades will likely show that most, if not all, meet criteria for the combined subtype of the disorder.

Additional changes in the *DSM–IV* are noteworthy. As shown in Table 20.1, symptoms of the disorder must cause some degree of impairment in multiple settings (e.g., both at home and at school). The intent of this criterion is to insure that children show pervasive as opposed to situational-based symptoms, the latter of which may suggest the presence of other clinical disorders or be due to a wide variety of environmental circumstances. A second criterion (see section E in Table 20.1) was added to highlight the fact that many children display behaviors suggestive of ADHD that are better accounted for by another disorder. For example, some form of or disturbance in attention and concentration are central to nearly all disorders of childhood, ranging from depression and anxiety to mental retardation and autism. A diagnosis of ADHD is not warranted in these cases.

Individuals with ADHD generally display some disturbance in each of the areas delineated in the *DSM–IV* and in most settings, but to varying degrees. Conversely, signs of the disorder may be minimal or even absent in novel settings (e.g., being examined in a doctor's office or clinical setting), when receiving individualized attention, or under conditions in which stimulation or interest level is relatively high.

At home, inattention is commonly displayed by frequent shifts from one uncompleted activity to another and a failure to follow through and/or comply with instructions. The impulsivity component is often expressed by acting without considering either the immediate or delayed consequences of one's actions (e.g., running into the street, accident proneness), interrupting the conversation of other household members, and grabbing objects (not with malevolent intent) in the store while on shopping trips. Problems with overactivity often are expressed by difficulty remaining seated during meals, while completing homework, or riding in the car, and excessive movement during sleep.

At school, inattention usually is evidenced by difficulty deploying and maintaining adequate attention (i.e., staying on-task), a failure to complete academic assignments, and deficient organizational and informational processing skills. Impulsivity is expressed in a variety of ways, such as interrupting others, beginning assignments be-

Table 20.1

DSM–IV Diagnostic Criteria for Attention Deficit Hyperactivity Disorder

A. Either (1) or (2):

(1) Six (or more) of the following symptoms of inattention have persisted for at least 6 months to a degree that is maladaptive and inconsistent with developmental level:

Inattention

(A) Often fails to give close attention to details or makes careless mistakes in schoolwork, work, or other activities.

(B) Often has difficulty sustaining attention in tasks or play activities.

(C) Often does not seem to listen when spoken to directly.

(D) Often does not follow through on instructions and fails to finish schoolwork, chores, or duties in the workplace (not due to oppositional behavior or failure to understand instructions).

(E) Often has difficulty organizing tasks and activities.

(F) Often avoids, dislikes, or is reluctant to engage in tasks that require sustained mental effort (such as schoolwork or home work).

(G) Often loses things necessary for tasks or activities (e.g., toys, school assignments, pencils, books, or tools).

(H) Is often easily distracted by extraneous stimuli.

(I) Is often forgetful in daily activities.

(2) Six (or more) of the following symptoms of hyperactivity–impulsivity have persisted for at least 6 months to a degree that is maladaptive and inconsistent with developmental level:

Hyperactivity

(A) Often fidgets with hands or feet or squirms in seat.

(B) Often leaves seat in classroom or in other situations in which remaining seated is expected.

(C) Often runs about or climbs excessively in situations in which it is inappropriate (in adolescents or adults, may be limited to subjective feelings of restlessness).

(D) Often has difficulty playing or engaging in leisure activities quietly.

(E) Is often "on the go" or often acts as if "driven by a motor."

(F) Often talks excessively.

Impulsivity

(G) Often blurts out answers before questions have been completed.

(H) Often has difficulty awaiting turn.

(I) Often interrupts or intrudes on others (e.g., butts into conversations or games).

B. Some hyperactive–impulsive or inattentive symptoms that caused impairment were present before age 7 years.

C. Some impairment from the symptoms is present in two or more settings (e.g., at school, work, and at home).

D. There must be clear evidence of clinically significant impairment in social, academic, or occupational functioning.

continued on next page

E. The symptoms do not occur exclusively during the course of a pervasive developmental disorder, schizophrenia, or other psychotic disorder and are not better accounted for by another mental disorder (e.g., mood disorder, anxiety disorder, dissociative disorder, or a personality disorder).

Code based on type:

Attention deficit hyperactivity disorder, combined type: If both criteria A1 and A2 are met for the past 6 months.

Attention deficit hyperactivity disorder, predominantly inattentive type: If Criterion A1 is met but criterion A2 is not met for the past 6 months.

Attention deficit hyperactivity disorder, predominantly hyperactive–impulsive type: If criterion A2 is met but criterion A1 is not met for the past 6 months.

For individuals (especially adolescents and adults) who currently have symptoms that no longer meet full criteria, "In Partial Remission" should be specified.

Note. Adapted from the *Diagnostic and Statistical Manual of Mental Disorders* (4th ed., [*DSM–IV*]; pp. 83–85) by the American Psychiatric Association, 1994, Washington, DC: Author. Reprinted by permission.

fore receiving (or understanding) complete instructions, making careless mistakes while completing assignments, blurting out answers in class, and having difficulty waiting one's turn in both small-group and organized sport activities. Hyperactivity frequently is manifested by fidgetiness, twisting and wiggling in one's seat or changing seat positions, dropping objects on the floor, and emitting noises or playing with objects during quiet assignment periods.

However, all of these behaviors may be diminished or exacerbated by subtle changes in the environment. Teachers frequently comment, for example, that an identified child with ADHD who is absorbed in a particular activity of high-interest value or who is working in a one-on-one situation with an adult can attend for normal time expectations and not move a muscle while doing so. Parents also report that their children with ADHD can sit perfectly still while engaged in highly stimulating activities such as watching movies (e.g., "Star Wars"), and while playing interactive computer or video games. This may have a direct bearing on the extant nature of the disorder.

Secondary Symptoms or Associated Features of ADHD

Secondary features are those behaviors and difficulties that occur at a greater than chance frequency in children with a particular disorder but are neither necessary nor sufficient to serve as formal diagnostic criteria. Many of these symptoms or behaviors are reported early in the developmental course of the disorder and may thus represent less prominent features of the disorder. These include lability of mood, temper tantrums, low frustration tolerance, social disinhibition, cognitive impairment with associated learning disability, and perceptual motor difficulties (Barkley, 1990). Other aspects of disturbance or behavioral difficulties may be secondary to or direct and indirect consequences of the disorder. For example, disturbed peer and interpersonal relationships, academic underachievement, school failure, decreased self-esteem, depressed mood, and conduct problems are characteristic of many children with ADHD. The presence or absence of attendant aggressive or conduct features is especially important and may be of both diagnostic and prognostic value.

CAUSES OF THE DISORDER

Speculations concerning the cause or causes of ADHD have proliferated in recent years, ranging from brain-based mechanisms to environmental toxins. Although definitive answers remain elusive, recent discoveries suggest several possible factors that may be related to the etiology of ADHD.

Environmental Toxins

A variety of environmental toxins and factors have been suggested as causal or contributing agents to the development of ADHD. The most popular of these include elevated blood lead levels, food additives (particularly salicylates, food dyes, and preservatives), sugar, cigarette smoking, or alcohol consumption during pregnancy, exposure to cool-white fluorescent lighting, and radioactive rays emitted from televisions. Although comprehensive coverage of these topics is beyond the scope of this chapter, it is worthwhile to point out that none of the environmental agents has received empirical support as an important contributing factor to the development of ADHD in a majority of children.

Neurological, Neurophysiological, and Neuroanatomical Factors

Results of routine neurological examinations usually are found to be normal in children with ADHD. Research investigating the presence of neuromaturational signs (i.e., signs that a person's brain represents a more immature form of development) has been equivocal but generally suggests either nonspecific or no increased frequency of soft signs in this population. Also, as noted previously, the overwhelming majority of children with ADHD do not have a history of brain injury or damage. More recent studies using advanced brain scanning techniques, such as computed tomography scan analysis, also have failed to reveal differences in brain structure. Preliminary findings using the higher resolution magnetic resonance imaging (MRI), however, have been more promising but await replication.

Neurochemical abnormalities, particularly those involving the monoamines—comprising the catecholamines (dopamine and norepinephrine) and an indoleamine (serotonin)—have been implicated as potential contributing factors in the pathophysiology of ADHD. The evidence to date remains speculative but suggests a possible selective deficiency in the availability of dopamine, norepinephrine, or both.

More promising results have emerged in three studies. Lou (1990), using single photon emission computed tomography to measure cerebral blood flow in the brain, reported hypoperfusion (reduced) and low neural activity in the striatal and orbital prefrontal regions of children with ADHD compared with controls, whereas the primary sensory and sensorimotor regions were hyperperfused (overly active). Ongoing studies by Satterfield (1990), using EEG brain electrical activity mapping techniques, have been relatively consistent with Lou's findings in showing abnormality in information processing in the frontal lobes of children with ADHD. Finally, Zametkin et al. (1990), in studying adults who had been hyperactive since childhood, reported reduced glucose metabolism in various areas of the brain, particularly the premotor and superior prefrontal regions—areas known to be associated with the regulation of attention, motor activity, and information processing.

Recent findings buttress those derived from earlier works in showing neurophysiological dysfunction in children with ADHD, particularly within the cortical and subcortical structures that serve the frontal–striatal system. Quantitative electro-encephalogram profile comparisons between 407 children with ADHD and 310 normal children revealed two major neurophysiological subtypes among children with ADHD (Chabot & Serfontein, 1996). The first subtype evidences varying degrees of EEG slowing, whereas the second shows an increase in EEG activity. Both abnormalities are particular to the frontal regions. The subtypes are thought to reflect the interaction of the cortical and subcortical structures contained within the frontal–striatal system and affect the range of attention, hyperactivity, and learning problems evidenced by the children. Interhemispheric power asymmetry (i.e., imbalance in neuroactivity between the right and left hemispheres) was also common among the ADHD sample, indicating abnormal right hemisphere function as well as interhemispheric communication between the two regions.

Results from the first comprehensive morphometric analysis are consistent with hypothesized dysfunction of right-sided prefrontal–striatal systems in ADHD. Castellanos et al. (1996) compared volumetric measures of both prefrontal (attention) and basal ganglia (motor control) structures in 57 boys with ADHD and 55 healthy matched control children using MRI scans. Both the caudate nucleus and globus pallidus, but not the putamen, were reported to be significantly smaller (predominantly in the right hemisphere) in ADHD children. Response inhibition measures derived from three attentional tasks were correlated with anatomical measures of frontostriatal brain structures in a complementary study (Casey et al., 1997). The results suggest that the distractability and impulsivity characteristic of children with ADHD reflects deficits in response inhibition. A nontechnical explanation of these findings involves understanding that the prefrontal cortex, located in the frontal lobe just behind the forehead, serves as the brain's command center. Commands emanating from this area are translated into action by the caudate nucleus and globus pallidus, both of which are located near the middle of the brain. By analogy, the prefrontal cortex can be viewed as the steering wheel and the caudate and globus as the accelerator and brakes, respectively. It is the braking or inhibitory function that appears to be dysfunctional or different in children with ADHD.

Collectively, results from positron emission tomography, MRI, and regional cerebral blood flow studies provide compelling evidence that ADHD results from a developmental abnormality in the frontal–cortical, striatal, and thalamic circuits, particularly with respect to the right hemisphere. The findings are also consistent with speculations concerning a possible selective deficiency in the availability of two of the brain's neurotransmitter systems: dopamine and norepinephrine. Prefrontal-limbic connections are known to contain relatively high amounts of these neurotransmitters. Psychostimulants (the primary pharmacological treatment for children with ADHD) are known agonists (they increase neurotransmitter function) of these systems. Finally, the brain areas implicated are thought to underlie several aspects of inattention, behavioral inhibition (impulsivity, executive planning abilities), emotion, and learning. Thus, findings to date highlight several possibilities concerning the pathogenesis of and treatment response observed in children with ADHD.

Before leaving this section, one may wonder what role a child's gross motor activity plays in the theoretical speculation proffered in the preceding paragraphs. For example, we know that brain–behavior relationships are not unidirectional. Ongoing activity within the human brain clearly affects how we behave, and our behavior also affects brain functioning. One example of this phenomenon is the well-documented finding that higher activity level increases the level or availability of dopamine in the human brain. Following this logic, one might speculate that the higher than average gross motor activity observed in children with ADHD while they attempt to concentrate on schoolwork or learning tasks represents the body's attempt to "self-medicate" itself by increasing dopamine availability to the brain. Conversely, normal levels of gross motor activity usually are observed in children with ADHD when they are actively engaged in highly stimulating activities, such as playing computer games or watching exciting videos.

Anecdotally, this phenomenon is readily observed in normal adults during periods of boredom (e.g., movement in chairs, leg movements, and doodling while sitting in a lecture for 45 minutes).

Psychological Theories

Three psychological theories of ADHD proposed in recent years are evaluated with respect to their conceptualization of brain–cognitive behavior relations and degree of empirical support. Quay's (1988) neuropsychological inhibition model and Sergeant's (1996) energetic–cognitive model are reviewed initially, as both contribute to features of Barkley's (1997) behavioral inhibition theory.

Quay (1988) used Gray's (1982) neuropsychological model of anxiety to explain the origin of poor impulse control or inhibition in children with ADHD. Implicit to the model is the basic hypothesis that brain function underlies various aspects of behavior and learning in humans. The three basic systems hypothesized to regulate human behavior include the (a) behavioral reward system (REW), (b) behavioral inhibition system (BIS), and (c) fight–flight system. The REW and BIS are of particular interest as they are interactive and control different forms of instrumental learning and behavior.

Quay's model postulates that ADHD is a result of an underreactive BIS whose anatomical location is in the septo–hippocampal region, with connections to the frontal cortex. The system operates by means of its dependence on noradrenergic inputs from the locus coeruleus, and serotonergic inputs from the raphe nucleus. The BIS responds to signals of conditioned punishment and nonreward as well as novelty and innate fear stimuli, resulting in passive avoidance and extinction. Quay emphasized that it is not that children with ADHD fail to respond to punishment but that they are less responsive to cues and signals, indicating that punishment or nonreward is dependent or contingent on their behavior. Measurement of these characteristics typically is derived from experimental paradigms such as the Continuous Performance Task (CPT) and the Stop–Signal Test (e.g., commission errors and ability to withhold responses, respectively). Collectively, results have been relatively consistent in demonstrating that impulsive errors and the ability to withhold responses on laboratory paradigms are highly characteristic of children with ADHD. Whether these proclivities are unique to children with ADHD or constitute a shared feature of other psychopathological disorders of childhood await empirical testing.

Quay's (1988) theory hypothesizes brain–behavior relations by specifying a relatively well-studied behavioral inhibition system based on experimental animal, anatomical, and pharmacological research. A rationale concerning why the BIS is under reactive in children with ADHD has not been proffered, and it is unclear whether BIS functioning in humans is best characterized as a continuum or categorically. In the latter case, only children exceeding a particular threshold would display behaviors characteristic of ADHD. The necessary conceptual framework specifying what is inhibited or disinhibited, the manner in which this irregularity arises, and the mechanisms through which it produces the cognitive and behavioral features of ADHD await empirical study.

The foundation of Sergeant's (1996) energetic–cognitive model of ADHD is derived from Sternberg's (1975) additive factor method (AFM) and Sander's (1983) cognitive–energetic model. Sternberg postulated that human information processing consists of four components or stages. These include encoding, serial comparison, decision making, and response organization. Tasks requiring attention typically require that the four processing stages be executed accurately and in proper sequence. The time to respond in an attention-demanding task is the sum of the times required to carry out each of the four components (i.e., the process is serial) as depicted in the top portion of Fig. 20.1. The AFM infers stages by determining the mutual relationships between the effects of task variables and reaction time. Additive effects typically are interpreted to mean that separate stages are affected, whereas significant interactions imply that two variables affect at least one common stage. Criticisms concerning basic assumptions underling the AFM include the proposed unidimensional nature of cognitive processing, the strict serial processing between stages, lack of feedback loops during the reaction process, and the designation of a constant stage output.

Sanders (1983) addressed several of the aforementioned criticisms by proposing a cognitive–energetic model that combines Sternberg's (1975) computational information processing model with Pribram and McGuinness's (1975) three suboptimal environmental or organismic conditions to explain attentional processing. These latter conditions include an arousal system as a phasic response to input, an activation system as a tonic readiness to respond, and an effort mechanism as a coordinating and organizing principle. Effort is thought to coordinate the activity of arousal and activation and has the additional function of promoting the proficiency of the information processing system (see bottom portion of Fig. 20.1).

Sergeant's (1996) energetic–cognitive model of ADHD focuses on explaining differences between children with ADHD and normal controls. His initial series of investigations sought to determine whether differences exist between children with ADHD and normal controls during the three primary information processing stages proposed by Sternberg (1975) that are thought to reflect arousal resources. Results suggest that arousal and primary information processing abilities are intact and that effort and activation (the motor presetting stage) may be responsible for deficient processing in ADHD (Sergeant & van der Meere, 1994; see bottom portion of Fig. 20.1). Sergeant's dependent measures are derived from signal detection theory. According to this theory, beta (response bias) is thought to reflect an individual's tendency to respond that a signal occurred instead of responding that no signal has occurred, or, stated differently, the subjective response criterion of the subject. Children's ability to detect the signal itself independent of their response tendencies is assessed by d–prime (d'). The distinction between d–prime and beta is purported to differentiate attentional and arousal factors from impulsiveness, motivational, and response style factors in vigilance.

In a series of subsequent articles, Sergeant and van der Meere (1990) challenged the notion that children with ADHD experience difficulties with sustained attention—a core feature of the disorder. They argued that a diagnostic grouping by time interaction must occur to demonstrate a specific deficit in sustained attention, that is, children with ADHD should show a pattern of responding characterized by a significantly steeper decline in performance (d') over time compared to normal control children. This type of response pattern failed to emerge in their series of investigations using an automatic (vs. controlled processing type) version of the continuous performance test (e.g., respond whenever the letter "X" immediately follows the letter "A" on the computer screen). Differences between children with ADHD and nor-

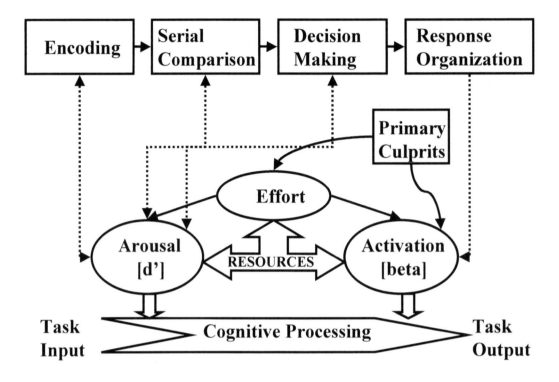

FIG. 20.1. A visual schematic of Sergeant's (1996) energetic–cognitive model of ADHD indicates that the time to respond in an attention-demanding task is the sum of the times required to carry out each of the four components shown at the top of the figure. Effort is required to modulate the two energetic pools (arousal, activation) that influence cognitive processing. Arousal and activation are measured by d–prime (d') and beta, respectively, and are intrinsically linked to the four serial processing components at the top of the figure.

mal controls were found on the beta but not d' index. Based on these results, Sergeant postulated that energetic resources involving effort and activation are responsible for the poor performance of children with ADHD. This suggests that the primary deficit in ADHD is not due to the attentional (arousal) or information processing stage but to the motor presetting stage involved in motor preparedness to act.

Although an intriguing model, the conceptual linkages between signal detection indexes, cognitive–energetic constructs, and primary features of ADHD they are presumed to explain have not been empirically validated. Criticisms of the state theory of human information processing remain largely unanswered. Use of simple, automatic processing tasks as indicators of cognitive functioning in broader domains limits the theory's applicability. Furthermore, recent reviews of the CPT literature reveal significant two-way interactions wherein children with ADHD exhibit steeper performance declines over time (i.e., deficits in sustained attention) compared to their normal peers.

Barkley's (1997) theory of behavioral inhibition emphasizes the role of cognitive processes described as executive functions in the regulation of behavior. He argued that these processes serve to organize elements of behavior such that their expression is orderly and in keeping with environmental demands. This view postulates that behavioral inhibition—the ability to stop expression of behavioral elements until and unless properly organized—is a necessary facet of behavioral control. These seemingly simple premises are formalized into a hierarchical, multidimensional model as shown in Figure 20.2. The illustration shows that deficiencies in behavioral inhibition represent the core pathology in ADHD. This deficit is presumed to emerge early in development and to interfere with the operation and development of four executive functions (prolongation/working memory, self-regulation of affect/motivation/arousal, internalization of speech, and reconstitution) that are responsible for the fluency with which behavioral sequences are executed. This view also postulates a positive feedback cycle in which poor executive functioning exacerbates deficient behavioral inhibition over time. Consequently, over the course of development, these interacting deficits give rise to the myriad cognitive and behavioral features characterizing ADHD.

Barkley (1997) attempted to provide a basic conceptual link between the postulated inhibitory functions, brain anatomy, genetics, and socialization. For example, the anatomical location of inhibitory functions is posited to reside in the orbital–frontal regions of the prefrontal cortex and its reciprocal interconnections with the

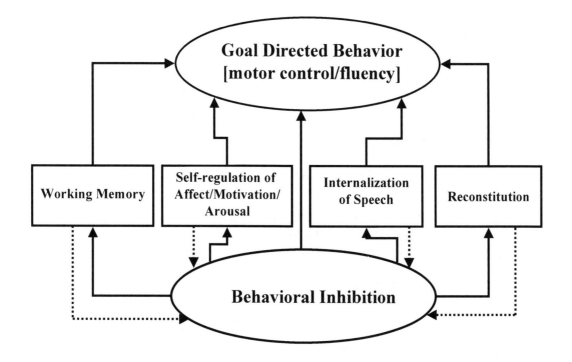

FIG. 20.2.   A visual schematic depicts Barkley's (1997) behavioral inhibition model of ADHD. Behavioral inhibition exerts a direct controlling influence over the motor control system (designated by solid lines with arrows), and sets the occasion for executive functions (working memory, self-regulation, internalization of speech, reconstitution). Executive functions produce direct effects on goal-directed behavior (motor control and fluency) in addition to having feedback loops (shown as dotted lines with arrows) to behavioral inhibition.

ventromedial region of the striatum. Executive functions are thought to arise from the development of neural networks in the prefrontal regions of the brain and are modifiable by socialization and experience. A deficit in behavioral inhibition, which is thought to emerge first during development, impairs executive functions and arises principally from genetic and neurodevelopmental origins.

Barkley (1997) proposed a hierarchical, multidimensional model with behavioral inhibition at the bottom, four executive functions in the middle (which are assumed to be interdependent, interactive, and critical for self-regulation and goal-directed persistence), and goal-directed behavior at the top. Anatomical origins are postulated for the various functions, and punctilious explanations are offered concerning how deficiencies in the system may account for various cognitive and behavioral difficulties experienced by children with ADHD. The model is clearly the most comprehensive and complex offered to date. For this reason, it is susceptible to multiple conceptual weaknesses. First, although much of the language of the model concerns itself with distinctions between children with ADHD and their normal peers (necessarily a correlational notion), the core assertion at issue is that alternation of the ability to inhibit will have measurable effects on the efficiency and precision with which the executive functions are carried out. The latter is necessarily a causal argument and therefore only can be evaluated definitively using experimental manipulations. Herein lies the primary problem. How does one measure disinhibition independently of task performance on instruments designed to measure executive functioning? Furthermore, if disinhibition cannot be operationally separated from the executive functions at issue, does it make conceptual sense to argue for disinhibition as a cause of executive functioning?

Second, the model fails to specify exactly what is inhibited. If, as Barkley (1997) argued, behavioral inhibition refers to the ability to stop a "prepotent response," does this refer to the level of the response's cognitive representation, its motoric execution, or both? If the latter is correct, how is disinhibition different from motor control and fluency?

Finally, the theory relies on assumed constructs (e.g., inhibition, executive functions) that have not been subjected to psychometric scrutiny, and brain–behavior inferences fail to meet basic criteria concerning behavioral pathology outlined by von Eckardt (1986):

1. Pathology outlined must be correctly interpreted as a failure of some specific and well-understood behavioral function.
2. Normal parameters of the specific behavior should be thoroughly understood a priori.
3. There should be a good model of the normal functional path for brain–behavior connections leading to the specific behavior (in which the pathology has been noted).
4. A specific deficit in this modeled pathway should be hypothesized as the source for the behavioral impairment.
5. There should be no better competing explanation for the phenomenon of impairment.

Comment

A comprehensive theory of ADHD must account for the plethora of findings derived from studies focusing on genetic, neurophysiological, anatomical, and early temperament differences in children. The way in which these factors affect cognitive function and behavior also must be hypothesized such that they can be empirically evaluated. A model of hypothesized interaction is depicted in Figure 20.3. Genetic, neuronal, and temperament influences are hypothesized to result in different brain states in children. Brain states, in turn, are postulated to result in different cognitive states (labeled C-1 through C-6), which produce a wide array of observable behavioral outcomes (labeled B-1 through B-6) in children. Interaction of the organism with the environment is known to alter brain growth and functioning, particularly during early years of development. This dynamic interplay will prove difficult to evaluate experimentally but must be taken into account in formulating a comprehensive theory of ADHD. It also may help to

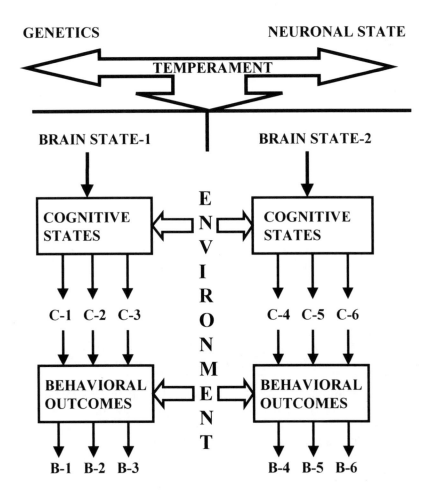

FIG. 20.3.   A visual schematic depicts a theoretical model of ADHD. Genetic, neuronal, and temperament factors at birth influence brain development, which, in turn, result in widely different cognitive and behavioral outcomes in children.

explain the myriad cognitive and behavioral difficulties that characterize the disorder and accentuate similar and unique features observed in children.

COURSE OF THE DISORDER

Early Childhood

Several well-controlled studies indicate that difficulties with attention and overactivity are relatively common among preschoolers. Only a small subset of these children continues to manifest symptoms characteristic of ADHD by the time they are 4 to 5 years of age. These symptoms are strongly predictive of continued difficulties and a probable clinical diagnosis by ages 6 and 9 (Campbell, 1990). Thus, the necessity of considering both the degree and duration of behavioral disturbance cannot be over-emphasized, particularly in very young children.

Parents describe children in this age group—who continue to exhibit a durable pattern of ADHD symptoms—as always on the go, fearless, restless, continually getting into things, not obeying parental commands, obstreperous, highly curious about their environment, and requiring high levels of adult supervision. Other problems, such as perceptual motor difficulties, sleep and eating difficulties, accident proneness, speech and language difficulties, and toilet training difficulties are reported in a subset of these children. Those with advanced intellectual and cognitive skills and who tend not to be aggressive are generally easier to manage both at home and in preschool settings. The parents of these children are under enormous daily stress in their caregiver roles, the reciprocal interaction of which not infrequently results in psychiatric disability, marital problems, alcoholism, and increased risk for child abuse.

Middle Childhood

Between the ages of 6 and 12 years, children with ADHD continue to demonstrate difficulties with attention, impulsivity, overactivity, and compliance with adult requests. These difficulties are exacerbated after they enter elementary school, with a subsequent increase in outpatient referral rates owing to two primary factors. Classroom teachers are more familiar with age-appropriate norms for behavior. Furthermore, children are expected to sit still, pay attention, and engage in more difficult academic tasks and organized activities for longer periods of time. In some cases, children are excused as "immature" by well-meaning school personnel and forced to repeat the grade or passed marginally with the expectation that "maturation" will occur over the summer months.

Increasing social and academic demands will affect their already handicapping condition to an even greater extent during these primary school years and cause greater stress to already overburdened parents and teachers. Homework assignments add an additional source of conflict to the familial environment, as 25% or more of the children experience significant difficulties with reading, develop other academic skill disorders, or both. Their inattention, impulsivity, and higher than normal activity level predestines them to develop poor peer and interpersonal relationships, with a resulting pattern of social isolation and low self-esteem in later years.

Adolescence

One of the prevailing myths about children with ADHD is that they "outgrow" the disorder when they reach adolescence. Follow-up and long-term outcome studies, however, inform us that approximately 70% of children diagnosed as having ADHD in childhood continue to display symptoms of and meet diagnostic criteria for ADHD as adolescents. Primary difficulties with attention–concentration, impulsivity, and difficulty following directions remain, whereas the overactivity component of the disorder diminishes somewhat and transitions into fidgeting and restlessness with increasing age.

Perhaps more unsettling are the findings that between 40% and 60% of adolescents with ADHD also meet diagnostic criteria for conduct disorder (CD)—a disorder characterized by serious and pervasive antisocial behavior. These comorbid adolescents, in turn, are also more likely to engage in substance use (e.g., cigarette smoking) and abuse (e.g., alcohol and marijuana).

One of the strongest predictors during early childhood for becoming a well-functioning, stable, successful adult is academic achievement. Follow-up studies of children with ADHD during their adolescent years, particularly those comorbid for CD, have been alarmingly negative with regard to academic outcome. They are significantly more likely to have been suspended or expelled from school, three times more likely to have failed at least one grade, and their standardized achievement test scores are below normal in math, reading, and spelling. Of even greater concern is that 25% to 31% fail to complete high school. Overall, adolescents with ADHD, and particularly those carrying a dual diagnosis of CD, represent a population at high risk for a variety of negative outcomes associated with psychiatric disability, social, and adult occupational functioning.

Adult Outcome and Long-Term Prognosis

Three trajectories have been postulated concerning the long-term outcome of children with ADHD: developmental delay, developmental decay, and continuous display. The first trajectory presumes that ADHD is a neuromaturational problem and that associated difficulties eventually will diminish with age. The developmental decay trajectory holds that the primary symptom picture will worsen with increasing age, and that specific clinical features will be manifested somewhat differently in older children. The continuous display trajectory posits that the primary symptom picture will continue to be manifested with increasing age to a more or less similar degree of severity. But, similar to the decay model, the topography of clinical features (e.g., inattention, impulsivity) will change to reflect difficulties associated with adolescence and adulthood.

Each of the three outcome trajectories is supported in part by the existing, albeit scant, literature concerning adults diagnosed during childhood as having ADHD. Between 50% and 65% of diagnosed children continue to experience difficulties with core clinical symptoms and related behavioral problems as adults; only 11% are estimated to be free of any psychiatric diagnosis and considered well-functioning adults. These rather bleak estimates are tempered somewhat when one considers that only about a third of the "normal" population of children are free of psychiatric disability as adults.

Other areas of adult functioning are equally impaired. Relatively few adults with a childhood diagnosis of ADHD go on to complete a university degree program (approximately 5% vs 41% of control children). Significant minorities of them (20% to 25%) continue to display a persistent pattern of antisocial behavior. Poor work records, lower job status, difficulties getting along with supervisors and overall lower socioeconomic status attainment are common. And, greater difficulties with social skills, unstable marriages, and lower self-esteem prevail. Conversely, other adults with ADHD appear to function normally and even exceptionally well as adults. The limited evidence available indicates that a supportive, stable family environment; milder ADHD symptoms; higher intelligence; greater emotional stability; and no concomitant CD, especially aggression during childhood, are the best predictors of positive adult outcome.

FAMILIAL CONTRIBUTIONS

Studies examining the families of children with ADHD represent an important avenue of inquiry concerning the heritability of the disorder. Although one cannot completely separate the role of genetics from that of deviant childrearing practices, family–genetic studies can nevertheless improve our understanding of the psychobiology of ADHD and specifically address whether ADHD tends to run in families (i.e., by establishing familial risk).

In the most comprehensive and methodologically eloquent study conducted to date, Biederman, Faraone, Keenan, Knee, and Tsuang (1990) evaluated family–genetic and psychosocial risk factors for ADHD among 457 first-degree relatives of clinically referred children and adolescents with ADHD compared with psychiatric and normal controls. Age-corrected rates of illness, termed *morbidity risks,* were used to adjust upwards the degree to which an individual was counted as "healthy" as a function of increasing age. Use of this technique has been woefully absent in a majority of family–genetic studies, but it is necessary because many psychiatric disorders have a variable age of onset (e.g., major depression). Consequently, the fact that one may not have lived through the "risk period" must be taken into account and corrected for statistically.

Several important findings emerged from the Biederman et al. (1990) study. The first of these was that parents of children with ADHD were significantly more likely to be separated or divorced relative to the psychiatric and normal comparison groups. This finding, however, must be interpreted cautiously. It could indicate a greater degree of psychopathology among the parents, or, alternatively, it could reflect the strain placed on a marriage in raising a child with ADHD. A second major finding of the study was that the probability or risk of having ADHD among relatives of ADHD children were 7.6 and 4.6 times the odds for having ADHD among the relatives of normal or psychiatric control groups, respectively. In examining these odds ratios, it was found that nearly 65% of the children with ADHD had at least one relative with ADHD, compared with 24% and 15% of the psychiatric and normal control groups, respectively. Relatives of ADHD children were also at higher risk for both antisocial disorder and mood disorders—These disorders were significantly more prevalent in the families of children with ADHD. Finally, both parents as well as brothers of children with ADHD had a significantly higher risk for ADHD compared to relatives of control groups: 44% of the fathers, 19% of the mothers, and 39% of the brothers of ADHD children also had ADHD. Finally, all of the aforementioned findings remained significant after controlling for social class and intactness of families among the different groups.

The conclusion that can be drawn from this and other studies is that ADHD is a highly familial disorder that places affected individuals at significant risk for adult psychopathology and dysfunctional marriages.

PSYCHOPHYSIOLOGICAL AND GENETIC INFLUENCES

Psychophysiological Influences

Psychophysiological functions in children with ADHD have been investigated in numerous studies over the past 20 years. Investigations in this field generally have sought to examine topics related to general autonomic arousal of the nervous system and cortical electrical activity of the brain, using measures such as galvanic skin response and EEG, respectively. Although popular several years ago, theories purporting that children with ADHD experience a general pattern of nervous system underarousal have not been supported by recent, better controlled studies.

More recent work in the field essentially has abandoned the notion of a simple difference model of brain activity and has sought instead to investigate brain activity while children are actively engaged in cognitive tasks known to differentiate them from normal children. This line of inquiry may prove more informative, as it recognizes the accepted fact that the difficulties experienced by children with ADHD are not static but dynamic and depend on a panoply of prevailing environmental conditions. (Related advances in the field are described previously in "Neurological, Neurophysiological and Neuroanatomical Factors.")

Genetic Factors

The role of hereditary transmission of ADHD has been investigated in several studies over the past 30 years. Unfortunately, the bulk of this research is uninterpretable because of numerous methodological problems and poorly defined diagnostic groups of children. Two recent twin studies, however, indicate significantly greater concordance (agreement) for hyperactive symptoms between identical than between fraternal twins, with heritability of ADHD estimated to be .73 to .91. Both studies (Gjone, Stevenson, & Sundet, 1996; Levy, Hay, McStephen, Wood, & Waldman, 1997) included large cohorts of children (915 and 1,938 participants, respectively). Estimated heritability was based on the extent to which cotwins of identical probands had scores more similar to their deviant proband and more different from the mean for the total population than cotwins of fraternal probands. Of perhaps greater significance were the findings in both studies suggesting that ADHD is best viewed as the extreme of a behavior that varies genetically throughout the entire population rather than as a disorder with discrete determinants.

Comment

ADHD is an inheritable condition, the symptomatology of which may be diminished or exacerbated by prevailing environmental conditions. There is also evidence to indicate that different etiological factors involving pregnancy, birth complications, exposure to lead or drugs, and a variety of CNS insults may be the primary culprit in a small subset of these children. The majority, however, inherit the disorder through some yet unknown mechanism, with resulting underactivity of the prefrontal–striatal–limbic regions of the brain. A different and admittedly speculative view of the disorder is that the brains of children with ADHD are not abnormal. Rather, they operate differently under certain environmental conditions, primarily conditions that involve sustained concentration for routine and nonstimulating tasks, as is the case with the majority of classroom learning. From a biological evolutionary perspective, it could be argued that many of the behavioral characteristics that typify children with ADHD may have had high adaptive value in earlier societies and cultures that relied on acting and shifting attention quickly without undue reflection.

CURRENT TREATMENTS

Current treatments for children with ADHD fall within two broad categories: behavioral and pharmacological. In a majority of cases, variants of these treatments must be combined to obtain optimal results, particularly for children with more severe ADHD symptoms.

Behavioral Treatment

A wide variety of behavioral interventions had been used to treat children with ADHD. Most focused on improving classroom functioning and school-based behavior, whereas more recent interventions emphasized the development of peer relationships and social skills. The discussion below focuses exclusively on classroom interventions.

Historical Overview of Behavioral Interventions.   Early behavioral interventions focused on decreasing disruptive behavior in children with ADHD. These eventually were abandoned when it was discovered that reducing disruptive behavior did not necessarily translate into improved academic performance. This was an important finding, because academic achievement is one of the best indicators of a good prognosis and favorable long-term outcome in children. It also was found that many of the behavioral interventions that required teachers to deliver positive feedback (using verbal praise or by administering points, stars, or checks on a sheet containing descriptions of desirable behavior) involved several drawbacks. One drawback was that the systems required a disproportionate amount of teacher time and thus was not "cost-effective." A second criticism was that many children with ADHD tended to be drawn off-task by the delivery of positive feedback and experienced difficulty getting back on-task—an effect opposite of that intended by the intervention.

Empirical studies examining the relative efficacy of behavioral interventions beginning in the early 1970s and continuing through the 1980s revealed a rather interesting finding. If the behavioral intervention directly targeted improved academic performance as its main goal (i.e., by making consequences specific for completing academic work successfully), disruptive behavior nearly always showed a concomitant decline in frequency. The "incompatible response approach" was subsequently coined to refer to these procedures. It implied that increased academic performance was incompatible with disruptive conduct in the classroom and should be the primary target of intervention efforts.

During the 1980s and continuing to present, the most successful classroom interventions followed this general principle and focused on developing incentive and feedback systems that directed the child's attention to the completion of his or her schoolwork. It was also established that a combination of positive and mild aversive corrective feedback worked better than either one alone. This type of intervention relies on a behavioral principle termed *response cost*. Children earn points that can be traded in for structured free-time or specific classroom activities and lose points for not attending to their academic assignments.

Newly Developed Behavioral Interventions.   A prototypical example of the response cost procedure for classroom use is the recently developed Attentional Training System (ATS). A small electronic device is placed on the child's desk during periods of in-seat academic work (see Fig. 20.4). Children receive basic instruction concerning how the system works and what they need to do to earn points during the ensuing academic period. The device is activated and points (one per minute) are accumulated on the display counter while children attend to their academic assignments. The classroom teacher possesses a hand-held remote control device (see Figure 2.4), which can be used anywhere within the classroom to control up to four different student units. This allows the teacher to work with other students throughout the academic period, either in small groups or individually, while monitoring ADHD children's behavior. The teacher glances periodically at the targeted children to determine whether they are on-task. If students are attending to their classroom assignment, the teacher does nothing. The students' desk module awards points on a cumulative basis throughout the academic assignment period for appropriate behavior. The teacher activates the hand held device on occasions when students are not attending to their assignments, signaling them that they are off-task. The red dome on the student's desk module is illuminated for 15-seconds, and one point is electronically deducted from the accumulated point total. The teacher immediately returns to whatever he or she was doing and checks the student's progress again in a minute or two. At the end of the academic period, the accumulated point total is transferred to a recording sheet. Students are permitted to engage in desirable learning activities (e.g., listening to tapes, art projects, using the computer) for an amount of time equivalent to the number of points earned during the preceding academic period (i.e., 15 points earns 15 minutes). In some cases, a leaner point to earned free

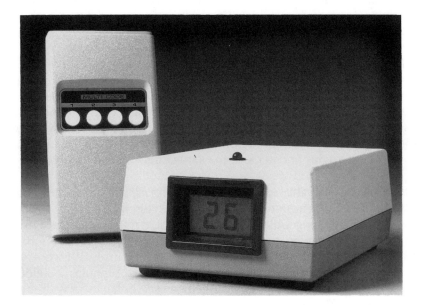

FIG. 20.4.   The Attentional Training System. Invented by M. D. Rapport (see Rapport, Murphy, & Bailey, 1982) for treating children with ADHD. Manufactured and distributed for commercial use by Gordon Systems, DeWitt, NY.

time ratio is employed (e.g., 2:1). The desk module is subsequently set aside until the next scheduled academic period. (An empirical demonstration and case example using the ATS is provided below under the pharmacological treatment section.)

Pharmacological Treatment

Pharmacological treatment of children with ADHD usually involves the use of psychostimulants and, less frequently, clonidine or one of the tricyclic antidepressants. In this section, the focus is exclusively on discussing one of the psychostimulants, methylphenidate (Ritalin). Methylphenidate (MPH) is used in approximately 90% of the cases for which medication is indicated, represents the "first-line defense" in treating children with ADHD, and is by far the best studied of the medications.

Overview and Rationale. Most students studying psychopathology, among children with ADHD raise serious questions concerning the use of medications with children. The topic is often "moralized," and children are viewed as "being medicated or drugged" unnecessarily, with blame placed on the adults (parents and teachers) who cannot cope with their behavior or academic difficulties. A useful analogy, however, might be to contrast the use of medication with that of using eyeglasses for reading. Eyeglasses or contact lenses, like medication, represent an unnatural intervention and clearly do not cure visual problems. They do, however, allow one who is experiencing visual problems to read or view the environment more normally. When they are removed, the original vision problems are as they were before. Like the child with ADHD, individuals with vision problems (e.g., farightedness) could in fact alter their environment so that they did not require glasses, for example, by having all written material they come in contact with printed in very large letters. This would require a great deal of cooperation and effort by those in the individual's environment, and, as with similar to the child with ADHD, it is not considered a cost-effective alternative. It is much easier and just as effective to simply wear one's glasses.

The ADHD brain simply does not work optimally in a variety of situations, particularly those requiring sustained concentration and the ability to reflectively approach and complete difficult tasks that characterize much of schoolwork. Thus, two alternatives exist. One can dramatically alter the child's academic environment by asking teachers to provide feedback, create a different curriculum, and supply unnatural incentives for the child throughout the day. Alternatively, the child can ingest a small tablet once or twice a day and achieve the same effect in a majority of cases.

Titrating and Assessing Psychostimulant Response in Children With ADHD. Using MPH as an ongoing (i.e., maintenance) treatment intervention for children with ADHD requires careful attention by a knowledgeable professional. First, it must be established that the child is a "positive responder" to the medication, which holds true in approximately 80% of the cases. This is relatively easy to accomplish, because MPH is not what is referred to as a steady–state medication, that is, it does not require a buildup in the bloodstream for several days or weeks. Rather, it affects behavior as well as cognitive performance within 30 to 45 minutes following ingestion, and the effects of a single tablet last approximately 4 hours. Thus, positive treatment effects are easily recognized on the first day of treatment, and the degree of change may be quantified using a variety of behavioral, medication-sensitive rating scales completed by the child's classroom teacher or by means of direct observation.

The second step is more difficult and somewhat controversial. It involves establishing the appropriate dosage for a particular child. The primary difficulty is that, unlike other medications, a child's gross body weight is not a useful determinant of how much MPH to administer. In fact, body weight has been found to be unrelated to behavioral response (Rapport & Denney, 1997; Rapport, DuPaul, & Kelly, 1989). The task is further complicated by the fact that children with ADHD cannot be relied on to provide useful information concerning medication response. Positive and even dramatic changes in their behavior and cognitive performance that are glaringly obvious to others are frequently unrecognized by the ADHD child. As a result, two alternatives remain. One is to request that parents and teachers complete standardized rating scales on a weekly basis as a means to adjust dosage. The second is to attempt to establish optimal dosage in the clinic. This is usually accomplished by observing children under a range of dosages while they undergo neurocognitive evaluation with instruments that attempt to mirror the cognitive demands associated with successful school performance and learning.

Teacher rating scales are by far the more cost-effective and traditional method for titrating dosage. Their primary drawback, with the lone exception being the recently developed Academic Performance Rating Scale (DuPaul, Rapport, & Perriello, 1991), is that the scales target changes in children's behavior and fail to consider changes in academic performance or learning. This has become a highly controversial issue over the years, as some have demonstrated that behavior and cognitive performance (or learning) may be optimized at different *dosages* (Sprague & Sleator, 1977). More recent investigations, however, have failed to confirm these findings (see Rapport & Kelly, 1991, for a comprehensive review). Nevertheless, it would be prudent to obtain some measure of a child's academic and learning performance when establishing optimal dosage.

Use of a dose-sensitive neurocognitive battery that mimics children's school performance is highly desirable. Various computer-administered instruments have been developed to assist with clinical titration in recent years, but they await standardization and empirical validation.

CASE ILLUSTRATION

Mitch was an 8-year-old boy with a chronic history of multiple behavioral and academic problems. His mother, following a school conference in which issues were raised concerning his ability to perform on grade level and "immature" behavior, brought him to an outpatient mental health facility for evaluation.

Assessment. A semistructured clinical interview was conducted with Mitch's mother, during which her son's developmental, medical, educational, and mental health history were reviewed. Age, onset, course, and duration of the symptoms or behaviors related to each of the clinical disorders described in the *DSM–IV* were reviewed for diagnostic formulation purposes. Following the clinical interview, a battery of standardized, age-appropriate teacher and parent rating scales was administered and scored to help quantify the degree and pervasiveness of difficulties experienced by Mitch. Finally, a standardized battery of intelligence and academic achievement tests was administered to assess Mitch's abilities and current level of functioning (see Rapport, 1993, for a review of appropriate instruments). Results were compared to academic records obtained from the school.

Diagnosis.   The results obtained from the assessment workup indicated that Mitch met diagnostic criteria for ADHD, combined type, as well as for a developmental arithmetic disorder (considered a "learning disability" in his state). Problems also were noted with peer relationships, compliance with adults, following oral and written directions, short-term memory, and self-esteem.

Treatment.   A meeting was scheduled with Mitch's parents, and treatment recommendations were offered that specifically targeted their son's behavior and academic performance in school. It was felt that Mitch's academic problems, low self-esteem, and at least some interpersonal problems were directly related to his difficulties paying attention and completing academic assignments correctly in school on a consistent basis. The parents consented to an alternating trial of MPH and attentional training to determine their relative benefits. As with most parents, they were concerned about having their son on medication.

Pharmacological treatment consisted of a closely monitored trial of MPH (Ritalin) at each of four doses: 5-mg (.23 mg/kg), 10-mg (.46 mg/kg), 15-mg (.64 mg/kg) and 20-mg (.92 mg/kg) following baseline (no medication) assessment. Each dose was tried for a minimum of 2 weeks before dosage was increased. The behavioral intervention (attentional training using response cost technology) was used during two of Mitch's most difficult morning academic periods (phonics and math) and instituted for a 3-week period initially, then a 4-week period during the last experimental condition (see Figs. 20.5 and 20.6). Teacher ratings were obtained weekly, with the teacher blind to medication conditions.

Results of Treatment.   An ABACBC (reversal) within-participant design was used to compare the effects of MPH at different doses with no-medication conditions (baseline) and then to contrast the most effective MPH dose with the behavioral intervention. Direct observation of Mitch's attention and completion of academic assignments were conducted daily and at the same time each morning—approximately 45 minutes after ingestion of the morning medication and at the same time on no-medication days (see Figs. 20.5 and 20.6).

Prior to any intervention (see first baseline condition in Fig. 20.5), Mitch experienced significant difficulty paying attention, as evidenced by his 40% to 48% on-task rate during the two morning academic assignment periods. Consistent with this low rate of attention, he completed between 35% and 60% of his academic assignments on a daily basis during the initial 3-week baseline (no-intervention) period (Fig. 20.6). A clear and somewhat dramatic increase in attention was observed under each of the medication conditions, with a concomitant increase in the percent of academic assignments completed (see .23 through .92 mg/kg MPH dose conditions in Figs. 20.5 and 20.6). Academic assignment accuracy remained relatively high and stable throughout the course of both interventions, which is noteworthy given his increase in academic productivity. Teacher ratings using the Abbreviated Conners Teacher Rating Scale (Werry, Sprague, & Cohen, 1975) generally paralleled changes observed in attention and academic performance (see Figs. 20.5 and 20.6).

A return to baseline (no-intervention) conditions was initiated following the medication trial to insure that observed changes were due to the active drug as opposed to some other phenomenon (e.g., developmental maturity in which improvement might be observed with the passage of time regardless of intervention). Clearly, this was not the case. Mitch's attention and academic productivity returned to near pretreatment levels (see second baseline in Figs. 20.5 and 20.6).

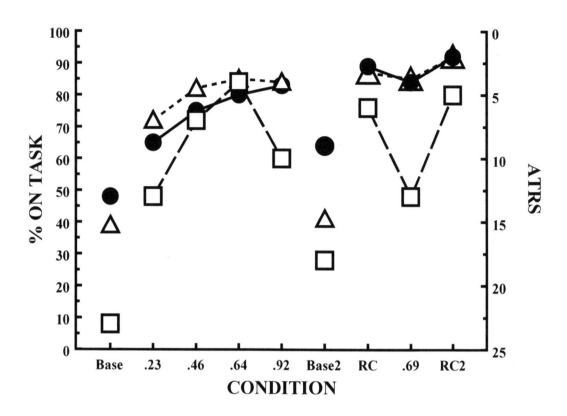

FIG. 20.5.   Mean percentage of daily observations in which Mitch was on-task (left-hand ordinate) during the two morning academic assignments periods (math = closed circles; phonics = open circles) during no-treatment (baseline), methylphenidate treatment (.23 mg/kg through .92 mg/kg doses), and behavioral treatment (response cost) conditions. Weekly teacher ratings are shown as open triangles and interpreted using the right-hand ordinate. Upward movement on the vertical axis indicates improvement on all measures.

The second stage of the evaluation was established such that the MPH dose deemed most therapeutic during the initial titration trials could be directly compared with the attentional training program. The 15-mg (.69 mg/kg) dose was selected instead of the 20-mg dose because Mitch's academic performance showed a decline under the higher dose condition, despite slightly higher levels of attention (see "% on-task" compared with "% completed" under the .92 mg/kg dose condition in Figs. 20.5 and 20.6)

Introduction of attentional training (for details, see the previous section titled Newly Developed Behavioral Interventions) resulted in clear and sustained increases in Mitch's attention and academic performance, as well as improved teacher ratings during the ensuing 3-week period. These effects, when contrasted with the 15-mg (.69 mg/kg) MPH condition, indicate that both interventions affected Mitch's attention to a similar degree, with somewhat higher rates of academic performance associated with attentional training. Discontinuation of MPH and a return to the attentional training intervention for the final 4 weeks of observation essentially replicated the effects observed previously.

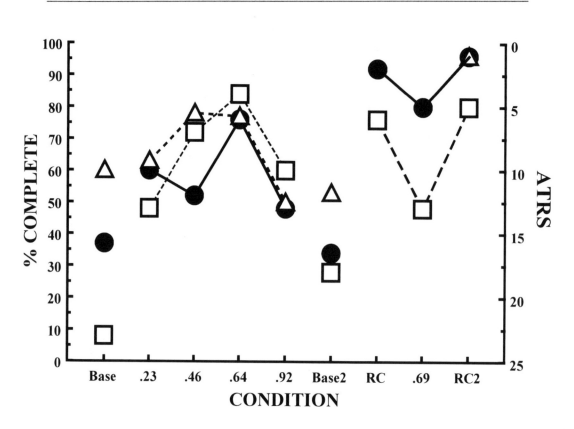

FIG. 20.6. Mean percentage of academic assignments completed daily (left-hand ordinate) during the two morning academic assignments periods (math = closed circles; phonics = open circles) during no-treatment (baseline), methylphenidate treatment (.23 mg/kg through .92 mg/kg doses), and behavioral treatment (response cost) conditions. Weekly teacher ratings are shown as open triangles and interpreted using the right-hand ordinate. Upward movement on the vertical axis indicates improvement on all measures.

The results were shared with both Mitch's parents and his classroom teacher. It was agreed that he would continue with the attentional training intervention for the remainder of the school year. The training apparatus was removed approximately 4 weeks later according to suggestions provided in the manual. A free-time product completion contingency was instituted in which Mitch completed all of his academic work with an established degree of accuracy in exchange for a fixed amount of in-class structured free time (approximately 10 minutes following each academic period).

Follow-up at the end of the school year indicated that Mitch maintained the therapeutic gains made during the formal assessment period of the evaluation and was promoted to the third grade. His third-grade teacher, however, was not interested in establishing an ongoing behavioral management system in the classroom. He was subsequently prescribed a regimen of MPH (15-mg twice a day) by his pediatrician, which proved to be relatively successful throughout the course of the school year.

Comment. Several points are worth noting. First, a combined behavioral and medication intervention are nearly always required for more severe cases of ADHD. Second, just as medication must be carefully titrated to achieve optimal results, behavioral interventions must be created using great care and attention to detail, and they nearly always require periodic adjustment to maintain their effectiveness. Finally, a host of parameters must be considered when creating a behavioral program. Questions concerning what will serve as an effective incentive for the child, how well the teacher will cooperate given the existing classroom demands, and how to intervene at other times during the day when the program is not operative must be addressed.

SUMMARY

In this chapter, it is argued that ADHD is a complex and chronic disorder of brain, behavior, and development whose behavioral and cognitive consequences affect multiple areas of functioning. Mounting evidence suggests that the disorder is significantly more common in certain families and is probably inherited through some yet unknown mechanism, with resulting underactivity of the prefrontal–striatal–limbic regions of the brain. Differences in the neurophysiological functioning of the brain, particularly executive and regulatory functioning, may help explain why these children experience profound difficulties in maintaining attention, regulating their arousal, inhibiting themselves in accordance with environmental demands, and getting along with others, yet only at specific times and under certain conditions. Behavioral and pharmacological interventions, both alone and in combination, represent the most efficacious treatments currently available for children with ADHD. They must be viewed as "maintenance" therapies, however, because neither cures the disorder. Indeed, both must be maintained on an ongoing, long-term basis. Alternative therapies, computerized assessment instruments, and dramatic changes in classroom instructional design are evolving and represent only a part of the developments expected during the next decade.

REFERENCES

American Psychiatric Association. (1968). *Diagnostic and statistical manual of mental disorders* (2nd ed.). Washington, DC: Author.

American Psychiatric Association. (1980). *Diagnostic and statistical manual of mental disorders* (3rd ed.). Washington, DC: Author.

American Psychiatric Association. (1987). *Diagnostic and statistical manual of mental disorders* (3rd. ed., rev). Washington, DC: Author.

American Psychiatric Association. (1994). *Diagnostic and statistical manual of mental disorders* (4th ed.). Washington, DC: Author.

Barkley, R. A. (1990). *Attention deficit hyperactivity disorder: A handbook for diagnosis and treatment*. New York: Guilford.

Barkley, R. A. (1997). Behavioral inhibition, sustained attention, and executive functions: Constructing a unifying theory of ADHD. *Psychological Bulletin, 121,* 65–94.

Biederman, J., Faraone, S. V., Keenan, K., Knee, D., & Tsuang, M. T. (1990). Family–genetic and psychosocial risk factors in *DSM–III* attention deficit disorder. *Journal of the American Academy of Child and Adolescent Psychiatry, 29,* 526–533.

Campbell, S. B. (1990). *Behavior problems in preschoolers: Clinical and developmental issues.* New York: Guilford.

Casey, B. J., Castellanos, F. X., Giedd, J. N., Marsh, W. L., Hamburger, S. D., Schubert, A. B., Vauss, Y. C., Vaituzis, A. C., Dickstein, D. P., Sarfatti, S. E., & Rapoport, J. L. (1997). Implication of right frontostriatal circuitry in response inhibition and attention-deficit/hyperactivity disorder. *Journal of the American Academy of Child and Adolescent Psychiatry, 36,* 374–383.

Castellanos, F. X., Giedd, J. N., Marsh, W. L., Hamburger, S. D., Vaituzis, A. C., Dickstein, D. P., Sarfatti, S. E., Vauss, Y. C., Snell, J. W., Lange, N., Kaysen, D., Krain, A. L., Ritchie, G. F., Rajapakse, J. C., & Rapoport, J. L. (1996). Quantitative brain magnetic resonance imaging in attention-deficit hyperactivity disorder. *Archives of General Psychiatry, 53,* 607–616.

Chabot, R. J., & Serfontein, G. (1996). Quantitative electroencephalographic profiles of children with attention deficit disorder. *Biological Psychiatry, 40,* 951–963.

DuPaul, G. J., Rapport, M. D., & Perriello, L. M. (1991). Teacher ratings of academic skills: The development of the Academic Performance Rating Scale. *School Psychology Review, 20,* 284–300.

Gjone, H., Stevenson, J., & Sundet, J. M. (1996). Genetic influence on parent-reported attention-related problems in a Norwegian general population twin sample. *Journal of the American Academy of Child and Adolescent Psychiatry, 35,* 588–596.

Gray, J. A. (1982). The neuropsychology of anxiety: An inquiry into the functions of the Septo-Hippocampal system. New York: Oxford University Press.

Levy, F. Hay, D. A., McStephen, M., Wood, C., & Waldman, I. (1997). Attention-deficit hyperactivity disorder: A category or a continuum? Genetic analysis of a large-scale twin study. *Journal of the American Academy of Child and Adolescent Psychiatry, 36,* 737–744.

Lou, H. C. (1990). Methylphenidate reversible hypoperfusion of striatal regions in ADHD. In K. Conners & M. Kinsbourne (Eds.), *Attention deficit hyperactivity disorder: ADHD; clinical, experimental and demographic issues* (pp. 137–148). Munich, Germany: Medizin Verlag.

Pibram, K. H., & McGuinness, D. (1975). Arousal, activation and effort in the control of attention. *Psychological Review, 82,* 116–149.

Quay, H. C. (1988). Attention deficit disorder and the behavioral inhibition system: The relevance of the neuropsychological theory of Jeffrey A. Gray. In L. M. Bloomingdale & J. Sergeant (Eds.), *Attention deficit disorder: Criteria, cognition, intervention* (pp. 117–126). New York: Pergamon.

Rapport, M. D. (1993). Attention deficit hyperactivity disorder. In T. H. Ollendick & M. Hersen (Eds.), *Handbook of child and adolescent assessment* (pp. 269–291). Allyn & Bacon.

Rapport, M. D., & Denney, C. (1997). Titrating methylphenidate in children with attention-deficit/hyperactivity disorder: Is body mass predictive of clinical response? *Journal of the American Academy of Child and Adolescent Psychiatry, 36,* 523–530.

Rapport, M. D., DuPaul, G. J., & Kelly, K. L. (1989). Attention-deficit/hyperactivity disorder and methylphenidate: The relationship between gross body weight and drug response in children. *Psychopharmacology Bulletin, 25,* 285–290.

Rapport, M. D., & Kelly, K. L. (1991). Psychostimulant effects on learning and cognitive function: Findings and implications for children with attention deficit hyperactivity disorder. *Clinical Psychology Review, 11,* 61–92.

Rapport, M. D., Murphy, H. A., & Bailey, J. S. (1982). Ritalin vs. response cost in the control of hyperactive children: A within-subject comparison. *Journal of Applied Behavior Analysis, 15,* 205–216.

Sanders, A. F. (1983). Towards a model of stress and human performance. *Acta Psychologica, 53,* 61–97.

Satterfield, J. H. (1990). BEAM studies in ADD boys. In C. K. Conners & M. Kinsbourne (Eds.), *Attention deficit hyperactivity disorder* (pp. 127–136). Munich, Germany: Medizin Verlag.

Sergeant, J. A. (1996, January). *The cognitive–energetic model of ADHD.* Paper presented at the annual meeting of the International Society of Research in Child and Adolescent Psychopathology, Los Angeles.

Sergeant, J. A., & van der Mere, J. (1990). Converging approaches on localizing the hyperactivity deficit. In B. B. Lahey & A. E. Kazdin (Eds.), *Advances in clinical child psychology* (Vol. 13, pp. 207–245). New York: Plenum.

Sergeant, J. A., & van der Meere, J. (1994). Toward an empirical child psychopathology. In D. K. Routh (Ed.), *Disruptive behavior disorders in childhood* (pp. 59–85). New York: Plenum.

Sprague, R. L., & Sleator, E. K. (1977). Methylphenidate in hyperkinetic children: Differences in dose effects on learning and social behavior. *Science, 198,* 1274–1276.

Sternberg, S. (1975). Memory scanning: New findings and current observations. *Quarterly Journal of Experimental Psychology, 27,* 1–42.

von Eckardt, B. (1986, June). Criteria for brain–behavior models. In D. Caplan (Chair), *Inferring normal cognitive function from pathological cases.* Symposium conducted at the annual meeting of the society for Philosophy and Psychology, Johns Hopkins University, Baltimore.

Werry, J. S., Sprague, R. L., & Cohen, M. N. (1975). Conners Teacher Rating Scale for use in drug studies with children: An empirical study. *Journal of Abnormal Child Psychology, 3,* 217–229.

Zametkin, A. J., Nordahl, T. E., Gross, M., King, A. C., Semple, W. E., Rumsey, J., Hamburger, S., & Cohen, R. M. (1990). Cerebral glucose metabolism in adults with hyperactivity of childhood onset. *New England Journal of Medicine, 323,* 1361–1366.

Eating Disorders

J. Scott Mizes
West Chester University

Katherine J. Miller
Philadelphia College of Osteopathic Medicine

DESCRIPTION OF THE DISORDERS

Few official psychological problems have captured as much national attention and concern as the eating disorders of anorexia nervosa and bulimia nervosa, and, to a lesser extent, binge eating disorder. There are likely a multitude of reasons for this, such as the fact that the essential pathology and struggles of eating-disordered persons touch on less intense, though very prevalent struggles in the vast majority of Westernized girls and women. Concerns about weight in Westernized cultures are almost impossible to escape. Another factor may be the celebrities who have revealed their own struggles with eating disorders. The tragedy of the untimely, gruesome death of Diana Spencer, Princess of Wales, focused the world's spotlight on not only her death, but also on her long years of suffering in a life of unhappiness, low self-esteem, and bulimia. Indeed, the December 1997 issue of the *International Journal of Eating Disorders* was dedicated to Princess Diana, noting that, "As part of her tireless and passionate quest to assist those in need, she also brought fresh urgency to the study and treatment of eating disorders."

Perhaps another reason eating disorders have garnered so much attention is that many adolescent and young adult women know someone with an eating disorder, whether it is a friend, family member, or casual acquaintance. That knowledge often elicits deep concern, a sense of helplessness, and fear. The first author, while director of an eating disorders clinic, received the following unsolicited letter :

Dear Dr. Mizes,

We are 15 years old and are in the ninth grade. The reason we are writing you is because we are deeply concerned about one of our close friends. She is also 15 years old and extremely underweight. Her ideal weight for her height and age is 125 lbs. She weighs only about 93 lbs. In the past few months she has lost about 25–30 lbs. She is an ice skater so we know that healthy eating is important, but she is taking it to an extreme. She is on a constant fat-free diet and we feel she is not getting the nutrients she needs. She has eaten so little for so long we are afraid that she may end up in the hospital or even worse. When she does eat, she binges on low fat pretzels and rice. She is always counting her calories and telling us what she eats, as if she needs our permission. She often complains of headaches and stomach aches and pains. We are afraid this is because she doesn't eat the food her body needs. She is always moody and depressed over the littlest things. She doesn't get her period any more and we think it is because of too much exercise and low food intake. Between school and skating, she puts herself under a lot of stress that she does not need. She is always so tired and constantly sick.

We think part of her problem is how she was treated in grade school. People would always tell her how fat they thought she was. What she didn't realize was that kids are cruel and once they find a fault in you they'll make it worse than it really is. If people keep telling you that something is wrong with you then you start believing it. We tried to explain to her that what other people think is not important and what really matters is what you think about yourself.

We have confronted her a couple of times about this and she always denies having a problem. She always says that her doctor says that she is okay and that she eats. We told her that she lost too much weight and that we are afraid that she could hurt herself even more, but she still thinks that she is fat.

It is like this disease is not only affecting her, but it is also affecting all of her family and friends. She is not even herself anymore. Her face is so long and thin and she is about as tiny as you could imagine. It is getting to the point where she does not even look healthy anymore.

We have the following questions. How can we help our friend recover? How can we help her to realize that we think she has a serious problem? How do we show her help is available for this serious disease?

Sincerely,

Sally and Susie

These young girls have articulately described the symptoms of eating disorders, as well as the impact on friends and family. Additionally, they have described some of the core pathology of eating disorders and a few of the key etiologic elements in their development. These are among the topics that are addressed in this chapter.

Eating disorders are relatively common disorders among adolescent and young adult women. Among this group, approximately 4% will develop bulimia nervosa sometime in their lives, and another 4% will develop subclinical bulimia nervosa (Kendler et al., 1991). Anorexia nervosa is less common; it is estimated that the incidence per year is 1.6 cases per 100,000 population. However, it is estimated that as many as 5% of young adolescent women may have some form of subclinical anorexia nervosa (Szmukler, 1985). Prevalence rates for binge eating disorder have varied substantially according to the sample assessed, from 2.6% of college students, 4.6% in community samples, 29.9% in weight-loss groups, to 71.2% in Overeaters Anonymous (de Zwaan, Mitchell, Raymond, & Spitzer, 1994). As compared to anorexia and bulimia nervosa, where approximately 90% of the afflicted people are female, the overall gender ratio for binge eating disorder is more nearly equal (65% female, 35% male; Hudson, Carter, & Pope, 1996).

There has been little study of boys and men with eating disorders. Nonetheless, initial research suggests that clinical features between the two genders are very similar (Olivardia, Pope, Mangueth, & Hudson, 1995). Preliminary research among male eating-disordered patients suggests that homosexuality or bisexuality may be a risk factor, more strongly so for male bulimia nervosa patients (Carlat, Camargo, & Herzog, 1997).

In addition to the suffering associated with clinical eating disorders, many adolescent and young adult women struggle with deep-seated unhappiness with what they perceive to be a fat body, are preoccupied with food and weight, and are endlessly struggling to eat less and exercise more. Reflective of this, Klesges, Mizes, and Klesges (1987) found that among university students, 89% of the women and 54% of the men had engaged in some form of dieting in the previous 6 months. This was the case despite the fact that only 20% were overweight from a medical perspective. Also, 80% of the women had been engaged in some form of physical activity to lose weight, as compared with 46% of the men. Indeed, several studies have reported similar findings beginning as early as the later elementary school years and continuing into adulthood. On a more positive note, there is some evidence indicating a trend toward some abatement over the past several years. In a study of a college population in 1982 and 1992, decreases were observed in the prevalence of bulimia nervosa, as well as corresponding decreases in binge eating, vomiting, and use of diet pills and diuretics. Increases in adaptive behavior also were noted in terms of healthier eating habits, less dieting, and improved body image (Heatherton, Nichols, Mahamed, & Keel, 1995). Despite improvement, problematic eating behaviors continued to be significant problems.

In the *Diagnostic and Statistical Manual of Mental Disorders* (4th ed., [*DSM–IV*] American Psychological Association [APA], 1994), severe weight loss is the most prominent feature of anorexia nervosa and must represent a weight loss of at least 15% of expected weight. Amenorrhea (cessation of menstruation) for at least 3 consecutive months in postmenarchial females is another crucial diagnostic feature. Despite being clearly underweight, persons with anorexia nervosa intensely fear weight gain or obesity and explicitly refuse to gain weight. Moreover, body weight becomes almost the sole determinant of self-worth and self-evaluation, and there is an intensely felt body dissatisfaction. They often seek to weigh 30 pounds less than their medically accepted ideal weight, and often their actual weight is a few pounds below this dangerously low self-ideal weight (Mizes, 1992). There are two subtypes of anorexia: a restrictor subtype, which is characterized by extreme calorie restriction in order to achieve weight loss (often consuming as few as 500 calories a day); and a binge–purge subtype, which also restricts calorie intake, but additionally experiences binges and, in particular, purging episodes via vomiting, abuse of laxatives, or diuretics.

The ICD–10 Classification of Mental and Behavioral Disorders: Clinical Descriptions and Diagnostic Guidelines (ICD–10, World Health Organization [WHO], 1992) diagnostic criteria for anorexia nervosa have significant differences from those in *DSM–IV*, and perhaps advantages. Key among those is the specification of weight loss of 15% below expected weight, or a Quetelet's body mass index (BMI) of 17.5 or less. This latter criterion creates a more black-and-white diagnostic criterion and avoids some problems associated with determining what is "expected weight" for a given individual. These problems include, for example, differences in definitions of ideal weight based on what weight chart is utilized, as well as individual differences in expected weight due to normal variations in relative weight.

The essential features of bulimia nervosa are frequent binge eating and purging or compensatory behaviors to prevent weight gain (APA, 1994). A frequency and duration of binge eating and inappropriate weight control behaviors of, on average, at least twice weekly for a minimum of 3 months is necessary for the diagnosis. In addition, for an episode of overeating to be considered a "binge," two criteria must be met: (a) the amount of food eaten must be more than what most people would eat in similar circumstances and in a similar time period; and (b) the person feels that the eating is out of control. Despite these seeming objective criteria, the definition of a binge has remained an elusive construct. W. G. Johnson, Carr-Nangle, Nangle, Antony, and Zayfert (1997) found marked differences in what eating behavior was considered a binge by binge eaters and noneating-disordered peers and dieticians. Of note, the binge eaters relied more on the perception of loss of control rather than objective amount consumed and duration of eating in deciding what constituted a binge. These researchers questioned the usefulness of the objective quantity and duration criteria in the diagnostic criteria.

In addition to binging, persons with bulimia attempt to control their weight by inappropriate means, such as skipping meals or fasting, self-induced vomiting, excessive exercise, or abuse of laxatives and diuretics. The type of compensatory behavior determines the diagnostic subtype of bulimia nervosa, that is, either purging or nonpurging subtype. Marked overconcern with body weight and shape are also part of the clinical picture. Whereas normal women on average wish to weigh 11 pounds less than their medically accepted ideal weight, bulimic women want to weigh nearly 18 pounds less (Mizes, 1992).

The third category among the eating disorder diagnoses is Eating Disorder Not Otherwise Specified (EDNOS; APA, 1994). EDNOS describes persons who have an eating disorder of clinical severity but who do not meet the diagnostic criteria for another specific eating disorder, that is, anorexia or bulimia nervosa. Persons with EDNOS are common in clinical samples, with several studies reporting that 25% of eating-disordered patients are diagnosed with EDNOS (cf. Mizes & Sloan, 1998). Early research suggested the EDNOS patients clustered into two groups, —"near bulimics" and "near anorectics" (Mitchell, Pyle, Hatsukami, & Eckert, 1986). The near bulimics were a group that ate small amounts of food prior to purging, rather than having binges of large amounts of food. The near anorectics continued to have their periods, did not quite meet the weight loss criterion, or both.

More recent research has suggested that another subgroup of EDNOS is persons who are overweight binge eaters. Williamson, Gleaves, and Savin (1992) and Mizes and Sloan (1998) both empirically found a subgroup of obese binge eaters among persons diagnosed with EDNOS. Binge Eating Disorder (BED) is listed as an example of an EDNOS and in the Appendix of the *DSM–IV* as a provisional diagnosis requiring further study (APA, 1994). BED is characterized by binge episodes that occur, on average, at least 2 days a week over a 6-month period, and the absence of regular compensatory behaviors (such a self-induced vomiting) as is seen in bulimia nervosa. In addition to eating a large amount of food, the binge must reflect behavioral indicators of feeling a loss of control over eating, such as eating rapidly, or feeling disgusted or depressed after the binge. Although not necessary for the diagnosis, most persons with BED are overweight to obese (de Zwaan et al., 1994).

Robin, Gilroy, and Dennis (1998) noted that the current diagnostic criteria for anorexia and bulimia nervosa are not developmentally sensitive to unique factors in the expression of eating-disorders in young adolescents or children. They described several important problems. Determination of expected weight can be difficult because of the normally wide variation in the rate and amount of increase in height and weight due to puberty, which begins at different times for different people. In fact, some young eating-disordered persons will not experience weight loss, but rather a lack of weight gain, during a time of anticipated growth. Use of the diagnostic criterion of a BMI of 17.5 or below is representative of a state of starvation of people age 18 and over. However, lower BMI values are more applicable to children and younger adolescents. Robin et al. (1998) also noted that the criterion of loss of three consecutive menstrual periods may be difficult to apply to persons who have developed anorexia prior to puberty and menstruation. Because anorexia nervosa may delay onset of puberty, it is impossible to determine when normal menstrual periods would have started for a specific patient. Finally, children with eating disorders may not report fear of weight gain or fatness or body image dissatisfaction. These symptom reports may require intellectual capabilities that children do not have, and which usually develop only in adolescence.

CAUSES OF THE DISORDERS

Research into the causes of eating disorders is in its infancy, but the breadth of contributory factors indicates that eating disorders are multidetermined by sociocultural, psychological, and biological factors. This section examines cultural expectations, life events, and psychological variables, including the onset of dieting, body dissatisfaction, and psychological distress. Contributions of family functioning, genetics, and biologic risk factors are discussed in later sections.

Western societies seem to be the most fertile ground for eating disorders, although they are not unknown in other nations. Because in most cultures a woman is valued according to her appearance, whereas a man is valued according to his prowess, physical appearance is a larger issue for females (Fallon, 1990). Some cultures value beauty more than others, and definitions of what is attractive vary according to time and place.

Given this context, a primary factor in making eating disordered behaviors attractive to young women in particular is the cultural expectation for thinness in an unnatural extreme at the same time that the material culture provides unprecedented access to food. Women in other times and places have been valued for their generous curves, which bespeak their husbands' or families' ability to provide for them generously, but Western ideals for women have shrunk even over the last 40 years (Wiseman, Gray, Mosimann, & Ahrens, 1992). Furthermore, our society denigrates men and women of large size in general, making them the butt of cruel jokes and the object of discrimination (Rothblum, 1994).

Some women may be protected from the expectations of dominant society by the ideals and values of their subcultures. For example, African American culture is accepting and even welcoming of large body size in women, valuing a distinctive look rather than conforming to a stereotyped image (Parker et al., 1995). However, women of color and immigrants are, in effect, bicultural, having two sets of standards to negotiate in some way (Root, 1990). Those wanting to succeed in the dominant culture may try to emulate ideals of thinness to become more acceptable.

Many writers have addressed the changing gender role expectations for women and suggested that the confusion experienced by young women in fashioning their identities makes them more vulnerable to eating disorders (Worell & Todd, 1996). They must negotiate the traditional ideas that women should be caretakers, including feeding and nurturing of others, subserve their own needs to others', and stay in a subordinate position to men; and yet they must develop their intelligence and skills, hold a wider range of occupations, and compete for more status in the world.

Steiner-Adair (1986) found that high school girls with the "Super Woman" ideal of total independence scored high on eating-disordered thoughts and behaviors; those who valued relationships and self-fulfilment were not in the eating-disordered range.

Internalization of a too-thin ideal has resulted in body dissatisfaction and dieting being normative for women in the dominant Western culture (Rodin, Silberstein, & Striegel-Moore, 1985). The question, then, is why some develop full-blown eating disorders and others do not, and why some men develop eating disorders also.

Dieting is commonly a precursor to development of an eating disorder, even though not all dieters develop an eating disorder. A large prospective study of ninth-grade girls followed for 4 years found that weight concerns, including worry about over weight and body shape, diet history, and perceived fatness, best predicted eating disorder symptoms among adolescent girls (Killan et al., 1996).

Although early puberty was previously thought to be a risk factor for eating disorders, recent studies support the synchrony hypothesis: Middle school girls who begin dating and menstruation in the same year are more at risk for body dissatisfaction and disturbed eating attitudes and behaviors than those who begin one or none, and the early synchronous girls are the most at risk (Smolak, Levine, & Gralen, 1993). Furthermore, if the girls are also experiencing academic threat and have a thin body image ideal, they are even more vulnerable to disordered eating (Levine, Smolak, Moodey, Shuman, & Hessen, 1994). Keel, Fulkerson, and Leon (1997) reported that among fifth- and sixth-grade girls, heavier girls who were at earlier stages of puberty were more likely to have disordered eating a year later. For boys, only body image predicted disordered eating a year later.

It has been observed that those in certain occupations are particularly at risk for eating disorders, such as athletes, dancers, and models. For example, a study of female athletes in eight sports at a university (Williamson et al., 1995) suggested that eating disorder symptoms were significantly influenced by an interaction of the sociocultural pressure for thinness, athletic performance anxiety, and negative self-appraisal of athletic achievement, which converged in overconcern with body size and shape. Smolak, Murnen, and Ruble (1998) did a meta-analysis that found a significant but extremely small overall difference between athletes and nonathletes. Differences were greater for elite athletes than nonelite athletes, and for those in sports that emphasize leanness than "nonlean" sports.

Teasing about weight and shape while growing up is a predictor of eating disturbances at least from childhood into early adulthood (Fairburn et al., 1997; Thelen, Lawrence, & Powell, 1992), whereas generalized teasing about appearance is not. In addition, the importance of others as comparison targets regarding weight and size correlates with body image and eating disturbances (J. K. Thompson & Heinberg, 1993). Thompson and colleagues (Cattarin & Thompson, 1994; J. K. Thompson & Heinberg, 1993) found empirical support for their causal model of eating disturbances: Level of obesity predicts teasing about weight and shape and body dissatisfaction; teasing predicts overall appearance dissatisfaction; and body dissatisfaction predicts eating disturbances.

In a study of students initially in grades 7 to 10, Leon, Keel, Klump, and Fulkerson (1997) followed students for 3 or 4 years and found that the single best predictor of eating disturbances for both girls and boys was negative affect–esteem, which was an aggregate of negative emotionality, depression, ineffectiveness, and body dissatisfaction. Rosen, Tacy, and Howell (1990), on the other hand, found that dieting predicted future psychological symptoms. Although media influences such as magazine ads, articles, and TV have a direct effect on eating-disordered behavior, effects are also mediated by arousing negative feelings and low self-esteem (Stice & Shaw, 1994; Stice, Schupak-Neuberg, Shaw, & Stein, 1994).

Nevertheless, "fat phobia" is not always a factor in the development of eating disorders. For example, 58.6% of anorexics in a Hong Kong study (Lee, Ho, & Hsu, 1993) and most in a Singapore study by Kok and Tian in 1994 (cited by Katzman & Lee, 1997) reported little fear of fatness. Eating disorder symptoms can serve as a way of coping with psychological distress caused by a wide range of factors, and they may serve to shore up inadequate coping methods related to attachment difficulties, faulty cognitive schemata, or developmental delays. Katzman and Lee saw the broader message of food refusal as powerlessness, with eating-disordered behavior an attempt to free oneself from the control of others. Thus, eating disorders may be responses to changing gender–role expectations, to the transition from childhood to adolescence, to adapting to a new culture, and to various forms of oppression. Research on life events addresses these areas.

Welch, Doll, and Fairburn (1997) found in a community sample that women with bulimia nervosa had experienced significantly more negative life events in the year before onset of significantly disordered eating than did the control group matched for age and parental class. The most influential events involved general disruption (a significant house move, change in family structure) or threat to the sense of bodily integrity and safety (physical illness, pregnancy, sexual or physical abuse). Loss or threat of loss, such as bereavement or end of a relationship, were not associated with bulimia nervosa. However, the stress of life events was cumulative—the greater the number of events, the greater the likelihood of disordered eating. Schmidt, Tiller, Blanchard, Andrews, and Treasure (1997) found more major life difficulties among anorexic and bulimic patients than among community controls, with the most common serious stresses before onset concerning close relationships with family and friends.

Although there is a long list of risk factors for bulimia nervosa that contrast to healthy controls, finding risk factors specific to eating disorders requires comparisons to a psychiatric control group. The specific risk factors (Fairburn, Welch, Doll, Davies, & O'Connor, 1997) likely to increase the risk of bulimia, found in a community study with psychiatric controls, were negative self-evaluation and perfectionism in childhood, premorbid major depression, marked conduct problems and truancy, repeated severe sexual assault, and childhood obesity. (Additional family variables are discussed in the section on Familial Contributions.)

The literature on childhood sexual abuse and physical abuse shows they are frequently associated with eating disorders, but there are debates about whether the abuse is causal, contributes to severity, or is simply co-occurring and predictive of some comorbid disorders. A rigorous literature review by Wonderlich, Brewerton, Jocic, Dansky, and Abbott (1997) examined six common hypotheses about childhood sexual abuse and eating disorders; they concluded that childhood sexual abuse is a risk factor for bulimia nervosa but not for anorexia nervosa. The history of sexual abuse was not associated with greater eating symptomatology, except when certain other factors were also present: more severe sexual abuse (Hastings & Kern, 1994), features of posttraumatic stress (Wonderlich, Klein, & Council, 1996), and perceived negative response to disclosure of the abuse (Everill & Waller, 1995). Other factors that worsen eating disturbance after sexual abuse include decreased social competence and perception of a poor maternal relationship (Mallinckrodt, McCreary, & Robertson, 1995), unreliable parenting (Hastings & Kern, 1994; Smolak, Levine, & Sullins, 1990), and lower level of perceived personal control (Waller, 1998).

There are other types of trauma that have been associated with eating disorders, including childhood physical abuse (Rorty, Yager, & Rossotto, 1995), refugee status (Adjukovic & Adjukovic, 1993), acculturation (Dolan, 1991), and racism, poverty, and heterosexism (B. Thompson, 1994). Eating problems often co-occur with other dysfunctional ways of regulating the intolerable feelings and extreme physiological arousal involved in posttraumatic stress (van der Kolk, 1996). An eating disorder may be seen as a comfort and a reliable "friend" in the absence of interpersonal support (Root & Fallon, 1989).

COURSE OF THE DISORDERS

Anorexia and bulimia nervosa have fluctuating courses, and many people move between these disorders over time. The good news is that psychotherapy can help, but recovery is often lengthy, fraught with relapses, and incomplete, and there are often long-term consequences of the disorders.

Bulimia nervosa begins on the average at 19 years, according to a community sample (Fairburn et al., 1997), and it is unusual for binge eating to begin after age 25 (Woodside & Garfinkel, 1992). Those with the purging subtype have earlier age of onset than the nonpurging subtype (Garfinkel et al., 1996; Mussell et al., 1997). When left untreated, it appears that bulimia tends to worsen and abate over several years (Drewnowski & Garn, 1987), and there is some anecdotal evidence that at least some people have brief, time-limited bulimia of moderate levels.

Fichter and Quadflieg (1997) reported outcome of bulimia nervosa over 6 years among 196 consecutively treated women. They found substantial improvement during therapy, a slight decline during the first 2 years after treatment, and further improvement and stabilization from 3 to 6 years posttreatment. After 6 years, 71.1% showed no major *DSM–IV* eating disorder. A global outcome score composed of eating disorder symptoms, other psychopathology, and social behavioral problems demonstrated that 59.9% achieved a good outcome, 29.4% an intermediate outcome, 9.6% a poor outcome, and 2 were deceased. Fichter and Quadflieg (1996) reported on a 2-year outcome of bulimic adolescents and found that at the 2-year follow-up, half of the bulimics had no major eating disorder. Collings and King (1994) followed bulimia patients over 10 years and found that 52% had recovered fully, 39% continued to experience some symptoms, and 9% had the full syndrome; predictors of favorable outcome were younger age at onset, higher social class, and a family history of alcohol abuse.

Predictors of the duration and severity of bulimia are unclear at this time, particularly because those who do not receive treatment are seldom studied. Patients with multi-impulsive bulimia (purgers with additional impulsive behaviors; Fichter, Quadflieg, & Rief, 1994), borderline personality disorder (Wonderlich, 1992), substance abuse, and severe body image disturbance (Mizes, 1994) tend to have more general psychopathology and a less favorable course of illness. Depression is inconsistently related to treatment outcome. In general, duration of bulimia, frequency of binge eating and purging, and history of anorexia have not been associated with response to treatment.

To get the patients' point of view, Rossotto, Rorty-Greenfield, and Yager (1996) interviewed recovered and nonrecovered bulimic women about what had caused and maintained their bulimia. Both groups believed that it was maintained by a sense of addiction, the belief that purging would control weight, and pervasive negative emotions. Half of the nonrecovered women also mentioned positive effects of bulimia such as giving them a sense of power and escape.

Average age of onset of anorexia nervosa is 17 years, with 68% beginning between ages 14 and 20 (Willi, Giacometti, & Limacher, 1990). Pike (1998) reviewed data from landmark and recent studies on the long-term course of anorexia nervosa and concluded that the factors that determine the course and outcome are largely unknown, partly because of methodological difficulties. Most studies found that 50% to 70% achieve a good to intermediate outcome, the vast majority recovering within 12 years, and 15% to 25% are chronically symptomatic. Over a 30-year period, Theander (1985) found that 18% of anorexics had died, two thirds from anorexia and one third from suicide.

The factors which appear to predict relapse are vomiting, low body weight at time of referral, longer duration of eating problems before treatment, long duration of illness, later age of onset, and anorexic attitudes about weight and shape (Pike, 1998). According to Schork, Eckert, and Halmi (1994), comorbid general psychopathology was significantly associated with continued eating disorder pathology, whereas those who had recovered reported no general psychopathology.

The study reporting the best outcome (Strober, Freeman, & Morrell, 1997) followed 95 adolescent anorexic patients from an eating disorder treatment program for 10 to 15 years. Nearly 30% had relapses following hospital discharge, and 30% developed binge eating within 5 years of intake, but by the end, nearly 76% had fully recovered. The best predictors of outcome were hostile attitudes toward family and lack of parental empathy and affection for the patient. Recovery time ranged from 57 to 79 months, and length was predicted by hostile attitudes toward family and extreme compulsivity in daily routines. Chronic outcome was predicted by extreme, compulsive need to exercise reported at discharge and history of poor social relationships before onset of the illness.

Both anorexia and bulimia nervosa are heterogeneous disorders with many comorbid conditions, and outcomes are poorer when looking at the bigger picture of psychological and somatic well-being than only at eating disorder symptoms. Disturbances in psychosocial functioning indicate a lower chance of recovery. For example, Rastam, Gillberg, and Gillberg (1996) found that empathy disorder, a combination of ritualistic behaviors, obsessive–compulsive phenomena, and social interaction problems found in 29% of anorexic patients predicted outcome better than the eating disorder or comorbid Axis I disorders.

Binge eating disorder begins on the average at age 25 years, but this conceals the fact that there are two distinct subgroups (Spurrell, Wilfley, Tanofsky, & Brownell, 1997). Those who reported binge eating before dieting began binge eating at 12 years, became overweight at 16, and first dieted at 18; binge eating disorder was diagnosable by 19. Those who dieted before binging started at 17, became overweight at 18, and began binge eating at 25; full-blown binge eating disorder developed by 33. Significantly more of the binge-first group had Axis II personality disorder, a history of substance abuse, or a higher cumulative number of lifetime Axis I diagnoses. A 6-year follow-up study (Fichter, Quadflieg, & Gnutzmann, 1998) reported significant improvement in binge eating disorder symptoms during treatment, a slight deterioration in the next 3 years, and stability or improvement in years 4 to 6. After 6 years, 79% had no *DSM–IV* eating disorder, although half of these were obese, and in terms of eating disorder symptoms, 57.4% had good outcome, 35.3% intermediate, 5.9% poor; 1.4% had died. There were also significant improvements in dimensions of general psychopathology and comorbid psychiatric conditions over that time, but affective disorder and anxiety disorder were still common at the end of 6 years (51.6% and 40.3%), especially among those with eating disorder symptoms.

FAMILIAL CONSIDERATIONS

Early accounts of the clinical presentation of anorexia nervosa vividly described pathological patterns in these patients' families and attempted to relate that pathology to the etiology of anorexia nervosa. Influential writings by psychodynamic and family systems theorists emphasized the difficulties of anorectic adolescents in the developmental task of separating from the family and becoming autonomous (Strober & Humphrey, 1987). Families of anorectics were described as enmeshed (overly close and lacking in boundaries and differentiation) with mothers, in particular, intrusively overinvolved in their daughters' lives, laying the groundwork for deficits in the daughters' development of autonomy and identity. Minuchin, Rosman, and Baker (1978) found that the anorectic's symptoms seemed to divert attention toward her problems and away from parental conflicts. These families also overfocused on bodily functions and avoided conflict rather than resolved it.

More recently, some of these issues have been examined using attachment theory, which hypothesizes that the degree of security and self-esteem fostered in the repeated interactions with early caregivers creates internal representations that influence identity, autonomy, and later relationships. A recent review of studies on attachment and eating disorders by O'Kearney (1996) demonstrated that, although there is no evidence that insecure attachment directly causes eating disorders, attachment problems are common in women with eating disorders, including anxiety, insecure attachment, fear of abandonment, and difficulty with autonomy. Mothers are not reported to be intrusive or overprotective in most studies (O'Kearney, 1996), although fathers have been seen as overprotective in some bulimic samples. Beliefs about having poor emotional relationships to parents and low parental support for autonomy correlate with higher drive for thinness and bulimic behavior.

Recent studies of anorexia nervosa have reported a number of familial correlates. Humphrey (1988, 1989) demonstrated that anorectics' families have less overt conflict and hostility than do families of bulimics or normal controls, and they tend to deny problems in the parent–child relationship. However, parents of anorectics give a double message of nurturant affection yet neglect of their daughters' needs for self-expression, whereas the daughters are ambivalent about disclosing their feelings or submitting to their parents. Humphrey also found high marital dissatisfaction in anorexic families.

Bulimic families have been characterized in theory and research as rather hostile environments in which relationships offer less understanding, nurturance, and support than normal families, even though the family members may be enmeshed. Relationships are characterized by mutual neglect, rejection, and blame, and many studies (e.g., Humphrey, 1988, 1989; Wonderlich et al., 1996) have found more conflict and hostility in families of bulimic patients than in families of anorectic patients or normal controls. Bulimic women also have reported significantly more physical punishment in childhood and perceived their discipline to have been more harsh and capricious than have women in a control group (Rorty et al., 1995). Increased levels of physical punishment were associated with greater global family pathology in the bulimic group, as well as with poorer functioning in specific areas. Pike (1995) found that lack of satisfaction with family cohesion contributed to a small but significant effect on bulimic symptomatology among high school girls.

In a community study (Fairburn et al., 1997), bulimics, as compared to healthy and psychiatric controls, had experienced more parental problems, such as parental depression, alcoholism, and drug abuse; parental arguments, criticism, underinvolvement, and high expectations; and low parental contact. In addition, bulimic families were more likely to diet and to give critical comments about shape, weight, or eating. Burge et al. (1997) found the extent of alienation in parental relationships to be a significant correlate of eating disorder symptomatology in late adolescent women. On follow-up a year later, low mutual trust and poor quality of communication with parents was a predictor of eating disorder symptomatology.

Families of persons with BED have been described as high in conflict, similar to bulimic families, but lower in expression of feelings (Hodges, Cochrane, & Brewerton, 1998). They reported less structure and predictability than anorectics or bulimics, and less cohesion than anorectics; compared with normal families, they saw their families as less supportive, cohesive, and open in expression of feelings. Fowler and Bulik (1997) compared women with BED to obese controls. The women with BED reported higher parental protection and lower scores on parental care, cohesion, expressiveness, and independence.

There is wide variability in patterns of pathology among families of eating-disordered persons, and some of these families are normal in their level of functioning (Blouin, Zuro, & Blouin, 1990). Among those families suffering with dysfunctional patterns, some may have had pathology that predated the development of the eating disorder, whereas in others the pathology may be, in part, a response to it. For example, many parents, particularly those of anorectics, are frightened by the potentially dire consequences of their daughter's disorder. Not knowing what to do, they resort to ineffective and often hostile and coercive strategies to try to get their child to eat.

The question of a causal role for family pathology in the eating disorders remains. Some studies have demonstrated that family functioning is more correlated with comorbid borderline personality disorder (Head & Williamson, 1990; C. Johnson, Tobin, & Enright, 1989; Steiger, Liquornik, Chapman, & Hussain, 1991; Wonderlich & Swift, 1990) or depression (Blouin et al., 1990) than with level of eating pathology. Thus, at least some types of family pathology may be more causally related to the presence of associated psychopathology or comorbid conditions rather than to the core eating disorder symptoms per se.

It is possible that other family variables, such as specific attitudes and behaviors regarding food and weight, are directly related to the development of eating disorder symptoms, and a few studies in addition to the community study of Fairburn et al. (1997) have investigated these effects. For example, Keel, Heatherton, Harnden, and Hornig (1997) found that junior high and high school girls were more likely to diet if their mothers described them as overweight and commented on the daughter's weight. Having a father who was unhappy with his weight and who commented on his daughter's weight was correlated to her weight dissatisfaction but not to her dieting. Sanftner, Crowther, Crawford, and Watts (1996) found that, before puberty, there was no association between girls and their mothers on weight preoccupation or eating psychopathology variables. However, a small but statistically significant relation emerged for girls in puberty, perhaps indicating that girls look to their mothers for modeling when learning to cope with a maturing body.

In summary, the family's behaviors and attitudes about eating, weight, and shape may affect eating disorder symptoms specifically, whereas other family interactions influence associated psychopathology.

PSYCHOPHYSIOLOGICAL AND GENETIC INFLUENCES

Persons suffering with bulimia nervosa can have a variety of physical complications of the disorder (for summaries, see Mitchell, 1995; Mitchell, Specker, & de Zwann, 1991). Although the medical consequences can be marked in some cases, it appears that many patients have few or only mild medical problems, and their physical examinations with their physicians are often generally normal. Some of the more common general problems are fatigue, lethargy, general weakness, and bloating while eating. Most of the more serious potential medical problems are due to vomiting or abuse of laxative or diuretics. Perhaps the most serious potential medical complication is a significant loss of potassium, a condition known as *hypokalemia*. At mild levels, hypokalemia results in fatigue and lethargy. However, at severe levels, it can be life-threatening. These problems can include muscle weakness, irregular heartbeats (arrhythmias), and potential heart failure. There has been some controversy as to how frequently hypokalemia, as well as other electrolyte disturbances, occur in eating-disordered patients. In a study of nearly 1,000 eating-disordered outpatients, only 4.6% were found to be hypokalemic (Greenfeld, Mickley, Quinlan, & Roloff, 1995). Hypokalemia was more common among those who abused laxatives, and among those who were low-weight, including low-weight bulimia nervosa patients or those with anorexia, binge–purge subtype.

Another significant complication of vomiting is loss of enamel, particularly on the inside surfaces of the upper teeth. Some bulimia patients brush their teeth after vomiting, either as a way to eliminate a bad taste in the mouth or as an attempt to prevent tooth enamel loss. Unfortunately, this makes the enamel loss worse as the acid in the stomach softens the enamel and brushing accelerates its wearing away. Patients are advised to rinse their mouths after vomiting, perhaps with an alkaline rinse or a teaspoon of baking soda dissolved in water. Chronic vomiting can, in some patients, lead to irritation of the esophagus. There may also be calluses or cuts on the back of the fingers from patients using their fingers to gag and self-induce vomiting.

Some patients have puffy cheeks, with a "chipmunk" appearance, due to enlargement of the parotid glands, the cause of which is unknown. Purging, especially frequent use of laxatives or diuretics, can result in dehydration. Dehydration can result in dry skin or, of more concern, low blood pressure, or orthostatic hypotension. Long-term use of stimulant laxatives can result in chronic constipation and laxative dependence such that normal bowel activity does not occur unless laxatives are taken.

Persons with anorexia nervosa, binge–purge subtype, can develop the problems associated with purging in bulimia nervosa patients. Additionally, persons with both the restrictor and binge–purge subtypes of anorexia nervosa suffer from the complications of semistarvation (for a summary, see Goldbloom & Kennedy, 1995). The diagnostic symptom of amenorrhea, or loss of menstrual periods, is one of the prominent effects of semistarvation. Significant weight loss results in the reproductive hormones reverting back to patterns seen prior to puberty. For young patients who have not yet reached menarche, low weight prevents the development of adult reproductive hormone patterns. Amenorrhea is associated with problems in the bone, including osteoporosis, stunting of growth, and easy fractures. Unfortunately, some degree of bone loss may be irreversible, even after weight restoration (Siemers, Chakmakjian, & Gench, 1996). Other problems of semistarvation include decreased body temperature, which results in coldness in the hands and feet, as well as intolerance to cold. Due to the loss of muscle tissue, muscle weakness is sometimes present. Starvation, in addition to laxative abuse, can result in constipation. Especially on refeeding, anorexia nervosa patients often report stomach bloating and abdominal pain. This may be due to the slowed emptying of the stomach and intestines. Patients also may have markedly slowed heart rate, which may indicate a serious medical situation possibly requiring hospitalization to improve food intake. Starvation can also produce low blood pressure and orthostatic hypotension. There can also be a loss of muscle mass in the heart, which may contribute to sudden death due to heart failure. Persons with anorexia also have shown atrophy of the brain. Although it generally has been thought that this atrophy is reversible with normalization of weight, there is some evidence that some of the structural changes in the brain may persist even after weight recovery (Lambe, Katzman, Mikulis, Kennedy, & Zipursky, 1997). Finally, skin changes can occur, including dry skin; a yellow or orange cast to the skin; development of a fine, downy body hair known as lanugo hair; and hair loss.

Genetic factors play an important role in the risk of developing an eating disorder. The potential role of genetic factors is supported by the consistent observation that eating disorders tend to run in families (Strober, 1991). For example, approximately 3% to 10% of the female siblings of anorectics also will develop the disorder, which is much higher than the expected rate among girls and women in general. The genetic vulnerability for anorexia and bulimia appears to be at least partially shared, rather than being separate genetic risk factors. First-degree relatives of anorectics have an increased risk of both disorders, approximately 2% to 4% each for anorexia and bulimia. Conversely, first-degree relatives of bulimics have shown an increased risk for both bulimia (9.6%) and anorexia nervosa (2.2%; Kassett, Gershon, & Maxwell, 1989).

Twin studies strongly support the role of a genetic vulnerability to eating disorders. For female identical (monozygotic) twins, both sisters have anorexia nervosa approximately 44% to 50% of the time. Nonidentical fraternal (dizygotic) twins both have the disorder about 7% of the time, similiar to the rate for nontwin sisters. In a study of bulimia nervosa in a large sample of female twins, monozygotic twins both had the disorder 29% of the time, as compared with the dizygotic twins, who both had the disorder 9% of the time (Kendler et al., 1991). It was estimated that 55% of the risk for bulimia came from genetic factors, with the remaining causes being due to the person's individual psychological experiences. The genetic vulnerability to bulimia does not appear to be specific to this disorder, nor does it seem to be due to a general risk factor for developing psychological problems. Using the same female twin registry, Kendler et al. (1995) examined the genetic and environmental risk factors for six psychological disorders. They found evidence that one set of genetic factors is related to phobias, panic disorder, and bulimia, whereas a second set of genetic factors is related to major depression and generalized anxiety disorder. The authors reported that approximately 30% of the risk of bulimia came from genetic factors, mainly from a common set of factors conferring genetic risk for phobias, panic, and bulimia. Of note, this study found that bulimia was the only one of the disorders studied in which the family environment (such as parental rearing style) represented a significant proportion of the risk for the disorder (i.e., 41%). Finally, 29% of the risk was due to individual psychological experiences that increased the risk of bulimia specifically, as opposed to increasing the risk of psychological distress generally.

CURRENT TREATMENTS

Research on the treatment of bulimia nervosa has focused primarily on young adult women as opposed to adolescents. This is no doubt due in part to the fact that the average age of onset is in the early adult years (age 21), although it is clear that initial onset of bulimia nervosa does occur in the adolescent years for many persons. It is an assumption that successful treatments of adults can be directly applied to adolescents. At present, the psychological treatment of choice is specific cognitive behavior therapy (CBT) for bulimia nervosa, provided in either an individual or group treatment format. Wilson and Fairburn (1998), in summarizing nine recent controlled studies of CBT, found a mean reduction in binge eating of 79%, with 62% becoming abstinent from binge eating. The mean reduction in purging was 83.5%, with a 47.5% remission rate. CBT treatment does not benefit all patients, as 17.6% dropped out of treatment prematurely. In general, CBT treatment appears to be associated with long-term maintenance of treatment gains. In a 6-year follow-up after initial treatment, Fairburn et al. (1995) found that the effects of CBT had been maintained, with 50% being abstinent. In addition to showing improvement in binge eating and purging, CBT has demonstrated improvements in other features of bulimia nervosa, including restrictive dieting, body dissatisfaction, and cognitive distortions about eating, body shape, and weight. CBT also positively affects associated psychological problems, including low self-esteem, depression, anxiety, and social functioning.

The vast majority of bulimia nervosa patients can be treated on an outpatient basis, with no more than 5% needing inpatient care, either for severe binge eating and purging, medical complications, or other psychological problems such as suicidality (Fairburn, Marcus, & Wilson, 1993). Moreover, there is some suggestion that bulimia nervosa patients may improve more quickly during inpatient treatment but may relapse more frequently (Williamson et al., 1989). Partial hospitalization is a less intense treatment option for severe bulimia nervosa patients who need a level of care more intense than regular outpatient treatment. Partial programs for eating disorders typically have programming 7 to 10 hours a day, including a variety of therapies as well as structured meal times. Patients return home in the evenings and on weekends. Partial hospitalization has been shown to be effective for adult bulimia nervosa patients (Maddocks, Kaplan, Woodside, Langdon, & Piran, 1992).

There has been little study of family therapy for bulimia nervosa. In a study of family therapy for anorexia and bulimia nervosa, a subgroup of bulimia patients received either individual or family therapy. By the end of the follow-up treatment period, only a few had improved enough to be classified as having a good or intermediate outcome, and there were similar results for individual and family therapy (Russell, Szumkler, Dare, & Eisler, 1987). In the only study of family therapy with bulimic adolescents, 8 patients were treated with family therapy. Although there was significant improvement from pre- to posttreatment, most of the patients had an intermediate outcome (Dodge, Hodes, Eisler, & Dare, 1995). Thus, at this point, family therapy has not been established as an effective therapy for bulimia nervosa, although further investigation is warranted.

Antidepressants have been used successfully for bulimia nervosa, including the monoamine oxidase inhibitors, tricylics, and selective serotonin reuptake inhibitors (SSRIs; Walsh, 1991). Most experts regard the antidepressants as a second choice, with CBT being the preferred initial treatment. Shortcomings of antidepressants include side effects that lead to drug discontinuation, relapse after drug withdrawal, and improvement in some but not all of the features of bulimia nervosa. In general, use of SSRIs as the first drug tried is preferred due to their fewer side effects as compared with other antidepressant agents. Among the SSRIs, fluoxetine (Prozac) has been studied extensively and has been shown to be effective in short-term treatment (8 weeks; Fluoxetine Bulimia Nervosa Collaborative Study Group, 1992) and somewhat longer treatment (16 weeks; Goldstein, Wilson, Thompson, Potvin, & Rampey,

1995). There is preliminary evidence from pilot studies that other SSRIs may be effective, including paroxetine (Paxil; Prats, Diez-Quevado, & Avila, 1994) and sertraline (Zoloft; Mizes, Sloan, Ruderich, Freiheit, & Silverman, 1996). It is unclear whether there is any benefit to combining CBT and antidepressant treatment. Combined treatment has not shown better outcome than CBT alone in some studies (e.g., Goldbloom et al., 1997), whereas combination treatment has shown modest additional benefit in other studies (Walsh et al., 1997).

The various CBT treatment packages for bulimia nervosa have several common features. Self-monitoring of food intake is important in identifying situational and emotional triggers to binge eating and purging. This allows for the development of alternative coping strategies (such as calling a friend when lonely rather than binge eating) or specific planning to avoid high-risk situations. CBT uses a strong psychoeducational component, such as reviewing how relative body weight is not under complete voluntary control, how extreme dieting can increase uncontrolled eating, and the ineffectiveness of purging as a weight-control strategy. Specific interventions for eating behavior are used, including establishing a regular pattern of three meals and a planned snack, reducing rigid dieting, and eating "forbidden foods" that were seen as off-limits due to their presumed fattening characteristics. Cognitive restructuring addresses characteristic cognitive distortions in bulimia nervosa, including inaccurate beliefs about body weight and approval from others, rigid control of eating behavior and fear of weight gain, and self-esteem being based on excessive self-control of eating and body weight (Mizes, 1992). Specific treatment of body image dissatisfaction, including the use of exposure-based treatments, is also an important component of CBT. Finally, CBT includes relapse prevention training, which helps patients identify high-risk situations and prepare for them, as well as how to handle brief relapses when they inevitably occur.

Recently, interpersonal psychotherapy (IPT) has been shown to be effective with bulimia nervosa. IPT is a short-term therapy that focuses on specific areas of interpersonal problems and was originally designed for treatment of depression (Klerman, Weissman, Rounsaville, & Chevron, 1984). It recently has been adapted for use with bulimia nervosa (Fairburn et al., 1991; Fairburn, Jones, Peveler, Hope, & O'Connor, 1993). IPT is very different from CBT in that the former does not focus directly on changing eating behavior or on the direct modification of dysfunctional cognitions regarding food, shape, and weight. Comparison of CBT and IPT has found that the two treatments are equally effective at the end of treatment in reducing binge eating; however, CBT is slightly more effective in reducing vomiting and dietary restraint and in improving cognitive distortions regarding food, shape, and weight. However, during the year after treatment, IPT-treated patients continued to improve such that their outcome was equivalent to those receiving CBT.

The case of Erica illustrates the use of cognitive behavior therapy in treating bulimia nervosa. Erica (age 27) began binge eating at age 15 and vomiting at 16. She averaged four binge episodes per week, and she vomited twice a month. She also would fast two to three times a week by skipping meals for a day after having a binge episode. Although she was currently normal weight, she wanted to weigh 14 pounds less than her medically accepted average weight. In the previous year, she had been treated for moderate depression with psychotherapy and antidepressant medication. Her depression was due in part to her self-criticism for being, in her mind, "fat," and loneliness due to her withdrawal from others because of her embarrassment about her weight.

During treatment, Erica began by keeping self-monitoring records of her eating behavior. They showed that she was more likely to binge and purge when she violated one of her rigid food rules, such as having a candy bar at work. She would criticize herself for being "weak and a failure" and would come home and binge. Binge eating often occurred on nights her husband worked, and she reduced her eating in anticipation of this. The main changes in her eating behavior were to stop reducing food intake prior to an anticipated binge, to regularly eat forbidden foods such as candy bars in moderation via planned snacks, and to practice eating larger meals to increase her tolerance for feeling full without the urge to vomit. Several strategies were utilized to change her eating-disordered cognitions. She was given correct nutritional information, for example, on the importance in genetics in determining relative body weight and shape. She was also helped to value herself for her desirable personal characteristics rather than for weight and appearance. Toward the end of treatment, she began to think that her current weight was acceptable and her body image dissatisfaction had lessened. Her binges and purges decreased to zero by the end of treatment, and her depression improved. She was continuing to be free of binges and purges at a 2-month follow-up visit.

As compared with bulimia nervosa, much less is known from the research literature about the treatment of anorexia nervosa. More is known about techniques for achieving short-term weight restoration, whereas much less is known about effective psychotherapy approaches. In general, techniques for restoration of weight in an inpatient hospital setting are successful with about 80% of patients over the short term (Hsu, 1986). However, relapse occurs in about 50% of patients. Also, although weight may have improved, many aspects of the disorder often continue to persist. A typical treatment program includes a behavior modification component where weekly weight gain of 2 to 3 pounds per week is needed to earn various privileges on the ward, such as visiting privileges, access to social activities, or access to moderate physical activities (Yates, 1990). Occasionally, contingent bed rest for not gaining weight is used (Hsu, 1986). Patients are usually weighed a few times to once a week, in a hospital gown, after voiding and before breakfast. This minimizes patients' efforts to manipulate their weight. The nutritional plan has the patient initially eating 1,200 to 1,500 calories per day, with a gradual increase in daily intake of 500 to 750 calorie increments (Yates, 1990). Often, patients eventually need to eat 3,500 to 5,000 calories per day in order to show steady weight gain. Such a high level of calories is needed due to substantial increases in resting energy expenditure during refeeding (Obarzanek, Lesem, & Jimerson, 1994), as well as increased diet-induced thermogenesis (Moukaddem, Boulier, Apfelbaum, & Rigaud, 1997). It is desirable to set a discharge weight that represents a substantial restoration of expected body weight, although this is often not possible due to the limitations of managed care. Research has shown that restoration on average of 96% of expected body weight results in more favorable outcome and reduced rehospitalization (Baran, Weltzin, & Kaye, 1995).

Due to the influence of managed care, outpatient options for anorexia nervosa are increasingly used. For example, creating a structured refeeding program at home is one treatment option (Robin et al., 1998). Partial hospitalization treatment of adolescents with anorexia nervosa also has been shown to result in significant improvement (Danziger, Carcl, Varsono, Tyano, & Mimoumi, 1988).

Although psychotherapy is seen as an important part of comprehensive treatment of anorexia nervosa, there is little controlled research on effective treatments (Pike, 1998). Moreover, due to the effects of semistarvation on cognition, psychotherapy usually must wait until there has been some normalization of eating and improvement in weight. Long-term psychodynamic therapy is frequently used in clinical practice, although it is not well studied. One study of anorectic adolescents found that outpatient ego-oriented individual therapy (which included separate sessions with parents) led to significant clinical improvement (Robin, Siegel, Koepke, Moye, & Tice, 1994).

Due to the success of CBT with bulimia nervosa, this treatment has been adapted for use with anorexia nervosa. One early study suggested that CBT was helpful for at least some anorectic patients (Cooper & Fairburn, 1984). In a pilot study of cognitive analytical therapy compared with educational behavior therapy for anorexia nervosa, both treatments were found to have a favorable outcome for two thirds of the patients (Treasure et al., 1995). Pike (1997) found, in a pilot study of anorectic patients, that treatment gains achieved via hospitalization were successfully maintained during year-long outpatient CBT. In contrast to these encouraging studies, an early study did not find any benefit of cognitive behavioral or behavioral treatment of anorexia as compared with a no-treatment control (Channon, DeSilva, Hemsley, & Perkins, 1989). CBT has much potential in terms of treatment of anorexia nervosa in a variety of treatment settings.

Research has suggested that family treatment can be effective for anorexia nervosa. Although approaches to family treatment vary, some common themes emerge: (a) the family is assisted to not blame themselves or the patient for having anorexia nervosa; (b) parents are shown how to take charge of the adolescent's eating; (c) a structured behavioral weight-gain contract is implemented; (d) as the adolescent's eating and weight improves, there is a gradual return of control over eating to the adolescent; and (e) later treatment shifts from a focus on eating and weight to family problems, growth and autonomy issues, and parent–child conflict (Robin et al., 1998). Patients with early onset of anorexia (under age 18) of less than 3 years' duration have been found to improve more with family therapy than with individual therapy. Conversely, those over 18 have better outcomes with individual therapy (Russell et al., 1987). The style of family therapy has been shown to not have an effect on treatment outcome. In a study of adolescents with anorexia nervosa, those receiving conjoint family therapy (all the family seen together in sessions) did as well as those receiving family counseling (adolescent seen individually and parents seen separately; le Grange, Eisler, Dare, & Russell, 1992). A version of family therapy called Behavioral Family Systems Therapy has been shown to be effective with adolescents with restricting anorexia nervosa (Robin et al., 1994). This study is notable because it reported 4-year follow-up for some patients and showed that treatment gains had been maintained.

Several medications have been tried for anorexia nervosa, with no benefit (Pike, 1998). Recently, there has been evidence that the SSRI fluoxetine (Prozac) may benefit weight maintenance and gain after hospitalization (Kaye et al., 1996). Although three studies have found benefit in fluoxetine, one study did not find any benefit of this drug for patients in restricting anorexia nervosa (Strober, Freeman, DeAntonio, Lampert, & Diamond, in press).

The case of Becky, a severe anorectic, illustrates some of the difficulties in treating these patients. Becky (age 16) had suffered from anorexia nervosa for 3 years. She was 5'3" tall, and weighed 75 pounds, as compared to an expected weight of 115 pounds. Her eating was limited to a small breakfast, an apple for lunch, and a piece of bread and some vegetables for dinner. She had seen several previous therapists and had been hospitalized twice without any weight gain. Previous outpatient therapy had not been helpful. In fact, she had refused to talk to her last therapist and terminated therapy prematurely (as she had done with all previous therapists). Becky was a straight-A student and previously had been a competitive gymnast. Her parents were concerned that she pushed herself too hard in school and encouraged her to have more social activities. Although not currently showing evidence of psychological disorder, one parent had previously suffered from major depression. Interestingly, her older sister, who was "driven" scholastically, also had suffered a brief period of near-anorexia nervosa.

Despite their initial resistance, the parents reluctantly agreed to an outpatient behavioral treatment contract for their daughter to achieve weight gain. The contract specified two pounds as the weekly weight goal, with a goal weight of 92 pounds. The contract was presented as a trial to see if outpatient treatment could be effective, in lieu of more intensive inpatient treatment. Not reaching the weekly weight goal was presented as evidence that outpatient treatment was not working and that hospitalization was needed. She initially started on 1,500 calories per day, which was gradually increased to 3,000 calories. She was seen twice weekly in individual treatment and her parents once weekly in separate collateral sessions. The patient's weight increased from 78 to 90 pounds. However, she did not meet the final goal of 92 pounds in the last week of the contract. In part, this was because her parents wavered in their commitment to hospitalize her, and they refused to write a new outpatient contract to continue weight gain. As had happened previously, the patient and her parents terminated prematurely and switched to yet another therapist.

Treatment of BED has only recently received research attention. Drawing from the successful treatment of bulimia nervosa, CBT has been adapted for BED and been found to be successful (Wilson & Fairburn, 1998). IPT also has been shown to be effective. In a study that compared CBT and IPT (Wilfley et al., 1993), the two treatments were found to be equally effective. Behavioral weight-loss treatment also has been used with BED. Marcus, Wing, and Fairburn (1995) compared CBT for binge eating with behavioral weight-loss treatment, and found that both treatments led to equivalent decreases in binge eating. Weight-loss treatment, as compared with CBT, led to substantial weight loss at the end of treatment, although those receiving weight-loss treatment had begun to regain weight 1 year after treatment. Although research is preliminary, antidepressant medication (including the tricyclics and SSRIs) may be beneficial in reducing binges (Hudson et al., 1996). There is initial evidence that the SSRIs may enhance weight loss, although the tricyclics do not.

SUMMARY

Anorexia nervosa, bulimia nervosa, and the recently described binge eating disorder are fascinating psychological problems that have received much media attention. It seems that every few months, there are media reports or speculation about an eating disorder in an actress, athlete, or high-profile personality. Perhaps such heightened media focus is a reflection of our own fears about weight and appearance and insecurities in self-esteem. This allows us to identify more keenly with the struggles of a person with an eating disorder than with, for example, a schizophrenic whose experiences are foreign to our own.

The eating disorders appear to be chronic conditions among the population that seeks treatment. There appears to be a gradual improvement over the years, although this improvement does not usually result in remission. A substantial minority has very chronic symptoms with little improvement, and for anorectics, the outcome can be death. Eating disorders are multidetermined, with societal, psychological, and biological risk factors. Recent research suggests a much stronger role for a genetic predisposition to eating disorders than previously thought. Progress has been made in indentifying psychological risk factors for eating disorders. Risk factors that appear to be related to eating disorders include negative life events, dieting and body dissatisfaction, and psychological distress. Developmental factors, such as early puberty and early dating, may increase the risk for eating disorders. Teasing about appearance, which may be influenced by early puberty, is also a risk factor. Sexual abuse appears to be a risk factor for bulimia, but not for anorexia nervosa. There is debate regarding whether sexual abuse is a general risk factor for psychological problems (including bulimia), or if it is a specific risk factor for bulimia.

Research on treatments for bulimia nervosa and BED has been very encouraging. CBT for bulimia results in remission for approximately half of patients treated, with good maintenance of treatment gains. A new treatment, IPT, has shown excellent promise, and appears to have treatment outcomes similar to those of CBT despite being very different in its underlying theory and its therapy techniques. Research on BED is in its early development. However, both CBT and IPT have shown treatment outcomes similar to those seen for bulimia nervosa. Antidepressant medications appear to benefit both bulimia and BED. Much less is known from the research regarding treatment of anorexia nervosa. Research has shown the effectiveness of behavioral approaches for weight gain over the short term during hospitalization. However, little is known regarding long-term treatment. There is some evidence that adolescent anorexia nervosa patients may benefit from family treatment. CBT is used frequently. In general, medications have not been shown to be helpful for anorexia. One exception is use of the SSRI antidepressants, which recent research has suggested may be beneficial.

REFERENCES

Ajdukovic, M., & Ajdukovic, D. (1993). Psychological well-being of refugee children. *Child Abuse & Neglect, 17,* 843–854.

American Psychiatric Association. (1994). *Diagnostic and statistical manual of mental disorders* (4th ed.). Washington, DC: Author.

Baran, S. A., Weltzin, T. E., & Kaye, W. H. (1995). Low discharge weight and outcome in anorexia nervosa. *American Journal of Psychiatry, 152,* 1070–1072.

Blouin, A. G., Zuro, C., & Blouin, J. H. (1990). Family environment in bulimia nervosa: The role of depression. *International Journal of Eating Disorders, 9,* 649–658.

Burge, D., Hammen, C., Davila, J., Daley, S. E., Paley, B., Lindberg, N., Herzberg, D., & Rudolph, K. D. (1997). The relationship between attachment cognitions and psychological adjustment in late adolescent women. *Development and Psychopathology, 9,* 151–167.

Carlat, D. J., Camargo, C. A., & Herzog, D. B. (1997). Eating disorders in males: A report on 135 patients. *American Journal of Psychiatry, 154,* 1127–1132.

Cattarin, J. A., & Thompson, J. K. (1994). A three-year longitudinal study of body image, eating disturbance, and general psychological functioning in adolescent females. *Eating Disorders: The Journal of Treatment and Prevention, 2,* 114–125.

Channon, S., DeSilva, P., Hemsley, D., & Perkins, R. (1989). A controlled trial of cognitive–behavioural and behavioural treatment of anorexia nervosa. *Behavior Research and Therapy, 27,* 529–535.

Collings, S., & King, M. (1994). Ten-year follow-up of 50 patients with bulimia nervosa. *British Journal of Psychiatry, 164,* 80–87.

Cooper, P. J., & Fairburn, C. G. (1984). Cognitive behavior therapy for anorexia nervosa: Some preliminary findings. *Journal of Psychosomatic Research, 28,* 493–499.

Danziger, Y., Carcl, C. A., Varsono, I., Tyano, S., & Mimoumi, M. (1988). Parental involvement in treatment of patients with anorexia nervosa in a pediatric day-care unit. *Pediatrics, 81,* 159–162.

Dodge, E., Hodes, M., Eisler, I., & Dare, C. (1995). Family therapy for bulimia nervosa in adolescents: An exploratory study. *Journal of Family Therapy, 17,* 59–77.

Dolan, B. (1991). Cross cultural aspects of anorexia nervosa and bulimia: A review. *International Journal of Eating Disorders, 10,* 67–79.

Drewnowski, A., & Garn, S. M. (1987). Concerning the use of weight tables to categorize patients with eating disorders. *International Journal of Eating Disorders, 6,* 639–646.

Everill, J., & Waller, G. (1995). Disclosure of sexual abuse and psychological adjustment in female undergraduates. *Child Abuse & Neglect, 19,* 93–100.

Fairburn, C. G., Jones, R., Peveler, R. C., Carr, S. J., Solomon, R. A., O'Connor, M. E., Burton, J., & Hope, R. A. (1991). Three psychological treatments for bulimia nervosa: A comparative trial. *Archives of General Psychiatry, 48,* 463–469.

Fairburn, C. G., Jones, R., Peveler, R. C., Hope, R. A., & O'Connor, M. (1993). Psychotherapy and bulimia nervosa: The longer-term effects of interpersonal psychotherapy, behaviour therapy and cognitive behaviour therapy. *Archives of General Psychiatry, 50,* 419–428.

Fairburn, C. G., Marcus, M. D., & Wilson, G. T. (1993). Cognitive–behavioral therapy for binge eating and bulimia nervosa: A comprehensive treatment manual. In C. G. Fairburn & G. T. Wilson (Eds.), *Binge eating: Nature, assessment and treatment* (pp. 361–404). New York: Guilford.

Fairburn, C. G., Norman, P. A., Welch, S. L., O'Connor, M. E., Doll, H. A., & Peveler, R. C. (1995). A prospective study of outcome in bulimia nervosa and the long-term effects of three psychological treatments. *Archives of General Psychiatry, 52,* 304–312.

Fairburn, C. G., Welch, S. L., Doll, H. A., Davies, B. A., & O'Connor, M. E. (1997). Risk factors for bulimia nervosa: A community-based case-control study. *Archives of General Psychiatry, 54,* 509–517.

Fallon, A. (1990). Culture in the mirror: Sociocultural determinants of body image. In T. F. Cash & T. Pruzinsky (Eds.), *Body images* (pp. 80–109). New York: Guilford.

Fichter, M. M., & Quadflieg, N. (1996). Course and two-year outcome in anorexic and bulimic adolescents. *Journal of Youth and Adolescence, 25,* 545–562.

Fichter, M. M., & Quadflieg, N. (1997). Six-year course of bulimia nervosa. *International Journal of Eating Disorders, 22,* 361–384.

Fichter, M. M., Quadflieg, N., & Gnutzmann, A. (1998). Binge eating disorder: Treatment outcome over a 6-year course. *Journal of Psychosomatic Research, 44,* 385–405.

Fichter, M. M., Quadflieg, N., & Rief, W. (1994). Course of multi-impulsive bulimia. *Psychological Medicine, 24,* 591–604.

Fowler, S. J., & Bulik, C. M. (1997). Family environment and psychiatric history in women with binge-eating disorder and obese controls. *Behaviour Change, 14,* 106–112.

Fluoxetine Bulimia Nervosa Collaborative Study Group. (1992). Fluoxetine in the treatment of bulimia nervosa: A multicenter, placebo-controlled, double-blind study. *Archives of General Psychiatry, 49,* 139–147.

Garfinkel, P. E., Lin, E., Goering, P., Spegg, C., Goldbloom, D. S., Kennedy, S., Kaplan, A. S., & Woodside, D. B. (1996). Purging and nonpurging forms of bulimia nervosa in a community sample. *International Journal of Eating Disorders, 20,* 231–238.

Goldbloom, D. S., & Kennedy, S. H. (1995). Medical complications of anorexia nervosa. In K. D. Brownell & C. G. Fairburn (Eds.), *Eating disorders and obesity: A comprehensive handbook* (pp. 266–270). New York: Guilford.

Goldbloom, D. S., Olmsted, M., Davis, R., Clewes, J., Heinmaa, M., Rockert, W., & Shaw, B. (1997). A randomized controlled trial of fluoxetine and cognitive behavioral therapy for bulimia nervosa: Short-term outcome. *Behavior Research and Therapy, 35,* 803–811.

Goldstein, D. J., Wilson, M. G., Thompson, V. L., Potvin, J. H., & Rampey, A. H. (1995). Long-term fluoxetine treatment of bulimia nervosa. *British Journal of Psychiatry, 166,* 660–666.

le Grange, D., Eisler, I., Dare, C., & Russell, G.F.M. (1992). Evaluation of family treatments in adolescent anorexia nervosa: A pilot study. *International Journal of Eating Disorders, 12,* 347–357.

Greenfeld, D., Mickley, D., Quinlan, D. M., & Roloff, P. (1995). Hypokalemia in outpatients with eating disorders. *American Journal of Psychiatry, 152,* 60–63.

Hastings, T., & Kern, J. M. (1994). Relationship between bulimia, childhood sexual abuse, and family environment. *International Journal of Eating Disorders, 15,* 103–111.

Head, S. B., & Williamson, D. A. (1990). Association of family environment and personality disturbances in bulimia nervosa. *International Journal of Eating Disorders, 9,* 667–674.

Heatherton, T. F., Nichols, P., Mahamedi, F., & Keel, P. (1995). Body weight, dieting, and eating disorder symptoms among college students, 1982 to 1992. *American Journal of Psychiatry, 152,* 1623–1629.

Hodges, E. L., Cochrane, C. E., & Brewerton, T. D. (1998). Family characteristics of binge-eating disorder patients. *International Journal of Eating Disorders, 23,* 145–151.

Hsu, L.K.G. (1986). The treatment of anorexia nervosa. *American Journal of Psychiatry, 143,* 573–581.

Hudson, J. I., Carter, W. P., & Pope, H. G. (1996). Antidepressant treatment of binge-eating disorder: Research findings and clinical guidelines. *Journal of Clinical Psychiatry, 57,* 73–79.

Humphrey, L. L. (1988). Relationships within subtypes of anorexic, bulimic, and normal families. *Journal of the American Academy of Child and Adolescent Psychiatry, 27,* 544–551.

Humphrey, L. L. (1989). Observed family interactions among subtypes of eating disorders using structural analysis of social behavior. *Journal of Consulting & Clinical Psychology, 57,* 206–214.

Johnson, C., Tobin, D., & Enright, A. (1989). Prevalence and clinical characteristics of borderline patients in an eating disordered population. *Journal of Clinical Psychiatry, 50,* 9–15.

Johnson, W. G., Carr-Nangle, R. E., Nangle, D. W., Antony, M. M., & Zayfert, C. (1997). What is binge eating? A comparison of binge eater, peer, and professional judgments of eating episodes. *Addictive Behaviors, 22,* 631–635.

Kassett, J. A., Gershon, E. S., & Maxwell, M. E. (1989). Psychiatric disorders in the first-degree relatives of probands with bulimia nervosa. *American Journal of Psychiatry, 146,* 1468–1471.

Katzman, M., & Lee, S. (1997). Beyond body image: The integration of feminist and transcultural theories in the understanding of self starvation. *International Journal of Eating Disorders, 22,* 385–394.

Kaye, W. H., McConaha, C., Nagata, T., Plotmicov, K. H., Sokol, M. S., Weltzin, T. E., Hsu, L.K.G., & LaVia, M. C. (1996, November). *Flouxetine prevents relapse in a majority of patients with anorexia nervosa: A double-blind placeba controlled study.* Presented at the meeting of the Eating Disorders Research Society, Pittsburg, PA.

Keel, P. K., Fulkerson, J. A., & Leon, G. R. (1997). Disordered eating presursors in pre- and early adolescent girls and boys. *Journal of Youth and Adolescence, 26,* 203–216.

Keel, P. K., Heatherton, T. F., Harnden, J. L., & Hornig, C. D. (1997). Mothers, fathers, and daughters: Dieting and disordered eating. *Eating Disorders: The Journal of Treatment and Prevention, 5,* 216–228.

Kendler, K. S., MacLean, C., Neale, M., Kessler, R., Heath, A., & Eaves, L. (1991). The genetic epidemiology of bulimia nervosa. *American Journal of Psychiatry, 148,* 1627–1637.

Kendler, K. S., Walters, E. E., Neale, M. C., Kessler, R. C., Heath, A. C., & Eaves, L. J. (1995). The structure of the genetic and environmental risk factors for six major psychiatric disorders in women. *Archives of General Psychiatry, 52,* 374–383.

Killan, J. D., Taylor, C. B., Hayward, C., Haydel, K. F., Wilson, D. M., Hammer, L., Kraemer, H., Blair-Greener, A., & Strachowski, D. (1996). Weight concerns influence the development of eating disorders: A 4-year prospective study. *Journal of Consulting and Clinical Psychology, 4,* 936–940.

Klerman, G. L., Weissman, M. M., Rounsaville, B. J., & Chevron, E. S. (1984). *Interpersonal psychotherapy of depression.* New York: Basic Books.

Klesges, R. C., Mizes, J. S., & Klesges, L. M. (1987). Self-help dieting strategies in college males and females. *International Journal of Eating Disorders, 6,* 409–417.

van der Kolk, B. A. (1996). The complexity of adaptation to trauma: Self-regulation, stimulus discrimination, and characterological development. In B. A. van der Kolk, A. C. McFarlane, & Weisaeth (Eds.), *Traumatic stress: The effects of overwhelming experience on mind, body, and society* (pp. 182–213). New York: Guilford.

Lambe, E. K., Katzman, D. K., Mikulis, D. J., Kennedy, S. H., & Zipursky, R. B. (1997). Cerebral gray matter volume deficits after weight recovery from anorexia nervosa. *Archives of General Psychiatry, 54,* 537–542.

Lee, S., Ho, T. P., & Hsu, L.K.G. (1993). Fat phobic and non-fat phobic anorexia nervosa: A comparative study of 70 Chinese patients in Hong Kong. *Psychological Medicine, 23,* 999–1017.

Leon, G. R., Keel, P. K., Klump, K. L., & Fulkerson, J. A. (1997). The future of risk factor research in understanding the etiology of eating disorders. *Psychopharmacology Bulletin, 33,* 405–411.

Levine, M. P., Smolak, L., Moodey, A., Shuman, M. D., & Hessen, L. D. (1994). Normative developmental challenges and dieting and eating disturbance in middle school girls. *International Journal of Eating Disorders, 15,* 11–20.

Maddocks, S. E., Kaplan, A. S., Woodside, D. B., Langdon, L., & Piran, N. (1992). Two year follow-up of bulimia nervosa: The importance of abstinence as the criterion of outcome. *International Journal of Eating Disorders, 12,* 133–141.

Mallinckrodt, B., McCreary, B. A., & Robertson, A. K. (1995). Co-occurrence of eating disorders and incest: The role of attachment, family environment, and social competencies. *Journal of Counseling Psychology, 42,* 178–186.

Marcus, M. D., Wing, R. R., & Fairburn, C. G. (1995). Cognitive treatment of binge eating versus behavioral weight control in the treatment of binge eating disorder. *Annals of Behavioral Medicine, 17,* S090.

Minuchin, S., Rosman, B. L., & Baker, L. (1978). *Psychosomatic families: Anorexia nervosa in context.* Cambridge, MA: Harvard University Press.

Mitchell, J. E. (1995). Medical complications of bulimia nervosa. In K. D. Brownell & C. G. Fairburn (Eds.), *Eating disorders and obesity: A comprehensive handbook* (pp. 271–277). New York: Guilford.

Mitchell, J. E., Pyle, R. L., Hatsukami, D., & Eckert, E. D. (1986). What are atypical eating disorders? *Psychosomatics, 27,* 21–28.

Mitchell, J. E., Specker, S. M., & de Zwaan, M. (1991). Comorbidity and medical complications of bulimia nervosa. *Journal of Clinical Psychiatry, 52*(Suppl. 10), 13–20.

Mizes, J. S. (1992). The Body Image Detection Device versus subjective measures of weight dissatisfaction: A validity comparison. *Addictive Behaviors, 17,* 125–136.

Mizes, J. S. (1994). Eating disorders. In V. B. Van Hasselt & M. Hersen (Eds.), *Advanced abnormal psychology* (pp. 253–270). New York: Plenum.

Mizes, J. S., & Sloan, D. M. (1998). An empirical analysis of eating disorder, not otherwise specified: Preliminary support for a distinct subgroup. *International Journal of Eating Disorders, 23,* 233–242.

Mizes, J. S., Sloan, D. M., Ruderich, S., Freiheit, & Silverman, E. (1996, November). *The efficacy of sertraline in bulimia nervosa patients: A preliminary report.* Pater presented at the annual meeting of the Eating Disorders Research Society, Pittsburgh, PA.

Moukaddem, M., Boulier, A., Apfelbaum, M., & Rigaud, D. (1997). Increase in diet-induced thermogenesis at the start of refeeding in severely malnourished anorexia nervosa patients. *American Journal of Clinical Nutrition, 66,* 133–140.

Mussell, M. P., Mitchell, J. E., Fenna, C. J., Crosby, R. D., Miller, J. P., & Hoberman, H. M. (1997). A comparison of the onset binge eating versus dieting in the development of bulimia nervosa. *International Journal of Eating Disorders, 21,* 353–360.

Obarzanek, E., Lesem, M. D., & Jimerson, D. C. (1994). Resting metabolic rate of anorexia nervosa patients during weight gain. *American Journal of Clinical Nutrition, 60,* 666–675.

O'Kearney, R. (1996). Attachment disruption in anorexia nervos and bulimia nervosa: A review of theory and empirical research. *International Journal of Eating Disorders, 20,* 115–127.

Olivardia, R., Pope, H. G., Mangweth, B., & Hudson, J. I. (1995). Eating disorders in college men. *American Journal of Psychiatry, 152,* 1279–1285.

Parker, S., Nichter, M., Nichter, M., Vuckovic, N., Sims, C., & Ritenbaugh, C. (1995). Body image and weight concerns among African-American and White adolescent females: Differences that make a difference. *Human Organization, 54,* 103–110.

Pike, K. M. (1995). Bulimic symptomatology in high school girls: Toward a model of cumulative risk. *Psychology of Women Quarterly, 19,* 373–396.

Pike, K. M. (1997, April). *Sequencing treatment for anorexia nervosa: Inpatient hospitalization followed by outpatient behavioral therapy.* Paper presented at the Third London International Conference on Eating Disorders, London.

Pike, K. M. (1998). Long-term course of anorexia nervosa: Response, relapse, remission, and recovery. *Clinical Psychology Review, 18,* 447–475.

Prats, M., Diez-Quevedo, C., & Avila, C. (1994, April). *Paroxetine treatment for bulimia nervosa and binge eating disorder.* Abstract 308 of the sixth international Conference on Eating Disorders, New York.

Rastam, M., Gillberg, C., & Gillberg, I. C. (1996). A six-year follow-up study of anorexia nervosa subjects with teenage onset. *Journal of Youth and Adolescence, 25,* 439–453.

Robin, A. L., Gilroy, M., & Dennis, A. B. (1998). Treatment of eating disorders in children and adolescents. *Clinical Psychology Review, 18,* 1–57.

Robin, A. L., Siegel, P. T., Koepke, T., Moye, A. W., & Tice, S. (1994). Family therapy versus individual therapy for adolescent females with anorexia nervosa. *Journal of Developmental and Behavioral Pediatrics, 15,* 111–116.

Rodin, J., Silberstein, L., & Striegel-Moore, R. (1985). Women and weight: A normative discontent. In T. Sonderegger (Ed.), *Nebraska Symposium on Motivation: Vol. 32. Psychology and gender* (pp. 267–307). Lincoln: University of Nebraska Press.

Root, M.P.P. (1990). Disordered eating in women of color. *Sex Roles, 22,* 525–536.

Root, M.P.P., & Fallon, P. (1989). Treating the victimized bulimic: The functions of binge–purge behavior. *Journal of Interpersonal Violence, 4,* 90–100.

Rorty, M., Yager, J., & Rossotto, E. (1995). Aspects of childhood physical punishment and family environment correlates in bulimia nervosa. *Child Abuse & Neglect, 19,* 659–667.

Rosen, J. C., Tacy, B., & Howell, D. (1990). Life stress, psychological symptoms and weight reducing behavior in adolescent girls: A prospective analysis. *International Journal of Eating Disorders, 9,* 17–26.

Rossotto, E., Rorty-Greenfield, M., & Yager, J. (1996). What causes and maintains bulimia nervosa? Recovered and nonrecovered women's reflections on the disorder. *Eating Disorders: The Journal of Treatment and Prevention, 4,* 128–138.

Rothblum, E. D. (1994). "I'll die for the revolution but don't ask me not to diet": Feminism and the continuing stigmatization of obesity. In P. Fallon, M. A. Katzman & S. C. Wolley (Eds.), *Feminist perspectives on eating disorders* (pp. 53–76). New York: Guilford.

Russell, G F.M., Szmukler, G. I., Dare, C., & Eisler, I. (1987). An evaluation of family therapy in anorexia nervosa and bulimia nervosa. *Archives of General Psychiatry, 44,* 1047–1056.

Sanftner, J. L., Crowther, J. H., Crawford, P. A., & Watts, D. D. (1996). Maternal influences (or lack thereof) on daughters' eating attitudes and behavior. *Eating Disorders: The Journal of Treatment and Prevention, 4,* 147–159.

Schmidt, U., Tiller, J., Blanchard, M., Andrews, B., & Treasure, J. (1997). Is there a specific trauma precipitating anorexia nervosa? *Psychological Medicine, 27,* 523–530.

Schork, E. J., Eckert, E. D., & Halmi, K. A. (1994). The relationship between psychopathology, eating disorder diagnosis, and clinical outcome at 10-year follow-up in anorexia nervosa. *Comprehensive Psychiatry, 35,* 113–123.

Siemers, B., Chakmakjian, Z., & Gench, B. (1996). Bone density patterns in women with anorexia nervosa. *International Journal of Eating Disorders, 19,* 179–186.

Smolak, L., Levine, M. P., & Gralen, S. (1993). The impact of puberty and dating on eating problems among middle school girls. *Journal of Youth and Adolescence, 22,* 355–368.

Smolak, L., Levine, M. P., & Sullins, E. (1990). Are child sexual experiences related to eating-disordered attitudes and behaviors in college sample? *International Journal of Eating Disorders, 9,* 167–178.

Smolak, L., Murnen, S. K., & Ruble, A. E. (1998, April). *Athletes and eating disorders: A meta-analysis.* Poster session presented at the International Conference on Eating Disorders, New York.

Spurrell, E. B., Wilfley, D. E., Tanofsky, M. B., & Brownell, K. D. (1997). Age of onset for binge eating: Are there different pathways to binge eating? *International Journal of Eating Disorders, 21,* 55–65.

Steiger, H., Liquornik, K., Chapman, J., & Hussain, N. (1991). Personality and family disturbances in eating-disorder patients: Comparison of "restricters" and "bingers" to normal controls. *International Journal of Eating Disorders, 10,* 501–512.

Steiner-Adair, C. (1986). The body politic: Normal female adolescent development and the development of eating disorders. *Journal of the American Academy of Psychoanalysis, 14,* 95–114.

Stice, E., Schupak-Neuberg, E., Shaw, H. E., & Stein, R. I. (1994). Relation of media exposure to eating disorder symptomatology: An examination of mediating mechanisms. *Journal of Abnormal Psychology, 103,* 836–840.

Stice, E., & Shaw, H. E. (1994). Adverse effects of the media portrayed thin-ideal on women and linkages to bulimic symptomatology. *Journal of Social and Clinical Psychology, 13,* 288–308.

Strober, M. (1991). Family–genetic studies of eating disorders. *Journal of Clinical Psychiatry, 52*(Suppl. 10), 9–12.

Strober, M., Freeman, R., DeAntonio, M. D., Lampert, C., & Diamond, J. (in press). Does adjunctive fluoxetine influence the post-hospital course of anorexia nervosa? A 24-month prospective, longitudinal follow-up and comparison with historical controls. *Psychopharmacology Bulletin.*

Strober, M., Freeman, R., & Morrell, W. (1997). The long-term course of severe anorexia nervosa in adolescents: Survival analysis of recovery, relapse, and outcome predictors over 10–15 years in a prospective study. *International Journal of Eating Disorders, 22,* 339–360.

Strober, M., & Humphrey, L. L. (1987). Familial contributions to the etiology and course of anorexia nervosa and bulimia. *Journal of Consulting and Clinical Psychology, 55,* 654–659.

Szmukler, G. I. (1985). The epidemiology of anorexia nervosa and bulimia. *Journal of Psychiatric Research, 19,* 143–153.

Theander, S. (1985). Outcome and prognosis in anorexia nervosa and bulimia: Some results of previous investigations, compared with those of a Swedish long-term study. *Journal of Psychiatric Research, 19,* 493–508.

Thelen, M. H., Lawrence, C. M., & Powell, A. L. (1992). Body image, weight control, and eating disorders among children. In J. H. Crowther, D. L. Tennenbaum, S. E. Hobfoll, & M.A.P. Stephens (Eds.), *The etiology of bulimia nervosa: The individual and family context* (pp. 81–101). Washington, DC: Hemisphere.

Thompson, B. (1994). Food, bodies, and growing up female: Childhood lessons about culture, race, and class. In P. Fallon, M. A. Katzment, & S. C. Wooley (Eds.), *Feminist perspectives on eating disorders* (pp. 355–378). New York: Guilford.

Thompson, J. K., & Heinberg, L. J. (1993). Preliminary test of two hypotheses of body image disturbance. *International Journal of Eating Disorders, 14,* 59–63.

Treasure, J., Todd, G., Brolly, M., Tiller, J., Nehmed, A., & Denman, F. (1995). A pilot study of a randomised trial of cognitive analytical therapy vs. educational behavioral therapy for adult anorexia nervosa. *Behavior Research and Therapy, 33,* 363–367.

Waller, G. (1998). Perceived control in eating disorders: Relationship with reported sexual abuse. *International Journal of Eating Disorders, 23,* 213–216.

Walsh, B. T. (1991). Psychopharmacological treatments of bulimia nervosa. *Journal of Clinical Psychiatry, 52,* 34–38.

Walsh, B. T., Wilson, G. T., Loeb, K. L., Devlin, M. J., Pike, K. M., Roose, S. P., Fleiss, J., & Waternaux, C. (1997). Medication and psychotherapy in the treatment of bulimia nervosa. *American Journal of Psychiatry, 154,* 523–531.

Welch, S. L., Doll, H. D., & Fairburn, C. G. (1997). Life events and the onset of bulimia: A controlled study. *Psychological Medicine, 27,* 515–522.

Wilfley, D. E., Agras, W. S., Telch, C. F., Rossiter, E. M., Schneider, J. A., Cole, A. G., Sifford, L., & Raeburn, S. D. (1993). Group cognitive–behavioral therapy and group interpersonal psychotherapy for the nonpurging bulimic individual: A controlled comparison. *Journal of Consulting and Clinical Psychology, 61,* 296–305.

Willi, J., Giacometti, G., & Limacher, B. (1990). Update on the epidemiology of anorexia nervosa in a defined region of Switzerland. *American Journal of Psychiatry, 147,* 1514–1517.

Williamson, D. A., Gleaves, D. H., & Savin, S. S. (1992). Empirical classification of eating disorder not otherwise specified: Support for *DSM–IV* changes. *Journal of Psychopathology and Behavioral Assessment, 14,* 201–216.

Williamson, D. A., Mitchell, R. G., Weller, C. L., Raymond, N. C., Crow, S. J., & Crosby, R. D. (1995). Structural equation modeling of risk factors for the development of eating disorder symptoms in female athletes. *International Journal of Eating Disorders, 17,* 387–393.

Williamson, D. A., Prather, R. C., Bennett, S. M., Davis, C. J., Watkins, P. C., & Grenier, C. E. (1989). An uncontrolled evaluation of inpatient and outpatient cognitive–behavior therapy for bulimia nervosa. *Behavior Modification, 13,* 340–360.

Wilson, G. T., & Fairburn, C. G. (1998). Treatments for eating disorders. In P. E. Nathan & J. M. Gorman (Eds.), *Guide to Treatments That Work* (pp. 501–530). New York: Oxford University Press.

Wiseman, C. V., Gray, J. J., Mosimann, J. E., Ahrens, A. H. (1992). Cultural expectations of thinness in women: An update. *International Journal of Eating Disorders, 11,* 85–89.

Wonderlich, S. (1992). Relationship of family and personality factors in bulimia. In J. H. Crowther, D. L. Tennenbaum, S. E. Hobfoll, & M..A.P. Stephens (Eds.), *The etiology of bulimia nervosa: The individual and family context* (pp. 103–126). Washington, DC: Hemisphere.

Wonderlich, S. A., Brewerton, T. D., Jocic, Z., Dansky, B. S., & Abbott, D. W. (1997). Relationship of childhood sexual abuse and eating disorders. *Journal of the American Academy of Child and Adolescent Psychiatry, 36,* 1107–1115.

Wonderlich, S., Klein, M. H., & Council, J. R. (1996). Relationship of social perceptions and self-concept in bulimia nervosa. *Journal of Consulting and Clinical Psychology, 64,* 1231–1237.

Wonderlich, S. A., & Swift, W. J. (1990). Borderline versus other personality disorders in the eating disorders: Clinical description. *International Journal of Eating Disorders, 9,* 629–638.

Woodside, D. B., & Garfinkel, P. E. (1992). Age of onset in eating disorders. *International Journal of Eating Disorders, 12,* 31–36.

Worell, J., & Todd, J. (1996). Development of the gendered self. In L. Smolak, M. T. Levine, & R. Striegel-Moore (Eds.), *The developmental psychopathology of eating disorders: Implications for research, prevention and treatment* (pp. 135–156). Mahwah, NJ: Lawrence Erlbaum Associates.

World Health Organization. (1992). *ICD–10 classification of mental and behavioral disorders: Clinical descriptions and diagnostic guidelines.* Geneva, Switzerland: Author.

Yates, A. (1990). Current perspectives on the eating disorders: II. Treatment, outcome, and research directions. *Journal of the American Academy of Child and Adolescent Psychiatry, 29,* 1–9.

de Zwaan, M., Mitchell, J. E., Raymond, N. C., & Spitzer, R. L. (1994). Binge eating disorder: Clinical features and treatment of a new diagnosis. *Harvard Review of Psychiatry, 1,* 310–325.

Substance Use Disorders

Michael D. Newcomb
University of Southern California

Mark A. Richardson
Boston University School of Medicine

CLINICAL DESCRIPTION

Substance use disorders are unlike most other mental disorders in at least two ways. First, drug abuse and dependence are pathoplastic disorders: Their existence and prevalence are dependent on an external agent (the drug) and vary depending on the availability of drugs (Newcomb, 1995b). Second, drug abuse disorders always involve a willing host (the abuser), who is an active instigator and participant in creating the disorder (Newcomb & Earleywine, 1996). If children and adolescents did not choose to ingest these substances and the drugs were not available, there would be no disorder. Nevertheless, many types of drugs are widely available, and there are many individuals willing to use them.

The leading cause of death among teenagers in the United States is drunk driving, accounting for more than 20% of all mortalities (Julien, 1998). Tobacco smoking is the leading cause of death among all Americans, accounting for over 400,000 lost lives each year, and probably will be responsible for killing more current children and teenagers later in their life than any other single cause (Julien, 1998). Up to 3,000 youngsters initiate smoking cigarettes each day (Julien, 1998). There are substantial reasons for concern regarding the abuse of cigarettes and alcohol among children and teenagers. Until very recently, clear focus on these drugs was conspicuously missing in this nation's "War on Drugs" that began in 1986. Primary attention has been devoted to the youthful use of illicit drugs, such as marijuana and cocaine (Newcomb, 1992a), even though the tobacco industry seems to have targeted children and teenagers as the next generation of nicotine addicts.

From the outset, we must emphasize the controversies surrounding definitions of drug use, misuse, abuse, and disorders among children and teenagers. There is no one accepted criterion for deciding whether the use of a drug by a youngster represents benign experimentation with proscribed behaviors that is viewed by some as a defining feature of adolescence (e.g., Newcomb, 1996a; Peele, 1987). There also is no criterion to decide whether drug involvement constitutes abuse, dependence, or a disorder that may be destructive to all aspects of this person's life. Furthermore, systematic research on adolescent abuse is limited, likely a function of the relatively low prevalence of substance abuse among adolescents (estimated at 6% to 10% of those adolescents currently using alcohol or illicit drugs at any given time).

Several critical issues must be kept in mind when trying to study, understand, or intervene in the use of drugs by children and teenagers. These include: (a) what should be considered a substance use disorder of children and teenagers; (b) the ramifications of treating such a disorder (however defined); and (c) an appreciation of the larger context of attitudes and behaviors within which youthful drug use occurs. The first and second issues are addressed in the Clinical Description and Current treatments sections of this chapter (respectively), and the third must be confronted from the outset.

Attempts to describe substance use disorders among children and teenagers are fraught with disagreement and controversy. For instance, addiction to tobacco is not considered a disorder by formal diagnostic criteria, although it is a significant problem among children and adolescents. Alcohol abuse (high quantities ingested per occasion and adverse consequences) is probably the most prevalent drug disorder among teenagers but is often overlooked. Furthermore, political mandates have defined illicit drug use by a teenager, even if only one experimental episode, as "abuse." In this chapter, we focus on drug disorders that create problems for youths that may be demonstrated in physically, psychologically, or socially adverse consequences or reactions.

Extent and Patterns of Teenage Drug Use

The most extensive surveys of drug use among U.S. children and teenagers are annual assessments of national samples. *Monitoring the Future* (Johnston, O'Malley, & Bachman, 1998) summarizes reports by 8th graders, 10th graders, and high school seniors of their prior and recent use of alcohol and other drugs, whereas the *National Household Survey on Drug Abuse* (Substance Abuse and Mental Health Services Administration, 1997) assesses drug use among respondents who range from 12 to 17 years old. These national and other local studies yield a fairly clear understanding of drug use patterns among children and teenagers. Although these data are illuminating, several problems cloud their descriptive clarity, including: (a) the exclusion of high school dropouts, who are expected to be heavier drug users; (b) limitations on the ability to identify and include adolescents considered at particularly high risk for substance abuse (e.g., inner-city gang members); and (c) the absence of generally recognized measures of drug abuse or dependence. Concern over these surveys' reliance on self-report of drug use (an illegal behavior among children and teenagers) has been addressed. The scales have demonstrated validity and reliability, particularly for recent drug use, when they are utilized under anonymous reporting conditions (e.g., Oetting & Beauvais, 1990).

There is irrefutable evidence attesting to the widespread use of tobacco (64% lifetime prevalence in 1997) and alcohol (82%) among high school seniors

(Johnston et al., 1998) and evidence that abuse of these substances is relatively common. For instance, nearly one third of American high school seniors reported having five or more drinks on at least one occasion in the past 2 weeks, and over 14% of this same group leave high school addicted to cigarettes, smoking a half-pack or more per day.

The use and abuse of all other drugs currently lag far behind these socially approved drugs. Marijuana is by far the most commonly used illicit substance among adolescent respondents to national surveys, with a 40% lifetime prevalence rate among high school seniors in 1997; over one-third (38%) reported marijuana use within 12 months, and 24% reported use within 30 days of the survey. In turn, 10% of high school seniors also reported that they had tried inhalants, stimulants, cocaine (powder or crack), or hallucinogens at some time in their lives (Johnston et al., 1998).

National survey data suggest that a fairly steady decrease in lifetime, annual, and 30-day prevalence rates was seen for most types of illicit drugs since the 1980s (including marijuana, cocaine, stimulants, & sedatives), with limited changes in cigarette and alcohol prevalence trends (Johnston et al., 1998). However, during the 1990s, there has been a steady increase in use of many illicit drugs among children and teenagers. For instance, the lifetime use of crack cocaine more than doubled for eighth grade students from 1991 (1.3%) to 1996 (2.9%). Similarly, lifetime use of marijuana more than doubled among these students over the same time period, from 10.2% in 1991 to 23.1% in 1996. However, the most recent surveys indicate that this alarming escalation may be leveling off for younger respondents, although this trend was less apparent among high school seniors where increases are still occurring (Johnston et al., 1998). Nevertheless, a disturbingly high number of young people continue to experiment with both "legal" and illicit drugs at very early ages, many of whom will progress to drug abuse and dependence.

The prevalence and incidence of a significant amount of drug use during the first decade of life is not documented to the degree to which it has been among teenagers. Nonetheless, both retrospective and cross-sectional (small-scale) surveys report very little use of illicit drugs at any level by Grade 6 (4% to 10% lifetime prevalence). At least one third of the same respondents indicate that they have at least tried cigarettes or alcohol by the sixth grade, and that by eighth grade over half (54%) of this nation's youth had tried alcohol and nearly half (47%) had tried cigarettes (Johnston et al., 1998; Oetting & Beauvais, 1990). These reports attest to appreciable risk for significant involvement with addictive substances very early in life.

Reports also suggest interesting differences and similarities in substance use related to demographic characteristics (e.g., Kandel, 1980). Roughly equivalent rates of use are reported across all social classes in many surveys (e.g., Brook, Whiteman, & Gordon, 1983; Johnston et al., 1998). Nonetheless, socioeconomic status (SES) is thought to function as a mediating variable, such that lower SES adolescents are at greater risk because lower SES increases the impact of other negative influences (Tolan, 1988). Available evidence regarding the impact of family structure (i.e., intact vs. broken families), however, is more equivocal; still, most investigators argue that greater adolescent drug use is observed within the context of family disruption (e.g., Needle, Su, & Doherty, 1990; Newcomb & Bentler, 1988c). National surveys suggest some reduction in regional differences in drug use in the mid-1990s. Yet, there is still greater use in the West and Northeast, compared with the north central and southern United States. There are only marginal differences in reported rates of drug use in rural compared to urban settings, although drugs of choice may differ dramatically in rural and urban contexts (Johnston et al., 1998).

Gender differences in rates of use typically are found in these surveys. Except for cigarettes, boys tend to initiate drug use before girls and to use slightly greater quantities, a differential that is maintained throughout high school (Johnston et al., 1998; Newcomb, Maddahian, Skager, & Bentler, 1987). Girls, however, tend to surpass the boys' use of pills with age.

Finally, although African Americans and Hispanics are reportedly overrepresented among adult drug-abusing populations (e.g., Medina, Wallace, Ralph, & Goldstein, 1982), this may represent an artifact of the type of patients and public health service facilities studied, and little similar data are readily available for children or teenagers. Most recent local and national surveys of adolescents suggest moderately higher rates of illicit drug use among White and Hispanic, when compared to African American and Asian, adolescent respondents (e.g., Johnston et al., 1998; Maddahian, Newcomb, & Bentler, 1986). These trends, however, may reflect differential school dropout rates as a function of ethnicity. Students enrolled in regular classroom settings generally report less drug use than do same-age peers in alternative education programs, wherein ethnic minority groups are overrepresented (Johnston et al., 1998; Oetting & Beauvais, 1990). Furthermore, Kandel (1995) noted that although African American and Hispanic youth may report lower drug use prevalence rates than Whites, those who do use drugs have greater problems from such use in these minority groups. Such differential vulnerability among these ethnic groups may arise due to issues related to acculturation, cultural identity, and perceived discrimination (e.g., Felix-Ortiz, Newcomb, & Myers, 1994) or other differences in risk or protective factors (Newcomb, 1995a). Therefore, we may wish to conclude that, nationwide, there are no clear differences in overall patterns of drug use and abuse as a function of ethnicity. Nonetheless, ethnic minorities (particularly African Americans and Hispanics) are currently far more likely than other adolescent groups to be targeted for attention from law enforcement officials as a function of drug involvement, and, if they are drug users, may be more likely to develop problems as a result (Kandel, 1995).

Assessment of Drug Use Disorders

Measurement and assessment of drug use, abuse, dependence, and addiction are not simple procedures and are plagued by several threats to reliability and validity. It is illegal for any child or teenager to use any drug without a prescription or for nonmedical purposes (including cigarettes, alcohol, or illicit substances); therefore, such use may not be reliably disclosed. Also, denial is a common feature of addiction (e.g., Miller & Gold, 1989). Both of these factors may undermine the truthfulness of self-report or interview data. These and other methodological issues and problems in the assessment of drug use have been reviewed by Carroll (1995).

The most widely used, though problematic, clinical description of substance use disorders is provided in the *Diagnostic and Statistical Manual of Mental Disorder* (4th ed., [*DSM–IV*] ; American Psychiatric Association [APA], 1994). There are no specific criteria for describing substance use disorders among children and teenagers within this system. Therefore, the only commonly used criteria for describing and assessing substance use disorders among children and teenagers are based on descriptions of adult mental disorders related to drug use and may be less appropriate or irrelevant for younger individuals.

Substance-related disorders in the *DSM–IV* are grouped into two general classes of phenomena and included as features of several other diagnostic groupings. One group involves diagnoses specifically related to acute effects of drug use, discontinuation of drug use, or persisting residual effects of drug use. These typically involve acute intoxication states, withdrawal syndromes, and recurrent events attributable to the drug and are not addressed in this chapter. Another group of disorders represents potential consequences of substance use, such as delirium, dementia, amnesia, psychosis, mood disorders, anxiety disorders, sexual dysfunction, and sleep disorders. This diverse group of disorders also is not described in this section. The final group represents maladaptive use of alcohol, illicit drugs, and prescription medications. Most classifications distinguish between two levels of the latter disorders: abuse (the lesser form) and dependence (the more serious form).

According to the *DSM–IV*, a diagnosis of substance dependence is met by meeting three or more (of seven) symptoms during a single 12-month period. The seven symptoms are: (a) tolerance to the drug (increased amounts required to achieve the same effects or diminished effects resulting from continued ingestion of the same amount of the drug); (b) withdrawal effects from the drug; (c) drug often taken in larger amounts or over a longer period of time than was intended; (d) persistent desire or unsuccessful efforts to cut down or control substance use; (e) a great deal of time spent in activities necessary to obtain, use, or recover from the effects of the drug; (f) important social, occupational, or recreational activities given up or reduced because of drug use; or (g) continued drug use despite knowledge of persistent or recurrent physical or psychological problems that were likely to have been caused or exacerbated by the drug use. All substance dependence diagnoses should include specification of the presence or absence of physiological dependence and course specifiers (extent of possible remission, use of agonist medications, and whether living in a controlled environment).

The less serious diagnosis of psychoactive substance abuse is met by not meeting the criteria for substance dependence (an exclusionary criteria) and by having one or more symptoms occur at any time within a 12-month period. The symptom criteria include any one of the following: (a) repeated drug use causing a failure to fulfill major role obligations at work, school, or home; (b) recurrent substance use in situations that are physically hazardous; and (c) recurrent legal problems related to drug use, or continued drug use despite persistent or repeated social or interpersonal problems related to the effects of the drug.

Several criticisms have been raised regarding the *DSM* criteria for diagnoses of alcohol and other drug disorders. Miller and Gold (1989) made general suggestions for improving all classifications of drug use disorders within formal diagnostic systems. They advocate that the term *drug* be used instead of *substance* (which is too broad and inclusive), that *addiction* should be used instead of *dependence* (which should be used only for physical dependence), and that greater attention should be given to polydrug problems, which is a common pattern for teenagers (e.g., Clayton & Ritter, 1985; Newcomb & Bentler, 1988a, 1988b). Winters, Latimer, and Stinchfield (in press) contrasted the two most recent versions of *DSM* (the 3rd ed., rev., [*DSM–III–R*]; APA, 1987; *DSM–IV*) for abuse and dependence among adolescents. They found that the most recent version allowed higher rates of abuse and lower rates of dependence compared to its predecessor. They and others (e.g., Bukstein & Kaminer, 1994) have concluded that it is critical to develop diagnostic criteria for drug use disorders that are unique to children and adolescents, because these developmental periods are so dissimilar to later life and adult roles (e.g., Newcomb, 1996a, 1996b).

For instance, Newcomb and Bentler (1989) noted that typical descriptions of drug abuse may be too narrow and adult-oriented to capture problems related to drug abuse among children and teenagers. They suggest that additional criteria be considered for young age groups. For instance, ingestion of drugs in inappropriate settings such as the workplace, classroom, driver's seat, or in isolation may be considered abuse, even though potential adverse consequences may not yet have occurred (e.g., a crash after drinking and driving). For every drug, consuming large quantities on any one occasion or moderate amounts regularly over prolonged time periods may be abuse, again because of the potential for psychological or physiological harm. Regular use of drugs at developmentally critical age periods, such as when very young or prior to puberty can be considered abuse because of the potential for interfering with crucial growth and adjustment tasks.

Wolraich (1996) attempted to develop unique diagnostic criteria and categories for adolescents. This work emerged from the needs of primary care providers to describe more accurately drug use patterns among children and teenagers. Although in its preliminary stage of development, this system allows for much greater and realistic variation in drug use styles and behaviors among children and teenagers. For instance, a section on developmental variation is included that allows a diagnosis of substance use variation, characterized by "occasional use of illegal substances in the context of experimentation" (Wolraich, 1996, p. 137).

Examples of questionnaires designed to identify potentially problematic drug use among children and adolescents include the Problem Oriented Screening Instrument for Teenagers (POSIT), the Personal Experience Screen Questionnaire (PESQ), and the Personal Experience Inventory (PEI). The POSIT is a 139-item, self-administered questionnaire designed to identify teens who need more focused assessment in any of 10 domains, including: (a) substance use and abuse; (b) physical health status; (c) mental health status; (d) family relations; (e) peer relation; (f) educational status; (g) vocational status; (h) social skills; (i) leisure and recreation; and (j) aggressive behaviors and delinquency (Rahdert, 1991). An important aspect of the POSIT is that it is imbedded in a comprehensive assessment and referral system designed specifically for adolescents. The PESQ is a 38-item tool designed to screen for the severity of adolescents' drug involvement (see Chatlos, 1991a). The PEI is a 300-item questionnaire designed to provide a more thorough assessment of teenagers' substance use history, patterns, and consequences (Winters, 1992). The PEI has been shown to have good convergent and predictive validity (Winters, Stinchfield, & Henley, 1996). Recent attempts also have been made to rescale adolescent drug use measures to be more appropriate for children and young teenagers (e.g., Williams, Toomey, McGovern, & Wagenaar, 1995).

Alternatively, Anglin (1987) offered excellent recommendations for clinical interview strategies specifically tailored to teens, which included a thorough exploration of home and family relationships, peer relationships, school functioning, leisure activity and employment history (with older adolescents), self-perception, stage drug of use (experimental, sensation-seeking, preoccupation, or abuse), and a detailed drug use history (particularly to describe initial use, past and present drug use settings and circumstances, and functional and emotional consequences of use). In addition, the Adolescent Diagnostic Interview is an example of a *DSM*-based structured diagnostic interview designed to assess six classes of Axis I disorders, as well as chemical abuse (see Chatlos, 1991a).

Drug Use and Other Problem Behaviors

Drug use and abuse do not occur as isolated events or as distinct aspects of an individual's behavior. They are typically only components of a cluster of behaviors and attitudes that form a syndrome or lifestyle of problem behavior or general deviance. Problem Behavior theory (Jessor & Jessor, 1977) provides a valuable conceptualization of teenage drug use as only one aspect of a deviance-prone lifestyle among some children and teenagers. Adolescent substance use is viewed as one facet of a constellation of attitudes and behavior that are considered problematic, unconventional, or nontraditional for a specific developmental stage, "behavior that is socially defined as a problem, a source of concern, or as undesirable by the norms of conventional society ... and its occurrence usually elicits some kind of social control response" (Jessor & Jessor, 1977, p. 33). For adolescents, these deviant behaviors also include academic problems, precocious sexual involvement, frequency of various sexual activities, deviant attitudes, and delinquent behavior.

Problem Behavior theory has been tested in several confirmatory factor analysis studies (Donovan & Jessor, 1985; McGee & Newcomb, 1992; Newcomb & Bentler, 1988a; Newcomb & McGee, 1991). These studies have identified a syndrome of problem behaviors among adolescents and young adults and revealed that either one common latent factor accounted for the correlations among the several indicators of problem behavior or that all of these constructs were highly correlated. For instance, Newcomb and Bentler (1988a) found that teenage polydrug use was highly correlated with low social conformity, criminal activities, deviant friendship network, early sexual involvement, and low academic potential. McGee and Newcomb (1992) used higher order confirmatory factor analyses to examine the construct of general deviance at four ages, from early adolescence to adulthood, and found that the construct was highly reliable at early and late adolescence. In short, the concept of problem behavior appears to adequately describe factors that encourage and correlate with adolescent drug use. Nonetheless, these strong relations may weaken or disappear in adulthood, where other types of deviance become more prominent and characteristic of older developmental periods of life (e.g., Newcomb, 1993).

Dealing with the risk of HIV infection has become particularly critical for adolescents, who tend to feel they are immune from life's illnesses and plagues. Engaging in risky AIDS behaviors has been associated with other problem behaviors and general deviance, including drug use (Stein, Newcomb, & Bentler, 1994). Many adolescents acknowledge their lack of concern, attention, and use of self-protective, safe sex practices, and this is particularly true for those teenagers who abuse drugs (e.g., Langer & Tubman, 1997).

CAUSES OF THE DISORDER

Factors that influence drug use and abuse are many, varied, and far from clearly understood. Although most drug use initiation occurs with friends or peers also using drugs, the stage for this event has been set much earlier by parents, the community, and society (e.g., Newcomb, 1994). We need to examine more closely how earlier childhood experiences, parenting practices, and general attitudes of this society contribute to the choice of using drugs or not.

Hundreds of variables have been studied for their ability to predict youthful drug involvement. These can be conceptualized as reflecting several areas (e.g., Lettieri, 1985): (a) cultural–societal environment; (b) interpersonal forces (i.e., school, peers, and family); (c) psychobehavioral factors (these may take several forms, including personality, attitudes, and activities); and (d) biogenetic influences. An individual can be considered at risk because of factors or forces within each of these areas (e.g,.

Newcomb, 1995b). A great deal of attention has been devoted to each of these possible influences and can be reviewed from both theoretical and empirical perspectives in several sources (e.g., Hawkins, Catalano, & Miller, 1992; Lettieri, 1985).

Hawkins et al. (1992) reviewed possible risk factors for youthful drug use and identified 17 potential causes that reflect the four general areas listed previously. Included among cultural–societal factors are laws and norms favorable toward drug use, availability of drugs, extreme economic deprivation, and neighborhood disorganization. Interpersonal forces include family alcohol and drug behavior and attitudes, poor and inconsistent family management practices, family conflict (see Family Contributions section), peer rejection in elementary grades, and association with drug-using peers. Psychobehavioral influences include early and persistent problem behaviors, academic failure, low degree of commitment to school, alienation and rebelliousness, attitudes favorable to drug use, and early onset of drug use. Finally, biogenetic factors include potential heritability of drug abuse and psychophysiological susceptibility to the effects of drugs (see Psychophysiological and Genetic Influences section). Additional influences not directly addressed in their review include psychological and emotional factors such as anxiety, need for excitement, depression, or antisocial personality, and contextual factors such as physical or sexual abuse or stressful life events (e.g, Harrison, Hoffmann, & Edwall, 1989; Newcomb & Harlow, 1986; Newcomb & McGee, 1991; Zucker & Gomberg, 1986).

Although not specifically mentioned by Hawkins et al. (1992), certainly the best predictor of future behavior is past behavior; this is no less true for drug use and abuse. Therefore, the strongest predictor of current drug use is past drug use. Peer influences, such as modeling drug use, provision of drugs, and attitudes and behavior that encourage drug use, generally are viewed as secondary only to prior experience with drugs. All other potential psychosocial predictors must exhibit a unique influence on altering drug use or abuse beyond that accounted for by prior involvement with drugs and peer influences.

Another obvious factor related to drug use initiation is age of the youngster. The risk for initiating drug use increases for most drugs to a peak during mid- to late adolescence and decreases thereafter (Kandel & Logan, 1984). Tobacco has the youngest age of peak vulnerability at about age 16 years. Increased likelihood for beginning use of alcohol, marijuana, and psychedelics occurs during the next 2 years of life. Although initial cocaine use typically occurs in young adulthood, this pattern may be changing due to the insurgence of crack, the inexpensive and smokable form of cocaine, which may be more alluring and available to teenagers.

Some types of alcohol and drug abuse may have a genetic component (see Psychophysiological and Genetic Influences). However, for initiation of drug use and progression to drug abuse, environmental, social, and psychological factors have received the most attention. Although biogenetic influences certainly affect the potential emergence of drug use disorders, they clearly are shaped and modified by other personal attributes and environmental conditions (e.g., Marlatt, Baer, Donovan, & Kivlahan, 1988).

Establishing correlates of substance use has been the primary basis for inferring etiological variables, although this approach is seriously flawed for inferring causal effects (Newcomb, 1990). Despite the compelling idea that the causes of drug use may be different from the causes of abuse, little systematic research exists to support such a notion (Glantz & Pickens, 1992). Nevertheless, several investigators have found that most drug use occurs due to social influences, whereas the abuse of drugs is more strongly tied to psychological factors and processes (i.e., self-medication against emotional distress; Carman, 1979; Newcomb & Bentler, 1990; Paton, Kessler & Kandel, 1977).

Indeed, contemporary biopsychosocial characterizations of alcohol and drug abuse (addiction) generally emphasize both the strong psychological and physical dependence, resulting in a withdrawal syndrome when use of the drug is halted. These dependencies are reflected in the driving forces behind addiction, the reinforcing properties of drugs. Of particular import is the biopsychosocial habit model (Marlatt, 1992), which posits that addiction reflects a learned, maladaptive habit pattern, maladaptive to the extent to which it becomes a central means of coping with distressing physical or mood states. Most excessive behaviors are those that are reinforced by immediate consequences. This model holds that two reinforcing principals are critical to addiction: *positive reinforcement* is produced by a stimulus that brings pleasure (e.g., the euphoric rush or "high" when a substance is used) to an individual who is in a "normal" mood state; *negative reinforcement* is produced by a stimulus that provides relief from negative mood states or from physical distress (i.e., withdrawal syndrome), returning the individual to a "normal" mood state.

Four alternative models of addiction remain influential within both conceptualizations of the addictive process and intervention (Hughes, 1989; Marlatt, 1992). Moral models view substance abuse as a sign of character weakness, a reflection of one's personal shortcomings and lack of willpower. The disease model is popular within various circles and holds that drug addiction is caused by an underlying pathology or disease process, such as metabolic or genetic abnormality, or an expression of an elevated biological vulnerability, triggered by critical exposure to addictive substances. Spiritually oriented models favored by self-help organizations such as Alcoholics Anonymous appear to be a combination of the moralistic and disease models, in that drug addiction is conceptualized as a disease from which an individual can never be "cured." However, recovery from such addiction is viewed as possible on admitting one's lack of personal power over the allure and influence of drugs and turning his or her life over to a higher power for help. Psychological models, such as those that describe substance abusers as having an addictive personality, characterize drug abuse as but one example of a range of behavior patterns to which such an individual is susceptible as a means of coping with unmet psychological needs. These conceptualizations are based on research and clinical evidence from animal and human adult subjects but also should apply to child and adolescent drug addiction as well, although such confirmation is currently lacking. Further discussion of the myriad sociopolitical influences on these definitions of drug abuse and addiction may be found in the section in this chapter entitled Course of the Disorder.

W. R. Miller (1993) proposed that a public health perspective may help integrate these disparate views of drug addiction. In this model, drug use is seen as the product of three interacting factors: the host (drug user), the agent (drug itself), and the environment (including social, physical, and attitudinal). This perspective avoids the tendency to blame one component of the biopsychosocial model for generating drug use more than the other. All three factors contribute and can be risk-inducing or protective against producing drug use, abuse, or dependence in an individual.

At younger ages, the major correlates of use are also the correlates of heavy use, and, by implication, of abuse. Because of the inevitable correlation of other problem behaviors with drug use, many predictors of drug involvement are similar to predictors of general problem behavior or deviance (Jessor & Jessor, 1977). The main mechanism for establishing these etiological factors has been the use of longitudinal studies, with statistical controls substituted for the more desirable experimental control, such as is represented by structural equation modeling methods (e.g., Bentler & Dudgeon, 1996; Newcomb, 1990, 1997).

Many and more of these varied influences have been related to involvement with drug use or abuse, but none has ever been found to be the primary factor that causes drug use or abuse. Because the range of variables leading to initial involvement in drug use is so large, recent views of this phenomenon have emphasized the risk factor notion that is often used in medical epidemiology (Bry, McKeon, & Pandina, 1982; Newcomb, Maddahian, & Bentler, 1986; Newcomb et al., 1987; Scheier & Newcomb, 1991). As might be expected, these risk factors include environmental, behavioral, psychological, and social attributes. Still, at this time, it seems highly unlikely that any one factor or even a few factors will ever be found that account fully and totally for all variations of drug involvement. Rather, adolescent drug involvement is multiply determined. This approach suggests that the more risk factors someone is exposed to that encourage drug use the more likely he or she will use or abuse drugs. Exposure to more risk factors is not only a reliable correlate of drug use, but predicts increases in drug use over time as well, implying a true etiological role for these influences (Newcomb et al., 1986; Scheier & Newcomb, 1991). This approach implies that drug use is but one of many coping responses for when the individual is exposed to an increasing number of vulnerability conditions. The particular risk factors appear less important than the accumulation of vulnerability factors in the person's life.

The flip side of risk factor modeling for drug use is that set of protective factors that reduce the likelihood and level of drug use and abuse. Protective factors are those psychosocial influences that have a direct effect on limiting or reducing drug involvement (Newcomb, 1992b). Recently, the risk factors approach to the study of drug use and abuse has been expanded to test for multiple protective factors as well (Newcomb, 1992b; Newcomb & Felix-Ortiz, 1992).

Protective factors may operate in a different manner or process than simply a direct effect on reducing drug involvement. Protective factors, in fact, may buffer or moderate the association between risk factors and drug use and abuse (Brook, Cohen, Whiteman, & Gordon, 1992; Newcomb & Felix-Ortiz, 1992; Stacy, Newcomb, & Bentler, 1992). Protective factors that moderate the relation between risk for drug use and drug use or abuse can involve aspects of the environment (e.g., maternal affection) or the individual (e.g., introversion or self-acceptance). For instance, Stacy et al. found a high degree of self-acceptance moderated the relation between peer use of hard drugs and self-use of hard drugs; a strong relation between these variables existed for those low in self-acceptance, and little association was found between these variables for those with high self-acceptance. Newcomb and Felix-Ortiz (1992) also tested the buffering effects of multiple protective factors on the relation between multiple risk factors and drug use and abuse. Several significant effects were noted, primarily for illicit drugs.

COURSE OF THE DISORDER

We now turn our attention to the course of drug involvement, once drug use has been initiated by children or teenagers. The particular cause of drug use may directly influence or shape the course of drug use disorders, in that specific reasons for drug involvement may differentially affect outcomes related to the drug use.

Despite significant opposition (e.g., Fingarette, 1988), many who believe that drug abuse and dependence are biogenetically determined also prefer to consider such disorders diseases (e.g., Vaillant, 1983). Such a perspective conforms to the overarching tenet of many antidrug use, self-help support groups (i.e., Alcoholics Anonymous) that any abuse of mood-altering substances represents a chronic, progressive, degenerative disease that can never be cured and at best can be controlled through abstinence, in a state of recovery (O'Neill & Barnes, 1987).

Such a strong position obviously creates problems for how to characterize drug use and even abuse among children and teenagers. There is also a major sociopolitical aspect to this dilemma. For instance, under President and Mrs. Reagan's leadership of this country, any use of a drug by a teenager was defined as abuse, requiring severe and intrusive intervention. Little distinction was allowed between those who may have had a beer at a party or tried marijuana once from those children and teenagers who drank alcohol or used illicit drugs daily, may be dependent on these drugs, and those who failed to function adequately in their lives as a result of their use. Conspicuously missing from such clearly biased categorizations of drug users and drug abusers have been those addicted to tobacco, who ultimately experience quite severe, direct, long-term consequences of their use in the form of disease and premature mortality. More recently, the tobacco industry has been targeted for seducing children and teenagers into using cigarettes. Drug abuse in this nation is certainly a devastating problem, but how it is described, characterized, treated, who is targeted, and which drugs are the "evil ones" are largely a function of how these problems get constructed (Humphreys & Rappaport, 1993). We have a choice of addressing drug problems as a defect in the person and a failing of moral willpower, or as a community and public health problem that is rooted both in the individual and the environment, including oppression of minorities.

These philosophical positions can be addressed with empirical evidence. The defect model has some support, because we know that certain personal characteristics contribute to drug use and abuse (e.g., Hawkins et al., 1992; Newcomb, 1995b). But this is not the whole story. At one extreme, those youngsters who abstain or who limit themselves to experimentation with various drugs typically do not develop a lifelong addiction nor do they suffer severe adverse consequences due to this use later in life (e.g., Kandel, Davies, Karus, & Yamaguchi, 1986; Newcomb & Bentler, 1988a, 1988b). In fact, Shedler and Block (1990) showed in a small sample of adolescents with varying histories of substance use that the well-adjusted teenagers were those who experimented with drugs. Abstainers were found to have worse life outcomes, and heavy drug users suffered the most negative consequences. These results support the position that drug use by teenagers is a typical and largely benign manifestation of adolescent growth experiences and quest for experimentation (Peele, 1987). They also suggest that youngsters who refrain from such experimentation may be overly restrained, inflexible, and unable to cope with challenges of later life (e.g., Newcomb, 1996a). This is certainly a controversial position that is blatantly at odds with the sociopolitical reality of the Reagan and Bush presidencies in the 1980s (and their associated domestic policies), but also suggests a considered and restrained emphasis on intervention with drug use among children and teenagers. Furthermore, drug abuse and dependence may be related to social conditions as well as personal vulnerability (Humphreys & Rappaport, 1993). These influences need much greater attention in future research, prevention, and treatment efforts.

Consistent across most studies of the course of youthful drug use is the finding that those children and adolescents who develop a lifestyle involving regular and heavy drug use will experience severe and even tragic outcomes attributable to this abuse, immediately or later in life. Newcomb and Bentler (1987, 1988a, 1988b) demonstrated direct linear relations between the level of teenage drug use and later negative consequences. In other words, the more seriously teenagers are involved with drugs, the more adverse are the consequences they experience in later life across several domains, including educational pursuits, work and job conditions, emotional health, social integration, criminal activities, and family establishment and stability. The only exception to this general pattern was that early use of alcohol to the exclusion of all other drugs had a few positive effects on later life that were limited to social relationships and self-feelings, a finding corroborated in other research (e.g., Kandel et al., 1986).

Overwhelming empirical evidence indicates that most teenage users of alcohol or other substances do not become addicts or abusers (Johnston et al., 1998; Kandel & Logan, 1984; Newcomb, 1995b, 1997). Even most of those who indulge heavily as teenagers do not develop substance use disorders later in life. In one study, the magnitude of association between level of consumption and amount of abuse (negative consequences) was examined for alcohol, marijuana, and cocaine (Newcomb, 1992b). There was a substantial association between amount of consumption and abuse consequences for alcohol, a higher degree of association for marijuana, and a perfect association for cocaine. Although no similar study has been conducted for tobacco, it may also rank quite high for addictive, if not abuse, potential.

In their review of adolescent drug use studies, Clayton and Ritter (1985) found that, "More often than not, the persons who are using drugs frequently, are multiple drug users" (p. 83). For instance, cocaine users reported significantly higher prevalence rates for all other types of drugs, including cigarettes, alcohol, cannabis, over-the-counter medications, hypnotics, stimulants, psychedelics, inhalants, narcotics, and phencyclidine (PCP), compared with those who had not used cocaine (Newcomb & Bentler, 1986a). These large differences were found for both female and male respondents, and were evident during adolescence and young adulthood (Newcomb & Bentler, 1986b). The association between various types of drug use is so high that latent constructs of general polydrug use (Bentler & Newcomb, 1986) and polydrug use in the workplace (Newcomb, 1988) have been identified distinctly and reliably.

Another way to understand drug involvement has been with the progression or stage theory. Kandel (1975) was one of the first researchers to investigate this hypothesis. In general, she found that teenagers initiate use with beer, wine, or cigarettes, progress to the use of hard liquor, may then transition to marijuana, and finally may proceed to the use of other illicit drugs. Of course, these shifts from a lower stage to a higher stage are not guaranteed, but are probabilistic (Newcomb & Bentler, 1989). Involvement at one stage does not necessarily lead to involvement at the next stage, but, rather, involvement at the next stage is unlikely without prior involvement at the previous stage. This notion has been tested in various cross-sectional and longitudinal studies (Donovan & Jessor, 1983; Ellickson, Hays, & Bell, 1992; Newcomb & Bentler, 1986a, 1986c), with results that generally confirm Kandel's hypotheses, despite some important variations. Donovan and Jessor (1983) found that problem drinking occurred higher in the progression than general alcohol use. Ellickson et al. (1992) found that weekly alcohol use occurred subsequent to marijuana use for Whites, Latinos, and African Americans, and followed illicit drug use for Asians. Newcomb and Bentler (1986c) found that several minisequences accounted for drug involvement from early adolescence to young adulthood, when the role of cigarettes and nonprescription medications was included. The mechanism that drives such staging, such as availability, anxiety reduction, peer groups norms, or physiological vulnerability perhaps associated with learning to appreciate the positive effects of a drug, are not known, although there are some hints that these factors may not be the same at all stages. For example, psychopathology has been implicated primarily at later stages or higher levels of drug involvement and not at initiation.

Ultimately, we must conclude that the course of youthful drug use is varied and largely unknown, due to different types of drugs, drug use pattern, biological vulnerability, and exposure to psychosocial risk and protective factors. It seems prudent that we directly confront the use of drugs by youths but perhaps not overreact to what may be a normal and benign experimentation with experiences that characterizes adolescence. We must not forget that most adult alcoholics and drug abusers began their patterns of abuse in their youth, whereas most youths who try drugs do not progress to abuse nor suffer severe consequences of their ingestion.

FAMILY CONTRIBUTIONS

Although biogenetic factors (discussed in the next section) certainly represent parental influences on the drug abuse susceptibility of their children, parents and other family members affect drug use patterns in other important ways. These factors typically represent socialization processes related to parental modeling of drug-using behaviors, youths' imitation of parents' behaviors, social reinforcement related to internalization of values and behaviors within the family, and social control aspects of parenting and disciplinary activities of parents. Considerable attention has been given to the important factors of family disruption, quality of parent–child relationships, parental support, parents as socialization agents and value inculcators, and parent use of and attitudes toward drugs (e.g., Johnson & Pandina, 1991; Needle et al., 1990; Newcomb & Bentler, 1988b, 1988c).

In general, family factors have a greater influence on drug-using behavior during preadolescence; in adolescence, peer and friendship networks become more prominent factors (Huba & Bentler, 1980). However, many suggest that parental influences contribute in a substantial manner even at later ages, because they create the basis on which the child constructs his or her social life. Therefore, even though parents may lose their direct effect on their child's drug use as he or she matures through adolescence, they, in fact, have established the trajectory of their child's evolution and can be considered to have an indirect influence on nearly all later outcomes of the child's development.

This mechanism of intergenerational transmission can be seen in the process of parents as models of drug-using behavior. For instance, parental alcohol and tobacco use seem to have an indirect effect on their child's use of these drugs as mediated by the child's perception of adult alcohol use (Newcomb, Huba, & Bentler, 1983) and of their peers' use of cigarettes (Hansen et al., 1987). However, during early adolescence, parental use of illicit substances may have indirect or direct effects on their child's use of these drugs. For example, Newcomb and Bentler (1988c) found that more maternal drug use was associated with more socially deviant attitudes and drug use in their children. In addition to actual drug use behavior in the parents, parents' attitudes and restrictions regarding drug use also can affect drug use in their children.

Nondrug aspects of parent and family behavior and functioning also may affect the likelihood of child drug use. Hawkins et al. (1992) categorized these more general family conditions into three groups: (a) poor and inconsistent family management practices, (b) family conflict, and (c) low bonding to family. Numerous factors related to inconsistent disciplinary and authoritarian parenting practices, low and poor quality of parent interaction and involvement with their children, and low aspirations and expectations for their children all reflect poor family management qualities that increase the chances of adolescent involvement with drugs. Family conflict as reflected in marital discord, divorce and separation, and general family conflict also increases the likelihood that children may turn to drugs in attempts to cope with such stress and unreliability (Newcomb & Harlow, 1986; Richardson, 1993). These family characteristics often prevent secure bonding of the child to the family, and as a result, also may contribute to youthful drug use, as evidenced by higher drug use among those families that lack closeness, maternal involvement, and positive parent–child relationships (Jessor & Jessor, 1977; Kandel, 1980). Conversely, close, supportive, involved, but not overly intrusive family relationships may protect children from the allure of drug use.

It is clear that many factors associated with family functioning and behaviors affect children's risk of drug use; other factors serve to protect youth from influences that serve to encourage drug use. Although the child's first use of drugs typically occurs in peer or social settings, the emergence of this event has been established many years earlier in the interactions and connections with parents and other family members (Newcomb, 1992a).

PSYCHOPHYSIOLOGICAL AND GENETIC INFLUENCES

Although literature exists regarding genetic factors related to substance use, the focus of this work is decidedly on the heritability of alcoholism. Our overview certainly reflects that bias. Psychophysiological influences, in turn, relate particularly to the hedonic effects of drug use that encourage continued and accelerated use.

Wise (1988) presented a comprehensive review of psychomotor stimulant theory, arguing that drug-induced stimulant effects are common to a wide array of popular drugs of addiction, including amphetamine, opiates, cannabis, alcohol, barbiturates, and PCP. Psychomotor effects are distinguished from simple motoric responses in that environmental cues shape both the behavior and affective response to the ingestion of addictive substances. The common physiologic mechanism of addiction for all of these is positive reinforcement (as described in Causes of the Disorder) and extant evidence suggests that the same mechanism mediates the positive reinforcing effects of these drugs. Positive reinforcement refers to the activation of brain dopamine systems such that the metabolism or reuptake of dopamine within the medial forebrain bundle is inhibited, producing a magnification of the intensity of most pleasurable sensations. Such effects may be of varying duration but generally are remembered for a long time and highly rewarding.

Negative reinforcing effects, in turn, depend on the aftereffects of stimulation but appear to be of relatively brief duration and may not depend on dopaminergic activation, but rather depletion. Furthermore, negative reinforcement may result from a wider array of drug actions (e.g., anxiolytic, analgesic, sedative) not necessarily linked to physical dependence and independent of positive reinforcement.

There is substantial evidence that certain patterns of alcohol abuse are influenced by genetic or biophysiological substrates (e.g., Goodwin, 1976; Vaillant, 1983). However, the magnitude and mechanism of such factors have not been clearly established. A growing body of literature also has shown that biogenetic factors play an important role in the use and abuse of drugs other than alcohol, in both animal (e.g., Crabbe, McSwigan, & Belknap, 1985) and human studies (e.g., Cadoret, 1992; Merikangas, Rounsaville, & Prusoff, 1992).

Genetic influences clearly play an important, but not exclusive, role in the etiology of alcoholism (Crabbe et al., 1985; Zucker & Gomberg, 1986). Among the best known is the work of Goodwin (1976, 1985). Studying adoptees from alcoholic and nonalcoholic fathers in Denmark, he determined that sons of alcoholics were at four times greater risk for developing alcoholism than were their peers with a nonalcoholic father. Twin and animal studies also have demonstrated a genetic factor for alcoholism. Nevertheless, even monozygotic twins exhibit far from 100% concordance for alcoholism (Crabbe et al., 1985), establishing that alcoholism is not totally genetic and that other personal, environmental, and societal factors play important roles (Newcomb, 1995b).

Two patterns of genetic transmission of alcoholism are described (Bohman, Sigvardsson, & Cloninger, 1981; Cloninger, Bohman, & Sigvardsson, 1981). Type I is called *milieu limited* and involves both genetic and environmental factors, affects both men and women, has a late onset, and is associated with few or no alcohol or criminal problems in the parents. Type II is called *male limited* and is affected little by the environment, is restricted to male transmission and early onset, is associated with criminal behavior, and is related to fathers with severe alcoholism, extensive treatment, and extensive criminality. Although these heritability patterns are interesting and informative, they have received substantial criticism on methodological bases (e.g., Searles, 1988) and must be considered with caution. They also tell us little about biogenetic causes of women's drug abuse (Lex, 1991).

Important questions concern what precisely is inherited there is a genetic influence for alcoholism or other drug abuse (e.g., Tarter & Vnyukov, 1994) and does this interact with environmental influences? Research evidence, primarily but not exclusively based on animal models, suggests at least two mechanisms (e.g., Bardo & Risner, 1985). Those at genetic risk for drug abuse may inherit a biological vulnerability to the hedonic affects of the drug, so for them the drug effect is more attractive than for others. On the other hand, those at genetic risk for drug abuse may not experience withdrawal effects as severely as those not at risk (e.g., less likelihood of hangover). However, these and other proposed mechanisms must be evaluated more conclusively in further research.

CURRENT TREATMENTS

The primary efforts at intervention for drugs among teenagers are primary prevention of both drug use and drug abuse and treatment of drug problems should they occur. Clearly, the best way to deal with a problem is to prevent it before it occurs. Therefore, extensive efforts have been devoted to the primary prevention of drug use and abuse among children and adolescents.

Primary Prevention

There exists an array of programs aimed at reducing the probability of drug and alcohol use and abuse among children and adolescents. These include programs designed to address critical family- and community-based risk factors, social influence approaches to drug use prevention, and interventions with teenagers at highest risk for addiction. Programs vary dramatically in their structure, leadership, and perceived impact (see comprehensive overview in Stoil & Hill, 1996).

The most widely known and distributed of early intervention programs is the Drug Abuse Resistance Education (DARE) program, typically cosponsored by local school and law enforcement officials and taught by active police officers. The core curricula is designed for preadolescents (fifth- to seventh-grade students), an attempt to reduce the probability of early experimentation with drugs or alcohol. Weekly classes over a 4-month period focus on four groups of issues and skills, including: the nature and consequences of drug use; resistance techniques; making decisions about risk-taking behaviors and critical analysis of media messages about drugs and violence; positive role models and choosing drug and violence-free activities. Program evaluation studies indicate that such programs frequently produce immediate attitudinal changes (e.g., lower expectations to use alcohol or other drugs in the future), but are less likely to produce lasting behavioral changes (Ennett et al., 1994; Palumbo & Ferguson, 1995; Stoil & Hill, 1996; Wysong, Aniskiewicz, & Wright, 1994). Given a rather extensive and consistent body of research that does not support the efficacy of the DARE program (e.g., Dukes, Ullman, & Stein, 1996) for reducing either drug use or drug abuse, the vast amount of money expended on this program would be spent more wisely elsewhere on more promising interventions. Unfortunately, the political and social construction of drug problems often favors a simplistic and personal deficit model of drug use (e.g., Humphreys & Rappaport, 1993) that leads to ineffective approaches such as DARE rather than to more comprehensive and ecologically based interventions that may have a greater likelihood of success (Newcomb, 1992a).

Adolescent respondents tell us that the success of any prevention program is at least partially dependent on the audience's initial beliefs about drugs, drug-using behavior, and what type of message will best encourage their resistance of drug use. They indicate that a focus on life-skills development is critical to foster change in drug-using behavior, whereas scare tactics are best suited for those who view drug use as a moral failing (Eiser, Eiser, Claxton-Oldfield, & Pritchard, 1988). Responses to punitive sanctions built into drug prevention programs for drug and alcohol use have been more varied (Carlson, 1994). Those aimed at the most serious drug offenses were universally supported, whereas punishments for common alcohol violations were viewed as excessive. Carlson (1994) also found that attitudes toward such sanctions were inversely associated with age and viewed as not helpful by the majority of older students.

Peer-directed prevention programs tend to have the greatest impact on cognitive risk factors (e.g., perceived consequences of drug use, normative beliefs, resistance self-efficacy, expectations of future use, knowledge about drugs) and on drug use itself (Bangert-Drowns, 1988; Ellickson, Bell & McGuigan, 1993; Tobler, 1986). In contrast, adult-directed programs taught without credible peer facilitators frequently produce early beneficial effects that quickly fade (Ellickson et al., 1993). Programs aimed at affecting the availability of drugs and the consequences for their use tend to produce modest, short-term declines in patterns of adolescent use, as do those designed to change social norms, such as media saturation designed to increase the development of antidrug and antialcohol attitudes among high-risk teens (Stoil & Hill, 1996).

Finally, a number of innovative programs designed to target early (family-based) risk factors have been examined. These include community- and school-based parenting skills training, early childhood, and family support programs (DeMarsh & Kumpfer, 1986; Perry et al., 1996), and are increasingly designed to address culture-specific needs and risks for teen drug use (Botvin, Schinke, Epstein, & Diaz, 1995; Myers et al., 1992; Schinke et al., 1988; Tobler, 1986). Unfortunately, these may not attract participation by parents of adolescents at highest risk for use (Cohen & Litton, 1995).

Treatment

Treatment models vary as widely as do prevention programs and may be distinguished by their duration, intensity, goals, degree of restrictiveness, and participant membership. An alternative view distinguishes between traditional and nontraditional treatment approaches (Institute of Medicine, 1990, cited in Jenson, Howard, & Yaffe, 1995). Traditional therapeutic models use many of the same techniques as adult programs and tend to view young clients as drug- or alcohol-addicted. Nontraditional approaches avoid such labeling and view substance abuse as an expression of normal developmental processes (gone awry) and are more likely to acknowledge that treatment must address underlying causes as well as manifest behavior.

Contemporary treatments may be viewed on a continuum that ranges from brief outpatient therapy to intensive inpatient treatment. Many experts believe that some form of outpatient therapy should be considered for all adolescents for whom regular drug use or early signs of abuse are evident. In addition, integrating family members into the treatment process is preferred, given the prominence of the family in shaping adolescents' attitudes and behavior. Candidates for such treatment should have no acute or chronic comorbid medical or psychiatric conditions that require intensive hospital treatment or preclude outpatient therapy, and should have no prior outpatient treatment failures (Chatlos, 1991b). A number of conceptually distinct models of family therapy have demonstrated utility for adolescent substance abuse, including: behavioral family therapy (e.g., Bry & Krinsley, 1992); family systems therapy (e.g., Joanning, Thomas, Newfield & Lamun, 1991); functional family therapy (e.g., A. S. Friedman, Granick, Kreisher, & Terras, 1993); multidimensional family therapies (e.g., Liddle & Diamond, 1991; Schmidt, Liddle, & Dakof, 1996); and strategic family systems therapy (e.g., Szapocznik et al., 1988). Treatment duration may range from several weeks to 12 months and may incorporate nontraditional efforts such as home visits (e.g., Henggeler, Pickrel, Brondino, & Crouch, 1996; Szapocznik et al., 1989). Although there is no clear evidence at present of the superiority of any particular therapeutic model, family therapy has demonstrated superiority to other forms of outpatient treatment with adolescents who abuse alcohol or drugs (e.g., Joanning, Quinn, Thomas, & Mullen, 1992). Furthermore, outpatient therapy with adolescent substance abusers is complicated not only by the typical problem of denial of the problem by the client, by the family, or both, but also by adolescents' basic mistrust of adult authority, their continued association with drug-using peers, their unwillingness to abstain from use, and lack of motivation. These factors must be considered in selecting an appropriate treatment (Chatlos, 1991b); practitioners might find useful a recent overview of strategies for enlisting family involvement in treatment (Morris, Gawinski, & Joanning, 1991).

Additional components across modes of therapy include: social skills training, posttreatment support and aftercare (e.g., self-help groups, relapse prevention); adjunctive modules to enhance the relevancy and scope of treatment for special populations (e.g., ethnic minority groups; teens at enhanced risk for exposure to HIV/AIDS).

No comprehensive reviews of the use of pharmacological agents in the treatment of adolescents are currently available, in part because of the limited scope of such research. This literature is primarily represented by single-case or small-group studies; no controlled clinical trials could be identified. Nonetheless, surveys of adolescents in treatment for drug-related disorders indicate that they view pharmacological therapy for substance-related disorders as a less-preferred therapeutic option (Kaminer, Tarter, Bukstein, & Kabene, 1992). In contrast, both adolescent patients and their treatment teams view participation in therapy group meetings and educational counseling as important components of successful completion of treatment. Kaminer (1995) further argued that, as with adult patients, multimodal therapeutic approaches are likely superior to drug treatment alone. In the absence of extensive clinical trials, however, it is not clear that drug therapies produce a clinically meaningful supplemental effect above and beyond that realized via current psychosocial therapies.

Most adolescent inpatient drug programs build on the experience of the Minnesota model of adult drug treatment programs. As such, they emphasize: (a) structured, residential stays (generally 21 to 60 days); (b) the understanding of dependency as a disease based on the idiosyncratic response of the adolescent rather than on the extent of his or her use; (c) commitment to an Alcoholics Anonymous-like 12-step recovery support system (with lectures and group sharing sessions as primary components) and abstinence from all mood-altering substances (with the conspicuous exclusion of tobacco and caffeine) and appropriately prescribed medications; (d) parent or family participation (parent education, family therapy, multifamily therapy, or support groups and attendance at Al-Anon or similar self-help support groups); and (e) extensive participation (typically 6 months or longer) in affiliated outpatient aftercare programs immediately following discharge. Such programs are best limited to hardcore abusers, the approximately 6% to 10% of adolescent drug users who meet criteria for dependence. Less frequently employed are a range of structured, long-term drug treatment options that range from highly structured inpatient treatment to therapeutic communities. The latter are often used as halfway homes between inpatient treatment and return to the family home or to the community (see Wheeler & Malmquist, 1987).

It is critical to remember that adolescents with drug-related disorders are not a homogeneous group. Extant literature clearly supports the proliferation of therapeutic models currently in use or under investigation, as a variety of different models may serve as effective deterrents or treatments for different segments of this population.

Critique

Many challenges to contemporary inpatient drug treatment programs for adolescents have been offered, some charging that more harm than good may result from the diagnosis and treatment of chemically addicted teenagers (R. M. Friedman, 1992; Peele, 1987). This position gains support from evidence that drug use typically declines during the late teens and early 20s, at least among achievement-oriented adolescents (e.g., Johnston et al., 1998; Newcomb & Bentler, 1986a). Minnesota-model drug treatment programs emphasize powerlessness and interdependence, phenomena not well matched to the social and emotional development of adolescents (Newcomb, 1996a, 1996b). Furthermore, a preoccupation with lifelong drug abstinence is not necessarily a realistic goal for adolescents and may detract from the development of coping skills that would improve their relationships within their primary social environments. A more advantageous goal may be the reduction of children's and adolescents' exposure to factors that increase the risk for later drug use (Jenson et al., 1995; Peele, 1987) and the development of social skills and competencies for them to handle a wide range of life problems and challenges (Newcomb, 1996a).

Treatment Efficacy

Few systematic reviews of treatment efficacy with drug-abusing adolescents are available. Extant literature, however, suggests a range of characteristics of both patients and models of therapy that are predictive of favorable outcomes. More positive outcomes are predicted for patients who are female, have a lower delinquency history, evidence less psychopathology, have higher verbal intelligence, and who are motivated for change (A. S. Friedman, Granick, & Kreisher, 1994; Knapp, Templer, Cannon, & Dobson, 1991). Coincidentally, these factors are consistent with predictors of patterns of drug use among young adults several years after discharge (Feigelman, Hyman, Amann, & Feigelman, 1990).

A lack of appropriate comparison precludes the direct contrast of different family therapy approaches (e.g., behavioral vs. family systems), but reports consistently suggest their superiority to drug education or supportive counseling (e.g., Azrin, Donahue, Besalel, & Kagen, 1994; Joanning et al., 1992). Recent publications also have dealt with concerns such as how clients lost to follow-up are dealt with when assessing long-term treatment effects (Stinchfield, Niforopulos, & Feder, 1994). Posttreatment booster sessions may enhance the long-range effects of outpatient family therapy (e.g., Bry & Krinsley, 1992). Long-term outpatient therapy may be superior to short-term inpatient treatment for patients who acknowledge significant social and occupational problems, as well as for patients with more severe psychiatric problems (e.g., A. S. Friedman et al., 1993). Finally, early studies of HMO-based treatment options suggest limited treatment effects (Freeborn, Polen, & Mullooly, 1995), which may result from restrictions in the range or duration of treatment options. For instance, even though family therapy may be the treatment of choice for adolescent drug abusers, there is limited access to such modalities among managed-care providers.

Although it is clear that further research in this area is needed to understand more completely the impact of treatment on adolescent patients, these outcomes are generally consistent with previous descriptions of long-term consequences of adolescent drug use (Newcomb & Bentler, 1989).

SUMMARY

Use and abuse of mood-altering drugs by children and adolescents are related to a wide array of various risk factors. Even though very few children experiment to any extent with abusable substances prior to the sixth grade, such drug involvement by these children and older teenagers is of grave concern, given the serious risks that such behaviors represent. Most adolescents experiment with alcohol prior to age 18; nearly half also experiment with at least one illicit drug by this age. However, despite common lore and differential media coverage, there are no unequivocal ethnic differences in rates of use, although drug of choice may vary as a function of SES, gender, ethnicity, regional setting, and population density. National surveys indicate that most types of drug use have decreased since the early 1980s, and even rates of cocaine use have decreased consistently since the mid-1980s, although there is significant concern that these patterns may not reflect all segments of the population (inner-city youth, school dropouts, gang members).

Considerable controversy rages as to the definition of the use and abuse of licit and illicit drugs among children and adolescents, fueled by contemporary politics. The diagnostic criteria outlined in the *DSM–IV* describe adult drug-using behavior and consequences, yet these typically are used to define drug abuse among adolescents as well.

   Drug-using behavior is clearly a multidetermined set of behaviors. Certainly, previous experience with drugs is the best predictor of later drug use. Peer influences (such as modeling of attitudes favorable to drug use) are consistently described as the second-most powerful psychosocial predictor of adolescent use. Other factors are clearly important, are certainly interrelated, and may be specific predictors of drug use, other problem behaviors, or both, as reflected in a syndrome of general deviance.

   Family influences primarily affect the emergence of drug abuse and occur most directly at younger ages (i.e., children) in the form of biogenetic vulnerability, modeling of drug use, and socialization experiences. At older ages, family influences continue to affect drug use of adolescents, but primarily indirectly via personality, attitudes, and behavior of the teenager, and their perceptions of and response to their larger social environment, particularly peers.

   Stage theories, which suggest that youthful drug use progresses from experimental use of licit substances (beer, wine, or cigarettes), through hard liquor, to marijuana, to illicit drugs other than marijuana, and to polydrug use, have received strong research support. Such a pattern is neither rigidly defined nor linear in nature. Indeed, many who are fairly regular or heavy users in adolescence discontinue that use early in adulthood. Nonetheless, as indicated previously, prior behavior is the best predictor of later drug-using behavior.

   Intervention occurs at many levels or stages in the course of an adolescent's history of drug use. Prevention strategies are aimed both at the nonusers at risk for later drug exposure and at those who already have been exposed to drug use at some level and who could benefit from additional information or skills development to arrest their progression short of more serious consequences. Peer-directed approaches appear to be the most promising of these strategies. Both outpatient and inpatient treatment strategies are limited both by the degree to which parents or primary guardians become active (and supportive) participants in the process and by the degree to which the adolescent patient is able and willing to accept the concept of himself or herself as helpless over the influence of a mood-altering substance (a critical underlying assumption of all 12-step treatment and support programs). A consistent criticism of adolescent drug treatment regards the fact that many who are subjected to treatment and coercive interventions may not, in fact, be in need of this attention. As a result, they may suffer long-term consequences of inappropriate manipulation and exposure to true drug abusers and general adolescent deviants. Such intrusive interventions may be drastically more harmful than the presumed cause or need for treatment (Peele, 1987).

   In short, despite evidence suggestive of a consistent decline in adolescent drug use since the early- to mid-1980s, most continue to experiment with and use both licit and illicit drugs at some time before their 19th birthday. Future directions in research and intervention need to include (a) precise identification of at risk populations; (b) clear delineation of protective factors; (c) descriptive and diagnostic criteria tailored specifically to adolescent populations (such that behavioral norms and political and economic realities are considered); (d) criteria gauged to the true need for intervention; and (e) efforts to tailor prevention and treatment strategies to specific populations (as a function of ethnicity, age, gender, and regional factors).

ACKNOWLEDGMENTS

Preparation of this chapter was supported by Grant DA 01070 from the National Institute on Drug Abuse. Manuscript preparation assistance of Gisele Pham is warmly acknowledged. Please address correspondence to: Dr. Michael Newcomb, Professor and Chairperson, Division of Counseling Psychology, University of Southern California, Los Angeles, CA 90089-0031.

REFERENCES

American Psychiatric Association. (1987). *Diagnostic and statistical manual of mental disorders* (3rd ed., rev.). Washington, DC: Author.

American Psychiatric Association. (1994). *Diagnostic and statistical manual of mental disorders* (4th ed.). Washington, DC: Author.

Anglin, T. M. (1987). Interviewing guidelines for the clinical evaluation of adolescent substance abuse. *Pediatric Clinics of North America, 34,* 381–397.

Azrin, N. H., Donohue, B., Besalel, V. A., & Kogan, E. S. (1994). Youth drug abuse treatment: A controlled outcome study. *Journal of Child and Adolescent Substance Abuse, 3,* 1–16.

Bangert-Drowns, R. L. (1988). The effects of school-based substance abuse education: A meta-analysis. *Journal of Drug Education, 18,* 243–264.

Bardo, M. T., & Risner, M. E. (1985). Biochemical substrates of drug abuse. In M. Galizio & S. A. Maisto (Eds.), *Determinants of substance abuse: Biological, psychological, and environmental factors* (pp. 65–99). New York: Plenum.

Bentler, P. M., & Dudgeon, P. (1996). Covariance structure analysis: Statistical practice, theory, directions. *Annual Review of Psychology, 47,* 563–592.

Bentler, P. M., & Newcomb, M. D. (1986). Personality, sexual behavior, and drug use revealed through latent variable methods. *Clinical Psychology Review, 6,* 363–385.

Bohman, M., Sigvardsson, S., & Cloninger, C. R. (1981). Maternal inheritance of alcohol abuse: Cross fostering analysis of adopted women. *Archives of General Psychiatry, 38,* 965–969.

Botvin, G. J., Schinke, S. P., Epstein, J. A., & Diaz, T. (1995). Effectiveness of culturally focused and generic skills training approaches to alcohol and drug abuse prevention among minority adolescents: Two-year follow-up results. *Psychology of Addictive Behaviors, 9,* 183–194.

Brook, J. S., Cohen, P., Whiteman, M., & Gordon, A. S. (1992). Psychosocial risk factors in the transition from moderate to heavy use or abuse of drugs. In M. D. Glantz and R. Pickens (Eds.), *Vulnerability to drug abuse* (pp. 359–388). Washington, DC: American Psychological Association.

Brook, J. S., Whiteman, M., & Gordon, A. S. (1983). Stages of drug use in adolescence: Personality, peer, and family correlates. *Developmental Psychology, 19,* 269–277.

Bry, B. H., & Krinsley, K. E. (1992). Booster sessions and long-term effects of behavioral family therapy on adolescent substance use and school performance. *Journal of Behavior Therapy and Experimental Psychiatry, 23,* 183–189.

Bry, B. H., McKeon, P., & Pandina, R. (1982). Extent of drug use as a function of number of risk factors. *Journal of Abnormal Psychology, 91,* 273–279.

Bukstein, O., & Kaminer, Y. (1994). The nosology of adolescent substance abuse. *American Journal on Addictions, 3,* 1–13.

Cadoret, R. J. (1992). Genetic and environmental factors in initiation of drug use and the transition to abuse. In M. D. Glantz & R. Pickens (Eds.), *Vulnerability to drug abuse* (pp. 99–114). Washington, DC: American Psychological Association.

Carlson, K. A. (1994). Prevention in its social context: Student views. *Journal of Alcohol and Drug Education, 40,* 26–35.

Carman, R. S. (1979). Motivations for drug use and problematic outcomes among rural junior high school students. *Addictive Behaviors, 4,* 91–93.

Carroll, K. M. (1995). Methodological issues and problems in the assessment of substance use. *Psychological Assessment, 7,* 349–358.

Chatlos, J. C. (1991a). Adolescent drug and alcohol addiction: Diagnosis and assessment. In N. S. Miller (Ed.), *Comprehensive handbook of drug and alcohol addiction* (pp. 211–233). New York: Marcel Dekker.

Chatlos, J. C. (1991b). Adolescent drug and alcohol addiction: Intervention and treatment. In N. S. Miller (Ed.), *Comprehensive handbook of drug and alcohol addiction* (pp. 235–253). New York: Marcel Dekker.

Clayton, R. R., & Ritter, C. (1985). The epidemiology of alcohol and drug abuse among adolescents. *Advances in Alcohol and Substance Abuse, 4,* 69–97.

Cloninger, C. R., Bohman, M., & Sigvardsson, S. (1981). Inheritance of alcohol abuse: Cross fostering analysis of adopted men. *Archives of General Psychiatry, 38,* 861–868.

Cohen, D. A., & Litton, K.L.P. (1995). Parent participation in an adolescent drug abuse prevention program. *Journal of Drug Education, 25,* 159–169.

Crabbe, J. C., McSwigan, J. D., & Belknap, J. K. (1985). The role of genetics in substance abuse. In M. Galizio & S. A. Maisto (Eds.), *Determinants of substance abuse: Biological, psychological, and environmental factors* (pp. 13–64). New York: Plenum.

DeMarsh, J., & Kumpfer, K. L. (1986). Family-oriented interventions for the prevention of chemical dependency in children and adolescents. In S. Griswold-Ezekoye, K. L. Kumpfer, & W. J. Bukoski (Eds.), *Childhood and chemical abuse: Prevention and intervention* (pp. 117–151). Binghamton, NY: Haworth.

Donovan, J. E., & Jessor, R. (1983). Problem drinking and the dimensions of involvement with drugs: A Guttman scalogram analysis of adolescent drug use. *American Journal of Public Health, 73,* 543–552.

Donovan, J. E., & Jessor, R. (1985). Structure of problem behavior in adolescence and young adulthood. *Journal of Consulting and Clinical Psychology, 53,* 890–904.

Dukes, R. L., Ullman, J. B., & Stein, J. S. (1996). Three-year follow-up of Drug Abuse Resistance Education (D.A.R.E.). *Evaluation Review, 20,* 49–66.

Eiser, C., Eiser, J. R., Claxton-Oldfield, S., & Pritchard, M. (1988). Attitudes, attributions, and persuasion: How young people's ideas about drugs relate to their preferences of different strategies of prevention. *Journal of Substance Abuse, 1,* 35–44.

Ellickson, P. L., Bell, R. M., & McGuigan, K. (1993). Preventing adolescent drug use: Long-term results of a junior high program. *American Journal of Public Health, 86,* 856–861.

Ellickson, P. L., Hays, R. D., & Bell, R. M. (1992). Stepping through the drug use sequence: Longitudinal scalogram analysis of initiation and regular use. *Journal of Abnormal Psychology, 101,* 441–451.

Ennett, S. T., Rosenbaum, D. P., Flewelling, R. L., Bieler, G. S., Ringwalt, C. L., & Bailey, S. L. (1994). Long-term evaluation of Drug Abuse Resistance Education. *Addictive Behaviors, 19,* 113–125.

Feigelman, W., Hyman, M. M., Amann, K., & Feigelman, B. (1990). Correlates of persisting drug use among former youth multiple drug abuse patients. *Journal of Psychoactive Drugs, 22,* 63–75

Felix-Ortiz, M., Newcomb, M. D., & Myers, H. (1994). A multidimensional measure of cultural identity for Latino and Latina adolescents. *Hispanic Journal of Behavioral Sciences, 16,* 99–115.

Fingarette, H. (1988). *Heavy drinking: The myth of alcoholism as a disease.* Berkeley: University of California Press.

Freeborn, D. K., Polen, M. R., & Mulooly, J. P. (1995). Adolescent drug misuse treatment and use of medical care services. *International Journal of the Addictions, 30,* 795–822.

Friedman, A. S., Granick, S., & Kreisher, C. (1994). Motivation of adolescent drug abusers for help and treatment. *Journal of Child and Adolescent Substance Abuse, 3,* 69–88.

Friedman, A. S., Granick, S., Kreisher, C., & Terras, A. (1993). Matching adolescents who abuse drugs to treatment. *American Journal on Addictions, 2,* 232–237.

Friedman, R. M. (1992). Mental health and substance abuse services for adolescents: Clinical and service system issues. *Administration and Policy in Mental Health, 19,* 159–178.

Glantz, M., & Pickens, R. (Eds.). (1992). *Vulnerability to drug abuse.* Washington, DC: American Psychological Association.

Goodwin, D. W. (1976). *Is alcoholism hereditary?* New York: Oxford University Press.

Goodwin, D. W. (1985). Alcoholism and genetics: The sins of the fathers. *Archives of General Psychiatry, 42,* 171–174.

Hansen, W. B., Graham, J. W., Sobel, J. L., Shelton, D. R., Flay, B. R., & Johnson, C. A. (1987). The consistency of peer and parent influences on tobacco, alcohol, and marijuana use among young adolescents. *Journal of Behavioral Medicine, 10,* 559–579.

Harrison, P., Hoffmann, N. G., & Edwall, G. E. (1989). Sexual abuse correlates: Similarities between male and female adolescents in chemical dependency treatment. *Journal of Adolescent Research, 4,* 385–399.

Hawkins, J. D., Catalano, R. F., & Miller, J. Y. (1992). Risk and protective factors for alcohol and other drug problems in adolescence and early adulthood: Implications for substance abuse problems. *Psychological Bulletin, 112,* 64–105.

Henggeler, S. W., Pickrel, S. G., Brondino, M. J., & Crouch, J. L. (1996). Eliminating (almost) treatment dropout of substance abusing or dependent delinquents through home-based multisystemic therapy. *American Journal of Psychiatry, 153,* 427–428.

Huba, G. J., & Bentler, P. M. (1980). The role of peer and adult models for drug taking at different stages in adolescence. *Journal of Youth and Adolescence, 9,* 449–465.

Hughes, T. L. (1989). Models and perspectives of addiction: Implications for treatment. *Nursing Clinics of North America, 24,* 1–12.

Humphreys, K., & Rappaport, J. (1993). From the community mental health movement to the war on drugs: A study in the definition of social problems. *American Psychologist, 48,* 892–901.

Jenson, J. M., Howard, M. O., & Yaffe, J. (1995). Treatment of adolescent substance abusers: Issues for practice and research. *Social Work in Health Care, 21,* 1–18.

Jessor, R., & Jessor, S. L. (1977). *Problem behavior and psychosocial development.* New York: Academic Press.

Joanning, H., Quinn, W., Thomas, F., & Mullen, R. (1992). Treating adolescent drug abuse: A comparison of family systems therapy, group therapy, and family drug education. *Journal of Marital and Family Therapy, 18,* 345–356.

Joanning, H., Thomas, F., Newfield, N., & Lamun, B. (1991). Organizing a coordinated family treatment model for the inpatient and outpatient treatment of adolescent drug abuse. *Journal of Family Psychotherapy, 1,* 29–47.

Johnson, V., & Pandina, R. J. (1991). Effects of the family environment on adolescent substance use, delinquency, and coping styles. *American Journal of Drug and Alcohol Abuse, 17,* 71–88.

Johnston, L. D., O'Malley, P. M., & Bachman, J. G. (1998). *National survey results on drug use from monitoring the future study, 1975–1997: Volume I. Secondary school students.* Rockville, MD: National Institute on Drug Abuse.

Julien, R. M. (1998). *A primer of drug action* (8th ed.). San Francisco: Freeman.

Kaminer, Y. (1995). Issues in the pharmacological treatment of adolescent substance abuse. *Journal of Child and Adolescent Psychopharmacology, 5,* 93–106.

Kaminer, Y., Tarter, R. E., Bukstein, O. G., & Kabene, M. (1992). Adolescent substance abuse treatment: Staff, treatment completers', and noncompleters' perceptions of the value of treatment variables. *American Journal on Addiction, 1,* 115–120.

Kandel, D. B. (1975). Stages in adolescent involvement in drug use. *Science, 190,* 912–914.

Kandel, D. B. (1980). Drug and drinking behavior among youth. *Annual Review of Sociology, 6,* 235–285.

Kandel, D. B. (1995). Ethnic differences in drug use: Patterns and paradoxes. In G. Botvin, S. Schinke, & M. Orlandi (Eds.), *Drug abuse prevention with multi-ethnic youth* (pp. 81–104). Newbury Park, CA: Sage.

Kandel, D. B., Davies, M., Karus, D., & Yamaguchi, K. (1986). The consequences in young adulthood of adolescent drug involvement. *Archives of General Psychiatry, 43,* 746–754.

Kandel, D. B., & Logan, J. A. (1984). Patterns of drug use from adolescence to young adulthood: I. Periods of risk for initiation, continued use, and discontinuation. *American Journal of Public Health, 74,* 660–666.

Knapp, J. E., Templer, D. I., Cannon, W. G., & Dobson, S. (1991). Variables associated with success in an adolescent drug treatment program. *Adolescence, 26,* 305–317.

Langer, L. M., & Tubman, J. G. (1997). Risky sexual behavior among substance-abusing adolescents: Psychosocial and contextual factors. *American Journal of Orthopsychiatry, 67,* 315–322;

Lettieri, D. J. (1985). Drug abuse: A review of explanations and models of explanation. *Advances in Alcohol and Substance Abuse, 4,* 9–40.

Lex, B. W. (1991). Some gender differences in alcohol and polysubstance users. *Health Psychology, 10,* 121–132.

Liddle, H. A., & Diamond, G. (1991). Adolescent substance abusers in family therapy: The critical initial phase of treatment. *Family Dynamics of Addiction Quarterly, 1,* 55–68.

Maddahian, E., Newcomb, M. D., & Bentler, P. M. (1986). Adolescent's substance use: Impact of ethnicity, income, and availability. *Advances in Alcohol and Substance Abuse, 5,* 63–78.

Marlatt, G. A. (1992). Substance abuse: Implications of a biopsychosocial model for prevention, treatment, and relapse prevention. In J. Grabowski & G. R. VandenBos (Eds.), *Psychopharmacology: Basic mechanisms and applied interventions* (pp. 127–162). Washington, DC: American Psychological Association.

Marlatt, G. A., Baer, J. S., Donovan, D. M., & Kivlahan, D. R. (1988). Addictive behaviors: Etiology and treatment. *Annual Review of Psychology, 39,* 223–252.

McGee, L., & Newcomb, M. D. (1992). General deviance syndrome: Expanded hierarchical evaluations at four ages from early adolescence to adulthood. *Journal of Consulting and Clinical Psychology, 60,* 766–776.

Medina, A. S., Wallace, H. M., Ralph, N. R., & Goldstein, H. (1982). Adolescent health in Alameda county. *Journal of Adolescent Health Care, 2,* 175–182.

Merikangas, K. R., Rounsaville, B. J., & Prusoff, B. A. (1992). Familial factors in vulnerability to substance abuse. In M. D. Glantz & R. Pickens (Eds.), *Vulnerability to drug abuse* (pp. 75–98). Washington, DC: American Psychological Association.

Miller, N. S., & Gold, M. S. (1989). Suggestions for changes in *DSM III–R* criteria for substance use disorders. *American Journal of Drug and Alcohol Abuse, 15,* 223–230.

Miller, W. R. (1993). Alcoholism: Toward a better disease model. *Psychology of Addictive Behaviors, 7,* 129–136.

Morris, J., Gawinski, B. A., & Joanning, H. (1991). Five strategies for enlisting family involvement in adolescent substance abuse treatment. *Journal of Family Psychotherapy, 2,* 41–52.

Myers, H. F., Alvy, K. T., Arrington, A., Richardson, M. A., Marigna, M., Robbin, H., Main, M., & Newcomb, M. D. (1992). The impact of a parent training program on inner-city African-American families. *Journal of Community Psychology, 20,* 132–147.

Needle, R. H., Su, S. S., & Doherty, W. J. (1990). Divorce, remarriage, and adolescent substance use: A prospective longitudinal study. *Journal of Marriage and the Family, 52,* 157–169.

Newcomb, M. D. (1988). *Drug use in the workplace: Risk factors for disruptive substance use among young adults.* Dover, MA: Auburn House.

Newcomb, M. D. (1990). What structural equation modeling can tell us about social support. In B. R. Sarason, I. G. Sarason, & G. R. Pierce (Eds.), *Social support: An interactional view* (pp. 26–63). New York: Wiley.

Newcomb, M. D. (1992a). Substance abuse and control in the United States: Ethical and legal issues. *Social Science and Medicine, 35,* 471–479.

Newcomb, M. D. (1992b). Understanding the multidimensional nature of drug use and abuse: The role of consumption, risk factors, and protective factors. In M. D. Glantz & R. Pickens (Eds.), *Vulnerability to drug abuse* (pp. 255–297). Washington, DC: American Psychological Association.

Newcomb, M. D. (1993). Problem behavior theory and perhaps a little beyond [Review of the book *Beyond adolescence: Problem behavior and young adult development*]. *Contemporary Psychology, 38,* 895–898.

Newcomb, M. D. (1994). Families, peers, and adolescent alcohol abuse: A paradigm to study multiple causes, mechanisms, and outcomes. In R. A. Zucker, G. M. Boyd, & J. Howard (Eds.), *Development of alcohol problems: Exploring the biopsychosocial matrix of risk* (pp. 157–168). Rockville, MD: National Institute on Alcoholism and Alcohol Abuse.

Newcomb, M. D. (1995a). Drug use etiology among ethnic minority adolescents: Risk and protective factors. In G. Botvin, S. Schinke, & M. Orlandi (Eds.), *Drug abuse prevention with multi-ethnic youth* (pp. 105–129). Newbury Park, CA: Sage.

Newcomb, M. D. (1995b). Identifying high-risk youth: Prevalence and patterns of adolescent drug abuse. In E. Rahdert, D. Czechowicz, & I. Amsel (Eds.), *Adolescent drug abuse: Clinical assessment and therapeutic intervention* (pp. 7–38). Rockville, MD: National Institute on Drug Abuse.

Newcomb, M. D. (1996a). Adolescence: Pathologizing a normal process. *The Counseling Psychologist, 24,* 482–490.

Newcomb, M. D. (1996b). Pseudomaturity among adolescents: Construct validation, sex differences, and associations in adulthood. *Journal of Drug Issues, 26,* 477–504.

Newcomb, M. D. (1997). Psychosocial predictors and consequences of drug use: A developmental perspective within a prospective study. *Journal of Addictive Diseases, 16,* 51–89.

Newcomb, M. D., & Bentler, P. M. (1986a). Cocaine use among adolescents: Longitudinal associations with social context, psychopathology, and use of other substances. *Addictive Behaviors, 11,* 263273.

Newcomb, M. D., & Bentler, P. M. (1986b). Cocaine use among young adults. *Advances in Alcohol and Substance Abuse, 6,* 7396.

Newcomb, M. D., & Bentler, P. M. (1986c). Frequency and sequence of drug use: A longitudinal study from early adolescence to young adulthood. *Journal of Drug Education, 16,* 101–120.

Newcomb, M. D., & Bentler, P. M. (1987). The impact of late adolescent substance use on young adult health status and utilization of health services: A structural equation model over four years. *Social Science and Medicine, 24,* 7182.

Newcomb, M. D., & Bentler, P. M. (1988a). *Consequences of adolescent drug use: Impact on the lives of young adults.* Beverly Hills, CA: Sage.

Newcomb, M. D., & Bentler, P. M. (1988b). Impact of adolescent drug use and social support on problems of young adults: A longitudinal study. *Journal of Abnormal Psychology, 97,* 64–75.

Newcomb, M. D., & Bentler, P. M. (1988c). The impact of family context, deviant attitudes, and emotional distress on adolescent drug use: Longitudinal latent variable analyses of mothers and their children. *Journal of Research in Personality, 22,* 154176.

Newcomb, M. D., & Bentler, P. M. (1989). Substance use and abuse among children and teenagers. *American Psychologist, 44,* 242–248.

Newcomb, M. D., & Bentler, P. M. (1990). Antecedents and consequences of cocaine use: An eight-year study from early adolescence to young adulthood. In L. Robins (Ed.), *Straight and devious pathways from childhood to adulthood* (pp. 158181). New York: Cambridge University Press.

Newcomb, M. D., & Earleywine, M. (1996). Intrapersonal contributors to drug use: The willing host. *American Behavioral Scientist, 39,* 823–837.

Newcomb, M. D., & Felix-Ortiz, M. (1992). Multiple protective and risk factors for drug use and abuse: Cross-sectional and prospective findings. *Journal of Personality and Social Psychology, 63,* 280–296.

Newcomb, M. D., & Harlow, L. L. (1986). Life events and substance use among adolescents: Mediating effects of perceived loss of control and meaninglessness in life. *Journal of Personality and Social Psychology, 51,* 564–577.

Newcomb, M. D., Huba, G. J., & Bentler, P. M. (1983). Mother's influence on the drug use of their children: Confirmatory tests of direct modeling and mediational theories. *Developmental Psychology, 19,* 714–726.

Newcomb, M. D., Maddahian, E., & Bentler, P. M. (1986). Risk factor for drug use among adolescents: Concurrent and longitudinal analyses. *American Journal of Public Health, 76,* 525–531.

Newcomb, M. D., Maddahian, E., Skager, R., & Bentler, P. M. (1987). Substance abuse and psychosocial risk factors among teenagers: Associations with sex, age, ethnicity, and type of school. *American Journal of Drug and Alcohol Abuse, 13,* 413433.

Newcomb, M. D., & McGee, L. (1991). The influence of sensation seeking on general deviance and specific problem behaviors from adolescence to young adulthood. *Journal of Personality and Social Psychology, 61,* 614–628.

Oetting, E. R., & Beauvais, F. (1990). Adolescent drug use: Findings of national and local surveys. *Journal of Consulting and Clinical Psychology, 58,* 385–394.

O'Neill, S. F., & Barnes, H. N. (1987). Alcoholics Anonymous. In H. N. Barnes, M. D. Aronoan, & T. L. Delbanco (Eds.), *Alcoholism: A guide to the primary care physician* (pp. 93–101). New York: Springer-Verlag.

Palumbo, D. J., & Ferguson, J. L. (1995). Evaluation of Gang Resistance Education and Training (GREAT): Is the impact the same as that of Drug Abuse Resistance Education (D.A.R.E.)? *Evaluation Review, 19,* 597–619.

Paton, S., Kessler, R. C., & Kandel, D. B. (1977). Depressive mood and illegal drug use: A longitudinal analysis. *Journal of Genetic Psychology, 131,* 267–289.

Peele, S. (1987). What can we expect from treatment of adolescent drug and alcohol abuse? *Pediatrician, 14,* 62–69.

Perry, C. L., Williams, C. L., Velben-Mortenson, S., Toomey, T. L., Komro, K. A., Anstine, P.I.S., McGovern, P. G., Finnegan, J. R., Forster, J. L., Wagennaar, A. C., & Wolfson, M. (1996). Project Northland: Outcomes of a communitywide alcohol use prevention program during early adolescence. *American Journal of Public Health, 86,* 956–965.

Rahdert, E. R. (1991). *The adolescent assessment/referral system: Manual.* Rockville, MD: National Institute on Drug Abuse.

Richardson, M. A. (1993). *Psychosocial predictors and consequences of recent drug use among Anglo and Hispanic children and adolescents: An evaluation of social development theory.* Unpublished doctoral dissertation, University of California, Los Angeles.

Scheier, L. M., & Newcomb, M. D. (1991). Psychosocial predictors of drug use initiation and escalation: An expansion of the multiple risk factors hypothesis using longitudinal data. *Contemporary Drug Problems, 18,* 31–73.

Schinke, S. P., Botvin, G. J., Trimble, J. E., Orlandi, M. A., Gilchrist, L. D., & Locklear, V. S. (1988). Preventing substance abuse among American-Indian adolescents: A bicultural competence skills approach. *Journal of Counseling Psychology, 35,* 87–90.

Schmidt, S. E., Liddle, H. A., & Dakof, G. A. (1996). Changes in parenting practices in adolescent drug abuse during multidimensional family therapy. *Journal of Family Psychology, 10,* 12–27.

Searles, J. S. (1988). The role of genetics in the pathogenesis of alcoholism. *Journal of Abnormal Psychology, 97,* 153–167.

Shedler, J., & Block, J. (1990). Adolescent drug use and psychological health: A longitudinal inquiry. *American Psychologist, 45,* 612–630.

Stacy, A. W., Newcomb, M. D., & Bentler, P. M. (1992). Interactive and higher-order effects on social influences on drug use. *Journal of Health and Social Behavior, 33,* 226–241.

Stein, J. A., Newcomb, M. D., & Bentler, P. M. (1994). Psychosocial correlates and predictors of AIDS risk behaviors, abortion, and drug use among a community sample of young adult women. *Health Psychology, 13,* 303–318.

Stinchfield, R. D., Niforopulos, L., & Feder, S. H. (1994). Follow-up contact bias in adolescent substance abuse treatment outcome research. *Journal of Studies on Alcohol, 55,* 285–289.

Stoil, M. J., & Hill, G. (1996). *Preventing substance abuse: Interventions that work.* New York: Plenum.

Substance Abuse and Mental Health Services Administration. (1997). *National household survey on drug abuse main findings 1995.* Rockville, MD: Author.

Szapocznik, J., Perez-Vidal, A., Brickman, A. L., Foote, F. H., Santisteban, D., & Hervis, O. (1988). Engaging adolescent drug abusers and their families in treatment: A strategic structural systems approach. *Journal of Consulting and Clinical Psychology, 56,* 552–557.

Szapocznik, J., Rio, A., Murray, E., Cohen, R., Scopetta, M., Rivas-Vasquez, A., Hervis, O., Posada, V., & Kurtines, W. (1989). Structural family versus psychodynamic child therapy for problematic Hispanic boys. *Journal of Consulting and Clinical Psychology, 57,* 571–578.

Tarter, R. E., & Vanyukov, M. (1994). Alcoholism: A developmental disorder. *Journal of Consulting and Clinical Psychology, 62,* 1096–1107.

Tobler, N. (1986). Meta-analysis of 143 adolescent drug prevention programs: Quantitative outcome results of program participants compared to control or comparison group. *Journal of Drug Issues, 4,* 537–567.

Tolan, P. (1988). Socioeconomic, family, and social stress correlates of adolescent antisocial and delinquent behavior. *Journal of Abnormal Child Psychology, 16,* 317–331.

Vaillant, G. E. (1983). *The natural history of alcoholism: Causes, patterns, and paths to recovery.* Cambridge, MA: Harvard University Press.

Wheeler, K., & Malmquist, J. (1987). Treatment approaches in adolescent chemical dependency. *Pediatric Clinics of North America, 34,* 437–447.

Williams, C. L., Toomey, T. L., McGovern, P., & Wagenaar, A. C. (1995). Development, reliability, and validity of self-report alcohol-use measures with young adolescents. *Journal of Child and Adolescent Substance Abuse, 4,* 17–40.

Winters, K. C. (1992). Development of an adolescent alcohol and other drug abuse screening scale: Personal experience screening questionnaire. *Addictive Behavior, 17,* 479–490.

Winters, K. C., Latimer, W., & Stinchfield, R. D. (in press). The *DSM–IV* criteria for adolescent alcohol and cocaine use disorders. *Journal of Studies on Alcohol.*

Winters, K. C., Stinchfield, R. D., & Henley, G. A. (1996). Convergent and predictive validity of scales measuring adolescent substance abuse. *Journal of Child and Adolescent Substance Abuse, 5,* 37–55.

Wise, R. A. (1988). The neurobiology of craving: Implications for the understanding and treatment of addiction. *Journal of Abnormal Psychology, 97,* 118–132.

Wolraich, M. L. (1996). *The classification of child and adolescent mental diagnoses in primary care.* Elk Grove, IL: American Academy of Pediatrics.

Wysong, E., Aniskiewicz, R., & Wright, D. (1994). Truth and DARE: Tracking drug education to graduation and as symbolic politics. *Social Problems, 41,* 448–472.

Zucker, R. A., & Gomberg, E.S.L. (1986). Etiology of alcoholism reconsidered: The case for a biopsychosocial process. *American Psychologist, 41,* 783–793.

Author Index

Subject Index